DICTIONARY

of Daily Life

IN BIBLICAL & POST-BIBLICAL ANTIQUITY

DICTIONARY

of Daily Life

IN BIBLICAL & POST-BIBLICAL ANTIQUITY

Volume II
De-H

Edwin M. Yamauchi & Marvin R. Wilson

Dictionary of Daily Life in Biblical and Post-Biblical Antiquity
Volume II, De-H
© 2015 by Hendrickson Publishers Marketing, LLC
P. O. Box 3473
Peabody, Massachusetts 01961-3473

ISBN 978-1-61970-640-8

Printed in the United States of America

First Printing — August 2015

Library of Congress Cataloging-in-Publication Data

Yamauchi, Edwin M.
    Dictionary of daily life in biblical and post-biblical antiquity /
Edwin M. Yamauchi and Marvin R. Wilson.
        volumes cm
    Includes bibliographical references.
    Contents: Volume I. A-Da.
    ISBN 978-1-61970-460-2 (v. 1)
    1. Bible—Dictionaries. I. Title.
BS440.Y37 2014
220.95—dc23
                2014017152

TABLE OF CONTENTS

CONTRIBUTORS

RB-L   BAILLEUL-LESUER, Rozenn. ABD, University of Chicago.

ALB   BEAN, Adam L. ABD, Johns Hopkins University.

RGB   BRANCH, Robin G. PhD, Extraordinary Associate Professor, North-West University, Potchefstroom, South Africa.

STC   CARROLL, Scott T. PhD, Director, Manuscript Research Group.

ACC   CHAMBERS, Adam C. PhD.

DJC   CHILDS, David J. PhD, Assistant Professor of Social Studies Education, Northern Kentucky University.

JJD   DAVIS, John J. ThD, Professor of Old Testament and Hebrew emeritus, Grace Theological Seminary.

JFD   DEFELICE, John F., Jr. PhD, Associate Professor of History, University of Maine Presque Isle.

LMF   FIELDS, Lee M. PhD, Professor of Biblical Studies, Mid-Atlantic Christian University.

LPG   GRIMSLEY, Lucas P. ABD, Southwestern Baptist Theological Seminary.

RKH   *HARRISON, Roland K. PhD, Professor of Old Testament, Wycliffe College, University of Toronto. *Deceased.

RSH   HESS, Richard S. PhD, Professor of Old Testament, Denver Seminary.

DLH   HOFFMAN, Daniel L. PhD, Senior Adjunct Professor of History, Lee University.

CSK   KEENER, Craig S. PhD, Professor of New Testament, Asbury Theological Seminary.

GLL   LINTON, Gregory L. PhD, Professor of New Testament, Johnson University.

PLM   MAIER, Paul L. PhD, Russell H. Seibert Professor of Ancient History emeritus, Western Michigan University.

GLM   MATTINGLY, Gerald L. PhD, Professor of Biblical Studies, Johnson University.

LJN   NESS, Lester J. PhD, Foreign Expert, Yunnan University, China.

JAP   PATTENGALE, Jerry A. PhD, University Professor, Indiana Wesleyan University.

HP   PEHLKE, Helmuth. ThD, Professor of Old Testament, Southwestern Baptist Theological Seminary, and Professor of Old Testament at Bibelseminar Bonn, Germany.

EBP   POWERY, Emerson B. PhD, Associate Professor of New Testament, Lee University.

TR   RATA, Tiberius. PhD, Professor of Old Testament, Grace College and Seminary.

WJR   REED, William J. ABD, Johns Hopkins University.

SMR   RODRIQUEZ, Seth M. PhD, Adjunct Professor of Old Testament Interpretation, The Southern Baptist Theological Seminary.

FDS   SCALF, Foy D. PhD, Head of Research Archives, The Oriental Institute, University of Chicago.

KNS   SCHOVILLE, Keith N. PhD, Professor of Hebrew and Semitic Studies emeritus, University of Wisconsin.

TMS   SIGLER, Tim M. PhD, Professor of Hebrew and Biblical Studies, Moody Bible Institute.

RWS   SMITH, Robert W. PhD, Professor of Bible and History, Mid-Atlantic Christian University.

PMS   SPRINKLE, Preston M. PhD, Vice President, Eternity Bible College, Boise Extension.

GCT   TUCKER, Gordon C. Professor of Biological Sciences, Eastern Illinois University.

MRW   WILSON, Marvin R. PhD, Harold J. Ockenga Professor of Biblical and Theological Studies, Gordon College.

JDW   WINELAND, John D. PhD, Professor of History and Archaeology, Kentucky Christian University.

EMY   YAMAUCHI, Edwin M. PhD, Professor of History emeritus, Miami University.

MSZ   ZIESE, Mark S. PhD, Professor of Old Testament, Johnson University.

ABBREVIATIONS

GENERAL

#(#)	number(s)
‖	parallel to
AD	*anno domini*, in the year of the Lord
Akk.	Akkadian
Arab.	Arabic
Aram.	Aramaic
ASV	American Standard Version
AV	Authorized Version (i.e., KJV = King James Version)
b.	*ben*, Hebrew "son"; born
b.	Babylonian Talmud
BC	before Christ
c.	century
C	centigrade
ca.	*circa*, about
CE	Codex Eshnunna
cf.	*confer*, compare
ch(s).	chapter(s)
CH	Code of Hammurabi
cm.	centimeter
col(s).	column(s)
d.	died
Dyn.	Dynasty
EA	El Amarna (designation of texts from)
ed.	editor(s), edition
e.g.	*exempli gratia*, for example
Egy.	Egyptian
Eng.	English

Ep.	epistle, letter
esp.	especially
et al.	*et alia*, and others
ESV	English Standard Version
Eth.	Ethiopic
F	Fahrenheit
fig.	figure
fl.	*floruit*, flourished
frag.	fragment
ft.	foot, feet
gal.	gallon(s)
Gk.	Greek
ha.	hectare (about 2.5 acres)
Heb.	Hebrew
i.e.	*id est*, that is
ibid.	*ibidem,* in the same place
in.	inch(es)
JB	Jerusalem Bible
KJV	King James Version
km.	kilometer
Lat.	Latin
lb(s).	pound(s)
LCL	Loeb Classical Library
lit.	literally
LXX	Septuagint
m.	meter(s)
m.	Mishnah
MAL	Middle Assyrian Law Code
MASCA	Museum Applied Science Center for Archaeology
mi.	mile(s)
MK	Middle Kingdom (of Egypt)
Mt.	mount, mountain
MT	Masoretic Text
n.	(foot/end)note
NAB	New American Bible
NASB	New American Standard Bible
NEB	New English Bible
NEV	New English Version
NHC	Nag Hammadi codices
NIV	New International Version
NJPS	*Tanakh: The Holy Scriptures: The New JPS Translation according to the Traditional Hebrew Text*

NK	New Kingdom (of Egypt)
no(s).	number(s)
NRSV	New Revised Standard Version
n.s.	new series (of journals)
NT	New Testament
OB	Old Babylonian
OK	Old Kingdom (Egypt)
Old Pers.	Old Persian
OT	Old Testament
Oxy.	Oxyrhynchus
Pap.	Papyrus
Phoen.	Phoenician
pl.	plate
pl.	plural
R.	rabbi
r.	reigned
REB	Revised English Bible
repr.	reprint(ed)
rev.	revised
RSV	Revised Standard Version
sing.	singular
sq.	square
St.	saint
Sum.	Sumerian
Suppl.	Supplement
t.	Tosefta
tr.	translated
trans.	translator(s)
Ugar.	Ugaritic
vol(s).	volume(s)
vs(s).	verse(s)
Vulg	Vulgate
y.	Jerusalem (*Yerushalmi*) Talmud
YLT	Young's Literal Translation

ANCIENT SOURCES

Hebrew Bible/Old Testament

Gen	Genesis
Exod	Exodus
Lev	Leviticus

Num	Numbers
Deut	Deuteronomy
Josh	Joshua
Judg	Judges
Ruth	Ruth
1–2 Sam	1–2 Samuel
1–2 Kgs	1–2 Kings
1–2 Chr	1–2 Chronicles
Ezra	Ezra
Neh	Nehemiah
Esth	Esther
Job	Job
Ps(s)	Psalm(s)
Prov	Proverbs
Eccl	Ecclesiastes
Song	Song of Songs
Isa	Isaiah
Jer	Jeremiah
Lam	Lamentations
Ezek	Ezekiel
Dan	Daniel
Hos	Hosea
Joel	Joel
Amos	Amos
Obad	Obadiah
Jonah	Jonah
Mic	Micah
Nah	Nahum
Hab	Habakkuk
Zeph	Zephaniah
Hag	Haggai
Zech	Zechariah
Mal	Malachi

New Testament

Matt	Matthew
Mark	Mark
Luke	Luke
John	John
Acts	Acts
Rom	Romans

1–2 Cor	1–2 Corinthians
Gal	Galatians
Eph	Ephesians
Phil	Philippians
Col	Colossians
1–2 Thess	1–2 Thessalonians
1–2 Tim	1–Timothy
Titus	Titus
Phlm	Philemon
Heb	Hebrews
Jas	James
1–2 Pet	1–2 Peter
1–3 John	1–3 John
Jude	Jude
Rev	Revelation

Apocrypha and Septuagint

1–2 Esd	1–2 Esdras
1–4 Macc	1–4 Maccabees
Add Esth	Addition to Esther
Bar	Baruch
Bel	Bel and the Dragon
Ep Jer	Epistle of Jeremiah
Jdt	Judith
Pr Azar	Prayer of Azariah
Pr Man	Prayer of Manasseh
Sg Three	Song of the Three Young Men
Sir	Sirach/Ecclesiasticus
Sus	Susanna
Tob	Tobias
Wis	Wisdom of Solomon

Old Testament Pseudepigrapha

2 Bar.	2 Baruch
1 En.	1 Enoch
4 Ezra	4 Ezra
Jos. Asen.	Joseph and Aseneth
Jub.	Jubilees
Lad. Jac.	Ladder of Jacob

Let. Aris.	*Letter of Aristeas*
Pss. Sol.	*Psalms of Solomon*
Sib. Or.	*Sibylline Oracles*
T. Ash.	*Testament of Asher*
T. Benj.	*Testament of Benjamin*
T. Isaac	*Testament of Isaac*
T. Jac.	*Testament of Jacob*
T. Levi	*Testament of Levi*
T. Naph.	*Testament of Naphtali*
T. Zeb.	*Testament of Zebulun*
Vis. Ezra	*Vision of Ezra*

New Testament Pseudepigrapha

Acts John	*Acts of John*

Dead Sea Scrolls and Cairo Geniza

CD	*Damascus Document*
1QH[a,b] (=1Q35)	*Hodayot* (Thanksgiving Hymns)
1QS	*Serek Hayaḥad* (Rule of the Community)
1QSa	1Q28a (Rule of the Congregation)
4QMMT (=4Q394–399)	(*Miqṣat Maʿaśê ha-Torah*)
11QTemple[a,b]	11Q19–20 (Temple Scroll)

Judaica

ʿAbod. Zar.	*ʿAbodah Zarah*
ʾAbot	*ʾAbot*
ʿArak.	*ʿArakin*
B. Bat.	*Baba Batra*
B. Meṣ.	*Baba Meṣiʿa*
B. Qam.	*Baba Qamma*
Bek.	*Bekorot*
Ber.	*Berakot*
Beṣah	*Beṣah (Yom Ṭob)*
ʿEd.	*ʿEduyyot*
ʿErub.	*ʿErubin*
Exod. Rab.	*Exodus Rabbah*
Gen. Rab.	*Genesis Rabbah*
Giṭ.	*Giṭṭin*

Ḥag.	*Ḥagigah*
Ḥul.	*Ḥullin*
Kelim	*Kelim*
Ker.	*Keritot*
Ketub.	*Ketubbot*
Kil.	*Kil'ayim*
Lev. Rab.	*Leviticus Rabbah*
Mak.	*Makkot*
Makš.	*Makširin*
Meg.	*Megillah*
Mek.	*Mekilta*
Menaḥ.	*Menaḥot*
Mid.	*Middot*
Miqw.	*Miqwa'ot*
Moʿed Qaṭ.	*Moʿed Qaṭan*
Naz.	*Nazir*
Ned.	*Nedarim*
Neg.	*Negaʿim*
Nez.	*Neziqin*
Nid.	*Niddah*
Num. Rab.	*Numbers Rabbah*
'Ohol.	*'Oholot*
Pe'ah	*Pe'ah*
Pesaḥ.	*Pesaḥim*
Qidd.	*Qiddušin*
Qod.	*Qodašim*
Roš Haš.	*Roš Haššanah*
Šabb.	*Šabbat*
Sanh.	*Sanhedrin*
Šeb.	*Šebiʿit*
Šeqal.	*Šeqalim*
Sifre Num	*Sifre (to Numbers)*
Sifre Deut	*Sifre (to Deuteronomy)*
Soṭah	*Soṭah*
Sukkah	*Sukkah*
Ṭ. Yom	*Ṭebul Yom*
Taʿan.	*Taʿanit*
Tamid	*Tamid*
Ṭehar.	*Ṭeharot*
Tem.	*Temurah*
Ter.	*Terumot*

'Uq.	*Uqṣin*
Yad.	*Yadayim*
Yebam.	*Yebamot*
Yoma	*Yoma (=Kippurim)*

Apostolic Fathers

1–2 Clem.	*1–2 Clement*
Did.	*Didache*
Herm. Mand.	*Shepherd of Hermas, Mandate(s)*
Herm. Simil.	*Shepherd of Hermas, Similitude(s)*
Herm. Vis.	*Shepherd of Hermas, Vision(s)*
Ign. *Eph.*	Ignatius, *To the Ephesians*
Ign. *Magn.*	Ignatius, *To the Magnesians*
Ign. *Phld.*	Ignatius, *To the Philadelphians*
Ign. *Pol.*	Ignatius, *To Polycarp*
Mart. Pol.	*Martyrdom of Polycarp*
Pol. *Phil.*	Polycarp, *To the Philippians*

Ancient Authors

Aelian (ca. AD 170–235)
    Nat. an.   *De natura animalium (Nature of Animals)*
Aeschines (ca. 397–ca. 322 BC)
    Tim.   *In Timarchum (Against Timarchus)*
Aeschylus (ca. 525–455 BC)
    Eum.   *Eumenides (Eumenides)*
    Suppl.   *Supplices (Suppliant Women)*
Ambrose (AD 339–397)
    Hex.   *Hexaemeron libri sex (Six Days of Creation)*
Ammianus Marcellinus (ca. AD 330–395)
    Res G.   *Res Gestae (Roman History)*
Anonymous
    H.A.   *Historia Augusta*
Apuleius (fl. ca. AD 155)
    Apol.   *Apology (Pro se de magia) (Apology)*
    Metam.   *Metamorphoses (The Golden Ass)*
Aristophanes [Aristoph.] (ca. 446–ca. 386 BC)
    Eq.   *Equites (Knights)*
    Nub.   *Nubes (Clouds)*
    Ran.   *Ranae (Frogs)*
    Thesm.   *Thesmophoriazusae*
    Vesp.   *Vespae (Wasps)*

Aristotle [Arist.] (384–322 BC)

Ath. pol.	*Athēnaiōn politeia (Constitution of Athens)*
Div. somn.	*De divination per somnum (Prophesying by Dreams)*
Eth. Nic.	*Ethica Nichomachea (Nichomachean Ethics)*
Hist. an.	*Historia animalium (History of Animals)*
Part. an.	*De partibus animalium (Parts of Animals)*
Pol.	*Politics*
Rhet.	*Rhetorica (Rhetoric)*

Artemidorus Daldianus (mid/late 2nd c. AD)

Oneir.	*Oneirocritica*

Athanasius (ca. AD 295–373)

C. Gent.	*Contra gentes (Against the Pagans)*
Vit. Ant.	*Vita Antonii (Life of Antony)*

Athenaeus (fl. ca. AD 200)

Deipn.	*Deipnosophistae (The Learned Banqueters)*

Athenagoras (fl. ca. AD 180)

Leg.	*Legatio pro Christianis (Embassy for the Christians)*

Augustine (AD 354–430)

Bon. conj.	*De bono conjugali (The Good of Marriage)*
Civ.	*De civitate Dei (The City of God)*
Conf.	*Confessionum (Confessions)*
Cons.	*De consensu evangelistarum (Harmony of the Gospels)*
De mend.	*De mendacio (On Lying)*
Doctr. chr.	*De doctrina christiana (Christian Instruction)*
Ennarat. Ps.	*Ennarationes in Psalmos (Expositions of the Psalms)*
Ep.	*Epistulae (Letters)*
Faust.	*Contra Faustum Manichaeum (Against Faustus the Manichaean)*
Haer.	*De haeresibus (Heresies)*
Incomp. nupt.	*Incompetentibus nuptiis (Adulterous Marriages)*
Man.	*De moribus Manichaeorum (On the Morals of the Manichaeans)*
Nupt.	*De nuptiis et concupiscentia ad Valerium comitem (Marriage and Concupiscence)*
Op. mon.	*De opere monachorum (On the Work of Monks)*
Quaest. ev.	*Quaestionum evangelicarum*
Tract. Ev. Jo.	*In Evangelium Johannis tractatus (Tractates on the Gospel of John)*

Aulus Cornelius Celsus (fl. ca. AD 25)

Med.	*De medicina*

Aulus Gellius

Noct. Att.	*Noctes atticae (Attic Nights)*

Basil (AD 330–379)
| *Ep.* | *Epistulae* |
| *Hex.* | *Hexaemeron* |

Caesar, Julius (100–44 BC)
| *Bell. gall.* | *Bellum gallicum (Gallic War)* |

Cassius Dio (ca. AD 155–235)
| *Hist. rom.* | *Historia romana (Roman History)* |

Cato (234–149 BC)
| *Agr.* | *De agricultura (Agriculture)* |

Cicero [Cic.] (106–43 BC)
Att.	*Epistulae ad Atticum (Letters to Atticus)*
De or.	*De oratore (On the Orator)*
Div.	*De divinatione (On Divination)*
Dom.	*De domo suo (On His House)*
Flac.	*Pro Flacco (In Defense of Lucius Valerius Flaccus)*
Font.	*Pro Fonteio (In Defense of Marcus Fonteius)*
Leg.	*De Legibus (On the Laws)*
Mur.	*Pro Murena (In Defence of Lucius Licinius Murena)*
Parad.	*Paradoxa Stoicorum (Stoic Paradoxes)*
Rep.	*De republica (On the Republic)*

Clement of Alexandria [Clem.] (d. ca. AD 214)
Paed.	*Paedagogus (Christ the Educator)*
Protr.	*Protrepticus (Exhortation to the Greeks)*
Strom.	*Stromateis (Miscellanies)*

Clement of Rome (fl. ca. AD 96) (see *1–2 Clement*)

Columella (fl. AD 60–65)
| *Rust.* | *De re rustica (On Farming)* |

Cyprian (ca. AD 200–258)
| *Unit. eccl.* | *De catholicae ecclesiae unitate (The Unity of the Catholic Church)* |

Demosthenes (384–322 BC)
| *1–3 Olynth.* | *Olynthiaca i–iii (1–3 Olynthiac)* |
| *Cor.* | *De corona (On the Crown)* |

Dio Chrysostom (ca. AD 40–after 110)
| *2 Fort* | *De fortuna ii (Fortune 2)* |
| *Rhod.* | *Rhodiaca (To the People of Rhodes)* |

Diodorus Siculus [Diod. Sic.] (fl. ca. 60–39 BC)
| *Bib. hist.* | *Bibliotheca historica (Library of History)* |

Dionysius of Halicarnassus
| *Ant. rom.* | *Antiquitates romanae* |

Dioscorides Pedanius (fl. 1st c. AD)
| *Mat. med.* | *De materia medica* |

Epictetus
    Disc.   *Dissertationes (Discourses)*
Epiphanius (ca. AD 315–403)
    Pan.   *Panarion (Adversus haereses) (Refutation of All Heresies)*
Euripides (ca. 485–406 BC)
    Bacch.   *Bacchae (Bacchanals)*
    Med.   *Medea*
Eusebius of Caesarea [Eus.] (AD ca. 260–ca. 339)
    Coet. sanct.   *Ad coetum sanctorum (Oration of the Emperor*
                    Constantine to the Assembly of the Saints)
    Hist. eccl.   *Historia ecclesiastica (Ecclesiastical History)*
    Prep. ev.   *Praeparatio evangelica (Preparation for the Gospel)*
    Vit. Const.   *Vita Constantini (Life of Constantine)*
Gaius (ca. AD 130–180)
    Dig.   *Digest*
Gregory of Nazianzus (ca. 330–390)
    Or. Bas.   *Oratio in laudem Basilii (Oration in Praise of Basil)*
Herodotus [Her.] (ca. 484–ca. 425 BC)
    Hist.   *Historiae*
Hesiod [Hes.] (ca. 700 BC)
    Op.   *Opera et dies (Works and Days)*
    Theog.   *Theogonia (Theogony)*
Hippocrates (ca. 460–ca. 370 BC)
    Aph.   *Aphorismata (Aphorisms)*
    Artic.   *De articulis reponendis (Joints)*
    Carn.   *De carne (Fleshes)*
    Epid.   *Epidemiae (Epidemics)*
    Morb.   *De morbis (Diseases)*
    Nat. hom.   *De natura hominis (Nature of Man)*
Hippolytus (ca. AD 160–235)
    Haer.   *Refutatio omnium haeresium (Refutation of All Heresies)*
    Trad. ap.   *Traditio apostolica (The Apostolic Tradition)*
Homer [Hom.] (8th c. BC)
    Il.   *Ilias (Iliad)*
    Od.   *Odyssea (Odyssey)*
Horace (65–8 BC)
    Ep.   *Epistulae (Epistles)*
    Sat.   *Satirae (Satires)*
Ignatius of Antioch (d. ca. AD 115) (see under *Apostolic Fathers*)
Irenaeus (ca. AD 130–ca. 200)
    Epid.   *Epideixis tou apostolikou kērygmatos (Demonstration*
                    of Apostolic Preaching)

Haer.	*Adversus haereses (Against Heresies)*

Jerome (ca. AD 347–ca. 420)

Comm. Ezech.	*Commentariorum in Ezechielem*
Epist.	*Epistulae*
Jov.	*Adversus Jovinianum*
Qu. hebr. Gen.	*Liber Quaestionum hebraicarum in Genesim*
Vigil.	*Adversus Vigilantium*
Vir. ill.	*De viris illustribus (On Illustrious Men)*
Vit. Malch.	*Vita Malchi monachi* ("The Life of Malchus the Monk")

John Chrysostom (AD 347–407)

Hom. Col.	*Homiliae in epistulam ad Colossenses*
Hom. 1 Cor.	*Homiliae in epistulam i ad Corinthios*
Hom. Eph.	*Homiliae in epistulam ad Ephesios*
Hom. Matt.	*Homiliae in Mattaeum*
Hom. 1 Tim.	*Homiliae in epistulam i ad Timotheum*
Inan. glor.	*De inani gloria (On Vainglory)*
Laz.	*De Lazaro*

Josephus [Jos.] (AD 37–after 93)

Ag. Ap.	*Against Apion*
Ant.	*Jewish Antiquities*
J.W.	*Jewish War*
Life	*Life*

Justin Martyr (d. AD 165)

1 Apol.	*Apologia 1 (First Apology)*
2 Apol.	*Apologia 2 (Second Apology)*
Dial.	*Dialoges cum Tryphone (Dialogue with Trypho)*

Justinian (ca. AD 463–565)

Corp.	*Corpus Iuris (Codex of Justinian)*
Dig. Just.	*Digest of Justinian*
Nov.	*Novellae*

Juvenal [Juv.] (fl. 2nd c. AD)

Sat.	*Satirae (Satires)*

Lactantius [Lac.] (ca. AD 240–ca. 320)

Inst.	*Divinarum Institutionum Libri VII (The Divine Institutes)*
Mort.	*De morte persecutorum (The Death of the Persecutors)*

Livy (59 BC–AD 17)

Ira	*De ira*
Rom. Hist.	*Ab urbe condita libri (Books from the Foundation of the City)*

Lucian of Samosata (ca. AD 120–180)

Alex.	*Alexander (Pseudomantis) (Alexander the False Prophet)*

Nav.	*Navigium (The Ship* or *The Wishes)*
Nigr.	*Nigrinus*
Peregr.	*De morte Peregrini (The Passing of Peregrinus)*
Philops.	*Philopseudes (The Lover of Lies)*
Salt.	*De saltatione (The Dance)*

Macrobius (fl. early 5th c. AD)

Sat.	*Saturnalia*

Martial (ca. AD 40–103)

Ep.	*Epigrammaton*

Methodius (d. ca. AD 311)

Symp.	*Symposium (Convivium decem virginum) (Banquet of the Ten Virgins)*

Minucius Felix (fl. ca. AD 200)

Oct.	*Octavius*

Musonius Rufus (ca. AD 30–100)

Lec.	*Lectures*

Origen [Orig.] (ca. AD 185–254)

Cels.	*Contra Celsum (Against Celsus)*
Comm. Matt.	*Commentarium in evangelium Matthaei*
Prin.	*De principiis (First Principles)*

Ovid [Ov.] (43 BC–AD 14)

Ars	*Ars amatoria (The Art of Love)*
Med.	*Medicamina faciei femineae (Drugs for the Female Face, i.e., Cosmetics)*
Metam.	*Metamorphoses*
Rem. am.	*Remedia amoris (Remedies of Love)*

Palladius of Galatia (fl. AD 420)

Hist. Laus.	*Historia Lausiaca (Lausiac History)*

Palladius (Rutilius Palladius) (fl. ca. 4th–5th c. AD)

Rust.	*De re rustica (On Farming)*

Pausanias (fl. ca. AD 160)

Descr.	*Graeciae descriptio (Description of Greece)*

Pedanius

Mat. med.	*De materia medica*

Persius (AD 34–62)

Sat.	*Satirae (Satires)*

Petronius (d. AD 66)

Sat.	*Satyricon*

Philo (ca. 20 BC–ca. AD 50)

Abr.	*De Abrahamo (On the Life of Abraham)*
Agr.	*De agricultura (On Agriculture)*
Cher.	*De cherubim (On the Cherubim)*

Contempl.	*De vita contemplativa (On the Contemplative Life)*
Decal.	*De decalogo (On the Decalogue)*
Ebr.	*De ebrietate (On Drunkenness)*
Flacc.	*In Flaccum (Against Flaccus)*
Gig.	*De gigantibus (On Giants)*
Her.	*Quis rerum divinarum heres sit (Who Is the Heir of Divine Things?)*
Hypoth.	*Hypothetica (Apology for the Jews)*
Ios.	*De Iosepho (On the Life of Joseph)*
Leg. 1–3	*Legum allegoriae 1–3 (Allegorical Interpretation 1–3)*
Legat.	*Legatio ad Gaium (On the Embassy to Gaius)*
Migr.	*De migratione Abrahami (On the Migration of Abraham)*
Mos. 1, 2	*De vita Mosis I, II (On the Life of Moses 1, 2)*
Mut.	*De mutatione nominum (On the Change of Names)*
Opif.	*De opificio mundi (On the Creation of the World)*
Post.	*De posteritate Caini (On the Posterity of Cain)*
QG	*Quaestiones et solutiones in Genesim (Questions and Answers on Genesis)*
Somn.	*De somniis (On Dreams 1–2)*
Spec.	*De specialibus legibus (On the Special Laws)*
Virt.	*De virtutibus (On the Virtues)*

Philostratus (fl. 3rd c. AD)

Vit. Apoll.	*Vita Apollonii (The Life of Apollonius [of Tyana])*

Pindar

Pyth.	*Pythionikai (Pythian Odes)*

Plato (ca. 429–347 BC)

Apol.	*Apologia (Apology of Socrates)*
Ep.	*Epistulae (Letters)*
Gorg.	*Gorgias*
Leg.	*Leges (Laws)*
Phaed.	*Phaedo*
Phaedr.	*Phaedrus*
Resp.	*Respublica (Republic)*
Symp.	*Symposium*
Theaet.	*Theaetetus*
Tim.	*Timaeus*

Plautus (ca. 250–184 BC)

Aul.	*Aulularia (The Pot of Gold)*
Trin.	*Trinimmus (Three-Dollar Day)*

Pliny the Elder [Pliny] (AD 23–79)

Nat.	*Naturalis historia (Natural History)*

Pliny the Younger (AD 61–113)

Ep.	*Epistulae*
Ep. Tra.	*Epistulae ad Trajanum*
Pan.	*Panegyricus Traiani (Praise of Trajan)*

Plutarch [Plu.] (ca. AD 50–129)

Aem.	*Aemilius Paulus*
Alc.	*Alcibiades*
Arist.	*Aristides*
Caes.	*Caesar*
Cat. Maj.	*Cato Major (Cato the Elder)*
Def. orac.	*De defectu oraculorum (Obsolence of Oracles)*
Luc.	*Lucullus*
Lyc.	*Lycurgus*
Lys.	*Lysander*
Mor.	*Moralia*
Pomp.	*Pompeius*
Quaest. conv.	*Quaestiones convivialum (Table Talk)*
Quaest. rom.	*Quaestiones romanae et graecae (Roman and Greek Questions)*
Rom.	*Romulus*
Sull.	*Sulla*
Tim.	*Timoleon*

Polybius [Polyb.] (ca. 200–118 BC)

Hist.	*Historiae (Histories)*

Polycarp (ca. AD 69–155) (see under *Apostolic Fathers*)

Possidius

Vita Aug.	*Vita Augustini*

Quintilian

Inst.	*Institutio oratoria (The Orator's Education)*

Seneca (ca. 4 BC–AD 65)

Apoc.	*Apocolocyntosis (The Gourdification [of Claudius])*
Ben.	*De beneficiis (Benefits)*
Ep.	*Epistulae morales (Moral Essays)*
Helv.	*Consolationem ad Helviam Matrem (Consolation to His Mother Helvia)*
Ira	*De ira (On Anger)*
Tranq.	*De tranquillitate animi*

Servius (Maurus Servius Honoratus)

Aen.	commentary on Virgil's *Aeneid*

Sextus Empiricus

Pyr.	*Pyrrhoniae hypotyposes (Outlines of Pyrrhonism)*
Math.	*Adversus mathematicos (Against the Mathematicians)*

Socrates Scholasticus (ca. AD 379–ca. 450)
  Eccl. Hist.   *Ecclesiastical History*
Sophocles (ca. 496–406 BC)
  Aj.   *Ajax*
Soranus (fl. 2nd c. AD)
  Gyn.   *Gynaecology*
Sozomen (ca. AD 375–ca. 447)
  Eccl. Hist.   *Ecclesiastical History*
Strabo [Str.] (64 BC–ca. AD 24)
  Geogr.   *Geographica (Geography)*
Suetonius [Suet.] (ca. AD 75–ca. 140)
  Aug.   *Divus Augustus*
  Cal.   *Gaius Caligula*
  Claud.   *Claudius*
  Dom.   *Domitianus*
  Gramm.   *De grammaticis*
  Jul.   *Divus Julius*
  Nero   *Nero*
  Tib.   *Tiberius*
  Vesp.   *Vespasian*
  Vit.   *Vitellius*
Tacitus [Tac.] (AD 56–ca. 117)
  Ann.   *Annales*
  Germ.   *Germania*
  Hist.   *Historiae*
Tatian
  Or.   *Oratio ad Graecos*
Tertullian (ca. AD 160–225)
  An.   *De anima (The Soul)*
  Apol.   *Apologeticus (Apology)*
  Bapt.   *De baptismo (On Baptism)*
  Carn.   *De carne Christi (The Flesh of Christ)*
  Cor.   *De corona militis (The Crown)*
  Cult. fem.   *De cultu feminarum (The Apparel of Women)*
  Fug.   *De fuga in persecution (Flight in Persecution)*
  Idol.   *De idololatria (Idolatry)*
  Jejun.   *De jejunio, adversus Psychicos (On Fasting, against the Psychics)*
  Marc.   *Adversus Marcionem (Against Marcion)*
  Mart.   *Ad martyras (To the Martyrs)*
  Mon.   *De monogamia (Monogamy)*
  Nat.   *Ad nationes (To the Heathen)*

Or.	*De oratione (On Prayer)*
Paen.	*De paenitentia (Repentance)*
Praescr.	*De praescriptione haereticorum (Prescription against Heretics)*
Res.	*De resurrectione carnis (The Resurrection of the Flesh)*
Scap.	*Ad Scapulam (To Scapula)*
Scorp.	*Scorpiace (Against the Scorpion's Sting)*
Spec.	*De spectaculis (The Shows)*
Ux.	*Ad uxorem (To His Wife)*
Virg.	*De virginibus velandis (The Veiling of Virgins)*

Theocritus (fl. early 3rd c. BC)

Id.	*Idylls*

Theodosius

Cod. Theod.	*Codex Theodosianus (Theodosian Code)*

Theophilus (fl. late 2nd c. AD)

Autol.	*Ad Autolycum (To Autolycus)*

Theophrastus (ca. 276–ca. 287 BC)

Char.	*Characteres (Characters)*
Hist. plan.	*Historia plantarum (History of Plants)*

Thucydides (ca. 455–400 BC)

Hist.	*History of the Peloponnesian War*

Varro (116–27 BC)

Rust.	*De re rustica (On Farming)*

Virgil (70–19 BC)

Aen.	*Aeneid*
Georg.	*Georgica (Georgics)*

Xenophon (ca. 428–354 BC)

Anab.	*Anabasis*
Cyr.	*Cyropaedia*
Mem.	*Memorabilia*
Oec.	*Oeconomicus*
Symp.	*Symposium*

Journals and Reference Works

ABD	*Anchor Bible Dictionary*. Edited by D. N. Freedman. 6 vols. New York: Doubleday, 1992
ABR	*Australian Biblical Review*
AcOr	*Acta Orientalia*
AEL	*Ancient Egyptian Literature*. M. Lichtheim. 3 vols. Berkeley: University of California, 1971–1980
AER	*American Ecclesiastical Review*

AF	*Altorientalische Forschungen*
AfO	*Archiv für Orientforschung*
AHB	*Ancient History Bulletin*
AJA	*American Journal of Archaeology*
AJAH	*American Journal of Ancient History*
AJBA	*Australian Journal of Biblical Archaeology*
AJP	*American Journal of Philology*
ANEP	*The Ancient Near East in Pictures Relating to the Old Testament.* Edited by J. B. Pritchard. Princeton: Princeton University, 1954
ANES	*Ancient Near Eastern Studies*
ANESTP	*The Ancient Near East: Supplementary Texts and Pictures Relating to the Old Testament.* Edited by J. B. Pritchard. Princeton: Princeton University, 1969
ANET	*Ancient Near Eastern Texts Relating to the Old Testament.* Edited by J. B. Pritchard. Princeton: Princeton University, Princeton: Princeton University, 1955
ANRW	*Aufstieg und Niedergang der römischen Welt: Geschichte und Kultur Roms im Spiegel der neueren Forschung.* Edited by H. Temporini and W. Haase. Berlin: W. de Gruyter, 1972–
AnSt	*Anatolian Studies*
AntCl	*Antiquité Classique*
Antiq	*Antiquity*
AR	*Archiv für Religionswissenschaft*
ARAB	*Ancient Records of Assyria and Babylonia.* Edited by D. D. Luckenbill. 2 vols. Chicago: University of Chicago, 1926–1927
Arch	*Archaeology*
ArchOd	*Archaeology Odyssey*
ARE	*Ancient Records of Egypt.* Edited by J. H. Breasted. 5 vols. Chicago, 1905–1907. Reprint, New York, 1962
ARMT	Archives royales de Mari, transcrite et traduite
AThR	*Anglican Theological Review*
Aug	*Augustinianum*
AUSS	*Andrews University Seminary Studies*
AW	*Ancient World*
BA	*Biblical Archaeologist*
BAR	*Biblical Archaeology Review*
Barrett	*The New Testament Background: Selected Documents.* Edited by C. K. Barrett. Rev. ed. San Francisco: Harper & Row, 1987
BASOR	*Bulletin of the American Schools of Oriental Research*

BASP	*Bulletin of the American Society of Papyrologists*
BBR	*Bulletin for Biblical Research*
Ber	*Berytus*
BHM	*Bulletin of the History of Medicine*
BI	*Biblical Illustrator*
Bib	*Biblica*
BibInt	*Biblical Interpretation*
BICS	*Bulletin of the Institute of Classical Studies*
BN	*Biblische Notizen*
BRev	*Bible Review*
BSac	*Bibliotheca Sacra*
BT	*The Bible Translator*
BTB	*Biblical Theology Bulletin*
BurH	*Buried History*
BWL	*Babylonian Wisdom Literature.* Edited by W. G. Lambert. Oxford: Clarendon Press, 1960
BZ	*Biblische Zeitschrift*
CAD	*The Assyrian Dictionary of the Oriental Institute of the University of Chicago.* Edited by I. J. Gelb et al. 1956–2010
CAM	*Civilization of the Ancient Mediterranean: Greece and Rome.* Edited by M. Grant and R. Kitzinger. 3 vols. New York, 1988
CANE	*Civilizations of the Ancient Near East.* Edited by J. Sasson. 4 vols. New York: Scribners, 1995. Repr., Peabody, MA: Hendrickson, 2000
CBQ	*Catholic Biblical Quarterly*
CCSL	*Corpus Christianorum Series Latina*
CH	*Church History*
ChrÉg	*Chronique d'Égypte*
CIG	*Corpus inscriptionum graecarum.* Edited by A. Boechth. 4 vols. Berlin, 1828–1877
CIL	*Corpus inscriptionum latinarum*
CJ	*Classical Journal*
CML	*Canaanite Myths and Legends.* Edited by G. R. Driver. Edinburgh: T&T Clark, 1956
COS	*The Context of Scripture: Canonical Compositions from the Biblical World.* 3 vols. Edited by W. W. Hallo and K. L. Younger Jr. Leiden: Brill, 1997–2002, 2003
CP	*Classical Philology*
CQ	*Classical Quarterly*
CSR	*Christian Scholar's Review*
CT	*Christianity Today*

CTA   *Corpus des tablettes en cunéiformes alphabétiques décou-vertes à Ras Shamra-Ugarit de 1929 à 1939.* Edited by A. Herdner. Mission de Ras Shamra 10. Paris: P. Geuthner, 1963

CurTM   *Currents in Theology and Mission*

DANE   *Dictionary of the Ancient Near East.* Edited by P. Bienkowski and A. Millard. Philadelphia: University of Pennsylvania, 2000

DDD   *Dictionary of Deities and Demons in the Bible.* Edited by K. van der Toorn, B. Becking, and P. W. van der Horst. 2nd rev. ed. Leiden: Brill, 1999

DJBA   *A Dictionary of Jewish Babylonian Aramaic.* Edited by M. Sokoloff. Ramat-Gan: Bar Ilan University / Baltimore: Johns Hopkins University, 2002

DOP   *Dumbarton Oaks Papers*

DOTHB   *Dictionary of the Old Testament: Historical Books.* Edited by B. T. Arnold and H. G. M. Williamson. Downers Grove, IL: InterVarsity, 2003

DPL   *Dictionary of Paul and His Letters.* Edited by G. F. Hawthorne, R. P. Martin, and D. G. Reid. Downers Grove, IL: InterVarsity, 1993

DRev   *Downside Review*

EAC   *Encyclopedia of Ancient Christianity.* Edited by A. Di Berardino. 3 vols. Downers Grove, IL: IVP Academic, 2014

EAEHL   *Encyclopedia of Archaeological Excavations in the Holy Land.* Edited by M. Avi-Yonah. 4 vols. London: Oxford University Press, 1975

EDB   *Eerdmans Dictionary of the Bible.* Edited by D. N. Freedman, A. C. Myers, and A. B. Beck. Grand Rapids: Eerdmans, 2000

EDEJ   *The Eerdmans Dictionary of Early Judaism.* Edited by J. J. Collins and D. C. Harlow. Grand Rapids: Eerdmans, 2010

EGA   *Egypt's Golden Age: The Art of Living in the New Kingdom, 1558–1085 B.C.* Edited by E. Brovarski, S. K. Doll, and R. Freed. Boston: Museum of Fine Arts, 1982

EGL & MWBS   *Eastern Great Lakes and Midwest Biblical Societies*

EncJud   *Encyclopaedia Judaica.* Edited by F. Skolnik. 22 vols. Detroit: Macmillan Reference, 2007

EMQ   *Evangelical Missions Quarterly*

ErIsr   *Eretz-Israel*

ETL   *Ephemerides theologicae lovanienses*

EvQ	*Evangelical Quarterly*
Exped	*Expedition*
ExpTim	*Expository Times*
FGrH	*Die Fragmente der griechischen Historiker.* Edited by F. Jacoby. Berlin: Weidmann, 1923
FiHi	*Fides et Historia*
GCS	Die griechische christliche Schriftsteller der ersten [drei] Jahrhunderte
Gibson	John C. L. Gibson. *Canaanite Myths and Legends.* 2nd ed. London: T&T Clark, 2004
GOTR	*Greek Orthodox Theological Review*
GR	*Greece and Rome*
Grant	Galen. *Galen on Food and Diet.* Translated by M. Grant. London: Routledge, 2000
GRBS	*Greek, Roman, and Byzantine Studies*
HAR	*Hebrew Annual Review*
HR	*History of Religions*
HSS	*Harvard Semitic Studies*
HTR	*Harvard Theological Review*
HUCA	*Hebrew Union College Annual*
IBD	*The Illustrated Bible Dictionary.* Edited by J. D. Douglas. 3 vols. Leicester, England: Inter-Varsity, 1980
IDB	*The Interpreter's Dictionary of the Bible.* Edited by G. A. Buttrick. 4 vols. New York: Abingdon, 1962
IEJ	*Israel Exploration Journal*
IJNA	*International Journal of Nautical Archaeology and Underwater Exploration*
Int	*Interpretation*
IOS	*Israel Oriental Studies*
ISBE	*The International Standard Bible Encyclopedia.* Edited by G. W. Bromiley et al. 4 vols. Grand Rapids: Eerdmans, 1979–1988
JAC	Jahrbuch für Antike und Christentum
JANESCU	*Journal of the Ancient Near Eastern Society of Columbia University*
JAOS	*Journal of the American Oriental Society*
JARCE	*Journal of the American Research Center in Egypt*
JASA	*Journal of the American Scientific Affiliation*
JATS	*Journal of the Adventist Theological Society*
JBL	*Journal of Biblical Literature*
JBQ	*Jewish Bible Quarterly*
JCS	*Journal of Cuneiform Studies*

JE	*The Jewish Encyclopedia*. Edited by I. Singer. 12 vols. New York: Funk & Wagnalls, 1907
JEA	*Journal of Egyptian Archaeology*
JECS	*Journal of Early Christian Studies*
JEgH	*Journal of Egyptian History*
JEH	*Journal of Ecclesiastical History*
JESHO	*Journal of the Economic and Social History of the Orient*
JETS	*Journal of the Evangelical Theological Society*
JFA	*Journal of Field Archaeology*
JHI	*Journal of the History of Ideas*
JHIL	*Journal of the History of International Law*
JHS	*Journal of Hellenic Studies*
JJP	*Journal of Juristic Papyrology*
JJS	*Journal of Jewish Studies*
JLH	*Journal of Library History*
JMA	*Journal of Mediterranean Archaeology*
JNES	*Journal of Near Eastern Studies*
JNSL	*Journal of Northwest Semitic Languages*
JQR	*Jewish Quarterly Review*
JRA	*Journal of Roman Archaeology*
JRE	*Journal of Religious Ethics*
JRS	*Journal of Roman Studies*
JSJ	*Journal for the Study of Judaism in the Persian, Hellenistic, and Roman Period*
JSNT	*Journal for the Study of the New Testament*
JSOT	*Journal for the Study of the Old Testament*
JSP	*Journal for the Study of the Pseudepigrapha*
JSS	*Journal of Semitic Studies*
JSSEA	*Journal of the Society for the Study of Egyptian Antiquities*
JTS	*Journal of Theological Studies*
King	*Musonius Rufus: Lectures and Sayings,* rev. ed. Translated by C. King. Createspace, 2011
LAE	*Literature of Ancient Egypt*. W. K. Simpson. New Haven: Yale University, 1972
LS	*Louvain Studies*
MARI	*Mari: Annales de recherches interdisciplinaires*
MDOG	Mitteilungen der Deutschen Orient-Gesellschaft
Meyer	*The Nag Hammadi Scriptures*. Edited by M. Meyer. New York: HarperOne, 2007
MGWJ	*Monatsschrift für Geschichte und Wissenschaft des Judentums*
NEA	*Near Eastern Archaeology*
NEASB	*Near East Archaeological Society Bulletin*

Neot	*Neotestamentica*
Neusner-T	*The Tosefta.* Translated by Jacob Neusner. 2 vols. Peabody: Hendrickson, 2002
Neusner-Y	*The Jerusalem Talmud.* Translated by Jacob Neusner. CD. Peabody: Hendrickson, 2009
NewDocs	*New Documents Illustrating Early Christianity*
NIDNTT	*New International Dictionary of New Testament Theology.* Edited by C. Brown. 4 vols. Grand Rapids: Zondervan, 1975–1985
NIDOTTE	*New International Dictionary of Old Testament Theology & Exegesis.* Edited by W. A. VanGemeren. 5 vols. Grand Rapids: Zondervan, 1997
NovT	*Novum Testamentum*
NTA	E. Hennecke. *New Testament Apocrypha.* Edited by W. Schneemelcher and R. McL. Wilson. Translated by E. Best et al. 2 vols. Philadelphia: Westminster Press, 1965
NTS	*New Testament Studies*
OCD	*The Oxford Classical Dictionary.* Edited by S. Hornblower and A. Spawforth. 3rd ed. Oxford: Oxford University, 1996
ODCC	*The Oxford Dictionary of the Christian Church.* Edited by F. L. Cross and E. A. Livingstone. 3rd ed. Oxford: Oxford University, 1997
OEANE	*The Oxford Encyclopedia of Archaeology in the Near East.* Edited by E. M. Meyers. New York: Oxford University, 1997
OEBA	*The Oxford Encyclopedia of the Bible and Archaeology.* Edited by D. M. Master. 2 vols. Oxford: Oxford University, 2013
OHJDL	*The Oxford Handbook of Jewish Daily Life in Roman Palestine.* Edited by C. Hezser. Oxford: Oxford University, 2010
Or	*Orientalia* (NS)
OrAnt	*Oriens antiquus*
OTP	*Old Testament Pseudepigrapha.* Edited by J. H. Charlesworth. 2 vols. New York, 1983, 1985
PAAJR	*Proceedings of the American Academy of Jewish Research*
PAPS	*Proceedings of the American Philosophical Society*
PEQ	*Palestine Exploration Quarterly*
PGM	*Papyri graecae magicae: Die griechischen Zauberpapyri.* Edited by K. Preisendanz. Berlin, 1928
PloS ONE	Public Library of Science One (http://www.plosone.org/)
PRSt	*Perspectives in Religious Studies*
PSBA	*Proceedings of the Society of Biblical Archaeology*

PSCF	*Perspectives on Science and Christian Faith*
PSTJ	*Perkins School of Theology Journal*
PTS	Patristische Texte und Studien
RA	*Revue d'assyriologie et d'archéologie orientale*
RB	*Revue biblique*
REAug	*Revue des études augustiniennes*
REJ	*Revue des études juives*
RelSRev	*Religious Studies Review*
ResQ	*Restoration Quarterly*
RevExp	*Review and Expositor*
RevQ	*Revue de Qumran (DC Qumrân)*
RHPR	*Revue d'histoire et de philosophie religieuses*
RHR	*Revue de l'histoire des religions*
RIDA	*Revue internationale des droits de l'antiquité*
SciAmer	*Scientific American*
SCJ	*Stone-Campbell Journal*
SecCent	*Second Century*
S.H.A.	*Scriptores Historiae Augustae (Augustan History)*
SJOT	*Scandinavian Journal of the Old Testament*
SJT	*Scottish Journal of Theology*
SPhilo	*Studia Philonica*
SR	*Studies in Religion*
ST	*Studia Theologica*
StPatr	Studia patristica
STRev	*Sewanee Theological Review*
TA	*Tel Aviv*
TAPA	*Transactions of the American Philological Association*
TDNT	*Theological Dictionary of the New Testament.* Edited by G. Kittel and G. Friedrich. Translated by G. W. Bromiley. 10 vols. Grand Rapids: Eerdmans, 1964–1976
TDOT	*Theological Dictionary of the Old Testament.* Edited by G. J. Botterweck and H. Ringgren. Translated by J. T. Willis, G. W. Bromiley, and D. E. Green. 15 vols. Grand Rapids: Eerdmans, 1974–
Them	*Themelios*
TJ	*Trinity Journal*
TS	*Theological Studies*
TSFB	*Theological Students Fellowship Bulletin*
TWOT	*Theological Wordbook of the Old Testament.* Edited by R. L. Harris, G. L. Archer, Jr., and B. K. Waltke. 2 vols. Chicago: Moody Press, 1980
TynBul	*Tyndale Bulletin*

TZ	*Theologische Zeitschrift*
UF	*Ugarit-Forschungen*
USQR	*Union Seminary Quarterly Review*
VC	*Vigiliae Christianae*
VT	*Vetus Testamentum*
WO	*Die Welt des Orients*
WTJ	*Westminster Theological Journal*
YBC	Yale Babylonian Collection
YOS	Yale Oriental Series
ZA	*Zeitschrift für Assyriologie*
ZABR	*Zeitschrift für altorientalische und biblische Rechtsgeschichte*
ZÄS	*Zeitschrift für ägyptische Sprache und Altertumskunde*
ZAW	*Zeitschrift für die alttestamentliche Wissenschaft*
ZDMG	*Zeitschrift der deutschen morgenländischen Gesellschaft*
ZNW	*Zeitschrift für die neutestamentliche Wissenschaft und die Kunde der älteren Kirche*
ZPE	*Zeitschrift für Papyrologie und Epigraphik*

PERIODS, AGES, AND DATES

Aside from a few passages that deal with "beginnings" or "origins" (e.g., Genesis 1–11; Psalm 104; John 1:1–5), the Bible, as received, recounts events in the lives of individuals, tribes, and nations located primarily in the ancient Near East that appear to have occurred over a period of approximately 1800 years, that is, from about 1700 BC to AD 100. The events portrayed in the Bible span a period that saw the development of technology from the use of bronze to the use of iron in the ancient Near East from Anatolia to Mesopotamia to Egypt. This same period saw political development from tribal cultures to the rise (and fall) of major empires—Egypt, Assyria, Babylon, Persia, Greece, and Rome, among others that figure less prominently in the biblical text. Numerous major religions flourished (and many fell out of use) during this same period (e.g., Egyptian, Assyrian, Babylonian, Persian, Greek, and Roman religions as well as Judaism and Christianity), not to mention other religions more local or tribal in character (e.g., Philistine, Aramean, Edomite, and Ammonite).

There is little evidence of how the passage of extended periods of time was marked in pre-history. With the advent of major empires, the reigns of kings and dynasties and the rule of nations began to be used to mark the passage of extended periods of time. Modern convention, of course, marks the passage of time using calendrical dates, which in the Western world are marked as BC (or BCE) and AD (or CE) surrounding the approximate date of the birth of Jesus of Nazareth during the period of the Roman Empire. But it is also a modern convention to use the development of technology to mark long periods of time, e.g., the various Stone Ages, the Copper or Chalcolithic Age, the Bronze Ages, and the Iron Ages. And, further, it remains a convention to mark some periods of time by the rule of political leaders, dynasties, and nations.

The various terms used for periods of time found in this Dictionary are often defined by approximate dates within the articles where they are used and, in the case of periods that covered millennia, closer approximations of the dates of events within a given period are provided. For convenience, however, the following tables provide a list of these periods and ages, as well as the durations of major empires (or dynasties within an empire) marking significant time periods in the ancient Near East, accompanied by their approximate and commonly associated dates.

Technological Ages

Technological ages vary widely from place to place, even within the ancient Near East. The following dates encompassing a given technology should be seen as highly approximate, as representing the ancient Near East generally, and as subject to ongoing scholarly debate. The dates below are intended to provide a general sense of time and are not to be used as a precise guide, simply because technological development is seldom linear.

Neolithic (Late Stone Age)	8500–4500 BC
Chalcolithic (Copper Age)	4500–3500 BC
Early Bronze Age	3500–2250 BC
Intermediate Bronze Age	2250–1950 BC
Middle Bronze Age	1950–1550 BC
Late Bronze Age	1550–1200 BC
Iron Age I (Early Iron Age)	1200–985 BC
Iron Age II (Late Iron Age)	985–586 BC

Political Ages

The dates of empires and dynasties are likewise subject to scholarly debate, which not infrequently includes proposals of "high chronologies" and "low chronologies" or sometimes even of "middle chronologies." Moreover, there was significant overlap among the various empires and dynasties, some of which rose in place of or fell to another, but which more often contested various geographic areas with varying degrees of hegemony at any given time as the politics of a given moment were usually in flux.

Egypt

Predynastic	4000–3150 BC
Early Dynastic (1st to 2nd Dynasties)	3150–2545 BC
Old Kingdom (3rd to 8th Dynasties)	2545–2120 BC
First Intermediate (9th to 10th Dynasties)	2120–1980 BC
Middle Kingdom (11th to 12th Dynasties)	1980–1760 BC

Second Intermediate (13th to 17th Dynasties)	1760–1540 BC
New Kingdom (18th to 20th Dynasties)	1540–1075 BC
Third Intermediate (21st to 24th Dynasties)	1075–722 BC
Late Period (25th to 30th Dynasties)	722–332 BC
Ptolemaic Dynasty	332–30 BC
Roman Period	30 BC–AD 395

Assyria
Old Assyrian Period	1850–1700 BC
Middle Assyrian Period	1360–1060 BC
Neo-Assyrian Period	910–612 BC

Babylon
Old Babylonian Period	1900–1590 BC
Middle Babylonian Period	1590–1100 BC
Neo-Babylonian Period	605–539 BC

Persia   550–331 BC

Greece
Minoan Era	2000–1500 BC
Mycenaean Era	1500–1200 BC
Dark Age	1200–800 BC
Archaic Age	800–500 BC
Classical Era	500–338 BC
Philip II & Alexander of Macedon	338–323 BC

Rome
Founding of Rome	753 BC
Etruscan kings of Rome	753–510 BC
Roman Republic	509–27 BC
Roman Empire	27 BC–AD 476
Roman control of Palestine	63 BC–AD 337

Biblical Chronology

There are two competing chronologies for the period before the monarchy, which are based upon a choice of either an early date for the Exodus of ca. 1450 BC, or a late date for the Exodus of ca. 1250 BC.

	Early Dates	Late Dates
Patriarchs (Abraham–Joseph)	ca. 2150–1850 BC	ca. 1950–1700 BC
Sojourn in Egypt	ca. 1850–1450 BC	ca. 1650–1250 BC
Conquest of Canaan	ca. 1400 BC	ca. 1200 BC
Period of the Judges	1400–1050 BC	1200–1050 BC

The United Monarchy
    Saul   1050–1010 BC
    David   1010–970 BC
    Solomon   970–930 BC

The Divided Kingdoms
    Northern   930–722 BC
    Southern   930–586 BC

The Exilic Period
    Restoration of Jews from Mesopotamia   537 BC
    Rebuilding of the Temple   515 BC
    Return of Ezra   458 BC
    Return of Nehemiah   445 BC
    Malachi, the last prophet   ca. 400 BC

Birth of Jesus   ca. 5 BC

Crucifixion of Jesus   AD 30 or 33

Execution of Paul and Peter   AD 64

Destruction of Jerusalem temple by Rome   AD 70

For the early dates for OT chronology, see G. L. Archer Jr., "The Chronology of the Old Testament," in *The Expositor's Bible Commentary* (ed. F. Gaebelein. Grand Rapids: Zondervan, 1979), 359–74. For the late dates, see K. A. Kitchen, *On the Reliability of the Old Testament* (Grand Rapids: Eerdmans, 2003). For a summary of the arguments, see E. M. Yamauchi, *The Stones and the Scriptures* (Philadelphia: J. B. Lippincott, 1972), 46–50. For more recent bibliography on the ongoing debate, see E. M. Yamauchi, "Akhenaten, Moses, and Monotheism," *NEASB* 55 (2010): 1–15.

For NT chronology, see H. Hoehner, "The Chronology of the New Testament," in *The Expositor's Bible Commentary* (ed. F. Gaebelein. Grand Rapids: Zondervan, 1979), 593–607 and H. Hoehner, *Chronological Aspects of the Life of Christ* (Grand Rapids: Zondervan, 1977). See also J. M. Vardaman and E. M. Yamauchi, eds., *Chronos, Kairos, Christos: Nativity and Chronological Studies Presented to Jack Finegan* (Winona Lake: Eisenbrauns, 1989).

For a detailed general reference see J. Finegan, *Handbook of Biblical Chronology* (rev. ed., Peabody: Hendrickson, 1998).

INTRODUCTION

The *Dictionary of Daily Life in Biblical and Post-Biblical Antiquity* (*DDL*), to be issued in three volumes, was a project begun 30 years ago with the collaboration of the distinguished Old Testament scholar Roland K. Harrison (1920–1993), to whom Marvin Wilson and I dedicate this reference work. In the original conception of the project, Harrison, Wilson, and I were to write all the articles for a work entitled *Dictionary of Bible Manners and Customs.* It subsequently became expedient to engage the research and writing skills of other select scholars of the ancient world.

While there are many excellent Bible dictionaries and encyclopedias, and popular books on biblical backgrounds available, I had noticed a serious deficiency. I noted that while every one of these had an entry on "Abomination," none (with the exception of the six-volume *Anchor Bible Dictionary*) had an entry on "Abortion." Why was this the case? It was because these references were keyed to the words which occurred in the Bible.

From my 40 years of teaching the history of ancient Mesopotamia, Egypt, Greece, Rome, early Judaism, and early Christianity, I was well aware of the widespread practice of abortion, contraception, and infanticide in these societies and epochs. I therefore proposed a new framework for the *DDL*, one based on the Human Relations Area Files, an anthropological grid of human society, which would systematically and comparatively survey different aspects of culture, whether they were highlighted in the Bible or not.

The biblical texts were not intended to give us a complete representation of their worlds. In fact, they take for granted what was well known to both the writers and readers, but of which we are not aware. It is as though we hear the vocalization of an operatic libretto, but do not see the scenery and the costumes of the singers. Thanks, however, to extra-biblical texts and archaeology, we are able to recreate much of the background for the Bible.

For example, what did ancient people eat and drink? In the essay on FOOD PRODUCTION, one will learn that before the introduction of rotary mills, housewives had to labor on hands and knees about four hours a day to grind wheat and barley for their daily bread. Most of the bread in the ancient world was flat (unleavened) bread, because the predominant emmer wheat and the barley in Mesopotamia, Egypt, and Greece did not have the gluten necessary to cause bread to rise.

From the articles on CLOTHING, DYEING, LAUNDRY & FULLERS, and TEXTILES, one would learn that white linen was the preferred textile in Egypt, and was worn by Israelite priests and New Testament angels. How was Jesus dressed? Jesus' sole garments, except for his burial shroud, were woolen. As wool was not easily laundered, his clothes would have been dirty except for the moment of his transfiguration.

How did Jesus appear? From the article on BARBERS & BEARDS, we can conclude with near certainty that Jesus had a beard. Why? Men in antiquity could not shave themselves. They had to resort either to slaves or to barbers for a shave. Moreover, beards were a symbol of masculinity and seniority. The Old Testament word for "elders" is literally "bearded ones."

Where did people live? This would have varied from place to place and from one time period to another. From the article on DWELLINGS, one would learn that in the Old Testament era in Palestine most would have lived in houses with flat roofs and courtyards full of animals. In Rome, 95% of the people would have lived in *insulae*, crowded tenements without kitchens or bathrooms.

What about the relations between men and women? From the articles on EDUCATION and MARRIAGE, one would learn a striking fact, which is missing from both the Old and the New Testaments—the average age of spouses. We learn from our extra-biblical evidence that the bride would have certainly been a young teenager, and the groom several years her senior. The early marriage of girls, to preserve their purity, meant that they had only at best a primary education, with the exception of those from wealthy Roman families, which could afford private tutors for their daughters.

The *DDL* is also quite unique in attempting to trace the developments of the features of the biblical world along what the French historians of the Annales School have called the *longue durée*, that is, over the centuries *after* the New Testament era. It is instructive to understand how the Jewish rabbis, in following the traditions of the Pharisees, debated over the application of biblical laws in changing circumstances, and how the Church Fathers also responded to these same developments.

Rather than attempting to cover all possible topics, we have chosen to concentrate on 120 subjects, not because of their prominence in the biblical text but because of their significant roles in the ancient world. For example, ASTROLOGY, DREAMS, MAGIC, and DIVINATION & SORTITION (i.e., the casting of lots) are mentioned sparingly in the biblical texts themselves but they were dominant facets of life in antiquity.

The outline each contributor has followed is to briefly summarize references to his or her subject in: (1) the Old Testament and (2) the New Testament; followed by (3) the Near Eastern world, primarily Mesopotamia and Egypt, with some references to Anatolia and Persia; (4) the Greco-Roman world, from the Minoans and Mycenaeans, Homer, through the Hellenistic era, the Roman Republic, and the Roman Empire; (5) the Jewish world, including the Old Testament Apocrypha, Pseudepigrapha, Philo, Josephus, the Dead Sea Scrolls, the Mishnah, and the Talmuds (Babylonian and Jerusalem); and (6) the Christian world, including the church fathers up to Chrysostom and Augustine, as well as the early Byzantine empire to Justinian. Each article closes with a bibliography providing both source material for the article and material for further study. Further, the articles are carefully cross-referenced with other articles in print or planned.

The citations from the Old Testament and the New Testament, unless otherwise marked, are from the New International Version. Citations from the Septuagint (LXX) are taken from A. Pietersma and B. G. Wright, trans., *A New English Translation of the Septuagint* (New York: Oxford University Press, 2007). Citations from the Tosefta are taken from J. Neusner, *The Tosefta* (2 vols.; Peabody, MA: Hendrickson, 2013 repr.). Citations from the Midrashim are from the *Soncino Midrash Rabba for Macintosh* (Copyright Institute for Computers in Jewish Life and Davka Corporation, 2008). Citations from the Old Testament Apocrypha are from the Revised Standard Version; those from the Old Testament Pseudepigrapha are from James H. Charlesworth, ed., *The Old Testament Pseudepigrapha* (2 vols.; Garden City, NY: Doubleday, 1983, 1985). The classical citations (including Philo and Josephus) are from the Loeb Classical Library. References to the Dead Sea Scrolls are from *The Dead Sea Scrolls: A New Translation* by Michael Wise, Martin Abegg Jr., and Edward Cook (rev. ed., New York: HarperSanFrancisco, 2005). Citations from the Mishnah are from Herbert Danby, trans., *The Mishnah* (Oxford: Oxford University Press, 1933). Citations from the Babylonian Talmud are from *The Soncino Talmud* (Institute for Computers in Jewish Life and Davka Corporation, 2007); those from the Jerusalem Talmud are from *The Jerusalem Talmud, A Translation and Commentary*, ed. Jacob Neusner (Peabody, MA: Hendrickson Publishers, 2009). With the exception of citations from Michael W. Holmes, *The Apostolic Fathers: Greek Texts and English Translations* (3rd. ed.; Grand Rapids: Baker Academic, 2007), patristic references are from the New Advent, *Fathers of the Church* (www. NewAdvent.org; 2007; © Kevin Knight). Citations from the Nag Hammadi texts are cited from Marvin Meyer, ed., *The Nag Hammadi Scriptures* (New York: HarperOne, 2007).

My deepest gratitude is first of all to Marvin R. Wilson, and to his former student, Andrew Pottorf, who have carefully examined all the essays and provided innumerable edits and corrections. I thank Graham Harrison for allowing us to update and expand his late father's excellent entries. I wish to express my appreciation to all of the contributors, many of whom were my history PhD students at Miami University. My thanks go also to my wife, Kimi, who spent countless hours photocopying pages from books and journals. I am grateful also to Sue Cameron, who has checked the biblical and apocryphal references for me.

My profound thanks go to Allan Emery, senior editor at Hendrickson, for spending much of the final two years before his retirement overseeing this project, and also to Hannah Brown and Carl Nellis. Our appreciation also goes to John F. Kutsko, who assisted with some of the research in the earliest stages of this dictionary project. Special thanks to Foy D. Scalf, Chief Archivist of the Oriental Institute, for supplying me with the sources of many Near Eastern quotations.

Finally, our profound thanks to Jonathan Kline, our new editor at Hendrickson, for his painstaking and meticulous supervision of the work on Volume 2, and to Andrew Pottorf and Rory Crawley for their help.

Edwin M. Yamauchi
April 2015

DEATH & THE AFTERLIFE

Death is the termination of physical life and earthly existence. From time immemorial, the ambiguities and incongruities of death, including the fear it evokes and its finality, have baffled human minds. The search for understanding of this mystery by both the uneducated and the wise has seldom led to a fully satisfying grasp of the meaning of life and human mortality. The ancient world was especially rife with speculations, superstitions, and rituals about death. In our modern, often death-denying world, people do not always have to confront death as the ancients did. In Bible times, families and communities were usually personally and intimately involved in caring for the needs of the dying and the dead. Today, professional specialists are called upon to render these services, thus permitting a certain degree of detachment on the part of the next of kin.

The present discussion focuses on the phenomenon of death in the ancient world. Special attention is given to how peoples of the biblical world coped with the presence of death, what their attitudes were toward it, and any belief they may have had about life after death.

A. THE OLD TESTAMENT

The Hebrew Scriptures point out that death is inescapable: "Like water spilled on the ground, which cannot be recovered, so we must die" (2 Sam 14:14). To die is "to go the way of all the earth" (Josh 23:14; 1 Kgs 2:2). Ideally, people expected to "die a natural death and suffer the fate of all mankind" (Num 16:29), and this, hopefully, at a "good old age" (Judg 8:32; 1 Chr 29:28).

Nevertheless, the OT describes many situations that could bring about an early death. Plagues of locusts brought death through starvation (cf. the book of Joel). Drought and famine were also greatly feared (Gen 41:54–57). Warfare also brought numerous casualties in its wake. Military campaigns were common and were one of the leading causes of death among adult males. The flight of war refugees and the wholesale movement of captives took its toll on life through starvation, dehydration, and exposure. The above two factors—warfare and natural forces—tended to retard the growth of populations in those areas affected. The widespread practice of polygamy, however, helped to compensate for the imbalance of females to males in many lands devastated by war.

Sudden or violent death was also a common occurrence. Death could come by the poisoning of food (2 Kgs 4:40), by stabbing (Judg 3:21), or by an arrow (2 Chr 35:23–24). Some people were stoned to death (Josh 7:25), others burned to death (Dan 3:11; cf. Gen 38:24). A person could be killed by a tent peg and hammer (Judg 4:21), an oxgoad (Judg 3:31), or by the collapse of a building (Judg 16:30). Elisha restored life to a child who apparently had died from sunstroke (2 Kgs 4:19–20).

Israel's concept of death stood in sharp contrast to those of the peoples around her. The Hebrew term for death is *māwet*. Unlike the literature of Ugarit, the Hebrew Bible does not subscribe to nature-worship or to the teaching that death is a deity. Though at various times in Israel's history certain individuals and groups acknowledged the existence of other gods and demonic forces, Yahweh alone claimed Israel's unrestricted gratitude and allegiance. The faith of Israel was monotheistic, set in the context of covenant. In every area of life, Israel was to be dependent on Yahweh, set apart and accountable to him. Since Israel considered Yahweh alone to be sovereign Lord, he, ultimately, was seen to be responsible for an individual's life and death (Deut 32:39). The Lord turns men "back to dust" (Ps 90:3). According to the creation account, death came into the world as punishment for human sin (Gen 3).

The Hebrew Bible declares that humankind was created mortal (Gen 3:19) and that only God is immortal (Isa 43:10). Thus, in contrast to her neighbors, there was no need for Israel to become excessively preoccupied with death and with performing incantations for the dead. Indeed, for everything—including death—there is a season (Eccl 3:1–2).

The Hebrews viewed death as the destiny of all creatures, the end of their life on earth (1 Kgs 2:2; Ps 49:12, 20). Like a ravenous monster, death is described as devouring its helpless victims (Job 18:13; cf. Ps 49:14). In Hebrew thought, death occurs when a person's life-giving forces are gone, his breath ceases, and his vitality has drained away. According to the Hebrew Bible, a living person possesses an animated body. At death, the vital power or "breath" (Heb. *nepeš*) disappears (Gen 35:18; 1 Kgs 17:21), and the "spirit" or "wind" (Heb. *rûaḥ*) returns to God, while the "dust" of the body returns to the earth (Eccl 12:7). The above two Hebrew terms are often used synonymously in the OT. For the Hebrews, the loss of breath is not to be thought of in terms of Greek dualism, which held that at death a "soul" existed in detachment from the corpse. Rather, a human being was considered to be a holistic creature; death was simply the removal of a person's vitality. It was the very opposite of life.

Death is never described in the Hebrew Bible as a pleasant experience or one that leaves the deceased "better off." However, a long life, upright character ("Surely the righteous will never be shaken; they will be remembered forever," Ps 112:6; cf. Num 23:10), and the attentive presence of one's extended family certainly would have helped ease the thought, and inevitable experience, of death. In old age, when one faced the imminent prospect of death, children—especially sons—were an important asset. They would become heirs to the family property (Ruth 4:5, 10), be responsible for carrying on the family name (Gen 30:1), and see that burial and mourning rites were attended to (Gen 50:1–13). Though death was understood to cut one off from serving God and from community relationships, the strong sense of corporate solidarity and mutual dependence among the Hebrews normally allowed them to place the importance of group survival above that of the individual. By any standard, death was painful, for it was seen as separation (Ruth 1:17). Yet people could affirm God's comfort even in the presence of death (Ps 73:23–28; cf. 23:4).

According to the OT, the dead inhabit a region separated from earthly existence known as Sheol (šĕʾôl). This netherworld is where the deceased person "went to his fathers," i.e., ancestors, or was "gathered to his people" (Gen 15:15; 25:8; 35:29). The dead are described as descending to Sheol, which was considered to be located below the earth (Pss 63:9; 139:8; Prov 2:18). This abode of the dead is described as dusty (Job 17:16; 21:26), dark (Ps 143:3; Lam 3:6), and silent (Pss 94:17; 115:17). In this dismal dwelling place people find rest from the weariness and turmoils of life (Job 3:17; Jer 51:39, 57). No earthly splendor or rewards are found there (Ps 49:17; Eccl 9:5). Sheol is the "realm of the dead" (Jonah 2:2); but sometimes the word is found in contexts where it is parallel to "Pit" (Ps 16:10, NJPS).

In Sheol, the dead are described as "shades" (Isa 14:9; 26:14, JPS), ghosts or gloomy shadows of their former earthly existence. They are mere echoes of the living. Sheol, a far-off "land of oblivion" (Ps 88:12), is described as the collecting place for the vast company of the dead (Prov 21:16; cf. Deut 31:16). Some of these "spirits" are recognized as leaders, a distinction seemingly made on the basis of their earthly position (Isa 14:9; Ezek 32:21–32). Though several passages affirm that the power of God reaches even to Sheol (Ps 139:7–8; Amos 9:2), people who have died are also said to be cut off from God's faithful, daily care (Ps 88:5; Isa 38:18). In this dreary existence, the dead have no memory (Ps 6:5; Eccl 9:5) and are not able to praise God (Pss 30:9; 88:10; 115:17). It was widely believed that the dead had no prospect of escape from this "place of no return" (Job 10:21; cf. 2 Sam 12:23).

Despite the general gloominess associated with the netherworld in OT times, there are some hints that the Hebrews believed death did not leave the righteous utterly hopeless. Certain passages suggest that in the future they would yet experience God's redeeming presence in some concrete way (Pss 17:15; 49:15; 73:24; cf. Job 19:25–26). The expression "sleep in death" (Ps 13:3) may suggest an eventual awakening to something different. The explicit development of the Jewish ideas of an afterlife and resurrection, however, came late in OT history. Prior to this, both Enoch (Gen 5:24) and Elijah (2 Kgs 2:10) were taken away to the presence of God without dying. In addition, dead people were restored to life (1 Kgs 17:22; 2 Kgs 4:32–37). While the primary meaning of the Valley of Dry Bones passage in Ezek 37 is that of Israel's national restoration, some scholars take this text as implying a version of resurrection belief (cf. Isa 26:19). In Isaiah's apocalyptic discourse on the universal reign of God (chs. 24–27), the prophet states that Sheol does not terminate God's relationship to his people. Indeed, the Sovereign Lord will "swallow up death forever" (Isa 25:8).

Likewise, Daniel affirms God's ability to conquer death, for both the righteous and the wicked dead: "Multitudes who sleep in the dust of the earth will awake: some to everlasting life, others to shame and everlasting contempt" (Dan 12:2).

It is difficult to say to what extent Jewish belief in resurrection and an afterlife may have been influenced by Zoroastrian teachings. In the sixth and fifth centuries BC, Jews living in Babylonia and other regions were certainly exposed to Persian beliefs, including that of a general resurrection of the dead. It is possible that the decisive impulse on the part of the Jews to articulate their own views on life after death may have come from this Persian setting, with a further refinement of these views occurring during the Hellenistic period. One problem with such an assumption, however, is the late date (9th c. AD) of the Zoroastrian texts that deal with an afterlife.

B. THE NEW TESTAMENT

In the NT, the Greek word *hadēs* ("Hades") is generally similar in meaning to Hebrew *šĕʾôl*. However, it is not always clear from the NT whether Hades was thought to be the location for all the dead, or only of the wicked. Hades is mentioned in the NT as the interim place of the dead between death and resurrection (Luke 16:23; Rev 6:8; cf. 1 Cor 15:55). In John's depiction of the last judgment, "death and Hades were thrown into the lake of fire" (Rev 20:14).

The NT has much to say about death. The emphasis, however, is not so much on coping with the problem of the termination of human life as it is on understanding death as a spiritual problem. Like the OT, the NT considers only God to be immortal (1 Tim 6:16). He alone has the ability to give eternal life to others. The NT teaches that Adam's fall brought physical and spiritual death to the human race (Rom 5:12–19) and that Adam's disobedience has separated humankind from God. Through faith in Christ, the new "Adam," sin is countered and humans are made spiritually alive. By his death, Christ broke the power of sin and death. Christ's resurrection from the dead demonstrated his victory over death (1 Cor 15:26, 54–57; 2 Tim 1:10). Because of this event, those who believe in him have spiritually passed from death to life (John 5:24). The righteous go to "paradise" (Luke 23:43) or to be "with the Lord" (2 Cor 5:8). They also have the assurance that to die "in Christ" means that their physical bodies will one day rise (1 Thess 4:16). In God's new order, in the new Jerusalem coming down out of heaven, "there will be no more death" (Rev 21:4).

Because of the great confidence in Jesus's triumph over death, the term "sleep" (Gk. *koimaō*, the root of *koimētērion*, "cemetery"; see CHRISTIAN WORLD) was sometimes used to express the temporary nature of death. Prior to reviving Lazarus, Jesus says that he "has fallen asleep; but I am going there to wake him up" (John 11:11). Paul also refers, several times, to death as sleep (1 Cor 7:39; 11:30; 15:6, 18, 20, 51), especially to instill in believers the hope of the resurrection: "Brothers and sisters, we do not want you to be uninformed about those who sleep in death, so that you do not grieve like the rest of mankind, who have no hope. For we believe that Jesus died and rose again, and so we believe that God will bring with Jesus those who have fallen asleep in him" (1 Thess 4:13–14).

C. THE NEAR EASTERN WORLD

Mesopotamia

According to scholarly estimates, the average life span in the ancient Near East around the start of the first millennium BC was about forty years, the age of a generation in the biblical estimate (cf. Ps 95:10). Catastrophes of nature claimed many lives. Floods (especially in Mesopotamia) brought drowning.

According to Babylonian creation accounts, the gods created humans in order to relieve themselves of the labor required to maintain the physical world. Humans were created to be servants of the gods, a productive labor force to build temples and offer sacrifices to these deities. These creation accounts suggest that humans were never intended to be immortal. In the

Babylonian flood account found in the *Gilgamesh Epic*, Gilgamesh, ruler of Uruk, sets out on a long and difficult journey to discover the secret of escaping death. Before he locates Utnapishtim, the flood-hero who had received immortality from the gods, he meets the tavern-keeper Siduri, who informs Gilgamesh that his quest is hopeless; humans, she says, are mere mortals whose deaths are ordained by the gods.

> Gilgamesh, whither rovest thou?
> The life thou pursuest thou shalt not find.
> When the gods created mankind,
> Death for mankind they set aside,
> Life in their own hands retaining.
>   (*ANET*, 90)

Gilgamesh tells the immortal one about his fear of death. He asks Utnapishtim what he can do and where he can go because "the Bereaver," death, is lurking in his bedchamber. The troubled Gilgamesh moans to him, "Wherever I se[t my foot], there is death!" (*ANET*, 96).

Mesopotamian mythology also reflects the idea of a cosmic struggle against death. In the Canaanite mythology of Ugarit, *mwt* (Mot) is the god of the netherworld responsible for drought and death, often swallowing his victims (cf. Ps 49:14; 1 Sam 25:8). He puts to death Baal, the god of fertility, forcing the latter to descend to the underworld. Anat, Baal's sister, avenges his death by killing Mot. Baal then comes back from the underworld, effecting the rainy season and the fertility of earth. The death of Death (Mot) springs Baal to life.

Egypt

The Egyptians had a strong preoccupation with death and the afterlife. This fact is probably one of the reasons why the Hebrews, in direct reaction against the beliefs and practices of those in neighboring countries, never developed a detailed system of thought regarding the "age to come" (Heb. *hāʿôlām habbāʾ*). A great desire of every Egyptian was the attaining of a good burial. Even more ideal was to have this take place at a ripe old age, which in Egyptian society was considered to be the age of 110 (cf. Gen 50:26). The gods were believed to allot life or death as they willed. Particularly feared was the goddess Sekhmet, Lady of the Messenger of Death, who knew how to kill by bringing epidemics.

Some scholars argue that when the Egyptians thought of death they may have had in their minds the image of a personified being of horrific form. That is, the Egyptians imagined death as being due to an attack of some evil demon or other awful being. This conclusion is based on a selection of texts, including the following passage from the Coffin Texts of the Middle Kingdom (ca. 2134–1786 BC): "Save me from the claws of him who takes for himself what he sees: may the glowing breath of his mouth not take me away" (Spell 1106; cited in Zandee, 185). A further reason why Egyptians may have viewed the process of dying as the consequence of some hostile attack is found in the fact that the usual hieroglyphic term meaning "to die," *mwt*, had as its determinative sign the picture of a man falling on his knees, with blood streaming from his head. If, however, the Egyptians did think of death in these frightening terms, the actual death-event seems to be omitted from any depiction in Egyptian art.

In Egyptian society, anyone of authority was allowed to prepare a tomb at his own expense. The Egyptians believed that the dead did everything people normally do while alive on earth—ploughing, reaping, eating, drinking, and making love (*The Book of the Dead*, 110). Upon death, great pains were taken to ensure that the grave was well stocked with food and other provisions for the deceased. The body was also carefully preserved through mummification.

Egyptians believed that the spirit of a deceased person continued to live in close relation with the corpse. The cell of the tomb where the corpse was placed became the eternal abiding place of the soul. The soul found rest in this underworld existence, fed by the worship given by the living. Belief in the paradises of gods such as Osiris, and belief in a paradise of the Sun, also provided an attractive escape from the underground existence of the tomb. The cults associated with such beliefs promised their followers great joy in the presence of the deities they had served during their earthly life. The fates of souls were never tied to such paradisaical options, however: each person was free to opt for one of these alternatives of posthumous existence or not.

The Egyptians also believed that entry into paradise was dependent upon successfully passing the judgment of the dead. The recitation of various magic spells or incantations from *The Book of the Dead* by a priest at the funeral ceremony was believed to persuade the divine judges of the person's innocence and to confer on the person a happy life.

Anatolia

In 2008 the University of Chicago expedition led by David Schloen discovered the Katumuwa Stela at the site of Zincirli in southeastern Turkey, at a mound of the ancient city of Samʾal, the capital of a Syro-Hittite kingdom that flourished from 900 to 700 BC. This basalt monument was set up by Katumuwa, an official under King Panamuwa II (r. 743/732–ca. 713/710 BC).

At the arched top of the stela is a damaged image of a winged sun-disk, which represents the god Šamš. Katamuwa, who sits on a straight-backed chair, rests his feet on a footstool. He has a conical cap and wears a fringed garment. His right hand grasps a large drinking bowl and his left hand holds a curved staff with a cone from a coniferous tree. Before him, to the right, is a table that has on it a covered pyxis, perhaps containing spices, a platter with a duck, and another platter with loaves of bread.

In the upper-right register is a well-preserved, thirteen-line inscription in Aramaic that reads as follows:

> I am Katumuwa, servant of Panamuwa, who commissioned for myself (this) stele while still living. I placed it in my eternal chamber and established a feast (at) this chamber: a bull for Hadad Qarpatalli, a ram for NGD/R ŞWD/RN, a ram for Šamš, a ram for Hadad of the Vineyards, a ram for Kubaba, and a ram for my 'soul' [*nbš* = *nabsh*] that (will be) in this stele. Henceforth, whoever of my sons or of the sons of anybody (else) should come into possession of this chamber, let him take from the best (produce) of this vineyard (as) a (presentation)-offering year by year. He is also to perform the slaughter (prescribed above) in (proximity to) my 'soul' and is to apportion for me a haunch [*šq* = *shuq*]. (Pardee, 45)

The god Hadad Qarpatalli may correspond to a Luwian deity. Kubaba was the well-known goddess of the nearby city of Carchemish to the east on the Euphrates River. Quite striking is Katumuwa's reference to his "soul" residing in the stela. "This is the first mention in a West Semitic context of the concept of a soul that was separable from the body" (Herrmann, 17). This stela is a vivid testimony to the widespread concern for establishing rites that would provide nourishment for the dead in the afterlife.

D. THE GRECO-ROMAN WORLD

Greece

Not all Greeks thought exactly the same about death and the afterlife. Views on this subject developed over a number of centuries. We may identify, however, some common ideas that influenced popular beliefs in this area. The Greeks viewed death essentially as a natural event in the cycle of life. They saw no need to explain the origin of death, nor did they view it as a theological problem. If there is an accepted perspective on the afterlife that succinctly presents the passage from death to another world, the epic work of Homer presents this. In order to consult with the deceased Theban prophet Tiresias about Poseidon and their challenges to get home,

Odysseus and his crew carry out libations and sacrifices at the River Ocea-nus in the land of the Cimmerians to attract souls of the dead from Hades. Besides Tiresias, they encounter several other souls, including Odysseus's mother. Upon rushing to embrace her, Odysseus finds that she is no more than a disembodied spirit. She says, "this is the appointed way with mor-tals when one dies. For the sinews no longer hold the flesh and the bones together, but the strong might of blazing fire [the funeral pyre] destroys these, as soon as the life leaves the white bones, and the spirit [*psychē*], like a dream, flits away, and hovers to and fro" (*Od.* 11.218–222). After death, the soul was thus thought to be on its own to join the community of the dead. The dichotomy between body and soul is also mentioned at the very opening of the *Iliad*, Homer's epic account of the Trojan War. According to the poet, Achilles's feud with his fellow captain Agamemnon incurs the wrath of the gods, who afflict the Achaean army with a plague that sends the souls of many warriors to Hades while their selves (i.e., bodies) became spoil for dogs and birds (*Il.* 1.1–5). In contrast, the soul's peaceful separation from the body is generally described in epic and tragic litera-ture as being the result of a proper funeral. Souls of people whose bod-ies were desecrated or left unburied are often described as restless or in pain: see, for example, Patroclus (Hom. *Il.* 23.65–74) and Elpenor (Hom. *Od.* 11.51–80).

In Greek thought, Thanatos is the god of death and darkness, and Hades is the god of the underworld. In order to enter the gates of Hades's realm, the soul of the deceased had to cross a barrier of dark water, a river known as Styx (Hom. *Od.* 10.513). The soul's guide to this strange world of the dead is depicted as the god Hermes, who is assisted by the ferryman Charon. Cerberus, a jagged-toothed hound, is frequently depicted guard-ing the gates of Hades. In Greek literature, the environs of Hades are dark, bleak, and misty. The bodiless souls there have the capacity to speak, but in a weakened and fatigued state because of their separation from the body. The Greeks never envisioned a resurrection of the body. In Aeschylus, the god Apollo observes, "But when once a man has died, and the dust has sucked up his blood, there is no rising again" (*Eumenides* 647–648).

The concept of the soul being immortal in its stay in Hades is found in Homer, especially in the accounts where immortality is conferred upon such famous, legendary heroes as Achilles and Agamemnon. During the sixth to fourth centuries BC, however, the possibility of personal immor-tality was extended to those who lived virtuous, self-critical lives, and to those involved with a closed sect or mystery cult. In the late sixth century BC, belief in the immortality of the soul was found among the followers of Pythagoras of Samos and followers of the poet Orpheus, who apparently considered the soul to be divine and hence immortal.

The classic expression of the immortality of the soul is found in the fourth-century BC works of Plato (*Apol.* 40b–41e; *Phaed.* 66–70, 107–114). According to Plato, the soul has three parts: the rational, the spirited, and the appetitive. He compared the soul to a charioteer (reason) yoked to two horses, one good (courage) and one bad (bodily desires) (*Phaedr.* 246a–d). In its rational element, the soul is divine and preexistent (*Tim.* 69a–e) and eternal (*Resp.* 10.610e–612a). If the body has ruled the soul and polluted it, the soul after death must do penance in a state of bodilessness before being reborn in three further incarnations (*Phaedr.* 249a–b), with a period of one thousand years in between each birth. After a final *katharsis* ("purification"), the soul will enter into the realm of the divine. According to Plato, the incorporeal soul is conscious and retains its self-identity after death (*Resp.* 10.611a).

Aristotle distinguished three types of living organisms that all possess a *psychē* ("soul"). All organisms possess a vegetative or nutritive soul; animals also have the sensitive or appetitive soul; but only man, who has both of the former, additionally has the rational soul with its intellect (*nous*). After death, according to Aristotle, the *nous* loses consciousness.

Homer, Pythagoras, Orpheus, and Plato each refer to judges in the underworld who declare their judgment upon the deeds of the departed. Pythagoras, Orpheus, and Plato refer to various forms of bodily punishment for the wicked, envisaging the basest criminals as undergoing torture.

The possibility that one could leave the gloomy confines of Hades and be mysteriously translated to a blissful life in paradise is attested as early as the seventh century BC. This transfer to the "Isles of the Blessed" (the poet Hesiod's term), however, was at first thought to be a possibility only for heroes, and only later one that could be attained by those who "lived the good life." The *Odyssey* refers to this ocean-bounded, magical land of immortals as "the Elysian field" at the ends of the earth (Hom. *Od.* 4.563–564). This paradise, where "life is easiest for men," has no snow, heavy storms, or rain (Hom. *Od.* 4.565). Later Greek poets such as Pindar elaborated further on the description of this blissful land open to the blessed dead.

The Hellenistic Epicurean and Stoic systems were, for the most part, skeptical about belief in the immortality of the soul. The Epicureans believed that everything is made up of small material "atoms." Upon death these disintegrate and therefore there is no afterlife. The Stoics, who were pantheists, believed that the divine soul survives death but will be absorbed into the Divine. Although the earlier Stoics believed that there is no individual immortality, the later Stoics were willing to believe that at least some souls survive death and continue to exist until the *ekpyrosis*, the final conflagration when everything will be absorbed in the All. It is therefore not surprising that Paul's mention in his speech before the Areopagus of God's raising Christ from the dead (Acts 17:31) caused the Stoics and Epicureans in his audience to sneer at him. Greek intellectuals did not believe a resurrection was possible, and they would not have believed it to be something desirable even if it were.

Rome

Roman beliefs about death and the afterlife, like those of the Greeks, manifested considerable variety, as evidenced from literary texts, funerary art, and funerary inscriptions. By the time of Cicero and Virgil (1st c. BC), many Greek ideas on death had already impacted Roman thought, especially in educated circles. Furthermore, Romans living in the Greek cities of southern Italy drew inspiration concerning the survival of the soul from various groups that followed the Greek thinkers Pythagoras and Orpheus. The Orphics (8th–6th c. BC) were followers of Dionysus. They believed in the divinity of the soul and held that the body is a prison for the soul, expressed in the formula *sōma sēma* ("the body is the tomb").

The early Romans believed in the continuing influence of the dead. During several public festivals, rituals for the dead were performed. Offerings were made to placate the deceased, for it was widely believed that the spirits of the dead had power to harm the living. The dead were often buried with valuable presents. At the tomb, it was common for the living to eat a meal and share some of it with the dead, thereby venerating them.

The average person of the Roman age—especially those of the lower orders—probably had very undefined notions about the afterlife. Since Roman religion espoused no single, accepted position regarding the afterlife, it is quite understandable why the common laboring class was frequently agnostic when it came to otherworldly beliefs. Such people were largely immune from the lofty philosophical speculations of the learned, views that tended to have the greatest impact on small sects.

Nevertheless, belief in an afterlife is expressed in various literary texts. Plautus (ca. 250–184 BC), for example, suggests that departed spirits are able to haunt the homes of the living. He also refers to paintings that depict the tortures of Hades. In Virgil's great Roman epic, the *Aeneid* (*Aen.* 6.426–893), the poet describes the divisions of the underworld. Just inside the gates of Hades is the region where infants, fallen warriors, and others who met a premature death are relegated. Later, this region became known as "Limbo," from the Latin *limbus*, "edge, border," hence the region on the border of Hades. To round out his tripartite division, Virgil tells of one pathway that divides to the left and leads to Tartarus, the region of eternal punishment, and another that veers to the right and leads to the field of

Elysium. From this and other Roman literary texts it is clear that the belief existed—at least in some circles—that a person's conduct in this world had some relation to his destiny beyond the grave. Individuals are responsible for their actions, and they will be judged accordingly. Dying people did fear falling into the hands of various gods who were reputed to be just but vengeful.

The imagery of funerary art, however, tends to be generally optimistic about what awaits the soul in the afterlife. Various depictions of Bacchus, a favorite god of the grave, frequently decorated tombs—especially those of children. Even though people may not have always personally believed the affirmations depicted in both funerary art and inscriptions, these things may have brought consolation and allayed certain fears concerning death. During the Roman period, the figural language of sarcophagi and numerous tombs reflected various uplifting themes of a richer and happier life. These include idyllic countryside scenes with flocks, herds, birds, palm trees, fruit trees, and flower gardens. Other popular motifs were scenes of hunting or of the slaying of savage beasts or enemies. Many tombs contain images of travelers on horses or in carriages, or pictures of ships. These relate to this world, not the life to come. They are reminders that life is a journey or a voyage, and that the weary traveler may be consoled to know that rest awaits him when his trip is over.

E. THE JEWISH WORLD

The OT does not emphasize the immortality of the soul. This concept was eventually picked up by various groups within Judaism from contact with Greek thought, chiefly Platonic philosophy. The dualistic notion of the body being a burden to the soul finds no support in the biblical presentation of the traditional Hebrew anthropology, a perspective that largely upholds the unity of the human person.

Philo expressed a Greek perspective on the soul, which he based on the Genesis account of the creation of Adam:

> For there are two things of which we consist, soul and body. The body, then, has been formed out of earth, but the soul is of the upper air, a particle detached from the Deity: "for God breathed into his face a breath of life, and man became a living soul" (Gen. ii. 7). It is in accordance with reason, therefore, that the body fashioned out of earth has food akin to it which earth yields, while the soul being a portion of an ethereal nature has on the contrary ethereal and divine food; for it is fed by knowledge in its various forms and not by meat and drink, of which the body stands in need. (*Leg.* 3.161)

Philo thought that the soul exists before entering the body. He agreed with the Orphic maxim that "the body is a tomb" (*Leg.* 1.32). As the body is "by nature . . . wicked and a plotter against the soul," there could, according to Philo, be no resurrection of the body (*Leg.* 3.71; cf. *Migr.* 2). Death, for him, is the separation of body and soul (*Leg.* 1.105). At death the soul is liberated from the body and returns to God, where it lives in perpetual contemplation of him.

According to Josephus, the Pharisees believed "that souls have power to survive death and that there are rewards and punishments under the earth for those who have led lives of virtue or vice" (*Ant.* 18.14). Evil souls, according to the Pharisees, are punished in an everlasting prison, while righteous souls can rise from the intermediate place under earth to inhabit other bodies (*J.W.* 2.163). Josephus himself made a philosophical case to his comrades for not committing suicide, basing his argument on the concept of the transmigration (or resurrection) of the soul (*J.W.* 3.361–382). As for the Essenes, Josephus reports that they also believed in the immortality of the soul, though, according to them, virtuous souls do not reenter bodies once they are freed from them through death (*J.W.* 2.154–158). In contrast to the Pharisees and Essenes, the Sadducees did not believe in the afterlife (*J.W.* 2.165).

The apocryphal Wisdom of Solomon also reflects a Hellenistic perspective. According to Wis 2:23–24 (JB), "Yet God did make man imperishable, he made him in the image of his own nature; it was the devil's envy that brought death into the world, as those who are his partners will discover" (cf. also Wis 1:15; 3:4; 8:13, 17; 15:3). While the righteous pass to the fullness of immortality and their souls rest in peace in the presence of God (Wis 3:1–9), the ungodly face the reality of divine punishment they had denied (Wis 4:16–5:2).

A belief in the resurrection of the body was strongly affirmed by the martyrs who died under the persecution of Antiochus IV, as recounted in 2 Maccabees (2 Macc 6:18–7:42). A mother of seven sons encouraged them with the promise that God would restore their bodies, which had been tortured and killed (2 Macc 7:9–29). As he committed suicide, the elderly Razis "tore out his entrails, took them with both hands and hurled them at the crowd, calling upon the Lord of life and spirit to give them back to him again" (2 Macc 14:46). Meanwhile, the tyrant Antiochus was destined to be punished (2 Macc 9:1–12).

The "Book of the Watchers," *1 Enoch* 1–36 (3rd–2nd c. BC), gives the most detailed Jewish description of the afterlife. Enoch is taken on a guided tour of and shown the various abodes of the dead in the west. According to *1 Enoch*, God will awake the spirits of righteous Israelites who await the resurrection:

> The Righteous One shall awaken from his sleep; he shall rise and walk in the ways of righteousness; and all the way of his conduct shall be in goodness and generosity forever. He [God?] will be generous to the Righteous One, and give him eternal uprightness; he will give authority and judge in kindness and righteousness; and they [or "he"] shall walk in eternal light. Sin and darkness shall perish forever, and shall no more be seen from that day forevermore.
> (*1 En.* 92:3–5)

The righteous will live on a transformed earth (*1 En.* 45:4–5). There is a fiery prison for the fallen angels (*1 En.* 21), who will be cast into an abyss of fire (*1 En.* 54:6). And there is an abode for the wicked (*1 En.* 22:9–14), who after judgment will be condemned to eternal punishment in Sheol, now regarded as hell (*1 En.* 103:7).

Fourth Ezra looks for a general resurrection of all the dead, followed by different fates for the righteous and the unrighteous. For the righteous, "death is hidden; hell [*Hades*] has fled and corruption has been forgotten; sorrows have passed away, and in the end the treasure of immortality is made manifest" (*4 Ezra* 8:53–54). After the judgment, "the furnace of Hell shall be disclosed, and opposite it the Paradise of delight" (*4 Ezra* 7:36).

Second Baruch likewise looks for a general resurrection and a judgment after the messiah returns in glory to heaven. The earth "receives them [i.e., the dead] now in order to keep them, not changing anything in their form. But as it has received them so it will give them back" (*2 Bar.* 50:2). After the judgment, "the shape of those who now act wickedly will be made more evil than it is (now) so that they shall suffer torment" (*2 Bar.* 51:2), but as for the righteous, "their splendor will then be glorifed by transformations, and the shape of their face will be changed into the light of their beauty so that they may acquire and receive the undying world which is promised to them" (*2 Bar.* 51:3). Furthermore, "they will be like the angels and be equal to the stars" (*2 Bar.* 51:10).

For much of the time since the discovery of the Dead Sea Scrolls, scholars were not certain whether the Qumran community believed in the resurrection of the dead or not. But the publication of the text 4Q521 now confirms that the members of this community believed that the messiah would be able to raise the dead: "In his mercy he will judge, and the reward of good deeds shall be withheld from no-one. The Lord will perform wonderful deeds such as have never been, as he said: for he will heal the wounded, make the dead live (*umtym yhyh*), proclaim good news to the meek, give generously to the needy, lead out the captive and feed the hungry" (4Q521 2 II, 9–13; cited in Davies, 208).

It is well known that the Sadducees denied the resurrection (Matt 22:23‖Mark 12:18; Acts 23:8), holding the law of Moses (which omits specific mention of the resurrection) as the only authoritative part of the Hebrew Bible (cf. *b. Sanh.* 90a).

The Pharisees, on the other hand, affirmed the fundamental doctrine of bodily resurrection (cf. Acts 23:6–7; 24:14–15). They believed that the ungodly were punished and the righteous rewarded (cf. *Pss. Sol.* 14:9–10; 15:11–13). The Mishnah declares forcefully, "All Israelites have a share in the world to come. . . . And these are they that have no share in the world to come; he that says that there is no resurrection of the dead prescribed in the Law" (*m. Sanh.* 10.1).

The Talmud states that "nine hundred and three forms of death have been created in this world," a number derived from the numerical value of the Hebrew word *tôṣāʾôt*, which in Ps 68:21 (Eng. 68:20) refers to "exits" or "escapes" from death (*b. Ber.* 8a). In this passage the rabbis make a midrashic diversion from the exegetical meaning of "escape" or "deliverance" from death (v. 21[20]), suggesting a different layer of meaning that emphasizes the many ways of death, some methods peaceful and others painful or violent. According to the rabbis, an easy death is referred to as "kind (death) by a kiss" (ibid).

Elsewhere in the Talmud (*b. Sanh.* 90b) it is recorded that Rabbi Simai reasoned: "How do we know that the resurrection of the dead can be derived from the Torah? From the verse, 'I also established My covenant with them [that is, Abraham, Isaac, and Jacob], to give them the land of Canaan' (Exod 6:4). 'To you' is not written but 'to them.' Hence, resurrection of the dead can be derived from the Torah" (Levenson, 28). In another place, Rab declared: "The future world is not like this world. In the future world there is no eating nor drinking nor propagation nor business nor jealousy nor hatred nor competition, but the righteous sit with their crowns on their heads feasting on the brightness of the divine presence, as it says, 'And they beheld God, and did eat and drink' (Exod 24:11)" (*b. Ber.* 17a).

In the important daily prayer called the *Shemoneh Esreh* (Eighteen Benedictions), or the *Amidah* (Standing Prayer), which was established in the first century of the Common Era and is recited three times each day and four times on the Sabbath, the pious Jew repeats four times: "You are mighty forever, my Lord. You are the one who revives the dead, powerful to save" (cited in Levenson, 3).

In the period prior to the destruction of the temple in AD 70, Jews in Israel practiced the secondary reburial of bones, a year after a person's death, in ossuaries, which took the form of decorated limestone boxes. Many of these are inscribed with names, including that of Caiaphas the high priest and names that may be identified with the Cyrenians mentioned in the NT. (See BONES & OBJECTS OF BONE.)

In Beth She'arim in Galilee a large Jewish necropolis with numerous catacombs was uncovered in excavations in the 1930s and 1950s. During the second through the fourth centuries AD, the site became the central burying place for Jewish leaders not only from Israel but also from the Diaspora. The catacombs are richly decorated with Jewish symbols such as the Torah ark, the menorah, and the shofar, and also with images from Greco-Roman mythology. Catacomb 20 contained over 130 limestone sarcophagi. Catacomb 14 contained inscriptions that mention Rabbi Simon, Rabbi Gamaliel, and Rabbi Hanina; it is possible that Rabbi Judah (*ha-Nasi*, "The Prince"), who compiled the Mishnah, was also interred in this catacomb.

Six Jewish catacombs were located in Rome: the catacomb of Monteverde, one at the Vigna Randanini, two at the Villa Torlonia, and two smaller hypogea at the Villa Labicana and at the Vigna Cimarra.

F. THE CHRISTIAN WORLD

The NT reaffirms the Jewish belief in the resurrection of man as an embodied spirit as God's gracious gift, following the firstfruits of Christ's resurrection (1 Cor 15:20). Early Christians proclaimed their faith in their funerary inscriptions, such as one that reads: "Here rests my flesh; but at the last day, through Christ, I believe it will be raised from the dead" (Withrow, 432). In denial of the finality of death, another inscription reads: "You, well-deserving one, having left your (relations), lie asleep in peace—you will arise—a temporary rest is granted you" (Withrow, 432). Such funerary inscriptions contrast starkly with the despair sometimes exhibited in pagan inscriptions, such as: "Neither to you nor to us was it granted to live forever" (Withrow, 438).

The Platonic idea of the immortality of the soul and the worthlessness of the body influenced some strains of early Christianity. The Coptic *Gospel of Thomas* declares that "Whoever finds the meaning of these words will not taste death" (logion 1; Bethge et al., 7) and promises that "Whoever has come to know the world has found a corpse. And whoever has found (this) corpse, of him the world is not worthy" (logion 56; Bethge et al., 20). This reflects the dualistic view that the body is inherently evil. The Valentinian *Gospel of Philip* declares (56.26–30), "Some are afraid lest they rise naked. Because of this they wish to rise in the flesh, and [they] do not know that it is those who wear the [flesh] who are naked" (Isenberg, 144). The Valentinian *Treatise on the Resurrection* (*Epistle to Rheginus*) teaches that the body is destined to die, but, for the Gnostic, the "true self" never dies, since it ascends to God when it is separated from the body (45.14–48.3).

The Gnostic in life already has the "resurrection" (49.9–36; cf. 2 Tim 2:18). Epiphanius reports that according to a gnostic sect called the Archontics, "there is no resurrection of the flesh, only of the soul" (*Pan.* 40.2–5; Williams, 263).

Unlike the gnostics, the apologist Justin Martyr denied the immortality of the soul. He believed in the reward and punishment of souls in the intermediate period between death and resurrection. The wicked, in his view, would be punished in everlasting fire. Justin's student Tatian declared: "The soul is not in itself immortal, O Greeks, but mortal. Yet it is possible for it not to die. If, indeed, it knows not the truth, it dies, and is dissolved with the body, but rises again at last at the end of the world with the body, receiving death by punishment in immortality" (*Oratio ad Graecos* 13.1).

Origen, who was heavily influenced by Middle Platonic ideas, espoused some unconventional ideas about the soul. He believed that souls are preexistent (*Prin.* 1.7.4), that they are immortal (*Cels.* 3.60, 81), and that they will undergo transmigration into different bodies (*Cels.* 7.32; *Comm. Matt.* 11.17; Jerome, *Epist.* 124.7). He believed that both angels and demons have an ethereal, luminous body, an *ochēma*, or "vehicle," of the soul (*Comm. Matt.* 17.30; *Prin.* Preface, 8). The resurrected body, in his view, will not be a physical body but rather a similar, luminous body (*Prin.* 2.2.1–2; 3.6.3–5). In his *Dialogue with Heraclides* (10–27), Origen disputes the view of the Thnetopsychics, who identified the soul with the blood and held that the soul dies when the body does. Origen's reading of such NT passages as 1 Cor 3:12–15 led him to believe that immediately upon death the just enter into paradise to be with Christ (*Prin.* 2.11.6). Origen was also universalistic, believing that all of the wicked in hell would eventually be redeemed, after being refined by fire. Likewise, he considered it possible for Satan himself to repent (*Prin.* 3.6.5–6).

Gregory of Nyssa, who was influenced by Origen, held that the resurrection will return the just to the original state of grace, and that the resurrected body will be transformed from its crass construction into something more fine and delicate. Unlike Origen, Basil held that it is only after the saints have become the "children of the resurrection" (see Luke 20:36) that they can share the face-to-face intimacy with God enjoyed by the angels (*Homily* 16:11).

Origen's views were condemned as heretical by Methodius of Olympus for denying the resurrection. Methodius affirmed the identity of the resurrected body with the previous material body of the deceased. Like most church fathers, he believed in an intermediate period before the righteous achieve complete salvation at the day of the final resurrection.

According to Irenaeus,

the souls of His disciples also, upon whose account the Lord underwent these things [i.e., descended to the dead], shall go away into the invisible place allotted to them by God, and there remain until the resurrection, awaiting that event; then receiving their bodies, and rising in their entirety, that is bodily, just as the Lord arose, they shall come thus into the presence of God. (*Haer.* 5.31.2)

Tertullian and other church fathers made an exception for martyrs, who, they believed, bypass Hades and immediately enter the presence of Christ. Time spent in Hades is remedial, as souls undergo "some compensatory discipline" (*An.* 58). According to Tertullian (*Mon.* 10), the prayers of the living can bring relief to the souls of the righteous.

Augustine held that mankind can be divided into three classes: the good, the bad, and those in between. For the evil, judgment and punishment begin immediately after death. The faithful can enjoy the beatifying presence of God even before their souls are reunited with their bodies. Augustine's belief in the efficacy of prayers for those who die in the communion of the church (*Civ.* 21.24) and his belief in the purifying fire after death (*Civ.* 21.26) eventually led to the development, in the Middle Ages, of the doctrine of Purgatory.

In conformity with Jewish practice and in contrast to the Roman custom of cremation, the Christians practiced inhumation (i.e., burial of the dead). The word "cemetery" is derived from Lat. *coemeterium*, which in turn is derived from the Greek word *koimētērion*, which originally meant a "place to sleep." In the early stages of Christianity believers were buried according to family traditions and in common burial plots. Beginning with the martyrdom of Polycarp (d. 156), special care was given to the remains of martyrs. Polycarp's body was cremated by his executioners. The account of his martyrdom relates: "We afterwards took up his bones, as being more precious than the most exquisite jewels, and more purified than gold, and deposited them in a fitting place, whither, being gathered together, as opportunity is allowed us, with joy and rejoicing, the Lord shall grant us to celebrate the anniversary of his martyrdom" (*Mart. Pol.* 18). Special shrines, or *martyria*, were built over the remains of the martyrs.

Pagans attacked Christian burials. As Tertullian remarked, "With the very frenzy of the Bacchanals, they do not even spare the Christian dead, but tear them, now sadly changed, no longer entire, from the rest of the tomb, from the asylum we might say of death, cutting them in pieces, rending them asunder" (*Apol.* 37.2). After the persecution and killing of Christians at Lugdunum (Lyons) in Gaul (modern-day France), the governor had their bodies burned and their ashes thrown into the Rhone River. As Eusebius explained:

And this they did, as if able to conquer God, and prevent their new birth; "that," as they said, "they may have no hope of a resurrection, through trust in which they bring to us this foreign and new religion, and despise terrible things, and are ready even to go to death with joy. Now let us see if they will rise again, and if their God is able to help them, and to deliver them out of our hands." (*Hist. eccl.* 5.1.63)

The word "catacomb" comes from the Greek phrase *kata kymbas*, "at the hollows." Burials of early Christians in the catacombs of Rome began in the second century. There are seven pre-Constantinian Christian catacombs in Rome. An additional thirty-five hypogeas were dug, all outside of the walls of the city. One of these, which was located in an area known as the "*scalone* of 1897," has four hundred tombs in underground galleries that extend 135 meters. Another, associated with the Flavii Aurelii, contained about 250 burials. A famous catacomb is that associated with Domitilla, niece of the emperor Domitian. The catacomb of the Via Latina was only discovered in 1956. It has been estimated that, all told, the catacombs contained thirty thousand to fifty thousand burials. The catacombs contain some of the earliest examples of Christian art; a popular motif is the visit of the magi.

After the conversion of Constantine and the cessation of martyrdom, Christians focused their veneration upon the relics of the martyrs, in some cases going so far as to exhume and dismember the bodies of martyrs, as we learn from legislation issued by the emperor Theodosius in 386, which forbade the practice. (See Rebillard, 65–66.)

St. Peter's Basilica in the Vatican was built over the traditional site of the martyrdom of Peter, which was believed to have taken place during the Neronian persecution of AD 64. Excavations under the altar area in the 1930s revealed remains of the *aedicula*, or memorial, erected to St. Peter about AD 160, which was mentioned by Gaius around the year 200. Bones that were uncovered in 1965 were declared to be Peter's by Pope Paul VI in 1968, based on M. Guarducci's interpretation of graffiti located nearby. Paul's traditional burial place is at a church by the Via Ostiense.

BIBLIOGRAPHY: B. Alster, ed., *Death in Mesopotamia* (1980); J. Assmann, *Death and Salvation in Ancient Egypt* (2005); A. J. Avery-Peck and J. Neusner, ed., *Judaism in Late Antiquity IV: Death, Life-After-Death, Resurrection and the World-to-Come in the Judaisms of Antiquity* (2000); N. Avigad and B. Mazar, "Beth She'arim," *EAEHL* 1.229–47; L. R. Bailey, *Biblical Perspectives on Death* (1979); R. Bauckham, *The Fate of the Dead: Studies on the Jewish and Christian Apocalypses* (1998); A. Bernstein, *The Formation of Hell: Death and Retribution in the Ancient and Early Christian World* (1993);

H.-G. Bethge et al., trans., *The Fifth Gospel: The Gospel of Thomas Comes of Age*, with contributions by S. J. Patterson and J. M. Robinson (1998); E. Bloch-Smith, "Death and Burial, Bronze and Iron Age," *OEBA* 1.254–62; E. Bloch-Smith, *Judahite Burial Practices and Beliefs about the Dead* (1992); S. Campbell and A. Green, ed., *The Archaeology of Death in the Ancient Near East* (1995); D. K. Cassell and R. C. Salinas, ed., *The Encyclopedia of Death* (2003); J. Clark-Soles, *Death and the Afterlife in the New Testament* (2006); P. R. Davies, "Death, Resurrection, and Life After Death in the Qumran Scrolls," in *Judaism in Late Antiquity*, ed. J. Neusner, A. J. Avery-Peck, and B. Chilton (2001), 3:189–211; A. de Buck, *The Egyptian Coffin Texts* vol. VII (1961); N. Denzey-Lewis, "Death and Burial in the Roman World," *OEBA* 1.280–86; F. Dunand and R. Lichtenberg, *Mummies and Death in Egypt* (2006); J. H. Ellens, ed., *Heaven, Hell, and the Afterlife: Eternity in Judaism, Christianity, and Islam* (3 vols., 2013); M. Erasmo, *Reading Death in Ancient Rome* (2008); R. Garland, *The Greek Way of Death* (1985); L. A. Greenberg, *"My Share of God's Reward": Exploring the Roles and Formulations of the Afterlife in Early Christian Martyrdom* (2009); J. Griffin, *Homer on Life and Death* (1980); M. Guarducci, *The Tomb of St. Peter: The New Discoveries in the Sacred Grottoes of the Vatican* (1960); R. S. Hallote, *Death, Burial, and Afterlife in the Biblical World* (2001); L. R. Hennessey, "Origen of Alexandria: The Fate of the Soul and the Body after Death," *SC* 8.3 (1991), 163–78; V. R. Herrmann and J. D. Schloen, ed., *In Remembrance of Me: Feasting with the Dead in the Ancient Middle East* (2014); M. Himmelfarb, *Ascent to Heaven in Jewish and Christian Apocalypses* (1993); M. Himmelfarb, *Tours of Hell: An Apocalyptic Form in Jewish and Christian Literature* (1983); V. M. Hope, *Roman Death: Dying with the Dead in Ancient Rome* (2009); E. Hornung, *The Ancient Egyptian Books of the Afterlife* (1999); K. J. Illman, *Old Testament Formulas about Death* (1979); W. W. Isenberg, trans., "The Gospel of Philip (*II, 3*)," in *The Nag Hammadi Library in English*, ed. J. M. Robinson (3rd ed., 1988), 139–60; S. Jellicoe, "Hebrew-Greek Equivalents for the Nether-World, Its Milieu and Inhabitants, in the Old Testament," *Textus* 8 (1973), 1–19; P. Johnston, *Shades of Sheol* (2002); M. King and G. J. Oliver, ed., *The Epigraphy of Death: Studies in the History and Society of Greece and Rome* (2000); P. Kousoulis, ed., *Ancient Egyptian Demonology* (2011); M. Lamm, *The Jewish Way in Death and Mourning* (1969); B. Lang, *Life After Death in the Prophetic Promises* (1986); J. D. Levenson, *Resurrection and Restoration of Israel* (2006); T. J. Lewis, *Cults of the Dead in Ancient Israel and Ugarit* (1989); R. Longenecker, ed., *Life in the Face of Death* (1998); J. H. Marks and R. M. Good, ed., *Love and Death in the Ancient Near East* [Marvin Pope Festschrift] (1982); R. Martin-Achard, *From Death to Life* (1960); B. R. McCane, "Death and Burial, Hellenistic and Roman Period, Palestine," *OEBA* 1.262–70; L. Mills, ed., *Perspectives on Death* (1966); M. S. Mirto, *Death in the Greek World: From Homer to the Classical Age* (2012); G. W. Nickelsburg, *Resurrection, Immortality and Eternal Life in Inter-Testamental Judaism* (1972); R. J. Osborn, *Death Before the Fall: Biblical Literalism and the Problem of Animal Suffering* (2014); D. Pardee, "The Katumuwa Inscription," in Herrmann and Schloen, 45–48; É. Rebillard, *The Care of the Dead in Late Antiquity*, trans. E. T. Rawlings and J. Routier-Pucci (2009); I. A. Richmond, *Archaeology and the After-Life in Pagan and Christian Imagery* (1950); B. Schmidt, *Israel's Beneficent Dead* (1994); J. A. Scurlock, "Death and the Afterlife in Ancient Mesopotamian Thought," *CANE* 4.1883–93; K. Spronk, *Beatific Afterlife in Ancient Israel and the Ancient Near East* (1986); K. B. Stern, "Death and Burial in the Jewish Diaspora," *OEBA* 1.270–80; J. Stevenson, *The Catacombs: Life and Death in Early Christianity* (1978); J. H. Taylor, ed., *Journey Through the Afterlife: Ancient Egyptian Book of the Dead* (2010); J. M. C. Toynbee, *Death and Burial in the Roman World* (1971); N. J. Tromp, *Primitive Conceptions of Death and the Nether World in the Old Testament* (1969); F. Williams, trans., *The Panarion of Epiphanius of Salamis* (rev. ed., 1997); W. H. Withrow, *The Catacombs of Rome: And Their Testimony Relative to Primitive Christianity* (6th ed., 1895); J. Zandee, *Death as an Enemy according to Ancient Egyptian Conceptions*, trans. W. F. Klasens (1960).

MRW

See also AGE & THE AGED, DEMONS, DISEASES & PLAGUES and MOURNING & WEEPING.

D̄EMONS

The belief in evil spirits or demons, who at times possessed humans and caused illnesses, was widely held in the ancient world.

A. THE OLD TESTAMENT

In general, the demonology of the OT is quite restrained. There are no cases of exorcism recorded. Both good and evil spirits are depicted as under the control of Yahweh. Examples of such evil spirits are the one that tormented Saul after the "Spirit of the LORD had departed" from him (1 Sam 16:14–23) and the lying spirit that deceived Ahab (1 Kgs 22:19–23||2 Chr 18:18–22). Even Satan, a word that appears in only three books in the OT, is described as being under the control of Yahweh. The word *śāṭān*, "accuser" or "adversary," occurs as a descriptive term fourteen times in Job (1:6–9, 12; 2:1–4, 6–7), where it appears with the definite article. In Zechariah the prophet sees a vision in which the *śāṭān* accuses a high priest named Joshua (Zech 3:1–2). In 1 Chr 21:1 Satan (without the definite article, hence a proper name) incites David to take a census of Israel.

The name of the god of Ekron, Baal-Zebub (2 Kgs 1:2–3, 6, 16), "lord of the flies," is probably a pejorative Hebrew play on Baal-Zebul, "princely lord" (cf. Ugaritic). Later, in Judaism (as reflected, for example, in the NT), Beelzebul became the prince of demons.

The *šēdîm* (sing. *šēd*; only the pl. is used in the Bible), which were considered to be protective genii by the Babylonians and Assyrians, were worshipped by the apostate Israelites (Deut 32:17; Ps 106:37–38). In Ps 106:37 the LXX (Ps 105:37) translates *šēdîm* as *daimoniois*, "demons." Another Hebrew word that some have considered to denote demons is *śĕ'îrîm* (sing. *śā'îr*). The LXX translates *śĕ'îrîm* in 2 Chr 11:15 as *tois eidōlois kai tois mataiois*, "idols and worthless things" (cf. Lev 17:7, where the NIV translates *śĕ'îrîm* "goat idols"). In some texts, such as Isa 13:21 and 34:14, the terms *śā'îr/śě'îrîm* may represent either wild animals or "hairy demons" (cf. RSV "satyrs"; LXX *daimonia*).

Another interesting case of the use of a Mesopotamian name for a demon in Israel is the reference to the *lîlît* in Isa 34:14, which the KJV translators rendered as "screech owl" (NIV, "night creatures"). The RSV has rendered the word "night hag"; the NJPS has "the lilith." One problem, however, with interpreting the words *śā'îr* and *lîlît* in Isa 34:14 as referring to demons is that other words in the context that describe the creatures that inhabit the ruins of Edom appear to denote real animals.

The following assurances of Ps 91:5–6 were regarded by later Jews and Christians as a protection against demons: "You will not fear the terror [*pahad*] of night, nor the arrow [*ḥēṣ*] that flies by day, nor the pestilence [*deber*] that stalks in the darkness, nor the plague [*qeṭeb*] that destroys at midday." In Hab 3:5, we read: "Plague [*deber*] went before him; pestilence [*rešep*] followed his steps." At Ebla, Deber was a demon who caused pestilence; and at Ugarit, Resheph was a plague god.

B. THE NEW TESTAMENT

The central place of Satan (*satanas*), or the devil (*diabolos*, the "Accuser"), in the NT as the adversary of Christ can hardly be gainsaid (see Matt 4:1–11; Mark 1:13; Luke 4:1–13; Rev 20:2). He who is named Beelzebul (Matt 10:25) is the "prince of demons" (Matt 12:24; Mark 3:22; Luke 11:15). He is also called *ho ponēros*, "the evil one" (Matt 13:19), and *ho peirazōn*, "the tempter" (1 Thess 3:5).

The usual Greek word for demon, *daimōn*, is used but once in the NT (Matt 8:31). In its stead is used the diminutive form *daimonion*, which occurs over fifty times in the Gospels (Matt 11x, Mark 13x, Luke 3x, and John 6x) and Acts. The phrase *pneuma akatharton* ("unclean spirit") and related phrases occur about two dozen times in the NT, with slightly fewer than half the occurrences in Mark. The word *ponēros* ("evil") is used with "spirit" eight times. The verb *daimonizomai* ("to be demon-possessed") is used thirteen times. Mary Magdalene is said to have had seven demons (Luke 8:2). The so-called Gadarene (Gergesene or Gerasene) demoniac says his name is "Legion," because so many demons inhabit him (Mark 5:9||Luke 8:30). A Roman legion had from five thousand to six thousand soldiers.

Among the most striking miracles Jesus performed were his numerous exorcisms, described in the Synoptic Gospels. Of the thirteen healing stories in Mark, four deal with exorcisms. John's Gospel does not record any exorcisms, but does report accusations that Jesus was "demon-possessed"

(John 7:20; 8:48–52; 10:20–21). Another (unnamed) exorcist is mentioned in the Synoptic Gospels (Mark 9:38 ||Luke 9:49), as is the fact that the Jews practiced exorcisms (Matt 12:27||Luke 11:19).

In NT times, demon possession was sometimes associated with epilepsy, a disease that is described in the Gospels (Matt 17:14–18||Mark 9:14–27||Luke 9:37–43). Jesus's repeated peremptory command *exelthe* ("Come out!"; Mark 1:25; 5:8–9; 9:25) has some parallels in the late *Papyri Graecae Magicae* (*PGM* IV.1243, 1245, 3013; V.158). In the Gospels, the exorcisms of Jesus serve to prepare for his coming triumph over Satan and his demons. Matthew 25:41 records Jesus's teaching that there will be a special place of punishment for these beings.

Satan, or the devil, is mentioned in only four places in the book of Acts. When Peter confronts Ananias and Sapphira, he says that their hearts have been filled by Satan (Acts 5:3). Peter preaches to Cornelius about how Jesus healed those under the power of the devil (Acts 10:38). Later, Elymas is called a "child of the devil" (Acts 13:10) by Paul. Paul also recounts how he was called to go as an ambassador to deliver Gentiles from the power of Satan (Acts 26:18). In addition, Paul exorcises a slave girl with a *pneuma pythōna*, or "spirit of divination," at Philippi (Acts 16:16–18). At Ephesus some Jews, including the seven sons of Sceva, were exorcising evil spirits "in the name of Jesus" (Acts 19:13–16).

The NT epistles use many different terms to describe spiritual forces that oppose the church. In 2 Cor 6:15 Paul asks: "What harmony is there between Christ and Belial [Gk. *Beliar*]?" Demons as such are mentioned in the Pauline corpus in 1 Cor 10:18–21, where those who sacrifice to idols are said to actually sacrifice to demons (cf. Deut 32:17 LXX), and in 1 Tim 4:1, where Paul warns of heretics who will follow "things taught by demons."

Paul also mentions *stoicheia*, translated "elemental spiritual forces" (Gal 4:3, 9; Col 2:8, 20), which were probably believed to be hostile spirits, as indicated by the later, apocryphal *Testament of Solomon*. Paul speaks of Satan as "the ruler of the kingdom of the air" (Eph 2:2). In Eph 6:12 Paul declares: "For our struggle is not against flesh and blood, but against the rulers [*archas*], against the authorities [*exousias*], against the powers of this dark world [*kosmokratoras*] and against the spiritual forces of evil in the heavenly realms [*epouraniois*]." Paul promises, "Then the end will come, when [Christ] hands over the kingdom to God the Father after he has destroyed all dominion, authority and power" (1 Cor 15:24).

James, remarking that faith without works is vain, asserts, "You believe that there is one God. Good! Even the demons believe that—and shudder" (Jas 2:19). He contrasts God's wisdom with the earthly wisdom that is "demonic" (Jas 3:15).

Passages that reflect the interpretation of "the sons of God" mentioned in Gen 6:2 as fallen angels, which was developed in intertestamental Jewish sources such as *Enoch* and *Jubilees*, are found in a number of the Catholic Epistles (e.g., 1 Pet 3:18–20; 2 Pet 2:4; Jude 6). Jude 14 explicitly cites *Enoch*.

In the Apocalypse of John the *drakōn* ("dragon") who is mentioned thirteen times is identified with "that ancient serpent called the devil, or Satan" (Rev 12:9). The worship of idols is equated with the worship of demons (Rev 9:20). Reflecting the words of the prophet Isaiah, the author writes that the future fallen city of Babylon (i.e., Rome) will become "a dwelling for demons and a haunt for every impure spirit, a haunt for every unclean bird, a haunt for every unclean and detestable animal" (Rev 18:2).

C. THE NEAR EASTERN WORLD

Every Near Eastern culture believed in different demons who punished mankind with diseases and disasters. This was most notably the case in Mesopotamia, and less so in Egypt. In Mesopotamia demons are not prominent in mythological texts but are mainly referred to in magical texts. Humans who were not accorded a proper burial could, it was believed, become restless demons.

The earliest evidence for belief in demons, who were thought to be the cast-off progeny of the gods, appears in Sumerian and Akkadian incantations of the late third and early second millennia BC. Demons or demon-like beings also appear in art from this time either as dog, snake, or scorpion figures or as mythological creatures with animal features.

Some of these minor deities were believed to be benevolent. For example, statues of the Shedu (Akk. sing. *šēdu*) or Lamassu (Akk. sing. *lamassu*) in the form of colossal winged bulls protected the palaces of Assyria. The most common form of protection for pregnant women was a bronze amulet of Pazuzu (Akk. *pazūzu*), a winged figure with bulging eyes, wings, and talons. The *kūbu*, an amulet of a divinized premature birth, also served to ward off danger.

Most often, however, demons and spirits are represented as malevolent in ancient Near Eastern art and writing. They are often described as having a grudge against the human race. Of particular danger to women in childbirth and infants was Lamashtu (Akk. *lamaštu*), the daughter of Anu, who had been thrown out of heaven because of her bad disposition. She is depicted with the head of a lion, a hairy body, and hands stained with blood. She was thought to live in deserts, swamps, and mountains with wild animals.

Ancient Near Eastern cultures also feared demons who attacked while people slept, such as the *lilû*, an incubus (demon in male form) who sexually assaulted women, and the *lilītu* (lilith), or *ardat* ("maiden of") *lilî*, a succubus (demon in female form) who slept with men. According to M. Hutter, "the female demon—*lilitu*, (*w*)*ardat lilî*—can be considered a young girl who has not reached maturity and thus has to stroll about ceaselessly in search of a male companion. Sexually unfulfilled, she is the perpetual seductress of men" (*DDD*, 521). According to the *Atraḫasis Epic*, in order to control overpopulation, the god Enki advised, "Let there be among the peoples the *Pashittu*-demon to snatch the baby from the lap of her who bore it" (3.7.3–4; Lambert and Millard, 103).

Another group of dreaded beings were the ghosts (Akk. sing. *eṭemmu*) of people who had died without proper burial. These performed the wishes of various gods who controlled the netherworld. They were thought to emerge from tombs or the underworld as disembodied apparitions. These ghosts could attack people if offerings had not been regularly brought to their tombs. In the *Descent of Ishtar to the Nether World*, the goddess threatens to bring an attack of ghosts: "I will raise up the dead, eating the living, so that the dead will outnumber the living" (*ANET*, 107).

Namtaru was a plague demon who was the messenger of Nergal, the god of the underworld. Among other evil spirits were the *alû*, a demon who hid in dark corners, waiting for the unwary; the *ekkēmu*, a departed spirit; the *gallû*, a spirit of the underworld; and the *ilu lemnu*, an evil god. One of the most important incantation texts (Sum. UDUG HUL; Akk. *Utukkū Lemnūtu*, "Evil Spirits") describes the ubiquity of such demons:

> On high roofs and broad roofs, they whirl like a flood.
> They are not held back either by the door or bolt,
> But they slither through the door like a snake.
> They carry off the wife from the husband's lap,
> They remove the son from the father's knee,
> They take the bridegroom from his father-in-law's house.
>   (lines 368–373; Geller, 40–41)

As even the gods themselves were thought to be vulnerable to attack by demons, all kinds of efforts were made to defend against these ubiquitous dangers. These include great collections of magical texts such as *Utukkū Lemnūtu*, the *Namburbi* series, and other incantations. Apotropaic figures were also placed around the home, including those of armed warriors and dogs, one of which from Nineveh has the inscription: "Don't stop to think, bite him [i.e., the demon]" (Mallowan, 57).

The ancient Mesopotamians ascribed many ailments and diseases to demons. It was when a man's own protective *šēdu* abandoned him that he was vulnerable to attack from evil demons.

To cure these ailments the demon had to be exorcised—by such formulas as "By Ea, the lord of all, be ye exorcised!" (Jastrow, 303)—and the protective spirit had to be invited back: "As for the man, the son of his god, may the evil demon who has seized him stand aside. May the favorable spirit stand at his head" (Thompson, I.205).

In Egypt it was especially internal diseases that had no obvious etiology that were ascribed to demons or spirits. As the demons were thought to come unobtrusively, one Egyptian incantation declares: "You will break out, you who have come in the darkness, who have entered stealthily—his nose turned backwards, his face averted—having failed in what he came for!" (Borghouts, 41).

In addition to the intrusion of demons or spirits, the Egyptians also believed in the *mt* or *mt.t*, male or female ghosts of the dead who had the power to enter into a person's body. Bloody urine was blamed on the presence of a god or a ghost in the abdomen of an individual.

The most notable example of possession from Egypt is the story of the daughter of the Prince of Bekhten inscribed at Thebes during the reign of Ramesses II. The inscription reads: "The god Khonsu went to the place where Bent-ent-resht was, and, having performed a magical ceremony over her, the demon departed from her and she was cured straightway. Then the demon addressed the Egyptian god, saying 'Grateful and welcome is thy coming unto us, O great god, thou vanquisher of the hosts of darkness!'" (Budge, 212).

Berlin Papyrus 3027 records an Egyptian charm to protect an infant from demons. The text reads: "Hast thou come to kiss this child? I will not let thee kiss him! . . . I have made his magical protection against thee" (*ANET*, 328). Nibamon of Thebes, a famous exorcist, cured migraine headaches, which he diagnosed as caused by a ghost who visited the afflicted every night.

The most popular deity to protect pregnant women was the dwarfish, bandy-legged god Bes, who had an ugly face, ears, and a tail like a lion. He danced, played music, and brandished a sword.

D. THE GRECO-ROMAN WORLD

Greece

The word *daimōn*, from which we derive the English word "demon," did not simply signify an evil spirit to the Greeks but assumed a variety of meanings for different writers through the ages. In Homer the word is used to describe a god five times in the *Iliad* (e.g., *Il.* 3.420) and once in the *Odyssey*. Werner Foerster quotes F. Andres's opinion that "'in Homer a god is called δαίμων when he meets man in his power and activity, whereas θεός is used for the divine personality itself.' ... Andres emphasises that already in the Iliad δαίμων has more of a hostile character and that in the Odyssey it sends evil" (Foerster, 2n.5). The *daimōn* never takes any visible form nor does it reside in a human body. The plural form *daimones* is used in Hesiod to describe heroes of the past who have been transformed into supernatural beings (*Op.* 122–124): "They are fine spirits [*daimones*] upon the earth, guardians of mortal human beings; they watch over judgments and cruel deeds, clad in invisibility, walking everywhere upon the earth, givers of wealth and this kingly honor they received" (*Op.* 122–126).

The word *daimōn* can also refer generally to "the god," not a particular deity but a divine force. It is found in the dramatists (e.g., Sophocles, *Aj.* 1214–1215) as the equivalent of Fate. Oedipus blames his circumstances on a *daimōn*.

The Greeks also believed in particular *daimones* that might protect or threaten human beings. The phrase *agathos daimōn* ("the good protective spirit"), which designated the household god, is first recorded by Aristophanes. It was customary to pour a libation to it at a meal or banquet. Seductive creatures such as *empousai* were also prominent in Greek drama. They were sent by Hecate to frighten travelers. They were said to lure young men to bed by transforming themselves into beautiful women; they then sucked the blood and ate the flesh of their victims. The Greeks also spoke of a creature called the *lamia*, whose face was distorted and who killed and ate children. The *lamiai* had serpentine tails in place of legs. The *kēres* were the bringers of death and other ills, including old age and illness. The *alastores* were vengeful wandering spirits. An *alastor* possesses Clytemnestra in Aeschylus's *Agamemnon*.

The pre-Socratic philosopher Empedocles conceived of the *daimones* as former gods who had been expelled from the ranks of immortals and who had to purify themselves of sin through a cycle of reincarnations. Later, *daimones* were thought of by the Pythagorean school as intermediaries between gods and men who were more akin to *angeloi* ("messengers"). According to Pythagoras, "The whole air is full of souls which are called genii [*daimones*] or heroes; these are they who send men dreams and signs of future disease and health, ... and it is to them that purifications and lustrations, all divination, omens and the like, have reference" (Diogenes Laertius, *Lives of Eminent Philosophers* 8.32).

Socrates claimed to have a personal *daimonion* who guided him from childhood (Plato, *Apol.* 24b, 40a). Socrates's disciple Plato maintained that *daimones* as well as gods were worthy of worship (*Leg.* 4.717; cf. *Apol.* 27e–28a). Plato expands and interprets the Pythagorean view in his *Symposium*, where he claims that all intercourse between gods and men takes place through the race of *daimones* (*Symp.* 202e–203a). According to the later writer Plutarch, Plato's successor Xenocrates held that both good and bad *daimones* live in the air thought to exist between the earth and the moon, and that they are "guardians of sacred rites of the gods and prompters in the mysteries, while others go about as avengers of arrogant and grievous cases of injustice" (Plu. *Mor.* 417a–b).

Rome

Roman belief in ghosts and spirits was of great antiquity. The *manes* were the shades of the dead; the *larvae* were evil ghosts. In order to placate the *lemures*, or spirits of the dead, the Romans celebrated the festival of Lemuria in May.

The Roman Stoics regarded demons as supervisory spirits. According to Epictetus, "He [Zeus] has stationed by each man's side as guardian his particular genius,—and has committed the man to his care,—and that too a guardian who never sleeps and is not to be beguiled" (*Disc.* 1.14.12).

Like the Greeks, some Roman philosophers believed that certain human souls could become divine after death. Plutarch, a Greek who wrote in the early Roman Empire, held that "from men into heroes and from heroes into demigods [*daimonas*] the better souls obtain their transmutation. But from the demigods a few souls still, in the long reach of time, because of supreme excellence, come, after being purified, to share completely in divine qualities" (Plu. *Mor.* 415b–c).

In his defense against the charge of magic, Apuleius of Madaura (in northern Africa) declared: "I believe Plato when he asserts that there are certain divine powers holding a position and possessing a character midway between gods and men, and that all divination and the miracles of magicians are controlled by them" (*Apol.* 43; Butler, 39). In his *De deo Socratis*, Apuleius also mentioned Plato's views (*Symp.* 202), and he was later cited in Augustine's *City of God* (books 8 and 9) for a belief in demons as *mediae potestates*, "mediating powers." These *daemones* were always without bodies.

These mediating spirits might be influenced to help or harm humans. In his novel *The Golden Ass*, Apuleius describes a baker's wife who, upon being divorced, went to a witch "requesting one of two alternatives: either to soften her husband's anger and bring about a reconciliation; or, if that were impossible, to send some ghoul [*certe larva*] or dreadful power [*diro numine*] to attack and destroy his life's breath" (*Metam.* 9.29).

Lucian, in his satire "The Pathological Liar," responds to the question "What about those people who exorcize ghosts and cure victims of demonic possession?" as follows:

Everyone knows about the Syrian from Palestine, the adept in it, how many he takes in hand who fall down in the light of the moon and roll their eyes and fill their mouths with foam; nevertheless, he restores them to health and sends them away normal in mind, delivering them from their straits for a large fee. ... Indeed, I actually saw one [i.e., a demon] coming out, black and smoky in colour. (*Philops.* 16)

E. THE JEWISH WORLD

The development of demonology in Judaism is often attributed to Iranian influences. The conquest of Mesopotamia by Cyrus in 539 BC certainly did expose the Jewish exiles to Iranian culture. We have a wealth of data on demons from late Zoroastrian texts such as the *Vendidad* and Manichaean sources. According to the *Avesta*, diseases are attributable to demons. But whether Sasanian and post-Islamic Zoroastrian sources can be used to re-create the pre-Christian demonology of Israel is highly dubious.

One specific piece of evidence that can, however, be attributed to Iranian influence is the name of the demon Asmodeus in the book of Tobit, which seems clearly to be derived from the Iranian *Aeshma* (*aēšma daēua*, "demon of wrath"), who is, significantly, the only demon mentioned in the early Gathas (Zoroastrian hymns). In the book of Tobit, Asmodeus in his jealousy kills the seven successive husbands of Sarah, each on the wedding night (Tob 3:7–8). The angel Raphael provides the remedy for her eighth husband, Tobias, by censing the room with the smoke from the burning heart and liver of a fish (Tob 8:3), whereupon Asmodeus departs to Egypt, where he is bound by Raphael.

The Septuagint translates the word *šēdîm* in Deut 32:17 as *daimoniois*, and translates the word *ʾĕlîlîm* ("idols") in Ps 96:5 (LXX 95:5) as *daimonia* ("demons"). It renders "the plague [*qeṭeb*] that destroys at midday" in Ps 91:6 (LXX 90:6) as *daimoniou mesēmbrinou*, "midday demon." The Wisdom of Solomon declares: "But through the devil's [*diabolou*] envy death entered the world" (Wis 2:24).

Later Jewish authors also use the Greek word *daimōn* in a more ambiguous sense. Philo, who was heavily influenced by Middle Platonism, interpreted the Scriptures allegorically. He conceived of angels as *daimones* or *psychai* ("souls") who fill the air. Philo rejected *Enoch*'s view of the "sons of God" of Gen 6:2 as fallen angels who became demons, interpreting them as souls who had fallen into bodies:

These are the evil ones who, cloaking themselves under the name of angels, know not the daughters of right reason, the sciences and virtues, but court the pleasures which are born of men, pleasures mortal as their parents—pleasures

endowed not with the true beauty, which the mind alone can discern, but
with the false comeliness, by which the senses are deceived.
  (*Gig.* 17; see Brenk, 2104–5)

Josephus also follows the Greek practice of using the word *daimones*
in both positive and negative senses. Josephus (*Ant.* 6.166; *J.W.* 3.485;
cf. *J.W.* 7.120) relates how persons could be overtaken by demons, who
could cause frenzy and strangle them. On the other hand, he records a
speech of Titus that claims that Roman soldiers who die in battle become
daimones agathoi, "good genii" (*J.W.* 6.46). Josephus also describes the
exorcism of an evil demon by Eleazar, a Jew, in the presence of Vespasian
as follows: "He put to the nose of the possessed man a ring which had
under its seal one of the roots prescribed by Solomon, and then, as the
man smelled it, drew out the demon through his nostrils, and, when the
man at once fell down, adjured the demon never to come back into him"
(*Ant.* 8.46–47).

The Dead Sea Scrolls from Qumran describe the present age as the
Kingdom of Belial (*mmšlt blyꜤl*). In *The War Scroll* we read: "You yourself
made Belial for the pit, an angel of malevolence" (1QM XIII, 10–11). One
psalm reads: "Let Satan have no dominion over me, nor an unclean spirit;
let neither pain nor the will to evil rule in me" (11Q5 XIX, 15–16). According to the Meditation of the Sage, the community was exhorted: "Fortify yourself with the statutes of God, and in order to battle evil spirits"
(4Q444 1–5 I, 4)

In the "Songs of the Sage for Protection Against Evil Spirits," perhaps
an apotropaic liturgy, we read:

> And I, the Instructor, proclaim His glorious splendor so as to frighten and to
> te[rrify] all the spirits of the destroying angels, spirits of the bastards, demons,
> Lilith, howlers, and [desert dwellers . . .] and those which fall upon men with-
> out warning to lead them astray from a spirit of understanding and to make
> their heart and their [. . .] desolate. (4Q510 1, 4–6)

Another Qumran text, "An Exorcism," reads: "[. . . I adjure you, all who
en]ter into the body: the male Wasting-demon and the female Wasting-
demon . . . O Fever-demon and Chills-demon and Chest Pain-demon . . .
O male Shrine-spirit and female Shrine-spirit" (4Q560 I, 3).

In the *Genesis Apocryphon* the pharaoh asks Abraham to pray that an
evil spirit might be rebuked. Abraham obliges by laying his hands upon
the pharaoh's head, whereupon the plague is removed and the evil spirit is
rebuked (1Qap Gen XX, 28–29).

The most important text for the development of demonology in the
intertestamental period is the book of *1 Enoch*. Aramaic fragments of this

text, which was highly regarded at Qumran, were found among the Dead Sea Scrolls (4Q208–211). The complete text has been preserved only in an Ethiopic version. The "Book of the Watchers" (*1 En.* 1–36) provides an interpretation of "the sons of God" in Gen 6 as fallen angels that was influential for both Jewish and Christian interpreters. According to *1 En.* 6:2, "The angels, the children of heaven, saw them and desired them; and they said to one another, 'Come, let us choose wives for ourselves from among the daughters of man and beget us children.'" Two hundred of these "Watchers," led by Semyaz, took human wives on Mount Hermon and sired giants. They also imparted the knowledge of astrology and magic to humans, and caused the violence and havoc that led to the great flood. Archangels were sent to imprison the Watchers under the earth to await judgment. The ghosts of the dead giants became evil spirits (*1 En.* 15:8–16:1).

The OT pseudepigraphical book of *Jubilees*, another popular work at Qumran, borrows from the Enoch traditions about fallen angels but with some differences. According to *Jubilees*, the Watchers originally came down to teach men what is right (*Jub.* 4:15); only later were they corrupted when they beheld the daughters of men (*Jub.* 5:1). The leader of the demons, Mastema, persuaded God to leave one-tenth of the evil spirits on earth to corrupt men (*Jub.* 10:8–9). Mastema corresponds with Azazel, the leader of the fallen angels in *1 Enoch* (55:4).

It is rather surprising that there is but one reference to demons in the Mishnah, which records that according to some "evil spirits" (*mzykyn*) were among the things created on the sixth day (*m.* ʾ*Abot* 5:6). References to demons are relatively rare in the Jerusalem Talmud. The later Babylonian Talmud claims that Hillel's great disciple, R. Johanan B. Zakkai, was reputed to know "the speech of the (evil) spirits" (*b. Sukkah* 28a).

The Babylonian Talmud and the later midrashim are replete with references to demons, who are referred to as *šēdîm, mazzîkîm,* or simply *rûḥôt* ("spirits"). According to *b. Ber.* 6a: "It has been taught: Abba Benjamin says, If the eye had the power to see them, no creature could endure the demons. Abaye says: They are more numerous than we are and they surround us like the ridge round a field. R. Huna says: Every one among us has a thousand on his left hand and ten thousand on his right hand." Jews were warned: "'One should not go out alone at night,' i.e., on the nights of neither Wednesday nor Sabbaths, because Igrath the daughter of Mahalath, she and 180,000 destroying angels go forth, and each has permission to wreak destruction independently" (*b. Pesaḥ.* 112b).

The Babylonian demon Lilith, who in later midrash is identified as Adam's first wife, appears in the Babylonian Talmud as a succubus who preyed on sleeping men. According to R. Hanina, "One may not sleep in a house alone, and whoever sleeps in a house alone is seized by Lilith" (*b. Šabb.* 151b). Lilith was believed to have long hair (*b. ʿErub.* 100b) and wings (*b. Nid.* 24b).

Demons were believed especially to haunt narrow paths, the shades of trees, rooftops, bath houses, and privies. There were morning, midday, and night demons. As protection against them the rabbis recommended, in addition to Torah observance, the recital of Ps 91, the use of *tefillin* (phylacteries), the *mĕzûzâ* on the doorpost, the burning of incense, the blowing of the shofar, and amulets.

F. THE CHRISTIAN WORLD

Christians held to the reality of a "spirit world" in the sense that there were beings that were very real that existed outside the normal bounds of the physical world. Their sense of what this non-natural world and its inhabitants were like varied considerably over a period of centuries and discussions of this non-material world and its inhabitants are wide-ranging.

In the early Christian period, classical accounts of demons and the gods were blended with ideas found within the Jewish and Christian Scriptures in the form of what came to be known as gnostic Christianity. Gnostics, who were, in due time, deemed to be heretical Christians, claimed that they alone had *gnōsis*, "secret knowledge" mediated to them by the risen Christ. They believed that the material world, which they understood to be evil, was created by a lesser deity known as the demiurge (originally a Platonic term), Yaldabaoth, who is also known as Sakla and Samael according to the *Apocryphon* (or *Secret Book*) *of John* (NHC II,1; III,1; IV,1). Marvin Meyer comments, "In Aramaic Yaldabaoth probably means 'child or chaos' or 'child of (S)abaoth,' Sakla means 'fool,' and Samael means 'blind god'" (Meyer, 116n.53). The earthly realm was thought to be populated with spirits that serve this lesser deity. The heavenly spheres were thought to be controlled by hostile *archōn*s, literally, "rulers" (cf. *tas archas*, Eph 6:12). Only perfect gnostics could defend themselves against the persecution of demons.

The word *daimōn* appears forty times in the Nag Hammadi texts. According to *The Apocryphon of John* (NHC II,1 [= *Ap. John*] 19), the material body of Adam was created by 365 angels, i.e., demons. Reflecting the Enochian tradition, in *The Apocryphon* Yaldabaoth, the chief *archōn*, sends his counterfeit angels to mate with the daughters of men (NHC II,1 16–30).

According to the Nag Hammadi text *On the Origin of the World*, the divine figure Sophia Zoe banished the *archontes* ("rulers") from the heavens and cast them down into the sinful world "so that they might dwell there as evil demons upon the earth" (NHC II,5 [= *Orig. World*] 121). They introduced mankind to magic, worship of idols, and blood sacrifices: "All people on earth served the demons from the creation until the end of the age—both the angels of justice and the people of injustice" (NHC II,5 123.17–21).

Gnostics often identified Jewish and Christian practices with demons and servants of the demiurge. One Nag Hammadi text, the *Paraphrase of Shem,* denounces water baptism as demonic: "At that time the demon [John the Baptist?] will also appear on the river to baptize with an imperfect baptism and to disturb the world with bondage of water" (NHC VII,1 [= *Paraph. Shem*] 30.24–27).

Although most orthodox Christian writers did not subscribe to the gnostics' "secret knowledge" about the origin of the world, they did affirm the existence of demons and evil spirits. The most significant early writer on the church's view of demons was the apologist Justin Martyr, who, based on the Septuagint rendering of Ps 95:5, held that all the Greco-Roman gods were demons. He was also influenced by the Enochian tradition, writing, "[God] committed the care of men and of all things under heaven to angels whom He appointed over them. But the angels transgressed this appointment, and were captivated by love of women, and begot children who are those that are called demons" (*2 Apol.* 5.2).

Justin maintained that the demons, who learned the prophecies about Christ, produced false fulfillments to lead people astray (*1 Apol.* 54), and that demons raised up false teachers (*1 Apol.* 26). He blames the persecution of Christians on "the evil demons, who hate us, and who keep such men as these subject to themselves, and serving them in the capacity of judges, incite them, as rulers actuated by evil spirits, to put us to death" (*2 Apol.* 1.2). He also cites Christians' power over demons as proof of the truth of their faith:

> For numberless demoniacs throughout the whole world, and in your city, many of our Christian men exorcising them in the name of Jesus Christ, who was crucified under Pontius Pilate, have healed and do heal, rendering helpless and driving the possessing devils out of the men, though they could not be cured by all the other exorcists, and those who used incantations and drugs. (*2 Apol.* 6)

Echoing the book of Revelation, Justin affirms that when Christ comes again, he will send the wicked "into everlasting fire with the wicked devils" (*1 Apol.* 52).

Like Justin, Clement of Alexandria regarded the Greco-Roman gods as evil and wicked *daimones.* Even the philosophers were suspect, since Greek philosophers (especially Socrates) sometimes derived their inspiration from *daimones*. Clement wrote: "How then can shades and demons be still reckoned gods, being in reality unclean and impure spirits, acknowledged by all to be of an earthly and watery nature, sinking downwards by their own weight, and flitting about graves and tombs, about which they appear dimly, being but shadowy phantasms?" (*Protr.* 4).

Unlike many of his contemporaries, Origen rejected the Enochian tradition on the origin of demons, as he did not consider *1 Enoch* scripture. Rather, Origen interpreted Gen 6:2 as an allegory about souls desiring corporeal existence. Like other Christian writers, he equated the fall of the king of Babylon (Isa 14:12–15) and the king of Tyre (Ezek 28:1–19) with the fall of Satan (*Cels.* 6.43). He believed that the devil, after becoming apostate, induced many angels to fall away (*Cels.* 7.69). According to Origen, "famine, blasting of the vine and fruit trees, pestilence among men and beasts: all these are the proper occupation of demons" (*Cels.* 8.31). In his *Dialogue with Candidus*, a gnostic teacher, Origen had stressed that even Satan had free will. This was taken by his critics, including Demetrius, the bishop of Alexander, to mean that Satan *would* be saved. In a letter to Alexander, bishop of Jerusalem, Origen explained that he only held that Satan *could* be saved. (See Trigg, 89.)

The early Latin apologist Minucius Felix describes demons inhabiting the shrines dedicated to pagan gods. According to him, the classical practice of divination was controlled by demons who intended to lead men astray. He writes,

> These impure spirits, therefore—the demons—as is shown by the Magi, by the philosophers, and by Plato, consecrated under statues and images, lurk there, and by their afflatus attain the authority as of a present deity; while in the meantime they are breathed into the prophets, while they dwell in the shrines, while sometimes they animate the fibres of the entrails, control the flights of birds, direct the lots, are the cause of oracles involved in many falsehoods. . . . Thus they weigh men downwards from heaven, and call them away from the true God to material things: they disturb the life, render all men unquiet; creeping also secretly into human bodies, with subtlety, as being spirits, they feign diseases, alarm the minds, wrench about the limbs; that they may constrain men to worship them, being gorged with the fumes of altars or the sacrifices of cattle, that, by remitting what they had bound, they may seem to have cured it. (*Oct.* 27)

Tertullian followed Justin and Clement in his account of the origin of evil spirits. He writes,

> We are instructed, moreover, by our sacred books how from certain angels, who fell of their own free will, there sprang a more wicked demon-brood, condemned of God along with the authors of their race, and their chief

[Satan]. . . . They inflict, accordingly, upon our bodies diseases and other grievous calamities, while by violent assaults they hurry the soul into sudden and extraordinary excesses. (*Apol.* 22)

Tertullian also added the detail: "Every spirit is possessed of wings. This is a common property of both angels and demons. So they are everywhere in a single moment; the whole world is as one place to them" (*Apol.* 22). Tertullian interpreted the fall of the king of Tyre in Ezekiel as the fall of Satan: "If you turn to the prophecy of Ezekiel, you will at once perceive that this angel was both by creation good and by choice corrupt. For in the person of the prince of Tyre it is said in reference to the devil" (*Marc.* 2.10). Addressing Scapula, the governor of Carthage, he wrote: "You think that others, too, are gods, whom we know to be devils" (*Scap.* 2). He held that Christians should avoid all pagan spectacles, such as drama in the theater, chariot races in the circus, and gladiatorial games in amphitheaters, as these were all the haunts of the devil and his demons (*Spect.*).

In his late Montanist phase, Tertullian encouraged Christians not to flee from persecution by reminding them that Christ has already overcome their true enemy, the devil. He writes, "We believe that persecution comes to pass, no question, by the devil's agency, but not by the devil's origination. Satan will not be at liberty to do anything against the servants of the living God unless the Lord grant leave" (*Fug.* 2). Tertullian's writings also exhibit the early Christian understanding of martyrdom as combat against demonic forces. According to him, even Christians in prison can trample the devil (*Mart.* 1). The famous martyr Perpetua, whose diary Tertullian may have edited, wrote, "[I] perceived that I was not to fight with beasts [in a gladiatorial spectacle], but against the devil. Still I knew that the victory was awaiting me" (*Passion of Perpetua* 10).

Tertullian also claims that ordinary Christians are able to exorcise demons: "So at our touch and breathing, overwhelmed by the thought and realization of those judgment fires, they leave at our command the bodies they have entered, unwilling, and distressed, and before your very eyes put to an open shame" (*Apol.* 23). Other church fathers claim that nothing more is needed to expel demons than to call on the name of Jesus, to recite prayers or verses, or to make the sign of the cross. It was only in the third century that a special order of "exorcists" was established.

When early Christians were baptized, they renounced "the devil, and his pomp, and his angels" (Tertullian, *Cor.* 3). By the second century a more elaborate exorcism had become part of the baptismal ritual. For many Christians deliverance from demons was as important as forgiveness of sins. An oil of exorcism (*oleum exorcismi*) was placed by the bishop on the catechumen's head, and then the bishop would exhale over the catechumen symbolically to drive out the evil spirits. In his *Catechical Lectures* to the newly baptized, Cyril of Jerusalem explains, "As the breathing of the saints, and the invocation of the Name of God, like fiercest flame, scorch and drive out evil spirits, so also this exorcised oil receives such virtue by the invocation of God and by prayer, as not only to burn and cleanse away the traces of sins, but also to chase away all the invisible powers of the evil one" (*Cat.* 20.3).

After the end of persecution in the fourth century, Christians also came to understand the monastic life as a kind of combat against demonic forces. Athanasius's influential *Life of Antony* describes the hermit's numerous conflicts with the devil. Athanasius records that "the devil, unhappy wight, one night even took upon him the shape of a woman and imitated all her acts simply to beguile Antony. But he, his mind filled with Christ and the nobility inspired by Him, and considering the spirituality of the soul, quenched the coal of the other's deceit" (*Vit. Ant.* 5). One of the *Apophthegmata* ("Sayings") of the Desert Fathers relates: "The devil appeared to a certain brother, transformed into an angel of light, and said to him, 'I am the angel Gabriel and I am sent unto thee.' But he said, 'Look to it that thou wast not sent to some other: for I am not worthy that an angel should be sent to me.' And the devil was no more seen" (Waddell, 169).

BIBLIOGRAPHY: L. Albinus, "Greek Demons and the Ambivalence of Clemens Alexandrinus," *Temenos: Studies in Comparative Religion* 31 (1995), 7–17; P. Alexander, "The Demonology of the Dead Sea Scrolls," in *The Dead Sea Scrolls after Fifty Years*, ed. P. W. Flint and J. C. VanderKam (1999), 2.331–53; C. E. Arnold, *Powers of Darkness: Principalities and Powers in Paul's Letters* (1992); M. Becker, *Wunder und Wundertäter im frührabbinischen Judentum: Studien zum Phänomen und seiner Überlieferung im Horizont von Magie und Dämonismus* (2002); J. A. Black and A. R. Green, *Gods, Demons and Symbols of Ancient Mesopotamia* (1992); J. F. Borghouts, trans., *Ancient Egyptian Magical Texts* (1978); F. E. Brenk, "In the Light of the Moon: Demonology in the Early Imperial Period," *ANRW* II, 16.3 (1986), 2068–2145; E. A. W. Budge, *Egyptian Magic* (1971); H. E. Butler, trans., *The Apologia and Florida of Apuleius of Madaura* (1909); P. L. Day, *An Adversary in Heaven: śāṭān in the Hebrew Bible* (1988); P.-E. Dion, "Raphaël l'Exorciste," *Bib* 57.3 (1976), 399–413; D. C. Duling, "Solomon, Exorcism, and the Son of David," *HTR* 68 (1975), 235–52; S. Eitrem, *Some Notes on the Demonology in the New Testament* (2nd ed., 1966); E. Ferguson, *Demonology of the Early Christian World* (1984); W. Foerster, "δαίμων," *TDNT* II, 1–20; C. Forbes, "Pauline Demonology and/or Cosmology? Principalities, Powers and the Elements of the World in Their Hellenistic

Context," *JSNT* 24.3 (2002), 51–73; H. Frey-Anthes, "Concepts of 'Demons' in Ancient Israel," *WO* 38 (2008), 38–52; J. H. Gaines, "Lilith: Seductress, Heroine or Murderer?," *BRev* 17.5 (2001), 12–20; M. J. Geller, *Forerunners to Udug-Hul: Sumerian Exorcistic Incantations* (1985); F. X. Gokey, *The Terminology for the Devil and Evil Spirits in the Apostolic Fathers* (1961); A. Green, "Beneficent Spirits and Malevolent Demons: The Iconography of Good and Evil in Ancient Assyria and Babylonia," *Visible Religion* 3 (1984), 80–105; M. J. Gruenthaner, "The Demonology of the Old Testament," *CBQ* 6 (1944), 6–27; N. P. Heessel, *Pazuzu* (2002); M. Jastrow, Jr., *Aspects of Religious Belief and Practice in Babylonia and Assyria* (1911); S. S. Jensen, *Dualism and Demonology: The Function of Demonology in Pythagorean and Platonic Thought* (1966); R. S. Kraemer, "Ecstasy and Possession," *HTR* 72 (1979), 55–80; W. G. Lambert and A. R. Millard, *Atra-ḫasīs, The Babylonian Story of the Flood* (1969); A. Lange, H. Lichtenberger, and K. F. D. Römheld, ed., *Demons: The Demonology of Israelite-Jewish and Early Christian Literature in Context of Their Environment* (2003); E. Langton, *Essentials of Demonology* (1949); R. Lebling, "Monsters from Mesopotamia," *Saudi Aramco World* 63.4 (2012), 10–17; J. Y. Lee, "Interpreting the Demonic Powers in Pauline Thought," *NovT* 12.1 (1970), 54–69; E. Leichty, "Demons and Population Control," *Exped* 13 (1971), 22–26; J. Lust, "Devils and Angels in the Old Testament," *LS* 5 (1974), 115–20; E. C. B. MacLaurin, "Beelzeboul," *NovT* 20 (1978), 156–60; M. Mallowan, *Twenty-Five Years of Mesopotamian Discovery, 1932–1956* (1956); D. B. Martin, "When Did Angels Become Demons?" *JBL* 129.4 (2010), 657–77; M. Meyer, ed., *The Nag Hammadi Scriptures* (2007); S. H. T. Page, *Powers of Evil: A Biblical Study of Satan and Demons* (1995); J. A. Marx, "Demonology in Rabbinic Literature," rabbinic thesis, Hebrew Union College-Jewish Institute of Religion (1983); A. Y. Reed, *Fallen Angels and the History of Judaism and Christianity: The Reception of Enochic Literature* (2005); A. Y. Reed, "The Trickery of the Fallen Angels and the Demonic Mimesis of the Divine: Aetiology, Demonology, and Polemics in the Writings of Justin Martyr," *JECS* 12.2 (2004), 141–71; J. E. Rexine, "*Daimon* in Classical Greek Literature," *GOTR* 30 (1985), 335–61; H. J. Rose, "Keres and Lemures," *HTR* 41 (1948), 217–28; J. Scurlock and B. R. Andersen, trans., *Diagnoses in Assyrian and Babylonian Medicine: Ancient Sources, Translations, and Modern Medical Analyses* (2005); J. Z. Smith, "Towards Interpreting Demonic Powers in Hellenistic and Roman Antiquity," *ANRW* II.16.1 (1978), 425–39; E. Sorensen, *Possession and Exorcism in the New Testament and Early Christianity* (2002); J. C. Thomas, *The Devil, Disease and Deliverance: Origins of Illness in New Testament Thought* (1998); R. C. Thompson, *The Devils and Evil Spirits of Babylonia* (2 vols., 1903–1904; repr. 1976); J. W. Trigg, *Origen: The Bible and Philosophy in the Third-Century Church* (1983); G. H.

Twelftree, *Jesus the Exorcist* (1993); K. van der Toorn, B. Becking, and P. W. van der Horst, ed., *Dictionary of Deities and Demons in the Bible* (rev. ed., 1999); H. Waddell, trans., *The Desert Fathers* (1936); F. A. M. Wiggerman, *Mesopotamian Protective Spirits: The Ritual Texts* (1992); C. Wahlen, *Jesus and the Impurity of Spirits in the Synoptic Gospels* (2004); A. T. Wright, *The Origin of Evil Spirits* (2005).

EMY

See also DISEASES & PLAGUES, DIVINATION & SORTITION, and MAGIC.

Dentistry & Teeth

Teeth are essential for mastication, articulation of speech, and appearance. Dentistry, or the care of teeth, was either rudimentary or nonexistent in antiquity, which meant that most persons, even royalty, would have been subject to toothaches and even the loss of teeth. As they are often among the best-preserved parts of the body after death, teeth are important archaeological evidence for the health and nutrition of ancient populations.

A. THE OLD TESTAMENT

The Hebrew word *šēn*, which occurs fifty-six times in the OT, is used to indicate human and animal teeth, and occasionally ivory. The well-known expression "tooth for tooth," which is similar to a phrase in the Code of Hammurabi, appears in the *lex talionis* ("law of retaliation") passages (Exod 21:23–25; Lev 24:20; Deut 19:21). Teeth were recognized as vital to one's health; if a master injured his slave, causing the loss of a tooth, he had to let the slave go free (Exod 21:27).

In Jacob's final blessing, Judah is promised that "His eyes will be darker than wine, his teeth whiter than milk" (Gen 49:12). In the Song of Songs, the lover says of his beloved, "Your teeth are like a flock of sheep just shorn, coming up from the washing. Each has its twin; not one of them is alone" (Song 4:2; cf. 6:6). Ecclesiastes's metaphorical description of the infirmities of old age, "when the grinders cease because they are few," is no doubt an allusion to the loss of teeth (Eccl 12:3).

Teeth appear in a number of wisdom sayings. Proverbs 10:26 declares, "As vinegar to the teeth and smoke to the eyes, so are sluggards to those who send them." Proverbs 25:19 warns, "Like a broken tooth or a lame foot is reliance on the unfaithful in a time of trouble." To highlight individual responsibility, the prophet Jeremiah declares that "in those days people will no longer say, 'The parents have eaten sour grapes, and the children's teeth are set on edge.' Instead, everyone will die for their own sin; whoever eats sour grapes—their own teeth will be set on edge" (Jer 31:29–30; cf. Ezek 18:2). The Lord declares through Amos, "I gave you empty stomachs [lit., "cleanness of teeth"] in every city and lack of bread in every town, yet you have not returned to me" (Amos 4:6). From Job we have the common expression, "I have escaped only by the skin of my teeth" (which the NIV note explains as "only my gums"; Job 19:20).

Teeth could also be a symbol of strength and rapaciousness. Job reminds his friends of his generosity to the poor, proclaiming, "I broke the fangs of the wicked and snatched the victims from their teeth" (Job 29:17). The psalmist declares, "I am in the midst of lions; I am forced to dwell among ravenous beasts—men whose teeth are spears and arrows, whose tongues are sharp swords" (Ps 57:4; cf. Prov 30:14). The author of Lamentations wails, "He has broken my teeth with gravel; he has trampled me in the dust" (Lam 3:16).

The phrase "gnashing of teeth" as an expression of strong anger occurs five times in the OT. For example, Job complains, "God assails me and tears me in his anger and gnashes his teeth at me" (Job 16:9; cf. Pss 35:16; 37:12; 112:10; Lam 2:16).

The mighty Leviathan's mouth is described as "ringed about with fearsome teeth" (Job 41:14). The second beast in Daniel's vision "had three ribs in its mouth between its teeth" (Dan 7:5); the fourth beast had "large iron teeth" (Dan 7:7).

B. THE NEW TESTAMENT

The Greek word for tooth, *odous*, occurs twelve times in the NT. With the exception of Jesus's reference to the OT *lex talionis* (Matt 5:38), and a reference to locust-like creatures whose teeth are like those of lions (Rev 9:8; cf. Joel 1:6), all references are to the "gnashing of teeth." A demon-possessed epileptic foams at the mouth and gnashes his teeth (Mark 9:18). The Jews who hear Stephen's speech accusing them of the death of Jesus "were furious and gnashed their teeth at him" (Acts 7:54). Descriptions of the "weeping and gnashing of teeth" of those condemned to eternal judgment also occur in seven passages (Matt 8:12; 13:42, 50; 22:13; 24:51; 25:30; Luke 13:28).

C. THE NEAR EASTERN WORLD

Mesopotamia

Though many people suffered from dental pain, and magical praxis and medications were prescribed as remedies, there were no dental specialists in ancient Mesopotamia. However, barbers (Akk. sing. *gallābu*) sometimes performed minor surgery, including dental operations such as extractions.

The Code of Hammurabi has two cases that describe *lex talionis* regarding teeth: "If a seignior has knocked out a tooth of a seignior of his own rank, they shall knock out his tooth" (CH 200; *ANET*, 175); "If he has knocked out a commoner's tooth, he shall pay one-third mina of silver" (CH 201; *ANET*, 175). The latter penalty, which amounted to twenty shekels of silver, or the equivalent of 20 months' labor, indicates the high value of a tooth.

We have numerous medical/magical texts from Mesopotamia, which fall broadly in two categories: (1) those that list symptoms and rituals to be followed by the *āšipu*, "exorcist priest," and (2) those that list plants and indicate their use by the *asû*, "physician or pharmacist." Some of these texts describe wobbly teeth and bloody gums. Dental decay and pain were ascribed to a "tooth worm," as a mythological text explains:

> After Anu [had created heaven], heaven had created [the earth], had created the rivers, the rivers had created the canals, the canals had created the marsh, (and) the marsh had created the worm—the worm went, weeping, before Shamash, his tears flowing before Ea: "What wilt thou give for my food? What wilt thou give me for my sucking?" "I shall give thee the ripe fig, (and) the apricot." "Of what use are they to me, the ripe fig and the apricot? Lift me up and among the teeth and the gums cause me to dwell! The blood of the tooth I will suck, and of the gum I will gnaw its *roots*!" *Fix the pin and seize its foot.* Because thou hast said this, O worm, may Ea smite thee with the might of his hand!
>
> (*A Cosmological Incantation: The Worm and the Toothache*; *ANET*, 100–101)

The foregoing incantation was to be recited three times as a mixture of beer, malt, and oil was placed on the teeth. This text, which comes from the Neo-Babylonian era, is based on an older original; a similar incantation in the Hurrian language from the Old Babylonian era was found at Mari.

A text that describes halitosis, bad breath caused by the infection of the gums and throat, reads as follows: "The earth created the tooth worm; the tooth worm created *buʾšānu* [lit., "stinking"]. Mighty is the affliction of *buʾšānu*. It [. . .] the breath like a lion; it seized the throat like a wolf. It seized the nose, the mucus from the nose; [it seized] the lungs. It set up its throne among the teeth" (Scurlock, 397).

Teeth are described in Mesopotamian texts as "yellow," "dark," or "shining," in some cases possibly because of fluorosis caused by excess fluoride in the water. Some medical prognoses were based on the principle that the color black was a portent of evil: "if his teeth are dark, his illness will be prolonged" (Scurlock, 55). One diagnosis of bruxism (teeth grinding) is remarkably perceptive: "[If a person] grinds his teeth in his sleep, [he is] worried" (Scurlock and Anderson, 368).

The following is a typical prescription for a toothache: "If a man's teeth hurt, thou shalt take a [name of some animal] . . . the white of its inside thou shalt enclose in wool, with oil. . . . male mandrake, ammi-root, . . . storax, gum of galbanum, vinegar . . . flour against his mouth (tooth) [thou shalt bind and he shall recover]" (Thompson, 58). A prescription for loose teeth and sore gums reads: "[If a man's teeth] are [all] loose and decay [sets in] . . . [thou shalt rub] . . . on his teeth until blood comes forth, [and he shall recover]" (Thompson, 61). One prescription called for the charring and crushing of another human tooth, which was then mixed with other ingredients and placed on the patient's aching tooth.

Another Mesopotamian prescription reads:

> If all of a person's teeth move and (the gums) have redness, you grind together "white plant," plant for *bu'šāni*, *nīnû*-mint and alum. You sprinkle a linen cloth with honey and soften (the plant mixture with it). You firmly rub (it) over his teeth until the blood comes out. He should eat either "lion fat" or "fox fat."
> (Scurlock, 401)

In some cases a plant was used to clean the teeth. Among plants used in prescriptions for toothache were ryegrass (*lolium*), thorn root (*lycium*), mandrake, cassia (*cinnamonum*), cumin, and especially henbane (*Hyoscyamus*).

Other treatments were based on imitation and correspondence. A medical text from Nippur (18th c. BC) reads: "If a man (has) a worm in his tooth, you crush 'sailor's excrement' in pressed oil; if it is a tooth on the right which aches, you pour (the oil) on a tooth on the left and he will get better. If it is a tooth on the left which aches, you pour (the oil) on a tooth on the right and he will get better" (Geller, 67). A unique model of a jaw with a grain of barley representing the painful tooth has been preserved. This was possibly used for curing the toothache by sympathetic magic.

We have an interesting letter, dating to about 668 BC, from a physician named Arad-Nana to the Assyrian king Esarhaddon: "As regards the cure of the aching teeth about which the king wrote to me, I will now begin with it; there is a great lot of remedies of aching teeth. I am collecting them" (cited by Paulissian, 109). Another letter, from Nabunasir to Esarhaddon, reads: "The truth to the king my lord I shall speak: the burning of his head, his hands, his feet (wherewith) he burns (is on account of his teeth)" (Denton, 314). The meaning of the next phrase, "his teeth are *a-na u-si-e* [lit., for coming out]," is disputed. Some scholars have rendered it as "the teeth should come out," anticipating the therapeutic extraction of teeth. But the more likely meaning is "the teeth are about to come out," inasmuch as the extraction of teeth for general health was not advocated until 1910, when William Hunter demonstrated the connection between oral sepsis and systemic disease caused by the spread of bacteria or toxins from infected teeth.

Egypt

It is from Egypt that we have the greatest artistic, textual, and archaeological evidence for the care of teeth and the practice of dentistry. The Egyptian word for tooth, *ibḥ*, could be represented by the hieroglyph of an elephant's tusk.

The ideal of feminine beauty is reflected in a love song dedicated to the goddess Mut at Karnak: "Blacker her hair than the black of night, than grapes of the riverbank. [Whiter] her teeth than bits of plaster" (Fox, 349).

Egypt was renowned throughout antiquity from Mesopotamia to Greece, from Homer to Herodotus, for its medical practitioners. Dentists were prominent, especially during the Old Kingdom or Pyramid Age. The first known *ibḥy*, or "dentist," Hesy-Re, is memorialized in a 3rd Dynasty tomb. In 2006 tombs of three other dentists were discovered at Saqqara, where the first pyramid was built for Djoser ca. 2700 BC. Six other individuals in Egyptian history are designated as "dentists," such as Khury, who was the "chief" of dentists, and Nyankhsekhmet, "chief of the dentists of the palace." All these, with the exception of an individual from the 26th Dynasty (7th c. BC), were from the Old Kingdom (3rd–6th Dyn.).

An examination of thousands of teeth from skulls and mummies gives us unique insight into the actual condition of the teeth of both commoners and royalty. Though there is relatively little evidence of caries (tooth decay), almost all individuals from the lowest peasant to the pharaoh had teeth that were affected by attrition, that is, the wear of the enamel crowns, especially of the molars, by the coarse grit that infiltrated flour and bread, both from the stone querns (mills) where the grain was ground and from windblown sand.

Dental problems and prescriptions for them are contained in the important Egyptian medical papyri: (1) the Edwin Smith Papyrus (1600 BC, a copy of a much older original), perhaps the most impressive medical document of antiquity for its objective diagnoses of fractures and its accurate prognoses of treatments; (2) the Kahun Papyrus (MK), which was recovered from Ilahun; and (3) the Ebers Magical Papyrus (NK), which is twenty meters long and contains nearly nine hundred prescriptions. As in Mesopotamia, the cause of dental pain was ascribed to a "tooth worm." A dispatch from an Egyptian official laments the suffering of one of his colleagues: "A *mns*-scribe is here with me, every muscle of whose face twitches . . . the worm gnaws into his tooth. I cannot leave him to his fate" (Papyrus Anastasi IV, 13.6–7; Caminos, 189).

The Edwin Smith Papyrus (case 25) describes the dislocation of a patient's mandible (lower jaw), and prescribes manipulation using the dentist's fingers, a procedure still used today. Case 7 describes a patient who may have suffered from tetanus: "He has developed toothache; his mouth is bound; he suffers stiffness of his neck—an ailment not to be treated" (Nunn, 182). The Kahun Papyrus (case 5), which is concerned with gynecological issues, also describes the case of "a woman who is afflicted in her teeth and gums and cannot open her mouth" (David, 62), perhaps as a result of trismus or lockjaw. The prescribed remedy was fumigation over a bowl containing oil and frankincense, and having the urine of a donkey poured into her vagina.

For halitosis, or foul breath, the Egyptians prescribed the first breath mints, a combination of pine nut, frankincense, myrrh, and cinnamon boiled with honey shaped into pellets. Teeth were cleaned with rags and sticks.

The great Ebers Papyrus contains about a dozen prescriptions for tooth problems, including:

No. 554: "Eliminating ulcers of the teeth, causing the flesh ($ḥ^ʿw$) of the teeth to grow: bsbs-plant 1; notched sycamore fig 1; lns·t-plant 1; honey 1; terebinth-resin (sntr) 1; left overnight in the dew; to be chewed around in the mouth." (Ghalioungui, 148)

No. 739: "Beginning of the remedies to consolidate (smn) a tooth: Flour of emmer seeds (mjmj) 1; ochre (stj) 1; honey 1; made into a mass; the tooth is filled with it." (Ghalioungui, 189)

No. 740: "Another: Scrapings of a millstone 1; ochre (stj) 1; honey 1; the tooth is filled therewith." (Ghalioungui, 189)

No. 741: "Elimination of a growth of pain-matter in the teeth: Notched sycamore-figs 1; beans 1; honey 1; malachite (w3ḏw) 1; ochre (stj) 1; ground; pulverized; applied to the tooth." (Ghalioungui, 189)

No. 742: "Another, to treat a tooth that is eating in the opening of the flesh ($ḥ^ʿ·w$): Cumin 1; terebinth-resin (sntr) 1; colocynth (ḏ3r·t) 1; made into a powder; applied to the tooth." (Ghalioungui, 189)

No. 745: "Another, to treat the teeth with masticatories: $^ʿm^ʿ$-part of cereal . . . 1; sweet beer 1; šw·t ḏḥwtj (potentilla reptans) 1; chewed; thrown down to earth (by spitting)." (Ghalioungui, 190)

The examination of over three thousand mummies and skulls has revealed, with few exceptions, almost no evidence of intervention to relieve pain from toothaches. A jaw found at Giza had holes that were possibly the result of natural processes rather than the result of drilling. Two molar teeth were found joined by gold wire, and a dental bridge from the 4th Dynasty was made by wrapping gold wire around four upper teeth.

X-rays of royal mummies have revealed the state of the dentition of some of the greatest pharaohs of the New Kingdom and their queens. Women of the late 17th and early 18th Dynasties suffered from malocclusion with severe maxillary prognathism, that is, markedly protruding upper teeth. The dentitions of Tuthmosis I, Tuthmosis II, and Tuthmosis III revealed bimaxillary protrusion of both upper and lower incisors. The teeth of Amenhotep III were heavily encrusted with tartar, a mineralized crust created from plaque. There was also evidence of extensive abscesses, which must have been very painful, as well as the loss of teeth.

The teeth of Seti I (19th Dyn./13th c. BC) were moderately worn, with one of his lower molars missing. Much worse was the dentition of the famous Ramesses II (the Great), whom advocates of the late date of the exodus identify as the pharaoh of the exodus. He was a long-reigning pharaoh and a prodigious builder of gigantic buildings and colossal statues of himself. Attrition had led to the exposure of the pulp chambers of his teeth, leading to extreme periodontitis (inflammation of gums) and severe abscesses of the roots of his teeth. Even worse was the dentition of his son, Merneptah, who by the time of his death had lost all his molars and premolars and suffered periodontal disease. Mutnodjmet, the queen of Horemheb, the last pharaoh of the 18th Dynasty, was almost toothless at her death.

Even in death magical spells provided protection for teeth. The *Book of the Dead* as represented in the Papyrus of Ani states, "The white teeth of Horus are presented unto thee so that they may fill thy mouth" (Budge, 212). Another passage promises, "The teeth of the Osiris Ani, whose word is truth, are the teeth of Serqet [a protective scorpion goddess]" (Budge, 597).

D. THE GRECO-ROMAN WORLD

Greece

We have some limited archaeological evidence of the status of dentition in the Aegean world from the Middle Bronze Age (2000–1500 BC) to the later Classical Age (5th c. BC). From the site of Kato Zakro in south-central Crete the 1,500 teeth of seventy-four skulls of the Middle Minoan population show relatively little incidence of caries (9 percent) but reveal widespread attrition of their molars from the use of stone querns (hand mills) and the consumption of coarse grains. Almost everyone over the age of forty was toothless.

Human remains from the Late Bronze Age (1500–1200 BC) begin to reflect the difference caused by the variance of food consumed by the aristocracy, on the one hand, and the rural folk, on the other. Among the former only 15 percent suffered from dental abrasions, but among the latter 28 percent did. Only 1 to 2 percent of the total population showed evidence of caries; their teeth may have been afforded protection by the fluoride in the fish they ate.

Aristotle's assumption of male superiority misled him to assert that "males have more numerous teeth than females, not only in mankind, but also in sheep, goats, and pig" (*Hist. an.* 501b.19–21).

The Hippocratic corpus, a collection of Greek medical treatises, includes detailed descriptions of teething and children's teeth. The Hippocratic *Aphorisms* observe that teething children suffered the following symptoms: "At the approach of dentition, irritation of the gums, fevers, convulsions, diarrhoea, especially when cutting the canine teeth, and in the case of very fat children, and if the bowels are hard" (*Aph.* 3.25). The treatise *De dentitione* ("Dentition"; Gk. *Peri odontophuiēs*) maintains that babies who eat solids while being breastfed bear weaning more easily. The treatise *De carne* observes:

> The primary teeth fall out when there have been seven years of the first regimen; in some cases this occurs earlier, if the children are being fed a regimen that is sickly—but in most cases when they are seven years old. The teeth that grow in afterwards grow old with the person, unless they are lost as the result of disease. (*Carn.* 12)

Greek medicine also prescribed various remedies for toothache, which ranged from the magical to the practical. The Homeric "Hymn to Demeter" refers to worms that were thought to be the cause of teething pains and toothache:

> And to you, also, lady, all hail, and may the gods give you good! Gladly will I take the boy to my breast, as you bid me, and will nurse him. Never, I ween, through any heedlessness of his nurse shall witchcraft hurt him nor the the the Undercutter [*hypotamnos*]: for I know a charm far stronger than the Woodcutter [*hylotomos*], and I know an excellent safeguard against woeful witchcraft. (lines 223–230)

Greek physicians recommended the massaging of gums, the rinsing of the mouth, and the use of a stick with frayed fibers on one end as a brush, and the other end sharpened as a toothpick. For the cleaning of teeth one could make use of the bare finger with a cloth or a round ball of wool dipped in honey. For a dentifrice (i.e., the equivalent of modern toothpaste) one could use carbonate of lime or chalk mixed with other ingredients. For a mouth wash either vinegar or a mixture of castorium and pepper was recommended.

In some cases, however, more serious measures were required. A Hippocratic treatise advises:

> Pains that arise about the teeth: if the tooth is decayed and loose, remove it; if it is not decayed or loose, but produces pain, dry it out by cautery; medications that are chewed are useful as well. These pains occur when phlegm invades beneath the roots of the teeth; some teeth are decayed by phlegm, others by foods, when they are weak by nature, have caries, and are poorly fixed in the gums. (*De affectionibus* 4)

Diocles (ca. 350 BC), who did not favor extraction, recommended treating the tooth with a mixture composed of saffron and cedar gum.

Aristotle mentions instruments such as scrapers and extractors. The Hippocratic treatise *Mechanics* described the use of dental forceps as follows:

> But the forceps are really two levers working in opposite directions, having the point at which the blades are joined together as the fulcrum; dentists use this instrument for extraction because they find it moves more easily ... but when he has moved it [the tooth] he can extract it more easily with the hand than with the instrument. (*Mech.* 21)

Erasistratus is said to have deposited in the temple of Apollo a forceps of lead for the extracting of teeth. Examples of such forceps are displayed in the Archaeological Museum in Athens.

The Hippocratic treatise *Epidemics* describes a dramatic case of osteomyelitis (inflammation of the marrow) as a result of caries: "In Cardia, Metrodorus' son had pain from the teeth, mortification of the jaw, and dreadful overgrowth of flesh on the gums. He was moderately purulent. His molars collapsed, or else his jawbone" (*Epid.* 7.113). Hippocratic treatises also discuss alveolar abscesses, necrosis of the gums, and the difficult eruption of wisdom molars.

Physicians also cared for their patients' teeth in the event of a fractured jaw. The Hippocratic treatise *On Joints* recommends: "If the teeth at the point of injury are displaced or loosened, when the bone is adjusted fasten them to one another, not merely the two but several, preferably with the gold wire, but failing that, with thread, till consolidation takes place" (*Artic.* 32).

Rome

The Romans in the Late Republic owed almost all aspects of their culture to the Greeks either through contact with the Greek colonies in Italy and Sicily or through their conquests in the Macedonian Wars (2nd c. BC). This included medicine and dentistry in particular.

Pliny the Elder (d. AD 79) followed Aristotle in maintaining that men have thirty-two teeth but that women have a lesser number. He furthermore maintained that the presence of two eye teeth (i.e., canines) "on the right side of the upper jaw are a promise of fortune's favours, as in the case of Domitius Nero's mother Agrippina; on the left side the opposite" (*Nat.* 7.15).

Aulus Cornelius Celsus (25 BC–AD 50), a physician who accompanied Claudius in the invasion of Britain, provides some of the most detailed texts on the care of teeth. He writes about toothache:

> Now in the case of pain in the teeth, which by itself also can be counted among the greatest of torments, wine must be entirely cut off. At first the patient must fast, then take sparingly of soft food, so as not to irritate the teeth when masticating; then externally steam from hot water is to be applied by a sponge, and an ointment put on made from Cyprus or iris oil, with a woolen bandage over it and the head must be wrapped up. (*Med.* 6.9)

Celsus continues:

> For more severe pain ... cinquefoil root may be boiled in diluted wine, and hyoscyamus root either in vinegar and water, or in wine, with the addition of a little salt, also poppy-head skins not too dry and mandragora root in the same condition. But with these three remedies, the patient should carefully avoid swallowing the fluid in the mouth. (*Med.* 6.9)

We also read in Celsus: "In children too if a second tooth is growing up before the first one has fallen out, the tooth which ought to come out must be freed all round and extracted; the tooth which has grown up in the place of the former one is to be pressed upwards with a finger every day until it has reached its proper height" (*Med.* 8.12). The fragrant roots of the iris were placed around the neck of a teething baby, partly as a talisman, and partly so the child could chew on it to ease teething pain.

Celsus described how, when it became necessary to extract a tooth, the tooth should be scraped free of the surrounding gum. He advocated pulling the tooth with fingers if possible, but if necessary using forceps to pull the tooth straight out lest the roots break. In the case of very hollow teeth, he recommended filling the tooth with lead lest the crown break in the grip of the forceps. He recommended binding loose teeth to other teeth with gold wire.

Even the most affluent members of society often resorted to this invasive remedy for toothache. According to Suetonius, while Vespasian was in Greece he dreamed that the beginning of good fortune for himself would come as soon as Nero had a tooth extracted. And then, "on the next day it came to pass that a physician walked into the hall and showed him a tooth which he had just then taken out" (*Vesp.* 5).

Scribonius Largus (ca. AD 47), the emperor Claudius's physician, advised,

> For pains of the teeth scissors are said to be the remedy by an exceedingly large number of people, however, I know many things to be useful in the case of this necessity. Therefore when indeed something has been consumed from this part, I do not persuade him immediately that it ought to be removed, but it ought to be cut out by a medicinal knife, which is careful, that it might be without pain: for the remaining solid part of him is preferable both for appearance and usefulness. (*Compositiones* 53; translation Hamilton)

Decay was attributed to *vermiculi*, "small worms." Scribonius Largus believed that fumigation of the burning seeds of henbane (*Hyoscyamus*) could drive out such worms. Dioscorides recommended *kankamon* (the gum of an Arabian tree) for the treatment of toothache and rotting gums.

Pliny the Elder's encyclopedic work *Natural History* includes many varied and in some cases bizarre prescriptions for problems with teeth. He recommends that the root of the mallow plant be placed around an aching tooth. In *Nat.* 30.8 he reports, "Toothache is also cured, the Magi tell us, by the ash of the burnt heads without any flesh of dogs that have died of madness." In *Nat.* 32.26, he writes: "Toothache is relieved by scraping the gums with the bones of the weaver fish, or by the brain of a dog-fish boiled down in oil and kept, so that the teeth may be washed with it once every year. To scrape the gums too with the ray of the sting ray is very beneficial for toothache." He further urges the eating of a mouse every two months to ward off pain in the teeth.

Archigenus (ca. AD 100) records drilling the crown of a tooth in its most discolored part to relieve pain. He invented a small drill to achieve this purpose. Actual examples of dental instruments have been found at Pompeii. Such instruments included, in addition to the forceps, a stylus and an *elevatorium* (bone lever).

Roman dentists were known as *medici artifices dentium* or simply *artifices dentium*. Martial refers to trudging the Aventine Hill, where "Cascellius extracts or restores an ailing tooth" (*Ep.* 10.56). Cascellius is the first western dentist known by name.

To counter halitosis (bad breath), Pliny the Elder (*Nat.* 20.5) counseled the use of such substances as hyssop, whose leaves have a camphorlike aroma. As a dentrifice he advised the use of dried whale's flesh and salt, as well as the use of pumice, and the ashes of dog's teeth mixed with honey (*Nat.* 32.26). Dioscorides recommended the use of emery as a tooth cleaner. Among other substances that were listed as dentrifices were powdered oyster shell, murex and crab shells, hartshorn (of the male red deer), and myrrh. The main purpose of tooth powder was to whiten teeth, not to cleanse them.

Scribonius Largus described a dentrifice as follows:

> Tooth powders, which make teeth shiny and strong: it is necessary to sprinkle a sixteenth of a peck of barley meal with vinegar and honey and to knead it for some time so as to divide it into six balls: into which spread out [and] mix half an ounce of mined salt, then bake in an oven, until it is reduced to charcoal. Then it will be necessary to grind up these globules and to mix in enough nard to give that odor; this is used by Augustus' sister Octavia.
> (*Compositiones* 59; translation Hamilton)

Messalina, wife of the Emperor, used this prescription: "One pint of burned staghorn, reduced to ashes in a new jar, mixed with one ounce of Chian mastic and one-half ounce of sal ammoniac" (*Compositiones* 60; translation Hamilton). Catullus noted that Celtiberians in Spain used stale urine to brush their teeth. (Modern toothpastes use urea.)

The Romans chewed mastic, a resinous gum from the bark of the tree *Pistachia lentiscus*, to sweeten their breath. Slips of wood from this tree could be used as toothpicks. Martial wrote: "Mastic is better; but if a leafy point [twig from a mastic tree] is not available, a quill can relieve your teeth" (*Ep.* 14.22). Pliny also recommended the bone of a hare as a toothpick. Some toiletry sets included a gold or silver toothpick.

As the title *artifices dentium* (lit., "makers of teeth") suggests, Roman dentistry was as much for cosmetic purposes as for medical ones. Good teeth were an especially valued feature of women's beauty, and some Roman women went to great lengths to mask the effects of dental disease. Ovid declared, "Nor should I approve your openly taking the mixed marrow of a hind, or cleaning your teeth for all to see" (*Ars* 3.216). He also advised ladies with bad teeth not to laugh. Martial has tooth powder personified addressing an old woman: "What have you to do with me? Let a girl take me. I am not in the habit of polishing purchased teeth" (*Ep.* 14.56).

Cosmetic dentistry could even be a symbol of high status in ancient Rome. It is quite remarkable that nearly twenty partial dentures, using gold wire, gold bands, and soldering, have been recovered from the pre-Roman era (7th–6th c. BC), at Orvieto, Tarquinia, Cerveteri, and other sites from Etruria north of Rome. Some included as many as five teeth. What is also unusual is that these prostheses replaced the healthy teeth (central incisors) of women to enhance their beauty.

Rome's earliest written laws, the *Twelve Tables* (449 BC), contain the following provision: "But him whose teeth shall have been fastened together with gold [*cui auro dentes iuncti escunt*], if a person shall bury or burn him along with that gold, it shall be with impunity" (X.8–9; Lewis and Reinhold, 115).

Gold teeth were a luxury not everyone could afford. The poet Martial's satirical epigrams afford a more realistic look at Roman cosmetic dentistry. In *Epigram* 12.23 he mocks a prostitute: "You use bought teeth and hair and you're not ashamed of it." In *Epigram* 1.72 he addresses a plagiarist, commenting: "Just so Aegle thinks she has teeth in virtue of purchased bones and Indian horn." In *Epigram* 9.37–38 he addresses an old woman: "You are at home yourself, Galla, but you are made up in the middle of Subura. Your hair is manufactured in your absence. You lay your teeth aside at night, as you do your silks, and lie stored in a hundred caskets." In *Epigram* 5.43 he writes: "Thais' teeth are black, Laecania's snow-white. The reason? The one has those she bought, the other her own." In *Epigram* 2.41, he remarks: "You are no girl, and you have but three teeth, Maximina, and they quite the color of pitch or boxwood."

Archaeological studies have confirmed Roman authors' descriptions of dentistry and the prevalence of dental disease. In 1984–1985 excavations were conducted in the Roman Forum at a *taberna*, or shop, in the podium of the Temple of Castor and Pollux that served as a barbershop and also a place where a dentist worked. Among the eighty-six teeth found there were decayed children's molars that had been extracted. Among the other objects discovered there were jars, bowls, scoops, picks, and spatulas. Excavations at Pompeii and Herculaneum revealed this dismaying evidence of general dental health: Though only 5 percent or fewer of the population had teeth with caries, at Pompeii 25 percent of the individuals had one or more abscesses, and 50 percent had periodontal disease. This means that most suffered from toothaches that could only have been cured by the extraction of the painful tooth. Older persons had teeth worn down by attrition from their coarse diet.

Lucian's professor of rhetoric claimed, "I went to live with an old woman and for a time got my victuals from her by pretending to love a hag of seventy with only four teeth still left, and those four fastened in with gold!" (Lucian, *Rhet. praec.* 24). Juvenal lamented the ravages of age: "But old men all look alike. Their voices are as shaky as their limbs, their heads without hair, their noses driveling as in childhood. Their bread, poor wretches, has to be munched by toothless gums; so offensive do they become to their wives, their children and themselves" (*Sat.* 10.198–201).

E. THE JEWISH WORLD

There are relatively few references to teeth in non-rabbinic Jewish texts. Ben Sirach warns, "Do not laugh with him [a child], lest you have sorrow with him, and in the end you will gnash your teeth" (Sir 30:10). The martyr

Eleazar, who was killed by Antiochus IV for refusing to eat pork, is praised as follows: "O priest, worthy of the priesthood, you neither defiled your sacred teeth nor profaned your stomach, which had room only for reverence and purity, by eating defiling foods" (4 Macc 7:6).

In commenting on *lex talionis* in the OT, Philo gives an extensive exposition on teeth:

> A further command is that if any one strike out a servant's tooth he must grant him his liberty. Why is this? Because life is precious and the means contrived by nature for the preservation of life are teeth by which the food is subjected to the processes necessary for dealing with it. Now the teeth are divided into the cutters and the grinders; the former do their part by cutting or biting the bread-stuffs and all other comestibles, whence their appropriate name of cutters, the latter by their capacity for reducing the bitten pieces into smaller particles. (*Spec.* 3.198)

There are abundant references to teeth and their care in the Talmud. Rabbi Meir taught, "Chew well with your teeth, and you will find it in your steps" (*b. Šabb.* 152a). There were discussions about the making and use of toothpicks on the Sabbath. Rabbi Eliezer said, "One may take a chip [lying] before him to pick his teeth therewith" (*b. Šabb.* 81b). There were also disputations about whether one could cut off a piece of hard or soft spicewood to use it as a toothpick: "It is forbidden; he may not cut off [a piece] in order to pick his teeth, but if he did cut off he is liable to a sin-offering!" (*b. Beṣah* 33b). One saying about a toothpick resembles one of Jesus's statements: "If the judge said to a man, 'Take the splinter from between your teeth,' he would retort, 'Take the beam from between your eyes'" (*b. B. Bat.* 15b).

Commenting on the implications of Exod 21:27, which requires a master to free his slave if he has damaged his teeth, the rabbis taught: "If his master is a doctor and he asks him ... to drill his tooth, and he knocks it out, he laughs at his master and goes out free" (*b. Qidd.* 24b).

The rabbis recommended chewing milt, that is, spleen, as good for the teeth: "Chew it well and then spit it out." Also, "Horse-beans are bad for the teeth but good for the bowels. What is the remedy?—To boil them well and swallow them" (*b. Ber.* 44b).

There is an extensive rabbinic discussion of a toothache that starts in the mouth but ends in the intestines. Rabbi Abaye ruled: "One who is troubled with his teeth must not rinse them with vinegar [on the Sabbath]" (*b. 'Abod. Zar.* 28a). Others said that if such a person's teeth troubled him very much, he could rinse them with vinegar. Rabbi Johanan was so bothered with scurvy that he went to a Gentile woman to get a secret remedy for his ailment.

The rabbis discussed the contradiction between popular advice about the use of vinegar for toothaches and the negative reference to vinegar in Prov 10:26. "There is no difficulty: the one refers to vinegar of fruit; the other to acid. Alternatively, both refer to acid: one means where there is a wound; the other, where there is no wound. If there is a wound it heals; if there is no wound it loosens [the teeth in the gums]" (b. Šabb. 111a). The Mishnah makes the distinction between using vinegar as food, which is permitted on the Sabbath, and its use for medicinal purposes, which is prohibited: "If his teeth pain him he may not suck vinegar through them but he may take vinegar after his usual fashion [i.e., during a meal], and if he is healed, he is healed" (m. Šabb. 14:4). Other recommended ingredients for the care of teeth and the mouth were salt, vinegar, oil of cloves, pepper, cinnamon, ginger, and fruit juices.

To combat halitosis, Jews were accustomed to keep a peppercorn or a grain of salt in their mouths. As to the practice of this custom on the Sabbath, the Mishnah indicates that if peppercorn or a piece of salt falls out of the mouth, a woman may not put it back (see m. Šabb. 6:5).

Rab advised his son Hiyya, "Do not take drugs . . . do not have a tooth extracted" (b. Pesaḥ. 113a). Women especially were accustomed to wearing artificial teeth, including "gold" teeth for the sake of appearance. In a discussion of what objects a woman could go out with on the Sabbath, we read, "Rabbi permits a false tooth or a gilded tooth; but the Sages forbid it" (m. Šabb. 6:5). The Gemara in the Talmud explains: "They taught this only of a gold [tooth], but as for a silver one, all agree that it is permitted" (b. Šabb. 65a). Elsewhere it is related that a woman who had an unsightly artificial tooth was rejected by the man to whom she was betrothed. Subsequently, Rabbi Ishmael made her a beautiful gold tooth at his own expense, with the result that she was then accepted (b. Ned. 66b).

The rabbis recognized that the loss of teeth was one of the inevitable effects of age. Rabbi Hinena observed: "As soon as a person's teeth fall out, his means of a livelihood are reduced" (b. Nid. 65a). This statement quotes out of context Amos 4:9, which reads, "And I also have given you cleanness of teeth in all your cities, and want of bread in all your places." An edentulous (toothless) priest was disqualified from temple service.

F. THE CHRISTIAN WORLD

There are relatively few references to teeth in patristic writings, except for commentaries on biblical passages that refer to teeth. Most patristic interpretations of these passages are allegorical in nature. For example, Irenaeus comments on Jacob's deathbed blessing on Judah (Gen 49:8–12), which ends as follows: "His eyes will be darker than wine, his teeth whiter than milk" (vs. 12). Interpreting this as a messianic prophecy, Irenaeus declares:

> Let those who have the reputation of investigating everything, inquire ... what was the ass's colt [referred to as] his, what the clothing, and what the eyes, what the teeth, and what the wine, and thus let them investigate every one of the points mentioned; and they shall find that there was none other announced than our Lord, Christ Jesus. (*Haer.* 4.10.2)

Origen, who rejected a literal interpretation of the Genesis account of the fall, asks:

> And who is found so ignorant as to suppose that God, as if He had been a husbandman, planted trees in paradise, in Eden towards the east, and a tree of life in it, i.e., a visible and palpable tree of wood, so that anyone eating of it with bodily teeth should obtain life, and, eating again of another tree, should come to the knowledge of good and evil? (*Prin.* 4.16)

Instead, in the beginning of his great theological work *De principiis* (*First Principles*), Origen argues that the physical functions of the body can symbolize activities of the soul:

> The names of the organs of sense are frequently applied to the soul, so that it may be said to see with the eyes of the heart, i.e., to perform an intellectual act by means of the power of intelligence. . . . So also we say that it makes use of teeth, when it chews and eats the bread of life which comes down from heaven. (*Prin.* 1.1)

Other church fathers also depict the tangible reality of eating in a positive light. Tertullian often referred to teeth to emphasize the physicality of both the resurrected Christ and resurrected Christians against the docetism of Marcion (who had claimed that Christ only appeared to have a body during his life). Tertullian mocked Marcion's docetic Christ as a phantom:

> Believe me, He chose rather to be born, than in any part to pretend—and that indeed to His own detriment—that He was bearing about a flesh hardened without bones, solid without muscles, bloody without blood, clothed without the tunic *of skin*, hungry without appetite, eating without teeth, speaking without a tongue, so that His word was a phantom to the ears through an imaginary voice. (*Carn.* 5)

Commenting on the appearance of the resurrected Christ in Luke 24:39–41, Tertullian challenges Marcion as follows:

Why, too, does He add, 'Know that it is I myself,' when they had before known Him to be corporeal? Else, if He were altogether a phantom, why did He upbraid them for supposing Him to be a phantom? But while they still believed not, He asked them for some meat, for the express purpose of showing them that He had teeth. (*Marc.* 4.43)

Critics challenged Tertullian on the question of Christians' resurrected bodies, saying: "What . . . will then be the use of the cavity of our mouth, and its rows of teeth, and the passage of the throat, and the branch-way of the stomach, and the gulf of the belly, and the entangled tissue of the bowels, when there shall no longer be room for eating and drinking?" (*Res.* 60). To this Tertullian responded,

Then, again, you received your teeth for the consumption of your meal: why not rather for wreathing your mouth with suitable defence on every opening thereof, small or wide? Why not, too, for moderating the impulses of your tongue, and guarding your articulate speech from failure and violence? Let me tell you, (if you do not know), that there are toothless persons in the world. Look at them, and ask whether even a cage of teeth be not an honor to the mouth. (*Res.* 61)

Although Tertullian affirmed the resurrection of the body, he was unsparing towards those who indulged in luxuries during this life. In his treatise on repentance, Tertullian rebukes those who eschew sackcloth and ashes: "Is it then becoming for us to supplicate for our sins in scarlet and purple? Hasten hither with the pin for panning the hair, and the powder for polishing the teeth, and some forked implement of steel or brass for cleaning the nails" (*Paen.* 11).

Augustine, who followed the Alexandrians (Clement, Origen) in establishing the allegorical approach to Scripture, commented on Song of Solomon 4:2 by taking "teeth like a flock of shorn ewes that have come up from the washing" as a reference to baptized Christians:

I don't know why, [but] I feel greater pleasure in contemplating holy men, when I view them as the teeth of the Church, tearing men away from their errors, and bringing them into the Church's body, with all their harshness softened down, just as if they had been torn off and masticated by the teeth. It is with the greatest pleasure, too, that I recognize them under the figure of sheep that have been shorn, laying down the burthens of the world like fleeces, and coming up from the washing, *i.e.*, from baptism, and all bearing twins, *i.e.*, the twin commandments of love, and none among them barren in that holy fruit. (*Doctr. chr.* 2.6.7)

As for his own teeth, Augustine was not immune from pain. In fact, shortly after his conversion, he suffered a terrible toothache:

Thou [God] at that time tortured me with toothache; and when it had become so exceeding great that I was not able to speak, it came into my heart to urge all my friends who were present to pray for me to You, the God of all manner of health. And I wrote it down on wax, and gave it to them to read. Presently, as with submissive desire we bowed our knees, that pain departed. But what pain? Or how did it depart? I confess to being much afraid, my Lord my God, seeing that from my earliest years I had not experienced such pain. And Your purposes were profoundly impressed upon me; and, rejoicing in faith, I praised Your name. (*Conf.* 9.4.12)

The great Basil of Caesarea (b. AD 330), who was instrumental in establishing the first hospital at his monastery in Cappadocia, wrote to Amphilochus, when he was but 46, that he had already lost all his teeth. Dionysius of Alexandria (AD 247–265) described the martyrdom of a virgin named Apollonia. Before she was killed the mob "knocked out all her teeth, and cut her jaws" (*Ep.* 3). In later centuries she became known as St. Apollonia and Christians prayed to her for relief from toothache. She was represented in art with pincers holding a tooth.

BIBLIOGRAPHY: T. Bardinet, *Dents et mâchoires dans les représentations religieuse et la pratique médicale de l'Égypte ancienne* (1990); M. J. Becker, "Early Dental Appliances in the Eastern Mediterranean," *Ber* 42 (1995), 71–102; M. J. Becker, "Etruscan Gold Dental Appliances: Three Newly 'Discovered' Examples," *AJA* 103.1 (1999), 103–11; L. Bliquez, "Prosthetics in Classical Antiquity: Greek, Etruscan, and Roman Prosthetics," *ANRW* 37.3 (1996), 2640–76; E. A. W. Budge, trans., *The Book of the Dead: The Papyrus of Ani* (2013); R. A. Caminos, trans. and ed., *Late-Egyptian Miscellanies* (1954); R. David, ed., *Egyptian Mummies and Modern Science* (2008); G. R. Denton, "A New Interpretation of a Well-Known Assyrian Letter," *JNES* 2.4 (1943), 314–15; G. T. Emery, "Dental Pathology and Archaeology," *Antiq* 37 (1963), 274–81; R. Forshaw, "Dental Health and Dentistry in Ancient Egypt," *Ancient Egypt* 9.6 (2009), 24–28; M. V. Fox, *The Song of Songs and the Ancient Egyptian Love Songs* (1985); M. J. Geller, *Ancient Babylonian Medicine* (2010); P. Ghalioungui, *The Ebers Papyrus: A New Translation with Commentaries* (1987); P. Ghalioungui and Z. el-Dawakhly, *Health and Healing in Ancient Egypt* (1963); B. Ginge, M. Becker, and P. Guldager, "Of Roman Extraction," *Arch* 42.4 (1989), 34–37; J. S. Hamilton, trans., *The Compositiones of Scribonius Largus* (1986); J. E. Harris and P. V. Ponitz, "Dental Health in Ancient Egypt," in *Mummies, Disease, and Ancient Cultures,* A. Cockburn and E. Cockburn, ed. (1980), 45–51; J. E. Harris, A. T. Storey, and P. V. Ponitz, "Dental Diseases in the Royal Mummies," in *An X-Ray Atlas of the Royal Mummies,* ed. J. E. Harris and E. Wente (1980), 328–45; J. E. Harris, Z. Iskander, and S. Farid, "Restorative Dentistry in

Ancient Egypt," *Journal of the Michigan Dental Association* 57.12 (1975), 401–4; J. E. Harris and K. R. Weeks, *X-Raying the Pharaohs* (1973); S. Hillson, *Teeth* (1986); S. Hillson, *Dental Anthropology* (1996); W. Hoffmann-Axthelm, *History of Dentistry* (1981); F. F. Leek, "Observations on the Dental Pathology Seen in Ancient Egyptian Skulls," *JEA* 52 (1966), 59–64; F. F. Leek, "The Practice of Dentistry in Ancient Egypt," *JEA* 53 (1967), 51–57; F. F. Leek, "A Technique for the Oral Examination of a Mummy," *JEA* 57 (1971), 105–9; F. F. Leek, "Teeth and Bread in Ancient Egypt," *JEA* 58 (1972), 126–32; N. Lewis and M. Reinhold, ed., *Roman Civilization I: The Republic and the Augustan Age* (3rd ed., 1990); J. Miller, "Dental Health and Disease in Ancient Egypt," in *Egyptian Mummies and Modern Science*, ed. R. David (2008), 52–78; J. Nunn, *Ancient Egyptian Medicine* (1996); R. Paulissian, "Dental Care in Ancient Assyria and Babylonia," *Journal of Assyrian Academic Studies* 7.2 (1993), 96–116; J. Scurlock, *Sourcebook for Ancient Mesopotamian Medicine* (2014); J. Scurlock and B. R. Andersen, trans., *Diagnoses in Assyrian and Babylonian Medicine: Ancient Sources, Translations, and Modern Medical Analyses* (2005), ch. 18, "Dental and Oral Diseases"; R. C. Thompson, *Assyrian Medical Texts* (1926); B. R. Townend, "An Assyrian Dental Diagnosis," *Iraq* 5 (1938), 82–84; B. R. Townend, "The Story of the Tooth-worm," *BHM* 15 (1944), 37–58; K. R. Weeks, "Ancient Egyptian Dentistry," in *An X-Ray Atlas of the Royal Mummies*, ed. J. E. Harris, and E. Wente (1980), 99–121; B. W. Weinberger, *An Introduction to the History of Dentistry* (1948); B. W. Weinberger, "Further Evidence That Dentistry Was Practiced in Ancient Egypt, Phoenicia, and Greece," *BHM* 20.2 (1946), 188–95; J. Zias and K. Numeroff, "Ancient Dentistry in the Eastern Mediterranean," *IEJ* 36.1/2 (1986), 65–67.

EMY

See also BONE & OBJECTS OF BONE, IVORY, and MEDICINE & PHYSICIANS.

D̲ISEASES & P̲LAGUES

In antiquity humans suffered from all kinds of illnesses that are still prevalent today. Ancient civilizations did not possess accurate knowledge about the causes of most ailments. In some cases, however, detailed records of symptoms preserved in ancient texts allow us to identify the ailments described as specific diseases, such as epilepsy and malaria. Scholars also use archeological evidence from graves and human remains to shed light on the meaning of ancient medical terminology and to provide a broader picture of physical health and medical practices in antiquity.

The threat of disease pervaded everyday life in the ancient world. Before the development of effective inoculations, contagious diseases caused plagues that killed large numbers of people in a short time. As the etiology (origin) of diseases was unknown, many were ascribed to divine influence or malevolent spirits.

A. THE OLD TESTAMENT

The general Hebrew words for "illness" (ḥŏlî) and "disease" (maḥălâ) are derived from the verbal root ḥlh, which means "to become weak." Some OT passages demonstrate the belief that God used diseases, including madness and blindness, as a punishment for Israel's disobedience (Lev 26:15–16; Num 14:12; Deut 28:22), or even for the sins of an individual, such as David (2 Sam 24:15–17). The churlish Nabal may have been struck with a heart attack (1 Sam 25:37–38). The proud Nebuchadnezzar may have been afflicted for a season with boanthropy, a mental disorder that led him to eat grass like a cow (Dan 4:33).

Blindness was one of the most common afflictions of antiquity, warranting special laws for those afflicted (Lev 19:14; Deut 27:18). External irritants such as sand could cause inflammation in the eyes; this was also true of the effect of bright sunlight on unshaded eyes. But the most common cause of blindness was trachoma, an infection spread by flies carrying

Chlamydia trachomatis. A priest who became blemished in his eyes was disqualified from serving (Lev 21:18).

Jehoram's "lingering disease of the bowels" (2 Chr 21:15) may have been colon cancer or bacillary dysentery. Archaeological evidence also sheds light on specific diseases, such as parasitic infections, that are not mentioned in Scripture. An examination of bricks from Bronze Age Jericho revealed the presence of a snail, *Bulinus truncatus*, that served as the intermediate host of *Schistosoma haematobium*. Evidence from coprolites (fecal remains) from latrines in Jerusalem at the time of the Babylonian siege (6th c. BC) revealed evidence of whipworm (*Trichuris trichiura*), a parasite ingested from eating poorly cooked beef.

The discharge from a man (that is, from his penis) that rendered him unclean (Lev 15:2) has been interpreted by some as evidence of gonorrhea. The book of Job describes the Lord allowing Satan to test Job with an affliction called *šĕḥîn*, "boils" (Job 2:7), which probably refers to an acute inflammatory skin condition; this has been interpreted as either eczema or impetigo. The itchy disease of the head or chin mentioned in Lev 13:30 is viewed as ringworm. The "boils of Egypt" (Deut 28:27) threatened as punishment for breaking the covenant may perhaps have denoted the itching rash scabies, which is caused by mites, or perhaps a staphylococcal infection. However, the sixth plague of Egypt, described as "festering boils" that affected both people and animals (Exod 9:9), may have been anthrax. The "sores on the head" foretold for the women of Judah in Isa 3:17 might refer to either favus or vitiligo, both of which affect the skin and hair. The threatened "fever (*qaddaḥat*) and inflammation (*dalleqet*)" described in Deut 28:22 (cf. Lev 26:16) may possibly be related to malaria. Hezekiah's boil, which was treated by a poultice of figs (2 Kgs 20:7; Isa 38:21), may have been a staphylococcal infection. Asa's foot ailment (1 Kgs 15:23||2 Chr 16:12) may have been gout, which is caused by the painful accumulation of uric acid, or it may have been a circulatory dysfunction that led to gangrene. Some, who have speculated that the word "foot" (*regel*) in this text is a euphemism for the penis, have also suggested sexual dysfunction.

The most prominent disease mentioned in the OT is *ṣāraʿat*, a word that occurs thirty-five times, twenty-nine of which are in Lev 13 and 14. This term has traditionally been translated "leprosy," following the rendering of the Hebrew word in the Septuagint by the Greek word *lepra* (derived from a root meaning "flake"). But it has become clear to biblical and medical scholars that the illness described is not true leprosy (called Hansen's disease after its identification by the Norwegian Gerhard Hansen in 1874), which did not make its appearance in the Mediterranean world until the Hellenistic age, when it was called *elephas* or *elephantiasis* by the Greek medical writers. (On Hansen's disease in the ancient world, see further below.)

Based on the descriptions of ṣāraʿat in the OT, we know that it was a flaking skin ailment that manifested itself in white patches of skin. Under the OT purity laws, a person suffering from ṣāraʿat was to show himself to the priest twice at an interval of a week (Lev 13:18–22). In contrast, Hansen's disease is much slower in its manifestation, taking years to develop into its extreme phase. If the whiteness of ṣāraʿat spread over the entire body, the individual was declared clean (Lev 13:12–13). In other cases of ṣāraʿat mentioned in the OT, such as those that afflicted Miriam (Num 12:10), Moses's hand (Exod 4:6), and Gehazi (2 Kgs 5:27), the skin is described as looking like "snow," although this may refer to the flakiness of the disease rather than to its white appearance. True leprous lesions, however, are not white. Moreover, Lev 13 and 14 describe a similar infection that could affect garments, perhaps indicating an outbreak of mold or fungus. Those who had ṣāraʿat were excluded from the army (Num 5:2). They were to isolate themselves from the community, wear torn garments, and cry out "Unclean! Unclean!" (Lev 13:45). Although lepers were regarded as social outcasts, high-ranking figures were not immune from the disease: King Azariah of Judah (2 Kgs 15:5), who is also called Uzziah (2 Chr 26:19), was punished for his impiety with "leprosy." Elisha cured the "leprosy" of the Syrian general Naaman by having him immerse himself seven times in the Jordan River (2 Kgs 5:14).

Large-scale plagues (sing. maggēpâ), which resulted in many deaths, are frequently recorded in the OT, such as the one following the rebellion of Korah that killed 14,700 (Num 16:49), the plague that led to the death of the 24,000 who were punished for worshipping Baal of Peor (Num 25:9), and the deber ("pestilence") that cost 70,000 lives as a result of David's sin in numbering his people (2 Sam 24:15). There is also an intriguing account of a plague outbreak in Philistine territory recorded in 1 Sam 5–6. This was interpreted as dysentery by Josephus (Ant. 6.3), following the interpretation of the ʿŏpālîm (1 Sam 5:6) as hemorrhoids (KJV "emerods"). Today some scholars interpret this word as a reference to buboes, or inflamed lymph nodes in the armpits and groin, which could suggest that the pestilence was the infamous "bubonic" plague that was later to ravage Europe as the Black Death. As the plague's Yersinia pestis organism is carried by fleas on rats (Rattus rattus), these scholars believe that the "mice" that are described infesting the Philistine cities (1 Sam 6:4, KJV) were in fact rats (so NIV). The disaster that befell Sennacherib's army and resulted in one hundred eighty-five thousand fatalities (2 Kgs 19:35||Isa 37:36) has also been interpreted as the bubonic plague, since Herodotus (Hist. 2.141) attributes Sennacherib's defeat to a legion of "mice" that gnawed the Assyrian weapons.

B. THE NEW TESTAMENT

The general Greek word for illness involving groups of people was *nosos*. Another word for disease, *astheneia* (Acts 28:9; Gal 4:13; 1 Tim 5:23), connoted "weakness," as did the word *malakia*, literally "softness" (Matt 9:35; 10:1). The word *mastix*, literally a "scourge," is also used in the NT to designate disease (Mark 3:10).

According to the NT, God can send illness as a punishment (Acts 12:23; 1 Cor 10:8; 11:30). Although the NT does not support a necessary connection between sin and disease (John 9:3), one man who is healed by Jesus is warned not to continue sinning lest something worse come upon him (John 5:14). James instructs those who are sick to ask the elders to pray for them and "anoint them with oil" (Jas 5:14).

Some illnesses in the NT are ascribed to Satan, as is the case of the woman, "a daughter of Abraham, whom Satan [had] kept bound for eighteen long years" (Luke 13:16; cf. Acts 10:38). She was bent over and could not straighten up, an affliction that is known as spondylitis, where the disks and vertebrae are fused to produce an abnormal curvature of the spine (kyphosis).

Other maladies are also associated with demons in the NT, most notably that of the epileptic boy (Matt 17:14–18; Mk 9:14–27). As his father explains the boy's condition to Jesus, he uses the Greek word *selēniazetai* (Matt 17:15), derived from the name of the moon goddess Selene, which reflects popular belief about the moon's influence on epileptics. In Mark's account, the boy convulses, rolls around, and foams at the mouth (Mark 9:20). He is possessed by a dumb (*alalos*) spirit (Mark 9:17; cf. Luke 9:39), whom Jesus exorcises. These details correspond to the phases of a tonic-clonic (formerly known as a grand mal) epileptic seizure: the tonic phase of muscular rigidity, the clonic phase of muscular jerking, and the postictal unconscious phase. Of the thirteen healing miracles in Mark's Gospel, six involve the exorcism of demons; in contrast, John's Gospel records no exorcisms.

Blindness was a common affliction in NT times (Matt 20:29–34; Mark 8:22–26). Those affected were forced to beg (Mark 10:46–52; John 9:1). Jesus healed the blind as well as a deaf mute (Mark 7:31–37). The woman with the flow of blood whom Jesus healed (Matt 9:20–22||Mark 5:25–34||Luke 8:43–48) suffered from menorrhagia, which may have been caused by a cancer of the uterus. The man with dropsy (edema; Gk. *hydrōpos*) mentioned in Luke 14:2–4 suffered from an effusion of fluid into his bodily cavities, particularly in his legs. The man with a shriveled (*xēros*) hand whom Jesus healed (Matt 12:9–14||Mark 3:1–6||Luke 6:6–11) may have suffered from acute anterior poliomyelitis in childhood. Many of the people whom Jesus and the disciples healed were *paralytikoi* (Matt 4:24), such as the servant of the centurion at Capernaum (Matt 8:6), the man who was carried on his "mat" (Matt 9:2||Mark 2:3), the man who sought help at the pool of Bethesda (John 5:5), the cripple at the temple gate (Acts 3:2), Aeneas, who was paralyzed in bed for eight years (Acts 9:33), and the cripple at Lystra (Acts 14:8).

Together, the Greek words *lepra* ("leprosy") and *lepros* ("leprous," "leper") occur thirteen times in the Gospels. Jesus healed a "leper" (Matt 8:2–4||Mark 1:40–45||Luke 5:12–16) and instructed him to show himself to the priest; on another occasion Jesus "cleansed" ten men who had "leprosy," of whom only one, a Samaritan, returned to thank him (Luke 17:12–19). The power to cleanse such diseases was a sign to John the Baptist that Jesus was the Messiah (Matt 11:5||Luke 7:22). Jesus dined at the house of "Simon the Leper" (Matt 26:6||Mark 14:3). The disciples were commanded to heal the sick and cleanse "those who have leprosy" (Matt 10:8). Jesus recounted the story of Naaman to those gathered at the synagogue in Nazareth (Luke 4:27). Though true leprosy (known as *elephas* or *elephantiasis*) had spread to the region by the Hellenistic era, the NT's use of the words *lepra* and *lepros* reflects the Septuagint's translation of Hebrew ṣāraʿat, which, as mentioned above, was not leprosy but a different skin disease. Thus, although it is possible, it is improbable that the words *lepra* and *lepros* in the NT refer to Hansen's disease.

The death of Herod Agrippa I in AD 44 is described by Luke (who was a physician) in graphic terms (Acts 12:23): "an angel of the Lord struck him down, and he was eaten by worms [*skōlēkobrōtos*] and died." Josephus (*Ant.* 19.343–350) offers a complementary account, which has led scholars to suggest that the king had suffered appendicitis, perforation of the bowels, infestation by tapeworms, or peritonitis.

Jesus healed Peter's mother-in-law, who suffered from *pyretos*, "fever" (Matt 8:14||Mark 1:30||Luke 4:38), and the official's son, who was close to death (John 4:47, 52). When Paul was shipwrecked at Malta, he learned that the official Publius's father was "sick in bed, suffering from fever [*pyretois*] and dysentery [*dysenteriō*]" (Acts 28:8). The use of the plural form of the word for fever may either connote its intensity or its intermittent nature, a sure sign of malaria. The island was also known for undulant Malta fever (*Brucella melitensis*), found in the milk of its goats. Dysentery is an inflammation of the colon by a bacillus, or amoeba, causing pain and diarrhea.

Paul's "thorn [or stake] in the flesh" (2 Cor 12:7) was apparently some severe ailment for which he unsuccessfully sought relief from the Lord, who assured him instead that his grace was sufficient. Some have suggested that this was malaria or migraine headaches. Others suggest that it was epilepsy, noting Paul's use in Gal 4:14 of the word *ekptyō*, "to despise," literally "to spit"—a popular defense against epileptics. Another attractive suggestion is that Paul's affliction was ophthalmia, a disfiguring disease of the eyes. Paul reminds the Galatians that it was because of "an illness" (Gal 4:13) that he preached to them, even though his condition was "a trial" to them (Gal 4:14). Several other passages in Galatians suggest that this illness was a disease of the eyes. Paul writes that the believers were willing to gouge out "their eyes" and give them to him (Gal 4:15), perhaps out of pity for his condition. At the end of the letter he remarks, "See what large letters I use as I write to you!" (Gal 6:11), which may indicate that his sight was failing. Later, before the Sanhedrin, he did not recognize the high priest (Acts 23:5).

C. THE NEAR EASTERN WORLD

Mesopotamia

We know practically nothing about Sumerian medicine, though Sumerian terms were used in later Akkadian texts. We do have an abundance of Akkadian texts from the Middle Assyrian and Middle Babylonian periods (ca. 1500–1200 BC), from Ashur, Nineveh, Sultantepe, Nippur, Sippar, Babylon, and Uruk.

Excavations in Mesopotamia have yielded about one thousand cuneiform texts dealing with diseases and their treatments by magical/medical methods. Especially valuable is the Diagnostic Handbook, a series of forty tablets known as *Sakikkû*, "Symptoms," with over three thousand entries that record diseases. According to tradition, this diagnostic and prognostic handbook was compiled by a scholar-physician named Esagil-kin-apli, under the patronage of king Adad-apla-iddina of Babylon (1068–1047 BC). We also have a list of ninety-five offenses that were believed to provoke the gods to send an illness as an intrusion to enter the body of the offender. Some ailments were ascribed to witchcraft, and many to the influence of demons or ghosts. Different demons were thought to attack different parts of the body:

> The *ašakku* attacks the head of the man.
> The *namtaru* attacks the life of the man.
> The bad *utukku* attacks the neck of the man.
> The bad *alû* attacks the breast of the man.
> The bad *gallû* attacks the hand of the man.
> The bad *ekimmu* attacks the stomach of the man.

The bad god attacks the foot of the man.
These seven together are found upon him.
(Thompson, II.29)

Epilepsy was believed to be caused by an attack of the "hand" (*qātu*) of Bennu, a deputy of Sin, the moon god (Scurlock, 200–3). The demon of epilepsy was also called Lugal-urra, "lord of the roof." One text describes a tonic-clonic (grand mal) seizure: "If his eye flutters, his lip(s) come apart, his spittle flows from his mouth, his hand, his foot, (and) his torso thrash around like (those of) a slaughtered sheep, AN.TA.ŠUB.BA (seizure) afflicts him" (Scurlock and Andersen, 317). The Code of Hammurabi guaranteed a refund for buying a slave who turned out to be an epileptic: "If a seignior purchased a male (or) female slave and when his month was not yet complete, epilepsy [*bennu*] attacked him, he shall return (him) to his seller and the purchaser shall get back the money which he paid out" (CH 278; *ANET*, 177).

The following text appears to be a case of Parkinson's disease: "If his head trembles, his neck and his spine are bent, he cannot stick out his tongue (?) or stretch out . . . his saliva continually flows from his mouth, his hands, his legs, and his feet all tremble at once, (and) when he walks, he falls forward . . . he will not get well" (Scurlock and Andersen, 336).

A stroke is described in one Assyrian text: "If he has a stroke and either his 'right' side or his 'left' side is affected (and) his shoulder is not released, . . . affliction by a ghost at the steppe: recovery in three (days)" (Scurlock, 208). A case of thrombosis is likely the subject of a Mari text (ARM 26.275): "The day I sent this tablet of mine to my lord, Sumhu-Rabi unfortunately fell ill. Not one day (had he felt any problem), not two days, on that day (he said), 'My foot hurts.' . . . And all of a sudden he laid down his life" (Heimpel, 281).

The following may describe asthma: "If a mighty illness afflicts him so that he has a reduced appetite for bread, his lungs sing like a reed flute (and) fever continually afflicts him daily in winter, he will die" (Scurlock and Andersen, 184). Another text may indicate tuberculosis: "If a person constantly has sick lungs so that he *guḫḫu* (brassy-coughs) (and) produces blood with his spittle . . ." (Scurlock and Andersen, 47). The cause of some illness was believed to be malevolent magic: "If a person's upper abdomen continually has mucus, his upper abdomen burns him hotly, he loses his appetite for bread and water/beer, (and) his flesh is tense, that person has eaten or drunk *kišpu* [witchcraft]" (Scurlock and Andersen, 357).

As Mesopotamia was a hot and dry environment with little shade, the population was always in danger of dehydration, with the high possibility of kidney stones, as described in this text: "If a person's kidney hurts him, his pelvic region continually hurts him intensely, and his urine is like the urine of a donkey (or) it is white (and) after his urine he shows blood, that person is sick with *mūṣu*" (Scurlock, 542).

In addition to epilepsy, the moon god Sin was also believed to cause *sinlurmā* (xerophthalmia), day or night blindness, which was probably caused by lack of vitamin A. A disease that affected the mouth was called *buʾšānu*, "stinking"; this may have described an acute infection of the tonsils, *Herpes simplex* infection of the palate, scurvy, or trench mouth disease.

Cases of jaundice, which is caused by elevated levels of bilirubin from an obstruction of the bile duct, were called *aḫḫāzu*: "If his face is yellow and the inner part of his eyes is yellow . . . *aḫḫāzu*" (Scurlock and Andersen, 139). "If *aḫḫāzu* rises to a person's eyes so that his eyes are covered with a network of yellow threads, his insides are puffed up . . . he will die" (Scurlock, 527).

Some scholars have interpreted the following text as referring to a case of leprosy: "If a man's body [*pagrum*] shows white spots [sing. *pūsum*] and is marked with dots [sing. *nuqdum*], that man is rejected by his god, he is rejected by mankind" (Scurlock and Andersen, 73). However, in the light of the epidemiological evidence that leprosy did not spread to the Near East until the Hellenistic age, this is not likely. Nor is *saḫarašubbû* (another skin disease) leprosy. *Garābu*, an ailment characterized by white marks on the head, may have been favus, a fungus infection, as it also affected sheep. *Epqu*, which covered a man with scales like a carp or snake and which was believed to be caused by the wrath of the moon god, may have been psoriasis.

Fever (*laʾbum* or *diʾû*) may possibly have been malaria. The ancients did not understand that malaria (from Italian *mal aria*, "bad air") was caused by mosquitoes, as this link was only discovered in the late nineteenth century. However, they did understand the connection between swampy areas and disease, as indicated by the following advice: "He must not go into the lowlands by the river or an infectious disease will infect him" (Scurlock and Andersen, 23). Though texts do not explicitly describe infestation by parasites such as *Schistosoma haematobium,* the evidence of its snail host as found in the bricks at Babylon make its presence in ancient Babylonia probable.

Plagues were ascribed to Nergal and his messenger Namtaru, gods of the underworld, in the Sumerian and Babylonian texts, and to Resheph in Eblaite, Ugaritic, and Phoenician texts. A Mari letter (ARM 26.259) reported:

> About the devouring of a god concerning which my lord wrote me—in Tuttul there are cases of illness. Death is rare. In Dunnum below Lasqum is a corpse

heap. Within two days about 20 men of the troops died. And the Dunnites left the city and went to the mountain of Lasqum. Muban, Manuhatan, in the vicinity of Dunnum, are well. Dunnum itself is diseased. Mari is well, the land is well. (Heimpel, 277)

A possible reference to the bubo of the bubonic plague may be found in the following text: "if the nature of the sore is that it is hard to the touch, he burns with fever, his spleen is very puffed up . . . its name is *šadānu*" (Scurlock and Andersen, 73–74).

That some Mesopotamians understood the contagious nature of disease—at least in terms of a possible magical transfer of disease—is illustrated by a letter of Zimri-Lim, the king of Mari, to his queen:

I have heard "Nanna has an infection (*simmum*)." Since she is often at the palace, it will infect the many women who are with her. Now give strict orders: No one is to drink from the cup she uses; no one is to sit on the seat she takes; no one is to lie on the bed she uses, lest it infect the many women who are with her. This is a very contagious infection! (ARM 10.129; cited in Sasson)

A particularly poignant record of a plague (either bubonic plague or typhus) that raged for twenty years is found in the prayer of the Hittite king Mursilis (14th c. BC), who recounted the advance of the army of his father Suppiluliumas into Egypt: "But when they brought back to the Hatti land the [Egyptian] prisoners which they had taken a plague broke out among the prisoners and they began to die. When they moved the prisoners to the Hatti land, these prisoners carried the plague into the Hatti land. From that day on, people have been dying in the Hatti land" (*ANET*, 395).

Egypt

From Egypt we have a wealth of information about illness and disease from three sources: (1) funerary art, (2) eight medical/magical papyri (Kahun, Edwin Smith, Ebers, Hearst, Erman, London, Berlin, and Chester Beatty) dating from 1900 to 1200 BC, and (3) more than thirty thousand mummies. In contrast to Mesopotamia, demons or evil spirits played a relatively minor role in the etiologies (i.e., attributed causes) of diseases in Egypt. A few cases exist, however, in which a figure called the Great Slanderer is described as commanding demons, the envoys of Sekhmet, to introduce diseases into a person's body.

Evidence of cancer in antiquity is relatively rare, in part perhaps because people did not live to advanced age. However, one skull from the Old Kingdom bears evidence of nasopharyngeal cancer. A possible example of uterine cancer is found in the following text from Egypt: "Instructions for a woman suffering in her uterus by wandering (sic). You shall say concerning it: What is the smell? If she says to you: I smell roast meat, then you shall say concerning it: it is the *nemsu* disorder of the uterus" (Nunn, 81).

The spongy bone structure of some skulls is an indication of anemia. An examination of the mummy of Ramesses II reveals the calcification of his temporal arteries; the aorta of his son, Merneptah, was similarly calcified. Examinations of lungs, which were removed from the body before embalming and placed in canopic jars, has revealed evidence of pneumoconiosis, which resulted from the inhalation of blown sand. Evidence of pneumonia has also been found.

The Egyptians believed that most disease was caused by a noxious substance called *wekhedu* (*wḥdw*), which was formed from residues of undigested food. They believed that this flowed backwards from the large intestine to the heart and was then distributed throughout the body by vessels known as the *mtw*. The *wḥdw* was also believed to turn into worms. All the ailments caused by this substance were countered by emetics, which caused vomiting, and by enemas.

Gallstones have been found in a mummy from the 21st Dynasty. Fishermen, boatmen, and papyrus gatherers, who had to wade into the Nile River, are portrayed with hernias or scrotal swellings, no doubt from an infestation of small parasites. These parasites were not identified until 1851, by Theodor Bilharz, after whom the disease, Bilharzia, has been named; it is also known as schistosomiasis, as it is caused by a fluke known as *Schistosoma*. The parasite, which flourishes in rivers, can infest humans who wade in their waters. Blood flukes and their eggs have been found in mummies from several different periods ranging from 3200 to 1250 BC. Papyri also mention haematuria, bloody urine, a prime symptom of the disease. The Ebers Papyrus has twenty prescriptions for haematuria, which the Egyptians thought was caused by a ghost in the abdomen.

There is striking archaeological evidence of tuberculosis, which is caused by *Mycobacterium tuberculosis*, probably originating from cattle. Tuberculosis of the spine causes Pott's disease, which results in the destruction of the lower thoracic and upper lumbar vertebrae and thus in a characteristic kyphotic, or bent, spine. About thirty cases have been discovered in mummies from as early as 3700 BC and up to 1000 BC.

Roma, the doorkeeper of the Lady Yamia (18th Dyn.), is depicted on a limestone stela from Saqqara with an atrophied right leg, no doubt after contracting polio, a viral infection of the central nervous system that atrophies the muscles of the leg. The pharaoh Siptah (19th Dyn.) had a congenital clubfoot. An examination of Tutankhamun's mummy in 2007 revealed that he suffered from Köhler disease, which resulted in diminished blood to his left leg, hence the presence of numerous walking sticks in his tomb.

The ultimate cause of his death was malaria, an affliction that had affected Egyptians since Predynastic times.

The Ebers Papyrus describes patients who suffered from reddish skin, a condition that was probably due to erysipelas, an inflammation caused by an acute infection of *Streptoccocus pyogenes*. There must also have been frequent cases of *neshu*, or eczema. The head of Ramesses V (19th Dyn.) and a mummy of the 20th Dynasty betray dense vesicular eruptions caused by the variola virus (smallpox). It is quite significant, however, that there is no evidence of leprosy from the pharaonic period of Egyptian history.

D. THE GRECO-ROMAN WORLD

Greece

In Greece prior to the Classical Age (5th c. BC) disease was widely attributed to divine causes. Every disease was interpreted as a *plēgē* ("stroke") or a *mastix* ("lash") by a god or demon. For example, Homer's *Iliad* opens with the enraged god Apollo sending a *loimos* ("pestilence") that kills Greek men and beasts alike (Hom. *Il.* 1.43–65). According to Hesiod (*Op.* 90–104), when Pandora unwisely opened the jar entrusted to her, among the evils that flew out were countless plagues and diseases.

Diseases were also believed to be caused by malign spirits such as the *kēres* and *alastores*. Madness was ascribed to possession by a god or by a nymph. The chthonic spirits of the underworld and the hounds of Hecate were feared as those who caused nervous disorders such as hysteria and epilepsy. The single reference in Homer (*Il.* 22.31) to fever (*pyretos*) brought on by "the Dog of Orion" (the star Sirius) may also be an indication that malaria was known in the Greek world by the eighth century BC.

The practice of medicine was also believed to be divinely influenced. The Greek pantheon including a god of healing, Asclepius, as well as other minor deities who were believed to aid ill or injured supplicants. The Greeks developed a strong tradition of healing centers at the shrines of Asclepius. The dedication of *anathēmata*, models made out of terra-cotta or other materials to represent diseased body parts that had been healed, is attested at various shrines, including those at Epidaurus and Corinth.

Beginning in the fifth century BC, however, Greek writers and physicians also began to investigate the natural causes of disease. This approach is credited to the physician Hippocrates (ca. 460–370 BC), who established his famous medical school on the island of Cos in the Aegean. About seventy books of the so-called Hippocratic Corpus, a series of treatises on specific diseases as well as the theory of medicine, have been preserved.

Physicians of the Hippocratic School rejected the supernatural etiology of diseases in favor of a doctrine of four "humors": (1) blood (*haima*), (2) yellow bile (*cholē*) from the liver, (3) black bile (*melan cholē*) from the spleen, and (4) phlegm (*phlegma*), a waste product. These were believed to correspond to the four seasons, the four basic elements (earth, fire, water, air), and the four basic *dynameis* ("qualities": hot, cold, moist, and dry). According to Hippocrates, "Now all our diseases arise either from things inside the body, bile and phlegm, or from things outside it: from exertions and wounds, and from heat that makes it too hot, and cold that makes it too cold" (*Morb.* 1.2). Perfect health depended on the right mixture (*eukrasis*) of hot, moist, cold, and dry elements; illness (*dyskrasia*) resulted from an imbalance of them. According to Hippocrates, it was the veins that carried the four humors; arteries carried the life-giving "breath," *pneuma*, from inhaled air.

The Hippocratic theory of humors quickly gained currency among Greek thinkers. Plato's dialogue *Timaeus* (c. 360 BC) follows Hippocrates in attributing diseases to an imbalance of humors or elements:

> The origin of disease is plain, of course, to everybody. For seeing that there are four elements of which the body is compacted,—earth, fire, water and air,—when, contrary to nature, there occurs either an excess or a deficiency of these elements, or a transference thereof from their native region to an alien region; or again, seeing that fire and the rest have each more than one variety, every time that the body admits an inappropriate variety, then these and all similar occurrences bring about internal disorders and disease. (*Tim.* 81e–82a)

In his treatise *The Sacred Disease* (*De morbo sacro*) Hippocrates refutes the then-common belief that epilepsy (*epilēpsis*) was caused by a god, and affirms rather that it is caused by a phlegmatic discharge that blocks the vessels to the brain. Many of the other diagnostic texts of the Hippocratic Corpus accurately describe diseases that are recognizable to modern readers. Hippocrates describes tuberculosis, which he calls *phthisis* ("consumption"), with its symptoms of shivering, acute fever, frequent coughing, and great wasting, which was often fatal. In another treatise he reports what was apparently an influenza outbreak at Perinthos.

Hippocrates describes typhoid fever, with its watery stools, abdominal pain, and delirium, which is caused by an infection of *Salmonella typhi*, a bacterium spread through contaminated feces. The Greek writers, including Aristotle, also knew about a variety of intestinal worms, including tapeworms (*Taenia*), roundworms (*Ascaris*), and pinworms (*Enterobius*).

The Hippocratic Corpus and other Greek texts also demonstrate a detailed knowledge of tumors and cancerous growths. The texts describe various kinds of tumors and swelling, such as *onkoi*, abnormal swellings or inflammations that they believed resulted from fluxes into tissue space, as well as *phymata* (benign tumors), *oidēmata* (soft tumors), and *oidēma* (dropsy). Malignant tumors are given the name *karkinōmata* (whence the English medical term carcinoma), which derives from the word for "crab," *karkinos* (Lat. *cancer*).

In the Hippocratic Corpus the Greek word *lepra*, which is related to *lepis* ("scale"), describes an itchy, scaly thickening of the skin caused by psoriasis or a fungal infection, and not true leprosy (Hansen's disease). An early Greek medical author, Straton (3rd c. BC), used the term *kakochymia* ("unhealthy state") to describe leprosy, and others employed the term *leontiasis* with reference to the faces of its victims, which resembled lions as their cheeks collapsed. Plutarch notes that *elephantiasis*—which appears to be yet another name for Hansen's disease—made its first appearance in Greece at the time of Asclepiades (100 BC; *Quaest. Conv.* 8.9). The early medieval theologian John of Damascus (AD 777–857) was the first to use the Greek word *lepra* to describe this disease (Hulse, 89).

Contrary to popular perception, true leprosy (Hansen's disease) is not a very contagious or fatal disease, but it can become extremely disfiguring. It has a long incubation period of between five and ten years before its effects are manifest. It is caused by *Mycobacterium leprae*, which affects the skin, the mucous membrane of the nose, lymph nodes, and peripheral nerves. In its extreme form it causes blindness, collapses the nose, leads to the loss of ears, and creates numbness in the extremities and deformities of the hands and legs. The skulls of victims clearly show its effects.

A description of the full range of traits of Hansen's disease, from its mild tuberculoid form to its extreme lepromatous form, is first found in texts from ancient India, the *Sushruta Samhita* (ca. 600 BC) and the *Manava Dharma Sástra* (*The Institutes of Manu*) (300 BC). It is now believed that it may have been the soldiers of Alexander the Great's army—or, more likely, Indian women sold as slaves to the Ptolemies—who first brought this disease west. The earliest skeletal evidence of leprosy from Ptolemaic Egypt was discovered in 1980 in the Dakhleh oasis and dates to 200 BC. The four afflicted individuals, who were of Caucasoid type (and therefore perhaps exiled from Alexandria), were buried in the midst of a Nubian cemetery.

It was the Greeks who accurately described the varieties of intermittent fevers characteristic of malaria, the disease that killed Alexander the Great in 323 BC. It was not until 1898 that Ronald Ross, an Englishman in India, discovered that malaria was conveyed by mosquitoes. We now know that malaria is caused by a parasite known as a *Plasmodium*, which is carried by the anopheles mosquito and which can also infect animals. There are four species of the parasite: *P. falciparum*, *P. vivax*, *P. malariae*, and *P. ovale*. The first is the most dangerous to humans.

The periodicity of malarial fevers is caused by the asexual reproduction of the malaria parasite in the host's red blood cells: these fevers recur either as tertian (every two days) or quartan (every three days) fevers. *P. falciparum* produces malignant tertian, *P. vivax* benign tertian, *P. malariae* quartan, and *P. ovale* benign tertian fevers. Hippocrates believed that quartan fevers were produced by black bile. Malaria that results in black blood, known as "Blackwater fever," is nearly always fatal. The Greeks were aware that marshy areas were unhealthy.

The Hippocratic treatise *Breaths* teaches that plagues (*loimoi*) are caused by foul air (*Breaths*, 6), a view later echoed by Diodorus Siculus (*Bib. hist.* 12.45). The most noteworthy plague in Greek history was the terrible pestilence that struck Athens at the beginning of the Peloponnesian War in 430 BC. It killed an estimated one-quarter to one-third of the population of Attica, which had crowded behind the long walls that connected the city to its harbor, the Piraeus. It also killed the great leader of Athens, Pericles. The disease is described in clinical detail by Thucydides (*Hist.* 47.3–49), who caught it himself and survived. The plague first began in the Piraeus, where it had probably been brought on a ship from Egypt. Several suggested candidates for this plague include anthrax, bubonic plague, ergotism (caused by rye infected with a fungus), malaria, measles, scarlet fever, and smallpox. Recent scholarship has favored typhus, a disease caused by *Ricksettsia prowaseki* bacteria transmitted by lice. (See Gourevitch, 65). In 1994 archaeologists found about 150 victims of this plague who had been dumped unceremoniously in a mass grave at the Kerameikos ("potter's field") outside of Athens.

Rome

As the Romans had no medical tradition of their own, they were entirely dependent on Greek doctors and traditions. In 293 BC, after a plague, the Romans sent to Epidaurus to obtain the snake sacred to Asclepius. When it was brought to Rome, the snake slithered onto the island of the Tiber, where a temple was established to the god (who became known in Latin as Aesculapius). Professional physicians and surgeons in the Roman Republic and the later empire were often Greek. Two of the most notable physicians whose writings survive from this period, Galen of Pergamum (AD 129–ca. 200) and Aretaeus of Cappadocia (ca. 1st c. AD), wrote in Greek.

Like their Greek counterparts, Roman medical authorities rejected the idea that diseases were caused by the gods or evil spirits, but their writings do reflect the older idea that external forces, such as the influence of the stars and the planets, caused diseases such as epilepsy. For example, according to Galen (*On Decisive Days*) the incidence of this disease was influenced by the waxing and waning of the moon. Aretaeus records that

> the sight of a paroxysm is disagreeable and its departure disgusting, with spontaneous evacuations of the urine and of the bowels. But also it is reckoned a disgraceful form of disease; for it is supposed that it is an infliction on persons who have sinned against the Moon, and hence some have called it the Sacred Disease, and that for more reasons than one. (Adams, 297)

Julius Caesar was known to have epileptic fits.

The Greek influence on Roman medicine is also reflected in non-medical records of Roman life. Seneca, the Stoic philosopher and adviser to Nero, complains about a breathing ailment in a letter to his friend Lucilius:

> I do not know why I should call it by its Greek name [*asthma*]; for it is well enough described as "shortness of breath." Its attack is of very brief duration, like that of a squall at sea; it usally ends within an hour. . . . I have passed through all the ills and dangers of the flesh; but nothing seems to me more troublesome than this. And naturally so; for anything else may be called illness; but this is a sort of continued "last gasp." Hence physicians call it, "practicing how to die." (*Ep.* 54.1–3)

Despite this dependence on Greek medicine, however, physicians in the Roman period did advance their understanding of certain diseases. Diabetes, a disease in which insulin from the pancreas is unable to process sugar, leading to excess sucrose in the blood (hyperglycemia), was first described by Aretaeus of Cappadocia: "Diabetes is an astonishing affection . . . being a melting down of the flesh . . . into urine. . . . The patients never stop making water. . . . The flow is incessant like the opening of aqueducts. . . . It is a chronic disease but the patient is short-lived . . . and his thirst unquenchable" (Adams, 297).

The Roman encyclopedist Celsus describes about fifty skin disorders in his work *De medicina*, including leprosy (Hansen's disease), which he calls *elephantiasis Graecorum*. In his great poem *De rerum natura*, the Epicurean poet Lucretius (1st c. BC) writes: "There is the elephant disease [*elephas morbus*] which is found by the river of Nile in mid-Egypt and nowhere else" (6.1114). Pliny the Elder reports that it was the troops of Pompey who brought leprosy back to Europe in 62–61 BC. Aretaeus of Cappadocia gives a clinical description of leprosy, as does Galen.

Romans were also familiar with epidemic diseases and plagues. Malaria became endemic in Italy by 50 BC, especially in the Pontine marshes south of Rome. We learn from Cicero's correspondence that in Athens Cicero's friend Atticus and his wife, Pilia, contracted quartan fever (*Att.* 6.9, #123) Celsus wrote extensively on malaria. There were three temples dedicated to Febris, the goddess of fever, in Rome in the first century AD. In the year AD 65 soldiers stationed in the unhealthy districts of the Vatican were overcome with an epidemic, possibly of malaria.

Earlier in the reign of Nero, in AD 54, a severe epidemic, perhaps of smallpox, resulted in thirty thousand deaths being recorded in the Temple of Libitina (Suet. *Nero*, 39). During the reign of Titus, there were multiple disasters, including a plague: "There were some dreadful disasters during his reign, such as the eruption of Mount Vesuvius in Campania, a fire at Rome which continued three days and as many nights, and a plague the like of which had hardly ever been known before" (Suet. *Titus*, 8).

In AD 125 the so-called "plague of Orosius" (named for the historian who described it in the most detail), probably smallpox, broke out in North Africa, where it killed over two hundred thousand, and then spread to Italy, where it killed thirty thousand Roman soldiers. A devastating smallpox plague (AD 165–180) broke out during the reign of the Antonine emperors, killing two of them—Lucius Verus in AD 169 and Marcus Aurelius in AD 180. Marcus Aurelius makes only a brief allusion to the pestilence in his *Meditations* (9.2). The plague was first encountered by soldiers fighting at Seleucia in Mesopotamia, and was then brought back to Rome, where as many as two thousand died daily. The disease killed about one-third of the population in some areas, and possibly a total of five million inhabitants.

Galen, the physician to Marcus Aurelius and his son Commodus, describes but two clinical cases in his *Methodus medendi* (5.12). The symptoms included high fever, cutaneous lesions, cough, diarrhea, internal hemorrhages, nausea, vomiting, and a foul smell. The most probable identification of this plague is smallpox, which was caused by *Poxviridae*. (See Gourevitch, 64–65.)

The later plague of Cyprian, which raged from AD 251 to 266 in North Africa and which spread to Syria and Italy and even to Scotland, may have been smallpox or, possibly, measles. It was characterized by redness of the eyes, fever, thirst, inflammation of the throat, diarrhea, paralysis of the lower extremities, and gangrene of the feet and legs.

E. THE JEWISH WORLD

Textual sources on diseases in the Jewish world have recently been supplemented by the scientific examination of archaeological finds. The most dramatic find thus far is the earliest confirmed case of leprosy (Hansen's disease) in the Jewish world. In 2009 DNA analysis of the deceased individual in the so-called "Tomb of the Shroud" in the lower Ben Hinnom Valley in Jerusalem, dated by radio-carbon dating to 50 BC–AD 16, revealed that the man who had been buried in the shroud suffered from both leprosy and tuberculosis. In addition, the examination of hair combs from Qumran and Masada has revealed the presence of *Pediculus humanus capitis*, that is, head lice, and their eggs. Coprolites (desiccated feces) from a cave near the Dead Sea in Nahal Mishmar yielded eggs of *Trichuris trichiura* (whipworm).

Jewish authors often interpreted illness as a punishment from God. Second Maccabees records that the Seleucid king and persecutor of the Jews Antiochus IV was smitten by the Lord with "an incurable and unseen blow. . . . He was seized with a pain in his bowels for which there was no relief and with sharp internal tortures—and that very justly, for he had tortured the bowels of others with many and strange inflictions" (2 Macc 9:5–6).

Herod died in 4 BC after suffering from a terrible disease that, according to Josephus (*Ant.* 17.168–172; *J. W.* 1.656–658), included inflammation in his lower abdomen and the putrefaction of his genital organs, which festered with worms. He possibly suffered from uremia, that is, kidney failure, and myiasis, or an infestation of fly maggots. Some scholars suspect that he had syphilis.

Disease could change a person's status in the Jewish community. Dead Sea Scrolls texts that mention the word ṣ-r-ʿ, "to have a skin blemish" (4Q394, 4Q396, 4Q397, 11Q19), or the word ṣrʿt, "skin blemish" (4Q266, 4Q270, 4Q272, 11Q19), expand on the directions provided in Leviticus in order to exclude those who had "leprosy" and any other disease from membership in the community. Since the Qumran community considered their members to be "priests," they interpreted the Levitical law strictly. In the *Rule of the Congregation*, we read: "No man with a physical handicap—crippled in both legs or hands, lame, blind, deaf, dumb, or possessed of a visible blemish in his flesh—or a doddering old man unable to do his share in the congregation—may en[ter] to take a place in the congregation of the m[e]n of reputation" (1QSa II, 5–8). The *War Scroll* declares: "No one crippled, blind, or lame, nor a man who has a permanent blemish on his skin, or a man affected with ritual uncleanness of his flesh; none of these shall go with them to battle" (1QM VII, 4–5). Likewise, the *Temple Scroll* rules that "no blind man may enter it as long as he lives, lest the city in whose midst I [i.e., YHWH] dwell be defiled" (11Q19 XLV, 12–14) and that "no leper or person afflicted with a skin disease is to enter the city until purified" (11Q19 XLV, 17–18).

According to the Talmud, disease could be sent by God as a punishment for sin (*b. Šabb.* 32b), but it could also arise from natural causes such as cold, heat, uncleanliness, improper food, worry, infections, and heredity. For example, the rabbis became aware of the hereditary nature of hemophilia (*b. Yebam.* 64b): According to Judah the Prince (also known simply as "Rabbi"), "If [a woman] circumcised her first child and he died [as a result of bleeding from the operation], and a second one who also died [similarly], she must not circumcise her third child." Rabban Simeon ben Gamaliel, however, said: "She circumcises the third, but must not circumcise the fourth child."

At the same time, many diseases, such as vertigo, delirium, headaches, and epilepsy, were ascribed to particular demons. Indecent behavior could, some believed, become the cause for epilepsy. "And do not stand naked in front of a lamp, for it was taught: 'He who stands naked in front of a lamp will be a epileptic'" (b. Pesaḥ. 112b). The rabbis banned marriage into families with epilepsy (b. Yebam. 64b).

According to the Talmud,

> It once happened to a maid-servant in Mar Samuel's house that her eye became inflamed on a Sabbath; she cried, but no one attended her and her eye dropped. On the morrow Mar Samuel went forth and propounded that if one's eye gets out of order it is permissible to paint it on the Sabbath, the reason being because the eyesight is connected with the mental faculties.
> (b. ʿAbod. Zar. 28b)

F. THE CHRISTIAN WORLD

Early Christians often attributed disease to God's action. They believed that God used diseases to punish their persecutors. At least one patristic text, Lactantius's *De mortibus persecutorum* (*The Death of the Persecutors*), is entirely dedicated to this theme. For example, Lactantius reports of the Roman emperor Galerius:

> In the eighteenth year of his reign, God struck him with an incurable plague. A malignant ulcer formed itself low down in his secret parts, and spread by degrees. . . . The ulcer began to be insensible to the remedies applied, and a gangrene seized all the neighbouring parts. . . . The stench was so foul as to pervade not only the palace, but even the whole city; and no wonder, for by that time his bladder and bowels, having been devoured by the worms, became indiscriminate, and his body, with intolerable anguish, was dissolved into one mass of corruption. (*Mort.* 33)

In addition to interpreting disease as God's punishment for misdeeds, the early Christian Fathers also believed in the demonic etiology of many diseases. Tertullian states that "[demons] inflict, accordingly, upon our bodies diseases and other grievous calamities" (*Apol.* 22). Origen argues that Christian exorcists benefit the Romans by their ministries, inasmuch as "wicked spirits . . . are the cause of plagues" (*Cels.* 1.31). In his *Commentary on Matthew*, Origen rejects the view of the Greek medical school that ascribed diseases like epilepsy to the influence of the moon and other astronomical bodies. Although this view seems to be reflected in the language of Matthew's Gospel, which uses the word *selēniazetai* (lit., "moon-struck") to describe the epileptic boy whom Jesus heals (Matt 17:14–17), Origen insists that "no star was formed by the God of the universe to work evil" (*Comm. Matt.* 13.6). Instead, he asserts that by those who "believe the Gospel . . . this sickness is viewed as having been effected by an impure dumb and deaf spirit in those who suffer from it" (*Comm. Matt.* 13.6). In appealing to the governor Scapula, Tertullian cites the curing of epileptics through the exorcism of their demons by Christians: "The clerk of one of them who was liable to be thrown upon the ground by an evil spirit, was set free from his affliction; as was also the relative of another, and the little boy of a third. How many men of rank (to say nothing of common people) have been delivered from devils, and healed of diseases!" (*Scap.* 4). In a sermon on Matthew, Chrysostom declares: "And if he call him a lunatic, trouble not yourself at all, for it is the father of the possessed who speaks the word. How then says the evangelist also, He healed many that were lunatic?" (*Hom. Matt.* 17:14–16). The Latin word *lunaticus*, "affected by the moon," is the equivalent of the Greek *selēniazetai* (Matt 17:15; cf. 4:24), which is derived from *selēnē*, "the moon." (See Dölger.) Since Christians considered epileptics to be possessed by a demon, those afflicted with this disease were considered unfit for communion and were barred from the priesthood, and they were also considered to be contagious.

Christians believed in the power of prayer to heal diseases, as illustrated in a letter from Valeria to the monk Paphnutius: "For I am overcome with a serious disease in the form of a terrible difficulty in breathing. For thus I have believed and I continue to believe that if you pray on my behalf I will receive healing" (P. Lond. VI.1926; Barrett-Lennard 1987, 246).

The sanctity of saints such as Basil of Caesarea did not spare them from diseases like malaria, nor did their belief in the efficacy of prayer prevent them from consulting doctors. Basil wrote to a physician: "Bouts of quartan ague have gone on for more than twenty turns. Now I do seem to be free from fever, but I am in such a feeble state that I am no stronger than a cobweb" (*Ep.* 193). Basil, who had studied medicine in Athens, established a hospital alongside the monastery in Caesarea in Cappadocia in 372.

After the conversion of Constantine in AD 312, Christians founded numerous hospitals to care for the sick, as well as hostels (*xenodocheia*) for pilgrims and travelers. Prominent among these charitable institutions were the *lepra asyla* for those afflicted with leprosy. Some Christians regarded lepers as having been chosen to suffer in this world so that they could attain a blessing in the world to come. In Judea, the monasteries of St. Martyrius, St. Gerasimus, and St. Theodosius housed lepers and cared for them.

It was even debated among some Christians whether avoiding epidemic disease was scripturally acceptable in view of the Church's teaching on the virtue of suffering. During the plague that struck the Empire during the reign of the emperor Maximinus II (r. AD 308–313), Christians distinguished themselves:

> They alone in the midst of such ills showed their sympathy and humanity by their deeds. Every day some continued caring for and burying the dead, for there were multitudes who had no one to care for them; others collected in one place those who were afflicted by the famine, throughout the entire city, and gave bread to them all. (Eus. *Hist. eccl.* 9.8)

When a plague struck Carthage and Alexandria in AD 252–253, pagans panicked, fleeing from the infection (*contagium*). Eusebius recounts the reaction of the populace to the plague as follows:

> Even those who were in the first stages of the disease they thrust away, and fled from their dearest. They would even cast them in the roads half-dead, and treat the unburied corpses as vile refuse, in their attempts to avoid the spreading and contagion of the death-plague; a thing which, for all their devices, it was not easy for them to escape. (*Hist. eccl.* 7.22)

According to Cyprian's treatise on *Mortality* (*Mort.* 8), Christians questioned why they as well as the pagans were affected. Cyprian vividly describes the symptoms, which included diarrhea, fever, vomiting, and burning eyes (*Mort.* 14). He urged Christians to consider this as a test and an opportunity to serve, even if it meant martyrdom in ministering to the sick (*Mort.* 16).

Dionysius, the bishop of Alexandria, reports in a letter:

> The most, at all events, of our brethren in their exceeding love and affection for the brotherhood were unsparing of themselves and clave to one another, visiting the sick without a thought as to the danger, assiduously ministering to them, tending them in Christ, and so most gladly departed this life along with them. (*H.E.* 7.22)

Even the apostate emperor Julian (AD 361–363) had to admire the Christians' compassion for the sick. He ordered pagan priests to imitate them and to establish *xenodocheia* in every city (*Ep.* 22).

BIBLIOGRAPHY: F. Adams, tr., *The Extant Works of Aretaeus, the Cappadocian* (1856; repr., 1990); J. Andersen and K. Grambling, "Leprosy and the Bible," *Tropical and Geographical Medicine* 2 (1958), 127–39; H. Avalos, "Nebuchadnezzar's Affliction: New Mesopotamian Parallels for Daniel 4," *JBL* 133 (2014), 497–507; R. J. S. Barrett-Lennard, "Request for Prayer in

Healing," in *NewDocs*, 4.245–50 (1987), ed. G. H. R. Horsley, IV.245–50; R. J. S. Barrett-Lennard, *Christian Healing after the New Testament* (1994); K. Berthelot, "La place des infermes et des 'lépreux' dans les texts de Qumrân et les Évangiles," *RB* 113 (2006), 211–41; D. Brothwell and A. T. Sandison, ed., *Diseases in Antiquity* (1967); S. G. Browne, "Leprosy in the Bible," in B. Palmer, ed., *Medicine and the Bible* (1986), 101–26; A. Cockburn, E. Cockburn, and T. A. Reyman, ed., *Mummies, Disease and Ancient Cultures* (1998); F. J. Dölger, "Der Einfluss des Origenes auf die Beurteilung der Epilepsie und Mondsucht im christlichen Altertum," *Antike und Christentum* 4 (1934), 95–109; W. Farber, "How to Marry a Disease: Epidemic Contagion and a Magic Ritual against the 'Hand of the Ghost,'" in *Magic and Rationality in Ancient Near Eastern and Graeco-Roman Medicine*, ed. H. F. J. Horstmanshoff, M. Stol, and C. R. van Tilburg (2004), 117–32; J. Filer, *Disease* (1996); I. L. Finel and M. J. Geller, ed., *Disease in Babylon* (2007); D. Gourevitch, "The Galenic Plague: A Breakdown of the Imperial Pathocoenosis," *History and Philosophy of the Life Sciences* 27 (2005), 57–69; M. D. Grmek, *Diseases in the Ancient Greek World* (1989); M. Heimpel, trans., *Letters to the King of Mari* (2003); V. M. Hope and E. Marshall, ed., *Death and Disease in the Ancient City* (2000); E. V. Hulse, "The Nature of the Biblical 'Leprosy' and the Use of Alternative Medical Terms in Modern Translations of the Bible," *PEQ* 107 (1975), 87–105; R. Jackson, *Doctors and Diseases in the Roman Empire* (1988); W. H. S. Jones, *Malaria and Greek History* (1909); C. S. Keener, "Fever and Dysentery in Acts 28:8 and Ancient Medicine," *BBR* 19 (2009), 393–402; N. Kiuchi, "A Paradox of the Skin Disease," *ZAW* 113 (2001), 505–14; J. O. Leiboivitz, *Some Aspects of Biblical and Talmudic Medicine* (1969); F. C. Lendrum, "The Name Leprosy," *The American Journal of Tropical Medicine and Hygiene* 1 (1952), 999–1008; K.-H. Leven, "*Athumia* and *Philanthrôpia*: Social Reactions to Plagues in Late Antiquity and Early Byzantine Society," in *Ancient Medicine in Its Socio-Cultural Context*, ed. P. J. van der Eijk, H. F. J. Horstmanshoff, and P. H. Schrijvers (1995), 393–407; J. Longrigg, "The Great Plague of Athens," *History of Science* 18 (1980), 209–25; J. Longrigg, *Death and Epidemic Disease in Classical Athens* (2000); K. Manchester, "Tuberculosis and Leprosy in Antiquity: An Interpretation," *Medical History* 28 (1984), 162–73; S. Mark, "Alexander the Great, Seafaring, and the Spread of Leprosy," *Journal of the History of Medicine and Allied Sciences* 57 (2002), 285–311; C. D. Matheson et al., "Molecular Exploration of the First-Century *Tomb of the Shroud* in Akeldama, Jerusalem," *PLoS ONE* 4(12): e8319, doi:10.1371/journal.pone.0008319, accessed September 12, 2013; D. Morse, D. Brothwell, and P. J. Ucko, "Tuberculosis in Ancient Egypt," *American Review of Respiratory Diseases* 90 (1964), 524–41; K. V. Mull and C. S. Mull, "Biblical Leprosy—Is It Really?" *BRev* 8.2 (1992), 32–39, 62; J. F. Nunn, *Ancient*

Egyptian Medicine (1996); J. Preuss, *Biblical and Talmudic Medicine* (1978); F. P. Retief and L. Cilliers, "Epidemics of the Roman Empire 27 BC–AD 467," *South African Medical Journal* 90 (2000), 267–72; O. Rimon et al., *Illness and Healing in Ancient Times* (1997); F. Rosner, *Medicine in the Bible and Talmud* (1995); R. Sallares, *Malaria and Rome* (2002); J. Sasson, *Mosaic of an Old Babylonian Culture: The Mari Archives* (forthcoming); W. Scheidel, *Death on the Nile: Disease and the Demography of Roman Egypt* (2001); J. Schipper, "Deuteronomy 24:5 and King Asa's Foot Disease in 1 Kings 15:23b," *JBL* 128 (2009), 643–48; J. Scurlock, *Sourcebook for Ancient Mesopotamian Medicine* (2014); J. Scurlock and B. R. Andersen, *Diagnoses in Assyrian and Babylonian Medicine* (2005); J. Shrewsbury, *The Plagues of the Philistines and Other Medical-Historical Essays* (1964); M. Stol, "Leprosy: New Light from Greek and Babylonian Sources," *Ex Oriente Lux* 30 (1989), 22–31; M. Stol, *Epilepsy in Babylon* (1993); M. Sussman, "Sickness and Disease," *ABD* VI, 6–15; O. Temkin, *The Falling Sickness: A History of Epilepsy from the Greeks to the Beginning of Modern Neurology* (1971); J. C. Thomas, *The Devil, Disease and Deliverance: Origins of Illness in New Testament Thought* (1998); R. C. Thompson, trans., *The Devils and Evil Spirits of Babylonia* (2 vols., 1903–1904); C. Wells, *Bones, Bodies and Disease* (1963); A. Weisenrieder, *Images of Illness in the Gospel of Luke: Insights of Ancient Medical Texts* (2003); J. Zias, "Death and Disease in Ancient Israel," *BA* 54 (1991), 146–59.

RKH and EMY

See also DEATH & THE AFTERLIFE, DEMONS, DENTISTRY & TEETH, and MEDICINE & PHYSICIANS.

DIVINATION & SORTITION

Divination is the attempt to foresee the future, discern the significance of given phenomena, or choose the right person in a certain circumstance or the right course of action. Sortition is the use of lots either to answer queries or to make assignments. Divination and sortition pervaded both public and private life in the ancient world. An omen is a phenomenon that is thought to portend a future event.

A. THE OLD TESTAMENT

The Hebrew Bible refers to a few sanctioned means of divination, but it more frequently condemns the many divinitory practices of Israel's neighbors. The instructions for the tabernacle in the book of Exodus assign a divinatory function to the priestly vestments. According to these instructions, the priest was always to "bear the means of making decisions for the Israelites over his heart" (Exod 28:30; cf. 28:15) in the form of a garment known as an ephod and of objects called the Urim and the Thummim. In the first place, the ephod was a garment, but in the second place, the ephod of the high priest, which had a pocket for the Urim and Thummim, was not just a garment but a special instrument for divination. Originally, the priest's ephod was probably meant to be used in connection with lots, to provide "yes" or "no" answers to questions. (On lots and cleromancy, see further below.) In the Septuagint version of 1 Sam 14:18, Saul asks that the ephod be brought (rather than the "ark"). David uses the ephod carried by Abiathar to ask God whether the men of Keilah, whom he has defended against the Philistines, will hand him over to Saul (1 Sam 23:13). On another occasion, after asking for Abiathar's ephod, David inquires of the Lord, "Shall I pursue this [Amalekite] raiding party? Will I overtake them?" The answer is: "Pursue them. You will certainly overtake them" (1 Sam 30:8). The OT also records idolatrous uses of the priestly ephod: Judg 17–18 relates the story of a man named Micah who makes himself "an ephod and some household gods [*těrāpîm*]" (Judg 17:5), which he uses as an oracle.

The Urim and Thummim (Heb. *'ûrîm wětummîm*, "lights and perfection"), which are mentioned in conjunction with the ephod in Exod 28, may have been objects like lots that the priests used to determine a "yes" or "no" answer (Exod 28:30; Num 27:21; Deut 33:8). The use of these divinatory objects is recorded in a dramatic scene during Saul's campaign against the Philistines. Looking for the cause of God's disfavor, Saul asks, "If the fault is in me or my son Jonathan, respond with Urim, but if the men of Israel are at fault, respond with Thummim" (1 Sam 14:41). When the lot falls on his family's side, Saul continues, "Cast the lot between me and Jonathan my son," and then we are told, "And Jonathan was taken" (1 Sam 14:42). That this method of divination later fell out of use is indicated by Ezra 2:63 (∥Neh 7:65), which records that priests who could not produce records to demonstrate their genealogy were ordered by the governor "not to eat any of the most sacred food until there was a priest ministering with the Urim and Thummim."

The OT also records that the ark of the covenant was consulted as an oracle in times of war. Judges 20 reports that the Israelites assembled before the ark to decide whether they would keep fighting after a defeat. They asked, " 'Shall we go up again to fight against the Benjamites, our fellow Israelites?' The LORD responded, 'Go, for tomorrow I will give them into your hands' " (Judg 20:28). It is possible that lots were cast in the presence of the ark.

The OT also occasionally mentions direct divination through the agency of an especially holy person. For example, to find the lost donkeys of his father Kish, Saul seeks information from Samuel, who is described as a *rō'ê*, or "seer" (1 Sam 9:9)—although in the same passage it is noted that the word "prophet" (*nābî'*) was used for this function later in Israel's history. Samuel assures Saul that the donkeys have been found, and then unexpectedly anoints him as the first king of Israel (1 Sam 10:1). Other seers/prophets were consulted about sickness (1 Kgs 14:1–17; 2 Kgs 1:2–17; 8:7–15) and military situations (1 Kgs 22:5–28; 2 Kgs 3:11–19).

Divination by lots, known as cleromancy (also called sortition), was used widely and for a variety of purposes. The Hebrew word *gôrāl* (pl. *gôrālôt*) is used seventy-eight times in the OT. Lots are, among other things, used (1) to identify a guilty individual, as in the case of Jonah (Jonah 1:7) and possibly also in the case of Achan (Josh 7:14–19); (2) to choose someone for an office, as in the choice of Saul to be king (1 Sam 10:17–24); (3) to divide up the conquered land of Canaan (Num 33:54); and (4) to determine who would bring up the wood offerings to burn on the altar (Neh 10:34). The faithful believed that God's providence guided the process: "The lot is cast into the lap, but its every decision is from the LORD" (Prov 16:33). The enemies of the Jews also used lots, as Haman did to determine a propitious day for attacking the Jews (Esth 3:7). Purim, the name of the festival that commemorates the deliverance of the Jews from Haman, comes from the Babylonian name for the lot, *pūru* (Esth 9:26).

The OT also records more obscure forms of divination. When Joseph's *gābîaʿ* ("drinking bowl") was discovered hidden in the sack of his brother Benjamin, his official asked, "Isn't this the cup my master drinks from and also uses for divination?" (Gen 44:5). This cup may have been used in the practice of lecanomancy, divination by observing (the shapes of oil on) the surface of water in a dish, basin, or cup. Mention of a "diviners' tree" in Judg 9:37 may allude to the practice of dendromancy, divination by interpreting the sound of rustling leaves.

Many of the divinatory practices described in the OT are associated with the nations surrounding Israel. Deuteronomy 18:10–11 condemns many forms of divination and idolatry in the same breath: "Let no one be found among you who sacrifices their son or daughter in the fire, who practices divination or sorcery, interprets omens, engages in witchcraft, or casts spells, or who is a medium or spiritist or who consults the dead." The best OT example of a non-Israelite diviner is Balaam, a Mesopotamian hired by the Moabite king Balak to curse the Israelites as they attempt to pass through his land (Num 22:2–24:25). What has been translated by some as Balaam's "fee for divination" (Num 22:7) may have been models of omens sent to him by the Moabite elders. Much to Balak's surprise, Balaam "did not resort to divination as at other times," but blessed Israel instead (Num 24:1–13). A remarkable eighth-century BC Aramaic inscription on plaster that records a prophecy by Balaam has been recovered from Tell Deir ʿAlla in Jordan.

Hosea 4:12 condemns Israel's practice of rhabdomancy, divination by a staff or stick of wood, as idolatrous. In Ezek 21:21 (MT vs. 26) Nebuchadnezzar is described as using three forms of divination to determine whether to attack Jerusalem or an Ammonite city: "He will cast lots with arrows, he will consult his idols, he will examine the liver." Some of these practices are attested in the archeological record from this area. Bronze arrowheads found in the Levant inscribed with archaic Phoenician and Hebrew script may have been used in belomancy, or divination by drawing arrows marked with the names of peoples or places from a quiver. "Inspecting the liver" refers to hepatoscopy, the examination of the liver of sacrificed sheep, which was the principal form of divination in Mesopotamia. Three clay liver models inscribed in cuneiform from the Middle Bronze Age have been found at Hazor, as well as one at Megiddo. The most common Hebrew word for divination, *qesem* (from the root *qsm*, "to cut," referring to the pieces of wood cut to form lots), also appears in Ezek 21:21.

The OT also contains several references to necromancy, divination by appealing to the spirits of the dead, which is specifically forbidden in Deut 18:11 (cf. Lev 19:31; 20:2, 6). In defiance of this ban, the wicked king Manasseh is said to have "sacrificed his own son in the fire, practiced divination, sought omens, and consulted mediums and spiritists" (2 Kgs 21:6). The reforming king Josiah put away "the mediums and spiritists, the household gods, [and] the idols" in Judah (2 Kgs 23:24). Isaiah (8:19; 19:3) also refers to the practice of necromancy.

The tragic career of Saul, who as time went on could no longer receive guidance from the Lord, ends with a desperate attempt to learn the future through necromancy. This is all the more ironic since Saul himself had earlier expelled the ʾôbôt, "mediums," and the yiddĕ ʿōnîm, "spiritists" (1 Sam 28:3, 9), from Israel. The medium at Endor raises the spirit of the prophet Samuel, who foretells Saul's defeat by the Philistines (1 Sam 28:8–19). Saul's action is condemned in 1 Chr 10:13: "Saul died because . . . he did not keep the word of the LORD and even consulted a medium for guidance."

B. THE NEW TESTAMENT

Although the NT repeatedly mentions prophets and dreams, it is remarkable that it contains only a few references to divination and sortition.

Luke 1:9 demonstrates familiarity with the organization of the priests who served in the temple when it notes that Zechariah, the father of John the Baptist, had been "chosen by lot" to burn incense in the temple while the priests of his division (the family of Abijah) were serving there. As there were more priests in Judah than were necessary, tables of priestly divisions called mišmārôt were prepared, examples of which have been found among the Dead Sea Scrolls and at Caesarea. Not only were the divisions chosen by lot, but the assignment of individual priests to specific duties was also determined by lot.

The apostles also used lots to appoint someone to replace Judas Iscariot. They nominated two candidates, Joseph called Barsabbas and Matthias, and after prayer used the casting of lots to select Matthias (Acts 1:23–26).

In one NT passage the power of divination is attributed to possession by a "spirit." Acts 16:16–19 reports Paul's encounter at Philippi with a slave girl who had a spirit of divination (pneuma pythōna) by which she earned a profit for her masters. A Greek myth relates that Apollo had killed a serpent that had guarded the site of Pythō, later named Delphi, where the god's most famous oracle was established, hence the association of the word with divination.

C. THE NEAR EASTERN WORLD

Mesopotamia

Most of our information on divination in Mesopotamia comes from royal archives, and highlights how essential divination was in determining public policies.

Compendia of omens were first compiled in the Old Babylonian era. Omens were recognized in many forms, from physical abnormalities in the organs of sacrificed animals to everyday situations. Written compilations, which diviners may have used as handbooks for interpreting omens, list possible phenomena with their significance. These omens are recorded in the handbooks using a traditional formula: the phenomenon is first described in the *protasis* clause, and the interpretation is given in the *apodosis*.

Initially collections of omens were based on the empirical observation of unusual phenomena, such as multiple births. But they were later expanded to an exaggerated degree, recording, for example, births not only of triplets but of octuplets and nonuplets, or a calf born not only with two tails but with up to six tails. One series of teratological (malformed birth) omens regarding both humans and animals is known as *šumma izbu* ("If a malformed . . ."). One example reads, "If a woman of the palace gives birth, and (the child) has the face of a lion—the king will have no opponent" (Leichty, 71). A letter from a governor to the king of Mari reports that the governer had found a lamb with one head but two bodies, which he had sent to the king for his inspection.

The behavior of animals and even the movement of a slaughtered animal's body were considered to be portentous.

After one poured water three times on the head of a reclining ox, if the ox got up, the answer was positive, but if he did not, the answer was negative. A large series of omens known as *šumma ālu* ("If a city . . .") sets forth the significance of encounters with animals, for example, of meeting a snake. "If, between the first and 30th of Nisannu, a snake turns from a man's right to the man's left in the street, harsh misery will carry that man off in the land of his enemy" (Tablet 22, 17; Freedman, 11). If a snake fell upon a man's shoulder, his supporters would die.

Another form of divination attested in Mesopotamia is the taking of auspices, or the observation of birds such as doves and swallows. One Old Babylonian text reads: "If on the upper side there is a red spot, it is a curse against his grandfather. . . . If on the right side of the bird, a red spot is found, it is a curse against the son" (author's translation of Durand, 275). Idrimi, while he was exiled from Alalakh (15th c. BC), released birds to observe their flight for seven years until Adad became favorable to him (*ANET*, 557). Among the Hittites, ornithomancy, divination by the observation of birds, was highly valued. They would at times observe birds by the riverside, as indicated by this text: "An *alliya* bird came back up from behind the river flying low; and it settled in a poplar tree; and while we watched it, another *alliya* bird attacked it from the vicinity and came up from behind the river from the good side" (Gurney, 155). These observations were made to decide such questions as "Have you, O gods, approved?" or "Have we nothing concerning him to fear from rebellion?" (Beal, 70).

The most important form of divination in Mesopotamia was extispicy (observation of the *exta*, the internal organs), and in particular hepatoscopy, the examination of livers, specifically those of sacrificed sheep. A myth describes how the gods Shamash and Adad gave Enmeduranki, the antediluvian king of Sippar, "the Tablet of the Gods [*ṭuppu ša ili*], the liver, a secret of heaven and nether world" (Lambert, 152). Of the nearly 2,700 attested omens, which are found in eighty-eight cuneiform texts, 80 percent are examples of extispicy. Special masters were known as *ummânū*, "experts." They learned their profession in a diviner's college, the *bīt bāri*. They studied tablets of *muštābiltū*, "interpretations," and of *mukallimtū*, "commentaries," that supplemented the compendia of omens.

The diviners worked primarily for the king and had to meet strict physical standards: "The diviner whose father is impure and who himself has any imperfection of limb or countenance, whose eyes are not sound, who has any teeth missing, who has lost a finger, whose countenance has a sickly look or who is pimpled, cannot be the keeper of the decrees of Shamash and Adad" (Contenau, 281).

In addition to the compendia of omens, hundreds of inscribed clay liver models (and a few lung models) showing great anatomical detail were kept on file to enable the experts to refer to prior liver types (listed in the omens' protases) in order to predict similar outcomes (listed in the omens' apodoses), which they did in a quasi-scientific fashion. Some features of the liver that were considered significant were the *ubānum* ("the finger," or caudate lobe), the *bāb ekallimi* ("the palace gate," the umbilical fissure, running vertically from the top of the liver), the *padānum* ("the path," a groove that ran horizontally in the upper part of the liver), and the papillaris. Also considered significant were the gallbladder (*martu*); the cystic, hepatic, and bile ducts; and the hepatic vein. In general, signs on the left side were negative, and signs on the right were positive. A swollen gallbladder signified an increase in the power of the king, a depression in the liver a decrease in his power. Holes, fissures, and scars portended death and defeat. Up to 40 percent of the apodoses in certain texts predict death.

Hepatoscopy in Mesopotamia was often performed after a ritual sacrifice. A series of *tamītu* tablets (2nd millennium BC) lists questions that were whispered into the ear of the sheep about to be sacrificed. They begin with the words, "Shamash, great Lord whom I ask, answer me with a reliable 'Yes'" (Lenzi, 52). The questions posed could deal with a great variety of issues, very often pertaining to the outcome of military ventures. One notable feature is the insertion of an *ezib*, a disclaimer to overcome in advance any fault in the procedure:

> Disregard that he who touches the forehead of the sheep (a) is dressed in his ordinary soiled garments, (b) has eaten, drunk, anointed himself with, touched or stepped upon anything unclean, (c) has seen fear and terror at night, (d) has touched the libation beer, the *maṣhatu*-flour, the water, the container and the fire, (e) has altered, added to, or changed the ritual proceedings, (f) or has jumbled the oracle query in his mouth. (Starr 1990, xxiv)

It is interesting to observe the candid complaints from the diviners about their salaries and, at times, their perception that they were not paid the respect they deserved. Some expressed dismay when the king doubted the validity of their observations, and ordered additional sacrifices to confirm their interpretations.

The practice of extispicy/hepatoscopy spread east to the Indo-Aryans, and west to Ugarit, Palestine, to the Hittites, and even to the Etruscans, and through the Etruscans to the Romans.

The Mesopotamians also made use of religious lots, with priests invoking Shamash, the god of oracles. After making an offering and asking a yes–no question, the priest would draw forth one of two stones for the answer. If the answer were to be positive, one text records, "May a stone of desire [*aban erēši*] jump up and may the hands catch (it)," but if it were to be negative, "May a stone of no desire [*aban lā erēši*] jump up and may the hands catch it" (Horowitz and Hurowitz, 101).

Minor forms of divination included libanomancy, the observation of smoke from burning incense, and lecanomancy, the observation of shapes formed by oil in a vessel of water. We have handbooks from the Old Babylonian period that explain the meanings of certain patterns in oil. Administrative texts also record deliveries of oil for diviners.

Necromancy is rarely attested in Mesopotamia. In the Epic of Gilgamesh (XIII.80–90; *ANET*, 98), Gilgamesh digs a pit and calls forth the spirit of his dead companion Enkidu to inquire about the state of the dead, much as Odysseus inquires of the shade of Achilles. One fragmentary text appeals to Shamash as follows: "May he (Shamash) bring up a ghost from the darkness for me! May he [put life back] into the dead man's limbs! I call [upon you], O skull of skulls, may he who is within the skull answer [me!]" (Finkel, 9).

Oracular prophets are attested as early as the Old Babylonian period, in the Mari texts. Ecstatic prophets and prophetesses (*muḫḫûm, muḫḫūtum*) were associated with the temple of Dagan at Terqa. On behalf of the god Adad from Aleppo, a prophet exhorted Zimri-Lim of Mari: "When a wronged man or woman cries out to you, stand and let his/her case be judged" (Malamat, 111). In the Neo-Assyrian period, prophets and prophetesses came from the three cult centers of Ishtar: Arbela, Calah, and Aššur. Esarhaddon claimed the support of diviners and ecstatic prophets: "Favorable signs in dreams and ominous utterances in order to secure the foundation of my throne and the length of my reign were portended on me" (Fales and Lanfranchi, 108). Esarhaddon was constantly asking questions of his diviners, such as:

> If Esarhaddon, king of [Assyria], gives him a royal daughter in marriage, will Bartatua, king of the Scythians, speak with [Esarhaddon, king of Assyria], in good faith, true and honest words of peace? Will he keep the treaty of [Esarhaddon, king of Assyria]? Will he do [whatever i]s pleasing to Esarhaddon, king of Assyria], in good faith, true and honest words of peace? (Starr 1990, 25)

Esarhaddon's successor, Ashurbanipal, who gathered the great library at Nineveh, boasted not only of his ability to read the texts found in it but even of his ability as a diviner:

> Marduk, master of the gods, granted me as a gift a receptive mind (*lit.*, wide ear) and ample (power of) thought. Nabû, the universal scribe, made me a present of his wisdom. . . . The art (*lit.*, work) of the Master Adapa I learned (*lit.*, acquired),—the hidden treasure of all scribal knowledge, the signs of heaven and earth. . . . I have studied (*lit.*, struggled with) the heavens with the learned masters of oil divination. (*ARAB*, 2.378–79)

Egypt

In Egypt the practice of divination, which was known as *pḥ nṯr*, "reaching the god," consisted in posing questions before an oracular statue of a god or pharaoh in a model of a ship borne by priests. A positive answer (*hn/hnn*) was indicated by a forward movement, while a negative answer (*nʿy n ḥ3*) was indicated by a backward movement. While the practice is first definitely attested only in the New Kingdom (after 1550 BC), some Middle Kingdom documents (ca. 2000 BC) proclaim that a god assented to an undertaking.

Hatshepsut received an oracle (*nḏwt-r3*) of Amun indicating that the ways to Punt should be searched out. Before his campaign against the Nubians, Tuthmosis IV came to the temple of Amun at Thebes to get the god's approval. Ramesses II read out a list of candidates for the position of high priest of Amun before this god, who indicated that Nebwennenef was his choice: "He was not satisfied with any of them, until I mentioned your name to him" (Kitchen, 46). Much later, divine oracles were even used to choose a new ruler. The last king of the 25th (Cushite) Dynasty was Aspelta (593–568 BC). In his Election Stela, he describes the gathering of the army at Napata (in modern-day Sudan) before the temple of Amun-Re: "Then they offered the King's Brothers before this god, (but) he did not take one of them. For a second time there was offered the King's Brother, Son of Amon, and Child of Mut, Lady of Heaven, the Son of Re: [Aspalta], living forever. Then this god, Amon-Re, Lord of the Thrones of the Two Lands, said: 'He is your king'" (*ANET*, 448).

The most extensive evidence for oracular questions comes from the workmen's village at Deir el-Medina. The deified ruler Amenhotep I's statue was carried in a litter by priests, who indicated his answer by their movement with the god. We have many ostraca covering a variety of subjects: "Will Seti be appointed to be prophet?" "Will we be given rations?" "Will they mention me to the vizier?" "Is it blame which will come to be against me?" (Ritner, 93). The adjudication of a case of the theft of several garments can be followed in some detail. The victim, Qaha, cried out: "My good lord, come out today! My two garments have been stolen!" (*CANE*, 3.1782). When the god indicated that a farmer, Pethauemdiamun, was the culprit, he protested his innocence. Though he attempted to bribe a second oracle by the offering of five loaves, he was again adjudged the guilty party. Only after his trial before a third god did he confess his crime. (See Blackman, 252–53; Černý, 40–41).

Over the course of time certain non-pharaonic humans were elevated to the rank of divine oracles, such as Amenhotep son of Hapu, a royal chancellor and architect. His statue proclaimed: "O people of Karnak, you who desire to see Amun, come to me. I will communicate your requests, for I am an intermediary for this god" (Ciraolo and Seidel, 90). Imhotep, the architect of the Step Pyramid of the 3rd Dynasty, who was known as the patron of medicine, also achieved divine status in the Late Egyptian period.

The Papyrus Nevill records a petitioner expressing his frustration at the lack of an answer from a god:

> I was looking for you to tell you of certain matters of mine, but you disappeared into your sanctuary and there was no one admitted. But as I was waiting I met Hori, the scribe of the Temple of Ramesses III, and he said to me, "I'm admitted." So I am sending him to you. Now look; you must discard mystery today, and come out in procession, and decide the case of the five garments of the Estate of Haremhab, also these two garments of the scribe of the Necropolis. (Ray, 181)

The Egyptians also used sacred animals, often associated with a particular god, for divination. The Apis (Egy. *Hapi*) bull was regarded as the incarnation of the god Ptah of Memphis. He was a specially marked bull (cf. Her. *Hist.* 3.28), who was pampered and whose movements in the courtyard at a fixed hour were interpreted as oracular signs. After the death of the Apis bull, a new successor would be identified. But we do have evidence from inscriptions dated to the time of the Persian conquest indicating that at this time there was an unusual overlap of a year and three months of the birth of a second Apis bull before the death of a preceding bull. (See Yamauchi 1990, 116–22.) The Apis bulls were buried in gigantic sarcophagi in the so-called Serapeum at Saqqara. In the nearby sacred necropolis for animal mummies were buried four million mummified ibises and five hundred baboons (both sacred to Thoth), five hundred thousand hawks (sacred to Horus), and a score of cows, representing Isis, the mother of the Apis bull. Oracular petitions were addressed to some of these creatures.

We do not have evidence from Egypt of typical examples of necromancy. What we have instead are so-called "Letters to the Dead" inscribed on bowls, ostraca, linen, and papyri, in which survivors address dead husbands and wives as spirits who can help or harm them. In one such letter the speaker asks: "How are you? Is the West [the land of the dead] taking care of you [according to] your desire? . . . Please become a spirit for me [before] my eyes so that I may see you in a dream fighting on my behalf" (Meltzer, 215). One man asks his deceased brother, "If one can hear me (in) the place where you are, tell the Lords of Eternity, 'Let (me) petition for my brother'" (McDowell, 106–7).

Located four hundred miles west of the Nile, in the Sahara near the modern border with Libya, was the oracle of Amun at the oasis of Siwa. The Persian conqueror Cambyses attempted in vain to send his army toward this oracle in 525 BC (Her. *Hist.* 3.25). The Greeks equated Amun with Zeus and held the oracle in high regard. Alexander the Great also visited the site. We do not know what the oracle told him, but thereafter he seems to have regarded himself as divine.

D. THE GRECO-ROMAN WORLD

In Greece the word for a diviner was *mantis*, and the words for divination were *manteia* and *mantikē*; all of these words are related to *mania*, "madness, ecstasy." The diviner looked for *sēmeia*, "signs" or "omens," which he or she could interpret. Xenophon regarded divination as among the greatest gifts given by the gods. To refute the claim that his teacher, Socrates, was an atheist, Xenophon (*Mem.* 1.2) noted that he offered sacrifices constantly and made use of divination (*manteia*).

The observation of omens from birds (*oiōnoi*), known as *oiōnomanteia*, is particularly well attested in Greek literature. Some birds were associated with certain gods: eagles with Zeus (Hom. *Il.* 24.315–316), for example, falcons with Apollo (Hom. *Il.* 15.525–528), and owls with Athena. In addition, Athena sent a heron to encourage Odysseus during a night raid (Hom. *Il.* 10.274–277), and disguised herself as a swallow (Hom. *Od.* 22.239–240). According to Pindar, the seer Mopsus dispatched Jason as well as Argonauts propitiously "divined by birds and holy lots" (*Pyth.* 4.190–191).

According to Steven Lonsdale:

> A fascinating historical document from Ephesus in the sixth century B.C. indicates that there was an attempt to codify the laws of augury. The fragmentary inscription can be restored to read as follows: Line of flight from right to left. If the bird disappeared from sight, the omen is favourable; but if it raised its left wing and then soared and disappeared, the omen is inauspicious. Line of flight from left to right. If it disappeared on a straight course, it is an ill omen, but if it raised its right wing and then soared and disappeared, the omen is good. (Lonsdale, 152–53)

The Greeks also practiced hydromancy, or divination by examining water, usually in a basin (*lekanē*), so the practice was also called lecanomancy. Catoptromancy, which involves the use of mirrors, was practiced at the oracle of Demeter, where a mirror was suspended over a spring. Pyromancy involved observing how the animal parts burned during sacrifice, while libanomancy involved observing the smoke of incense or the smoldering of laurel leaves or barley flour in the flames.

The Greeks believed in cledonomancy (from *klēdōn*, an aural sign), an omen from a sound such as a sneeze or a chance saying. Speaking of the oracle of Hermes at Pharae, Pausanias explained: "Coming at eventide, the inquirer of the god, having burnt incense upon the hearth, filled the lamps with oil and lighted them. . . . After that he stops his ears and leaves the marketplace. On coming outside he takes his hands from his ears, and whatever utterance he hears he considers oracular" (*Descr.* 7.22.3).

Necromancy is described in Greek literature. In a celebrated passage in the *Odyssey* (Hom. *Od.* 11.20–50), Odysseus digs a ditch at the border of the Underworld, pours libations to the dead, and sacrifices sheep so that the blood drips into the pit, thus attracting the shades of the dead like Elpenor and Achilles, who speak to him. In general, however, necromancy was rarely practiced in Greece.

In ancient Greece, many of these forms of divination were most commonly practiced at oracular shrines. Each shrine was sacred to a particular deity (for example, the shrine of Apollo at Delphi). Priests or priestesses who lived at the shrine were believed to interpret omens or other messages from the god for their supplicants. Everyone from common people to the rulers of city-states might visit an oracular shrine to learn the future or seek the god's favor.

The most ancient oracular shrine in Greece was the temple of Zeus in Dodona in the Peloponnesus, which was already functioning by the eighth century BC, as indicated by various bronze objects deposited there. The Selli (priests) and Peleiades (priestesses) interpreted the sound made by the wind as it blew through the leaves of the oak sacred to Zeus. Visitors wrote down their queries on strips of lead, more than 1,400 of which have been found.

The most renowned and influential oracle in the Greek world was that of Apollo at Delphi, situated on the slopes of Mount Parnassus, overlooking the Gulf of Corinth. Greeks seeking advice received their answers from the ecstatic utterances of a prophetess called the Pythia, who is usually described as an old woman. Prior to the consultation a sheep would be sacrificed, with water poured upon its head to get it to bow as though in assent. The priestess was then seated upon a tripod in the *manteion*, an underground chamber. Her unintelligible responses would be rendered into dactylic hexameter verses by the priests. According to Plutarch, who served as a priest at Delphi: "Those, however, who had reached the conclusion that the two are one and the same god very naturally dedicated the oracle to Apollo and Earth in common, thinking that the sun creates the disposition and temperament in the earth from which the prophet-inspiring vapours [*mantikas anathymiaseis*] are wafted forth" (*Def. orac.* 433).

Joseph Fontenrose dismissed Plutarch's statement: "Plutarch mentions *pneumata, dynameis, anathymiaseis,* and *atmoi* which affect the Pythia, inducing the *enthousiasmos* under which she speaks Apollo's oracles. These currents and exhalations are obviously not vapors; they are nothing visible nor otherwise perceptible to the senses, but entirely theoretical" (Fontenrose 1978, 197). Recent examinations, however, of the geology under the shrine have suggested that either naturally occurring ethylene fumes or the deprivation of oxygen may have affected the Pythia. (See de Boer, Hale, and Chanton; Etiope et al.)

Delphi became internationally famous. It was consulted by Amasis II, the pharaoh of Egypt (Her. *Hist.* 2.180). When Croesus, king of Lydia, consulted the oracle about whether he should fight the Persians, he was told that if he did, a great kingdom would be destroyed. The prediction came true—but unfortunately for Croesus, the kingdom that fell was his own (Her. *Hist.* 1.53–54, 86).

Herodotus records that prior to the Persian invasion of Greece led by Xerxes in 480 BC, the Delphic oracle advised the Athenians: "Wretches, why tarry ye thus? Nay, flee from your houses and city, flee to the ends of the earth" (Her. *Hist.* 7.140). The Athenians pleaded for a second oracle. The priestess responded: "All shall be taken and lost that the sacred border of Cecrops holds in keeping to-day, and the dales divine of Cithaeron; yet shall a wood-built wall [*teichos xylinon*] by Zeus all-seeing be granted" (Her. *Hist.* 7.141). Some of the older citizens incorrectly interpreted the "wooden wall" as the wooden palisade on the Acropolis, which proved no barrier against the Persian capture of Athens. Themistocles evacuated the city and cleverly interpreted the oracle to mean a fleet of triremes, which decisively defeated the Persian fleet in the Bay of Salamis.

Another important oracle of Apollo was located at Didyma, near Miletus in western Asia Minor. Its priests and priestesses were known as the Branchidae. Like Delphi, the oracle at Didyma was consulted both by Egyptian pharaohs like Necho II (Her. *Hist.* 2.159) and by Lydian kings like Croesus (Her. *Hist.* 1.92). After the Ionian Revolt, the Persians destroyed the archaic temple in 494 BC. Paionios, the same architect who designed the great temple of Artemis at Ephesus, also designed the new Hellenistic temple at Didyma. (See Yamauchi 1980, 129–34.) Later, the oracle foretold Alexander's victory at Issus.

In addition to consulting an oracle, generals and officials might also use their own methods of divination to determine appointments. *Klērōsis* (from *klēros,* "lot"), or casting lots, was widely used for this purpose in Greece. Lots could be knucklebones, dice, or black and white beans. In the *Iliad,* it was from the lot drawn from Agamemnon's helmet that the Greek warrior Ajax was designated to fight the Trojan Hector: "So spake they, and the horseman, Nestor of Gerenia, shook the helmet, and forth therefrom leapt the lot that themselves desired, even the lot of Aias [Ajax]" (Hom. *Il.* 7.181–183).

Sortition, the use of lots to choose officials, was the fundamental principle of Athenian democracy, inasmuch as its randomness provided poor citizens and wealthier citizens with equal opportunity to serve. Cleisthenes's democratic reform of 508 BC created ten new tribes; his *boulē,* or governing council, was made up of fifty men chosen by lot from each tribe. Beginning in 487 BC the choice of archons, the heads of various departments of government including the judiciary, was also determined by lot. Legal disputes were decided by large juries—for example, 501 jurors decided Socrates's trial—that were chosen by a sortition machine called the *klērōtērion.* This system, which chose men by chance rather than by ability, was condemned by Socrates and Plato.

Greek historians also describe generals on campaign relying on sacrificial omens for divine confirmation of their battle plans. The interpretation of sacrifices (*sphagia*) by diviners played a critical role in the battle of Plataea, in Greece, which took place between the Persians and the Greeks in

479 BC. At first, "the sacrifices boded good to the Greeks if they should but defend themselves, but evil if they should cross the Asopus and be the first to attack" (*Hist.* 9.36); but a similar interpretation of their sacrifices was offered to the Persians (*Hist.* 9.37). As a result, neither side attacked for ten days. But when the Persians discovered that the Greeks had been moving from their positions at night, they launched an attack against the Athenian position. The Spartans failed to join the battle, "as they could get no favourable omen from their sacrifices" (*Hist.* 9.61). In despair, the Spartan general Pausanias prayed earnestly to Hera for a favorable omen. When, "immediately after Pausanias' prayer the sacrifices of the Lacedaemonians grew to be favourable" (*Hist.* 9.62), the Spartans were able to come to the aid of the Athenians and win a decisive victory over the Persians.

The practice of extispicy (also known as haruspicy) was unknown to Homer, and may have been imported either from the East or from Etruria. Extispicy was a necessary practice for the Spartan army, which performed it before leaving on campaign, at the crossing of rivers, at the front lines, and after victories.

The examination of the organs of sacrificed sheep is also illustrated in Xenophon's account of the march of ten thousand Greek mercenaries against the Persians. If the first victim's omen proved to be unfavorable, a second and even a third sheep would be sacrificed (*Anab.* 6.4.16). When all the sheep had been sacrificed, they even resorted to sacrificing the cattle that should have drawn their wagons. The discovery of a liver with a missing lobe was thought to portend imminent death, as in the cases of Cimon, Agesilaus, and Alexander.

Rome

Both in the Roman Republic and in the Roman Empire no major act of public business, whether a meeting of the Assembly or of the Senate, or a battle, could proceed without divine sanction. Roman divination relied principally upon extispicy/haruspicy (cf. *haruspex*, lit., "gut gazer") or upon auspices (from Lat. *aves* + *spicere*), the observation of birds. The aim of Roman divination was not primarily to divine the future but to see if a proposed course of action was *fas*, "approved," or *nefas*, "disapproved." There were two types of signs: *auspicia oblativa*, "unsolicited signs," and *auspicia impetrativa*, "solicited signs." In his classic essay *De divinatione*, Cicero divides divination into two categories: practices that require *ars*, or technical skill (hepatoscopy, the interpretation of portents, lots, augury, and astrology), and omens produced by *natura* (dreams, ecstasy, and oracles) (*Div.* 1.6.12).

The pre-Roman Etruscans, who lived to the north of Rome, were influenced by traditions from the Near East and from the Greeks to develop a rich tradition of divination, which they passed on to the Romans. The so-called *Disciplina Etrusca*, a collection of Etruscan texts quoted in many later Roman works, included diviners' manuals such as the *Libri fulgurales*, which dealt with the interpretation of lightning flashes. The Etruscans divided the sky into four quarters, each of which they further subdivided into four sections, and assigned to each different significances.

Their tradition also included *Libri haruspicini*, which dealt with the examination of the organs of sacrificed sheep. A bronze Etruscan mirror (ca. 400 BC) depicts a diviner holding a liver in his hand. A bronze model of a sheep's liver from Piacenza (ca. 100 BC) is divided into forty-two sections, each marked in the Etruscan language, which has not yet been fully deciphered.

In Etruscan and Roman haruspicy, the liver was divided into three major parts: (1) the *caput*, "head"; (2) the *pars familiaris*, the part pertaining to the person sacrificing; and (3) the *pars hostilis*, the part pertaining to the enemy. If the *caput* was big this was a good sign, but if it was missing this portended death. If the skin around the liver was thick, this was a good sign; if thin, a bad sign. If the gallbladder was big, it signified a victory, as in the case of Augustus at Actium; if it was black, it was a bad sign.

Obtaining favorable omens was thought to be particularly important on the battlefield. Sixty *haruspices* were organized in an official body (*ordo haruspicium*, headed by a *maximus haruspex*). They accompanied troops into battle, offered sacrifice, and then reported the results of their examination to the commanders, conveying the gods' favor or disfavor for a planned action (Livy, *Rom. Hist.* 8.9.1–2).

The most important official diviners were priests known as *augures*, who would request propitious signs from the gods before any public action. At the beginning of the Republic (509 BC) there were only three, but their numbers were increased to nine by 300 BC, and then to sixteen under Julius Caesar. Augurs could not have any physical abnormalities. This was a prestigious position held by select senators for life. The augur's position was not purely ceremonial but had broad-reaching social influence. Cicero, who was himself an augur, declared: "Whatever an augur shall declare to be unjust, unholy, pernicious, or ill-omened, shall be null and void; and whoever yields not obedience shall be put to death" (*Leg.* 2.8).

With his head veiled, the augur would use a *lituus*, a curved staff derived from the Etruscans, to mark out the *templum*, the area from which he could watch for signs. When looking for meteorological signs at night (thunder and lightning), the augur would face south. Thunder and lightning to the east or left were favorable, to the west or right unfavorable.

The augur could also observe birds during the day. The Romans paid attention to the cries of birds including the raven, crow, night owl, and screech owl, and to the flight of the falcon, osprey, eagle, and vulture. According to Livy's account of Rome's founding myth (*Rom. Hist.* 1.6), the twins Romulus and Remus sought to decide who should have precedence in founding the city. Remus first saw six vultures from the Aventine Hill, but then Romulus saw twelve vultures from the Palatine Hill. Each claimed supremacy, which resulted in a clash in which Remus was killed. Surprisingly, the appearance of vultures is a positive omen in this story. Other birds were unfavorable omens: the cries of owls, for example, were always bad. Contrary to the Greeks, the Romans held that birds that appeared from the right were bad, whereas birds that appeared from the left were good.

Captive birds might also provide omens for an augur. The Roman army sometimes brought chickens (*pulli*) on campaign under the care of a *pullarius*, who would observe how they fed before a battle. If they ate so quickly that food fell out of their beaks, this was regarded as a favorable sign. Suetonius recounts that during the naval battle of Drepana during the First Punic War (249 BC), the consul Claudius Pulcher "took the auspices . . . off Sicily and, finding the sacred chickens had refused their feed, cried: 'If they will not eat, let them drink!'" (*Tib.* 2.2)—that is, he threw the birds into the sea. After his disregard of divinatory protocol, he lost ninety-three of his 123 warships to the Carthaginians.

The Romans were keenly sensitive to *prodigia*, extraordinary phenomena that they took as indications that the *pax deorum* ("the peace of the gods") had been broken, requiring a *procuratio*, or expiatory sacrifice. Such *omina* included streams running with blood, earthquakes, buildings and statues being struck by lightning, and more. Livy (*Rom. Hist.* 21.62–22.6) recounts a series of ominous events that presaged disaster for the consul Gaius Flaminius at the time of the Second Punic War. A calf that was to be sacrificed ran away, spattering bystanders with blood. When Gaius mounted his horse, it stumbled and threw him to the ground. The standard-bearer could not pull up the standard (the legionary eagle) from the ground. At the battle of Lake Trasimene in 217 BC, Gaius and fifteen thousand Romans were ambushed and slaughtered by Hannibal.

The most important official oracular source for the Roman government was the Sibylline Books, a semi-legendary work that does not survive. According to Roman tradition, the Sibyl was originally a prophetess from Asia Minor, either from Marpessus in the Troad or Erythrae in Ionia. An early prophetess with the title of Sibyl came to reside in a cave at Cumae north of Naples, and was then followed by her successors.

Roman legend recounts that the last Etruscan king, Tarquinius Superbus, purchased the original Sibylline Books from an old foreign woman, but only after she had destroyed two-thirds of the books, as the king at first declined to pay the price she was asking. The remaining books, which were said to record the Sibyl's utterances, were kept under guard at the temple of Jupiter on the Capitoline Hill.

Ten aristocratic priests, the *decemviri*, and later fifteen priests, the *quindecimviri*, were in charge of the books. Dionysius of Halicarnassus (4.62.5–6) reports:

> The others are not permitted to inspect the oracles. In short, there is no possession of the Romans, sacred or profane, which they guard so carefully as they do the Sibylline oracles. They consult them, by order of the senate, when the state is in the grip of party strife or some great misfortune has happened to them in war, or some important prodigies and apparitions have been seen which are difficult of interpretation, as has often happened. (*Ant. rom.* 4.62.5)

Between 496 and 100 BC, the Sibylline Books were consulted on fifty occasions. One such consultation that occurred during the Second Punic War even resulted in the founding of a new cult at Rome. When the Romans could get no aid from their own gods against the armies of Hannibal, which were winning victory after victory on the Italian peninsula, they ceremonially invited the *magna mater* goddess (Cybele) from Asia Minor to Rome in accordance with a text from the Sibylline Books.

In addition to consulting omens and oracles, the Romans used sortition, or lots (*sors*, pl. *sortes*), to make all kinds of appointments, such as the choice of Vestal Virgins and the allotment of armies to generals or provinces to proconsuls. Inscribed wooden lots would be placed into a vessel and then drawn out. In Cicero's dialogue *De divinatione*, Cicero's brother expresses Roman Stoicism's positive attitude toward divination: "Men capable of correctly interpreting all these signs [*sortes*] of the future seem to approach very near to the divine spirit of the gods whose will they interpret, just as scholars do when they interpret the poets" (*Div.* 1.18).

Lots were also used for divination. At the temple of Fortuna Primigenia at Praeneste, clients would approach with a query. A young boy would draw an inscribed lot from an urn, which would then be interpreted by a *sortilegus*. Similarly, one expert's book called the *Oracles of Astrampsychus*, which dates from the later Roman Empire (2nd–3rd c. AD), had a list of ninety-two questions and a table of ninety-two decades of possible answers. The petitioner would choose a certain numbered question and then be assigned by lot a number from one to ten, which he added to the number of the question. For example, Question 16 is *ei prokoptō*, "If I will advance?" (Browne 1983, 1; author's translation). If his lot number were five, he would add five to sixteen, resulting in twenty-one. There is a table in black with numbers in order and a second column with numbers in red in random order. Looking at this table, opposite the black number twenty-one is the red number eight. Finding the eighth decade, one will find that the answer five, which corresponds to his lot number, is *prokopteis meta chronon kathōs epithumeis*, "You will advance after a while, as you wish" (Stewart, 21; translation Browne 1970, 95).

The Romans did not suppress the older tradition of oracular shrines, and minor oracles were found throughout the larger Roman Empire. At the temple of Jupiter Heliopolitans at Baalbek in Lebanon, the oracle answered queries by the movement of a statue of the god carried in a procession, as in ancient Egypt. At Myra in Lycia fish in the fountain of Apollo Caria were called by flutes. If they ate the food thrown to them, it was a good sign; if they rejected it with their tails, it was a bad sign.

Oracles such as the one at Oxyrhynchus in Egypt continued to be popular during the Roman period. There survives from the third century AD a set of questions that were posed to it: "(85) Am I to become bankrupt? (86) Shall I become a refugee? . . . (88) Am I to become a senator?" (P. Oxy. 12 1477; Ferguson, 152). An affirmative answer to the last question would not have been welcome; by this period, such an office meant a ruinous financial obligation.

The popularity of oracles and their abuse led the Prefect of Egypt to issue the following order in AD 198:

> Encountering many who believed themselves to be deceived by the practices of divination I quickly considered it necessary, in order that no danger should ensue upon their foolishness, clearly herein to enjoin all people to abstain from this hazardous inquisitiveness. Therefore, let no man through oracles, that is, by means of written documents supposedly granted under divine influence, nor by means of the parade of images or suchlike charlatanry, pretend to know things beyond human ken and profess (to know) the obscurity of things to come, . . . let him be persuaded that he will be handed over to the extreme penalty. (Rea, 153)

The satirist Lucian (2nd c. AD) gives a detailed account of a certain Alexander who used chicanery to establish himself as a prophet at Abono-teichus in northern Asia Minor (Lucian, *Alex.* 26). Alexander fooled the gullible public to believe that a god had been born in the form of a snake. He made a long tube by joining the windpipes of several cranes, attached this to a mechanical snake head, and had an assistant in another room speak as the voice of the god. He also took sealed queries and carefully broke and reattached seals, so that he could "miraculously" provide apposite answers. Through Rutilianus, an important Roman official who was his devoted follower, Apollonius was even able to persuade the emperor Marcus Aurelius to heed his oracular declaration that two lions should be thrown into the Danube River in order to defeat the Marco-manni and the Quadi (*Alex.* 48).

E. THE JEWISH WORLD

The Jewish rabbis distinguished between *naḥaš*, "divination," which was condemned, and *sîimānîm*, "signs," which were permitted. For the rabbis, "divination" specifically included Greco-Roman practices such as augury. The *Sifra* forbade divination by the cries of birds. According to the Sibylline Books:

> There is a city . . . in the land of Ur of the Chaldeans, whence comes a race of most righteous men. They are always concerned with good counsel and noble works for they do not worry about the cyclic course of the sun or the moon . . . nor portents of sneezes, nor birds of augurers, nor seers. . . . Neither do they practice the astrological predictions of the Chaldeans nor astronomy.
> (*Sib. Or.* 3.218–228)

On the other hand, Rabbi Ilish distrusted the language of the raven, believing it to be a lying bird, but heeded the same message if it came from a dove (*b. Giṭ.* 45a). Josephus quotes the historian Hecataeus's recounting of an interesting tale of Mosollamus, a Jewish bowman serving in a Gentile army. When Mosollamus noticed that the army halted and marched according to the directions of a diviner who was watching the movement of a bird, Mosollamus shot the bird with an arrow. When the diviner and others became outraged at his action, Mosollamus took the bird in his hand and said: "Pray, how could any sound information about our march be given by this creature, which could not provide for its own safety? Had it been gifted with divination, it would not have come to this spot, for fear of being killed by an arrow of Mosollamus the Jew" (Jos. *Ag. Ap.* 1.204).

The use of lots played a major role in the assignment of duties to the priests in the temple. Before daybreak the supervisor cast lots to assign the priest who would remove the ashes from the altar of burnt offerings. He then cast lots to determine who would act as slaughterer, who would sprinkle the blood on the altar, who would trim the (lamps of the) candlestick, etc. Lots were also cast for the incense offering. (See *m. Yoma* 2:2–4; *m. Tamid* 1:2; 3:1; 5:2.)

Lots played a similarly important role in the life of the Qumran community. The word *gôrāl*, "lot," occurs over a hundred times in the Dead Sea Scrolls, often in the sense of "allotted membership." The Qumran texts describe God's predestination in terms of the lots he has cast for the good, who are called the Sons of Light, and for the evil, the Sons of Darkness. With regard to the former group, we read: "He has cast your lot and greatly increased your honor and has made you like a firstborn son for Him" (4Q418 81+81a, 5). With regard to the latter group, we read: "conversely, in proportion to bequest in the lot of evil, one will act wickedly and abominate truth" (1QS IV, 24–25). The oracle of the lot was used in the administration of the *yaḥad*, the community.

Josephus's history *The Jewish War* provides evidence for the practice of observing "signs" and the use of lots during his time. For example, Josephus records several premonitory omens that portended doom before the First Jewish Revolt broke out in AD 66, although some misinterpreted them in a positive fashion: "a star resembling a sword, stood over the city, and a comet which continued for a year" (*J.W.* 6.288–300); a cow gave birth to a lamb in the temple; the massive door of the inner court of the temple spontaneously opened; chariots were seen in the air, etc. Most disconcerting of all was the appearance in AD 66 of a rude peasant, Jesus son of Ananias, who cried out "Woe to Jerusalem!" day and night for seven years and five months, until he died in the Roman siege of Jerusalem (*J.W.* 6.301–308).

During the First Revolt against the Romans, at the siege of Jotapata, Josephus and about forty others drew lots to commit suicide. But then, when it came down to Josephus and one other survivor, they had a change of heart and surrendered to the Romans. It was quite different at the last siege at Masada in AD 74. According to Josephus, "then, having chosen by lot ten of their number to dispatch the rest, they laid themselves down each beside his prostrate wife and children, and, flinging their arms around them, offered their throats in readiness for the executants of the melancholy office" (*J.W.* 7.395–396). Yigael Yadin, after discovering eleven ostraca, commented:

> Had we indeed found the very ostraca which had been used in the casting of the lots? We shall never know for certain. But the probability is strengthened by the fact that among these eleven inscribed pieces of pottery was one bearing the name "Ben Ya'ir." The inscription of plain "Ben Ya'ir" on Masada at that particular time could have referred to no other than Eleazar ben Ya'ir. And it also seems possible that this final group were his ten commanders who had been left to the last, after the decision had been wholly carried out, and who had them cast lots amongst themselves. (Yadin, 201)

While Jews were forbidden to practice divination, some Jewish texts refer to the practices of the Jews' Greco-Roman neighbors. For example, the rabbis seem to have held that although necromancy was wicked, it was possible: "Our Rabbis taught: A *Ba'al ob* [necromancer] is one who speaks from between the joints of his body and his elbow joints. A *yidde'oni* [soothsayer] is one who places the bone of a *yidoa'* [an animal?] in his mouth and it speaks of itself" (*b. Sanh.* 65b). Furthermore,

Our Rabbis taught: *Ba'al ob* denotes both him who conjures up the dead by means of soothsaying and one who consults a skull. What is the difference between them?—The dead conjured up by soothsaying does not ascend naturally [but feet first], nor on the Sabbath; whilst if consulted by its skull it ascends naturally and on the Sabbath too. (*b. Sanh.* 65b)

The passage reports that some starved themselves and spent the night in a cemetery so that an unclean spirit would enable them to tell the future.

The phrase *ba'al 'ôb*, "necromancer," goes back to the biblical phrase *ba'ălat 'ôb*, which describes the woman of Endor who was asked by Saul to contact the dead Samuel (1 Sam 28:7). According to Harry Hoffner, the word *'ôb* originally designated a pit where offerings were placed to lure spirits from the Underworld.

F. THE CHRISTIAN WORLD

Early Christian writers opposed the Roman practice of divination on the basis of the OT prohibition of it and because of its inherent connection to polytheistic religion in their own day. All the patristic sources condemn divination, though Clement of Alexandria was willing to interpret the pre-Socratic philosopher Heraclitus's use of the word *manteuomai*, "to divine," in a positive light. Since divination was a feature of everyday life, many of these writers devote their efforts to disproving the idea that oracles and omens were caused by the gods. Many Christian writers attribute oracular phenomena and other types of divination to the power of demons, whom they identify with the gods of the Greco-Roman pantheon. This understanding of divination is even evident in early Christian readings of OT accounts of divination. For example, the church fathers were divided over how to interpret the incident of Saul at Endor in light of the OT's condemnation of necromancy: (1) some (Justin Martyr, Origen, Ambrose, Augustine) believed that the medium did actually resuscitate Samuel; (2) others (e.g., John Chrysostom) believed that either Samuel or a demon in his shape appeared at God's command; (3) and still others (Pionius, Tertullian, Ephraem the Syrian, Gregory of Nyssa, Jerome) believed that a demon deceived Saul and gave him a forged prophecy.

Christian opponents of divination had to account for widely believed instances of Greek and Roman oracles correctly predicting the outcome of events. The pagan philosopher Celsus rebuked Christians for believing in prophets rather than oracles. He maintained:

What need is there to collect all the oracular responses, which have been delivered with a divine voice by priests and priestesses, as well as by others,

whether men or women, who were under a divine influence?—all the wonderful things that have been heard issuing from the inner sanctuary?—all the
revelations that have been made to those who consulted the sacrificial victims? (Origen, *Cels.* 8.45)

In his work refuting Celsus, Origen was willing to concede that oracles
were sometimes successful, but he maintained that they were inspired by
demons (*Cels.* 8.47).

The same concession was made by the early Christian apologist Minucius Felix, who granted that "sometimes, it is true, even auspices or oracles
have touched the truth" (*Oct.* 26.7). He held that demons were behind all
sorts of divination: "They are breathed into the prophets, while they dwell
in the shrines, while sometimes they animate the fibres of the entrails, control the flights of birds, direct the lots, are the cause of oracles involved
in many falsehoods." He continued: "Raging maniacs also, whom you see
rush about in public, are moreover themselves prophets without a temple;
thus they rage, thus they rave, thus they are whirled around. In them also
there is a like instigation of the demon" (*Oct.* 27.4). Minucius Felix also
pointed out that those who disobey auguries do not encounter disaster and
that those who obey them do not find success.

Lactantius repeated the charge that demons

> brought to light astrology, and augury, and divination; and though these
> things are in themselves false, yet they themselves, the authors of evils, so gov-
> ern and regulate them that they are believed to be true. . . . They themselves
> invented necromancies, responses, and oracles, to delude the minds of men
> with lying divination by means of ambiguous issues. (*Epit.* 28)

This new explanation of oracles provoked non-Christian thinkers to
defend their traditional practices more vigorously than before. Porphyry,
the great Neo-Platonist philosopher, defended divination in his *Philosophy of Oracles*. The debate continued even after Christianity became an
officially tolerated religion in the Empire. The church historian Eusebius,
who was a friend of Constantine, devoted the whole of the fourth book
and much of the fifth book of his *Praeparatio Evangelica* to discrediting the
pagan oracles.

The issue of divination also became a major bone of contention between the Roman emperors and the Christians. Eusebius claims that when
Diocletian consulted Delphi, the oracle refused to answer because of the
presence of Christians (*Vit. Const.* 2.50–54). Lactantius reports that when
Diocletian was at Antioch in AD 304, he

> began to slay victims, that from their livers he might obtain a prognostic of
> events; and while he sacrificed, some attendants of his, who were Christians,

stood by, and they put the immortal sign [i.e., of the cross] on their foreheads. At this the demons were chased away, and the holy rites interrupted. The soothsayers trembled, unable to investigate the wonted marks on the entrails of the victims. (Lac. *Mort.* 10; cf. Lac. *Inst.* 4.27)

This infuriated the emperor. A year later, in 305, he and his colleague Galerius unleashed the last great persecution against the Christians.

When the emperor Constantine converted to Christianity in AD 312, he enacted laws that made private forms of divination illegal; these are found in section 9 of the Theodosian Code, entitled *De maleficis et mathematicis et ceteris similibus* ("Magicians, Astrologers, and All Other Like Criminals"), the beginning of which reads: "That soothsayer shall be burned alive who approaches the home of another, and the person who has summoned him by persuasion or rewards shall be exiled to an island, after the confiscation of his property" (*Cod. Theod.*, 9.16.1; Pharr, Davidson, and Pharr, 237). At the same time, Constantine allowed public forms of divination: "But you who think that this art is advantageous to you, go to the public altars and shrines and celebrate the rites of your custom; for We do not prohibit the ceremonies of a bygone perversion to be conducted openly" (*Cod. Theod.*, 9.16.2; Pharr, Davidson, and Pharr, 237).

Constantine's son Constantius II was much more severe against all forms of divination. He declared:

No person shall consult a soothsayer [*haruspex*] or an astrologer [*mathematicus*] or a diviner [*hariolus*]. The wicked doctrines of augurs and seers [*vates*] shall become silent. The Chaldeans and wizards [*magi*] and all the rest whom the common people call magicians [*malefici*], because of the magnitude of their crimes, shall not attempt anything in this direction. The inquisitiveness of all men for divination shall cease forever. For if any person should deny obedience to these orders, he shall suffer capital punishment, felled by the avenging sword. (*Cod. Theod.*, 9.16.4; Pharr, Davidson, and Pharr, 237)

Until AD 357, diviners were condemned to death and their clients were deported, but after 357 clients themselves were also subject to the death penalty. In 359 the emperor sent his envoy to shut down the popular oracular shrine of Bes at Abydos in Egypt.

Divination and other pagan rites experienced a brief revival in the reign of Julian "the Apostate" (AD 361–363). Like Diocletian, he consulted the oracle at Delphi, but to no avail. When he failed to get a good response from the oracle of Apollo at Daphne, a suburb of Antioch, he had the relics of St. Babylas removed from a nearby site, an action that was later denounced by John Chrysostom.

The great pagan historian Ammianus Marcellinus accompanied Julian and admired him, but was critical of his excessive devotion to divination:

"Julian in the midst of his many occupations in Illyricum was constantly prying into the entrails of victims and watching the flight of birds in his eagerness to foreknow the result of events; but he was perplexed by ambiguous and obscure predictions and continued to be uncertain of the future" (*Res G.* 22.1.1).

Later on, John Chrysostom accused Julian of sacrificing infants for the purpose of examining human entrails for divination (as the Druids did). The fact that Julian received a fatal wound in his liver from a Sasanian (Persian) soldier seemed to Gregory of Nazianzus to be poetic justice:

> He receives a wound truly seasonable (or mortal) and salutary for the whole world, and by a single cut from his slaughterer he pays the penalty for the many entrails of victims to which he had trusted (to his own destruction); but what surprises me, is how the vain man that fancied he learnt the future from that means, knew nothing of the wound about to be inflicted on his own entrails! (*Invective Against Julian*, 2.13; King, 96–97)

Nevertheless, even Christian emperors might occasionally resort to divination. The emperor Theodosius I (AD 379–395) ruled that if the palace were struck by lightning, the haruspices must be consulted. But in 391, probably under the influence of Ambrose, the formidable bishop of Milan, Theodosius closed all pagan temples and banned all forms of pagan worship. In 408 Etruscan diviners offered their services as Rome was being threatened by the Goths. Innocent, then bishop of Rome, said that he would not object, if the consultations were kept secret. Alas, Rome was sacked in 410.

Early Christians believed that some ancient oracles could be interpreted as foretelling the coming of Christ. This view was influenced by *The Sibylline Oracles*, a collection of prophecies that appear to describe a messianic figure. These oracles were in fact partly composed by Christians, as Celsus had suspected, but they were accepted as genuine pagan prophecies of Christianity by many Christians, including Lactantius, who quoted them often. Eusebius records that Constantine cited book 8, on the day of judgment, in an oration, and declared:

> It is evident that the virgin [Sybil] uttered these verses under the influence of divine inspiration. And I cannot but esteem her blessed, whom the Saviour thus selected to unfold his gracious purpose towards us. Many, however, who admit that the Erythræan Sibyl was really a prophetess, yet refuse to credit this prediction, and imagine that some one professing our faith, and not unacquainted with the poetic art, was the composer of these verses.
> (Eus. *Coet. sanct.* 18–19)

Augustine (d. 430) was converted by hearing the eloquent sermons of Ambrose at Milan, and by a form of cledonomancy, when he heeded the voices of children crying *tolle, lege, tolle, lege* ("Take, read, take, read"). He opened the NT to Rom 13:13 and was convicted and dramatically converted (*Conf.* 8.12.29). As for the *Sibylline Oracles*, Augustine remarked:

> But this sibyl, whether she is the Erythræan, or, as some rather believe, the Cumæan, in her whole poem, of which this is a very small portion, not only has nothing that can relate to the worship of the false or feigned gods, but rather speaks against them and their worshippers in such a way that we might even think she ought to be reckoned among those who belong to the city of God. (*Civ.* 18.23)

In the fifth century, sortilege (from Lat. *sortilegium*) as a form of divination remained popular in Gaul, as we learn from the Council of Vannes (ca. 465):

> Some clergy are devoted to the interpretation of signs (*auguria*), and under the label of what pretends to be religion—what they call Saints' Lots (*sanctorum sortes*)—they profess a knowledge of divination, or by looking into any kind of writings whatever they predict future events. Any cleric found either to have consulted or expounds this should be considered estranged from the church.
> (*Concilia Galliae*, A. 314–A. 506 [*CCSL* 148:156]; Klingshirn 2005, 100)

In an adaption of a much older practice, sacred books were also used for divination by selecting a passage at random. Gregory of Tours (538–594) reports that the Psalms and Gospels were used by clerics and others as a kind of *sortes biblicae*. New oracular texts were also written during this time: one such work, the *Sortes Sangallenses*, lists more than fifty possible answers to a query according to a triple throw of dice.

According to the sixth-century historian John Malalas, in 529,

> during the consulship of Decius, the emperor (Justinian) issued a decree and sent it to Athens ordering that no one should teach philosophy nor interpret astronomy nor in any city should there be lots cast using dice, for some who cast dice had been discovered in Byzantium indulging themselves in dreadful blasphemies. Their hands were cut off and they were paraded on camels.
> (*Chronicle* 18.47; cited in Watts, 171)

Procopius reported that astrologers were also punished and paraded on camels in Byzantium (Williamson, 99).

BIBLIOGRAPHY: A. Annus, ed., *Divination and Interpretation of Signs in the Ancient World* (2010); B. T. Arnold, "Necromancy and Cleomancy in 1 and 2 Samuel," *CBQ* 66 (2004), 199–213; R. Beal, "Hittite Oracles," in Ciraolo and Seidel, 57–81; A. M. Blackman, "Oracles in Ancient Egypt," *JEA* 11.3/4 (1925), 249–55; R. Borger, *Die Inschriften Asarhaddons, Königs von Assyrien* (1956); J. F. Borghouts, "Witchcraft, Magic, and Divination in Ancient Egypt," *CANE*, 3:1775–85; H. Bowden, *Classical Athens and the Delphic Oracle: Divination and Democracy* (2005); G. M. Browne, "The Composition of the Sortes Astrampsychi," *BICS* 17.1 (1970), 95–100; G. M. Browne, ed., *Sortes Astrampsychi*, vol. 1 (1983); J. Černý, "Egyptian Oracles," in R. A. Parker, trans. and ed., *A Saite Oracle Papyrus from Thebes in the Brooklyn Museum* (1962), 35–48; L. Ciraolo and J. Seidel, ed., *Magic and Divination in the Ancient World* (2002); G. Contenau, *Everyday Life in Babylon and Assyria* (1954); F. H. Cryer, *Divination in Ancient Israel and Its Near Eastern Environment* (1994); J. Z. de Boer, J. R. Hale, and J. Chanton, "New Evidence for the Geological Origins of the Ancient Delphic Oracle (Greece)," *Geology* 29.8 (2001), 707–10; M. Dillon, "The Importance of Oinomanteia in Greek Divination," in *Religion in the Ancient World*, ed. M. Dillon (1996), 99–121; A. Dinan, "Clement of Alexandria's Predication of the Verb *manteuomai* of Heraclitus," *JECS* 16.1 (2008), 31–60; J.-M. Durand, "La divination par les oiseaux," *MARI* 8 (1997), 273–82; G. Etiope et al. "The Geological Links of the Ancient Delphic Oracle (Greece): A Reappraisal of Natural Gas Occurrence and Origin," *Geology* 34.10 (2006), 821–24; F. M. Fales and G. B. Lanfranchi, "The Impact of Oracular Material on the Political Utterances and Political Action in the Royal Inscriptions of the Sargonid Dynasty," in *Oracles et prophéties dans l'antiquité*, ed. J.-G. Heintz (1997), 99–114; J. Ferguson, *The Religions of the Roman Empire* (1970); I. L. Finkel, "Necromancy in Ancient Mesopotamia," *AfO* 29/30 (1983–1984), 1–17; J. Fontenrose, *The Delphic Oracle: Its Responses and Operations, with a Catalogue of Responses* (1978); J. Fontenrose, *Python: A Study of Delphic Myth and Its Origins* (1980); S. M. Freedman, *If a City Is Set on a Height: The Akkadian Omen Series Šumma Alu ina Mēlê Šakin II: Tablets 22–40* (2006); M. Greenberg, "Nebuchadnezzar and the Parting of the Ways: Ezek 21:26–27," in *Ah, Assyria!*, ed. M. Cogan and I. Eph'al (1991), 267–71; R. A. Greer and M. M. Mitchell, trans., *The "Belly-Myther" of Endor: Interpretations of 1 Kingdoms 28 in the Early Church* (2007), 789–91; O. R. Gurney, "The Babylonians and Hittites," in Loewe and Blacker, 142–73; W. R. Halliday, *Greek Divination: A Study of Its Methods and Principles* (1967); E. J. Hamori, "The Prophet and the Necromancer: Women's Divination for Kings," *JBL* 132.4 (2013), 827–43; R. P. C. Hanson, "The Christian Attitude to Pagan Religions up to the Time of Constantine the Great," *ANRW* II.23.2 (1980), 910–73; H. A. Hoffner, "Second Millennium Antecedents of the Hebrew ʾōḇ," *JBL* 86.4 (1967), 385–401; W. Horowitz and V. Hurowitz, "Urim and Thummim in Light of a Psephomancy Ritual from Assur (*LKA* 137)," *JANESCU* 21 (1992), 95–115; H. B. Huffmon, "The Oracular Process: Delphi and the Near East," *VT* 57.4 (2007), 449–60; E. D. Huntsman, "And They Cast Lots: Divination, Democracy, and Josephus," in *Masada and the World of the New Testament*, ed. J. F. Hall and J. W. Welch (1997), 365–77; A. Jeffers, *Magic and Divination in Ancient Palestine and Syria* (1996); U. Jeyes, *Old Babylonian Extispicy* (1989); S. I. Johnston, *Ancient Greek Divination* (2008); S. I. Johnston and P. T. Struck, ed., *Mantikê: Studies in Ancient Divination* (2005); C. W. King, trans., *Julian the Emperor, Containing Gregory Nazianzen's Two Invectives and Libanius' Monody with Julian's Extant Theosophical Works* (1888); K. A. Kitchen, *Pharaoh Triumphant: The Life and Times of Ramesses II* (1982); W. E. Klingshirn, "Defining the Sortes Sanctorum: Gibbon, Du Cange, and Early Christian Lot Divination," *JECS* 10.1 (2002), 77–130; W. E. Klingshirn, "Christian Divination in Late Roman Gaul: The *Sortes Sangallenses*," in *Mantike: Studies in Ancient Divination*, ed. S. I. Johnston and P. T. Struck (2005), 99–128; U. S. Koch-Westenholz, *Babylonian Liver Omens* (2000); W. G. Lambert, "The Qualifications of Babylonian Diviners," in *Festschrift für Rykle Borger*, ed. S. M. Maul (1998), 141–58; A. Lange, "The Essene Position on Magic and Divination," in *Legal Texts and Legal Issues*, ed. M. Bernstein, F. García Martínez, and J. Kampen (1997), 377–435; A. Lange, "The Determination of Fate by the Oracle of the Lot in the Dead Sea Scrolls, the Hebrew Bible, and Ancient Mesopotamian Literature," in *Sapiential, Liturgical and Poetical Texts from Qumran*, ed. D. K. Falk, F. García Martínez, and E. M. Schuller (2000), 39–48; J. M. Lawrence, "Julian the Apostate and Sacrificial Divination," *NEASB* 18 (1981), 31–45; E. Leichty, *The Omen Series Šumma Izbu* (1970); A. Lenzi, ed., *Reading Akkadian Prayers and Hymns* (2011); J. Lindblom, "Lot-Casting in the Old Testament," *VT* 12.1 (1962), 164–78; J. Linderski, "Watching the Birds: Cicero the Augur and the Augural *Templa*," *CP* 81.4 (1986), 330–40; M. Loewe and C. Blacker, *Divination and Oracles* (1981); S. H. Lonsdale, "Attitudes towards Animals in Ancient Greece," *GR* 26.2 (1979), 146–59; A. Malamat, "A Forerunner of Biblical Prophecy: The Mari Documents," in *Ancient Israelite Religion*, ed. P. D. Miller, Jr., P. D. Hanson, and S. D. McBride (1987), 33–52; N. Marchetti, "Divination at Ebla during the Old Syrian Period: The Archaeological Evidence," in *Exploring the Longue Durée: Essays in Honor of Lawrence E. Stager*, ed. J. D. Schloen (2009), 279–95; A. G. McDowell, *Village Life in Ancient Egypt* (1999); E. S. Meltzer, ed., *Letters from Ancient Egypt*, trans. E. F. Wente (1990); J. A. North, "Diviners and Divination at Rome," in *Pagan Priests*, ed. M. Beard and J. A. North (1990), 51–71; D. Ogden, *Greek and Roman Necromancy* (2001); H. W. Parke, *Sibyls and Sibylline Prophecy in Classical Antiquity* (1988); C. Pharr, T. S. Davidson, and M. B. Pharr, ed., *The Theodosian Code and Novels, and the Sirmondian Constitutions* (2001); S. Price, "Delphi and Divination," in *Greek Religion and Society*, ed. P. E. Easterling and J. N. Muir (1985), 98–127; J. D. Ray, "Ancient Egypt," in Loewe and Blacker, 174–90; J. Rea, "A New Version of P. Yale Inv.

299," *ZPE* 27 (1977), 151–56; R. K. Ritner, "Necromancy in Ancient Egypt," in Ciraolo and Seidel, 89–96; F. Rochberg, "Empiricism in Babylonian Omen Texts and the Classification of Mesopotamian Divination as Science," *JAOS* 119.4 (1999), 559–69; N. Rosenstein, "Sorting Out the Lot in Republican Rome," *AJP* 116 (1995), 43–75; B. B. Schmidt, *Israel's Beneficent Dead: Ancestor Cult and Necromancy in Ancient Israelite Religion and Tradition* (1994); R. Schmitt, *Mantik im Alten Testament* (2014); M. Schofield, "Cicero for and against Divination," *JRS* 76 (1986), 47–65; K. Smelik, "The Witch of Endor: I Samuel 28 in Rabbinic and Christian Exegesis till 800 AD," *VC* 33.2 (1979), 160–79; D. E. Smith, " 'Pisser against a Wall': An Echo of Divination in Biblical Hebrew," *CBQ* 72.4 (2010), 699–717; I. Starr, *The Rituals of the Diviner* (1983); I. Starr, ed., *Queries to the Sungod: Divination and Politics in Sargonid Assyria* (1990); R. Stewart, ed., *Sortes Astrampsychi*, vol. 2 (2001); C. Van Dam, *The Urim and Thummim: A Means of Revelation in Ancient Israel* (1997); A. von Lieven, "Divination in Ägypten," *AF* 26.1 (1999), 77–126; E. Watts, "Justinian, Malalas, and the End of Athenian Philosophical Teaching in A.D. 529," *JRS* 94 (2004), 168–82; G. A. Williamson, trans., *Procopius, The Secret History* (1966); Y. Yadin, *Masada: Herod's Fortress and the Zealots' Last Stand* (1966); E. M. Yamauchi, *The Archaeology of New Testament Cities in Western Asia Minor* (1980); E. M. Yamauchi, *Persia and the Bible* (1990).

EMY

See also ASTROLOGY, DREAMS, GAMES & GAMBLING, and MAGIC.

DIVORCE

In the ancient world, the formal dissolution of a marriage was most often initiated by the husband, and only rarely by the initiation of the aggrieved wife.

A. THE OLD TESTAMENT

The OT does not legislate for divorce but clearly presupposes that it could occur. It was only the husband's prerogative to divorce his wife, though a woman might attempt to return to her father's home (cf. Judg 19:2, where the woman is a concubine).

From metaphorical passages in which Yahweh likens his relationship to Israel as that of a husband to his wife, we learn that the oral formula of divorce must have been "She is not my wife, and I am not her husband" (Hos 2:2). An adulterous woman could be shamed by being stripped bare and sent away (Hos 2:3).

The key passage on divorce in the Pentateuch is Deut 24:1–4a:

> If a man marries a woman who becomes displeasing to him because he finds something indecent [ʿerwat dābār] about her, and he writes her a certificate of divorce [sēper kĕrîtut], gives it to her and sends her from his house, and if after she leaves his house she becomes the wife of another man, and her second husband dislikes her and writes her a certificate of divorce [cf. Isa 50:1], gives it to her and sends her from his house, or if he dies, then her first husband, who divorced her, is not allowed to marry her again after she has been defiled.

This text, which prohibits the remarriage of the divorced wife to her first husband, presupposes the possibility of divorce. The certificate of divorce enabled the woman to remarry.

In cases where a man had shamed a bride by falsely claiming that she was not a virgin, or where he had raped a virgin, the man was not allowed ever to divorce the woman (Deut 22:13–19, 28–29). Priests were forbidden to marry divorced women (Lev 21:7, 14; Ezek 44:22). In the postexilic period, Ezra forced Jewish men who had married non-Jewish women to divorce them (Ezra 10:11), whereas Nehemiah seems to have only forbidden mixed marriages that had not already occurred (Neh 13:23–27).

Another key passage is Exod 21:7–11:

> If a man sells his daughter as a servant, she is not to go free as male servants do. If she does not please the master who has selected her for himself, he must let her be redeemed. He has no right to sell her to foreigners, because he has broken faith with her. . . . If he marries another woman, he must not deprive the first one of *her food, clothing* and *marital rights* [emphasis added]. If he does not provide her with these three things, she is to go free, without any payment of money.

This was later interpreted as specifying the three rights of a married woman, which the husband contracted to provide her; if he failed, this could lead to a divorce.

The prophet Malachi denounces Jewish men's marrying of foreign women who worship other gods, and men who divorce their wives, perhaps to marry such women:

> Judah has desecrated the sanctuary the LORD loves by marrying women who worship a foreign god. . . . Another thing you do: You flood the LORD's altar with tears. You weep and wail because he no longer looks with favor on your offerings or accepts them with pleasure from your hands. You ask, "Why?" It is because the LORD is the witness between you and the wife of your youth. You have been unfaithful to her, though she is your partner, the wife of your marriage covenant. . . . So be on your guard, and do not be unfaithful to the wife of your youth. "The man who hates and divorces his wife," says the LORD, the God of Israel, "does violence to the one he should protect," says the LORD Almighty. (Mal 2:11, 13–16)

In verse 16 the Hebrew text reads: *kî-śānēʾ šallaḥ*, literally, "for (or if) he hates divorce." A Qumran fragment of Malachi reads *ky ʾm śnth šlḥ*, "but if you hate [her], send [her] away" (4Q76 II, 4). Translations that understand Yahweh as the subject of the verb "hate" in this text have interpreted it to mean, "I (Yahweh) hate divorce."

B. THE NEW TESTAMENT

When Joseph found that his betrothed, Mary, was pregnant, he suspected that this was the result of an affair. "Because Joseph her husband was faithful to the law, and yet did not want to expose her to public disgrace, he had in mind to divorce her quietly" (Matt 1:19). As betrothal was a contractual agreement between two families, a divorce was necessary for the dissolution of the unconsummated marriage.

In commenting on God's purpose in creating marriage as a permanent relationship, Jesus cites Gen 2:24 (Matt 19:5||Mark 10:7–8). His response to the Pharisees about the legitimacy of divorce was no doubt framed in reaction to the dispute between the followers of the stricter rabbi Shammai and the more liberal rabbi Hillel about the allowable justification for a man to divorce his wife found in Deut 24:1–4. Jesus said that Moses had permitted divorce only as a concession for the hardness of men's hearts (see Matt 19:8). In Matt 19:9 the prohibition of divorce and remarriage contains an exception clause, "except for sexual immorality [*porneia*]." But in the Jewish world divorce always implied the right to remarry.

The parallels to Matt 19:9 in Mark 10:11–12 and Luke 16:18 do not include an "exception clause" allowing for divorce. Following Roman custom, Herodias divorced her husband, Philip, and married Herod Antipas, for which she was criticized by John the Baptist (Mark 6:17–18; cf. Jos. *Ant.* 18.5.1).

Some scholars view Jesus's strong statements against divorce as a reaction to the "no-fault," easy divorce popularized by Hillel and his followers, and as possibly a rhetorical overstatement of an ideal similar to statements made in the Sermon on the Mount.

In response to questions about marriage from the church in Corinth, Paul strongly indicated his preference for celibacy in order better to serve the Lord, especially in light of the difficult times. That said, he conceded the legitimacy of marriage for those who did not have a gift of celibacy. In speaking of divorce he assumed that a wife as well as a husband might initiate a divorce. He wrote in 1 Cor 7:12–16:

> To the rest I say this (I, not the Lord): If any brother has a wife who is not a believer and she is willing to live with him, he must not divorce her. And if a woman has a husband who is not a believer and he is willing to live with her, she must not divorce him. . . . But if the unbeliever leaves, let it be so. The brother or the sister is not bound in such circumstances; God has called us to live in peace.

Some church fathers restricted the so-called "Pauline privilege" of a believing wife to part from her unbelieving husband who had abandoned her, considering it to be "separation" and not divorce. But in the Greco-Roman world such a separation meant divorce and the privilege of remarriage. The Greek word *chōrizetai*, "to separate," used in 1 Cor 7:15 had come to mean "to divorce" by the fourth century BC. The phrase *ou dedoulōtai*, "he/she is not bound," in 1 Cor 7:15 (cf. Rom 7:3) implied the right to remarry another Christian, as was the case for a widow (1 Cor 7:39).

C. THE NEAR EASTERN WORLD

Mesopotamia

In Mesopotamian divorces, the husband would say to his wife *ul aššatī atti*, "You are not my wife," and the wife would say to her husband *ul mutī atta*, "You are not my husband." Some divorces in which the wife was at fault involved the cutting of the hem (*sissiktu*), which signified that the wife was prevented from recovering her dowry.

Some marriage contracts contained a clause imposing a specific penalty for divorce without grounds, ranging from ten shekels to a mina (sixty shekels). The shekel of silver was equivalent to a month's wage. A West Semitic marriage contract from Ḫana (16th c. BC) declared:

> If Kikkinu, her husband, to Bitti-Dagan, his wife, shall say: "thou art not my wife," empty handed she shall leave his house; with the oxen of the palace he shall herd her. And if Bitti-Dagan, his wife to Kikkinu, her husband, shall say: "thou art not my husband," she shall leave her bed; to the carriage house of the palace, he shall cause her to go [i.e., she will become a slave in the palace]. (cited in Clay, 51)

In some Old Asssyrian contracts the wife had the same right to divorce (*ezēbu*, "to leave") as the husband. The Old Babylonian Code of Hammurabi, from the eighteenth century BC, contains a number of cases that deal with divorce. CH 137 rules: "If a seignior has made up his mind to divorce a lay priestess, who bore him children, or a hierodule who provided him with children, they shall return her dowry to that woman and also give her half of the field, orchard and goods in order that she may rear her children" (*ANET*, 172). According to CH 138, "If a seignior wishes to divorce his wife who did not bear him children, he shall give her money to the full amount of her marriage-price and he shall also make good to her the dowry which she brought from her father's house and then he may divorce her" (*ANET*, 172). According to CH 141,

> If a seignior's wife, who was living in the house of the seignior, has made up her mind to leave in order that she may engage in business, thus neglecting her house (and) humiliating her husband, they shall prove it against her; and if her husband has then decided on her divorce, he may divorce her, with nothing to be given her as her divorce-settlement upon her departure. If her husband has not decided on her divorce, her husband may marry another woman, with the former woman [i.e., first wife] living in the house of her husband like a maidservant. (*ANET*, 172)

Only in rare cases could a woman initiate a divorce before the city council. According to CH 142,

If a woman so hated her husband that she has declared, "You may not have me," her record shall be investigated at her city council, and if she was careful and was not at fault, even though her husband has been going out and disparaging her greatly, that woman, without incurring any blame at all, may take her dowry and go off to her father's house. (*ANET*, 172)

On the other hand, CH 143 stipulates: "If she was not careful, but was a gadabout, thus neglecting her house (and) humiliating her husband, they shall throw that woman into the water" (*ANET*, 172).

Divorce was forbidden in certain circumstances. According to CH 148, "When a seignior married a woman and a fever has then seized her, if he has made up his mind to marry another, he may marry (her), without divorcing his wife whom the fever seized; she shall live in the house which he built and he shall continue to support her as long as she lives" (*ANET*, 172).

The somewhat earlier Laws of Eshnunna stipulate: "If a man divorces his wife after having made her bear children and takes [ano]ther wife, he shall be driven from his house and from whatever he owns and may go after him who will accept him" (CE 59; *ANET*, 163).

A text from Alalakh (15th c. BC) declares:

If Naidu has taken a dislike to Irihalpa and she continuously repels him, he (i.e., Irihalpa) shall retain the "bride-price" of the young girl (i.e., Naidu), but whatever was apportioned to her in her father's house (i.e., her dowry), she shall take and depart. If he (Irihalpa) "leads the young girl by the nose" (i.e., treats her with disrespect), he shall return the "bride-price," and whatever she brought from her father's house with her as her portion, she shall take and depart. (cited in Lipinski, 18)

At Nuzi (14th c. BC) a husband could send constables after a wife who had left his home. According to the Middle Assyrian Laws (12th c. BC), Assyrian men could divorce their wives at will and send them away without anything (MAL 37). An Assyrian wife could divorce her husband if he had been captured for two years or had deserted her for five years (MAL 36, 45).

Egypt

No law codes have been recovered from Egypt. The Demotic "Legal Code of Hermopolis," from the Ptolemaic era, a papyrus that was discovered in 1939 and published only in 1975, is a handbook for making decisions in disputes over property and inheritance and contains nothing concerning marriage or divorce. It is only from very late in Egyptian history that we have any surviving marriage or divorce documents. The earliest surviving Egyptian divorce document (542 BC) dates to the 26th Dynasty (7th–6th c. BC). There are ten Demotic divorce writs dating from the Persian and Hellenistic periods. These deeds guaranteed the divorced women the right to remarry.

The divorce document of an Egyptian named Amenhotpe/Amenhotep, dated to 282 BC, reads:

> I have abandoned thee (Taapi), I am removed from thee regarding the "law of wife." It is I who has said unto thee: "Make for thyself a husband," I shall not be able to stand before thee in any place where thou goest in order to make for thyself a husband there. I have no claim on earth against thee in the name of "wife" from today onward, instantly, without delay, without a blow.
>   (Reich, 138–39)

As VerSteeg observes, "Both husband and wife had the right to sue the other for divorce. The terms of the annuity [i.e., marriage] contracts (which generally seem to have presumed that a man might eventually desire a younger bride), however, probably had a normative effect, and, thus, discouraged some men from divorcing their wives" (VerSteeg, 155).

Some deeds stipulated that a rather high fine had to be paid by the husband who divorced his wife. A text from 230 BC fined a husband ten *deben* of silver for divorcing his wife and the same amount for marrying a second wife. (At this time, one *deben* represented between one day's and one week's pay for a laborer.) The husband had the right to use what the woman had brought into the marriage. If he divorced her and could not return her dowry or her household goods, he had to pay for her maintenance.

A 20th Dynasty papyrus (Turin 2021) contains a declaration by the children of a first marriage, which had ended in divorce, that they have received a proper share of their parents' estate and have no claim on the property their father intends to give to his second wife. The court affirms that he can give this property even to "a Syrian or a Nubian whom he loved" (cited in Černý and Peet, 32).

The Demotic *Instruction of Ankhsheshonq* counsels: "If you find your wife with her lover get yourself a bride to suit you" (13.12; cited in *AEL*, 3.169). It also advises: "Do not abandon a woman of your household when she has not conceived a child" (14.16; cited in *AEL*, 3.170). Childless wives sometimes brought up children their husbands had begotten by slave women.

D. THE GRECO-ROMAN WORLD

Greece

The *Code of Gortyn* (450 BC) from Crete stipulates: "If a husband and wife divorce, she is to keep her property, whatever she brought to the marriage, and one-half the produce (if there is any) from her own property, and half of whatever she has woven within the house" (cited in Lefkowitz and Fant, 56). If her husband was the cause of the divorce, she was awarded five staters. If the husband swore that he was not the cause, a judge would decide. If the woman had taken anything, she was obliged to return it to her husband. If she denied having taken anything, she had to swear this before the statue of Artemis.

Later, under Attic (Athenian) law, a couple could agree to separate simply to contract a more suitable union, as occurred in the case of Pericles and his wife. A husband had the right to divorce his wife without any reason. An adulterous wife had to be repudiated. In the usual procedure, the husband took back the keys of the house from his wife before witnesses and sent her back (the verbs used for this action are *ekballein, ekpempein,* and *apompein*) to her family with her dowry. If he did not pay back her dowry immediately, he was liable to pay 18 percent interest on it per year until it was repaid.

A wife whose husband had been flagrantly unfaithful could sue for divorce before the eponymous archon of Athens. In a fictional letter of Alciphron (2nd or 3rd c. AD), Panopē warns her philandering husband, Euthybolus: "Either cease playing the nabob and stop being a lecher and crazy about women or, let me tell you, I shall be off to my father. He will not overlook my plight, and he will prosecute you before the judges for ill-usage" (Letter 6).

A wife was legally unable to manage her affairs without a male guardian (*kyrios*) so she needed her father or brother to initiate divorce proceedings against an unwilling husband. This was not always easy to do, as Plutarch points out in his life of the notorious Alcibiades:

> Hipparete was a decorous and affectionate wife, but being distressed because her husband would consort with courtezans [*sic*], native and foreign, she left his house and went to live with her brother. Alcibiades did not mind this, but continued his wanton ways, and so she had to put in her plea for divorce to the magistrate, and that not by proxy but in her own person. On her appearing publicly to do this, as the law required, Alcibiades came up and seized her and carried her off home with him through the market place, no man daring to oppose him or take her from him. (*Alc.* 8)

Rome

Gaius, a jurist of the second century AD, defined divorce as follows: "The term *divortium* is derived either from the *difference* of minds (of the parties), or from the fact that the parties who are tearing the marriage asunder are going their *different* ways" (*Dig.* 24.2.2.pr; cited in Rabello, 79). Divorce, like marriage, was a private affair that required no state or religious ratification. As initially there were different types of marriages, so there were different types of divorces. The oldest and most solemn form of marriage, *confarreatio*, which was required of certain priesthoods, could only be dissolved by a similar religious ceremony, the *diffarreatio*.

According to Plutarch, Romulus, the first ruler of Rome,

> enacted certain laws, and among them one of severity, which forbids a wife to leave her husband, but permits a husband to put away his wife for using poisons, for substituting children, and for adultery; but if a man for any other reason sends his wife away, the law prescribes that half his substance shall belong to his wife, and the other half be consecrate [*sic*] to Ceres; and whosoever puts away his wife, shall make a sacrifice to the gods of the lower world. (*Rom.* 22)

In the early history of Rome divorce was rare. Nevertheless, despite the assertion of Aulus Gellius that there was not a single case of divorce until 230 BC, when Spurius Carvilius divorced his wife because she was barren, divorces are known from as early as the seventh century BC. The Twelve Tables of Law inscribed in 451 BC record the formula for divorce: *Res tuas tibi habeto*, "Take your things with you."

In 307 BC a senator who put away his wife without the judgment of a tribunal was penalized. In 268 BC a consul named Publius Sempronius Sophus divorced his wife because she had dared to attend the games without his knowledge. In 166 BC a consul named Gaius Sulpicius Gallus repudiated his wife because he had detected her in public with her head uncovered.

Society frowned upon the divorce of a virtuous woman who had provided her husband with children. Aemilus Paulus divorced his wife, Papira, who was the mother of very fine children, including the famous Scipio. When his friends berated him for this, he held out a good-looking shoe as an object lesson. He said, "Is it not new? But no one of you can tell me where it pinches my foot?" Plutarch goes on to explain this comment as follows:

> For, as a matter of fact, it is great and notorious faults that separate many wives from their husbands; but the slight and frequent frictions arising from some unpleasantness or incongruity of characters, unnoticed as they may be by everybody else, also produce incurable alienations in those whose lives are linked together. (Plu. *Aem.* 5.2)

In Plautus's play *Mercator*, a woman complains about a double standard:

> My, my! Women do live under hard conditions, so much more unfair, poor things, than the men's. Why, if a husband has brought home some strumpet [prostitute], unbeknown to his wife, and she finds it out, the husband goes

scot free. But once a wife steps out of the house unbeknown to her husband, he has his grounds and she's divorced. Oh, I wish there was the same rule for the husband as for the wife! (817–823)

In the late Republic (3rd c. BC), with the prevalence of "free" marriages a wife or her father acting on her behalf could secure a divorce. That is, when a wife married she did not become a part of her husband's family but was still under her own father's *patria potestas*. This enabled women, as well as men, to initiate a divorce, with the exception that if a man freed a slave to marry her, she could not divorce him.

By the late Roman Republic and early Empire divorces had become quite common among the upper classes, often for political and even trivial reasons. Seneca commented: "Is there any woman that blushes at divorce now that certain illustrious and noble ladies reckon their years, not by the number of consuls, but by the number of their husbands, and leave home in order to marry, and marry in order to be divorced?" (*Ben.* 3.16.2). The satirist Juvenal railed at a woman who, "wearing out her bridal veil," had eight husbands in the course of five autumns (*Sat.* 6.224–230).

The scathing comments of the moralists create a somewhat misleading impression of the prevalence of divorce in the early Roman Empire. Actual divorces that can be documented in literary sources from 100 to 38 BC number thirty-two, and most of these were made for political reasons. A study of the senatorial aristocracy for the Augustan period to around AD 200 found only twenty-seven attested divorces out of 562 women, most from the Julio-Claudian period (31 BC–AD 68). However, this evidence comes only from historical accounts, and not from inscriptions, as tombstones did not record divorces.

Cicero divorced Terentia, his wife of thirty years, because he wanted to marry his wealthy ward, in order to use her wealth to pay off his debts. He then divorced his young wife because she failed to share his grief about the loss of his daughter Tullia. Pompey, who had five wives, was twice widowed and twice divorced. Caesar divorced his wife Pompeia because he suspected that Clodius had planned to meet her in disguise at a women's religious rite. He explained, "Caesar's wife must be above reproach" (Plu. *Caes.* 10.6). Augustus forced his stepson Tiberius to divorce his beloved wife Vipsania to marry his (Augustus's) own daughter Julia, whom Tiberius loathed (Suet. *Tib.* 7).

Augustus, who passed legislation to regulate morals, had himself divorced his wife Scribonia, because of her bad temper, in order to marry his mistress Livia, who was already pregnant at the time with Drusus. Scribonia was given away in marriage by her ex-husband, Tibierius Claudius Nero. In 18 BC Augustus, by the *lex Iulia de adulteriis*, made *adulterium* a public crime and required a husband to divorce his wife who had committed adultery. According to this law, if a husband did not divorce an adulterous wife he would be guilty of *lenocinium*, "pimping." The adulterous woman would lose half of her *dos* (dowry) and be exiled to an island, and she could not contract a valid marriage.

A wife could not prosecute her husband for adultery, but could divorce him and get her dowry back, and could also remarry. Under Augustan law she would have to remarry if she wanted to be eligible to receive legacies. Augustus's Julian law permitted a woman to wait six months after a divorce before remarriage, and his later Papian law extended that period to a year and six months. A man who divorced his wife who had committed adultery was obliged to remarry if he did not wish to diminish his ability to receive legacies.

Though no ceremony or even notification was necessary to effect a divorce, it was often customary to send a *repudium* by a messenger to inform the wife that she was divorced. Messalina celebrated her wedding with her lover, Silius, without sending Claudius a notice that she was divorcing him (Tac. *Ann.* 11.27; Suet. *Claud.* 26.2). In AD 293 Diocletian allowed women to dissolve their marriages by writing a bill of divorce without even giving it to their husbands or informing them.

Children, unless they were quite young, would remain with the father. Because of the frequency of divorces, many children lived with stepmothers. The case of Octavia, the sister of Octavian (Augustus) who was divorced by Mark Antony when the latter married Cleopatra, was quite remarkable. This noble woman cared not only for the three children she had borne to Antony but also for Antony's son from his previous wife, Fulvia, and for three of Cleopatra's children.

An unusually long inscription (*Laudatio Turiae*) records a moving tribute to a woman named Turia, the wife of the inscription's author, who was possibly the consul Q. Lucretius Vespillo (consul of 19 BC). Among other things, he praises his wife for her offer to divorce him because she is barren:

> Marriages as long as ours are rare, marriages that are ended by death and not broken by divorce. For we were fortunate enough to see our marriage last without disharmony for fully 40 years. . . . When you despaired of your ability to bear children and grieved over my childlessness, you became anxious lest by retaining you in marriage I might lose all hope of having children and be distressed for that reason. So you proposed a divorce outright and offered to yield our house free to another woman's fertility. Your intention was in fact that you yourself, relying on our well-known conformity of sentiment, would search out and provide for me a wife who was worthy and suitable for me. . . . I must admit that I flared up so that I almost lost control of myself; so horrified was I by what you tried to do that I found it difficult to retrieve my composure.

To think that separation should be considered between us before fate had so ordained, to think that you had been able to conceive in your mind the idea that you might cease to be my wife while I was still alive, although you had been utterly faithful to me when I was exiled and practically dead! (Laudatio Turiae 1.27–28; 2.31–34, 40–43; cited in Lefkowitz and Fant, 136, 138)

E. THE JEWISH WORLD

Among the Aramaic papyri from the Jewish mercenary colony serving the Persians at Elephantine, Egypt (5th c. BC), there are three marriage contracts (dated to 449, 440, and 420 BC). According to one of these:

> However, Jeh[oishma] does not have right [to] acquire another husband besi[des] Anani. And if she do thus, it is divorce; they shall apply to [her the provisions of div]orce. . . . Moreover, [Ananiah shall] n[ot be able to ta]ke [another] woman [besides Jehoishma his wife] in marriage. If he do [thus, it is divorce]. (Kraeling 7:33–34, 36–37; Porten, 57)

Another contract reads:

> Tomorrow or another day, should Anani stand up in an assembly and say, "I have divorced Tamut my wife" divorce money [*ksp śn'*, lit., "silver of hatred"] is on his head. . . . Tomorrow or another day, should Tamut stand up and say, "I have divorced my husband Anani" divorce money is on her head. She shall give Anani silver, 7 shekels 2 q(*uarters*) and she shall take out all that she brought in in her hand from straw to string. (Kraeling 2:8–10; Porten, 38–39)

Ben Sira (Ecclesiasticus) praises the blessings of a good and loyal wife (Sir 26:1–4), and decries the misery caused by an evil wife (Sir 25:16–26). He concludes, "If she does not accept your control, divorce her and send her away" (Sir 25:26 NEB).

The members of the Herodian family, whose lives Josephus chronicled, were nominally Jewish but lived according to Roman mores that allowed women to divorce their husbands. Josephus reports nine divorces among the Herodians, four by the husbands and five by the wives.

Herod the Great, who had multiple wives, divorced his first wife, Doris, to marry Mariamme, the daughter of the high priest (Jos. Ant. 14.300). Herod's sister Salome sent a "document dissolving their marriage" (*grammateion, apoluomenē ton gamon*) to her husband, Costobarus (Jos. Ant. 15.260). Josephus comments that this "was not in accordance with Jewish law."

Herod Antipas promised to divorce his wife, the daughter of the Nabatean king Aretas, in order to marry Herodias (Ant. 18.110–112). Herodias herself divorced her uncle Herod Philip to marry Antipas (Matt

14:3–6; Mark 6:17–19), a marriage that was denounced by John the Baptist, not because of the divorces that were involved but because Herodias had been married to Antipas's half-brother (Lev 18:16; 20:21), who was still alive when she remarried.

The three daughters of Herod Agrippa I (Acts 12:1–21) had multiple marriages: (1) Drusilla (Acts 24:24) divorced Azizus, king of Emesa (Homs) in Syria, to marry the Roman governor Felix (Jos. Ant. 20.141–143). (2) Bernice (Acts 25:13, 23; 26:30) married her uncle Herod of Chalcis, and after his death married Polemo, king of Cilicia, whom she divorced to live, it was said, in an incestuous relationship with her brother Herod Agrippa II, before she became the mistress of the Roman general and future emperor Titus (Jos. Ant. 20.146). (3) Mariamme divorced her husband Julius Archelaus to marry Demetrius, the alabarch of Alexandria (Jos. Ant. 20.147).

Commenting on Deut 24:1–4, Josephus writes: "He who desires to be divorced from the wife who is living with him for whatsoever cause—and with mortals many such may arise—must certify in writing that he will have no further intercourse with her" (*Ant.* 4.253). After he allied himself with the Romans, Josephus married, at the behest of Vespasian, "one of the women taken captive at Caesarea" (*Life* 414), but she left him. Then, when he went with Vespasian to Alexandria, he married again (*Life* 415). But as this wife did not please him, Josephus divorced her (*Life* 426). He later married a Jewish woman from Crete, who bore him two sons (*Life* 427).

Jewish marriages assumed the possibility of divorce, with rare exceptions. The Qumran *Temple Scroll* commands the king not to take another wife, for "she alone shall be with him as long as she lives. If she dies, then he may take himself another wife from his father's house, that is, his family" (11Q19 LVII, 18–19). This text thus proscribes both polygamy and divorce for the king. An ambiguous phrase (*bḥyyhm*, "in their lives") in the Damascus Document (CD IV, 20–21) has been interpreted by some scholars as a prohibition of polygamy, and by others as a prohibition of remarriage after divorce or the death of a spouse. But most Jews permitted remarriage after divorce. This same text requires one who would divorce his wife to consult with the *mbqr*, "supervisor" (CD XIII, 15–17). A different text fragment prohibits a man who has falsely accused his wife from divorcing her (4Q159 2–4, 8–10; cf. Deut 22:19).

In the first century BC, a celebrated debate occurred between the Pharisees Shammai and Hillel over the interpretation of the phrase ʿerwat dābār in Deut 24:1. According to the Mishnah,

> The School of Shammai say: A man may not divorce his wife unless he has found unchastity [*dbr ʿrwh*, lit., "matter of indecency"] in her, for it is written, *Because he hath found in her* indecency *in anything* [ʿrwt dbr]. And the School

of Hillel say: [He may divorce her] even if she spoiled a dish for him, for it is written, *Because he hath found in her indecency in* anything. (*m. Giṭ.* 9:10)

That is, Shammai inverted the original phrase *ʿerwat dābār*, turning it into *dābār ʿerwâ* (*dbr ʿrwh*), and explained it as "a matter of indecency (i.e., a matter of unchastity)," holding that divorce was permissible only for adultery. Hillel, on the other hand, interpreted the phrase *ʿerwat dābār* as referring to "indecency in (any) matter," and thus as encompassing any kind of defect that would cause her husband to be dissatisfied. Later, Rabbi Akiba held that a man might divorce his wife "even if he found another fairer than she, for it is written: 'if she find no favor in his eyes'" (*m. Giṭ.* 9:10). By Jesus's day, apparently the liberal, Hillelite "any matter" view of divorce had become dominant. According to David Instone-Brewer, "The Hillelite divorce was already common in the first century B.C.E. The reforms of Simeon ben Shetah in the previous century . . . were probably introduced mainly as a result of the Hillelite 'any matter' divorce, which effectively allowed divorce at the whim of the husband" (Instone-Brewer, 113). He adds: "the vast majority of first-century Jewish divorces were 'any matter' divorces in a Hillelite court" (ibid., 117).

The Mishnah and Talmud list myriad reasons that might cause a husband to divorce his wife. A serious reason was the lack of children, as the essential purpose of marriage was considered to be procreation.

> If he married a woman and lived with her ten years and she bare no child, it is not permitted him to abstain [i.e., from the command to be fruitful and multiply]. If he divorced her she may be married to another and the second husband may live with her for ten years [i.e., to see if she could still bear children]. If she had a miscarriage the space [of ten years] is reckoned from the time of the miscarriage. (*m. Yebam.* 6:6)

That is, this amount of time was taken to see if she could still bear children.

According to the Mishnah, these were some of the reasons that would justify a man divorcing his wife without giving her divorce money: "If she goes out with her hair unbound, or spins in the street, or speaks with any man. . . . Also if she curses his parents in his presence. R. Tarfon says: Also (if she is) a scolding woman. And who is deemed a scolding woman? Whoever speaks inside her house so that her neighbours hear her voice" (*m. Ketub.* 7:6). The Tosefta adds: "she [who] tells everybody about things which are between him and her . . . who goes out with her clothes in a mess . . . who washes and bathes in the public bath with just anyone" (*t. Ketub.* 7:6). On the Mishnaic phrase about spinning in the street, the Talmud comments: "Rab Judah stated in the name of Samuel: (The prohibition applies only) where she exposed her arms to the public. R. Hisda stated in the name of Abimi: (This applies only) where she spins rose (coloured materials, and holds them up) to her face" (*b. Ketub.* 72b). In cases where a woman has been suspected of having been seduced by a man, R. Judah the Patriarch declares: "When a pedlar leaves a house and the woman within is fastening her sinnar [petticoat], since the thing is ugly she must, said Rabbi, go. If spittle is found on the upper part of the curtained bed, since the thing is ugly, she must, said Rabbi, go" (*b. Yebam.* 24b). Divorce was obligatory if the wife had committed adultery.

The Mishnah reports that in former times three types of women were to be divorced but could take their *Ketubah*: those who say "'I am unclean to thee,' 'Heaven [knows what befalls] betwixt me and thee!' or 'I will remove me from all Jews!'" (*m. Ned.* 11:12). The second case refers to a woman who accuses her husband of being impotent and the third refers to a woman who is unable to stand intercourse.

According to *m. Yebam.* 14:1, it was only the husband's prerogative to divorce his spouse: "The man who divorces is not like to the woman that is divorced; for a woman is put away with her consent or without it, but a husband can put away his wife only with his own consent." A husband could not divorce a wife who was insane, who was too young to understand what a divorce means, or who was in captivity (*m. Ketub.* 4:9; *m. Giṭ.* 6:2–3). If the husband became mad, there was no possibility of divorce, as he would not be able to write a divorce document for his wife.

Under certain conditions a wife could apply to the rabbinical court to have her marriage dissolved. This included a husband's vowing "to abstain from his wife" for unreasonable periods of time, ranging from two days to a maximum of two months if he were a priest (*m. Ketub.* 7:2). Also, repulsive physical conditions or malodorous occupations could become a cause for divorce. According to *m. Ketub.* 6:10:

> And these are they that are compelled to put away their wives: he that is afflicted with boils, or that has a polypus, or that collects [dog's excrements], or that is a coppersmith or a tanner, whether these defects were in them before they married or whether they arose after they married. R. Meir said: Although the husband made it a condition with her [to marry him despite these defects], she may say, "I thought that I could endure it, but now I cannot endure it."

In all such circumstances it would not be likely that there would be successful conjugal relations that would result in children.

If a husband defied the court, the court could try to persuade him by gradually increasing the amount of the contract he would have to pay his wife, even up to the point of bankrupting him. Even physical force is countenanced in *m. Giṭ* 9:8: "A bill of divorce given under compulsion is valid if it is ordered by an Israelitish court, but if by a gentile court it is invalid; but if the gentiles beat a man, and say to him, 'Do what the Israelites bid thee,' it is valid."

All Jews were expected to marry and to have children, as the very first commandment given to Adam was to procreate. To validate a marriage the rabbis required a written agreement, a *ketubah* (plural *kĕtûbôt*; from the verb "to write"), between the groom and the father or other male guardian of the bride, who was often in her early teens. The contract would stipulate the legal rights and obligations of each partner, including a pledge payable to the wife in the case of divorce. The divorce payment was often set at 200 *zûzîn*, "sacred shekels," which would pay for his wife's sustenance for seven or eight months. A husband could use his wife's dowry while they were married, but had to return the dowry or its equivalent in the case of a divorce.

To make divorce more costly for the husband, Simeon ben Shetah (ca. 40 BC) ruled that all the property of a husband was liable for the payment of the divorce money (*m. Ketub.* 12:1). Only one actual *ketubah* has been recovered from Egypt. The divorced woman had to provide a receipt that she had received what was owed to her.

To validate a divorce, the husband had to give a *gēṭ*, "bill of divorce," to his wife and have the divorce registered in a Jewish court. Without such a certificate, a woman could neither get divorced nor remarry, even if her husband were missing. According to the Mishnah, "The essential formula in the bill of divorce is, 'Lo, thou art free to marry any man.' . . . The essential formula in a writ of emancipation is, 'Lo, thou art a freedwoman: lo, thou belongest to thyself'" (*m. Giṭ.* 9:3).

From the seven centuries of the Second Temple period, in addition to a single Greek Jewish divorce deed from Alexandria, we have recovered only one other *gēṭ*, which was written in Aramaic. The latter dates to AD 72 and was discovered at Wadi Murabbaʿat. A certain Joseph b. Naqsan issued this to his wife at Masada, declaring:

> You, Mariam, daughter of Yonatan of Hanablaṭa, resident at Masada, who have been my wife heretofore, . . . you are free on your part to go and to become the wife of any Jewish man whom you might desire [to marry]. And now, here on my part is the deed of repudiation [*spr trkyn*] and the letter of divorce [*gṭ šbqyn*]. (author's translation of Benoit, Milik, and de Vaux, 105–6)

From Murabbaʿat also comes a Greek text dating to AD 124 that presents the rare case of the remarriage of a husband to the wife whom he had originally divorced. Papyrus Ṣeʾelim 13 (AD 135), which a few have regarded as a *gēṭ*, is considered by most scholars to be a receipt of goods from Shelamzion to her divorced husband, Eleazar.

Despite these realistic provisions for divorce, some rabbis expressed sadness at such dissolutions of marriage. According to R. Eliezer, "For him who divorces the first wife, the very altar sheds tears" (*b. Sanh.* 2a; cf. *b. Giṭ* 90b).

F. THE CHRISTIAN WORLD

In interpreting the NT statements on divorce, the church fathers held that a husband could put away an adulterous wife and a wife could leave an adulterous husband. But most held that the innocent spouse could not remarry until the death of his or her former spouse. The Fathers were not disposed to broaden the grounds for separation beyond adultery, though Origen considered it a matter of inquiry whether Jesus would have forbidden the putting away of a wife for such heinous crimes as witchcraft, infanticide, and murder.

The earliest patristic comment on the subject of divorce is contained in a dialogue in the *Shepherd of Hermas*. Hermas asks what a believing husband should do if he finds that his wife is guilty of adultery. The Shepherd replies that he should separate from her: "But if the husband know [*sic*] that his wife has gone astray, and if the woman does not repent, but persists in her fornication [*porneia*], and yet the husband continues to live with her, he also is guilty of her crime, and a sharer in her adultery [*moicheia*]." But if she does repent, he is to receive her back: "Yes, if the husband does not receive her he sins and covers himself with a great sin; but it is necessary to receive the sinner who repents, but not often, for the servant of God has but one repentance. Therefore, for the sake of repentance the husband ought not to remarry" (*Herm. Mand.* 4.1).

Justin Martyr reports the case of a Christian woman married to a philandering unbeliever. Her friends counseled her to remain with her husband.

> But when her husband had gone into Alexandria, and was reported to be conducting himself worse than ever, she—that she might not, by continuing in matrimonial connection with him, and by sharing his table and his bed, become a partaker also in his wickednesses and impieties—gave him what you call a bill of divorce [*repoudion*], and was separated from him. (*2 Apol.* 2)

In retaliation, the husband accused the wife's Christian teacher of treason, resulting in his execution under the reign of Antoninus Pius.

Divorce based on the Pauline privilege of separating from an unbelieving partner was considered *divortium a mensa et toro*, "separation from bed and board," and conferred no liberty to enter a second union. Clement expressed the prevailing view that any second union while the other partner was still alive was not a valid marriage. According to Clement, "Now that the Scripture counsels marriage, and allows no release from the union, is expressly contained in the law, You shall not put away your wife, except for the cause of fornication" (*Strom.* 2.23). However, he implied that for those who did not have the gift of being a eunuch it was permissible to remarry after the death of a spouse. Epiphanius grudgingly allowed the remarriage of one who had divorced an adulterer, considering it a lesser sin than unchastity.

Origen wrote,

> But now contrary to what was written, some even of the rulers of the church have permitted a woman to marry, even when her husband was living, doing contrary to what was written . . . not indeed altogether without reason, for it is probable this concession was permitted in comparison with worse things, contrary to what was from the beginning ordained by law, and written. (*Comm. Matt.* 14.23)

He pointed out that a man may cause a divorce by the sexual neglect of his wife, and that there are other offenses worse than adultery, such as the attempted poisoning of a spouse or the murder of a child, that might legitimately lead to a divorce. In such disputable cases, he left the decision to divorce up to the individual conscience.

The antipope Hippolytus was scandalized by the lax behavior of Callistus, the bishop of Rome: "About the time of this man, bishops, priests, and deacons, who had been twice married, and thrice married, began to be allowed to retain their place among the clergy" (Hippolytus, *Haer.* 9.7).

The church council at Elvira, Spain (AD 305), issued several canons dealing with divorce among Christians:

> The 8th canon declared: "Again, women who, without any preceding cause, leave their husbands and take up with other men are not to receive communion even at the end." (Laeuchli, 127)

> The 9th canon stipulated: "Further, a baptized woman who leaves her adulterous baptized husband and marries another is forbidden to marry him; if she does she shall not receive communion until the death of her former husband unless, by chance, the pressure of illness demand that it be given." (ibid.)

> The 10th canon stated: "If a woman who has been deserted by her catechumen husband marries another man, she may be admitted to the font of baptism; this also applies to female catechumens. But if the man who leaves the innocent woman marries a Christian woman, and this woman knew he had a wife whom he had left without cause, communion may be given to her at death." (ibid.)

> Finally the 11th canon conceded: "If that female catechumen should grow seriously ill during the five-year period, baptism is not to be denied her." (ibid.)

These canons reveal a higher standard for wives than for husbands, and for baptized Christians than for catechumens. Husbands were ordered to dismiss wives who had committed adultery. But there were no sanctions against men who left their wives and remarried.

Basil's comments also reflect a double standard:

> The sentence of the Lord that it is unlawful to withdraw from wedlock, save on account of fornication, applies, according to the argument, to men and women alike. ... Yet custom ordains that men who commit adultery and are in fornication be retained by their wives. Consequently I do not know if the woman who lives with the man who has been dismissed can properly be called an adulteress; the charge in this case attaches to the woman who has put away her husband, and depends upon the cause for which she withdrew from wedlock. In the case of her being beaten, and refusing to submit, it would be better for her to endure than to be separated from her husband. (*Ep.* 188.9)

John Chrysostom, whose congregation included divorced women, likened them to runaway slaves:

> Just as escaped slaves, even if they have left the house of their master, still carry their chain, so wives, even if they have left their husbands, have the law in the form of a chain which condemns them, accusing them of adultery, accusing those who take them, and saying: "Your husband is still living and what you have done is adultery." (*De libello repudii* 1; cited in Harper, 164)

He stated further: "They are runaway slaves, who flee the master's house but drag their chains along. Women who leave their husbands carry around the condemnation of the law like a chain, and are accused of adultery . . . For she whose husband is alive becomes an adulteress" (ibid.).

At all times divorce by mutual consent was allowed by Roman law. But in AD 331 Constantine drastically revised the Roman law on unilateral divorce, severely restricting either partner's legitimate causes for divorce. The emperor decreed:

> It is Our pleasure that no woman, on account of her own depraved desires, shall be permitted to send a notice of divorce [*repudium*] to her husband on trumped up grounds, as, for instance, that he is a drunkard [*ebriosus*] or a gambler or a philanderer [*muliercularius*], nor indeed shall a husband be permitted to divorce his wife on every sort of pretext. But when a woman sends a notice of divorce, the following criminal charges only shall be investigated, that is, if she should prove that her husband is a homicide [*sic*], a sorcerer [*medicamentarius*], or a destroyer of tombs, so that the wife may thus earn commendation and at length recover her entire dowry. For if she should send a notice of divorce to her husband on grounds other than these criminal charges, she must leave everything, even to her last hairpin, in her husband's home, and as punishment for her supreme self confidence, she shall be deported to an island. (*Cod. Theod.* 3.16.1; Pharr, 76–77)

A husband could only divorce his wife if she were an adulteress, a poisoner, or a procuress (that is, a female pimp). If he divorced for any other reason, he was not to remarry. But if he did remarry, the first wife could enter his home and seize the second wife's dowry.

In a law passed in AD 337 just after Constantine's death, a woman was allowed to divorce a soldier from whom she had not heard for four or more years. From the two centuries between Constantine and Justinian only one actual divorce document (which is written on papyrus) has been preserved.

Ambrose warned his congregation not to avail themselves of civil law to divorce a Christian spouse. Nor, he said, should a Christian appeal to Deut 24, as that would be acting like a Jew. Only marriage between two Christians, he held, was a true marriage. For a Christian to seek a divorce from another Christian would be to deny that God was the author of their marriage.

Jerome wrote to Amandus, "A husband may be an adulterer or a sodomite, he may be stained with every crime and may have been left by his wife because of his sins; yet he is still her husband and, so long as he lives, she may not marry another" (*Epist.* 55.3). Fabiola, who in her youth had divorced her husband for his adultery, and then had remarried after the death of her second husband, did penance for her remarriage, which she had not known was against Christian teaching. In a letter Jerome wrote to her as follows:

> The laws of Caesar are different, it is true, from the laws of Christ: Papinianus commands one thing; our own Paul another. Earthly laws give a free rein to the unchastity of men, merely condemning seduction and adultery; lust is allowed to range unrestrained among brothels and slave girls, as if the guilt were constituted by the rank of the person assailed and not by the purpose of the assailant. But with us Christians what is unlawful for women is equally unlawful for men, and as both serve the same God both are bound by the same obligations. (*Epist.* 77.3)

Ambrose taught that "all sexual violation is adultery and what is not allowed to a woman is also not allowed to a man. The same chastity is demanded of the man, which is exacted of the woman. Whatever has been committed against her who is not a lawful wife is branded with the crime of adultery" (*De Abraham* 1.4.25; Dooley, 113–14). This was made explicit in a canon from the Council of Carthage (AD 407), which required the same standards of behavior from men as well as from women.

On the OT provision by Moses for a writ of divorce, Augustine comments:

> But, that the laws of the Gentiles are otherwise, who is there that knows not; where, by the interposition of divorce, without any offense of which man takes cognizance, both the woman is married to whom she will, and the man marries whom he will. And something like this custom, on account of the hardness of the Israelites, Moses seems to have allowed, concerning a bill of

divorcement. In which matter there appears rather a rebuke, than an approval, of divorce. (*Bon. conj.* 7)

Augustine stated further:

> This we now say, that, according to this condition of being born and dying, which we know, and in which we have been created, the marriage of male and female is some good; the compact whereof divine Scripture so commends, as that neither is it allowed one put away by her husband to marry, so long as her husband lives: nor is it allowed one put away by his wife to marry another, unless she who have separated from him be dead. (*Bon. conj.* 3)

In the only treatise from the first five centuries devoted solely to the subject of divorce and remarriage, Augustine declares:

> Moreover in the text, *Anyone who divorces his wife, except in the case of adultery, causes her to commit adultery* (Mt. 5:32), how are we to interpret what is said here except as saying that a man is forbidden to divorce his wife, if there is no adultery to justify it? We are even told why this is so, namely, that it is to avoid causing her to commit adultery; and this surely is because, even if she does not divorce him but is herself the one divorced, she will be guilty of adultery if she remarries. It is to avoid this great evil that a man is not allowed to divorce his wife unless it is for adultery. In that case he does not cause her to become an adulteress by divorcing her, but he divorces her because she is already an adulteress. (*Incomp. nupt.* 1.2.2–3; Kearney, 143)

Influenced by the Latin translation *sacramentum* of the Greek word *mystērion* in the expression "mystery of marriage" found in Eph 5:32, Augustine argued that, like the sacrament of baptism, which is our marriage to Christ, human marriage is irreversible. He maintained that divorce is not justified in the case of a wife's sterility or her chronic disease. Even in the case of an adulterous spouse, the innocent partner should, Augustine believed, forgive the spouse and take him or her back. In his *On Faith and Works*, Augustine wrote that the church should not agree to receive remarried divorced people to baptism and the Eucharist.

The anonymous commentator on the Pauline epistles known as "Ambrosiaster" was the first church father who specifically approved of the remarriage of an innocent wife after an unbeliever left her, as such desertion, in his view, breaks the bond of marriage. In the case of an innocent husband's divorce of an adulterous wife, Augustine permitted the husband to remarry. But in the reverse case, he did not permit the innocent wife to remarry: "This is so because the inferior party does not have the same rights under the law as the stronger one has" (*Commentary on 1 Corinthians 7:12*; Bray, 150–51).

BIBLIOGRAPHY: P. Benoit, J. T. Milik, and R. de Vaux, *Les Grottes de Murabba'ât* (*Discoveries in the Judaean Desert* 2, 1961); C. L. Blomberg, "Marriage, Divorce, Remarriage and Celibacy," *TJ* 11 (1990), 161–96; M. Bockmuehl, "Matthew 5.32; 19.9 in the Light of Pre-Rabbinic Halakhah," *NTS* 35 (1989), 291–95; G. L. Bray, trans. and ed., *Ambrosiaster: Commentaries on Romans and 1–2 Corinthians* (2009); R. Brody, "Evidence for Divorce by Jewish Women," *JJS* 50 (1999), 230–34; J. Černý and T. E. Peet, "A Marriage Settlement of the Twentieth Dynasty: An Unpublished Document from Turin," *JEA* 13 (1927), 30–39; E. Christian, "The 'Hard Sayings' of Jesus and Divorce: Not Commandments but Goals," *JATS* 12 (2001), 62–75; E. A. Clark, "Constraining the Body, Expanding the Text: The Exegesis of Divorce in the Later Latin Fathers," in *The Limits of Ancient Christianity*, ed. W. E. Klingshirn and M. Vessey (1999), 153–71; A. T. Clay, *Babylonian Records in the Library of J. Pierpont Morgan*, vol. IV (1923); L. H. Cohick, "Marriage, Divorce, and Discipleship: Jesus' Encounter with the Samaritan Woman," *IBR Library Review* 8 (2010), 20–36; A. E. Cowley, trans. and ed., *Aramaic Papyri of the Fifth Century B.C.* (1923); W. J. Dooley, *Marriage according to St. Ambrose* (1948); C. D. Elledge, "'From the Beginning It Was Not So . . .': Jesus, Divorce, and Remarriage in the Light of the Dead Sea Scrolls," *PRSt* 37 (2010), 371–90; J. J. Finkelstein, "Cutting the Sissiktu in Divorce Proceedings," *WO* 8 (1976), 236–40; J. A. Fitzmyer, "Divorce among First-Century Palestinian Jews," *EI* 14 (1978), 103–10; R. Gane, "Old Testament Principles Relating to Divorce and Remarriage," *JATS* 12 (2001), 35–61; B. Glazier-McDonald, "Intermarriage, Divorce, and the *bat-'ēl nēkār*: Insights into Mal 2:10–16," *JBL* 106 (1987), 603–11; J. E. Grubbs, *Law and Family in Late Antiquity: The Emperor Constantine's Marriage Legislation* (1995); J. E. Grubbs, "'Pagan' and 'Christian' Marriage: The State of the Question," *JECS* 2 (1994), 361–412; K. C. Hanson, "The Herodians and Mediterranean Kinship 2: Marriage and Divorce," *BTB* 19 (1989), 142–51; K. Harper, *From Shame to Sin: The Christian Transformation of Sexual Morality in Late Antiquity* (2013); A. Harrison, *The Law of Athens I: The Family and Property* (1968); W. Heth and G. J. Wenham, *Jesus & Divorce* (1984); G. P. Hugenberger, *Marriage as a Covenant* (1994); T. Ilan, "Notes and Observations on a Newly Published Divorce Bill from the Judaean Desert," *HTR* 89 (1996), 195–202; D. Instone-Brewer, *Divorce and Remarriage in the Bible: The Social and Literary Context* (2002); J. Kampen, "The Matthean Divorce Texts Reexamined," in *New Qumran Texts and Studies*, ed. G. J. Brooke (1994), 149–67; R. Kearney, trans., *Augustine: Marriage and Virginity*, ed. J. E. Rotelle (1999); C. S. Keener, *And Marries Another: Divorce and Remarriage in the Teaching of the New Testament* (1991); E. G. Kraeling, ed., *The Brooklyn Museum Aramaic Papyri* (1953); S. Laeuchli, *Power and Sexuality: The Emergence of Canon Law at the Synod of Elvira*

(1972); M. R. Lefkowitz and M. B. Fant, ed., *Women's Life in Greece and Rome: A Source Book in Translation* (1992); E. Lipinski, "The Wife's Right To Divorce in the Light of an Ancient Near Eastern Tradition," *The Jewish Law Annual* 4 (1981), 9–26; M. McDonnell, "Divorce Initiated by Women in Rome," *AJAH* 8 (1983), 54–80; J. Moiser, "A Reassessment of Paul's View of Marriage with Reference to 1 Cor 7," *JSNT* 18 (1983), 103–22; J. R. Mueller, "The Temple Scroll and the Gospel Divorce Texts," *RevQ* 10 (1980), 247–56; J. Murphy-O'Connor, "The Divorced Woman in I Cor. 7:10–11," *JBL* 100 (1981), 601–6; V. Noam, "Divorce in Qumran in Light of Early Halakha," *JJS* 56 (2005), 206–23; J. Nolland, "The Gospel Prohibition of Divorce: Tradition History and Meaning," *JSNT* 58 (1995), 19–35; C. Pharr, trans., *The Theodosian Code and Novels, and the Sirmondian Constitutions* (1952); B. Porten and J. C. Greenfield, trans., *Jews of Elephantine and Arameans of Syene* (1974); A. M. Rabello, "Divorce of Jews in the Roman Empire," The Jewish Law Annual 4 (1981), 79–102; B. Rawson, *Marriage, Divorce, and Children in Ancient Rome* (1996); N. J. Reich, "A Demotic Divorce," *Mizraim* 1 (1933), 135–39; A. Schremer, "Divorce in Papyri Se'elim 13 Once Again," *HTR* 91 (1998), 193–202; J. M. Sprinkle, "Old Testament Perspectives on Divorce and Remarriage," *JETS* 40 (1997), 529–50; R. H. Stein, "Is It Lawful for a Man to Divorce His Wife?" *JETS* 22 (1979), 115–21; S. Treggiari, *Roman Marriage* (1991); A. van Praag, *Droit matrimonial assyro-babylonien* (1945); R. VerSteeg, *Law in the Ancient World* (2002); J. von Allmen, *The Pauline Teachings on Marriage* (1963); A. Warren, "Did Moses Permit Divorce?" *TynBul* 49 (1998), 39–56; R. Westbrook, *Old Babylonian Marriage Law* (1988); R. Westbrook, "The Prohibition on Restoration of Marriage in Deuteronomy 24:1–4," *Scripta Hierosolymitana* 31 (1986), 387–405; B. Witherington III, "Matthew 5:32 and 19:9—Exception or Exceptional Situation?" *NTS 31* (1985), 571–76; H. Wolff, *Written and Unwritten Marriages in Hellenistic and Postclassical Roman Law* (1939); R. Yaron, "On Divorce in Old Testament Times," *RIDA* 4 (1957), 117–28.

EMY

See also ADULTERY, CELIBACY, and MARRIAGE.

DOGS

Man's "best friend," the dog (*Canis lupus familiaris*), was the earliest animal to be domesticated. The dog is descended from the gray wolf (*Canis lupus*), perhaps independently in more than one area. It has been suggested that domestication occurred when wolves gathering around hunters' encampments became tame and learned to live with these humans.

Dogs could be used to guard flocks. In some cultures they were sacrificed, but they were rarely eaten in antiquity. Some dogs were kept as pets, but many ownerless dogs roamed in packs through the streets as scavengers, even eating corpses. These pariah dogs were vicious and highly feared.

A. THE OLD TESTAMENT

In the OT the word dog (Heb. *keleb*) occurs twenty-one times in a literal sense and nine times metaphorically. The term "dog" in Deut 23:18 probably denotes a male cultic prostitute.

On the basis of Mesopotamian parallels, it has been suggested that the personal name Caleb (which in Hebrew is identical to the word for "dog"), which was the name of the only person besides Joshua who had faith that God could conquer the Canaanites after the Israelites had spied out the land (Num 13:2), is perhaps a shortened form of the name Caleb-El, "Dog of God."

Sheep were sometimes driven ahead of a shepherd with the aid of dogs (cf. Job 30:1), and in the Apocryphal book of Tobit a dog accompanies Tobias on his trip (Tob 11:4). However, dogs are often pictured in the OT roaming in pariah packs (Pss 22:16–21; 59:6, 14; 1 Kgs 14:11). Dogs appear generally to have not been held in high esteem in ancient Israel. "Dog" was an insulting term (1 Sam 17:43; 2 Sam 9:8), and it was a particular disgrace for a dead body to be eaten by dogs (2 Kgs 9:36–37). The book of Proverbs compares habitual folly with the dog's disgusting habit of returning to its vomit (Prov 26:11), and Eccl 9:4 proclaims that "even a live dog is better off than a dead lion!"

Isaiah 66:3 may contain an allusion to a dog sacrifice: "But whoever sacrifices a bull is like one who kills a person, and whoever offers a lamb is like one who breaks a dog's neck." Remains of canid bones at Tel Haror, Tel Miqne, and Tell el-Hesi point to the ritual killing of dogs.

B. THE NEW TESTAMENT

In response to Jesus's rebuff that "it is not right to take the children's bread and toss it to the dogs," the Syro-Phoenician woman declares that "even the dogs eat the crumbs that fall from their master's table" (Matt 15:26–27||Mark 7:27–28); this alludes to the common practice of throwing scraps of food to house dogs after a meal. The term used for "dog" in these texts, *kunarion* (a diminutive of the normal word for dog, *kyōn*), may refer to a little dog who was kept as a pet. Jesus warns his disciples not to give what is holy to dogs or pearls to swine (Matt 7:6). In a variant of this saying in the *Gospel of Thomas* Jesus declares, "Give not what is holy to the dogs, lest they cast it on the dung-heap" (logion 93). In his story about the heartless wealthy man, Jesus relates how dogs licked the sores of the beggar Lazarus (Luke 16:21). Second Peter 2:22 quotes Prov 26:11 about a dog returning to its own vomit. As in the OT, "dog" is used in the NT as an insulting epithet (Phil 3:2). Those who are excluded from the kingdom of Christ include "dogs," a metaphor for the wicked in general, along with sorcerers, fornicators, murderers, idolaters, and liars (Rev 22:15).

In the *Gospel of Thomas* Jesus says: "Woe to the Pharisees, for they are like a dog sleeping in the manger of oxen, for neither does he eat nor does he [let] the oxen eat" (logion 102).

C. THE NEAR EASTERN WORLD

Evidence from the Palegawra Cave in Iraq dating to ca. 10,000 BC indicates that dogs were among the earliest animals to be domesticated for use in hunting and as companions. Canid remains were found from the Natufian levels (10,000 BC) at Ein Mallaha in Palestine; a human skeleton was found with its arm lying on the chest of a puppy. Two adult dogs were found at another Natufian site, Hayonim. At a sanctuary at Gilat (ca. 4000 BC), a dog was buried with an offering.

In Mesopotamia the dog was associated with the shepherd god Dumuzi. In the Akkadian text "The Fable of the Fox," we read:

The Fox entered the bottom of his hole,
The Wolf crouched inside his hole,
The Dog kept guard of their entrances . . .
The Dog opened his mouth as he bayed,
Fearful to them was his bellow,
Their hearts were so overcome that they secreted gall. . . .
I sit like a beggar in front of the sheep,
Their lives are entrusted to me as to a herdsman and shepherd.
    (Lambert, 193)

Some Akkadian theophoric personal names contain the word for dog (*kalbum*)—e.g., Kalbi-Marduk, "The Dog of Marduk," Kalbi-Shamash, "The Dog of Shamash"—which implies that the individuals so named (or their parents) were loyal followers of the gods whose names they bore.

The Babylonians believed that dogs could lick away diseases. Dogs were used in sacrificial rites, especially those relating to the demon of sickness, Lamashtu. The temple of the healing god Gula (also known as Nintinuga) in Kassite Nippur (13th c. BC) contained figurines of dogs. Thirty dog burials were found at this deity's temple at Isin (10th c. BC). Nebuchadnezzar reports that he buried at the entrance to the temple of Gula "two golden dogs, two silver dogs, two bronze dogs, whose limbs were strong, whose bodily proportions were massive" (cited in Van Buren, 18). Figurines of dogs were also used in magic rites to transfer evil from humans; they were sometimes tossed into a river as a substitution ritual. The dedication of a sculpture of a healing dog reads as follows: "Lugal-murube . . . fashioned for Nintinuga Tuni-lusha ('her spell cures a man'), her messenger dog. On that account, a dog will always wag (his) tail for his mistress (and) nibble (at wounds?) for her" (*COS* 2.143:395).

The Assyrians used dogs for hunting lions, as is vividly rendered on the reliefs of Ashurbanipal from Nineveh. They also used dogs on military campaigns, and fed them the bodies of their enemies.

The Hittites valued dogs for hunting, shepherding, and guarding. Hittite Laws 87–89 (*ANET*, 193), which list the value of several kinds of dogs, indicate that an ordinary dog was worth one shekel and a herding dog was valued at twenty shekels. Young puppies were used in numerous prevention and purification rituals among the Hittites. The bodies of these puppies were severed and the persons involved passed between the parts (cf. Gen 15:9–10; Jer 34:18–20).

In Egypt depictions of dogs have survived from the Predynastic Amratian period. One of the earliest pharaohs, Djer, had his pet dogs buried at Abydos, with stelae bearing their names. The Egyptians raised four different kinds of dogs especially for hunting: the greyhound, the saluki, the pharaoh hound, and the Ibizan hound. At Amarna, the capital of Akhenaten, excavators discovered remains of kennels for the king's greyhounds. Like no other animal, dogs were prized as pets. We have records of about eighty dogs that were given names, such as "the Good Watcher."

Ancient Egypt also had its share of wild dogs. A Ramesside official complained of the danger from a pack of two hundred large dogs and three hundred jackals that menaced him and his faithful dog. In *The Tale of the Two Brothers*, the unfaithful wife is cast to the dogs.

The god of mummification, Anubis, was depicted as a lean black hound or a jackal (*Canis aureus*). In mythology Isis is accompanied by dogs in her search for the body of Osiris. The dog was associated with Sothis/Sirius, the star that announced the flooding of the Nile in the summer.

In the Amarna Letters (14th c. BC), the Levantine vassals of Amenhotep III and IV refer to themselves as "dogs" in the loyal service of these pharaohs. The phrase "evil dog" is also used by the king of Byblos against the king of Amurru. In the much later Lachish Letters (6th c. BC), an inferior greets his officer by writing, "Who is your servant (but) a dog" (*COS* 3.42A:79; 3.42D:80; 3.42E:80).

Many mummified dogs were found in a city that the Greeks called Cynopolis (superior), which means "Dog City." Thousands of dogs were also found mummified at Roda, Thebes, and Abydos. Dog catacombs at Saqqara dating to 747–730 BC that were dedicated to the god Anubis were discovered in 1897 but have only been explored since 2011. The excavator estimates that as many as eight million animals were buried here. These dogs, which must have been bred by the thousands in "puppy farms," were sacrificed to act as intermediaries between the donors and the gods.

The Persian Zoroastrians honored the dog as the noblest creature of Ahura-Mazda after man. They were to be fed even before the family. The food given to them was believed to nourish the dead. A funerary purification rite known as the *bareshnum* required the presence of a "four-eyed dog," that is, a dog with two spots under its eyes.

At the Palestinian coastal site of Ashkelon, 1,400 dog burials, mostly of puppies, were found dating from the Persian era (late 5th and early 4th c. BC). These dogs may possibly have been connected with a temple dedicated to a Phoenician healing cult.

At Sardis in western Turkey, twenty-seven buried pot clusters—each containing three different pots, a plate, and knives—were uncovered in Persian levels dating to 575–525 BC. Each assemblage also contained the remains of puppies, none older than three months of age. These dogs may have been dedicated to the Lydian god Kandaulas, who had the title "Dog Throttler," and may all have been sacrificed to avert the assault on Sardis by Cyrus (Harvey, 284).

D. THE GRECO-ROMAN WORLD

Evidence indicates that during the Early Bronze Age dogs were eaten in Greece and at Troy. The opening lines of the *Iliad* (*Il.* 1.4) speak of the "wrath" of Achilles, which causes many brave souls to become a feast for dogs and birds (i.e., vultures). Elsewhere in this work, dogs of the table (*trapezēes*), that is, pet dogs, are sacrificed at Patroklos's funeral: "Nine dogs had the prince, that fed beneath his table, and of these did Achilles cut the throats of twain, and cast them upon the pyre" (*Il.* 23.173–174).

The *Odyssey* relates the touching tale of Odysseus's dog Argos, who recognizes his disguised master even after the latter's twenty-year absence (*Od.* 17.292–322). The multiheaded dog Cerberus, whose epithet was "the hound of Hades," guarded the underworld (*Od.* 11.623–625).

Dogs are depicted in Mycenaean frescoes of wild-boar hunts. During the Mycenaean period, dogs were buried in chamber and tholos tombs to accompany their masters. This practice was continued on Crete in the Iron Age.

Dogs were thought to cure sickness by licking the afflicted areas, and were associated with the healing god, Asclepius. An inscription from this deity's sanctuary at Epidauros reads: "A dog cured a boy from Aigina. He had a growth on his neck. When he had come to the god, a dog from the sanctuary took care of him with its tongue while he was awake, and made him well" (LiDonnici, 105).

Dogs were found in the sanctuary of Hera at Samos. In Boeotia and Macedonia dogs were killed and then split, and armies purified themselves by marching between the halves. The Spartans sacrificed dogs to Ares/Enyalios in bloody healing rituals.

The Greek word for "hunter" was *kynagos*, literally, "leader of dogs," since dogs were used for hunting birds. They accompanied Artemis, the goddess of the hunt. A familiar scene on Greek vase paintings depicts Actaeon's hounds attacking their owner at the goddess's command for his temerity in gazing upon her as she bathed. A group of Hellenistic philosophers that included Diogenes were called "Cynics" as they appeared to live and function like dogs (*kynes*).

The Romans used watchdogs in their towers on their frontiers and also used messenger dogs for communication. A famous mosaic at Pompeii depicts a snarling watchdog with the inscription *cave canem*, "Beware of the dog!" Many dogs were kept as pets, including Issa, whose master, Publius, had a lifelike portrait made of her and who was memorialized by the poet Martial. According to Pliny the Elder, "There are some obscure diseases of the intestines, for which is prescribed a wonderful cure. If, before they can see, puppies are applied for three days, especially to the stomach and chest of a patient, and suck milk from his mouth, the power of the disease is transferred to them" (*Nat.* 30.20.64).

Dogs were sacrificed to appease the god Robigus, who was responsible for a blight called "rust," which affects plants. Dogs were also offered up to Juno, and also at the Lupercalia, a feast in February. Pliny also mentions that dogs were crucified annually between the temples of Juventas and of Summanus because, unlike Juno's sacred geese, they had failed to warn the Romans of the Gauls' attack upon the Capitoline Hill in 390 BC (*Nat.* 29.14.4).

Dog bones have been found at the altar to Artemis of Ephesus. The dog was especially associated with Hecate, the goddess of crossroads and magic. Dogs were often sacrificed to her in nocturnal rituals.

Dogs were not normally eaten, but the Roman medical authority Galen observed: "As for dogs, what can I say? In some countries they are often eaten when young and plump, and particularly after they have been castrated" (*On the Powers of Foods* 3.1; Grant, 2000).

To call a person a "dog" was the ultimate insult. In Petronius's novel *The Satyricon*, when Trimalchio shows overtly his affection for a young boy, his wife, Fortunata, reacts as follows: "Fortunata, to assert her rights at law, proceeded to abuse Trimalchio, and called him a dirty disgrace for not holding his lust in check. At last she even added, 'You hound [*canis*]'" (*Sat.* 74).

E. THE JEWISH WORLD

In the tale of *Joseph and Aseneth*, after the Egyptian princess converts to Judaism, she casts her non-kosher royal food out the window to "strange dogs," lest her own dogs eat of it (*Jos. Asen.* 10:13; 13:8).

In his exposition *On the Decalogue*, Philo holds up as examples for men to emulate dogs who will defend their master's house to the death and dogs who will fight on behalf of the flocks they guard (*Decal.* 23.114). But in another passage he describes drunkards who "bellow and rave like wild dogs, attack and bite each other and gnaw off noses, ears, fingers and some other parts of the body" (*Contempl.* 40).

Josephus describes two occasions during the Jewish War against the Romans on which corpses were thrown to the dogs. In the first, the Zealots and Idumaeans, who had seized Jerusalem, cast out the Jewish leaders Ananus and Jesus "to be devoured by dogs and beasts of prey" (*J.W.* 4.324). In the second, Jews who tried to escape the city "were all massacred and their bodies flung to the dogs" (*J.W.* 6.367).

According to the important Qumran document 4QMMT, "(Concerning dogs,) one may not bring dogs into the holy camp because they may eat some of the [b]ones from the sanc[tuary and] the meat which is still on them" (4Q394 8 IV, 8–9).

The Mishnah understands the term "dog" in Deut 23:18 literally rather than metaphorically (*m. Tem.* 6.3). Rabbi Eleazar declared that "he who breeds dogs is like him who breeds swine" (*b. B. Qam.* 83a). However, according to the rabbis dogs might be permitted in a frontier town, where one was to keep them chained during the day and loose them at night (*b. B. Qam.* 83a).

The Talmud discusses various symptoms, such as foaming at the mouth, that identify a rabid dog, as well as several remedies for the bite of such animals (*b. Yoma* 83b, 84a). The rabbis included rabid dogs among animals that could be killed on the Sabbath, and were of the opinion that the only safe way to kill them is by stoning (*b. Yoma* 83b, 84a).

F. THE CHRISTIAN WORLD

The *Didache* cites Matt 7:6 in connection with its comment that the unbaptized are unworthy of communion: "But let no one eat or drink of your Eucharist except those who have been baptized into the name of the Lord, for the Lord has also spoken concerning this: 'Do not give what is holy to dogs'" (*Did.* 9.5; Holmes, 359).

Ignatius likens false teachers to raving mad dogs "whom you must flee as you would wild beasts. For they are ravening dogs, who bite secretly" (*Eph.* 7.1). In an exhortation on modesty in eating, Clement of Alexandria wrote: "For you may see such people, liker swine or dogs for gluttony than men, in such a hurry to feed themselves full" (*Paed.* 1.2).

According to the *Acts of Thomas*, the proof that Thomas is an apostle is the fulfillment of Thomas's prediction that a wine-pourer who has struck him will have his hand "dragged about by dogs." This leads to the conversion of the Jewish flute-girl who overhears Thomas make this prediction. In late antiquity some Christians believed that demons could in some cases appear as dogs (e.g., *Acts of Andrew* 6).

In a homily on creation, Basil praises the faithful dog: "Does not the gratitude of the dog shame all who are ungrateful to their benefactors? Many are said to have fallen dead by their murdered masters in lonely places. Others, when a crime has just been committed, have led those who were searching for the murderers, and have caused the criminals to be brought to justice" (*Hex.* 9.4).

In his homily on Colossians, Chrysostom compares unfaithful Christians with dogs: "And the mention I have now made of dogs is happy, in regard of those who give thanks then only when they receive a benefit.

Take shame, I pray you, at the dogs, which when famishing still fawn upon their masters. But you, if you have haply heard that the Demon has cured anyone, straightway forsakest your Master; O more unreasoning than the dogs!" (*Hom. Col.* 1:7).

BIBLIOGRAPHY: D. Brewer, T. Clark, and A. Phillips, *Dogs in Antiquity: Anubis to Cerberus* (2001); J. B. Burns, "Devotee or Deviate: The 'Dog' (*keleb*) in Ancient Israel as a Symbol of Male Passivity and Perversion," *Journal of Religion & Society* 2 (2000), 1–10; E. E. Burris, "The Place of the Dog in Superstition as Revealed in Latin Literature," *CP* 30 (1935), 32–42; B. J. Collins, "The Puppy in Hittite Ritual," *JCS* 42 (1990), 211–26; J. Crawford, "Caleb the Dog: How a Biblical Good Guy Got a Bad Name," *BR* 20.2 (2004), 20–7, 45; L. P. Day, "Dog Burials in the Greek World," *AJA* 88 (1984), 21–32; B. Doyle, "Howling Like Dogs: Metaphorical Language in Psalm LIX," *VT* 54 (2004), 61–82; M. Edrey, "The Dog Burials at Achaemenid Ashkelon Revisited," *TA* 35 (2008), 267–82; M. W. Fox, *The Dog: Its Domestication and Behavior* (1978); J. M. Galán, "What is he, the dog?" *UF* 25 (1994), 173–80; E. A. Goodfriend, "Could *keleb* in Deuteronomy 23.19 Actually Refer to a Canine?" in *Pomegranates and Golden Bells*, ed. D. P. Wright, D. N. Freedman, and A. Hurvitz (1995), 386–91; M. Grant, ed., *Galen on Food and Diet* (2000); C. H. Greenewalt, Jr., *Ritual Dinners in Early Historic Sardis* (1976); B. Halpern, "The Canine Conundrum of Ashkelon: A Classical Connection?" in *The Archaeology of Jordan and Beyond*, ed. L. E. Stager, J. A. Greene, and M. D. Coogan (2000), 133–44; D. Harvey, "Lydian Specialties, Croesus' Golden Baking-Woman, and Dogs' Dinners," in *Food in Antiquity*, ed. J. Wilkins, D. Harvey, and M. Dobson (1995), 273–85; M. Hilzheimer, "Dogs," *Antiq* 6 (1932), 411–19; N. R. Howell, "'Going to the Dogs': Canid Ethology and Theological Reflection," *Zygon* 41.1 (2006), 59–69; M. O. Howey, *Cults of the Dog* (1972); C. Johns, *Dogs: History, Myth, Art* (2008); W. G. Lambert, *Babylonian Wisdom Literature* (1960); A. Livingstone, "The Isin 'Dog House' Revisited," *JCS* 40 (1988), 54–60; J. A. Lobell and E. A. Powell, "More Than Man's Best Friend," *Arch* 63.5 (2010), 26–35; O. Margalith, "*KELEB*: Homonym or Metaphor?" *VT* 33 (1983), 491–95; O. Margalith, "The K*eˉ*lābīm of Ahab," *VT* 34 (1984), 228–32; R. H. A. Merlen, *De Canibus: Dog and Hound in Antiquity* (1971); W. L. Moran, "Puppies in Proverbs," *ErIsr* 14 (1978), 32*–37*; M. D. Nanos, "Paul's Reversal of Jews Calling Gentiles 'Dogs' (Philippians 3:2): 1600 Years of an Ideological Tale Wagging an Exegetical Dog?" *Biblical Interpretation* 17 (2009), 448–82; E. Pennisi, "A Shaggy Dog History," *Science* 298 (Nov. 22, 2002), 1540–42; M. Rist, "The Fable of the Dog in the Manger in the Gospel of Thomas," *Iliff Review* 25.3 (1968), 13–26; S. Schreiber, "Cavete canes!" *BZ* 45 (2001), 170–92; J. Schwartz, "Dogs in Jewish Society in the

Second Temple Period and in the Time of the Mishnah and Talmud," *JJS* 55 (2004), 246–77; L. E. Stager, "Why Were Hundreds of Dogs Buried at Ashkelon?" *BAR* 17.3 (1991), 26–39, 42; R. Strelan, "'Outside are the dogs and the sorcerers. . . .' (Revelation 22:15)," *BTB* 33.4 (2003), 148–57; J. M. C. Toynbee, *Animals in Roman Life and Art* (1973); C. G. Trew, *The Story of the Dog and His Uses to Mankind* (1939); E. D. Van Buren, *The Fauna of Ancient Mesopotamia as Represented in Art* (1939); H. van de Sandt, "'Do not give what is holy to the dogs' (Did 9:5D and Matt 7:6A): The Eucharistic Food of the Didache in Its Jewish Purity Setting," *VC* 56 (2002), 223–46; P. Villard, "Le chien dans la documentation néo-Assyrienne," *Topoi*, Suppl. 2 (2000), 235–49; P. Wapnish and B. Hesse, "Pampered Pooches or Plain Pariahs? The Ashkelon Dog Burials," *BA* 56 (1993), 55–80; F. E. Zeuner, "Dog and Cat in the Neolithic of Early Jericho," *PEQ* 90 (1958), 52–55.

EMY

See also WILD ANIMALS & HUNTING.

DONKEYS & MULES

The animals used most commonly used for hauling goods and for transportation were the donkey (ass), the mule, the horse, and the camel. Of these, the donkey was the most common work animal; the mule was less common, since it was a hybrid animal.

Because these animals were beasts of burden, they were vulnerable to abuse and overuse. Practices of breeding donkeys and mules, the treatment of these animals, and the uses to which they were put varied from culture to culture in the ancient world. The Greeks were willing to eat donkey meat, for example, while Hebrew teaching forbade this practice and also prohibited the raising of mules through crossbreeding horses and donkeys.

Prescriptions for the treatment of beasts of burden were sometimes determined in part by the significance of the animals beyond their practical functions. Over time and across cultures a variety of religious associations, some favorable, some derogatory, were attached to the figure of the donkey, which played diverse roles in religious and literary narratives.

A. THE OLD TESTAMENT

The Hebrew word *ḥămôr*, "ass, donkey," occurs about one hundred times in the OT, and the word *ʾātôn*, "jenny, female donkey," about a third as many times. The word *ʿayir*, which occurs eight times, designates a male equid, usually a donkey. Its translation as "colt" in Zech 9:9 in most English versions has been influenced by the LXX translation *pōlos*.

The ass or the donkey—the terms are used interchangeably—was regarded as the day-to-day work animal and was used widely as a means of human and commercial transport. It was not uncommon for rulers and high officials to ride on ceremonially attired donkeys. The average householder would own one donkey. The Israelites were to redeem a firstborn donkey along with their firstborn lambs (Exod 13:13; 34:20). In numerous texts (Exod 21:33; 23:4; etc.) the donkey and the ox are paired together, possibly because these were the two primary animals one would own. Deuteronomy 22:10 bans plowing with an ox and a donkey yoked together. The book of Ezra reports that 6,720 donkeys accompanied the 42,360 persons returning from the Babylonian exile (Ezra 2:67).

According to Hebrew custom, all equids (donkeys, mules, and horses) and camels were unfit for consumption. It was a sign of desperation that during the famine that occurred on account of the Syrian siege of Samaria a donkey's head sold for eighty shekels of silver (2 Kgs 6:25).

In addition to their being forbidden as food, donkeys are viewed in some OT texts as having negative behavioral traits. For example, the donkey is characterized as licentious (Ezek 23:20) and as a stubborn or lazy animal (Prov 26:3). That donkeys were not treated respectfully in death is indicated by God's prediction that Josiah's son Jehoiakim "will have the burial of a donkey—dragged away and thrown outside the gates of Jerusalem" (Jer 22:19).

The Shechem tradition concerning the sons of Hamor found in Gen 33:18–34:31 seems to play on the fact that Hamor's name is identical to the Hebrew word for "donkey." The tale of the man of God from Judah in 1 Kgs 13 records the curious detail that the lion that killed the man was found, accompanied by the man's donkey, standing next to the corpse (vs. 34). The most vivid narrative depiction of a donkey in the OT is that of Baalam's jenny, who rebukes the hired prophet for beating her when he fails to see the angel of the Lord who stands in their path (Num 22:22–35).

Mules (Heb. masculine sing. *pered*, feminine sing. *pirdâ*) are mentioned occasionally in the OT, almost always in royal contexts (e.g., 1 Kgs 1:33, 38, 44). Mules appear, for example, as mounts for David's sons (2 Sam 13:29), and David sent his mule to Solomon as he prepared to name him as his successor (1 Kgs 1:33). As the breeding of mules was forbidden (Lev 19:19), these valuable hybrids were probably imported. Phoenicia imported mules from Togarmah, i.e., Armenia (Ezek 27:14). The prosperity of the Jewish exiles in Mesopotamia is attested by the fact that among the animals they brought with them on their trek back to Palestine were 245 mules (Ezra 2:66; cf. Neh 7:68).

B. THE NEW TESTAMENT

Donkeys are mentioned nine times in the NT, twice in statements made by Jesus about showing kindness to animals on the Sabbath (Luke 13:15; 14:5). In his warning about offending children, Jesus refers to the a "large millstone," literally, a *mylos onikos*, "millstone of a donkey" (Matt 18:6||Mark 9:42). On Palm Sunday, Jesus rode into Jerusalem riding on a "colt," that is, a young donkey (Matt 21:1–9||Mark 11:1–10||Luke 19:28–40;

John 12:12–15), thus fulfilling the prophecy of Zech 9:9. Matthew's reference to both a female donkey and its colt and his remark that Jesus sat upon "them" (vs. 7) has sometimes been ascribed to Matthew's misunderstanding of the grammatical parallelism in Zech 9:9; the "them" can, however, be understood as a reference to the "cloaks" placed on the beast. That this interpretation is possible is not clear from the NIV, in which Matt 21:7 reads, "They brought the donkey and the colt and placed their cloaks on them for Jesus to sit on," but the ambiguity of the Greek is reflected in other, more literal translations, such as the ESV: "They brought the donkey and the colt and put on them their cloaks, and he sat on them."

C. THE NEAR EASTERN WORLD

In Mesopotamia wild donkeys called onagers (*Equus hemionus*) were first utilized for pulling wagons, as depicted on the Standard of Ur (ca. 2500 BC), before the use of the domesticated ass (*Equus asinus*) became widespread. The earliest evidence of the domesticated donkey in Mesopotamia comes from the late fourth millennium BC at Uruk and Tell Rubeidheh.

Donkeys were frequently buried with their masters so they would be available to the latter in the afterlife. A passage in the Sumerian "Death of Ur-Namma" relates: "His donkeys were to be found with the king; they were buried with him" (lines 115–116; cited in Way 2011, 95). Sites in Mesopotamia (e.g., Tell Madhur, Tell Razuk, Tell Ababra, Kish, and Abu Salabikh), mainly from the 3rd millennium BC, have yielded the remains of equids, some of which can be interpreted as belonging to donkeys, who were buried with their masters (see Way 2011, 142–48).

The donkey is a marvelous beast of burden since it is sure footed, lives long, and is indefatigable. It can carry loads of about 220 pounds and travel up to twenty miles a day. Old Assyrian trading colonies in Cappadocia (19th–18th c. BC) were serviced by donkey caravans. A letter from Mari mentions about three thousand donkeys, and other texts from this site refer to the sacrifice of donkeys (using the phrase *ḥayarum qatālum*, "to kill a jackass") to seal pacts between tribes. The only other known textual reference to this custom is found some six hundred years later in Ugaritic ritual texts. A monumental donkey burial in a temple courtyard found at Tell Abu Hureireh, which burial was the object of ongoing veneration, may be evidence of an Amorite covenant ceremony performed at the founding of the temple.

The mule (*Equus asinus mulus*) is the offspring of a donkey stallion and a mare. A mule, which is stronger than a donkey, can carry loads up to four hundred pounds. The hinny, the hybrid resulting from the union of a horse stallion and a jenny, was quite rare. Both hybrids were sterile. Mules are first attested about 2200 BC. The mule is first mentioned in a Mari letter from the Old Babylonian era. In a letter to the king of Mari, an official named Baḫdi Lim advises: "[My lord] should not ride a horse. Let my [lord] ride in a chariot or on a mule and he will thereby honour his royal head!" (ARMT VI, 76:20–25; Malamat, 51). Law 180 of the Hittite Law Code (ca. 1500–1100 BC) stipulates: "If it is a draft-horse, its price is 20 shekels of silver. The price for 1 mule is 1 mina of silver" (*ANET*, 196); since a mina equaled sixty shekels, the worth of a mule, according to this law, was three times that of a horse. Mules are not attested in Egypt.

The donkey may have been first domesticated in the Nile Valley, as wild asses were indigenous to northeast Africa. Wild donkeys first appear in the archaeological record ca. 4500 BC. The domesticated donkey first appears in Egypt in the Predynastic period (3600–3000 BC) at Maadi, at the apex of the Delta in Lower Egypt (see Hoffman, 201). Domestic donkeys are depicted in several slate palettes, such as the so-called "Libyan Palette," which is now in the Cairo Museum (al-Miṣri, 20). In Egypt, the donkey was both the chief mode of transportation and the main beast of burden. Large numbers of this animal were required to carry food and water on long journeys into the desert regions, in the trade for gold in Nubia, for example. An expedition into the Sinai required five hundred asses. Harkhuf, the governor of Upper Egypt during the 6th Dynasty (ca. 2300 BC), made four journeys south into Kush (Nubia = Sudan). He reported that on one of his return journeys, "I came down (to Egypt) with three hundred donkeys laden with incense, ebony, *ḥnkw*-oil, *s3t*, panther skins, elephant's-tusks, throw sticks, and all sorts of good products" (*AEL*, 1.26). Another governor of Upper Egypt, Sebni, proceeded south with one hundred donkeys loaded with ointments, honey, clothing, oil, and other goods as gifts, to help him recover the body of his father, who had died in Wawat (Northern Nubia) (see *ARE*, 1.167).

In Egypt donkeys were also used to thresh grain. Donkeys are rarely depicted in Egyptian art being ridden. In the famed painting from Beni-Hasan, donkeys are ridden by "Asiatics," that is, Semites from Palestine, and a depiction of Hatshepsut's expedition to Punt includes a portly queen of that country riding a donkey.

We have numerous ostraca from the workmen's village at Deir el-Medina, near the Valley of the Kings, that describe the hiring and treatment (including, at times, the mistreatment) of donkeys. According to these ostraca, donkeys were used for hauling water and wood and for threshing. In Egyptian mythology the donkey was associated with the god Seth, the enemy of Osiris and Horus. The animal was also invoked as part of coarse imprecations.

D. THE GRECO-ROMAN WORLD

Donkeys and mules were abundant in Greece and were used for various tasks, such as turning stone mills, and for transport. The donkey's small size and sure-footedness made it the ideal animal for use in terraced vineyards. The *Iliad* presents the donkey as a symbol of noble stubbornness (11.558). Plato condemns orators who praise evil under the name of good by praising, as it were, "the shadow of an ass." He has Socrates say to Phaedrus: "If I tried to persuade you in all seriousness, composing a speech in praise of the ass, which I called a horse, and saying that the beast was a most valuable possession at home and in war, that you could use him as a mount in battle, and that he was able to carry baggage and was useful for many other purposes . . ."; and to this Phaedrus responds, "then it would be supremely ridiculous" (*Phaedr.* 260b–c).

The Greeks were not averse to eating donkey meat. The donkey was sacred to Dionysus; both the god and his companion Silenus are described in literature and depicted in visual art as riding on donkeys. According to Diodorus Siculus, the funeral carriage of Alexander the Great (died 323 BC) was pulled by a team of sixty-four mules (*hēmionoi*) (*Bib. hist.* 18.27).

In Rome the *carpentum*, a two-wheeled covered carriage pulled by mules, is one of the earliest vehicles mentioned (Livy, *Rom. Hist.* 1.34). Priestesses and matrons were granted the special privilege of riding in this vehicle during public festal processions (Livy, *Rom. Hist.* 5.25; Tac. *Ann.* 12.42). Mules also pulled carriages carrying official messages as part of the *cursus publicus*, the imperial postal and transportation system established by Augustus (Suet. *Aug.* 49). In a mosaic in the Baths of the Cisarii (drivers of gigs) at Ostia, mules are given such names as Pudes ("Bashful"), Podagrosus ("Gouty"), Potiscus ("Thirsty Fish"), and Barosus ("Mollycoddle"). The Romans used mules as military pack animals, as shown in the writings of Julius Caesar and on the columns of Trajan and Marcus Aurelius. According to Suetonius, Nero traveled with a thousand carriages drawn by mules shod with silver "hipposandals" (*Nero* 30).

The Romans generally considered donkeys to be strong but stupid animals, and they often treated them poorly. A common task of the donkey was to work on mills grinding grain. In a poem a donkey complains, "Why do you drive me, the slow-footed, braying ass, round and round . . . driven in a circle and blindfolded, I am forced to turn the heavy millstone?" (Toynbee, 195).

Apuleius's novel *The Golden Ass* tells the story of Lucius, who was accidentally transformed into a donkey. The author vividly describes the beatings and hard labor that were the lot of the donkey in his day.

Despite the donkey's overall low status among the Romans, the animal was sacred to Apollo and was also associated with Vesta. During the festivals of Consualia in honor of Consus, a god of the harvest, which took place on August 21 and December 15, horses, asses, and mules were garlanded and allowed to rest. According to Pliny the Elder, "Asses' milk is actually thought to contribute something to the whiteness in women's skin; at all events Domitius Nero's wife Poppaea used to drag five hundred she asses with foals about with her everywhere and actually soaked her whole body in a bath-tub with ass's milk, believing that it also smoothed out wrinkles" (*Nat.* 11.238; cf. Juv., *Sat.* 6.462–70).

E. THE JEWISH WORLD

The Mishnah lays down rules for the hiring of donkeys, the quality of their food, and the amount of their loads. Josephus remarks on how extremely useful asses were in agriculture (*Ag. Ap.* 2.87). The Talumud's statement "if one sees an ass in a dream, he may hope for salvation, as it says, 'Behold thy king cometh unto thee; he is triumphant and victorious, lowly and riding upon an ass'" (*b. Ber.* 56b), refers to the messianic prophecy of Zech 9:9. Though Jews were prohibited from producing mules, they were allowed to use them (*t. Kil.* 5.6).

Apion, an anti-Semite in Alexandria (ca. 25 BC–AD 45), was refuted by Josephus in the latter's work *Against Apion*. Mnaseas of Patara in Lycia (200 BC), who is quoted by Apion, according to Josephus (*Ag. Ap.* 2.114), was the first to mention the calumny that the Jews engaged in donkey worship. Apion cited the Stoic philosopher Posidonius (ca. 135–51 BC) as the source of his information. According to Josephus, "Within the sanctuary Apion has the effrontery to assert that the Jews kept an ass's head, worshipping that animal and deeming it worthy of the deepest reverence; the fact was disclosed, he maintains, on the occasion of the spoliation of the temple by Antiochus Epiphanes, when the head, made of gold and worth a high price, was discovered" (*Ag. Ap.* 2.80). Josephus sarcastically wrote: "May we not, on our side, suggest that Apion is overloading the pack-ass, that is to say himself, with a crushing pack of nonsense and lies?" (*Ag. Ap.* 2.115).

According to Diodorus Siculus, "Antiochus, called Epiphanes, on defeating the Jews had entered the innermost sanctuary of the god's temple. . . . Finding there a marble statue of a heavily bearded man seated on an ass, with a book in his hands, he supposed it to be an image of Moses" (*Bib. hist.* 34.1.3). Tacitus reported the tale that a herd of wild asses led Moses to a spring of water (*Hist.* 5.3.2). The calumny that the Jews worshipped the donkey may have originally arisen from the similarity between the name of the Hebrew God, *Yahu*, and the Egyptian word for "donkey," *iaw*. (For other scholarly speculations on this matter, see Feldman, 498–501.)

F. THE CHRISTIAN WORLD

Like Jews, Christians were accused of donkey worship. A notorious graffito found on the Palatine Hill in Rome that dates to ca. AD 200 depicts a crucified man with a donkey's head and the Greek inscription ALEXA-MENOC CEBETE THEON, "Alexamenos worships god" (Snyder, 27–28). The pagan interlocutor in Minucius Felix's *Octavius* reports, "I hear that they adore the head of an ass, that basest of creatures, consecrated by I know not what silly persuasion—a worthy and appropriate religion for such manners" (9). According to Tertullian,

> Report has introduced a new calumny respecting our God. Not so long ago, a most abandoned wretch in that city of yours, a man who had deserted indeed his own religion—a Jew, . . . carried about in public a caricature of us with this label: *Onocoetes* ["he who lies in an ass's manger"]. This (figure) had ass's ears, and was dressed in a *toga* with a book, having a hoof on one of his feet.
> (*Nat.* 1.14)

Tertullian also retorted to the pagans: "You will not, however, deny that all beasts of burden, and not parts of them, but the animals entire, are with their goddess Epona objects of worship with you. It is this, perhaps, which displeases you in us, that while your worship here is universal, we do homage only to the ass" (*Apol.* 16). Of Celsus, Origen commented, "And after these remarks, he goes on to speak in a way quite in harmony with the tone of those who have invented the fictions of lion-like, and ass-headed, and serpent-like ruling angels, and other similar absurdities, but which does not affect those who belong to the Church" (*Cels.* 6.37).

For Justin Martyr, the harnessed donkey is a symbol of the Jews, and the unharnessed colt is a symbol of the Gentiles. Clement of Alexandria compares Christians to the donkey colt, "And we who are little ones being such colts, are reared up by our divine colt-tamer" (*Paed.* 1.5). In his allegorical interpretation of the Parable of the Good Samaritan (Luke 10:29–37), Augustine writes of the donkey in Luke 10:34: "The *beast* is the flesh in which He deigned to come to us. The being *set upon the beast* is belief in the incarnation of Christ" (*Quaest. ev.* 2.19; cited in Dodd, 1–2).

Justin cites the mule in arguing that after the resurrection women need not bear children: "And we find that some even of the lower animals, though possessed of wombs, do not bear, such as the mule; and the male mules do not beget their kind. So that both in the case of men and the irrational animals we can see sexual intercourse abolished; and this, too, before the future world" (*On the Resurrection* 3).

In late fourth-century paintings found under the church of Santa Maria near Verona, Christ is portrayed entering Jerusalem on the back of a donkey. A sixth-century ivory throne at Ravenna depicts Mary traveling to Bethlehem seated on a donkey.

BIBLIOGRAPHY: W. F. Albright, "Midianite Donkey Caravans," in *Translating & Understanding the Old Testament*, ed. H. T. Frank and W. L. Reed (1970), 197–205; E. Bickermann, "Ritualmord und Eselkult," *MGWJ* 71 (1927), 171–87, 255–64, repr. in *Studies in Jewish and Christian History* (1980), II.225–55; O. Borowski, *Every Living Thing: Daily Use of Animals in Ancient Israel* (1998); B. Brentjes, "Onager und Esel im Alten Orient," in *Beiträge zu Geschichte, Kultur und Religion des alten Orients* (1971), 131–45; A. Dent, *Donkey: The Story of the Ass from East to West* (1972); C. H. Dodd, *The Parables of the Kingdom* (1961); L. H. Feldman, *Jew & Gentile in the Ancient World* (1993); A. Finet, "Le sacrifice de l'âne en Mésopotamie," in *Ritual and Sacrifice in the Ancient Near East*, ed. J. Quaegebeur (1993), 135–42; G. S. Cansdale, *All the Animals of the Bible Lands* (1970); M. Hoffman, *Egypt Before the Pharaohs* (1984); P. F. Houlihan, *The Animal World of the Pharaohs* (1996), 29–32; D. Instone-Brewer, "The Two Asses of Zechariah 9:9 in Matthew 21," *TynBul* 54 (2003), 87–98; A. Jacoby, "Der angebliche Eselkult der Juden und Christen," *AR* 25 (1927), 265–82; J. Janssen, *Donkeys at Deir el-Medina* (2005); G. A. Klingbeil, "Los mulos como indice de posicion social en los dias de David y durante el siglo X AC," *Theologika* 14 (1999), 232–71; A. Malamat, "Prophecy at Mari," in *"The Place Is Too Small for Us": The Israelite Prophets in Recent Scholarship*, ed. R. P. Gordon (1995), 50–73; M. al-Miṣri, *The Egyptian Museum in Cairo: A Walk through the Alleys of Ancient Egypt* (2005); A. Nibbi, "Some Remarks on Ass and Horse in Ancient Egypt and the Absence of the Mule," *ZÄS* 106 (1979), 148–68; E. Nielsen, "Ass and Ox in the Old Testament," in *Studia Orientalia Ioanni Pedersen* (1953), 263–74; G. Snyder, *Ante Pacem: Archaeological Evidence of Church Life before Constantine* (1985); J. M. C. Toynbee, *Animals in Roman Life and Art* (1996); United Bible Society, *Fauna and Flora of the Bible* (1972); L. Vischer, "Le prétendu 'culte de l'âne' dans l'Église primitive," *RHR* 139 (1951), 14–35; K. C. Way, "Animals in the Prophetic World: Literary Reflections on Numbers 22 and 1 Kings 13," *JSOT* 34 (2009), 47–62; K. C. Way, "Assessing Sacred Asses: Bronze Age Donkey Burials in the Near East," *Levant* 42 (2010), 210–25; K. C. Way, "Donkey Domain: Zechariah 9:9 and Lexical Semantics," *JBL* 129 (2010), 105–14; K. C. Way, *Donkeys in the Biblical World: Ceremony and Symbol* (2011).

EMY

See also CAMELS and HORSES.

DOORS & KEYS

In ancient times, the door was more than a movable barrier for opening and closing an entrance or for controlling light and ventilation. People of the biblical world tended to make their doors as attractive as possible. Various types of bolts, locks, and keys were developed to secure doors.

A. THE OLD TESTAMENT

In the Hebrew Bible, the door separated an outer world of darkness and danger from an inner sanctum of hospitality and security (Judg 19:27; 2 Kgs 6:32; Job 31:32). A special sanctity became associated with the threshold of the home.

The OT distinguishes between the terms the *petaḥ*, "entrance," to a house or tent (Gen 18:1; 43:19), and the *delet*, "door" (a term with cognates in, e.g., Akk., Ugar., and Phoen., including Punic, and which is likely related to the Heb. letter *dālet*, which possibly depicts a door), the mechanism for closing and opening the entrance (Gen 19:6, 9). Doors were usually made of planks of wood either studded with nails or bounded by strips of metal. In Solomon's temple, the doors for the courtyard of the priests were overlaid with bronze (2 Chr 4:9). Doorways had three parts: two doorposts, that is, the door's vertical sides, which in Hebrew are called *mĕzûzôt*; a lintel (Heb. *mašqôp*), the horizontal beam over the door; and a threshold (Heb. *sap*, *miptān*), a horizontal sill at the bottom of the doorway used to keep dirt and water out. In the OT, the term *delet* occurs twenty-three times in the dual (*dĕlātayim*), suggesting that two door leaves were used in wide doorways (cf. Isa 45:1). This necessitated a third vertical post between the doors. The doors came together on this third post when closed. Doors normally swung inward. The edge of the door next to the doorpost consisted of an upright wooden beam set in a socket or depression at the top in the lintel and at the bottom in the sill (cf. 1 Kgs 6:34; 7:50). Archaeologists have uncovered various sockets in the excavation of Palestinian homes.

At Passover during the time of the exodus, blood was smeared on the doorposts and lintel of the houses of the Israelites (Exod 12:7). A Hebrew slave who opted to remain a slave for life was required to have his master pierce his ear at the doorpost with an awl (Exod 21:6; Deut 15:17). Moses commanded the Israelites to write God's words upon the doorposts of their houses (Deut 6:9; 11:20). In later periods, up to today, Jews have fulfilled this last command by attaching *mĕzûzôt* (small metal or wooden cylinders into which passages from the Mosaic law are inserted) to their doorframes.

According to 1 Kgs 6:31–33, Solomon constructed the doors to the Holy of Holies and to the Holy Place of the temple according to these proportions:

> For the entrance to the inner sanctuary he made doors out of olive wood that were one fifth of the width of the sanctuary. And on the two olive-wood doors he carved cherubim, palm trees and open flowers, and overlaid the cherubim and palm trees with hammered gold. In the same way, for the entrance to the main hall he made doorframes out of olive wood that were one fourth of the width of the hall.

Since the temple was twenty cubits wide, the doors to the inner sanctuary would have been four cubits (about 2 m., or a little over 6 ft.) wide, and the outer doors would have been five cubits (2.5 m. or 7.5 ft.) wide.

Doors and gates could be locked by a bolt (2 Sam 13:17–18; Neh 3:3). Some keys (Heb. sing. *maptēaḥ*, lit., "that which opens") were more than a foot in length, perhaps an indication that Isa 22:22 may not be restricted merely to a figurative interpretation: "I will place on his shoulder the key to the house of David." Doors could be locked or unlocked from the outside (Judg 3:23–25; 2 Sam 13:17–18). Apparently, a large keyhole sometimes permitted a person to open a door by hand without use of a key (Song 5:4). At times a bar was used to secure a door from the inside. First Chronicles 9:26–27 describes the use of a key: "But the four principal gatekeepers, who were Levites, were entrusted with the responsibility for the rooms and treasuries in the house of God. They would spend the night stationed around the house of God, because they had to guard it; and they had charge of the key for opening it each morning." Though this was a lowly position, one psalmist proclaimed, "I would rather be a doorkeeper in the house of my God than dwell in the tents of the wicked" (Ps 84:10).

The NIV and other English versions translate Prov 26:14, "As a door turns on its hinges [Heb. *ṣîr*], so a sluggard turns on his bed." But as hinges were generally unknown in antiquity, a better translation would be "pivot." Sirach 21:23–24 comments: "A boor peers into the house from the door, but a cultivated man remains outside. It is ill-mannered for a man to listen at a door, and a discreet man is grieved by the disgrace."

B. THE NEW TESTAMENT

In a typical village, the door of a home remained open all day long as an invitation to sociability and visitation; at sunset, it was closed. The NT contains passages that speak of locked doors (Luke 11:7; John 20:26) and the necessity of knocking to enter (Matt 7:7–8; Rev 3:20). In two texts a female servant goes to open the door (John 18:15–16; Acts 12:13–15). In the latter case, Rhoda is so astonished at seeing Peter, who has been locked in jail, that she leaves him standing at the door knocking (Acts 12:16). People of influence or wealth often had doorkeepers who guarded the property and authorized people to enter (Mark 13:34). Keys are mentioned in numerous NT passages, always in a metaphorical sense; examples are "the keys of the kingdom of heaven" (Matt 16:19), "the key to knowledge" (Luke 11:52), "the keys of death and Hades" (Rev 1:18), "the key of David" (Rev 3:7), "the key to the shaft of the Abyss" (Rev 9:1), and "the key to the Abyss" (Rev 20:1).

C. THE NEAR EASTERN WORLD

Mesopotamia

Doors were at first made of reed matting, woven materials, or ox hides, but were later made of wood. Doors were generally less than one meter wide and less than two meters high. Brick arches frequently spanned doorways. The threshold was made of stone, and the two upright doorjambs and the lintel were made of stone or wood.

Doors and gates generally opened inward; raised edges on the threshold and lintel kept the door from swinging outward. In early Mesopotamia, doors were attached to, and swung on, vertical poles that extended just above and below the top and bottom edges of the door frame. The lower end of such poles rested in a hollow in the threshold or in a stone socket fixed in the floor of the doorway, which in some cases was protected with a bronze sheathing.

In the village of Hassuna in Assyria, a stone door socket was discovered that may date as early as ca. 4500 BC. Examples of such stone sockets for the lower pivot of doors are widely attested throughout Western Asia in later times. In temples and royal dwellings, door sockets often carried inscriptions. A door socket from ca. 2100 BC records the restoration of a temple by Gudea, the Sumerian governor at Lagash. One of the earliest examples of a lock and key comes from Khorsabad and dates to ca. 2000 BC.

Since stone was not abundant in Mesopotamia, stone sockets were valuable and usually moved from house to house when a family changed its place of residence. When a house, most of which were made of unbaked bricks, was abandoned, its wooden doors were removed and used in the next dwelling.

Doors were at times painted bright red to keep out evil spirits. Doors and gates could be locked from within with a bar or bolt. Wooden gates could be reinforced, or even covered, with metal. The most spectacular surviving examples of overlaid wooden gates are the monumental Neo-Assyrian gates from Balawat (9th c. BC), now in the British Museum. These were originally six feet wide and over twenty feet high. The wooden doors (probably of cedar) have not survived, but the bronze sheathing in eight bands that covered the doors has been recovered. These bronze-covered gates depict in extraordinary detail the campaigns of Shalmaneser III (858–824 BC), including scenes of camp life, animal sacrifice, siege warfare, and the payment of tribute. A Neo-Assyrian text (8th c. BC) lists the dimensions of thirty-six doors, perhaps for the palace of Sargon II at Khorsabad; one pair was four cubits (6 ft.) wide and thirteen cubits (21 ft.) high.

Numerous texts from the archives at Mari (18th c. BC) refer to the sealing and unsealing of storeroom and archive doors. André Parrot discovered a pottery disk (11 cm. in diameter) with a hole (2.7 cm) fixed on a doorpost 1.15 meters above the floor, which he facetiously called a "bouton de sonnette," i.e., a doorbell. The hole had once held a wooden peg. As A. Malamat explains: "The door was pierced at about the height of the 'doorbell,' and a cord knotted at one end was threaded out through it. In sealing the door, the cord was stretched to the peg, where it could be wound around several times. The peg and the cord coiled around it were then wrapped in an envelope of soft clay, which was stamped with a seal" (Malamat, 165).

Egypt

Ancient Egyptian doors made of cypress and, at times, of imported cedar were often beautifully decorated and built with a cornice above them. Doors were sometimes stained to imitate hard-to-find or foreign wood tones. In Egypt, as in Mesopotamia, doors might be painted red to repel hostile spirits. Doors swung on metal pins or sockets with projecting pivots. The two corners of the door with projecting cones were inserted into the sockets, which were fastened to the wood with nails. The pivot of the lower socket rested in a hole in the floor. Bronze sockets have been found in tombs at Thebes. In Egypt doors opened inwards. Some doors were of a folding style, bolted in the center. Some Egyptian officials had stone doorways with their names and titles incised in the jambs.

Since temples in Egypt were not meant to be buildings for worshippers, but were darkened sanctuaries accessible only to priests, their doors were not only narrow, but were often sealed, as we learn from the stela of

Piankhy or Piye (747–716 BC) from Kush (the Sudan), who conquered Egypt. When he had come to the city of On, he proceeded to the temple of Re. "Breaking the seals of the bolts, opening the doors; viewing his father Re in the holy Pyramidion House. . . . Closing the doors, applying the clay, sealing with the king's own seal, and instructing the priests: 'I have inspected the seal. No other king who may arise shall enter here' " (*AEL*, 3.77).

The locking device used in Egypt as early as 2000 BC was the forerunner of the modern pin-tumbler type of lock (devised by Linus Yale in the 19th c. AD). Made of wood, the lock consisted of a vertical housing that held several movable wooden pegs or pins. These fell naturally into holes bored in the top of a wooden bolt as it was moved through the housing into a socket in the doorpost. The pegs thus kept the bolt from being moved and the door from being opened. A long wooden key was used to lift the pegs out of the bolt, so the bolt could be drawn back to free the door. The tip of the key had pegs on one surface corresponding to the holes in the bolt. When the key was put into the hollow slot in the bolt and lifted, the sliding pegs were pushed up from their holes, unlocking the door. These keys were huge by today's standards, from six inches to two feet in length!

A frequent feature of Egyptian tombs was a "false" door, carved of stone, which served as a threshold between the land of the living and the next world. Offerings for the dead would be placed before the door. This door would be situated in the tomb so that it was oriented toward the west, since the setting sun was associated with the realm of the dead.

D. THE GRECO-ROMAN WORLD

Greece

The volcanic eruption of Thera buried the Minoan town of Akrotiri, where, as a result, rectangular doorways were preserved with their frames of wood and stone. Wooden doors had pivots that fitted into sockets in the lintel and in the threshold. In Minoan palaces double doors were common.

Our knowledge of doors (*thyrai*) in the later Greek world comes largely from the descriptions of classical authors and from depictions on murals, vases, and funerary art. Homer describes how Penelope "took the bent key in her strong hand—a goodly key of bronze, and on it was a handle of ivory" to unlock the chamber that contained Odysseus's special bow (*Od.* 21.6). The passage continues:

> Now when the fair lady had come to the store-room, and had stepped upon the threshold of oak, which of old the carpenter had skilfully planed and made straight to the line—thereon had he also fitted door-posts, and set on them

bright doors—straightway she quickly loosed the thong from the handle and thrust in the key, and with sure aim shot back the bolt. (*Od.* 21.42–48)

In Aristophanes's play *The Thesmophioriazusae*, a woman complains of the tyranny of husbands: "Then, because of this man, they install locks and bolts on the women's doors to guard them . . . our husbands now carry the house keys with them, complicated nasty things with triple teeth, imported from Sparta" (412–21).

From the sixth to the first century BC the Dorian batton door was widely used, especially in domestic architecture. This door was of simple style and featured little decoration. A batton consisted of vertical wooden planks held together by attaching horizontal or diagonal braces to them with nails. Several marble imitations of batton doors have been discovered in Macedonian tombs.

The more elaborate Ionian door was built with a rich frame, at times decorated with ivory and ebony. These doors would advertise the status of their owners. Objects were hung on the doors to announce special occasions: branches for weddings, wreaths for the birth of a son, and wool for the birth of a daughter.

Houses were constructed with a wall that provided protection and privacy and which had a single entrance to the outside. A *prothyron* or vestibule prevented passersby from looking in. As these doors opened outwards, before going out people would rap on them to prevent passersby from walking into a suddenly opened door.

Doors were secured by a bolt (*mochlos*) that passed through frames on the inner side of the door. The door was locked from the outside by pulling the bolt into position with a strap that passed to the outside. The door was unlocked by passing a key (*kleis*), which was a metal rod bent twice at a right angle, through another hole in the door, engaging the end of it in a groove in the bolt, and then pulling to release the bolt. More complex locks (sing. *kleistron*) and keys were developed in the fifth century BC. In these systems, slots were cut in the bolt and into these fell vertical pegs (*balanoi*, lit., "acorns"); a *balanagra*, "key, hook," was employed to lift up the *balanoi* so that the bolt could be freed. Some lock-and-key combinations required two hands to operate.

One of the earliest extant Greek keys dates from the sixth century BC and comes from the temple of Artemis in Lousoi. Bronze door plates at times decorated key holes in ancient Greece. Door handles were frequently constructed in the shape of a lion's head holding the pull-ring in its jaws. Bronze door knockers have been recovered from Olynthus.

The entrance to the temple of Zeus at Olympia had bronze doors (Pausanias, *Descr.* 5.10.10). An inscription records the construction materials and expenses of the fourth-century BC temple of Asclepius, the Greek god of healing, at Epidauros. It mentions hinge sockets, metal for nails, handles, and quantities of ivory and exotic woods—including lotus, elm, and box-wood—used for the detailed inlay work on the temple doors. The Hellenistic doors of the temple of Minerva are described by Cicero as having massive golden knobs and scenes exquisitely carved in ivory. In the Hellenistic age, Hero of Alexandria in his *Pneumatics* described an automatic trumpeting doorbell for a temple (16–17).

In the usual procedure for divorce, a husband would take back the keys of the house from his wife in the presence of witnesses. Priests and priestesses carried large, bulky keys as symbols of their dignity. Hecate was believed to hold the key of Hades, and Aeacus, one of the three judges in Hades, is depicted carrying a bunch of keys.

Rome

Wall paintings from the Villa Boscoreale (near Pompeii) that date to about 50 BC depict doors apparently made of ivory with inlays of tortoise shells. Representations in Roman funerary art (grave altars, urns, and sarcophagi) provide some of our most valuable evidence for the appearance of doors. However, since many of these depictions are symbolic, it is often difficult to determine whether they depict doors as they actually looked.

In the Roman world, doors (Lat. sing. *ianua*) were usually made of wood, though they could be reinforced by metal. Doors for both public buildings and houses generally opened inward, but exceptions could be made for those who garnered tremendous prestige, such as P. Valerius Publicola, one of the first consuls of the Roman republic (ca. 6th c. BC) (Dionysius of Halicarnassus, *Ant. Rom.* 5.39; Pliny, *Nat.* 36.24). In contrast to the guarded privacy of Greek houses, the houses of Roman patricians were kept open except at night or at times of mourning. Wealthy Romans wanted the public to see the grandeur of their public spaces (the atrium, *tablinum*, and peristyle). It was the expectation that the clients of a Roman senator would visit him in the morning to pay their respects in the act of *salutatio*. Before the doors of the house would be a *vestibulum*, where the waiting *salutatores* would stand before being admitted.

Wealthy Romans employed a doorkeeper (*ostiarius, ianitor*), often a slave who performed minimal responsibilities such as keeping the key at night. Seneca writes: "Who is that broken-down dotard? You have done well to place him at the entrance; for he is outward bound. Where did you get him? What pleasure did it give you to take up for burial some other man's dead?" (*Ep.* 12.3). We learn from Suetonius of an exceptional doorkeeper: "Lucius Voltacilius Plotus is said to have been a slave and even to have served as a doorkeeper in chains, according to the ancient custom, until he was set free because of his talent and interest in letters" (*De Rhetoribus* 3). Martial had occasion to complain: "What is worse still, Paulus, worn out after a thousand labors, I am told by your janitor [doorman] that you are not at home" (*Ep.* 5.22). At times a guard dog was also posted, as indicated by a famous mosaic from the House of the Mosaic Atrium at Pompeii, with the image of a snarling dog and the text *cave canem*, "Beware of the dog."

If a wife counterfeited the household keys, this would be a reason for divorce. Since the time of the Twelve Tables (ca. 450 BC) the taking back of the keys (sing. *clavis*, pl. *claves*) was an expression for divorce (as it was in Greece, as mentioned above).

The Romans were responsible for several major breakthroughs in the development of the lock and key. They were the first to use metal in lock-making; locks they made from iron and keys from bronze. Locks were de-signed in various shapes (round, square, and triangular), which lessened the possibility of an intruder making a duplicate key. Keys were reduced in size and often artistically decorated for wearing as pendants or for on the finger for safekeeping. Bronze springs were added to locks in order to achieve quicker action in moving the pins into the bolt. Locks were often camouflaged by designing them in the shape of horses, birds, or flowers.

In addition, the Romans invented warded locks. With warded locks, keys were made for turning in locks rather than for pushing and sliding into locks, which had been the former method. In a warded lock, a key has slots cut to match the projections (wards) inside the lock. When such a key is rotated, the bolt is released. Metal keys from the Roman period have been found at Pompeii and Herculaneum.

The dry conditions of Egypt have preserved many structures from the late Roman era (2nd–3rd c. AD) at Karanis in the Faiyum area. A wooden door with a latch has been preserved, for example. The door latch would have rested in an L-shaped bracket in the door's interior. A person stand-ing outside the building could unlatch the door by pulling on a string fed through a small hole in the door. Wooden keys found at Karanis range between six and twelve inches in length.

Three major doors from the Imperial period of Roman history are still in existence in the city of Rome. These are located at the Pantheon, the temple of Romulus in the Roman Forum, and the Diocletianic Curia. All three doors make use of thin sheets of bronze with numerous studs or bosses, some of them decorated.

In early Roman times three gods were assigned various responsibili-ties related to doors, a tradition that was later mocked by Augustine, who declaimed: "Every one sets a porter at the door of his house, and because he is a man, he is quite sufficient; but these people have set three gods,

Forculus to the doors [*fores*], Cardea to the hinge [*cardo*], Limentinus to the threshold [*limen*]. Thus Forculus could not at the same time take care also of the hinge and the threshold" (*Civ.* 4.8). The deity Portunus, who is regularly depicted holding a key, was originally a protector of doors (cf. Lat. *porta*, "gate") but later became a god of harbors (cf. Lat. *portus*, "harbor"). Janus, the Roman god of all beginnings (hence "January," the first month of the year), also served as god of doorways. Janus was often presented as having two faces, which looked in opposite directions, much as a door faces two different ways. Janus Patulcius was a manifestation of this deity who opened doors and Janus Clusivus was the manifestation who closed doors. Janus's small bronze shrine in the Forum consisted of passageways with doors at each end that were closed only in times of peace.

E. THE JEWISH WORLD

Jews adapted Roman architecture and devices using the materials at hand. In keeping with the OT perspective that doors separated an inner sanctum of hospitality and security from an outside world of darkness and danger, Jews held their privacy in high regard and considered their houses sacred spaces for Torah study and prayer (*b. Meg.* 29a). In interpreting Deut 24:10 ("When you make a loan of any kind to your neighbor, do not go into their house to get what is offered to you as a pledge"), Philo declared: "A creditor must not enter the houses of his debtors, to take with violence a pledge or surety for the loan, but must stand outside in the porch and quietly bid them bring it out" (*Virt.* 89). It was the custom for callers to announce their arrival at the entrance to a house. According to R. Shimon bar-Yohai, "There are four things which the Holy One, blessed be He, hates, and I too dislike them . . . one who enters his house suddenly—much more so his neighbour's house . . . When R. Johanan went to enquire about the welfare of R. Hanina he would knock at the door" (*Lev. Rab.* 21:8). The rabbis took a common phenomenon and made laws about it. It was important to them.

Doorways were often oriented to the south or east to maximize light and warmth from the sun. Josephus may allude to the law of writing God's words on the doorframes of one's house (see Deut 6:9) by stating that Jews "inscribe on their doors the greatest of the benefits which they have received from God" (Jos. *Ant.* 4.213). During the rabbinic period, it was common to affix a *mezuzah* (a small container of Scriptural parchments) to the right doorpost. The *mezuzah* was a reminder that, living in the privacy of a person's own home, the power of God was present to protect the one who obediently reveres him. Thus, R. Eliezer b. Jacob said, "Whoever has . . . the *mezuzah* on his doorpost, is in absolute security against sinning" (*b. Menaḥ.* 43b).

According to the Mishnah, "If a man let a house to his fellow he must provide it with a door, a bolt, a lock, and whatsoever is the work of a craftsman" (*m. B. Meṣ* 8:7). In the Mishnah, keys typically used in warded locks are referred to as *gamma* keys. The Mishnah distinguishes the *gamma*-shaped key from what it calls a "knee" or "elbow" key. The latter is known for the characteristic bent, teeth-like projections made of bronze that are found on its end. According to the Mishnah,

> If a knee-shaped key is broken at its joint it becomes insusceptible to uncleanness. R. Judah declares it susceptible since one may still open [the door] with the inner portion. If a *gamma*-shaped key was broken off at its bend it becomes insusceptible. If [what remained] still retained the teeth and gaps it remains susceptible. If a key has lost its teeth it is still susceptible because of the gaps; if the gaps were blocked up it is still susceptible because of the teeth. If the teeth were lost and the gaps blocked up or merged into one another, the key becomes insusceptible. (*m. Kelim* 14:8)

At Masada excavators found six small bronze slide keys (three of which were finger rings) that were used to open metal boxes. Keys have also been found in burial caves at Beth Shearim, Ein Gedi, Herodion, Jericho, and Meiron. The Tosefta (late 4th c. AD) forbids a woman from going out in public on the Sabbath with a key on her finger (*t. Šabb.* 4:11), as the rabbis considered it a tool.

F. THE CHRISTIAN WORLD

Roman keys for warded locks were popular in the Byzantine era, with the shaft of the key becoming more rod-like. The key panels contained open recesses. The keys were inserted through a vertical slit in the lock plate and rotated until they engaged the bolt. The keyhole could have a notch that would admit only a key with a corresponding groove.

After the end of the second century, when Christian congregations started to own houses for worship, they appointed *ostiarii*, "porters" (from Lat. *ostium*, "door"), to help administer the buildings. The first reference to such doorkeepers as minor clergy comes in a letter of Pope Cornelius to Bishop Fabius of Antioch in AD 251, which details the number of clergy at Rome. The *ostiarius* was the lowest rank among the minor clergy, and did not require literacy as a qualification. An *ostiarius* named Romanus died as a martyr in AD 258.

The *Rule of St. Benedict* (6th c. AD) stipulates:

> At the entrance to the monastery there should be a wise senior who is too mature in stability to think of wandering about and who can deal with inquiries

and give whatever help is needed. This official's room should be near the main door so that visitors will always find someone there to greet them. . . . If the porter or portress needs help, then a junior should be assigned to the task.
(*Saint Benedict's Rule*, ch. 66; translation Barry, 145)

Up to the third century, the bishops of Rome appealed to the tradition of Paul and Peter preaching in Rome to buttress their position. Stephen I (254–257) was the first to appeal explicitly to Matt 16:18–19 in this connection. Most early references to this passage stress the reference to Peter as the "rock" rather than to the *potestas clavium*, "power of the keys," except those that appear in the controversies between the Montanists and Novatians over who has the power to forgive sins. Pope Damasus (366–384) asserted Rome's primacy over other sees by virtue of these verses, a position also contained in the so-called *Decretum Gelasianum*, which was probably formulated under Damasus, perhaps in 382. Two crossed keys became the iconic symbol of the papacy.

BIBLIOGRAPHY: M. L. Allen, "The Keys of Masada," in *Masada and the World of the New Testament*, ed. J. F. Hall and J. W. Welch (1997), 154–68; A. Baumann, "*deleth*," *TDOT* III, 230–33; P. Barry, trans., *Saint Benedict's Rule* (2004); E. F. Bishop, "The Door of the Sheep," *ExpT* 71 (1959/60), 307–9; M. S. B. Danmerji, *The Development of the Architecture of Doors and Gates in Ancient Mesopotamia* (1987); V. J. M. Eras, *Locks and Keys throughout the Ages* (1957); Y. Garfinkel and M. Mumcuoglu, "Triglyphs and Recessed Doorframes on a Building Model from Khirbet Qeiyafa," *IEJ* 63 (2013), 135–63; B. Haarløv, *The Half-Open Door: A Common Symbolic Motif within Roman Sepulchral Sculpture* (1977); J. Jeremias, "θυρα," *TDNT* III, 173–80; J. Jeremias, "κλεις," *TDNT* III, 744–53; A. Malamat, "'Doorbells' at Mari," in *Cuneiform Archives and Libraries*, ed. K. R. Veenhof (1986), 160–67; D. K. McKim, "Door," *ISBE* (rev.), I, 983–84; A. R. Millard, "The Doorways of Solomon's Temple," *ErIsr* 20 (1989), 135*–39*; T. G. Palaima and J. C. Wright, "Ins and Outs of the Archive Rooms at Pylos: Form and Function in a Mycenaean Palace," *AJA* 89 (1985), 251–62; J. J. Pollitt, *The Art of Greece: Sources and Documents* (1965); A. Salonen, *Die Türen des alten Mesopotamien* (1961); D. Strong and D. Brown, *Roman Crafts* (1979); E. L. Tilton, "A Greek Door of Stone at the Argive Heraeum," *AJA* 7 (1903), 94–95; D. A. Walton, "Doors of the Greek and Roman World," *Arc* 36.1 (1983), 44–50; Y. Yadin, *Bar-Kokhba* (1971), 196–200; Z. Yeivin, "Door and Doorpost," *EncJud* VI, 170–72.

MRW

See also DWELLINGS and PALACES.

DRAMA & THEATERS

Drama is the representation by actors of stories about gods, heroes, or men. This was usually performed in theaters, structures where performances could be viewed by an audience, but which were also used for other purposes such as political assemblies. In the ancient Near East, theatrical performances were often closely linked to religious rituals. Later on, dramatic genres such as tragedy and comedy and acting through pantomiming and miming became important forms of entertainment among the Greeks and Romans, and theaters became an essential component of their cities. However, some Greco-Roman moralists and later Jewish and Christian writers associated popular performances with immoral behavior.

A. THE OLD TESTAMENT

There is little trace of drama in the OT. Some scholars have speculated that the Song of Solomon can be construed as a drama with a dialogue between the Lover and his Beloved, as well as a chorus of maidens. The book of Job also contains dialogues between Job and his three friends, with the final intervention of God himself at the end. Prophets like Jeremiah (Jer 13:1–11; 19:1–15) and Ezekiel (Ezek 5:1–4; 12:1–20) were called upon to act out certain visual performances to drive home their messages.

B. THE NEW TESTAMENT

Jesus alone strikingly uses the Greek word for "actor," *hypokritēs*, of the Pharisees seventeen times in the Synoptics (13 times in Matthew, once in Mark 7:6, and 3 times in Luke). He warns his disciples not to practice their piety as a public performance to be seen (*theathēnai*) by an audience (Matt 6:1).

Jesus describes the Pharisees as announcing their philanthropic acts with a trumpet, as actors did (Matt 6:2); as making up their faces, like tragic actors (Matt 6:16); and as attempting to remove a speck from some-one else's eye, as might occur in a farce (Matt 7:3).

It should be noted that the words *hypokritēs* and *hypokrinomai* ("to act") were already being used prior to the NT in a developed sense and not always in their original association with stage acting and actors. For example, Sir 32:15 reads, "He who seeks the law will be filled with it, but the *hypocrite* will stumble at it" (italics added). And Sir 33:2 states, "A wise man will not hate the law, but he who is *hypocritical* about it is like a boat in a storm" (italics added).

Some scholars suggest that Jesus may have become familiar with drama and actors from the theater at the city of Sepphoris, which was located less than four miles away from his hometown of Nazareth. Sepphoris, which is not mentioned in the NT, was established by Herod Antipas in 3 BC as his key city, before he moved his capital to Tiberias in AD 26. The remains of the theater, which was situated on a natural hill, have been uncovered in excavations. Eventually expanded to provide thirty-four rows of seats, it could hold an audience of four thousand to five thousand persons. This theater, however, may date to the late first century AD.

Acts 12:19–23 depicts the arrival of Herod (Agrippa I) at the port city of Caesarea. The people of Tyre and Sidon, who had a dispute with him, sought an audience with the Jewish king as they depended on him for food. According to Josephus's account of this event, Herod was "clad in a gar-ment woven completely of silver." When he entered the theater facing the audience and the morning sun, his robe became "wondrously radiant and by its glitter inspired fear and awe in those who gazed intently upon it." The audience called out that he was a god and immortal. He suddenly experi-enced excruciating pain in his chest and stomach, and died five days later (*Ant.* 19.343–350).

These events took place in the theater at Caesarea built by Herod the Great, grandfather of Agrippa I. Construction on the theater was begun in 19 BC and finished by 9 BC. The more than thirty rows of seats could have held up to four thousand spectators. A slab with a Latin dedication by Pontius Pilate in honor of Tiberius was found in a fourth-century AD reconstruction of the theater, which was used until the fifth century AD.

There was a theater in every Greco-Roman city where Paul preached in his missionary journeys in Asia Minor and in Greece. Near the theater at Corinth was found an important Latin inscription: *Erastus pro aedilit[at]e s(ua) p(ecunia) stravit*, "Erastus for his aedileship laid (the pavement) at his own expense" (Gill, 293). Erastus, who is described in Rom 16:23 as Corinth's *oikonomos* (= Lat. *aedile*), or "director of public works," was an influential and important co-worker with Paul (cf. Acts 19:22; 2 Tim 4:20). In 1 Cor 15:33 Paul quotes from Menander's play *Thais*: "Bad company corrupts good character." As this was a well-known quotation, this does not mean that Paul attended a theater performance.

According to Acts 19:9, when in Ephesus Paul had daily discussions for two years in the *scholē* ("lecture hall") of Tyrannus. The Western Text adds "from the fifth hour to the tenth," that is, from about 11 a.m. to 4 p.m., when laborers may have taken a noonday pause. This may have been in a small covered theater known in Greek as an *odeion* (Lat. *odeum*), where musical recitals were held. An early second-century AD Greek inscription found near the Library of Celsus at Ephesus contains the word *audeitōrion* (from Lat. *auditorium*), that is, a place for hearing a performance.

Alarmed at the loss of business because of Paul's preaching and the resultant conversions, the silversmiths, led by Demetrius, fomented a riot among the Ephesians, who "rushed with one accord into the theater" (Acts 19:29). According to Acts 19:31, "Even some of the officials of the province, friends of Paul, sent him a message begging him not to venture into the theater." These were the Asiarchs, wealthy men who had the honor of serving as the priests of the imperial cult.

The great theater at Ephesus, which was begun in the first century BC and expanded by Claudius and Nero, could hold twenty-four thousand spectators in its sixty-seven rows of seats. An inscription reports the donation of 120 statues of Cupids and of Nike (Victory), which embellished the stage building. The continuing popularity of drama at Ephesus in the third century AD is evidenced by the wall paintings uncovered in the upper-class residences found in the houses on the slope of the hill above Curetes Street, which depict four scenes: two from Euripides's plays and two from Menander's plays.

On his way back to Jerusalem, Paul bypassed Ephesus and landed at Miletus, summoning the Ephesian elders to meet him there (Acts 20:15–17). The theater at Miletus is situated on a high hill overlooking the Theater Harbor. With a frontage of 140 meters (460 ft.), the large theater could accommodate fifteen thousand spectators. An inscription from Miletus records that in AD 48 Claudius wrote to the sacred victors and performers devoted to Dionysus to assure the actors that he would not only preserve their rights and privileges but would try to increase them. Two columns supported an awning, which shaded Marcus Aurelius and his wife Faustina when they visited Miletus in AD 164.

Theaters have been uncovered in excavations from the Seven Cities of Revelation (chs. 1–2), for example, at Pergamum (Rev 1:11), where there was a steeply slanted theater that could have accommodated ten thousand people. The scene building was located 122 feet below the top row of seats. The panorama from the theater over the plain was (and remains) truly breathtaking.

Of the two theaters at Laodicea (Rev 1:11; 3:14; cf. Col 4:13–16), the larger, north theater built on a hillside with forty-six rows of seats could have accommodated twelve thousand spectators. Names of civic associations and leading families were carved in the front row of seats. Holes indicate that posts held up an awning to shield the honored spectators from the sun.

At nearby Hierapolis (cf. Col 4:13) the well-preserved theater had fifty rows of seats and included a royal box. The twelve-foot-high stage is decorated with reliefs depicting episodes from the lives of Dionysus, Artemis, and Apollo. One relief portrays Chrysoroas, who was the personification of the sulfurous fumes of Hierapolis.

C. THE NEAR EASTERN WORLD

Dramas in the ancient Near East were generally religious reenactments of myths, and were not intended as entertainment.

In ancient Mesopotamia the Sumerian kings of the Ur III Dynasty (21st c. BC) played the role of the god Dumuzi (Akk. Tammuz), while a hierodule, or sacred prostitute, played the role of the goddess Inanna (Akk. Ishtar). Highly erotic love songs express the love of Dumuzi and Inanna. Their sacred drama culminated in an act of copulation, which was intended to stimulate the fertility of crops and animals by sympathetic magic.

A "Mourning Drama" was enacted by a procession of musicians and singers to the desert to mourn the death of Dumuzi. This included a plea for proper funerary offerings for Dumuzi, and ended with his sister offering to be a mother for him. A "Search and Fetching Drama," which played out at Uruk, has Dumuzi escorted in a joyous procession as his worshippers sing hymns of praise to him as the bringer of prosperity. During the New Year's *akitu* festival at Babylon, there may have been a dramatic reenactment of the conflict between Marduk, the god of Babylon, and Tiamat.

From Egypt we have a number of religious texts that have been interpreted by some scholars as liturgical "drama." The triumph of Horus over Seth/Apophis was celebrated in festivals of Osiris at Abydos and rituals at Edfu. Two texts from the Ptolemaic era have women enacting the roles of Isis and her sister Nephthys. A text preserved on a papyrus now in Berlin was to be read by a lector-priest, while two women representing the goddesses simply sat. The Bremner-Rhind Papyrus has two women singing solos and duets. (See O'Rourke, 409.)

D. THE GRECO-ROMAN WORLD

Greece

It was the Greeks who invented drama as we know it, developing tragedies and comedies and the classic form of the outdoor theater. Drama was dedicated to the god Dionysus (Bacchus), the god of wine, and developed out of the emotional celebrations promoted by drinking and drunkenness, which was conceived of as *ekstasis*, "being outside of oneself," and *enthousiasmos*, "being indwelt by the god" Dionysus. In myth Dionysus was followed by females called maenads and by half-human satyrs. During festivals, the statue of Dionysus was carried out of his temple and brought into the theater to witness the drama. An altar (*thymelē*) was placed in the midst of the *orchestra*, the circular dancing floor for the chorus. The *orchestra* (from *orcheisthai*, "to dance") also had a stand for the image of the god. At Athens the priest of Dionysus was given the main seat of honor in the front row.

The word "tragedy" comes from the Greek word *tragoidos*, "goat song," perhaps because such songs were sung as an accompaniment to a goat being sacrificed. In myth, the maenads tore apart a living goat and ate its raw flesh. In his *Poetics*, Aristotle stated that the goal of tragedy was to arouse the audience's pity and fear in a way that purged these feelings and provided relief in a *katharsis*. Aristotle believed that drama arose from the dithyrambs, enthusiastic choral songs in honor of the god Dionysus. The word "comedy" is derived from *kōmoidos*, the song of the riotous *kōmos*, a Dionysian parade of men costumed as satyrs.

The earliest forms of drama involved a chorus (*choros*) of fifty men, who sang and danced in a circular motion (*choreia*) on the *orchestra* to the accompaniment of a double flute (*diaulos*). In Athens the eponymous archon chose a wealthy individual to receive the honor of *chorēgia*, a kind of *leitourgia*, or duty, which meant that as the *chorēgos* he was responsible for the recruiting, feeding, and costuming of the chorus, and its training, which could last almost a year. These expenses ranged from three hundred to five thousand drachmas (a drachma was a day's wage), and by the end of the fourth century BC had become so expensive as to result in the system of *synchorēgia*, or the sharing of the expenses. Choruses were led by a *chorodidaskalos*. Tragedies employed choruses of first twelve and then fifteen *choreutai*; comedies used choruses of twenty-four members.

The word *theatron* ("theater") is derived from *theasthai*, "to look at." The *theatron* was an essential building in every Greek city and was used not only used for the performance of drama but also for public assemblies and trials. Greek theaters were built on the slopes of hills, such as the theater on the south slope of the Athenian Acropolis near the temple of Dionysus. The viewers (*theatai*) at first sat on *ikria*, or wooden seats, which were later replaced by stone seats. The two outermost sections were reserved for foreigners and latecomers. Only the *proedria*, the front-row seats of honor for priests and dignitaries, had backs. In criticizing Demosthenes for his fawning behavior before Philip of Macedon, Aeschines recalls:

For Demosthenes, fellow citizens, was senator for a year, yet he will be found never to have invited any other embassy to the seat of honour—nay, that was the first and the only time; and he placed cushions and spread rugs; and at daybreak he came escorting the ambassadors into the theatre, so that he was actually hissed for his unseemly flattery. (*Against Ctesiphon*, 76)

At first admission was free and there were no assigned seats, which caused problems:

People would rush for seats and even occupy places during the night before the performance, there were shoving matches, battles, and beatings. They decided then to sell seats so that each spectator would have his own seat and not cause a disturbance by guarding places or occupying them in advance and so that those who came late would not be deprived of a spot.
(Philochorus, *FGrH* 328F)

Ushers called *rhabdouchoi* ("staff bearers") kept order. Tickets in bronze, ivory, or bone that were decorated with symbols and letters designating the "wedges" (i.e., sections) of seats in a theater were sold for only two obols (one-third of a drachma). For those who could not afford even this, a fund called the Theoric Fund was created to pay for their tickets. Those who were granted the honor of *proedria* were given free admission to the front-row seats for honored guests; included in this group were the nine archons (leading officials), the ten generals, athletic victors, and orphans of men who had fallen in battle.

The earliest stage, or *proskēnion*, was made of wood. Behind it was the *skēnē* ("tent"), a backdrop with a large central door and two small doors on either side. The sense of "scenery" only became attached to the word *skēnē* in 296 BC. The best preserved Greek theater is that found at Epidauros in the Peloponnesus, which had fifty rows of seats that could accommodate fourteen thousand spectators. With its perfect acoustics, this theater is still used today for the performance of Greek plays.

The most famous theater of Greek drama was the theater of Dionysus on the south slope of the Acropolis. The earliest theater (6th c. BC) consisted of the orchestra, the circular dancing floor, with temporary seating on the hillside. Pericles (5th c. BC) enlarged the theater with *ikria*, wooden seating. In the fourth century BC stone seats were provided that could seat about fourteen thousand spectators. A permanent stone *skēnē* ("stage building"), forty-six meters long, was built, and columnar structures called *paraskēnia* projected toward the seats at either end. Special backed seats for dignitaries such as the priest of Dionysos were set in the front row. (See Wycherley, 204–11.)

Pericles was also credited with the erection of a covered theater (the *Ōideion*, or *Odeum*), which was built for the presentation of musical odes.

This large covered building—which measured 62.4 meters (205 ft.) by 68.6 meters (225 ft.)—was erected at the east side of the theater. It represented the pinnacle of architectural achievement in covering the maximum space possible at the time.

The Greeks used a number of devices to enhance the performances of their dramas. Some theaters had a *theologeion*, an upper platform for the appearance of gods. They also used a *mēchanē* or *geranos* ("crane") for the introduction of celestial figures like Bellophoron on his winged horse Pegasus. The Greek phrase *theos apo mēchanē* was later translated into Latin as *deus ex machina* to indicate an unexpected solution to a problematic situation. The Greeks sometimes used an *ekkyklēma*, a platform on wheels to bring in a murdered victim who had been killed offstage. As there was no drop curtain to indicate a change of scenery, the Greeks used the *periaktos*, a device with triangular prisms that were rotated to indicate a change of scenery. A person carrying a lamp would indicate that it was night. The Greeks used a *bronteion*, an urn with pebbles, to create the sound of thunder.

In 534 BC, Thespis, the leader of a dithyrambic chorus, traveled from Icaria to Athens, where he was the first to win a prize at the newly established dramatic festival, the City Dionysia. He stepped out of the chorus and spoke in the guise of a god, thus becoming the first *hypokritēs* ("actor"), a word that originally meant "one who answers." He carried his belongings in a wagon shaped like a ship, which he could transform into an improvised stage.

It was the tyrant Peisistratus who had established the City (or Great) Dionysia, a festival held every April, which featured the competitive presentation of tragedies. These were a form of poetry sung or spoken in lyric meters or in iambic trimeters to the accompaniment of a flute.

The first day of the Dionysia began with a *pompē*, or procession, with a trumpeter at the head, followed by maidens, and a priest leading a bull to be sacrificed. Three authors of tragedies were invited to present a trilogy and a satyr play (*satyrikon*). The order of presentation was determined by lot. In 486 BC a competition for comedies was also instituted in the City Dionysia. Three days were devoted to tragedies and one to comedies. Normally five comedies were presented. Counting all the actors (*choreutai*) and musicians, about one thousand Athenian citizens took part.

On the seventh day an *ekklēsia* was convened to assemble the judges, who were ten citizens chosen by lot. They would award first, second, and third prizes to the trilogies of tragedies. Awards were also voted to the author, the *chorēgos*, and the leading actor. The City Dionysia eventually became an attraction for the entire Greek world, second only to the Olympics.

A less important festival was the Rural Dionysia, held in mid-winter (December), at which *kōmoi*, or revelries, were performed in honor of Dionysus. Tragedies that were performed at the City Dionysia could be repeated at the Rural Dionysia. In the fourth century BC comedies were also performed in this festival. Another festival was the Lenaea, which took place in January. Begun in 442 BC, it at first featured only comedies; in 432 BC tragedies were also added. Aristophanes presented some of his plays at this event. As overseas travel was not possible during the Mediterranean winter, only Athenians attended these two festivals.

At Athens, during the City Dionysia, the audience—which included women, boys, and slaves who were all relegated to the upper sections—came to watch for hours, from dawn to dusk. Each tragedy took about an hour and a half, the satyr play lasted fifty minutes, and a comedy took about two hours. Vendors sold food and drink. Aristotle observed that "people who eat sweets at the theatre do so especially when the acting is bad" (*Eth. nic.* 10.5.4). Audiences expressed their displeasure by catcalling, kicking their seats, and even throwing stones.

One of the earliest tragedians of note was Phrynichus, whose play *The Sack of Miletus* was presented in 493 BC and depicted the Persian suppression of the Ionian Revolt. The Athenians fined him a thousand drachmas and forbade the reproduction of this play as it was too painful a reminder of their kinsmen's sorrows (Her. *Hist.* 6.21.10).

The three greatest tragedians of Classical Greece were Aeschylus, Sophocles, and Euripides, a number of whose plays are still being performed. Aeschylus (ca. 525–456 BC) first submitted a play in 499 and first won a victory in 484. He won first prize thirteen times. He added a second actor, *deuteragonistēs*, and developed lavish costumes. He was associated with the democratic leader Pericles, and fought the Persians at Marathon in 490 BC and at Salamis in 480. He was invited by the tyrant Hieron of Gela to travel to Sicily, where he died. His epitaph mentioned only his fighting at Marathon and not his plays.

Only seven of Aeschylus's ninety plays have been preserved: *The Persians, Seven against Thebes, Suppliant Women, Agamemnon, The Libation Bearers, The Eumenides,* and *Prometheus Bound.* His play *The Persians,* which was presented in 472 BC, just eight years after the Greek victory over the Persian navy at the bay of Salamis, gives us a vivid eyewitness account of this decisive battle. In the play Persian counselors form the chorus, and Atossa, the mother of Xerxes, is the protagonist; with the ghost of his father, Darius, she laments the hubris of Xerxes, who caused such a disaster for the Persians.

The *Oresteia,* our only surviving trilogy, was performed in 458 BC. *Agamemnon, The Libation Bearers,* and *The Eumenides* (i.e., the Furies) recount how Agamemnon, the king of Mycenae, is slain by his wife, Clytemnestra, and her lover Aegisthus upon his (Agamemnon's) return from the expedition to Troy. This creates a moral dilemma for their son, Orestes, who is obliged to avenge his father's death by killing his mother and her lover. After being pursued by the Furies, Orestes is defended by Apollo before the Areopagus, with Athena casting the deciding vote for acquittal.

Sophocles (496–406 BC) was by far the most successful tragedian in his day, winning first prize twenty-four times and second prize seven times. In 480, at the age of sixteen, he was chosen to be the leader of the chorus and a soloist in the celebration of the victory at Salamis. He was later elected as the treasurer of the Delian League, and from 441 to 439 served as a general with Pericles in quelling the rebellion of Samos.

Sophocles first produced tragedies in 471 BC, defeated Aeschylus in 468, and thirty years later defeated Euripides. He introduced a third actor, increased the chorus from twelve to fifteen, and developed scenic painting. He stressed the importance of oracles and prophecies, and developed the personality of his characters. We have only seven of his 123 plays: *Ajax, Antigone, Women of Trachis, Oedipus the King, Electra, Philoctetes,* and *Oedipus at Colonus.* Fragments of one of his satyr plays, *The Trackers,* have also been preserved.

In *Antigone,* performed in 442 BC, the heroine defies Creon, her uncle and the king of Thebes, by burying her brother, the rebel Polyneices. The king's stubbornness leads to Antigone's execution and the tragic suicide of both his wife and his son, Haemon, who was betrothed to Antigone.

Oedipus the King, Sophocles's masterpiece, was considered by Aristotle to be the model drama. Oedipus ("Swollen Foot") had been abandoned by his father, King Laius, to be killed because of a prophecy that had foretold that in the future Oedipus would kill and supplant his father. But his life was spared and he rose to manhood. Oedipus seeks from the blind seer Tiresias the reason for the plague that had fallen upon the city of Thebes. To his horror, Oedipus comes to realize the ghastly truth, that he has unwittingly killed his father and married the queen Jocasta, his mother. Jocasta hangs herself and Oedipus blinds himself.

Euripides (484–406 BC), the least popular of the three great tragedians in his lifetime, became the most popular in later generations. He won only five first prizes, and one of these was a posthumous award. His ideas were too radical for his age. Having been influenced by philosophers, he was skeptical of traditional religion. He was opposed to the Peloponnesian civil war between Athens and Sparta (431–404 BC), and was also a recluse. When he was nearly eighty, he was invited to the court of King Archelaus in Macedonia, where he died.

Eighteen of Euripides's ninety-two plays have been preserved: *Alcestis, Medea, Children of Heracles, Hippolytus, Andromache, Hecuba, Suppliant Women, Electra, Heracles, Trojan Women, Iphigenia among the Taurians, Ion, Helen, Phoenician Women, Orestes, Bacchae, Iphigenia at Aulis,* and a satyr play, *Cyclops*. Euripides was especially interested in the characters and the psychology of women. In *Medea*, performed in 431 BC, the princess from Colchis, east of the Black Sea, who had helped Jason gain the golden fleece is so outraged that he has abandoned her for another woman that she kills their two children.

Trojan Women (415 BC) was produced after the Athenians massacred the inhabitants of the island of Melos, and vividly depicts the tragic fate faced by those, especially women, who live in times of war. *The Bacchae* was presented after Euripides's death. It describes how the flesh of King Pentheus, who has intruded into the maenads' *orgia* ("secret rites") disguised as a woman, is torn apart by his wife and mother. In 53 BC, after the Parthians' calamitous defeat of the Roman legions led by the general Crassus, Crassus's head was used as a prop during a performance of *The Bacchae* at the Parthian court.

Old Comedy of the Classical Age of Athens, which involved satirical criticism of contemporary figures, is represented solely by Aristophanes (446–386 BC). As a member of the conservative class, he was sharply critical of the new modes of education promoted by the Sophists, which emphasized rhetoric. He also condemned the militaristic policy of Athens that prolonged the Peloponnesian War (431–404 BC) with Sparta. He depicted the gods as foolish and cowardly, but did not deny their power or the validity of the worship due them.

Eleven of the forty-four plays Aristophanes authored are preserved: *Acharnians, Knights, Wasps, Peace, Clouds, Birds, Lysistrata, Thesmophoriazousai, Frogs, Ekklēsiazousai,* and *Wealth*. In the *Acharnians*, performed in 425 BC, an ordinary farmer named Dikaiopolis ("Just City") who fails to interest the Athenians in discussing peace arranges a private peace for himself and his family. Aristophanes criticized Cleon, the leader of the War Party in Athens. *Knights*, produced the following year, is also an attack against Cleon, who is depicted as a leather seller from Paphlagonia who has befuddled the senile Demos ("People"). Oracles predict that Cleon will be replaced by a sausage seller who will restore the "good old days."

Clouds, produced in 418 BC, unfairly depicts Socrates as a sophist who taught the art of rhetoric in his *Phrontistērion* ("Thinkery"). Aristophanes contrasts the good old education with the corrupting influence of the new education. Strepsiades, who has incurred debts because of his son Pheidippides's passion for gambling on horse races, has him enrolled in Socrates's school. At the performance it is said that Socrates stood, so that all could see him. In Plato's *Apology*, Socrates blamed this play for stirring up the enmity that led to his death in 399 BC.

Lysistrata, peformed at the Lenaea in 411 BC, offered Greeks their first comic heroine, who led both Athenian and Spartan wives to deny sex to their husbands so they could come to their senses and stop fighting. The *Ekklēsiazousai*, or "Assembly-women," has the heroine Praxagora ("Woman Effective in Public") lead women to disguise themselves so they can take over the government. They abolish private property and even eliminate the family—radical, "communistic" ideas that would be promoted a decade later by Plato in his *Republic*. *Wealth*, produced in 388 BC, asked what would happen if Wealth were cured of his blindness, so that he rewarded only the deserving.

With the rise of Alexander and his successors (the Ptolemies, Seleucids, and Antigonids), the Greek democratic city-states were absorbed into kingdoms, and it was no longer possible to criticize the state. New Comedy concentrated on humorous plots of mistaken identities, slaves outwitting their masters, and young impoverished men pining for their girlfriends. We have the names of sixty-four writers of New Comedy, who produced a total of 1,400 plays.

Our only substantial representative of New Comedy is Menander (342–292 BC), who wrote more than one hundred comedies over a period of thirty-three years and who earned an immense reputation. In 1905 a papyrus was discovered at Aphroditopolis in Egypt with fragments of five of his plays. Then, in 1957, another papyrus was discovered that contained his play *Dyskolos* (*The Sullen Man*). Many quotations from his plays became proverbial, including "We live not as we wish but as we can" (*Lady of Andros*, frag. 50) and "He whom the gods love dies young" (derived from *The Double Deceiver*, via Plautus's *Bacchides*). "Evil communications corrupt good manners," the saying quoted by Paul in 1 Cor 15:33, is from *Thaïs*.

A *hypothesis*, or introduction, would at times be given to outline the plot beforehand. All actors in Greek drama were males who wore masks and who could also represent females. The masks were made of leather or cloth. Comic masks were grotesque. Comic actors wore *somatia*, flesh-colored tights, and stuffed themselves with cushions behind and in front, with a penis appended. In addition to an attached penis, satyrs also had a horse's tail. Young men were depicted with white linen garments, old women with sky-blue clothing, and harlots with yellow dress. Actors and chorus members needed to have strong voices. Non-speaking extras were called *doryphorēmata*, "spear carriers."

Beginning in the third century BC, actors were organized into guilds (sing. *synodos*) of Dionysiac artists (*hoi peri tōn Dionysōn technitai*). This included not only actors but also musicians, dancers, stage managers, and others. The head of the guild, often a flutist, would also function as a priest of Dionysus. The most important guilds were those of Delos, Athens, Thebes, Isthmia, Nemea, and Teos in Greece, and Ptolemais in Egypt. The members of these guilds traveled to perform at the palaces of rulers, at sanctuaries, and at Panhellenic festivals such as the Olympic games and the Pythian games at Delphi. They received exemption from taxes (*ateleia*) and military service, and were granted personal immunity (*asphaleia*). Their officers had the right to wear honorific dress in public, including purple garments (*porphyrophoria*) and those decorated with gold (*chrysophoria*).

Rome

The Etruscans, who lived north of Rome, were accustomed to sing Fescennine verses, which included dialogues and jests, at joyous events such as weddings and harvests. Such *saturae* ("mixtures"), which combined dancing and acting, were performed in the countryside in honor of Liber or Bacchus. Because of a plague in Rome in 367 BC, this form of entertainment was imported into Rome as a kind of offering to the gods to ward off the plague. This early stage entertainment then became popular.

Theatrical presentations became part of the official state holidays known as *ludi* ("games"), which were given in honor of the gods under the supervision of the state. The festivities would begin with a *pompa*, a parade including dancers and musicians and wagons called *tensae* that carried the images of the gods. This procession ended with a sacrifice.

The oldest games were the *Ludi Romani*, which were held in honor of Jupiter and which began in 214 BC. These included four days of theatrical presentations before the chariot races and gladiatorial contests. Other festivals included the *Ludi Apollinares*, begun in 212, and the *Ludi Megalenses*, begun in 204. These entertainments were the responsibility of elected officials such as the *aediles* and the *praetor urbanus*. By 200 BC about fifteen days were devoted to such shows; by the reign of Augustus the number had increased to about forty-five. The *ludi* increased in number through the Early Empire as generals and emperors created new holidays to celebrate their victories and birthdays. Eventually, by the mid-fourth century AD, there were as many holidays as working days. Of 175 days of holidays, ten were devoted to gladiatorial games, sixty-four to chariot racing, and 101 to dramatic presentations.

The earliest literary Latin author was Livius Andronicus, a Greek slave who translated Sophocles, Euripides, and Greek New Comedy into Latin. Livius Andronicus is, in fact, the first known translator in Western literature. It was in 240 BC that he presented for the first time a Latin adaptation of a Greek play in Rome. Such adaptations became known as *fabulae palliatae*; later original plays based on life in Italy were known as *fabulae togatae*.

The most successful adaptors of Greek New Comedy, and the only ones from whom we have complete plays preserved, are Plautus and Terence, both of whom wrote at the end of the third century BC when Rome was fighting the Second Punic War against Hannibal (218–201 BC). The name of Titus Maccus Plautus (254–184 BC) includes two nicknames, Maccus ("Clown") and Plautus ("Flat-footed"), that indicate that he had been an actor in farces. He skillfully adapted plays of the Greek New Comedy (Menander, Diphilus, Demophilus, and Philemon) for his Roman audience. Twenty-one of his 130 plays have been preserved: *Amphitryon, Comedy of Asses, The Pot of Gold, The Two Bacchises, The Captive, Casina, The Casket, Curculio, Epidicus, The Brothers Menaechmus, The Merchant, The Braggart Warrior, The Haunted House, The Girl from Persia, The Little Carthaginian, Pseudolus, The Rope, Stichus, Three Penny Day, Truculentus,* and *The Traveling Bag,* which is fragmentary.

Plautus's stock characters included the *senex,* an old man who is easily deceived; the lovesick *adulescens;* and the faithful and clever *servus.* The actors in Roman comedy wore thirty different types of masks, made of light wood or linen, and also wore wigs, white for old men, black for youths, and red for slaves. The wealthy wore purple garments, the poor red ones. A common plot involved slaves who outwit their masters with lies and impersonations. Plautus's plays also poked fun at the Greeks. *The Brothers Menaechmus,* which involved twin masters with twin servants and all kinds of confusion, inspired Shakespeare's *Comedy of Errors.* The Broadway play *A Funny Thing Happened on the Way to the Forum* is based on the work of Plautus.

In the prologue to his play *The Little Carthaginian,* Plautus addresses the audience as follows: "Matrons are to view this play in silence, laugh in silence, temper here their tuneful chirping, take their prittle prattle home, and not be a nuisance to their husbands here as well as there" (*Poen.,* prologue 32–35).

Publius Terentius Afer (190–159 BC), known as Terence, was a slave from Carthage who was brought to Rome and then freed by his master. He also adapted plays from Greek New Comedy, especially those by Menander. Only six of his plays have been preserved: *The Woman of Andros, The Self-Tormentor, Eunuchus, Phormio, Adelphi,* and *The Mother-in-Law.* At the presentation of the latter play, Terence complained that twice his audience had deserted him, once to see boxers and tightrope dancers, and another time to see gladiators. Terence's plays avoided farce, and displayed refinement and realism, which attributes were much admired in the Middle Ages and the Renaissance.

The Romans did not have much interest in adaptations of Greek tragedy, and though some were performed as late as the reign of Claudius, none has survived. What has survived are "drawing room" tragedies ascribed to Seneca, Nero's tutor, including *Hercules Furens, Troades, Phoenissae, Medea, Phaedra, Oedipus, Agamemnon, Hercules Otaeus,* and *Thyestes.* Seneca was possibly also the author of the play *Octavia*, which is about Nero's innocent wife who was condemned to death by the emperor. Seneca scorned the *ludi scaenici*, as those who attended these theatrical performances absorbed all the degraded behavior depicted in them.

For the longest time the Romans were content to erect temporary wooden seats and stages for their theatrical performances. According to Pliny the Elder, in 58 BC Marcus Scaurus built a temporary theater large enough to hold eighty thousand spectators. After Sulla established a Roman colony at Pompeii, the Romans transformed the Greek theater there into a Roman one, making this the oldest Roman theater.

Three stone theaters were built in Rome close to each other in the Campus Martius near the Tiber River. Pompey the Great built his theater in 55 BC; this was, and remains, the largest theater ever built. Pompey dedicated it to Venus Victrix, for whom he erected a temple at the top of the theater. It became a kind of tourist attraction for visitors to Rome. It could seat twenty-seven thousand spectators and was adjoined by a large garden portico, where the audience could lounge. It was near this portico that Julius Caesar was assassinated on the Ides of March, 44 BC.

The nearby theater of Balbus, which was built in 13 BC, could hold 7,700 spectators. In 11 BC Augustus dedicated a theater next to the temple of Apollo to his nephew Marcellus. This theater could seat fourteen thousand spectators. Its remains have been incorporated into a modern apartment building.

Unlike Greek theaters, which were built on the slopes of hills, Roman theaters were freestanding structures. Around the exterior, vaults provided space for *tabernae*, or shops. The seating area, the *cavea*, was supported by a concrete structure that was pierced by vaulted entrances (*vomitoria*). Vertical stairs, the *scalae*, divided the seating areas into *cunei*, wedges. The *cavea* was divided from bottom to top into three zones at times separated by parapets: *ima*, *media*, and *summa*, with the most favored seats located in the *ima cavea*.

The rigid hierarchy of Roman society was reflected in the assignment of seats in the theaters. Boxes (*tribunalia*) were built for the sponsors of the plays, the imperial family, and the Vestal Virgins. The semicircular Roman orchestra was provided with *bisellia*, broad seats for senators, magistrates, and dignitaries. Chairs were also provided for the images of the gods. In some cases *vela* or *velaria*, awnings, were provided for the privileged few. By a law of 67 BC, the first fourteen rows of seats were reserved for the equestrian class. Admission was free but one needed a circular ticket that indicated the designated seating area. An usher, or *designator*, would show a spectator to his proper seat. A person who sat in the wrong section would be asked to move.

The *media cavea* was reserved for plebeian citizens, provided they wore their white togas. The *summa cavea* was occupied by women and poor men without togas (*pullati*). The respectable married women (*matronae*) sat separately from the prostitutes (*meretrices*). Slaves were admitted but could not sit. The audience did not remain passive, but reacted quite vocally to the performances they attended. According to Cicero, "If an actor makes a movement that is a little out of time with the music or recites a verse that is one syllable too short or too long, he is hissed and hooted off the stage" (*Parad.* 3.26).

A Roman theater had a raised stage (*pulpitum*). Behind the stage the Romans built a concrete facade known as a *scaenae frons*, which would be two to three stories high. A good example is found in the well-preserved theater at Sabratha in Libya, which has a three-story *scaena frons* that was decorated with a total of ninety-six columns and numerous statues. Other well-preserved Roman theaters are found at Leptis Magna in Libya, Arausio in France, and Aspendos in southern Turkey.

Vitruvius, a Roman authority on architecture, describes an ingenious device for amplifying the actors' voices:

> Hence in accordance with these enquiries, bronze vases are to be made in mathematical ratios corresponding with the size of the theatre. They are to be so made that, when they are touched, they can make a sound from one to another of a fourth, a fifth and so on the second octave. . . . Thus by this calculation the voice, spreading from the stage as from a centre and sriking by its contact the hollows of the several vases, will arouse an increased clearness of sound, and, by the concord, a consonance harmonising with itself.
> (Vitruvius, *De architectura* 5.5.1–3)

Beginning in about 200 BC, Roman actors (*histriones*) were organized into companies (*greges*, lit., "flocks") led by a *dominus gregis*. They would be under the patronage of Apollo. Their organization was known as the *Parasiti Apollinis* ("Guests of Apollo"). Actors, who on the whole were non-Romans and non-citizens, suffered legal *infamia* ("dishonor"). There were exceptions, however, such as Roscius, a friendly rival of Cicero, who was made into an equestrian by Sulla.

By the first century BC, a popular form of drama was the presentation of the *pantomimus* ("one who imitates all things"), which featured a male soloist who used masks to portray male and female roles. In a kind of ballet, these virtuosos danced without speaking or singing, and by their bodily gestures, particularly those made with their hands, they conveyed well-known mythological stories. They would be accompanied by singing and music played by trumpeters, cymbalists, flutists, and even foot-cymbal players (*scabellarii*).

Stars such as Pylades of Cilicia and Bathyllus of Alexandria attracted passionate and even fanatical fans. According to Tacitus (*Ann.* 1.77), a riot that broke out in AD 15 between partisans of these two pantomime actors resulted in the death of several soldiers and a centurion. Caligula admired the pantomime actor Mnester so much that if anyone made the slightest noise during his performance, Caligula would have the individual dragged from his seat and flogged. Mnester became the lover of the empress Messalina and was put to death by Claudius. Nero banned pantomime actors because of riots in AD 56, but then recalled them three years later. His jealousy of the leading pantomime actor, Paris, led to the latter's execution. A later Paris, another pantomime actor, who became the lover of the empress Domitia, was executed by Domitian.

Quite different from pantomime was mime (Gk. *mimos*, Lat. *mimus*), which presented a caricature of daily life and which was played by actors and actresses without masks. Mime became the most popular form of dramatic entertainment in the Roman world, and it persisted until the Byzantine era (6th c. AD). The costumes and characters were taken from the lower classes. The mimes presented coarse plots through monologues, dialogues, and dances. Actors were described as effeminate with wavy hair. A "second fiddle" (*secundarium partium*) would repeat and distort the jokes of the principal actor.

Originating among the Dorian Greeks of Sicily and southern Italy, mime reached Rome by 211 BC. It was first given literary form in the first century BC by Decimus Laberius. We have the titles of forty-two mimes, but no Latin mime has survived. The titles include *Wealthy Overnight* and *Love Locked Out*. In the performances of the mimes *Death of Hercules* and *Laureolus the Highwayman*, criminals were substituted for actors and were in the first case immolated and in the second crucified on stage.

Erotic plots about adultery were most popular. When in exile, Ovid, the author of a guide to seduction, the *Art of Love*, lamenting that this and other offenses had caused Augustus to exile him to the Black Sea region, wrote: "What if I had written foul-jesting mimes which always contain the sin of forbidden love, in which constantly a well-dressed adulterer appears and the artful wife fools her stupid husband?" (*Tristia* 2.497–500). We learn of the emperor Heliogabalus that "when adultery was represented on the stage, he would order what was usually done in pretence to be carried out in fact" (*H.A., Elagabalus* 25.4–5). The nudity displayed by actresses was a major element of this coarse form of entertainment.

The Roman rulers maintained an ambivalent attitude toward theater and its actors. On the one hand, they despised the lowborn status of actors and especially actresses. On the other hand, they, like their people, were fascinated with theatrical performances. It became an expected responsibility for them to provide not only *panis* ("bread") but also *circenses* ("circuses"), or entertainment, and also to attend such public performances, which offered a gauge for the moods of the people. Petitions and requests were presented to the emperors at assemblies gathered in theaters. In the provinces imperial letters would be read in the theaters.

Julius Caesar was criticized for doing his correspondence while attending a theatrical performance. Augustus was an enthusiastic fan of the theater. He even wrote a drama, *Ajax*, though he destroyed it. On his deathbed, he said to his friends, "Since well I've played my part, all clap your hands and from the stage dismiss me with applause" (Suet. *Aug.* 99).

Because of the violence between factions of the leading pantomimes in AD 15, Tiberius banished actors from Italy. According to Suetonius, "When a quarrel in the theatre ended in bloodshed, he banished the leaders of the factions as well as the actors who were the cause of the dissension; and no entreaties of the people could ever induce him to recall them" (*Tib.* 37.2). Tiberius's successor, Gaius Caligula, recalled the actors and lavished huge sums upon his favorite actors. When the masses at a performance clamored for lighter taxes, Caligula threatened to execute anybody who continued to shout.

The most ardent devotee of the theater was the philhellene Nero, who not only performed in public himself, as a lyre player, an actor, and a singer, but urged other noble Romans to do so. As Tacitus reported in disgust, "Neither rank, nor age, nor an official career debarred a man from practising the art of a Greek or Latin mummer, down to attitudes and melodies never meant for the male sex" (*Ann.* 14.15).

According to Suetonius, Nero "made his début at Naples, where he did not cease singing until he had finished the number which he had begun, even though the theatre was shaken by a sudden earthquake shock" (*Nero* 20). Suetonius reports further that

> while he was singing no one was allowed to leave the theatre even for the most urgent reasons. And so it is said that some women gave birth to children there, while many who were worn out with listening and applauding, secretly leaped from the wall, since the gates at the entrance were closed, or feigned death and were carried out as if for burial. (*Nero* 23)

Nero enrolled himself among the *tragoedi*, and played the roles of Creon, Orestes, and Attis, and even some female roles such as that of Canace, who was in an incestuous relationship with her brother Macareus. Nero was emboldened during his tour of Corinth in AD 67–68 to compete not only in athletic events but also in dramatic competitions. Nero was noted for his stage fright, as well as for his jealousy of rivals. According to Verus Philostratus, when an Epirote actor refused to yield the stage to Nero without a huge bribe, Nero sent his henchmen to smash the man's throat with writing tablets of ivory.

A particular infamous event involving Nero's acting occurred during the catastrophic fire of Rome in AD 64, which led to the persecution of Christians, who were made scapegoats. According to Suetonius, Nero, while "viewing the conflagration from the tower of Maecenas and exulting, as he said, in 'the beauty of the flames,' . . . sang the whole of the 'Sack of Ilium [i.e., Troy],' in his regular stage costume [*suo scaenico habitu*]" (*Nero* 38).

E. THE JEWISH WORLD

The Jews in the Diaspora were the first to encounter Greek drama, especially in the city of Alexandria, where they occupied two of the city's five districts. In the *Letter of Aristeas*, which relates the legendary tale of the miraculous translation of the Hebrew Scriptures into the Greek Septuagint under Ptolemy II, the king asks the Jewish translators who had come from Israel, "What must be one's conduct in relaxation and leisure?" They counsel the king, "Be a spectator of entertainments which exercise restraint and keep before your eyes things in life done with decency and moderation" (*Let. Aris.* 284).

A most remarkable and significant play, written by a Jewish author named Ezekiel the Tragedian in Alexandria in the second century BC, is the *Exagōgē*. Sizable excerpts of 269 lines of this work, which was written in iambic trimeter, are cited by later, Christian authors, including Eusebius (in his *Preparatio evangelica* 9, quoting from Alexander Polyhistor), Clement of Alexandria (*Strom.* 1.23.155–156), and Eustathius. Together, these fragments of the *Exagōgē* represent the most extensive remains of any Hellenistic drama that have survived. Ezekiel demonstrates his familiarity with Aeschylus, Sophocles, and Euripides. Scholars believe that the play originally had five acts: (1) Moses's monologue and his meeting with the daughters of Raguel, (2) Moses's dream and its interpretation, (3) the burning bush and God's appearance, (4) a messenger's speech about the crossing of the Red Sea, and (5) the scouting report at the oasis of Elim and a description of the legendary phoenix bird. Scholars debate whether the play was written for a purely Jewish audience or for a mixed audience of Jews and Gentiles.

Philo (ca. 20 BC–ca. AD 50), the famous Jewish writer who lived in Alexandria, was not only familiar with the tragedies of Aeschylus and Euripides, which he quotes, but also attended theatrical performances, and refers to them in his expositions. In his essay *On Drunkenness*, Philo reports, "I have often when I chanced to be in the theatre noticed the effect produced by some single tune sung by the actors on the stage or played by the musicians. Some of the audience are so moved, that in their excitement they cannot help raising their voices in a chorus of acclamation" (*Ebr.* 177).

Josephus reports that when he landed at Puteoli in Italy, "I formed a friendship with Aliturus, an actor who was a special favorite of Nero and of Jewish origin. Through him I was introduced to Poppaea, Caesar's consort" (*Life* 16). In a satire Martial described an actor as follows: "So large a sheath covers Menophilus' penis that it would be enough by itself for all our comic actors. . . . (we often bathe together). . . . But while he was in a game in the middle of the sportsground with everybody watching, the sheath slipped off the poor soul; he was circumcised" (*Ep.* 7.82).

It was Herod the Great who first built theaters in Palestine, which he did to honor Augustus, thus demonstrating his full allegiance to Roman culture. According to Josephus, "For in the first place he established athletic contests every fifth year in honor of Caesar, and he built a theater in Jerusalem, and after that a very large amphitheater in the plain, both being spectacularly lavish but foreign to Jewish custom, for the use of such buildings and the exhibition of such spectacles have not been traditional (with the Jews)" (*Ant.* 15.268). Some reused *scalaria* stones with inscribed Greek letters that were found near the southwestern area of the temple platform in Jerusalem may possibly have belonged to this theater, though some scholars believe that the theater in Jerusalem was a temporary structure, as it is never mentioned again. Two ornamented discs found in excavations in the nearby Upper City have been interpreted by some scholars as theater tickets.

According to Josephus, "Herod also built a theatre of stone in the city [of Caesarea], and on the south side of the harbour, farther back, an amphitheatre" (*Ant.* 15.341). He also built a small theater near his winter palace at Jericho, and another theater in Samaria. In 2008 a small royal theater was discovered halfway up the slope of Herodium. Excavators also uncovered a royal box with scenes painted by Italian artists of the Nile River with animals and trees.

Ruins of Roman theaters have been uncovered in twenty-three cities in Palestine and in the Transjordan, most of them built in the second and third centuries AD. Some of the cities, such as Scythopolis, Gadara, Amman, and Gerasa, had more than one theater. The theaters range from small ones that could hold up to 1,500 (Hammat Gader), to medium theaters that could accommodate up to four thousand (Sepphoris, Samaria, Gadara), to large theaters that could hold up to eight thousand (Scythopolis). A theater uncovered at Tiberias could have held seven thousand spectators. The audience had a view of Mt. Hermon to the northeast.

Carved in the fifth row at the theater in Miletus in Asia Minor is a remarkable Greek inscription from ca. AD 200 that reads: *topos Eioudeōn tōn kai theosebion* ("Place of the Jews, who are also called God-fearing") (Deissmann, 451). Its interpretation is not clear: does it refer to Jews who were also known as "God-fearers," or does it refer to Jews *and* Gentile proselytes who were sympathetic to Judaism? One proposed interpretative translation is: "The place of the Jews [real Jews], who are called [are part of] the group of θεοσέβιοι [followers of the Most High God]" (Baker, 416).

While there are indications that some Jews watched drama, and that some even participated as actors, the rabbinic authorities who are quoted in the Talmud were unanimously opposed to the theater. The earlier rabbinic generation of the Tannaim were adamantly opposed to this Gentile custom because of its implicit, if not its explicit, association with idolatry. According to the Babylonian Talmud, "Our Rabbis taught: One should not go to theaters or circuses because entertainments are arranged there in honor of the idols. This is the opinion of R. Meir" (*b. ʿAbod. Zar.* 18b). In the same passage, the third-century AD Rabbi Shimon ben Pazi, alluding to Psalm 1, says: "Happy is the man that has not gone to theaters and circuses of idolaters and had not stood in the way of sinners." The later rabbinic generation of the Amoraim softened their opposition, by focusing on the fact that preoccupation with dramatic entertainment diverted one's attention from the study of the Torah.

Rabbi Abbahu had a dream about an actor nicknamed Pentakaka ("Five Evils"), whom he summoned and asked about his profession. Pentakaka answered: "Five sins that man does [I] do every day, hiring whores, cleaning up the theater, bringing home their garments for washing, dancing, and banging cymbals before them." Pentakaka then added that one day, as he was cleaning the theater, a woman whose husband had been imprisoned pleaded with him for help. He thereupon sold his bedstead and its cover and gave the woman the money from the sale. Rabbi Abbahu then concluded, "You are worthy of praying [for rain] and having your prayers answered" (*y. Taʿan.* 1.3E). According to Z. Weiss: "Although participation of Jewish women in the theatre cannot be fully deduced from this story, it nevertheless provides some information about how actors found employment in the theatre as well as demonstrating the active participation of women in the public shows" (Weiss, 629).

Some of the mimes made fun of the Jews, as we learn from proem 17 of *Lamentations Rabbah*:

> *They that sit in the gate talk of me* (Psalms 69.13). This refers to the nations of the world who sit in theaters and circuses. . . . They then take a camel into their theaters, put their shirts upon it, and ask one another, "Why is it mourn-

ing?," to which they reply, "The Jews observe the law of the Sabbatical year and they have no vegetables, so they eat this camel's thorns, and that is why it is in mourning." (*Lam. Rab.*, *petiḥtah* 17)

The Jewish antipathy to the theater is expressed in the Jerusalem Talmud as follows:

I give thanks to thee, Lord my God, God of my fathers, that you cast my lot with those who sit in the study hall and the synagogues, and you did not cast my lot with those who sit in the theaters and circuses. For I toil and they toil. I arise early and they arise early. I toil so that I shall inherit [a share of] paradise [in the world to come] and they toil [and shall end up] in a pit of destruction. (*y. Ber.* 4:2)

F. THE CHRISTIAN WORLD

Christian preachers, bishops, and councils unanimously condemned drama, especially that of the popular mimes, both for its association with pagan gods and for the immorality that it portrayed. Nevertheless, these performances continued unabated, providing popular entertainment for the masses through the centuries.

It was Tertullian of Carthage, the first great Latin Father with a thorough knowledge of Greek drama, who offered the most vehement and systematic attack on all pagan spectacles, including the theater. In his *Apologeticus* (15.2–3), he denounced the retelling of myths in the theater. In his *De spectaculis* (17.23), he argued that even to attend theatrical performances, whether or not any explicitly idolatrous ceremony was involved, was to support *idolatria*. He noted that all the Roman *ludi* were originally religious ceremonies to placate the gods. He observed: "They resemble each other also in their pomp, having the same procession [*pompa*] to the scene of their display from temples and altars, and that mournful profusion of incense and blood, with music of pipes and trumpets" (*Spec.* 10).

According to Tertullian, the very practice of acting involved a lie: God, he said, "never will approve any putting on of voice, or sex, or age; He never will approve pretended loves, and wraths, and groans, and tears. Then, too, as in His law it is declared that the man is cursed who attires himself in female garments [Deut 22:5], what must be His judgment of the pantomime, who is even brought up to play the woman!" (*Spec.* 23).

The emperor Julian "the Apostate" (AD 361–363) rejected Christianity and briefly tried to revive paganism. Julian himself had a dim view of the popular theater. He commanded, "Therefore let no priest enter a theatre or have an actor or a chariot-driver for his friend; and let no dancer or mime even approach his door" (*Letter to a Priest*, 362c). According to Sozomen's *Ecclesiastical History*, when Julian banned Christians from teaching the pagan classics, since they did not believe in their gods. Apolinarius, a bishop of Syria, "employed his great learning and ingenuity in the production of a heroic epic on the antiquities of the Hebrews to the reign of Saul, as a substitute for the poem of Homer. . . . He also wrote comedies in imitation of Menander, tragedies resembling those of Euripides, and odes on the model of Pindar" (5.18).

In the east the most famed theater was at Antioch in Syria. It was in this city, and later at Constantinople, that the famed bishop and preacher John Chrysostom (354–407) tirelessly inveighed against the popular drama that so tempted many in his flock. Chrysostom rebuked their fawning enthusiasm:

> But if they be not abominable, go down unto the stage, imitate that which you praise, or rather, do thou merely take a walk with him that is exciting that laugh. Nay, you could not bear it. Why then bestow on him so great honor? Yea, while the laws that are enacted by the Gentiles would have them to be dishonored, you receive them with your whole city, like ambassadors and generals, and dost convoke all men, to receive dung in their ears. (*Hom. Matt.* 37.7)

He contrasted his listeners' listlessness in attending church when the church became too hot in the summer with the enthusiasm of those who went to the theater: "Do you not see those sitting in the theater, how they sweat as the sun beats down upon their bare heads?" (cited in Leyerle, 14).

Chrysostom considered theaters "abysses of vice" (*ta tēs ponērias barathra*). In particular, he condemned the lascivious mimes for their corrupting influence. As some in his flock talked and laughed during the service, John spoke out: "Excuse me, is this a theatrical show here?" and "Yes indeed, I think it is the theater that teaches such behavior" (*Hom. in Acta Apost.* 24.4; cited in Leyerle, 66). What was also insidious was that theater-going created a desire in churchgoers for entertainment rather than edification from the pulpit. When his own congregation began to applaud John's eloquence, he announced a rule enjoining silence, but even this announcement was greeted by great applause.

Augustine condemned the theater because it was rooted in paganism, it encouraged bad behavior, and it interfered with Christians' pursuit of God. However, in his *Confessions*, Augustine admitted his great enthusiasm for the theater as a young man, before his conversion. In his voluminous writings he refers to the theater about two hundred times, especially in *The City of God, Concerning the Teacher*, and *On Christian Doctrine*, in addition to his *Confessions*. In the *Confessions* he recalls that when in Carthage, "stage-plays [*spectacula theatrica*] also drew me away; sights full of representations of my miseries and of fuel to my fire" (*Conf.* 3.2.2). There was nothing that proved to Augustine the powerful hold of the theater on the populace more than the behavior of refugees from the sack of Rome in AD 410, who came to Carthage and were interested in nothing else but attending theatrical spectacles (*Civ.* 1.33).

Jacob of Serugh (451–521) produced a number of homilies in Syriac denouncing the theater. In Homily 3 he preached: "The fruits (of the spectacles of the theatre) are these as thou too hast learnt through the sight of them: dancing, amusement and music, the miming of lying tales; Teaching which destroys the mind; responses (or chorus chants) which are not true; troublesome and confused sounds" (Moss, 105).

In Homily 4 Jacob reports the following remark from a church member in defense of his attendance at the theater: "I do not go that I may believe, but I go that I may laugh. And what do I lose on account of this, since I laugh and do not believe? (As for) those things in the stories which are mimed concerning the tales of the idols, I know that they are false; and I see them—laughing. What shall I lose on account of this?" (Moss, 109).

Ecclesiastical councils condemned the theater and imperial laws regulated actors and actresses, though this had little effect on the popularity of drama among the masses. The fourth and fifth canons of the Council of Elvira (ca. AD 300), the fifth canon of Arles (AD 314), and the tenth canon of Nicaea (AD 325) all decreed that anyone connected with the pantomime must abandon this profession to be eligible for baptism. Canon 54 of the Council of Laodicea (AD 381) stipulated: "Members of the priesthood and of the clergy must not witness the plays at weddings or banquets; but, before the players enter, they must rise and depart." The Third Council of Carthage (AD 397) offered reconciliation for baptized stage players (*histriones*) who had seen the error of their ways. The Fourth Council of Carthage (AD 398) excommunicated those who went to the theater instead of to church on holy days. A law of 425 declared: "On the following occasions all amusements of the theaters and the circuses [*theatrorum adque circensium voluptas*] shall be denied throughout all cities to the people thereof, and the minds of Christians and of the faithful shall be wholly occupied in the worship of God: namely, on the Lord's day, which is the first day of the week, on the Natal Day and Epiphany of Christ, and on the day of Easter and of Pentecost" (*Cod. Theod.* 15.5.5; Pharr, 433).

Pagan mimes were used to mock Christians. During the Arian crisis, Eusebius reported:

> Not only the prelates of the churches … but the people themselves were completely divided, some adhering to one faction and others to another. Nay, so notorious did the scandal of these proceedings become, that the sacred

matters of inspired teaching were exposed to the most shameful ridicule in the very theaters of the unbelievers. (*Vit. Const.* 2.61.5)

The most frequent subject of parody was the rite of Christian baptism. In some such cases not a few mime actors were suddenly converted and became martyrs. The most renowned example is that of St. Gelasinos, later the patron saint of actors in the Middle Ages, who was converted during the performance of a mime in the third century AD at Heliopolis (Baalbek) in Phoenicia. Upon his confession of faith, the audience stoned him to death. St. Genesius experienced his dramatic conversion when performing in a mime before the emperor Diocletian in AD 305. Saint Porphyry, who was converted during a mime performance before Julian the Apostate (AD 361–363), was ordered to be executed by the emperor. Similar stories circulated about St. Ardalion, St. Babylas, and St. Gaianos.

By the late third century AD stage performers (*mimes, histriones, technitai Dionysiou*) were incorporated into *collegia necessaria* or *corpora obligata*, which performed a necessary public service. Their children were obliged to follow the vocations of their parents. To be baptized, a converted mime needed a certificate from the bishop and a public official. A decree of AD 381 stipulated the following for an actress who had been released from her profession because she had professed to become a Christian but had subsequently behaved in an unworthy manner: "She shall be dragged back to the stage, and without hope of any absolution she shall remain there, until, a ridiculous old woman, unsightly through old age [*donec anus ridicula senectute deformis*], she cannot, indeed, even then receive absolution, although she could not then be anything else than chaste" (*Cod. Theod.* 15.7.8; Pharr, 434).

Margarito, the leading mime actress of Antioch, was beautiful, wealthy, and much admired. When she came to church on Easter and heard the sermon of Nonnos, a bishop from Egypt, she was convicted of her sinfulness and begged to be baptized. Nonnos replied: "My daughter, the canons of the church require that one should not baptize a prostitute without her having some sponsors, otherwise she may continue in her old ways" (Brock and Harvey, 50). When a sponsor was found, she was baptized, assumed her birth name, Pelagia, put on a hair shirt, and lived as a monk. Her gender was not discovered until her death. That this may not simply be a legend is indicated by a sermon of Chrysostom that refers to the conversion of an outstanding actress for whom many men had, in trying to impress her, ruined themselves financially.

The most significant conversion of a mime actress was that of Theodora, who, according to the court historian Procopius's *Secret History*, began performing as a child of a theatrical family. When she was old enough, she not only brazenly bared herself completely, but performed sexual acts on the stage. She went to North Africa as the mistress of an official, who abandoned her. She then made her way to Egypt, where under the influence of Monophysites she experienced a conversion. Returning to Constantinople, Theodora met Justinian, a general, who fell in love with her. Augustus, in his *Leges Iulia et Papia Poppaea* (AD 9), had prohibited all freeborn Romans from marrying an actress or a woman who was the daughter of actors or actresses. To enable his nephew to marry a former actress, the emperor Justin repealed this law, allowing Theodora's marriage to Justinian in 525. Justinian and Theodora became the most significant rulers of the Byzantine era. It was Justinian who closed the theaters and other pagan institutions in AD 529.

BIBLIOGRAPHY: J. Allen, "Ezekiel the Tragedian on the Despoliation of Egypt," *JSP* 17 (2007), 3–19; P. Arnott, *Greek Scenic Conventions in the Fifth Century B.C.* (1962); P. Arnott, *An Introduction to the Greek Theatre* (1959); M. Baker, "Who Was Sitting in the Theatre at Miletos?" *JSJ* 36 (2005), 397–416; R. A. Batey, "Jesus and the Theatre," *NTS* 30 (1984), 563–74; M. T. Boatwright, "Theaters in the Roman Empire," *BA* 53 (1990), 184–92; S. P. Brock and S. A. Harvey, trans., *Holy Women of the Syrian Orient* (1998); R. Browning, *Justinian and Theodora* (1971); E. Csapo and W. J. Slater, *The Context of Ancient Drama* (1995); A. Deissmann, *Light from the Ancient East* (1965 repr. of 1922 ed.); D. Dox, *The Idea of the Theater in Latin Christian Thought: Augustine to the Fourteenth Century* (2004); G. Duckworth, *The Nature of Roman Comedy* (1952); P. Easterling and E. Hall, ed., *Greek and Roman Actors: Aspects of an Ancient Profession* (2002); D. Elm, "Mimes into Martyrs: Conversion on Stage," in *The Changing Face of Judaism, Christianity, and Other Greco-Roman Religions in Antiquity*, ed. I. Henderson and G. Oegema (2006), 87–100; M. Erasmo, *Roman Tragedy: Theatre to Theatricality* (2004); H. P. Foley, *Female Acts in Greek Tragedy* (2001); M. P. Foley, "A Spectacle to the World: The Theatrical Meaning of St. Augustine's *Soliloquies*," *JECS* 22 (2014), 243–60; D. W. J. Gill, "Erastus the Aedile," *TynBul* 40 (1989), 293–301; A. E. Haigh, *The Attic Theatre* (1968); J. Hanson, *Roman Theater-Temples* (1959); G. C. Izenour, *Roofed Theaters of Classical Antiquity* (1992); M. Jacobs, "Theatres and Performances as Reflected in the Talmud Yerushalmi," in *The Talmud Yerushalmi and Graeco-Roman Culture*, ed. P. Schäfer (1998), 327–47; T. Jacobsen, "Religious Drama in Ancient Mesopotamia," in *Unity and Diversity: Essays in the History, Literature, and Religion of the Ancient Near East*, ed. H. Goedicke and J. J. M. Roberts (1975), 65–97; H. Jacobson, *The Exagoge of Ezekiel* (1983); S. N. Kramer, *The Sacred Marriage Rite* (1969); P. Lanfranchi, *L'Exagoge d'Ezéchiel le Tragique* (2006); B. Leyerle, *Theatrical Shows and Ascetic Lives:*

John Chrysostom's Attack on Spiritual Marriage (2001); C. Moss, trans. and ed., *Jacob of Serugh's Homilies on the Spectacles of the Theatre* (2010); P. F. O'Rourke, "Drama," in *The Oxford Encyclopedia of Ancient Egypt*, ed. D. B. Redford (2001), 1.407–10; P. Petitmengin et al., *Pélagie la pénitente: Métamorphoses d'une légende* (1981); C. Pharr, trans., *The Theodosian Code and Novels, and the Sirmondian Constitutions* (2012 repr. of 1952 ed.); A. Pickard-Cambridge, *The Dramatic Festivals of Athens* (1968); A. Retzleff, "John Chrysostom's Sex Aquarium: Aquatic Metaphors for Theater in Homily 7 on Matthew," *JECS* 11 (2003), 195–207; C. Roueché, *Performers and Partisans at Aphrodisias in the Roman and Late Roman Periods* (1993); C. Schnurr, "The *lex Julia theatralis* of Augustus: Some Remarks on Seating Problems in Theatre, Amphitheatre and Circus," *Liverpool Classical Monthly* 17 (1992), 147–60; C. C. Schnusenberg, *The Relationship between the Church and the Theatre* (1988); F. Sear, *Roman Theatres: An Architectural Study* (2006); A. Segal, *Theatres in Roman Palestine and Provincia Arabia* (1995); G. M. Sifakis, *Studies in the History of Hellenistic Drama* (1967); M. S. Silk, *Aristophanes and the Definition of Comedy* (2001); W. J. Slater, ed., *Roman Theater and Society* (1996); A. Stock, "Jesus, Hypocrites, and Herodians," *BTB* 16.1 (1986), 3–7; J. M. Walton, *Greek Theatre Practice* (1980); T. B. L. Webster, *Greek Theatre Production* (1970); Z. Weiss, "Theatres, Hippodromes, Amphitheatres, and Performances," *OHJDL* 623–40; P. Wilson, *Athenian Institution of the Khoregia* (2000); R. E. Wycherley, *The Stones of Athens* (1978).

EMY

See also ATHLETICS, DANCE, and SPECTACLES.

D̲REAMS

Images or sequences of thoughts received during sleep and recalled upon wakening were believed to be significant by many ancient peoples. These could contain either clear messages from a supernatural source or enigmatic symbols that needed interpretation. Many societies did not clearly distinguish between dreams experienced at night and visions received during the day.

A. THE OLD TESTAMENT

The Hebrew word for "dream," *ḥălôm*, occurs over sixty times in the OT, and the cognate verb *ḥālam*, "to dream," occurs about thirty. Words for "vision" include *mar'ê* and *ḥāzôn*. Job 20:8 refers to "a vision of the night" (*ḥezyôn lāylâ*). Isaiah and Ezekiel see visions, but it is not reported that they experienced dreams. In contrast to Moses, with whom the Lord speaks "face to face," we read in Num 12:6, "When there is a prophet among you, I, the LORD, reveal myself to them in visions, I speak to them in dreams." According to Elihu, God gives his warnings in dreams (Job 33:15–16). Saul is distressed when God "did not answer him by dreams or Urim or prophets" (1 Sam 28:6).

Dreams figure prominently in the book of Genesis. God sends dreams to Abraham (Gen 15:1–6), Abimelek (Gen 20:3–7), Isaac (Gen 26:24), Jacob (Gen 28:10–22; 31:10–13; 46:1–5), Laban (Gen 31:24), Joseph (Gen 37:5–11), pharaoh's butler (Gen 40:5–14), pharaoh's baker (Gen 40:16–22), and pharaoh himself (Gen 41:5–8). Joseph is given the gift of interpretation to understand the significance of the dreams of the butler, the baker, and the pharaoh (Gen 40:8).

God appears to Balaam, the seer hired by Balak, king of Moab, to curse the Israelites (Num 22:20). The remarkable Aramaic inscription on a plaster wall from Tell Deir ʿAlla in Jordan refers to Balaam in this regard: "The gods came to him at night, And he beheld a vision [*mḥzh*] in accordance with El's utterance" (COS 2.27:142). An invading Midianite dreams of a round loaf of barley that tumbled into the camp and struck and overturned their tent, which his companion interprets to signify an attack led by Gideon (Judg 7:13–14). In a time when visions (ḥāzôn) were rare (1 Sam 3:1), the young boy Samuel receives a vision (marʾāh; 1 Sam 3:15) from God that reveals God's judgment against Eli's house.

The only account in the OT of activity that resembles a practice known from elsewhere in the ancient Near East that is referred to as "incubation" (which involves offering prayers and sacrifice and then sleeping in a sacred space to solicit a message from the deity) is the story of Solomon's dream at Gibeon (1 Kgs 3:4–15||2 Chr 1:6–12).

Dreams are prominent in the book of Daniel, including the dreams of Nebuchadnezzar (Dan 2 and 4), which the court "magicians, enchanters, sorcerers and astrologers" (Dan 2:2) cannot interpret, but which Daniel, by his God-given insight, can (Dan 2:27–28). Daniel himself has dreams and visions (Dan 7–8), including his famous "vision at night" (Dan 7:2), in which he sees "one like a son of man, coming with the clouds of heaven" (Dan 7:13), an important messianic reference.

The book of Isaiah describes a hungry man dreaming of eating and a thirsty man dreaming of drinking (Isa 29:8). In some biblical passages, dreams are characterized as evanescent and meaningless (Job 20:8; Ps 73:20; Eccl 5:7) or frightening (Job 4:13–15; 7:13–14; 33:15–16). Misleading dreams that encouraged apostasy are condemned by Deuteronomy (13:1–5). False dreams are repeatedly condemned by Jeremiah (Jer 23:25–27, 32; 27:9; 29:8), but the prophet himself records a prophetic dream (Jer 31:26). Though Zechariah condemns dreamers who speak lies (Zech 10:2), he himself has a vision in the night (Zech 1:8).

Joel prophesies that in the messianic age, after the pouring out of God's spirit, "Your sons and daughters will prophesy, your old men will dream dreams, and your young men will see visions" (2:28), a verse that is cited by Peter after the Holy Spirit comes upon the early Christians in Jerusalem on the day of Pentecost (Acts 2:17).

B. THE NEW TESTAMENT

While visions (Gk. horama, horasis, optasia) are mentioned in a number of NT books (Matthew, Luke, Acts, 2 Corinthians, and Revelation), the Greek word for "dream," onar, occurs only in Matthew—five times in the nativity narrative (with reference to dreams experienced by Joseph in which he is encouraged, warned, or given a command, and with reference to a dream in which the magi are warned; Matt 1:20; 2:12, 13, 19, 22), and once with respect to a dream that afflicts Pilate's wife and that prompts her to warn her husband to have nothing to do with Jesus, "that innocent man" (Matt 27:19).

The important call of the "man from Macedonia" bidding Paul and his companions to cross over from Asia to Europe comes in a vision (*horama*) in the night (Acts 16:9). When Paul is discouraged at the lack of response to his preaching at Corinth, the Lord appears to him at night in a vision to encourage him (Acts 18:9–10), with the result that he stays in the city for a year and a half (Acts 18:11). After Paul is rescued from a Jewish mob in the temple at Jerusalem, the Lord stands by him at night and promises that Paul will bear testimony to the Lord at Rome itself (Acts 23:11). During the frightening storm before the shipwreck at Malta, God's angel reassures Paul at night that no lives will be lost and that he will stand before Caesar, i.e., Nero (Acts 27:23–24).

C. THE NEAR EASTERN WORLD

Mesopotamia

The word for "dream" in Sumerian is MA.MÚ or Ù. The Akkadian word for "dream," *šuttu*, is related to the word for "sleep," *šittu*. The phrase *tabrīt mūši* designates a "nocturnal vision"; the word *munattu* designates a waking dream.

Dreams were thought to come from a variety of sources, including the dream gods Mamu and Zaqiqu, whose name is derived from the verb *zâqu*, "to blow." Dreams could come from demons, sorcery, and one's personal god, i.e., a deity who acted as a "guardian angel" to an individual. One text reads, "If a man cannot recall the dream which he sees (it means that) his personal god is angry with him" (Zgoll, 299). Another individual complained to his personal god, "While I dream of you constantly, you [act] as if we have never met or as if I don't exist. And you don't resolve my problem" (Sasson, 283n.2).

In the Akkadian versions of the *Gilgamesh Epic* the hero learns from a sequence of two dreams that the gods are sending the wild man Enkidu to tame him. Later, after the two adversaries have become friends, Enkidu makes a "house of Zaqiqu" so that Gilgamesh may obtain dreams from the gods (IV.42–54). The hero Atraḥasis learns through a dream that the gods are sending a great flood (XI.186–187).

Dreams are very prominent in royal inscriptions. The oldest example comes from the Sumerian "Stele of the Vultures" of Eanatum of Lagash

(25th c. BC). The most extensive Sumerian dream accounts come from Gudea of Lagash (22nd c. BC). For example, in one text it is recorded of Gudea: "On that day in a night vision (he saw) his king, Gudea saw the lord Ningirsu, (and) he commanded him to build his temple" (Gudea Cylinder A i.17–19; *COS* 2.155:419).

The rise of Sargon of Akkad (23rd c. BC) is narrated in a Sumerian text that relates that Sargon, who was the cupbearer for king Urzababa of Kish, had a premonitory dream. He dreamt that a goddess was drowning his master in a river of blood.

From the Old Babylonian period (18th c. BC) we have a series of letters from Mari reporting dreams to the king. The prominent role played by women in this connection is particularly interesting. Women called *šāʾilātu*, from the verbal root "to question," served as interpreters. The dreamers included women as well as men, royalty as well as commoners. As the interpretation of dreams was considered a secondary form of divination, dream reports had to be checked against the results of hepatoscopy, the examination of sheep livers. Most ominous was the dream of an elite woman, Addu-duri: "In my dream, I entered the chapel of the goddess Belet-ekallim; but Belet-ekallim was not in residence! Moreover, the statues before her were not there either. Seeing this, I broke into weeping" (Sasson, 286). When the king himself had a dream, he referred it to his expert dream interpreters.

A poignant example of the solicitation of information through a dream is found in the Hittite Plague Prayer of Mursili II (14th c. BC), in which the king asked for the cause of the plague that was ravaging his kingdom: "May the gods, my lords, manifest their providence, and may someone there see it in a dream. And may the reason that people are dying be discovered" (*ANET*, 394–96).

Neo-Assyrian kings placed a high regard on dreams. Esarhaddon proclaimed, "Favourable signs in dreams and ominous utterances (*egirrê*) in order to secure the foundation of my throne and the length of my reign were portended on me" (Fales and Lanfranchi, 108). When this king invaded Egypt, among the prisoners he brought back were Egyptian dream interpreters, *ḫardibi*. His successor, Ashurbanipal, reported that during an Elamite invasion, he lay prostrate at the foot of Ishtar in her temple, to plead for her help. "During the night in which I appeared before her, a *šabrû*-priest lay down and had a dream. He awoke with a start and then Ishtar caused him to see a nocturnal vision. He reported to me as follows ..." (*ANET*, 606).

The last Neo-Babylonian king, Nabonidus, recorded having had some notable dreams:

In the . . . dream, when my royal predecessor Nebuchadnezzar and one attendant (appeared to me) standing on a chariot, the attendant said to Nebuchadnezzar, "Do speak to Nabonidus, that he should report to you the dream he
has seen!" Nabonidus replied to Nebuchadnezzar, "In my dream I beheld with
joy the Great Star, the moon and Marduk (i.e., the planet Jupiter) high up on
the sky and it (the Great Star) called me by my name!" (*ANET*, 310)

Nabonidus and his remarkable mother, who lived to be over one hundred, both had dreams in which they were commanded to rebuild the
temple of Sin at Harran. In his first regnal year, Nabonidus had a dream
in which Marduk told him: "Nabonidus, king of Babylon, carry bricks on
your riding horse, rebuild Ehulhul and cause Sîn, the great lord, to establish his residence in its midst" (Sippar Cylinder; *COS* 2.123A:311).

Dream interpreters had available a reference work written on eleven
tablets called *Zaqiqu*, which contained a collection of dream omina (pl. of
Lat. omen, "prognostication"). Such reference works as this date from at
least 1700 BC. The omina consist of a protasis (an "if" clause) followed by
an apodosis ("then" clause). For example, "If his urine expands in front of
(his) penis [and] he does obeisance in front of his urine: he will beget a son
and he (i.e., the son) will be king" (Oppenheim, 265). Among nightmare
demons who were feared were the male *lilû* (an incubus) and the female
lilītu or *ardat lili* (a succubus), who seduced women and men, respectively,
in their sleep, and also attacked their babies.

A man asked the dream-god Anzagar: "Turn to good luck the evil
which you did to me (i.e., sending a bad dream)!" (Butler, 141). An evil
dream could be transferred to a clod of earth, and an incantation recited
over it: "Just as I will throw you (O Clod) into (running) water, and you
will be soaked, you will disintegrate . . . (so) may the evil of this dream
which [I] saw be thrown into water just like you!" (Butler, 180).

Egypt

In Egypt the word for "dream" was *rsw.t*, which is derived from the
verb *r(i)s*, "to be watchful" and which was written with the determinative
of an open eye. The *wrs*, "that which keeps awake," was a "wooden pillow,"
a headrest that the Egyptians believed facilitated dreaming. The ancient
Egyptians likened a sleeper to the sun in its diurnal rather than its nocturnal cycle. A person in his sleep was believed to reach the next world and
to mingle with the gods. Dreams were given by the gods: "He [the god]
made for them . . . dreams by night as well as day" (*The Instruction for King
Meri-ka-Re*; *ANET*, 417).

Almost all of the surviving records of specific dreams from Egypt are found in royal inscriptions. The earliest example comes from an inscription from Elephantine dating to the Middle Kingdom reign of Sesostris I (20th c. BC) and describes a dream in which the goddess Satet asked the pharaoh to look after her cult.

Amon, the god of Thebes, encouraged Amenhotep II (1427–1396 BC) with a dream that promised him victory in battle: "The majesty of this august god, Amon, Lord of the Throne of the Two Lands, came before his majesty in a dream to give valor to his son, Aa-khepru-Re" (*ANET*, 246).

One of the most famous dreams from ancient Egypt is that of Thutmose IV (r. 1396–1386 BC) in which he was commanded to clear the Sphinx of the encroaching sand:

> One of these days it happened that the King's Son Thut-mose came on an excursion at noon time. Then he rested in the shadow of this great god [i.e., the Sphinx]. Sleep took hold of him, slumbering at the time when the sun was at (its) peak. . . . [Then the god Harmarkhis, who was in the Sphinx declared:] "Behold, my state was like (that of) one who is in *need*, and my whole body was going to pieces. The sands of the desert, that upon which I had been, were encroaching upon me." (*ANET*, 449)

When Egypt was attacked by the Libyans and Sea Peoples in the reign of Merneptah (1213–1204 BC), this pharaoh was encouraged by the vision of a huge statue of the god Ptah, who handed him a sword. The last ruler of the 25th (Cushite) Dynasty, Tantamun (664–656 BC), was also encouraged by a dream: "In the year 1 . . . his majesty saw a dream by night: two serpents, one upon his right, the other upon his left. . . . Then they answered him saying, 'Thine is the Southland, take for thyself also the Northland. The Two Goddesses shine upon thy brow, the land is given to thee, in its length and breadth'" (*ARE*, 4.469). The two serpents or cobras (*uraei*) that adorned the Cushite crown represented the South (= Cush; that is, Nubia, or the Sudan) and the North (= Egypt).

The so-called "Famine Stela," which is from the Ptolemaic Era, purports to describe a dream seen by Djoser (ca. 2700 BC) after a period of seven years of famine:

> As I slept in life and satisfaction, I discovered the god standing over against me. . . . He revealed himself to me, his face being fresh. . . . "I am Khnum, thy fashioner. . . . The Nile will pour forth for thee, without a year of cessation or laxness for any land. Plants will grow, bowing down under the fruit. . . . The starvation year will have gone, and (people's) borrowing from their granaries will have departed." (*ANET*, 32)

The expert dream interpreters at the Egyptian royal court were the *ḥry-ḥb ḥry tp* (commonly abbreviated *ḥry tp*, from which is derived Hebrew *ḥarṭōm*, "soothsayer"), literally, "he who carries the festival scroll, who is at the top," that is, "chief lector priest" (see Ritner, 220). These individuals were able to consult so-called "dream books." The earliest preserved example is Chester Beatty Papyrus III (dated to the 13th c. BC), which contains about two hundred examples of dreams and their interpretations. In this dream manual, dreams are designated as either good or bad. The latter are marked in red, a color associated with the evil god Seth. While some of the interpretations (which are written as apodoses following the descriptions of the dreams) defy rational explanation, others seem to have been based on wordplay between words that sound similar but have different meanings. Some examples are:

[If a man sees himself in a dream and the following occurs:]

"his mouth full of earth—GOOD; eating (the possessions of) his townsfolk." (*Chester Beatty Papyrus III*, recto 2,20)

"eating donkey flesh (*iwf n ʿ3*)—GOOD; it means his promotion (*sʿ3.f*)." (ibid.)

"white (*ḥḏ*) bread being given to him—GOOD; it means something at which his face will brighten up (*ḥḏ*)." (ibid., 3,1)

"seeing a large cat (*my ʿ3*)—GOOD; it means a large (*šmw ʿ3*) harvest will come to [him]." (ibid., 4,1)

"seeing himself dead—GOOD; a long life [in] front of him." (ibid., 4,10)

On the other hand, the following dreams were evil portents:

"seeing his face in a mirror—BAD; it means another wife." (ibid., 7,10)

"he being bitten by a dog—BAD; cleaving fast to him of magic." (ibid., 7,15)

"his bed catching fire—BAD; it means driving away his wife." (ibid., 7,25)

"being given a harp (*bnt*)—BAD; it means something through which he fares ill (*bin*)." (ibid., 8,1)

"seeing a dwarf—BAD; the taking away of half of his life." (ibid., 8,10; cited in Gardiner, 12–18)

To counter bad dreams, one was to have one's face rubbed with herbs, beer, and myrrh, and was to recite this incantation: "Come to me, come to me, my mother Isis. . . . [The goddess replies:] 'Here am I, my son Horus, come out with what thou hast seen, in order that thy afflictions through thy dreams may vanish. . . . Driven forth are all evil filthy things which Seth, the son of Nut, has made'" (Gardiner, 19). In a so-called "Letter to the Dead," a husband wrote to his departed wife: "Remove the infirmity of my body! please become a spirit for me [before] my eyes so that I may see you in a dream fighting on my behalf" (Wente, 215).

The practice of incubation for the purpose of healing became popular in Egypt in the Ptolemaic Era, no doubt in imitation of the Greek cult of Asclepius. Numerous gods, such as Serapis, Isis, Ptah, Thoth, Harpocratis, the deified architect-physician Imhotep, and even the deified bull Osorapis, were addressed in temples at Canopis, Memphis, Dendera, Abydos, and Philae not only by Egyptians but by pilgrims from abroad seeking dreams from these gods to obtain healing for their various diseases.

A late (1st c. AD) demotic text known as the Papyrus Insinger states: "He [the Creator] created sleep to end weariness, waking for looking after food. . . . He created the dream to show the way to the dreamer in his blindness" (32.11, 13; *AEL*, 3.210–11).

D. THE GRECO-ROMAN WORLD

Greece

The Greek word for "dream," *oneiros*, from which come the word *oneiromancy*, "divination by dreams," and other cognate words, originally referred to a dream figure. Another word for "dream" was *enupnion*, literally, "in sleep" (*hypnos*). The word *horāma*, "sight, spectacle," could signify a predictive dream; *chrēmatismos* was a dream oracle, in which a god appeared to foretell a future event; and a *phantasma* was "an appearance" in one's sleep. According to Aeschylus's *Prometheus Bound*, dream interpretation was one of the most important gifts given to man. In the Homeric Hymns, Hermes is called the *hēgētōr oneirōn*, "guide of dreams."

Dreams are prominent in the Homeric epics. In the *Iliad* only dreams of men are recounted, in the *Odyssey* only dreams of women (as was later the case in tragedies). Dreams come from Zeus (Hom. *Il.* 1.63), but sometimes they are deceptive, as is the baneful dream (*oulon oneiron*) sent to Agamemnon in the guise of Nestor (Hom. *Il.* 2.6–34). At the end of its message urging Agamemnon to attack the Trojans, the dream concludes:

"But do thou keep this in thy heart, nor let forgetfulness lay hold of thee, whenso honey-hearted sleep shall let thee go."

In a famous passage Penelope comments to the Stranger (actually Odysseus in disguise) these thoughts about dreams:

> Stranger, dreams verily are baffling and unclear of meaning, and in no wise do they find fulfillment in all things for men. For two are the gates of shadowy dreams, and one is fashioned of horn and one of ivory. Those dreams that pass through the gate of sawn ivory deceive men, bringing words that find no fulfillment. But those that come forth through the gate of polished horn bring true issues to pass, when any mortal sees them. (*Od.* 19.560–567)

Dreams play a prominent role in Greek historical narratives. Herodotus relates that the Median king Astyages had alarming dreams about his daughter Mandane, whose son Cyrus was destined to overthrow him: first that enough water flowed from her to overflow all Asia, and second that a vine grew from her that covered all Asia (*Hist.* 1.107–108). Later Cyrus was to view in a dream "the eldest of the sons of Hystaspes [i.e., Darius] wearing wings on his shoulders, the one wing overshadowing Asia and the other Europe" (Her. *Hist.* 1.209). Xerxes dreamed that a tall young man urged him to invade Greece; his counselor Artabanus was skeptical until he had the identical dream (Her. *Hist.* 7.12–18).

When Alexander invaded India, the Indians shot poisoned arrows at his men, fatally wounding many of them. According to Diodorus Siculus,

> The king saw a vision [*opsin*] in his sleep. It seemed to him that a snake appeared carrying a plant in its mouth, and showed him its nature and efficacy and the place where it grew. When Alexander awoke, he sought out the plant, and grinding it up plastered it on Ptolemy's body. He also prepared an infusion of the plant and gave Ptolemy a drink of it. This restored him to health. (*Bib. hist.* 17.103.7–8)

Dreams played a major role in Greek medicine. *On Dreams* (Gk. *peri enypniōn*; Lat. *De victu*), the fourth book of the Hippocratic work *Regimen*, is devoted to the subject of dreams. Dreams that reflect a person's daytime activities are considered healthy. Symbolic dreams are interpreted by analogy: for example, the earth represents the patient's skin, the tree his penis, a cistern his bladder, rivers his blood, etc. A dream of the earth being flooded with water indicates that the patient has to get rid of excess moisture by emetics or by perspiration. The same dream can have a different significance according to the patient. Diving in a lake is evil for a healthy person but a good sign for a feverish person. Dreams can indicate to which god one should pray for healing.

The practice of incubation to solicit dreams, especially from Asklepios (Lat. Asclepius), the god of healing, was widespread in the Greco-Roman world, beginning in the fifth century BC. About four hundred inscriptions attest to how a deity healed the patient or prescribed a course of treatment for him or her. Sometimes the healing was effected by the animals sacred to Asklepios, including his serpent (*drakōn*) or his dog. Supplicants had to be ritually clean, offer a sacrifice, and also a payment in gratitude for their cures. Many *simulacra*, or models, of healed body parts were dedicated at these shrines. By the second century AD, there were more than four hundred incubation centers in the Roman Empire.

The most famous temple sites or *askliēpeia* were at Epidauros in the northeastern Peloponnesus and Pergamum in western Asia Minor. A large marble slab that relates about seventy cures has been preserved at Epidauros. For example, a man who had a dreadful wound on his toe was brought on a stretcher to the temple. "Sleep overtook him, and in that time a snake emerged from the adytum and healed the toe with its tongue, and after doing that it returned to the adytum. When he awoke he was well, and he said he had seen a vision: He dreamt that a young man of beautiful appearance sprinkled a drug on the toe" (cited by Lewis, 39).

As she saw the testimonies to the cures at Epidaurus by Asklepios, Ambrosia of Athens, who was blind in one eye, believed that they were impossible. "She dreamt the god appeared to her and said he would make her sound, and as his fee she would have to dedicate in the sanctuary a silver pig as a memorial of her ignorance; so saying, he cut open her diseased eyeball and poured in some drug. When day came she emerged healthy" (cited by Lewis, 37).

Greek philosophers held a variety of views as to the significance of dreams. A number of pre-Socratic scholars were quite skeptical. Xenophanes denied the objective reality of dreams, and Heraclitus held that dreams are private, subjective experiences. Democritus believed that dreams are caused by images that came through the pores of the skin. In similar fashion, the Epicureans believed that dreams are caused by the bombardment of the sense organs by atoms.

Socrates cited dreams as one source of his conviction that he had to continue his unpopular mission to the people of Athens (Plato, *Apol.* 33c). In a dream a woman dressed in white informed him of the day of his death (Plato, *Crito* 44a). Plato held that in every human being there are wild and unnatural desires that express themselves only in dreams (*Resp.* 572b). The dreams of uneducated persons he held to be wicked. On the other hand, the dreams of a man or woman in whom the reasoning element is dominant can, according to Plato, yield important truths.

Aristotle left two treatises on sleep and dreams: *De insomniis* (Gk. *Perienypniōn*) and *De divinatione per somnum* (Gk. *Peri tēs kath'hypnon mantikēs*). He believed that young children do not dream. He held that dreams are not sent by gods, else they would only be seen by the best and wisest men. Dreams, according to Aristotle, are *phantasia* ("appearances," "presentations," or "imaginings") caused by the lingering movement of sense impressions from the day. He maintained: "As for divination that takes place during periods of sleep and is said to be based on dreams, it is not easy either to despise it or to believe in it" (*Div. somn.* 1.1; Gallop, 103).

Rome

The Stoics, who were pantheists, believed in divination by dreams. According to Cicero, "Now Posidonius [135–51 BC] holds the view that there are three ways in which men dream as the result of divine impulse: first, the soul is clairvoyant of itself because of its kinship with the gods; second, the air is full of immortal souls, already clearly stamped, as it were, with the marks of truth; and third, the gods in person converse with men when they are asleep" (*Div.* 1.30.64).

Macrobius, who lived ca. AD 400, commenting on Cicero's *Somnium scipionis*, indicated that there were five Latin terms (corresponding to Greek words) designating types of dreams: (1) *somnium* (Gk. *oneiros*), "enigmatic dream"; (2) *visio* (Gk. *horama*), "prophetic vision"; (3) *oraculum* (Gk. *chrēmatismos*), "oracular dream"; (4) *insomnium* (Gk. *enuption*), "nightmare"; and (5) *visum* (Gk. *phantasma*), "apparition." (See Stahl.)

In his brilliant poem *On the Nature of Things* (*De rerum natura*), the Epicurean Lucretius denied that dreams are sent by the gods, as the gods do not concern themselves with human affairs. Nor, in his view, are dreams proof of the immortality of souls. Rather, all things, even the gods, continuously release vague images (*idola, imagines, simulacra*) that fly through space and then penetrate the sleeper as dreams. Dreams depict the repetition of human activities while awake (4.962–986) and the repetition of animal activities (4.987–1010). Lucretius vividly describes seven dreams of a sleeper (4.1011–1036): those in which (1) he screams as though he is about to be strangled, (2) he screams as though he is about to be devoured by an animal, (3) he divulges secrets in his sleep, (4) he dreams of falling from a high mountain, (5) he drinks a whole river but remains thirsty, (6) he dreams he is sitting on a latrine and wets the precious "Babylonian" sheets, and (7) he sees the image of a beautiful female body and spills floods of sperm.

The most substantial discussion of dreams among Roman authors is found in Cicero's *De divinatione*, which consists of a dialogue with Cicero's brother, Quintus, who, influenced by the Stoics, argues for the validity of dreams for divination (*Div.* 1.30.64). Cicero himself, influenced by the Academy (that is, Platonists), argues that dreams are not sent by a divine power. To believe in them is superstition.

In Virgil's *Aeneid* there are thirteen dreams and dream visions from a god or a deceased person. After Aeneas and his family flee Troy and land on Crete, the Penates (household gods) he has carried with him appear to him in a dream, directing him to go to Italy (*Aen.* 3.147–171). When Dido pleads with Virgil to stay with her in Carthage, he claims that dream visions from his father Anchises, his son Ascanius, and the gods themselves have impelled him to leave (*Aen.* 4.351–353).

There is very little evidence that dreams played a role in Roman political life before 300 BC. As a rule, dreams were not included in the officially recognized auspices or *prodigia*, "bad omens." However, in 90 BC the Senate ordered the repair of a temple as the result of a dream reported by the daughter of a consul.

During the Punic Wars, the Carthaginian general Hamilcar dreamed that he would dine in Syracuse, Sicily, on the following evening. He did so, but unfortunately for him, it was as a captive of the Romans (Cic., *Div.* 1.50). Scipio "Africanus," the victor over Hannibal, had a dream of Neptune, which he used to encourage his troops before the battle at Carthago Nova (Polyb. *Hist.* 10.11.7–8). Eunus, who led the slave revolt in Sicily in 135 BC, claimed that he was visited by the gods both in dreams and while he was awake (Diod. Sic. *Bib. hist.* 34–35). According to Plutarch, the dictator Sulla dreamed that Bellona handed him a thunderbolt to strike down his enemies (*Sull.* 6). Before a key battle against Caesar in 48 BC, Pompey dreamed that he would decorate the temple of Venus Victrix with trophies, which he did, but as the loser (Plu. *Pomp.* 68).

Suetonius's history *The Twelve Caesars* is replete with accounts of dreams that came to Julius Caesar and the Julio-Claudian emperors. Caesar's own commentaries *The Gallic War* and *The Civil War* are, however, devoid of any descriptions of his dreams. According to Suetonius, Caesar saw himself hovering over the clouds and stretching out his hand to Jupiter (*Jul.* 81.3). When he had a disturbing dream in which he raped his own mother, "the soothsayers inspired him with high hopes by their interpretation, which was: that he was destined to rule the world, since the mother whom he had seen in his power was none other than the earth, which is regarded as the common parent of all mankind" (*Jul.* 7.2). On the eve of his assassination on the Ides of March, 44 BC, Caesar's wife, Calpurnia, dreamed that the gable of their house collapsed and that Caesar was run through while in her arms. She begged him in vain not to go to the Senate.

Atia, the mother of Augustus, dreamed before his birth that her vital organs were borne up to the stars and spread over the whole extent of land and sea (Suet. *Aug.* 94.4). As for Augustus himself, "He was not indifferent to his own dreams or to those which others dreamed about him. . . . All through the spring his own dreams were very numerous and fearful, but idle and unfulfilled; during the rest of the year they were less frequent and more reliable" (Suet. *Aug.* 91.1–2).

The emperor Gaius Caligula was a madman. According to Suetonius, "He was especially tormented with sleeplessness; for he never rested more than three hours at night, and even for that length of time he did not sleep quietly, but was terrified by strange apparitions, once for example dreaming that the spirit of the Ocean talked with him" (Suet. *Cal.* 50.3). Before Caligula was assassinated, he dreamed that Jupiter threw him from heaven to earth (*Cal.* 57).

After he had ordered the murder of his meddling mother, Agrippina, Nero began to be tormented at night.

> Although he had never before been in the habit of dreaming, after he had killed his mother it seemed to him that he was steering a ship in his sleep and that the helm was wrenched from his hands; that he was dragged by his wife Octavia into thickest darkness, and that he was now covered with a swarm of winged ants. (Suet. *Nero* 46.1)

Vespasian was assured in a dream that he, and his sons, Titus and Domitian, would rule as long as Claudius and Nero combined (Suet. *Vesp.* 25). Before Domitian's assassination in AD 96, "he dreamed that Minerva, whom he worshipped with superstitious veneration, came forth from her shrine and declared that she could no longer protect him, since she had been disarmed by Jupiter" (Suet. *Dom.* 15.3).

Dio Cassius published a work on dreams that foretold the accession of Septimius Severus in AD 193. The emperor set up an equestrian statue of himself in the forum at the place where, in a dream, he had seen the horse of Pertinax, his predecessor, throw off his rider, who then acknowledged Severus as the new ruler.

The Stoic emperor Marcus Aurelius believed that the gods send dreams to help people, and he accepted cures given in dreams. His physician, Galen, also believed in the efficacy of dreams. It was a dream seen by Galen's father, Nikon, that led to Galen's medical apprenticeship at the age of sixteen at Pergamum. When Nikon was twenty, he suffered from a subdiaphragmatic abscess. Asklepios appeared to him in a dream and ordered him to open an artery in his hand, which operation seemed to have cured him. In his *Diagnosis from Dreams*, Galen indicated his belief that some dreams are caused by daytime thoughts and others by the excess and quality of the four bodily humors (blood, phlegm, black bile, and yellow bile). He claimed that it was the authority of a dream that prevented him from accompanying Marcus Aurelius to the Danube battlefront.

Aelius Aristides, a rhetorician who suffered from numerous ailments including respiratory problems and intestinal ailments, sought relief by the practice of incubation for seventeen years (AD 146–163) at the Asklepion at Pergamum. In his *Sacred Teachings* (*Hieroi logoi*), the only pagan autobiography from antiquity, he recounts no fewer than 163 dreams. In many of these dreams the god Asklepios gives him counterintuitive instructions. When he was feverish, the god commanded him to plunge into an ice-cold river; when he was asthmatic, the god commanded him to deliver public speeches; and when he had a painful swelling in his loins, the god commanded him to ride a horse. In other dreams, Aristides conversed with Athena, met Plato, shared a tomb with Alexander the Great, and heard others proclaim that he was a greater orator than Demosthenes.

In Rome there were *coniectores somniorum*, paid interpreters of dreams. This group, which included Jewish women, were satirized by Juvenal: "No sooner has he gone than a palsied Jewish woman will abandon her hay-lined chest and start begging into her private ear. . . . She too gets her hand filled, though with less, because Jews will sell you whatever dreams you like for the tiniest copper coin" (*Sat.* 6.542–547). There were also *Isiaci coniectores*, who interpreted the dreams of Isis worshippers.

The most influential dream book from antiquity was the *Oneirocritica*, which was written in Greek by Artemidorus from Daldis in Lydia (2nd c. AD). He considered an *enypnion*, a dream based on wish fulfillment or caused by anxiety, to have no predictive value. Dreams that correspond exactly to the predictive event he called *theorematic* (*theōrēmatikoi*); dreams that were symbolic or obscure he called *allegorical* (*allēgorikoi*).

Some of Artemidorus's interpretations were based upon plays on similarly sounding words. To dream one has a large head (*kephalē*) means one will accumulate capital (*kephalaia*). Eating goat meat (*chimairai*) means good luck to people in a storm (*cheimōn*). Asses (*onoi*) can indicate the getting of profit (*onasthai*).

The same dream could mean different things to different people:

> Being crucified is auspicious for all seafarers. For the cross, like a ship, is made of wood and nails, and the ship's mast resembles a cross. It is also auspicious for a poor man. For a crucified man is raised high and his substance is sufficient to keep many birds. But it means the betrayal of secrets. For a crucified

man can be seen by all. On the other hand, it signifies harm for rich men, since the crucified are stripped naked and lose their flesh. For a bachelor, the dream means marriage, because the connection between the victim and the cross is a bond, but it will not be a very easy one. (*Oneir.* 2.53; White, 127)

E. THE JEWISH WORLD

Dreams played a prominent role in many texts both during the Intertestamental period and the rabbinic era in books of the OT Apocrypha and Pseudepigrapha, Philo, Josephus, and the Talmud.

The Qumran *Temple Scroll* condemns misleading dream interpreters, recalling the warnings of Deuteronomy and of Jeremiah:

If a prophet or interpreter of dreams arises among you and promises you an omen or portent, and then the omen or portent that he has promised actually happens—if he says, "Let us go and serve other gods" that you have not known, you must not obey that prophet or dream interpreter. For I am testing you to know whether you really love the Lord. . . . That prophet or dream interpreter [*hwlm*] must be put to death. (11Q19–20 LIV, 8–12, 15)

Sirach (Ecclesiasticus) contains highly negative comments about dreams: "A man of no understanding has vain and false hopes, and dreams give wings to fools. As one who catches at a shadow and pursues the wind, so is he who gives heed to dreams" (Sir 34:1–2); "Divinations and omens and dreams are folly" (Sir 34:5); "For dreams have deceived many, and those who put their hope in them have failed" (Sir 34:7).

Before his decisive victory over Nicanor, Judas Maccabeus had a dream in which he saw the high priest Onias praying and then Jeremiah the prophet holding out a golden sword and saying, "Take this holy sword, a gift from God, with which you will strike down your adversaries" (2 Macc 15:16).

The book of *1 Enoch* consists largely of dreams and visions, including a tour by Enoch of heaven, earth, and Sheol (*1 En.* 13:7–36:4). Enoch recounts to his son, Methuselah, two dreams that he had in his grandfather Mahalel's house: a dream of the flood (*1 En.* 83), and the so-called "Animal Apocalypse" (*1 En.* 85–90), in which the history of Israel is recounted with Israel being represented by sheep oppressed by their enemies, the dogs and foxes.

In the book of *2 Enoch*, in a dream Enoch sees two huge men, who turn out to be angels and who take him on a tour through the seven heavens (*2 En.* 3–68). In the *Ladder of Jacob*, the archangel Sariel, who is "in charge of dreams" (*Lad. Jac.* 3), is sent to Jacob to explain his dream (cf. Gen

28:11–22). Sariel proclaims to Jacob: "You have seen a ladder with twelve steps, each step having two human faces which kept changing their appearance. The ladder is this age, and the twelve steps are the periods of this age. But the twenty-four faces are the kings of the ungodly nations of this age" (*Lad. Jac.* 5.1–5).

Philo's *De somniis* is a running commentary on the dreams of Genesis. Though he considered most dreams ephemeral, he seems to have been influenced by the Stoic Posidonius in considering that some dreams are God-sent (*theopemtoi oneiroi*). Another class of dreams that foretell the future result when a man's mind (*nous*), inspired with the Mind of the Universe, receives foreknowledge of the things to come. In his essay *On Joseph*, Philo contrasts Joseph, "the statesman" who accurately interpreted dreams, with "one of the praters who shew off their cleverness for hire and use their art of interpreting the visions given in sleep as a pretext for making money" (*Ios.* 125).

The writings of Josephus are replete with Greek words for dreams: *onar* or *oneiros* appear sixty-seven times; of the 174 occurrences of the word *opsis*, twenty-nine refer to dreams; *phantasmai* occurs eleven times. After receiving threats against his command in Galilee at the outbreak of the revolt against Rome, Josephus was encouraged to stay by a dream that admonished him, "Remember that thou must even battle with the Romans" (*Life* 212).

As the commander of the besieged city of Jotapata, Josephus, after others had committed suicide as they had agreed to do, had a change of heart:

> He was an interpreter of dreams and skilled in divining the meaning of ambiguous utterances of the Deity; a priest himself and of priestly descent, he was not ignorant of the prophecies in the sacred books. At that hour he was inspired to read their meaning, and recalling the dreadful images of his recent dreams, he offered up a silent prayer to God. . . . "I willingly surrender to the Romans and consent to live; but I take thee to witness that I go, not as a traitor, but as thy minister." (*J.W.* 3.351–354)

There are more than two hundred references to dreams in the Babylonian Talmud. In no dream in the Talmud does God himself appear. In some dreams a sacred text is seen.

> There are three prophets [of significance for dreams]. If one sees the Book of Kings, he may look forward to greatness; if Ezekiel, he may look forward to wisdom; if Isaiah he may look forward to consolation; if Jeremiah, let him fear for punishment. There are three larger books of the Hagiographa [which are significant for dreams]. If one sees the Book of Psalms, he may hope for piety; if the Book of Proverbs, he may hope for wisdom; if the Book of Job, let him

fear for punishment. There are three smaller books of the Hagiographa [significant for dreams]. If one sees the Songs of Songs in a dream, he may hope for piety; if Ecclesiastes, he may hope for wisdom; if Lamentations, let him fear for punishment; and one who sees the Scroll of Esther will have a miracle wrought for him. (*b. Ber.* 57b)

In what has been called the Jewish Dream Book (*b. Ber.* 55a–57b), we have a list of about a hundred different dream omina. Rabbi Ḥisda declared, "A dream which is not interpreted is like a letter which is not read" (*b. Ber.* 55a). Most dream interpreters were rabbis, and some of these (for example, R. Ishmael b. Jose, R. Jose b. Ḥalafta, and R. Aqiba) achieved fame in this regard.

According to R. Banaʾah, "there were twenty-four interpreters of dreams in Jerusalem. Once I had a dream and I went round to all of them, and they all gave different interpretations, and all were fulfilled, thus confirming that which is said, 'All dreams follow the mouth'" (*b. Ber.* 55b). That is, the dream is fulfilled according to its interpretation.

The Talmud relates the cautionary tale of a mercenary dream interpreter named Bar Hedya, who gave favorable interpretations to Abaye, who paid him, and unfavorable interpretations to Rava, who at first refused to pay him, even though both had identical dreams. Bar Hedya met a gruesome end in Rome (*b. Ber.* 56a).

Many of the rabbinic interpretations were based on paronomasia, a play on words with similar sounds but different meanings. "If one sees an elephant [*pyl*] in a dream, wonders [*plʾwt*] will be wrought for him" (*b. Ber.* 56b). At times an initial interpretation could be replaced by a more favorable one. Bar Kappar reported a dream that some interpreted as follows: "You will die in the month of Adar [*ʾdr*] and not see Nisan [*nysn*]." Rabbi Judah ha-Nasi, however, reinterpreted the dream to mean: "You will die with honor [*ʾdrwtʾ*], and not experience trials [*nsywn*]" (*b. Ber.* 56b).

Mar Samuel, who lived from the end of the second century to the middle of the third century AD, was the head of the important rabbinical academy at Nehardea, in Mesopotamia. "When Samuel had a bad dream, he used to say, 'The dreams speak falsely.' When he had a good dream, he used to say, 'Do the dreams speak falsely, seeing that it is written, I (God) do speak with him in a dream?' . . . There is no contradiction; in the one case it is through an angel, in the other through a demon" (*b. Ber.* 55b). The association of a favorable Scripture can anticipate and nullify the association with an unfavorable Scripture, as in the following example: "If one sees a lion in a dream he should rise early and say: *The lion hath roared, who will not fear?* (Amos 3.8), before another verse occurs to him, viz. *A lion is gone up from his thicket* (Jer 4.7)" (*b. Ber.* 56b).

The rabbis believed that one should ask for protection against evil dreams caused by demons such as the succubus Lilith. Therefore, Rabbi Hanina urged that men should not sleep alone, lest they be seduced by her (*b. Šabb.* 151b). But even if a man has a sexual emission because of an erotic dream, he was not considered guilty, because this was not actual sexual intercourse with another woman. Even dreams of incest could be interpreted in a favorable manner: "If one dreams that he has intercourse with his mother, he may expect to obtain understanding, since it says, *Yea, thou wilt call understanding 'mother.'* . . . If one dreams that he has had intercourse with his sister, he may expect to obtain wisdom, since it says, *Say to wisdom, thou art my sister*" (*b. Ber.* 57a).

According to the Talmud, one should ask for a good sleep:

> On going to bed one says from "Hear, oh Israel" to "And it shall come to pass if ye hearken diligently." Then he says: "Blessed is He who causes the bands of sleep to fall upon my eyes and slumber on my eyelids, and gives light to the apple of the eye. . . . And deliver me from evil hap and sore diseases, and let not evil dreams and evil thoughts disturb me, and may my couch be flawless before Thee, and enlighten mine eyes lest I sleep the sleep of death." (*b. Ber.* 60b)

F. THE CHRISTIAN WORLD

Because of the roles that dreams had played in both the OT and the NT, Christians believed in the validity of ongoing revelations from God through dreams, but they were also wary about the demonic origin of other dreams.

The *Shepherd of Hermas*, which dates to the end of the first century or the beginning of the second century, was a major work of the apostolic fathers and was regarded in some circles as inspired. Hermas has a series of visions (*horāseis*), some of which are explicitly identified as dreams. One of these visions is recorded close to the beginning of the work:

> Some time later, as I was going to Cumae and glorifying God's creatures for their greatness, splendor, and power, I fell asleep as I walked. And a spirit took me and carried me way through a pathless region . . . and I knelt down and began to pray to the Lord and to confess my sins. While I was praying the heavens opened and I saw that woman whom I had desired greeting me from heaven, saying, "Hello, Hermas." (*Herm. Vis.* 1.3–4)

In the Homilies of the Pseudo-Clementines, Simon Magus argues for the validity of dreams, but Peter counters that a dream messenger is not a trustworthy source, saying:

How many, in like manner, have been seen by others in dreams; and when they have met one another when awake, and compared them with what they saw in their dream, they have not accorded: so that the dream is not a manifestation, but is either the production of a demon or of the soul, giving forms to present fears and desire. (*Homily* 9.15)

Justin Martyr, addressing Romans, held that demons "strive to hold you their slaves and servants; and sometimes by appearances in dreams, and sometimes by magical impositions, they subdue all who make no strong opposing effort for their own salvation" (*1 Apol.* 14; cf. 18). His disciple Tatian echoed this same sentiment:

The demons do not cure, but by their art make men their captives. And the most admirable Justin has rightly denounced them as robbers. For, as it is the practice of some to capture persons . . . , so those who are esteemed gods, invading the bodies of certain persons, and producing a sense of their presence by dreams, command them to come forth into public, and in the sight of all. (*Or.* 18)

Among early Christian writers, the most extensive and perceptive observations on dreams were made by Tertullian in his essay on the soul. He held that some dreams are created by the soul (*ab anima*), others by demons (*a daemonio*), and some by God (*a deo*). In contrast to Aristotle, Tertullian commented,

As for those persons who suppose that infants do not dream, on the ground that all the functions of the soul throughout life are accomplished according to the capacity of age, they ought to observe attentively their tremors, and nods, and bright smiles as they sleep, and from such facts understand that they are the emotions of their soul as it dreams. (*An.* 49)

He asked, "Who is such a stranger to human experience as not sometimes to have perceived some truth in dreams?" (*An.* 46). He argued that we are not responsible for our actions in dreams: "In these dreams, indeed, good actions are useless, and crimes harmless; for we shall no more be condemned for visionary acts of sin, than we shall be crowned for imaginary martyrdom" (*An.* 45). He concluded: "We declare, then, that dreams are inflicted on us mainly by demons, although they sometimes turn out true and favorable to us." And he added: "It was, indeed, by an inspiration from God that Nebuchadnezzar dreamt his dreams; and almost the greater part of mankind get their knowledge of God from dreams" (*An.* 47).

A Montanist editor, who some suggest was Tertullian, introduced the remarkable *Passio sanctae Perpetuae*, the authentic diary of a twenty-two-year-old nursing mother, Perpetua, who was martyred at Carthage in

AD 203. It was claimed that the account of her martyrdom was based on Perpetua's own diary. Kraemer and Lander observe: "If true, as contemporary scholarship generally takes it to be, Perpetua is the first and only known Christian woman to write in her own name before the fourth century CE" (Kraemer and Lander, 2.1048). Perpetua records a series of four dreams she had while in prison. She writes that in the first dream,

> I saw a golden ladder of marvellous height, reaching up even to heaven, and very narrow, so that persons could only ascend it one by one; and on the sides of the ladder was fixed every kind of iron weapon. . . . And under the ladder itself was crouching a dragon of wonderful size, who lay in wait for those who ascended, and frightened them from the ascent. (*Passio sanctae Perpetuae* 1.3)

At the top of the ladder she was welcomed by a white-haired man dressed like a shepherd.

In the second dream she saw her deceased brother Dinocrates, whose childhood cancer had disfigured his face and killed him. In her third dream she prayed for him and saw him healed and happy. In her account of her fourth dream, she recalls: "Then there came forth against me a certain Egyptian, horrible in appearance, with his backers, to fight with me. And there came to me, as my helpers and encouragers, handsome youths; and I was stripped, and became a man" (*Passio sanctae Perpetuae* 3.2). In a violent combat, Perpetua defeated the Egyptian gladiator. "Then I awoke, and perceived that I was not to fight with beasts, but against the devil. Still I knew that the victory was awaiting me" (*Passio sanctae Perpetuae* 3.2).

Origen maintained,

> We nevertheless, so far as we can, shall support our position, maintaining that . . . it is a matter of belief that in a *dream* impressions have been brought before the minds of many, some relating to divine things, and others to future events of this life, and this either with clearness or in an enigmatic manner—a fact which is manifest to all who accept the doctrine of providence. (*Cels.* 1.48)

In his refutation of Celsus's attack against Christianity, Origen testifies that many pagans have been converted to Christ by waking visions and dreams of the night.

In his *Panarion* (30.4–12), Epiphanius relates the remarkable stories told to him by a Joseph(us) of Tiberias, a notable leader in the Jewish community. Joseph became intrigued with Christianity after finding Hebrew versions of Matthew, John, and Acts in a locked box in the home of the Jewish patriarch, who on his deathbed had been converted by a bishop. Jesus then appeared to Joseph in a dream, declaring: "I am Jesus, whom your forefathers crucified, but believe in me" (30.9.1; Williams, 137). Jesus appeared to Joseph in a dream a second time after he had become ill. Then, in another dream, Jesus granted Joseph miraculous powers to exorcise a demoniac, but he still refused to believe in Christ. Only after fellow Jews in Cilicia had nearly drowned Joseph did he convert. He became a friend of Constantine and was given imperial funds to build churches in Tiberias, Sepphoris, Nazareth, and Capernaum. (See Thornton.)

Arnobius, a pagan rhetorician teaching near Carthage, was led by a dream to seek Christ. His student Lactantius wrote *The Divine Institutes* to instruct Constantine. The most momentous dream in history was that seen by Constantine before the critical battle of the Milvian Bridge outside of Rome in AD 312, which led to his conversion. According to Lactantius's work *The Death of the Persecutors*, which was written only two or three years after the event,

> Constantine was directed in a dream to cause the heavenly sign to be delin-eated on the shields of his soldiers, and so to proceed to battle. He did as he had been commanded, and he marked on their shields the letter X, with a perpendicular line drawn through it and turned round thus at the top, being the cipher of Christ. Having this sign, his troops stood to arms. (*Mort.* 44.3–6)

Writing forty years later, the church historian Eusebius offered a vari-ant account, describing the vision as occurring at midday. But he adds that later at night, "in his sleep the Christ of God appeared to him [Constantine] with the same sign which he had seen in the heavens, and commanded him to make a likeness of that sign which he had seen in the heavens, and to use it as a safeguard in all engagements with his enemies" (*Vit. Const.* 1.29). The ecclesiastical histories written after Eusebius by Socrates Scholasticus (1.2) and some years later by Sozomen (1.3) also refer to a vision seen by Constantine rather than a dream.

Athanasius cited the fact that humans dream as proof that the soul is rational and immortal:

> Often when the body is quiet, and at rest and asleep, man moves inwardly, and beholds what is outside himself, travelling to other countries, walking about, meeting his acquaintances, and often by these means divining and forecasting the actions of the day. But to what can this be due save to the rational soul, in which man thinks of and perceives things beyond himself? (*C. Gent.* 31)

In his biography of St. Antony, Athanasius notes that demons can appear in the guise of monks in dreams: "They arouse us from our sleep to prayers; and this constantly, hardly allowing us to sleep at all. At another time they assume the appearance of monks and feign the speech of holy men, that by their similarity they may deceive and thus drag their victims where they will" (*Vit. Ant.* 25). Antony's counsel was: "When, therefore, they [the demons] come by night to you and wish to tell the future, or say, we are the angels, give no heed, for they lie . . . sign yourselves and your houses [with the cross], and pray, and you shall see them vanish" (*Vit. Ant.* 35).

Basil conceded that dreams could be a source of revelation, but he was embarrassed that he could not control them by his rational mind. He counseled monks not to sleep too much, because this would open the mind to wild dreams. He wrote, "Where then is the need of having recourse to dreams and of hiring their interpreters, and making matter for talk over the cups at public entertainments?" (*Ep.* 210.2).

Although Gregory of Nyssa was turned to a life of contemplation by a dream in which "forty martyrs" challenged him, he denigrated dreams as blurred *ainigmas*, which represent the sickness of the soul:

> We for our part say that it is only the conscious and sound action of the intellect which we ought to refer to mind; and as to the fantastic nonsense which occurs to us in sleep, we suppose that some appearances of the operations of the mind are accidentally moulded in the less rational part of the soul; for the soul, being by sleep dissociated from the senses, is also of necessity outside the range of the operations of the mind; for it is through the senses that the union of mind with man takes place; therefore when the senses are at rest, the intellect also must needs be inactive; and an evidence of this is the fact that the dreamer often seems to be in absurd and impossible situations, which would not happen if the soul were then guided by reason and intellect.
> (*On the Making of Man* 13.5)

In an autobiographical poem, Gregory of Nazianzus wrote that God called him in dreams during childhood. Together with Basil and Gregory of Nyssa, he refuted those who denied the deity of the Holy Spirit and influenced the adoption of the doctrine of the Trinity at the Council of Constantinople in 381. His devotion to the Trinity was given to him by his dreams.

Jerome, while living as a hermit in Syria, was troubled by dreams about his indulgent past as a young man: "How often, when I was living in the desert, in the vast solitude which gives to hermits a savage dwelling-place, parched by a burning sun, how often did I fancy myself among the pleasures of Rome!" (*Epist.* 22.7). A bibliophile and scholar, Jerome could not bear to leave his library behind, but would fast and then read his beloved Cicero. Then he had a most terrifying nightmare: "Suddenly I was caught up in the spirit and dragged before the judgment seat of the Judge; . . . Asked who and what I was I replied: I am a Christian. But He who presided said: Thou liest, you are a follower of Cicero and not of Christ" (*Epist.* 22.30). When he awoke, he could still feel the scourges on his back administered by the Judge.

Ambrose, the bishop of Milan, saw his deceased brother Satyrus in a dream. It was also in a dream that the location of the relics of the martyrs Gervasius and Protasius was revealed to him. Again, it was a dream that emboldened Ambrose to deny communion to the emperor Theodosius I:

> Lastly, I am writing with my own hand that which you alone may read. . . . I have been warned, not by man, nor through man, but plainly by Himself that this is forbidden me. For when I was anxious, in the very night in which I was preparing to set out, you appeared to me in a dream to have come into the Church, and I was not permitted to offer the sacrifice. (*Epist.* 51.14)

After he became a Manichaean, Augustine was refused welcome by his mother, Monica, until she had a dream in which

> she saw herself standing on a certain wooden rule, and a bright youth advancing towards her, joyous and smiling upon her, while she was grieving and bowed down with sorrow. But he having inquired of her the cause of her sorrow and daily weeping (he wishing to teach, as is their wont, and not to be taught), and she answering that it was my perdition she was lamenting, he bade her rest contented, and told her to behold and see that where she was, there was I also. And when she looked she saw me standing near her on the same rule. (*Conf.* 3.11.19)

It was not until nine years later that Augustine was dramatically converted to the Catholic faith in Milan.

Augustine admitted that he was troubled by lustful dreams: "But there still exist in my memory . . . the images of such things as my habits had fixed there; and these rush into my thoughts . . . when I am awake; but in sleep they do so not only so as to give pleasure, but even to obtain consent, and what very nearly resembles reality" (*Conf.* 10.30.41). Augustine commented:

> In fine, sleep itself, which is justly called repose, how little of repose there sometimes is in it when disturbed with dreams and visions; and with what terror is the wretched mind overwhelmed by the appearances of things which are so presented, and which, as it were so stand out before the senses, that we can not distinguish them from realities! How wretchedly do false appearances distract men in certain diseases! (*Civ.* 22.22)

He gave a specific example, as follows:

> A gouty doctor of the same city, when he had given in his name for baptism, and had been prohibited the day before his baptism from being baptized that year, by black woolly-haired boys who appeared to him in his dreams, and whom he understood to be devils, and when, though they trod on his feet,

and inflicted the acutest pain he had ever yet experienced, he refused to obey them, but overcame them, and would not defer being washed in the laver of regeneration, was relieved in the very act of baptism, not only of the extraordinary pain he was tortured with, but also of the disease itself, so that, though he lived a long time afterwards, he never suffered from gout. (*Civ.* 22.8)

At the same time, Augustine believed that God could reveal himself in dreams, citing the example of his physician friend Gennadius, who was skeptical about life after death until he saw two dreams of a youth and a heavenly city.

Augustine disapproved of the practice of Christians sleeping in *martyria* in order to solicit dreams from the martyrs. Due to his influence, the Council of Carthage condemned this practice in AD 401. Similarly, Athanasius denounced incubation of this kind that was practiced in Egypt at the shrines of Colluthus, Menas, Victor, John, Cyrus, Leontius, and Philoxenus.

BIBLIOGRAPHY: E. Alvstad, *Reading the Dream Text: A Nexus between Dreams and Texts in the Rabbinic Literature of Late Antiquity* (2010); S. Bar, *A Letter That Has Not Been Read: Dreams in the Hebrew Bible*, trans. L. J. Schramm (2001); P. Barlev, "Interpreting the Rabbis Interpreting the Dreams," rabbinic thesis, Hebrew Union College/Jewish Institute of Religion (2007); C. A. Behr, *Aelius Aristides and the Sacred Tales* (1968); R. M. Berchman, ed., *Mediators of the Divine: Horizons of Prophecy, Divination, Dreams and Theurgy in Mediterranean Antiquity* (1998); S. A. L. Butler, *Mesopotamian Conceptions of Dreams and Dream Rituals* (1998); J. S. Cooper, "Sargon and Joseph: Dreams Come True," in *Biblical and Related Studies*, ed. A. Kort and S. Morschauser (1985), 3–39; D. del Corno, "Dreams and Their Interpretation in Ancient Greece," *BICS* 29 (1982), 55–62; D. S. Dodson, "Philo's *De somniis* in the Context of Ancient Dream Theories and Classifications," *PRSt* 30 (2003), 299–312; M. Dulaey, *Le Rêve dans la vie et la pensée de saint Augustin* (1973); F. M. Fales and G. B. Lanfranchi, "The Impact of Oracular Material on the Political Utterances and Political Action in the Royal Inscriptions of the Sargonid Dynasty," in *Oracles et prophéties dans l'antiquité*, ed. J-G. Heintz (1997), 99–114; R. Fidler, " 'Here Comes This Dreamer' (Genesis 37:19): Towards a Typology of Dreams/Dreamers in the Hebrew Bible," *JANESCU* 32 (2012), 51–72; F. Flannery-Dailey, *Dreamers, Scribes, and Priests: Jewish Dreams in the Hellenistic and Roman Eras* (2004); D. Gallop, ed., *Aristotle on Sleep and Dreams* (1996); A. H. Gardiner, ed., *Hieratic Papyri in the British Museum: Third Series, Chester Beatty Gift I: Text* (1935); R. K. Gnuse, "Dream Genre in the Matthean Infancy Narratives," *NovT* 32 (1990), 97–120; R. K. Gnuse, *Dreams and Dream Reports in the Writings of Josephus* (1996); J. S. Hanson, "Dreams and Visions in the GraecoRoman World and Early Christianity," *ANRW* II.23.2 (1980), 1395–1427; M. Harris, *Studies in Jewish Dream Interpretation* (1994); W. V. Harris, *Dreams and Experience in Classical Antiquity* (2009); W. V. Harris, "Roman Opinions about the Truthfulness of Dreams," *JRS* 93 (2003), 18–34; J.-M. Husser, *Dreams and Dream Narratives in the Biblical World*, trans. J. M. Munro (1999); M. T. Kelsey, *God, Dreams, and Revelation: A Christian Interpretation of Dreams* (1974); B. J. Koet, *Dreams and Scriptures in Luke-Acts* (2006); R. S. Kraemer and S. L. Lander, "Perpetua and Felicitas," in *The Early Christian World*, ed. P. F. Esler (2000), 2.1048–68; K. H. Kudisch, *The Rabbinic Conception of Dreams and Dream Interpretation* (1971); N. Lewis, *The Interpretation of Dreams and Portents* (1976); L. LiDonnici, *The Epidaurian Miracle Inscriptions* (1995); D. Lipton, *Revisions of the Night: Politics and Promises in the Patriarchal Dreams of Genesis* (1999); B. M. Litfin, "Eusebius on Constantine: Truth and Hagiography at the Milvian Bridge," *JETS* 55 (2012), 773–92; P. C. Miller, *Dreams in Late Antiquity* (1994); G. Mussies, "Joseph's Dream (Matt 1, 18–23) and Comparable Stories," in *Text and Testimony*, ed. T. Baarda et al. (1988), 177–86; S. Noegel, *Nocturnal Ciphers: The Allusive Language of Dreams in the Ancient Near East* (2007); S. M. Oberhelman, "Dreams in Graeco-Roman Medicine," *ANRW* II.37.1 (1993), 121–56; A. L. Oppenheim, *The Interpretation of Dreams in the Ancient Near East* (1956); R. Ritner, *The Mechanics of Ancient Egyptian Magical Practice* (1993); S. Rossel, *Bible Dreams* (2003); R. Rousselle, "Healing Cults in Antiquity: The Dream Cures of Asclepius of Epidaurus," *Journal of Psychohistory* 12 (1985), 339–52; J. Sasson, "Mari Dreams," *JAOS* 103 (1983), 283–93; S. Sauneron, ed., *Les Songes et leur interpretation* (1959); D. Shulman and G. G. Stroumsa, ed., *Dream Cultures: Explorations in the Comparative History of Dreaming* (1999); N. Shupak, "A Fresh Look at the Dreams of the Officials and of the Pharaoh in the Story of Joseph (Genesis 40–41) in the Light of Egyptian Dreams," *JANESCU* 30 (2006), 103–38; G. Shushan, "Greek and Egyptian Dreams in Two Ptolemaic Archives: Individual and Cultural Layers of Meaning," *Dreaming* 16.2 (2006), 129–42; M. Slome, *Dreams in the Bible* (1987); W. H. Stahl, trans., *Macrobius, Commentary on the Dream of Scipio* (1952); K. Szpakowska, ed., *Through a Glass Darkly: Magic, Dreams and Prophecy in Ancient Egypt* (2006); T. C. G. Thornton, "The Stories of Joseph of Tiberias," *VC* 44 (1990), 54–63; R. Toueg, *Dreams and Visions in the Bible* (1992); G. G. Tribl, "Dream as a Constitutive Cultural Determinant—The Example of Ancient Egypt," *International Journal of Dream Research* 4 (2011), 24–30; R. G. A. van Lieshout, *Greeks on Dreams* (1980); G. H. Walter, "Dreams in the Literature of the Ancient Near East and the Babylonian Talmud," rabbinic thesis, Hebrew Union College/Jewish Institute of Religion (1974); E. Wente, trans., *Letters from Ancient Egypt*, ed. E. S. Meltzer (1990); R. White, trans., *The*

Interpretation of Dreams: The Oneirocritica of Artemidorus (1975); F. Williams, trans., *The Panarion of Epiphanius of Salamis, Book I (Sects 1–46)* (1987); A. Zgoll, "Dreams as Gods and Gods in Dreams: Dream-Realities in Ancient Mesopotamia from the 3rd to the 1st Millennium B.C.," in *He Has Opened Nisaba's House of Learning: Studies in Honor of Åke Waldemar Sjöberg*, ed. L. Sassmannshausen and G. Neumann (2013), 299–313.

EMY

See also ASTROLOGY and DIVINATION & SORTITION.

DWELLINGS

To dwell implies to reside in a fixed place. Dwellings are places in which people reside to protect themselves and their possessions. Early hunters and gatherers did not reside in fixed places. As wanderers in search of game and edible vegetation, they used materials at hand to make temporary windbreaks and to provide shade for themselves. Any of these temporary shelters and animal-hide tents, if used, have completely disappeared. Tents made of woven hair became possible only after the domestication of sheep and goats.

Archaeological evidence indicates that caves also served as early dwellings in terrain where they naturally occurred. Examples of caves that have been excavated in Israel, Lebanon, and Syria are the Tabun, Zuttiyeh, Jabrud, and Bezes caves. Caverns provide a dry environment with a stable, comfortable temperature, protection from the elements, and security from other threats. These advantages explain the continuing use of some caves in Israel and Jordan as dwellings into modern times.

A. THE OLD TESTAMENT

Dwellings mentioned in the OT include both primitive shelters such as caves and even the shade of plants as well as shelters both moveable and those of a more permanent nature ranging from ordinary to palatial in size. In addition to temporary shelter, caves were also used as places of hiding. After leaving Zoar, Lot and his two daughters lived in a cave (Gen 19:30). Elijah fled to a cave in Mount Horeb (1 Kgs 19:9). Because of the oppression of the Midianites, the Israelites hid in caves (Judg 6:2).

The first biblical reference to building is to Cain's building a city in the land to which he wandered east of Eden (Gen 4:17). As this was apparently in Mesopotamia, we can assume that he employed mud-brick construction techniques. Tents (Heb. sing. ʾōhel) are first mentioned in reference to Jabal, the progenitor of "those who live in tents and raise livestock" (Gen

4:20). The patriarchs Abraham (Gen 13:18) and Jacob (Gen 25:27) lived in tents. The Israelites lived in tents after they left Egypt and were on their way to the promised land (Num 1:52). Even after most of the people had settled in villages and towns, nomadic shepherds like the Rechabites remained tent dwellers (Jer 35:6–10).

Some Bedouin still dwell in black goat-hair tents similar to those used by the biblical patriarchs. These tents are made of panels of woven goat hair, wooden poles, guy ropes, and tent pegs. The panels are about one three feet wide and from thirty to fifty feet long, and are stitched together side by side to attain the width desired for the roof. The roof is raised on center poles six or more feet in height, and on lower side poles. The side panels are attached to the side poles, but the front is left open. The tent is erected with the front facing east, away from the prevailing wind. The guy ropes extend out several yards and are anchored to the tent pegs. A single-room tent is twelve to sixteen feet long; tents with multiple rooms may extend up to 150 feet. Such tents may last fifteen to twenty years before they wear out; the smaller the tent, the longer it will last.

The tent is ideal for those whose wealth is in small and large cattle and who must move as needed to access available forage. Such people do not live in individual isolation, but in encampments of families or clans associated with other tribal encampments. Available resources determine the size of camps, as in the case of Abraham and Lot (Gen 13:6–12). The tent remained in the consciousness of Israel long after the people were dwelling in houses, as is evident from the rallying cry "To your tents, O Israel!" (2 Sam 20:1).

God commanded Moses to build a tent called the "tabernacle," a word that comes from Latin *tabernaculum*, which simply means "tent." (The Hebrew term for the tabernacle, *miškān*, literally means "dwelling place.") It was appropriate for the deity of a nomadic people to dwell in a tent. The tabernacle was a grandiose, portable shrine protected by a goat-hair tent (Exod 26:7). The layout of the tent, with certain rooms curtained off from visitors to the holy encampment and access limited only to the servants (priests), coincided with that of a pastoralist's tent, in which access to some rooms was limited to the family only. In expressing his desire to build a more permanent dwelling for the Lord, David said to Nathan (2 Sam 7:2): "Here I am, living in a house of cedar, while the ark of God remains in a tent" (2 Sam 7:2).

The Hebrew word *bayit*, "house," which appears over two thousand times in the OT, has cognates in a number of other Semitic languages (e.g., Akk. *bītu*; Ugar. and Phoen. *bt*; Aram. *byt*; Eth. *bēt*; Arab. *bayt*), indicating the antiquity of the root in Semitic. In Hebrew the word has a broad range of meanings, including "palace," "temple," "household," "family," "dynasty," and other extended nuances.

Wooden beams from a variety of trees, such as oak, pine, and terebinth, were available in Palestine. More opulent homes, such as those of kings, or large buildings such as temples that required larger beams could make use of imported cypress or cedars from Lebanon (Isa 9:10). The primary building material was sun-dried mud-brick, which was vulnerable to erosion by wind and rain (Ezek 13:10–18). Baked bricks (Gen 11:3), which were used in Babylonian palaces, for example, were far too expensive to produce for general use.

In the earliest settlements associated with the Israelites, the occupational evidence consists of numerous storage pits. This suggests that at an early stage the Israelites still dwelled in tents. Next, early villages with up to twenty houses of the "pillared four-room" type, a building form that may have evolved from the tent, are evident. About 150 examples of this kind of four-room house, dating from the eleventh century BC to the end of the kingdom of Judah, i.e., the early sixth century BC, have been found at such sites as Tell Beit Mirsim, Beth Shemesh, Hazor, and Tel Beersheba. This type of house seems to be characteristic of the Israelites, with only a few examples found in Philistine territory.

Such houses consisted of a windowless outer wall penetrated by a single door opening that led into a courtyard that was divided into roofed and unroofed areas by four pillars. Depending on the local building materials, the structure might be made of stone or mud-brick set on a low stone foundation (so as to protect the lowest level of the building's mud-brick walls from erosion caused by runoff rain water). Two or three rooms might be partitioned beneath the roofed part of the building. Each house would accommodate one family, with other houses arranged in a circular pattern about a central open space so as to provide a perimeter wall for security and to allow a large open area within the enclosure for multipurpose uses. Animals including donkeys, sheep, goats, and cattle were kept in the courtyard of each house, which would provide a degree of heat during the winter cold.

Typically, such houses, which usually included a second floor, provided about 1,500 square feet of living space. Rooms would average between five feet by eight feet and eight feet by eight feet. The height of the rooms ranged from seven to twelve feet. The second floor (ʿăliyyâ) was reached by either wooden steps or ladders. Some houses had a guest chamber in the upper room such as those used by Elijah and Elisha (1 Kgs 17:19, 23; 2 Kgs 4:10).

The roofs of Israelite houses were flat, supported by wooden beams and made of slats covered with mud. They could be used for many activities such as the drying of figs, dates, and flax (cf. Josh 2:6–7), as well as for sleeping. As a safeguard from falling, Deut 22:8 stipulates, "When you build a new house, make a parapet around your roof so that you may not bring the guilt of bloodshed on your house if someone falls from the root." The prophets condemned the practice of worshiping pagan gods such as astral deities on roofs (Jer 19:13; 32:29; Zeph 1:5). After the rainy season, when leaks would develop (Prov 19:13; 27:15; Eccl 10:18), roofs had to be repaired by the addition of more mud, which would then be smoothed with stone rollers, some of which have been found. Seeds from the mud that was used would sprout on the roof (2 Kgs 19:26; Ps 129:6; Isa 37:27).

Windows were generally situated high up on walls. They were narrow, to keep out the heat in the summer and the cold in the winter, but large enough for a man to pass through (Josh 2:15; 1 Sam 19:12). Windows of the wealthier homes were covered with lattices (Judg 5:28; 2 Kgs 1:2; Prov 7:6; Song 2:9).

Various domestic tasks occurred in Israelite dwellings. Cooking was performed by using a small clay oven or a cooking pot. Fuel was provided by charcoal, dry twigs, or dried animal dung (Ezek 4:15). As Israelite houses had no chimney, the smoke generated from cooking escaped through the open door or a window (Hos 13:3). Houses were provided with cisterns to contain water for household use (2 Kgs 18:31).

The establishment of a strong central government during the period of the monarchy brought a transition from village life to city life at many locations. Within city walls, rectangular blocks of houses were built back-to-back with an alley separating them, as can be seen, for example, at Tel Beersheba. Each house had a single entrance into a courtyard, at least three rooms on a lower level, and additional rooms on an upper level. The construction of fortified gates and walls, governmental administrative buildings, and palaces in some cities reduced the available space for family homeswithin the city proper. Urban houses were smaller than rural ones, since city dwellers were not accustomed to keeping animals in their houses.

B. THE NEW TESTAMENT

Paul and his friends Aquila and Priscilla were *skēnopoioi*, "tentmakers" (Acts 18:3). The NT uses the word "tent" (Gk. *skēnos, skēnōma*) metaphorically to refer to the temporary habitation that is the human body (2 Cor 5:4; 2 Pet 1:13–14). The divine Logos "tabernacled" (cf. YLT), or, more literally, "pitched his tent" (*eskēnōsen*), among humankind (John 1:14).

The concept of "house" or "dwelling" is expressed in Greek by the words *oikos* and *oikia*, which basically overlap in meaning. In the LXX, *oikos* regularly translates Hebrew *bayit*, with its various nuances. The phrase "house

of God" can refer to the physical temple but it is also used metaphorically
to refer to the community of believers in both the old and new dispensa-
tions (Heb 3:2–6; 1 Pet 2:5). Residences for people in NT times varied according to social status, wealth, and regional location.

One of Jesus's parables discusses the necessity of building a house's
foundation not on sand but on rock, so that the house could withstand
storms, which occasioned runoff from rain that could cause damage to
or undermine the bottom of a building's outer wall (Matt 7:24–27). Jesus's
saying that no one lights a lamp and places it in a *kryptē*, "dark or hidden
place," i.e., a cellar (Luke 11:33), is an adaptation to a non-Palestinian setting, as there were no cellars in Palestinian homes. Jesus declares that in
his Father's house there are many *monai* (sing. *monē*) "rooms" (NIV) or
"dwelling places" (NRSV); the KJV translation "mansions" reflects a use
of the word "mansion" (which is derived from Lat. *mansio*, "abode") that
is now outdated and therefore misleading in this context. The word *monē*
occurs elsewhere in the NT only in John 14:23, where Jesus states that he
and his Father will "make our home [*monēn*]" with those who obey Jesus's
teaching. Walls in NT times were whitewashed (cf. Acts 23:3) and floors
were made of packed dirt or of cobblestones, among which small objects,
for example, coins, could easily be lost (Luke 15:8).

In Capernaum houses were made of basalt; in Judea they were made of
limestone. They were situated on either side of narrow lanes. Each house
included an entrance into a courtyard, which would have contained one or
more ovens near plastered cisterns, which were for storing rainwater. From
a house's courtyard a stairway would have led to a flat roof. One one occasion when four men carrying their friend on a litter could not get close
to Jesus because of the crowds, they tore a hole in the roof and lowered
him down into Jesus's presence (Mark 2:1–5). The mention of roof tiles
(*keramōn*) in Luke's version of this story (Luke 5:17–26, esp. vs. 19) is a
narrative adaptation reflecting a Roman architectural feature that was not
introduced into Palestine until after the Roman conquest in AD 70. Numerous ceramic tiles stamped "LEGIO X," a reference to the Tenth Legion
that occupied Jerusalem, have been found. At the home of Simon the Tanner in Joppa, Peter went up to the roof (*dōma*) to pray (Acts 10:9).

The upper room (*anagaion*) where Jesus and his disciples ate the Last
Supper was a *triclinium*, which would have contained three couches where
they could recline, as was the custom (Mark 14:12–18||Luke 22:7–14; John
13:23–25). After Jesus's ascension, the early disciples met for prayer and
fellowship in an upper room (*hyperōon*; Acts 1:13). When Paul kept talk-
ing through the night in a third-floor upper room at Troas, a youth named
Eutychus who was sitting in one of the room's window fell asleep and fell
out of the window to his death, but was revived by Paul (Acts 20:7–10).

Hospitality was crucial for the spread of the gospel. While Jesus embarked on an itinerant ministry, he stayed at the homes of his friends (Matt 8:20). No matter whether early Christians lived in poor or prosperous housing, they were to practice hospitality (Rom 12:13; 1 Pet 1:9). In the NT period and later, Christians assembled for worship and fellowship in "house churches" (cf. Acts 5:42), which were typically made available at the generosity of the wealthier members of the community of believers. The book of Acts mentions gatherings of believers at the house of Mary, the mother of John Mark (Acts 12:12), the house of Lydia at Philippi (Acts 16:15, 40), and the house of Titus Justus in Corinth (Acts 18:7). In his letters, Paul mentions churches in the house of Priscilla and Aquila at Ephesus (1 Cor 16:19–24), and also in their home at Rome (Rom 16:3–5), in the home of Philemon at Colosse (Phlm 2, 22), and in the house of Nympha at Laodicea (Col 4:15). Most house churches could probably have accommodated between thirty and forty persons. At Corinth there may have been six or more house churches. Before his conversion, Saul went from house to house to search out members of "the Way" (Acts 8:3; 9:2).

In the typical Roman house of Paul's day, an example of which is the Villa at Anaploga near Corinth, there were only two spaces available for a large group: (1) the *triclinium* or dining area (in the Villa at Anaploga this was 42.25 sq. m. = 455 sq. ft.), and (2) the atrium (in the Villa at Anaploga this was 30 sq. m. = 322 sq. ft.), whose space for activity was reduced by the *impluvium* or pool for rain water that it contained. The wealthy host would be inclined to invite his peers into the *triclinium*, while "the many" (*hoi polloi*) would be left to gather in the atrium. The Roman custom of offering different kinds of food to the guests in different rooms may be at the root of the tensions involved in the agape meal practices described in 1 Cor 11:17–34.

When Paul was under house arrest in Rome, he occupied a rented apartment (Gk. *misthōmati*, lit., "that which is rented"; Acts 28:30)—not "house," as in NIV—which was no doubt paid for by his friends. He had enough space and freedom to entertain visitors, both Christians and Jews (Acts 28:16–31).

C. THE NEAR EASTERN WORLD

Early hunters and gatherers lived in caves. The Neolithic revolution ushered in fundamental social changes. The domestication of plants and animals allowed for a settled way of life, including the construction of dwellings. The earliest houses, which date back to the eighth and seventh millennia BC, were oval, single-room structures. These early dwellings, which were clustered together, suggest small villages of related clan members in an apparently egalitarian society. The floors were often in pits dug within and below the foundation stones. This allowed for the construction of lower outside walls and roofs, which were probably constructed in reeds, branches, and mud plaster, according to what was available in the immediate environment.

Mesopotamia

Throughout the millennia, married children built houses next to their parents' home, as attested, for example, at Nippur. In time, dwellings came to reflect social stratification with larger structures for the elite as well as more humble residences for most. Each region of the ancient Near East developed its own characteristic housing based on the environment, the available building materials, and social patterns. With housing, as with all human artifices, form followed function and underwent modest change over time.

In the southern, marshy regions of Mesopotamia, dwellings constructed with reed bundles bent over at the top to form a tent-like structure followed a tradition that has been continued into modern times by the Marsh Arabs and Mandaeans in these areas.

The Sumerians established the first sophisticated sedentary culture. Climatic changes following the last Ice Age allowed meadow and shrub lands to emerge from earlier swamps and mudflats, and people moved out of the highlands into the valleys of Mesopotamia. The earliest structures show no ordered planning, and adjoining rooms were added as space allowed. Some third-millennium BC houses at Uruk and Fara enclosed four hundred square meters (4305 sq. ft.), while later, second-millennium BC Old Babylonian houses were smaller, measuring one hundred square meters (1076 sq. ft.). Only larger houses would have specialized rooms like kitchens, bathrooms, and household shrines. The typical Sumerian house was a two-story building surrounding a courtyard.

The basic building material of these structures was mud-brick and mud-plaster. In order to keep the bricks from cracking when they dried, the clay would be mixed with a temper made of finely chopped straw, animal dung, sand, or grit. After the winter rains and spring floods, the first summer month (May to June) was known as the "month of bricks." Brick structures would normally last for up to thirty years. Houses too damaged to repair would be razed and a new house would be built on the raised foundation of a previous house. As city walls circumscribed the available building area within the city, the result within the walls was the slow formation of hill-like tells.

In the fourth millennium BC, the Sumerians invented the corbeled arch, with two sets of bricks or stone slabs coming closer to each other as they rose till they met at the top of the apex of a triangle. A few small openings placed high in the walls served as windows for ventilation. These were covered either by wooden grills or perforated clay disks.

Earthen floors were likely covered with rush mats or carpets. Many houses would have shrines dedicated to protective deities. Apotropaic statues were also frequently installed. Family members buried their dead below their houses at Ur, Mari, Babylon, Ashur, and Ugarit.

The layout of the residential area of an Old Babylonian city has been described as a tangle of narrow lanes leading off from wider passages, with single-story poorer houses mixed with richer houses of two stories that were lighted by open courtyards, similar in many respects to structures still found in older cities of modern Iraq.

House walls were six to eight feet thick, providing a cool respite from the intensity of the sun. The walls were whitewashed to reflect sunlight. Houses were built around courtyards, which occupied one-fifth to one-quarter of the total area of the building. These courtyards often housed animals and provided storage space. The homes of some wealthy households had by the entrance to the courtyard a small room for a slave who served as a doorkeeper. Some houses had facilities for guests to wash their feet before entering. Courtyards contained hearths made of brick for cooking. These would be heated with charcoal made from palm wood. Large pottery jars full of water brought from the river would also be stored in the courtyard.

Courtyards in the south of the region were roofed with palm logs, while in the north poplar wood would be used for roofing. At the opposite end of the courtyard from the entrance would be a long reception room where visitors were entertained. Ladders gave access to second stories and to the roof. The smoke from the fire would escape through an opening in the roof. Roofs would need to be repaired from time to time. A man in a Mesopotamian proverb complained, "I dwell in a house of asphalt and bricks, yet some clay . . . pours over me" (*ANET*, 425). In the Ugaritic poem about Aqhat, the job of the sons of the family was to plaster the roof with mud to prevent seepage of water during the rainy season.

By the time of Nebuchadnezzar II (r. 605–562 BC), courtyards and floors would often be surfaced with fired bricks. Some floors were covered with a composite of bitumen and powdered limestone. Further to the north, in Assyria, where stone was more plentiful than in the alluvial plain, foundations of stone were used, but most construction was still of mud-brick.

Roofs were flat, made of horizontal timbers with layers of reeds, palm leaves, and mud, and at times also had roof drains running down through the walls to exit into the street. By the Old Babylonian period fired brick with bitumen mortar was used to keep water away from foundations.

Extensive cases regarding builders and their liabilities are recorded in the famous eighteenth-century BC Code of Hammurabi (CH). For example, CH 229 stipulates: "If a builder constructs a house for a man but does not make his work sound, and the house that he constructs collapses and causes the death of the householder, that builder shall be killed" (*COS* 2.131:349). CH 230 further states: "If it should cause the death of a son of the householder, they shall kill a son of that builder" (*COS* 2.131:349).

Egypt

We are exceptionally well informed about dwellings in Egypt, because of the widespread custom of providing tombs with elaborate paintings and even models of daily life as provisions for the afterlife. Sites that have preserved extensive remains of workmen's houses are the city of Lahun, the royal site of Amarna, and the village of Deir el-Medina.

Even before the Dynastic period began (ca. 3100 BC), Egyptians were building with mud-brick. Nile mud continued to be the construction material of choice for the peasant population, even into the modern era. Of interest is the fact that the word *adobe*, which refers to sun-dried mud used for construction, is ultimately derived from Egyptian *djebe*, "brick," which became Coptic *tōōbe*, Arabic *aṭ-ṭub*, and then Spanish *adobe*.

Mud would be mixed with water, then kneaded by workmen's feet. It was necessary to mix the mud with sand and chopped straw (cf. Exod 5:7–10). The process is illustrated from a famous scene in the tomb of Rekhmire (18th Dyn.). Workmen put the mud in wooden brick molds and allowed it to dry for a week or so. In the *Satire of the Trades*, a scribe describes professions other than his own pejoratively, including that of making mud-bricks: "The small building contractor carries mud. . . . He is *dirtier* than vines or pigs, *from treading* under his mud. His clothes are stiff with clay" (*ANET*, 433).

At Lahun the village of the workmen who built a 12th Dynasty pyramid was uncovered. It was a walled village with a broad avenue running north and south. It had a block of sixty-four small, three-room houses that were only fifty square meters (540 sq. ft.). There were also medium-sized houses with six rooms (100 sq. m. = 1,075 sq. ft.). A large mansion with thirty thousand square feet of space must have belonged to the mayor of the town.

At Akhenaten's new capital at Amarna (ca. 1350 BC), in addition to palaces a large variety of dwellings was discovered. In the South Suburb there were originally an estimated 2,400 houses. There were small dwellings (50–80 sq. m.) with four to six rooms, medium houses (80–150 sq. m.) with eight rooms, and large residences (150–200 sq. m.) with fifteen rooms. The largest was the palatial home of the vizier Nakht, which was eight hundred square meters and had thirty rooms. His house was decorated with a blue ceiling and brightly painted columns.

The typical house at Amarna, as well as elsewhere in Egypt in this period and for some centuries to follow, had at least four rooms: an outer hall, a living room with a column, a back bedroom, and a kitchen with stairs leading up to the roof. Some of the houses had shrines with reliefs of Akhenaten and Nefertiti worshipping the sun god Aten.

As an example of this, the workmen's village at Deir el-Medina, which was founded by Tuthmosis I (18th Dynasty, ca. 1500 BC), flourished for four centuries, until the 20th Dynasty. This village consisted of the homes of the workers who carved out the tombs in the nearby Valley of the Kings. The village was 50 meters x 130 meters (164 x 426 ft.) in size, was enclosed in a perimeter wall, and contained seventy houses. These houses were one-story dwellings each with four rooms. The entrance hall had the family's shrine to the gods. The middle room had a column that supported the roof, and served as the main living room. The next room was used for sleeping and storage. The kitchen was located at the rear of the house. It was walled but open to the sky. A staircase led to the flat roof; some houses had underground cellars.

Most homes in the cities would be enclosed by a mud-brick perimeter wall about three meters (10 ft.) high. The single entry would have faced north to take advantage of the prevailing winds. The outside of the wall would have been whitewashed, while the interior of the wall would have been colorfully decorated.

The courtyard of Egyptian homes contained adobe brick structures for the storage of grain. Around the court were workrooms for spinning, weaving, grinding grain, baking bread, and brewing beer. Homes of the wealthy might have a slaughterhouse where cows would be butchered and their meat hung to dry.

A typical inscription on the entrance door would read: "May Amun-Re, Lord of the Thrones of the Two Lands, give life, prosperity, health, joy, favor, and love." The first room was a foyer with an altar and related religious objects, including representations of the household's protective deity, Bes. The central room, with its higher ceiling, often supported by one or two colums, was illuminated by small windows with wooden lattices to keep the birds out. This room served as the social center for entertaining guests and as the main dining room. Tomb paintings depicting such rooms show large dining tables laden with loaves of bread, fruit, meat, and flowers.

One or more private bedrooms lay beyond this room. These rooms would be provided with niches for oil lamps, adobe benches, and raised alcoves for sleeping. Some homes had bedrooms on an upper story.

At the rear of the house was a kitchen and a stairway to the flat roof, which was surrounded by a parapet. The roof was used for storage, relaxing, and even sleeping. Some roofs were provided with awnings, and even scoops that caught the breezes from the north and circulated them through vents to the rooms below.

In addition to employing window lattices for keeping out birds, as noted above, the Egyptians, like householders from every age, are known to have used all kinds of concoctions, often in vain, to keep out unwanted visitors: a solution of natron for driving off insects, oriole grease against flies, fish spawn against fleas, and cat grease to drive off rats.

D. THE GRECO-ROMAN WORLD

Greece

The best evidence for dwellings in the Minoan Era (2000–1450 BC) comes from the town of Gournia east of Knossos on the north coast of Crete. In addition to a small palace, multistoried houses had lined a steep street. The houses were built with mud-bricks, which were coated with lime plaster. So-called "town mosaics" made of faience depict two-story houses with flat roofs. Wooden beams alternated with stones as a buffer against the earthquakes occurring in the region. Window frames were painted red. The volcanic eruption in the late Minoan period resulted in widespread destruction on the island of Santorini (Thera) and preserved the town of Akrotiri in much the same way that the eruption of Mt. Vesuvius preserved the city of Pompeii in Italy about 1500 years later. Some of the buildings in Akrotiri rose to three stories and had been built of ashlar (rectangular-stone) masonry, mud-brick, and rubble interspersed with timber. Magnificent frescoes depicting a naval battle scene, monkeys, and flowers have been recovered.

From the early Iron Age (10th–8th c. BC) come the earliest Greek houses, which were semi-circular, one-room dwellings that contained a hearth. Most activities must have taken place outdoors. From the eighth century BC, simple courtyard houses with two or three rooms were built at sites all around the Aegean. By the late fifth century BC, in order, apparently, to keep their women from the eyes of strangers, families built high walls around their houses.

In the Classical Age (5th c. BC), during which the Athenians erected magnificent temples in marble, domestic dwellings were surprisingly modest, as recounted by Pseudo-Dichaearchus: "Most of the houses are mean, the nice ones few. A stranger would doubt, on seeing it first, if this were really the renowned city of the Athenians" (Ault and Nevett, 141). In the fourth century BC Demosthenes declared: "Out of the wealth of the state they set up for our delight so many fair buildings . . . yet in private they were so modest, so careful to obey the spirit of the constitution, that the houses of their famous men, of Aristides or of Miltiades, as any of you can see that knows them, are not a whit more splendid than those of their neighbours" (3 *Olynth.* 25). In the third century BC a traveller remarked that, with only a few exceptions, almost all the houses were of very poor quality.

Greek houses were set upon stone foundations and built with mud-brick and timber framing. Some walls were so thin that burglars went directly through the walls and were thus known as *toichōrhychoi*, "wall piercers." Floors were earthen. Early Greek roofs were thatch roofs. The thatch was later replaced by large terra-cotta pantiles, two to three feet long and one and a half to two feet wide. The roof was slanted to direct rain water to an underground cistern in the court. Some houses had balconies that extended over the street, an extension that could be considered illegal.

The bedrooms, including the *thalamos* (master bedroom), were often located upstairs. The upstairs could be accessed by a *klimax*, an external wooden staircase. Texts speak of the *gynaikeion/gynaikōnitis*, or "women's quarters." In Xenophon's *Oeconomicus* (9.5), Ischomachus reports, "I also showed her the *gunaikonitis* ['women's apartments'], divided from the *andronitis* ['men's apartments'] by a bolted door, so that nothing can be taken from inside which should not be, and the inhabitants cannot have children without us knowing" (Nevett, 17). In a celebrated court case (Lysias, *On the Murder of Eratosthenes* 1.9), the defendant, Euphiletos, who strangled his wife's lover, explained: "My little house is on two floors, with equal space upstairs and down for the '*gunaikonitis*' ['women's quarters'] and the '*andronitis*' ['men's quarters']. When our child was born its mother fed it; so that she should not endanger herself going downstairs each time the baby had to be washed, I lived upstairs and the women below" (Nevett, 18). Although most of the time that women were indoors was spent in their quarters, the archaeological evidence indicates that they were also active in all areas of the house save in the one area reserved for men.

The most elaborately decorated room was the *andrōn*, or men's quarters, where three dining couches (*triklinai*) were placed in a U-shaped arrangement for the *symposion*, or evening banquet, for the entertainment of men who were accompanied not by their wives but by *hetairai*, female companions. Some large dining areas could hold as many as eleven couches.

In Athens itself only a few private dwellings have been excavated, including the so-called Cobbler's House, owned by Simo, a friend of Socrates. The house, which was 13 x 15 meters (42 x 49 ft.), had a modest courtyard (5.5 x 6.5 m. = 18 x 21 ft.). The houses of the sculptors Micon and Menon had ten rooms, with eight of them opening around a courtyard.

After the conquests of Alexander, the wealth acquired by the Macedonians and Greeks was manifested in the increasing elegance of Hellenistic houses. In the fourth century BC homes added a *peristyle*, that is, a garden space surrounded on four sides with columns. Also in this period mosaics, which were patterns originally made with black and white pebbles, were created with *tesserae*, carefully cut cubes of stone, to create geometric and figural patterns. Of certain wealthy Athenians Demosthenes writes: "today every man who takes part in public life enjoys such superfluity of wealth that some of them have built private dwelling-houses more magnificent than many public buildings" (*Against Aristocrates* 208).

The most extensive archaeological remains of Greek houses were uncovered at Olynthus in northeastern Greece, a city that was destroyed by Philip, the father of Alexander, in 348 BC. The community was laid out in blocks in the orthogonal Hippodamian plan, with each block (300 x 120 ft.) containing ten houses with common walls. Each block was bisected by a narrow alley, which was provided with a *stenōpos*, a drainage channel. The houses were centered on courtyards, which ranged from ten to one hundred square meters in size. These were paved with cobbles and were provided with cisterns to collect rain water. The living rooms were placed in the north. The lower floor was fronted by a wooden colonnade (*pasta*), with a gallery above; both of these were open to sunlight from the south. Only four of the more than forty houses uncovered at Olynthus (late 5th and early 4th c. BC) had peristyles. Later, peristyle courtyards became characteristic of Hellenistic houses.

Another type of Hellenistic house was uncovered at Priene (4th c. BC) in western Turkey. It is characterized by a *prostas* (lit., "standing in front"), which was a porch or anteroom with two columns. Also in the front was an *exedra*, or sitting room. The main room, which was shaded by a shallow porch, was placed on the north side of the court, so it could face south.

In the Hellenistic period a high-quality plaster named *stucco* (Gk. *koniama*) was developed. Made of slaked lime, quartz particles, and gypsum, its density and plasticity enabled artisans to smooth it or shape it into decorative patterns, using a *triptēr*, a board with a handle.

At the site of the Panhellenic games or at healing shrines that attracted many visitors, *katagōgia*, or hostels, were erected. The Leonidaion at Olympia was built around a central court. It extended 75 x 81 meters (247 x 266 ft.) and could accommodate fifty athletes. A smaller hostel at Nemea held fourteen rooms for athletes. At Epidaurus a hostel had seventy rooms for sick pilgrims seeking healing.

Some buildings had multiple occupancies (*synoikiai*). Apartments or houses could be rented. If the landlord was not paid, he could make life miserable for the tenants who refused to leave. He could deny them the use of the well, remove the front door from the house, and even strip off tiles from the roof.

Even in the golden age of Athens under Pericles, there were homeless people. When the weather turned cold, they would seek refuge in the baths, huddling near the furnaces. In the crisis of the Peloponnesian civil war between Athens and Sparta (431–404 BC), masses fled the countryside for refuge between the long walls that connected Athens to its harbor at the Piraeus. According to Thucydides, "they had to live in huts that were stifling [*kalybais pnigērais*] in the hot season" (*Hist.* 2.52). Diogenes, the famous Cynic, disdained the comfort of a home and lived in temples during the summer and in the public baths during the winter, and even for a time in a large jar.

Rome

In the early history of Rome, shepherds lived in huts made of wattle (interlocking branches) covered with daub (mud), under sloping thatched roofs. In time, these were replaced by mud-brick buildings with wooden roofs covered with fired clay tiles (*tegulae*). The joints between these flat-pan tiles were covered by semicylindrical cover tiles (*imbrices*).

Italy abounded in fir trees that grew to one hundred feet and pine trees that grew to sixty feet. These provided the most common timber for building. Cedar and juniper were valued for their resistance to rot.

The Romans had a variety of stones for construction, including limestone, volcanic tufa, and travertine, which, like stalactites and stalagmites, is formed through the deposition of calcium carbonate in water. The Romans' most important and versatile building material was cement, which was first developed in Campania during the third century BC from the local *pozzolana*, volcanic sand, which was mixed with lime and water to form a strong but versatile concrete. Cement was in general use in Rome by the second century BC.

The earliest types of walls were made in the *opus incertum* style, which used rough stones placed in cement. By the second century BC walls were made in the *opus reticulatum* style, which featured uniform stones set in concrete in a net-like pattern. From the first century BC through the imperial period a style called *opus latericium* or *opus testaceum*, which used baked bricks set in concrete, became dominant.

The eruption of Vesuvius in AD 79 preserved many homes at Pompeii and Herculaneum, some up to the second story, and also their furniture and stunning wall frescoes. The tourist guide books list seventy-eight homes in Pompeii and thirty-one in Herculaneum that have been uncovered and are open to tourists. The average home in Pompeii enclosed about 280 square meters (3,000 sq. ft.). Lead pipes provided running water to most houses.

The best-preserved house in Herculaneum is the *Opus Craticum*, or Trellis House, which occupied an entire block. Two families used opposite entrances. Its name comes from the use of thinly plastered partitions made of laths. Rooms along the streets were converted into shops and small dwellings (of about 10 x 10 ft.) for shopkeepers. Many shops at Herculaneum and Pompeii were food shops with counters equipped with large *dolia* (jugs) filled with a variety of foods. Customers either ate the food standing or took the food to their homes.

The most magnificent house at Herculaneum was the three-story House of Telephus, which was probably the house of Marcus Nonius Balbus, the proconsul of Crete and Libya. Its preserved roof permits the first full reconstruction of the timberwork of a Roman roof. Its magnificent dining room had a polychrome marble floor and a ceiling thirty feet high.

The typical home at Pompeii, such as the House of Sallust, contained both an *atrium* and a *peristyle*, an innovation introduced from the Greeks in the second century BC. The door from the street led through the *fauces* ("jaws") into the *atrium*, a large, lofty room with a square hole in the roof that was situated above a stone-lined *impluvium*, which channeled rainwater into a cistern below. Beyond the atrium was the *tablinum*, a small room that contained *tabulae*, the family records, and *imagines*, funeral portrait masks of the family's male ancestors. Behind this was the *peristyle*, a garden (*hortus*) surrounded on four sides by porticoes. The House of Menander had five reception rooms around its *peristyle*. In some homes a pool for fish was also included. Moreover, some houses, such as the House of the Faun, had a *balneum*, a private bath system.

Unlike the Greeks, who kept their homes private, aristocratic Romans deliberately kept their doors open so the public could view their wealth. Livius Drusus (the plebian tribune in 91 BC) instructed his architect, "Take ten [talents] and make the whole house open to view, that all the citizens may see how I live" (*Praecepta Gerendae Republicae* 4). Cicero declared, "My house stands in full view of virtually the whole city" (*Dom.* 100)

In 25 BC Vitruvius decreed, "Advocates and professors of rhetoric should be housed with distinction, and in sufficient space to accommodate their audiences. For persons of high rank who hold office and magistracies, and whose duty it is to serve the state, we must provide princely vestibules, lofty halls and very spacious peristyles" (*De Architectura* 6.5.2).

It was customary for clients (*clientes*) to pay a call to their patron (*patronus*). During this morning *salutation,* from the first to the second hours of the day, clients would visit their patrons to receive their *sportulae* (gifts and food portions). The head of the house would then leave the house to visit the forum and the baths, only to return for dinner at the ninth hour (about 3 p.m.).

The most elaborately decorated room would be the dining room, or *triclinium,* so called because it was provided with three couches, with each couch usually bearing three men, each of whom reclined on his left elbow, and a low, circular table in the middle. The dinner was served by slaves known as *servi triclinarii.* Slaves slept in small, dark, undecorated rooms (*cellae*); some slaves, such as the *cubicularii,* slept outside the bedroom (*cubicula*) door, so they could be on call at night. Some children slept with their slave nursemaids and tutors.

Wealthy Romans were fond of villas, elaborate country homes located originally in agricultural areas and later on the coast (*villae maritimae*). Away from the bustle of Rome, such people could enjoy *otium cum dignitate,* "quiet relaxation with culture."

Columella stated:

> The manor house should be divided in turn into winter apartments and summer apartments, in such a way that the winter bedrooms may face the sunrise at the winter solstice, and the winter dining-room face the sunset at the equinox. The summer bedrooms, on the other hand, should look toward the midday sun at the time of the equinox, but the dining-rooms of that season should look toward the rising sun of winter. The baths should face the setting sun of summer, that they may be lighted from midday up to evening. . . . It will be best that cubicles for unfettered slaves be built to admit the midday sun at the equinox; for those who are in chains there should be an underground prison, as wholesome as possible, receiving light through a number of narrow windows. (*Rust.* 1.6.1–3)

The villa at Boscoreale (two miles north of Pompeii) was a classic farm villa (*villa rustica*). Its central court separated the domestic section from the agricultural quarters. The major room of the residence was the *triclinium.* There were three small bedrooms; other bedrooms may have been located on an upper floor. The villa's facilities included a kitchen, furnace room, bakery, baths, and a toilet. An entrance led to the cellar. The farm was equipped with oil presses and winepresses. In the *cella olearia,* there would have been enough stone jars to hold 1,300 gallons of olive oil. In the large *cella vinaria*, there were numerous clay *dolia* (wine-storing jars) for the fermentation and storage of twenty-three thousand gallons of wine.

Pliny the Younger describes his villas in loving detail in his letters. His Tuscan villa had both an indoor and an outdoor swimming pool. It had a superb view of his vineyards and the mountains. Pliny declared, "I have now informed you why I prefer my Tuscan villa, to those which I possess at Tusculum, Tibur, and Praeneste" (*Ep.* 5.6). His villa at Laurentum was on the coast. It had extensive terraces, porticoes, libraries, baths, gardens, and exercise areas. Pliny wrote:

> Crowning the terrace, portico [*cryptoporticus*, a corridor formed by a portico walled on both sides], and garden, stands a detached building, which I call my *favourite*: and in truth I am extremely fond of it, as I erected it myself. It contains a very warm winter-room [*Heliocaminus*, a sun-parlor], one side of which looks upon the terrace, the other has a view of the sea, and both lie exposed to the sun. (*Ep.* 2.17)

The Villa of the Papyri at Herculaneum was explored by tunneling in the eighteenth century. Its extensive peristyle was provided with gardens and *piscinae*, pools. In addition to magnificent bronze and marble sculptures, remains of 1,800 carbonized papyrus rolls, including Epicurean writings, were recovered. The villa probably belonged to L. Calpurnius Piso, the father-in-law of Julius Caesar. The plan of the villa has been faithfully reproduced in the lavish Paul Getty Museum of Greek and Roman Antiquities in Malibu, California.

Perhaps the grandest villa of all at Pompeii is the Villa of Mysteries outside the city's Herculaneum gate. It covered more than an acre and included a residence that had sixty rooms. Its most famous feature is a unique painting that measures sixty-nine feet long and covers three sides of a room. This artwork depicts figures involved in the Dionysiac mysteries, including Silenus, a follower of Bacchus (Dionysus). A female Bacchante whirls in a dance, clicking castanets above her head. A figure with black wings raises a whip to scourge the back of a woman, who is a candidate for initiation into the mysteries.

Almost as well preserved as the buildings at Pompeii and Herculaneum are some of the buildings at Ostia, once a city of thirty thousand near the mouth of the Tiber River. Two-thirds of Ostia has been excavated. Some 184 buildings, which include multiple dwellings for all classes, have been unearthed, most dating to the Trajanic period (AD 123–128). The lower class lived in small apartments behind their shops. Both the middle and upper classes lived in apartments in two- to four-story *insulae* (lit., "islands"), or blocks of apartments (*cenacula*). The Garden Court featured

apartment buildings around a large court. These buildings contained between fifty and sixty apartments.

Many buildings at Ostia had their own well or cistern. The typical apartment measured about 35 square meters (377 sq. ft.). The *medianum*, a long
room, ran parallel to the street. At either end were *exedrae*, or dayrooms;
on the inner side away from the street were the *cubicula*, or bedrooms. As
only two kitchens were discovered, the majority of the occupants apparently used portable braziers or ate at the shops (*tabernae*).

The majority of apartments at Ostia were rentals. One announcement
reads: "The Insula Arriana Polliana, property of Gnaeus Alleius Nigidius
Maius. To rent from the first day of next July: shops with attached upper
rooms, gentlemen's quarters upstairs, and the main house. Prospective
tenants should apply to Primus, slave of Gnaeus Alleius Nigidius Maius"
(McKay, 82). The annual rent ranged from two thousand sesterces ($80)
to thirty thousand sesterces ($1,200). Leases were concluded in May; July
1 was the beginning of the rental year. Normally the rent was paid at the
end of the rental period. Often a tenant would sublet rooms of his apartment. The landlord provided bolts and keys, but the apartments were
unfurnished.

In Rome, with nearly a million inhabitants in the early Empire, the
vast majority of inhabitants lived in crowded *insulae*, four- to five-story
tenements that contained an average of forty apartments each. *Curiosum
Urbis Romae Regionum XIV*, the fourth-century AD catalogue of the fourteen regions of Rome, lists 46,602 insulae but only 1,797 private houses.
This means that only one out of twenty-six persons lived in a *domus* (a
private home).

Remains of one ancient *insula*, the Casa di Via Giulio Romano, dating
from ca. AD 100, have been uncovered. Built against the Capitoline Hill, it
had room for 380 occupants. Its many tiny rooms (10 sq. m. = 108 sq. ft.)
must have been dark. As there were no elevators, the higher up one went,
the cheaper and less desirable were the apartments. Water had to be carried
up by hand. As there were no fireplaces or chimneys, residents relied on
small portable braziers. Inhabitants went to bed fully clothed.

Unscrupulous landlords built shoddy buildings with weak foundations
and flimsy walls, which led to frequent collapses and fires. Crassus became
the richest citizen in the Late Republic by having his slaves buy up cheaply
numerous properties that had burned down. Augustus decreed that no *insula* was to be built higher than eighteen meters (60 ft.). It is clear that
many builders ignored this law, as Trajan had to pass another law limiting
buildings to the same height.

Martial, a satirist, wrote of his years as a tenant in a dark, drafty apartment. He complained about having to climb up two hundred steps to his

apartment and he noted that he never saw his next-door neighbor, Novius. Like Seneca, who lived above a gymnasium, Martial complained of the noise that made sleep difficult. Juvenal also complained of the noise of the city, which was aggravated by Julius Caesar's decree that agricultural wagons should come into the city at night.

Juvenal concluded,

> But here we inhabit a city supported for the most part by slender props: for that is how the bailiff holds up the tottering house, patches up gaping cracks in the old wall, bidding the inmate sleep at ease under a roof ready to tumble about their ears. No, no, I must live where there are no fires, no nightly alarms. Ucalegon [a neighbor] below is already shouting for water and shifting his chattels; smoke is pouring out of your third-floor attic, but you know nothing of it; for if the alarm begins in the ground-flour, the last man to burn will be he who has nothing to shelter him from the rain but the tiles, where the gentle doves lay their eggs. (*Sat.* 3.193–202)

The great fire of AD 64, which devastated much of Rome and caused Nero to persecute the Christians as scapegoats, was widely blamed on the emperor himself, but Rome was a tinderbox that any fire could ignite.

E. THE JEWISH WORLD

In rabbinic sources, the three most common building materials mentioned are stones, wood, and earth. Cypress, sycamore, and date palm were used as lumber for the construction of ceilings and doors. Sun-dried bricks were cheap and easy to make, though strong rains would cause cracks in walls, resulting in collapse. Whitewash made from lime was used to coat the walls. Mortar was made from burnt lime slaked with water. The rabbis ruled that a person may plaster his house but must leave a small area unplastered in remembrance of the destruction of the temple (*b. B. Bat.* 60b). Beginning in the second century BC, stucco plaster became characteristic of lavish Jewish houses in Palestine. Mosaic floors also became popular among the upper classes and among the Herodians.

Palestine had a great variety of stones for building. Volcanic basalt was abundant in the Hauran in the northeast. Hard limestone was used for the outer faces of walls; medium hard stones were used for pilasters, door and window frames; and soft limestone was used for the upper courses of the walls, arches, and vaults. The simplest floors were made of tamped earth; more elaborate floors were made of ground chalk, which could be covered with mats or rugs. Mosaic floors, such as the ones found at Tel Anafa in northern Israel, were first introduced in the second century BC.

The rabbis distinguished between the Tyrian window and the smaller Egyptian window, "through which a man's head cannot enter" (*m. B. Bat.* 3:6). Windows were covered with grills called *qînqallîn* (sing. *qînqāl*; from Gk. *kigklis*). The most important room in the house was the *ṭraqlîn* (from Lat. *triclinium*), which usually measured about five square meters (= 53 sq. ft.). The bedroom, *qîṭôn* (from Gk. *koitōn*), was usually behind the *ṭraqlîn*. Tacitus observed that one of the unusual customs of the Jews was that men and women slept apart (*Hist.* 5.5).

Ceilings were relatively low, about 1.7 meters (5.5 ft.) high. The lower level of the house was known as the *bayit*; the upper level, the *ʿăliyyâ*. The *maʿăzîbâ*, a layer of mortar that incorporated mats, served as the ceiling of the *bayit* and the floor of the *ʿăliyyâ*. According to the Mishnah, if two tenants share a house, "he that dwells below should provide the beams and he that dwells above the plastering" (*m. B. Meṣ.* 10:2).

In order to set an oven on the upper story, the flooring beneath needed to be three handbreadths (ca. 60 cm. = 24 in.) deep (*m. B. Bat.* 2.2). The upper story could be accessed by either a light, portable "Egyptian" ladder or a Tyrian ladder, which was a stationary staircase (*m. B. Bat.* 3.6).

According to the Mishnah: "If there was a house and an upper room belonging to two persons and the [floor of the] upper room was in part broken down, and the owner of the house below was not minded to mend it, he that occupies the upper room may come down and dwell below until the owner shall mend for him the [floor of the] upper room" (*m. B. Meṣ.* 10:2).

Clay roofs needed repair. A midrash speaks of "*the former rain* (*yoreh*)—so called because it comes down and instructs (*moreh*) people to bring in their produce, to plaster their roofs, and to attend to all their (other) needs" (*Sifre Deut* 42; Hammer 86). The stone roller used to repair roofs was stored on the roof, with sometimes fatal results. According to the Mishnah, "These must escape into exile: If a man killed a soul unwittingly—if he was rolling [the roof] with a roller and it fell on a man and killed him" (*Mak.* 2.1).

Flat roofs were used for a variety of activities, including the drying of raisins and figs, the eating of the Passover meal, and sleeping during the summer. The roof was to be surrounded by a protective parapet at least two cubits (= 36 in.) high (*m. B. Bat.* 4:1). As houses often shared a wall, it was possible to go from roof to roof (*b. B. Meṣ.* 88a).

Excavations in the Upper City of ancient Jerusalem to the west of the temple platform have uncovered two mansions that were destroyed in the Roman assault in AD 70. The so-called Burnt House, which revealed traces of its destruction by fire and which measured two hundred square meters (= 2150 sq. ft.), was probably a high priest's home. It had rooms arranged around the courtyard. The courtyard's beaten earth surface contained four sunken ovens. There was a small *miqwê*, or ritual bath, to the south of the courtyard. The walls of the house were coated with white lime plaster. Its living rooms were probably located on the second floor and did not survive the fire.

Nearby was the much larger Great Mansion, which measured six hundred square meters (= 6460 sq. ft.). The ground floor contained the main rooms, which surrounded a square courtyard paved with flagstones. The walls, which were built with ashlar stones, have survived to a height of three meters (10 ft.). The walls of one room were covered with red and yellow fresco panels that resemble the wall paintings of Pompeii. The Great Mansion contained a very large (6.5 x 11 m. = 21 x 36 ft.) banqueting hall whose walls and ceiling were covered with elaborate stucco decorations. The ground floor was used mainly for workshops and the storage of wine and oil. A staircase led to the living rooms on the upper floor. East of the courtyard was a room for a sunken bath that was decorated with a colored geometrical mosaic pattern. There were separated steps for a *miqwê*, one set for descending, and one for ascending after the ritual purification.

F. THE CHRISTIAN WORLD

Early Christians lived in dwellings that cannot be distinguished from those of their non-Christian neighbors. One possible exception is the House of the Bicentenary uncovered at Herculaneum. On the upper floor was a white stucco panel with the clear outline of a cross or crucifix above a wooden cabinet with a platform in front, which was possibly intended to be used by a kneeling worshipper.

As noted in the NT, early Christians customarily met in homes. By the end of the second century AD, existing homes were remodeled as what has been called a *domus ecclesiae* ("house of the church") to accommodate the increasing size of the congregations. In Greek this was called an *oikos ekklēsia* or *oikos kyriakou*, "house of the Lord." The term *kyriakou* became German *Kirche*, Dutch *kerk*, Anglo-Saxon *circe*, Middle English *chirche*, and, finally, English *church*.

At Capernaum, about eighty feet south of the synagogue, a house has been plausibly identified as Peter's house (Matt 8:14; Mark 2:1). The presence of fish hooks indicates that it was a fisherman's home. As early as the late first century AD, the floor, walls, and ceiling of the single large room of the house were plastered. From the second century AD, worshippers inscribed over one hundred graffiti, most in Greek, and others in Syriac, Aramaic, Latin, and Hebrew, two of which mention the name Peter. The pilgrim named Egeria (or Etheria) who visited Capernaum late in the fourth century AD observed, as reported by Peter the Deacon (12th c. AD), "In Capernaum, moreover, out of the house of the first of the apostles a church (*ecclesia*) has been made, the walls of which still stand just as they were. Here the Lord cured the paralytic" (*Liber de Locis Sanctis* 16; Finegan, 110).

In 2005 the Israel Antiquities Authority announced that inmates from the Megiddo Prison directed by Yotam Tepper had uncovered a Christian "prayer hall" in a Roman legionary building, which housed the officers and their families and also contained a bakery. The site of Kefar 'Othnay, where this discovery was made, is adjacent to Tel Megiddo and to Legio, the headquarters of the VI Ferrata Legion. While chapels at Roman military camps are commonplace, this is the first time that a Christian chapel at such a site has been discovered. The hall was a rectangle measuring five by ten meters. Fallen fresco fragments indicate that its walls were decorated in shades of red, pink, yellow, blue, and white. Located in the center of the room was a podium that probably functioned as a base for a ritual table. The mosaic floor included a medallion on which two fish are portrayed. The Christian character of the hall is unmistakably revealed by an inscription on the floor that reads: *prosēniken Akeptous hē philotheos tēn trapezan TH(e)ô I(ēso)u CH(rist)ô* "The god-loving Akeptous has offered the table to God Jesus Christ as a memorial" (Tepper and Di Segni, 36). The use of abbreviations for the divine names became common practice in the papyri; this is the earliest attestation of such abbreviations used in an inscription. Another inscription from the site reads: "Remember Primilla and Cyriaca and Dorothea, and moreover also Chreste" (Tepper and Di Segni, 41). A third inscription indicated that Gaianus, a centurion, had contributed funds for the building, which was constructed ca. AD 230 and was abandoned ca. 300 when the legion was transferred.

At the Roman frontier city of Dura Europos on the Euphrates River, three important religious structures have been found, including a Jewish synagogue, a Mithraeum, and a Christian church. The latter was built of mud-brick and rubble walls and had a flat roof. Externally it was indistinguishable from other houses. But ca. AD 250 a dining room was enlarged with the removal of a wall to create an assembly hall with a low platform at the eastern end. This hall, which measured 5.15 x 12.9 m. (17 x 42 ft.), could have accommodated a congregation of between sixty-five and one hundred persons. In another room a baptistery was created with tiles and a canopy. This was surrounded with walls painted with scenes of Jesus's ministry.

In Rome, Justin Martyr (2nd c. AD) worshiped in an apartment over some baths. Some of the earliest *tituli* churches (the score of the earliest churches in Rome each known by the title of the founder or owner of the building), such as the Church of San Giovanni e Paolo, began in *insulae* (apartment buildings). Some of these were developed into large assembly halls (*aulae ecclesiae*) by the third century AD.

BIBLIOGRAPHY: B. A. Ault and L. C. Nevett, ed., *Ancient Greek Houses and Households* (2005); N. Avigad, *Archaeological Discoveries in the Jewish Quarter of Jerusalem* (1976); R. Banks, *Paul's Idea of Community: The Early House Churches in Their Historical Setting* (1980); H. K. Beebe, "Ancient Palestinian Dwellings," *BA* 31 (1968), 38–58; H. K. Beebe, "Domestic Architecture in the New Testament," *BA* 38 (1975), 89–104; N. D. Cahill, *Household and City Organization at Olynthus* (2002); D. R. Clark, "Bricks, Sweat and Tears: The Human Investment in Constructing a 'Four-Room' House," *NEA* 66 (2003), 34–43; J. R. Clarke, *The Houses of Roman Italy, 100 B.C.–A.D. 250* (1991); J. J. Deiss, *Herculaneum* (1966); S. P. Ellis, *Roman Housing* (2000); A. Faust and S. Bunimovitz, "The Four-Room House: Embodying Iron Age Israelite Society," *NEA* 66 (2003), 22–31; A. Faust, "Domestic Architecture, Bronze and Iron Age," *OEBA* I.302–10; J. Finegan, *The Archeology of the New Testament* (rev. ed., 1992); B. W. Frier, *Landlords and Tenants in Imperial Rome* (1980); K. Galor, "Domestic Architecture," *OHJDL* 420–39; S. Hales, *The Roman House and Social Identity* (2003); R. Hammer, *Sifre: A Tannaitic Commentary on the Book of Deuteronomy* (1986); G. Hermansen, *Ostia: Aspects of Roman City Life* (1982); Y. Hirschfeld, *The Palestinian Dwelling in the Roman-Byzantine Period* (1995); J. S. Holladay, Jr., "Syro-Palestinian Houses," *OEANE* 3.94–114; B. J. Kemp, "The Character of the South Suburb at Tell el-Amarna," *MDOG* 113 (1981), 81–97; B. J. Kemp and S. Garfi, *A Survey of the Ancient City of el-'Amarna* (1993); A. Killebrew and S. Fine, "Qatzrin—Reconstructing Village Life in Talmudic Times," *BAR* 17 (1991), 44–56; A. Koltsida, "Domestic Space and Gender Roles in Ancient Egyptian Village Households: A View from Amarna Workmen's Village and Deir el-Medina," in *Building Communities: House, Settlement and Society in the Aegean and Beyond*, ed. R. Westgate, N. Fisher, and J. Whitley (2007), 121–27; C. Kraeling, *The Christian Building: The Excavations at Dura Europos* (1967); M. Krafeld-Daugherty, *Wohnen im Alten Orient* (1994); A. McKay, *Houses, Villas, and Palaces in the Roman World* (1975); O. Michel, "οἶκος," *TDNT* V.119–59; J. Morgan, *The Classical Greek House* (2010); L. C. Nevett, *House and Society in the Ancient Greek World* (1999); P. Oakes, "Domestic Architecture, Hellenistic and Roman Period," *OEBA* I.310–18; C. Osiek and D. Balch, ed., *Families in the New Testament World: Households and House Churches* (1997); J. Percival, *The Roman Villa* (1976); J. M. Petersen, "House-Churches in Rome," *VC* 23 (1969), 264–72; I. Shaw, "Ideal Homes in Ancient Egypt: The Archaeology of Social Aspiration," *Cambridge Archaeological Journal* 22 (1992), 147–66; R. W. Smith, "*Ante-Pacem* Christian Structures in the Levant," in *The Light of Discovery*, ed. J. D. Wineland (2007), 83–105; E. C. Stone, "Mesopotamian Houses," *OEANE* 3.90–94; J. Strange and H. Shanks, "Has the House Where Jesus Stayed in Capernaum Been Found?" *BAR* 8.6 (1982), 26–37; Y. Tepper and L. Di Segni, *A Christian Prayer Hall of the Third Century CE at Kefar ʿOthnay (Legio): Excavations at the Megiddo Prison 2005* (2006); K. R. Veenhof, ed., *Houses and Households in Ancient Mesopotamia* (1996); A. Wallace-Hadrill, *Houses and Society in Pompeii and Herculaneum* (1994); A. Webber, "Building Practice and Regulation in the Land of Israel in the Talmudic Age," PhD diss., South Bank University (1993); R. Westgate, N. Fisher, and J. Whitley, ed., *Building Communities: House, Settlement and Society in the Aegean and Beyond* (2007); L. M. White, *Building God's House in the Roman World* (1989).

KNS and EMY

See also BANQUETS, CITIES, DOORS & KEYS, PALACES, and SANITATION.

DYEING

The ability to apply substances to fabrics, skins, and other objects to impart colors to them for aesthetic reasons, and to mark them as status objects, was an important skill in antiquity. Except when the dye being used was indigo or woad (*Isaatis tinctoria*), textiles needed to be treated with a mordant, or chemical fixer, such as alum or iron salts, for the dye to be absorbed.

A. THE OLD TESTAMENT

A number of passages in the Bible refer to colors, dyed goods, and the dyeing industry. The common translation "coat of many colours" (KJV, Gen 37:3, 23, 32) for Joseph's famous garment is probably incorrect. The Hebrew expression here, *kĕtōnet passîm*, might better be rendered "multi-threaded garment," suggesting that this robe was full-length and long-sleeved rather than multicolored (see 2 Sam 13:18–19). The Septuagint and the Vulgate correctly read "multi-threaded."

Dyed goods were prized booty (Judg 5:30). Purples, scarlets, and blues decorated the tabernacle (Exod 26:1, 36; 35:35), the priestly vestments (Exod 38:23; 39:1–3, 29), and Solomon's temple, which was built with the help of Tyrian artisans (2 Chr 2:7, 14; 3:14; see also Exod 27:16, 27). The three colored wools mentioned in the OT are Heb. *tĕkēlet*, *'argāmān*, and *tôlā'*, which represent, respectively, "blue-purple," "red-purple," and "crimson."

Scarlet was used ritually and symbolically (Lev 14:4, 49, 51–52; Num 19:6; Josh 2:18, 21). Purple was a coveted color (Judg 8:26; Prov 31:21–22). The images of pagan gods were adorned with purple (Jer 10:9).

In Num 15:38 God tells Moses: "Speak to the Israelites and say to them: 'Throughout the generations to come you are to make tassels on the corners of your garments, with a blue [*tĕkēlet*] cord on each tassel [*ṣîṣit*].'"

In the first chapter of Isaiah, God promises Judah: "Though your sins are like scarlet [*šānîm*], they shall be as white as snow; though they are red as crimson [*tôlāʿ*], they shall be like wool" (Isa 1:18).

B. THE NEW TESTAMENT

According to the apocryphal *Protevangelium of James*, which is dated ca. AD 150, a priest said, "'Choose for me by lot who shall spin the gold, and the white, and the fine linen, and the silk, and the blue, and the scarlet, and the true purple.' And the true purple and the scarlet fell to the lot of Mary, and she took them, and went away to her house" (*Prot. Jas.* 10). According to the *Gospel of Pseudo-Matthew* (ca. AD 400): "For they cast lots among themselves what each virgin should do, and the purple for the veil of the temple of the Lord fell to the lot of Mary" (*Ps.-Mt.* ch. 8). In a parable contrasting the pitiable state of a beggar with a wealthy man, Jesus described the latter as "dressed in purple" (Luke 16:19).

Jesus was robed in a scarlet (Gk. *kokkinos*) cloak and mocked at his scourging (Matt 27:28, 31; in the parallel texts, Mark 15:17 and John 19:2, the color of the cloak is purple, Gk. *porphyra*). In the book of Revelation, Babylon the harlot, no doubt a veiled reference to Rome, is described as being robed in scarlet and purple (Rev 18:12, 16). John seems to contrast heavenly white raiment with dyed goods from Laodicea (Rev 3:18). Lydia, a seller of purple from Thyatira, was converted in Philippi (Acts 16:14). If Lydia was an ethnic cognomen, it may indicate that she was a freedwoman. Epigraphic evidence shows that both shop owners and freedmen traveled and sold dyed wares. There are other examples of women in the ancient world who sold dyed goods, and epigraphic evidence indicates that dyers were active in both Philippi and Thyatira. The herb madder (*Rubia tinctorum*) was used in Thyatira to imitate murex purple. An inscription illustrates an affiliation between the dyers of Thyatira and Macedonia.

C. THE NEAR EASTERN WORLD

In Mesopotamia wool garments dyed in red, blue, and purple are represented in artistic depictions, most notably from the wall paintings of the eighth-century BC Assyrian palace at Til Barsip (Tell Ahmar) (see Parrot, 100–11), and in some cases material remains of such garments have been discovered. Women buried in the Early Dynastic graves at Ur were clothed in garments of bright red. Texts from Ur mention red wool. Red dye may have been derived from madder. In the Neo-Babylonian period the root of the plant *Alkanna tinctoria* provided another source of red dye.

Orchil lichens from mountain trees may have been the source of a dye known as archil (or orseille), whose color was a blue tending toward violet. Indigo from India became known in Mesopotamia in the seventh century BC. Woad was not seriously cultivated until the Hellenistic era.

Yellow dye was extracted from ground pomegranate rinds. Yellow dye-stuff could have been produced from safflower (*Carthamus tinctorius*). Yellow may also have been produced from sumac.

Red-dyed leather and matting have been recovered from Predynastic Egyptian tombs. Dyeing of cloth is attested in mummy wrappings dated ca. 2500 BC. Indigo was known and used in Egypt as early as the 5th Dynasty (ca. 2500 BC).

The most coveted dye in antiquity was purple extracted from the murex mussel, as it was the most colorfast dye known. The Linear B tablets from Crete, the Ugaritic archives from Ras Shamra, and the Amarna tablets indicate that purple goods were important commercial items well before classical times. The earliest archaeological evidence for purple dyeing works was found on the island of Leuke (modern Konfonision) southeast of Crete and dates to ca. 2200 BC.

Literary and archaeological evidence indicates that the Phoenicians had a preeminent role in the purple dyeing industry. The name "Phoenician" is in fact derived from a word for "red-purple": the Greek word *phoinix* (first attested in Linear B as *po-ni-ki-ya* and possibly derived from Ugaritic *pwt*, "madder") refers to this color, as does the later Latin word *punicus*. Similarly, the Hurrian word for purple (*kinaḫḫu*) became "Canaan," the familiar name for the entire region. The Phoenicians produced two kinds of purple dye: a blue-purple or hyacinth and a red-purple or Tyrian purple. Tyre was the center of the Phoenician (red-)purple industry. Strabo reported, "Although the great number of dye-works makes the city unpleasant to live in, nevertheless it makes the city rich since its people are so enterprising" (*Geogr.* 16.2.23). A large mound of banded murex shells (*Phyllanotous murex trunculus*) used for blue-purple dye was found near Sidon, with each shell carefully broken above the chromogenic gland. Two other species used for red-purple, the spiny dye-murex (*Bolinus murex brandaris*) and the rock shell or oyster drill (*Thais haemastoma*), were found in a separate pile.

Murex dye was difficult and extremely expensive to produce, requiring thousands of mollusks for an ounce of dye. Sherds from a storage container covered with (blue) purple and located near a deposit of crushed mollusk shells were discovered at Sarepta (biblical Zarephath), which is located between Tyre and Sidon. Large mounds of murex shells have also been found at Tyre, Ugarit, Ashdod, Akko, and Shiqmona. An installation with pools and channels was found at Dor, which flourished as a dyeing center during the Persian era. To obtain the dye, one crushed the shells of the murex, extracted the organisms, and deposited them in vats carved out of rocks to putrefy. The dead murex secreted a yellowish liquid that provided the dye. Great quantities of water were necessary for this process, and it was extremely odoriferous; hence, dye works were situated at a distance in the leeside of towns.

A number of red, blue, yellow, and black dyes were also used in antiquity, most of which were derived from organic sources. The most important red dyes were extracted from the females of two similar types of insect, kermes and cochineal. Tiglath-pileser I (ca. 1100 BC) introduced a tree known as the kermes-oak to Assyria as a breeding ground for the kermes insect (*Coccus ilicis*). This insect's coloring matter was contained in its unhatched eggs, which were deposited in late spring on the leaves of oak trees. The eggs (or grains) were crushed, yielding a carmine-red soluble dye. Cochineal insects bred in certain kinds of grass near Ararat in Armenia and were introduced to Assyria by Sargon II after he invaded Urartu in 714.

A list of Tiglath-pileser III's booty from Syria and Palestine (8th c. BC) included "linen garments with multicolored trimmings, blue-dyed wool, purple-dyed wool, . . . also lambs whose stretched hides were dyed purple [Akk. *argamanu*], (and) wild birds whose spread-out wings were dyed blue [Akk. *takilte*]" (*ANET*, 283).

Gall-black, which is used in ink, was combined with a mordant to dye wool black. A black hair dye was made from myrtle and may have been used to dye cloth as well. Nut-brown dye was produced from the extracts of the nuts of the *Juqlans regia*. Dark dyes were also used to stain wood and parchment. According to an Akkadian text, grays were made by spinning black and white wool together.

Henna, or true alkanet (*Alkanna atinctoria*), was a red dye extracted from a root cultivated in Syria, Palestine, and Rome. It was used together with *asafoetida* to stain skin and dye hair. False alkanet (*Anchusa barrelieri*) was similarly extracted from a plant that was native to Europe.

Safflower, a soluble yellow dye, was extracted from the petals of the flower *Carthamus tinctorius*. Safflower was used to produce vegetable oil and its seeds were thought to have medicinal value, which may explain why stores of these have been found in stone jars in Mesopotamia and in Egyptian tombs. Mummy wrappings were dyed with safflower in order to repel fleas.

Saffron, a beautiful orange-yellow dye, was extracted from the dried stigmas of the crocus flower. Saffron (Heb. *karkōm*) is referred to once in the OT (Song 4:14). There is a famous "Saffron Gatherer" fresco from the Minoan palace at Knossos that depicts either a boy or a trained monkey gathering the precious flower. Saffron dye was not produced in Palestine but was used in Phoenicia, Syria, and Egypt.

Dyeing took place in small stone vats that were generally about two feet square and two feet deep, examples of which have been found in Palestine. Because dye was expensive, excess dye was carefully recovered after the dyeing process was completed. Wool was dyed before being made into cloth.

D. THE GRECO-ROMAN WORLD

Pliny the Elder and Vitruvius give useful descriptions of the purple dyeing process. The coloring matter was a secretion from the murex mussel. The mollusks, which bred in spring along the shallow, rocky coast, were caught in baited wicker baskets. The Phoenicians carefully broke the shells where the gland could be easily reached, but the Greeks crushed the shells, mixing the entire mollusk in a saline solution that was later strained. Classical writers complained about the putrid stench that surrounded dye works.

Plato uses dyeing as an extended analogy for the education of wise rulers:

> You are aware that dyers when they wish to dye wool so as to hold the purple hue begin by selecting from the many colours there be the one nature of the white and then give it a careful preparatory treatment so that it will take the hue in the best way, and after the treatment, then and then only, dip it in the dye. And things that are dyed by this process become fast-coloured and washing either with or without lyes cannot take away the sheen of their hues.
> (*Resp.* 4.429d–e)

While many ancient dyeing techniques were guarded as trade secrets, several books were written in the Hellenistic era on dyeing. Pliny the Elder and the authors of several so-called chemical papyri quote from these works. Seventy fragmentary recipes in the Papyrus Holmiensis (also known as the Stockholm papyrus) provide a survey of wool dyeing in Hellenistic times. Archaeological discoveries have also supplemented our understanding of the industry in the Greco-Roman world. A sign from the workshop of Verecundus, one of three Pompeiian dye shops, depicts scenes of the work done inside his shop.

At Pompeii, madder was used for red, whortleberry for blue, and, for purple, dyes from the murex mollusk, which in Latin was called *purpur* and which came from nearby Puteoli. The latter was probably produced by Tyrian craftsmen who settled there. Indigo for blue was probably imported from India. An ivory statue of the Indian goddess Lakshmi was found next to a dye house.

The dye houses at Pompeii were known as *tinctoria* or *infectoria*. In a dye house, wool was soaked in vats with mordants, such as alum or iron salts. Deep lead cauldrons were set over firepots to keep the dyes warm. The dyers stirred the wool with poles. A pound of wool required a pound of dye. To get deep colors, a garment needed to be dyed twice. Several dye works, which are identified by their distinctive furnaces, were also found at neighboring Herculaneum.

Dyers specialized in particular colors, for example, the *cerinarii* in yellow and the *violarii* in red. A humorous description of creditors relates:

> Wherever you go nowadays you can see more wagons in front of a city house than in the countryside when you go to a farmhouse. But this is still pleasant compared with when the women demand that you should pay their bills. There stands the launderer, the embroiderer, the goldsmith, and the woollen worker; the dealers in flounces and tunics; those who dye garments in flaming red, violet, and brown. (Plautus, *Aul.* 505–511)

Poor people in Greece and Rome wore blacks, browns, grays, and creams, which are the natural colors of wool. Roman senators were distinguished by their togas, which bore a broad purple stripe, while equestrians wore togas with narrow purple stripes. Nero issued an edict permitting only the emperor to wear purple garments. The later emperor Alexander Severus made the purple dyeing industry a state monopoly.

Our word for the color vermillion is a transliteration of a form of the Latin word *vermiculus*, "worm," which refers specifically to the larva of the kermes insect (*Coccus ilicis*). The Romans obtained the scarlet used for the cloaks of their military officers from carminic acid derived from this insect, which lives only on a special species of oak (*Quercus cocifera*).

Madder was an inexpensive red dye substitute extracted from the pulverized root of the plants *Rubia tinctorium* and *Rubia peregrina*, which grew throughout the Mediterranean. Strabo praised the wool from Colossae dyed with madder dye. He informs us, "The water at Hierapolis is also wonderfully suited to the dyeing of wools, so that the wool dyed with madder-root is comparable to the ones dyed with the kermes and with sea-purple" (*Geogr.* 13.4.14).

A popular blue dye came from the woad plant, which was known in the Near East, Egypt, the Greco-Roman world, and Celtic Britain. Woad leaves were ground into a paste, reduced to powder, and fermented to produce a blue dye that was later mixed with urine. Besides being used to dye fabric, woad was also used by the people of northern Europe as body paint. Caesar observed that Britons dyed their faces blue. Pliny reports that the British women stained their whole bodies with woad (*Nat.* 22.2–4). Indigo was extracted from a native Indian plant, which was imported to the Near East and cultivated in Roman Palestine.

E. THE JEWISH WORLD

In Greco-Roman times, Gaza, Luz, and Lydda were important dyeing centers in Palestine. A dye shop has been discovered in Jerusalem.

The pseudepigraphal text *1 Enoch* states that dyeing techniques were first introduced to mankind by fallen angels, based on a mythological interpretation of the "sons of God" mentioned in Gen 6 (a tradition also followed by several church fathers).

Deuteronomy 22:11 (cf. Lev 19:19) forbids the wearing of garments made of a mixture of wool and linen. Some examples of cloth made from blue linen and red wool have been found at Kuntillet Ajrud, while the many textiles found in the later Bar Kochba cave at Nahal Hever on the western shore of the Dead Sea were all unmixed. The thirty-four different shades of colored wool found in the Bar Kochba cave were all derived from three basic dyes: yellow, red, and blue. The yellow was obtained from saffron, the red from the madder plant, and the blue from indigo. A bundle of dyed, unspun wool found in the same cave was probably intended for the "blue cord" of the ritual tassels (Heb. *ṣîṣit*) prescribed by Num 15:38–39 (cf. Deut 22:12).

The problem of obtaining the correct blue dye for these tassels occupied the rabbis, as indicated by a long section in the Babylonian Talmud (*b. Menaḥ.* 38–52). By Talmudic times the *tĕkēlet* dye was no longer available (*b. Menaḥ.* 42b, 44a). Though rabbinic tradition generally held that this ancient color had been "sky blue," some scholars, based on a chemical analysis of dyed fabric from Masada, believe that it was a bluish-purple hue obtained from the *Murex trunculus* snail.

F. THE CHRISTIAN WORLD

Clement of Alexandria used the process of dyeing as an illustration to explain OT references to God censuring the Israelites: "He [God] uses the very bitter mordant of fear . . . repressing the people, and at the same time turning them to salvation; as also wool that is undergoing the process of dyeing is wont to be previously treated with mordants, in order to prepare it for taking on a fast color" (*Paed.* 1.9). Clement also decried the use of dyed clothing as an extravagance:

> Dyeing of clothes is also to be rejected. For it is remote both from necessity and truth, in addition to the fact that reproach in manners spring from it. For the use of colors is not beneficial, for they are of no service against cold; nor has it anything for covering more than other clothing, except the opprobrium alone. And the agreeableness of the color afflicts greedy eyes, inflaming them to senseless blindness. But for those who are white and unstained within, it is most suitable to use white and simple garments. (*Paed.* 2.11)

Tertullian, another church father known in part for his writings on practical matters such as dress and appearance, objected to cosmetics and dyed materials on the grounds that they were unnatural:

> For what legitimate honor can garments derive from adulteration with illegitimate colors? God is not pleased by what He Himself did not produce. We cannot suppose that God was unable to produce sheep with purple or sky-blue fleeces! If He was *able*, then plainly He was *unwilling*: what God willed not, of course ought not to be fashioned. (*Cult. fem.* 1.8)

Elsewhere in this essay (*On the Apparel of Women*), Tertullian writes sarcastically: "It was God, no doubt, who showed the way to dye wools with the juices of herbs and the humours of conchs! It had escaped Him, when He was bidding the universe to come into being, to issue a command for (the production of) purple and scarlet sheep!" (*Cult. fem.* 2.10).

Diocletian's Edict on Maximum Prices of AD 301, which was intended to counter inflation, listed luxury fabrics such as simple dyed purple, genuine Milesian purple, second-quality Milesian purple, archil (lichen) purple (of four different qualities), light purple, and bright Tyrian purple. The director of the Tyrian dye works during the reign of Diocletian was a Christian who was martyred for his faith.

BIBLIOGRAPHY: M. C. Astour, "The Origin of the Terms 'Canaan,' 'Phoenician,' and 'Purple,'" *JNES* 24 (1965), 346–50; J. T. Baker, "Tyrian Purple: An Ancient Dye, A Modern Problem," *Endeavor* 33 (1974), 11–17; H. Block, "The Missing Thread of Blue," *JBQ* 31 (2003), 245–48; F. Bruin, "Royal Purple and the Dye Industries of the Mycenaeans and Phoenicians," in *American University of Beirut Festival Book*, ed. F. Ṣarrūf and S. Tamim (1967), 295–325; M. Farnsworth, "Second Century B.C. Rose Madder from Corinth and Athens," *AJA* 55 (1951), 236–39; P. Faure, "La pourpre, invention égéenne," *Aegaeum* 7 (1991), 311–13; H. Fleming, "Facts and Conjectures as to the Beginnings of the Art of Dyeing," *Textile Colorist and Converter* 52 (1930), 696–703; R. J. Forbes, "Dyes and Dyeing," *Studies in*

Ancient Technology (1964), IV.98–150; F. H. Gerber, *Cochineal and the Insect Dyes* (1978); H. A. Hoffner, Jr., "Ugaritic *pwt*: A Term from the Early Canaanite Dyeing Industry," *JAOS* 87 (1967), 300–303; G. H. R. Horsley, ed., *New Documents Illustrating Early Christianity* II (1982), nos. 3, 14.2, and 68; and III (1983), nos. 17 and 104; J. W. Humphrey, J. P. Oleson, and A. N. Sherwood, ed., *Greek and Roman Technology: A Sourcebook* (1998), 356–62; J. B. Hurry, *The Woad Plant and Its Dye* (1930); L. B. Jensen, "Royal Purple of Tyre," *JNES* 22 (1963), 104–18; C. Kardara, "Dyeing and Weaving Works at Isthmia," *AJA* 65 (1961), 261–66; N. Karmon and E. Spanier, "Remains of a Purple Dye Industry Found at Tel Shiqmona," *IEJ* 38 (1988), 184–86; P. J. King and L. E. Stager, *Life in Biblical Israel* (2001), 159–62; H. Kurdian, "Kirmiz," *JAOS* 61 (1941), 105–7; F. G. Lang, "Neues über Lydia? Zur Deutung von 'Purpurhändlerin' in Apg 16,14," *ZNW* 100 (2009), 29–42; J. Laudermilk, "The Bug with the Crimson Past," *Natural History* 58 (1949), 114–18; W. F. Leggett, *Ancient and Medieval Dyes* (1944); A. Lucas and J. R. Harris, *Ancient Egyptian Materials and Industries* (1999), 150–54; P. E. McGovern and R. H. Michel, "Royal Purple Dye: Tracing Chemical Origins of the Industry," *Analytical Chemistry* 57 (1985), 1514A–1522A; P. E. McGovern and R. H. Michel, "Royal Purple and the Pre-Phoenician Dye Industry of Lebanon," *Museum Applied Science Center for Archaeology Journal* 3.3 (1984), 67–70; C. D. Mell, "The History and Economic Uses of Safflower," *Textile Colorist and Converter* 54 (1932), 97–99; A. Parrot, *The Arts of Assyria* (1961); D. S. Reese, "Industrial Exploitation of Murex Shells," *Society for Libyan Studies Annual Report* 11 (1979–80), 79–83; M. Reinhold, *History of Purple as a Status Symbol in Antiquity* (1970); E. Spanier, ed., *The Royal Purple and the Biblical Blue: Argaman and Tekhelet* (1987); R. Stieglitz, "The Minoan Origin of Tyrian Purple," *BA* 57 (1994), 46–54; Y. Yadin, *Bar-Kokhba* (1971), 66–85; Y. Yadin, *The Finds from the Bar Kokhba Period in the Cave of Letters* (1963); I. Ziderman, "First Identification of Authentic *Tĕkēlet*," *BASOR* 265 (1987), 25–33; I. Ziderman, "A Modern Miracle—Rediscovery of 'Blue' Dye for Tallit Tassels," *Israel Yearbook* 43 (1988), 287–92; I. Ziderman, "Purple Dyes Made from Shellfish in Antiquity," *Review of Progress in Coloration and Related Topics* 16 (1986), 46–52; I. Ziderman, "Seashells and Ancient Purple Dyeing," *BA* 53 (1990), 98–101.

STC

See also CLOTHING and COSMETICS.

EDUCATION

The instruction of children and youths in antiquity was, with a few exceptions, the responsibility of families, not of the state. Learning often involved rote memory and was enforced by the threat of beatings. Only a select few boys went on to acquire a secondary education, and an even smaller cadre went on to higher education. The learning process for most females stopped at puberty so that they could prepare for marriage, with the exception of girls from noble families, who could be privately tutored.

A. THE OLD TESTAMENT

The legacy of learning constitutes one of the weightiest dimensions of the Jewish heritage that has been bequeathed to modern civilization. The idea "to educate" is mainly conveyed in Hebrew by verbs that can be translated "to instruct," "to train," "to direct," "to teach," and "to learn," and by nouns denoting "insight," "wisdom," and "knowledge." Education in ancient Israel was quite diverse and mainly informal. However, before the close of the biblical period an extensive system of formal schooling began to develop.

The Bible declares that God is the teacher of his people (Deut 4:1; Pss 25:4–5; 94:10). Parents and others who teach are considered engaged in a sacred task, an extension of God's authority (cf., e.g., Deut 4:9–10; 11:19; Ps 78:5).

Among the Hebrews, education primarily had a religious aim. It was to train the whole person for lifelong, obedient service in the knowledge of God (Prov 1:7; Eccl 12:13; Hos 6:3, 6). Abraham, the "rock" from which all Israelites were hewn (Isa 51:1–2), was chosen that he might direct his children to "keep the way of the LORD" (Gen 18:19). Torah, literally, "direction," "instruction," "guidance," was the divine gift and means to keep one on this path (Josh 1:8; Pss 1:1–2; 119:105). This "education in holiness" meant for one to be separated unto God from the lifestyle of other peoples. It especially focused on knowledge of God's acts in history, hence the constant appeal to "remember" (Deut 4:9–10; 24:22). But this instructional heritage held in equal reverence the transmission of the *miṣwōt* ("commandments"), the ethical directives or laws for right living. In short, as ancient Israelite and, later, Jewish thought developed, learning became an act of worship; indeed, learning was life.

In addition to its all-encompassing process of teaching how to live, education also focused on how one should make a living. Craftsmen imparted technical skills and practical instruction. A son often learned a craft or trade as an apprentice to his father. But know-how was also acquired from serving in guilds that specialized in such occupations as metalworking, stonemasonry, pottery making, and merchandizing. The ultimate goal of all education was the recognition of the Lord's authority in every path and circumstance of life (Ps 16:8; Prov 3:5–6) so that the earth might be full of his knowledge (Isa 11:9; Hab 2:14).

The fountainhead of education in ancient Israel was the family. The father bore primary responsibility for the religious instruction of the children (Deut 11:19). The *Shema* (Deut 6:4–5) appears to have been taught as the first lesson of faith as soon as a child could speak. Parents were to impress God's teachings upon their children and talk about them freely at home and away (Deut 6:7). Various home festivals, such as Passover, provided opportunities to tell and vividly relive the great stories of redemptive history (Exod 12:26–27; 13:14). Furthermore, as children grew older, the phylacteries (Deut 6:8), the doorframes of the home (Deut 6:9), and the ṣîṣit ("fringes") they wore on their garments (Num 15:38) were additional, visual, pedagogical aids in recalling the commandments of God. Parents were expected to transmit this heritage so that even generations of the yet unborn would know God's words and his deeds (Ps 78:1–8). Education within the family sometimes provided the first steps to literacy. But even rudimentary learning was always viewed as a means to an end—the study of divine teaching, rather than "secular" subjects.

At home children were also taught the essential routines necessary for general family and community life. Sons learned from their father the skills of farming and sheep tending (1 Sam 16:11). Daughters, however, usually remained with their mother to learn domestic procedures, such as weaving and cooking (Prov 31:13–14, 19; Song 8:2). In many families children also learned music and dance. In addition, learning was acquired informally through family pilgrimages and by listening to elders at the gate and caravaneers at the wells.

Though the home remained the major source of education for most people, other important spokes filled out the educational wheel. Some scholars hold that a rather elaborate system of schools—elementary, regional, royal, priestly, and prophetic—operated in ancient Israel. Although biblical and epigraphic evidence suggests that literacy was not rare in ancient Israel, particularly from the time of the monarchy on, it would be incorrect to conclude that professional education was readily available to the masses or that a well-defined network of schools existed during OT times.

Some of the more important indications of literacy in ancient Israel are these: The Israelites were required to write the words of God on the doorframes and gates of their homes (Deut 6:9). The Gezer Calendar (10th c. BC) seems to reflect a schoolboy's writing exercise. Abecedaries have been discovered at several sites, including Lachish, Kadesh-Barnea, Khirbet el-Qom, Khirbet Qeiyafa, Tel Zayit, and Kuntillet-ʿAjrud. Various biblical passages mention the skill of writing, namely, Josh 18:4, Job 31:35, Isa 8:1, 10:19, and Hab 2:2. The Hebrew alphabet of twenty-two letters would have been quite simple to master compared with the writing systems of Egypt and Mesopotamia, which involved hundreds of complex signs. The statement in Isa 28:10 that the NIV renders "Do this, do that, a rule for this, a rule for that" is literally "ṣ after ṣ, ṣ after ṣ, q after q, q after q," referring to the teaching of the alphabet to a child. The young man of Judg 8:14 "wrote down" (not, as the KJV has it, "described") the names of the elders of Sukkoth. In addition, the archaeological evidence of monumental inscriptions, ostraca, seals, papyri, and the like indicates that the ability to read and write was more widespread in ancient Israel than many scholars have believed.

Jer 18:18 refers to three of the most influential classes of religious educators: "For the teaching of the law [tôrâ] by the priest will not cease, nor will counsel from the wise, nor the word from the prophets." The priests were custodians and expounders of the law (Deut 31:9–13). Periodically they would travel from town to town, gather the people together, and teach them (2 Chr 17:8–9). As ministers around the sanctuary, the priests were experts in sacrificial rites, laws of ritual purity, and liturgy (including music). Priests were sometimes called "father," which underscores the educational responsibility incumbent on both fathers and priests (Judg 17:10; 18:19).

The prophets called the people to repentance and righteous living, with particular stress on the ethical and inner, spiritual dimensions of the teachings of Moses (Jer 4:4; Amos 5:21–24; Mic 6:1–8). Many prophets had disciples, or "sons," who clustered around them to learn their teaching and observe their deeds (2 Kgs 2:3–8; Isa 8:16, 18; cf. Amos 7:14). These prophetic bands—sometimes called "schools"—attended to various needs of the prophet and passed on orally the sayings of the prophet before they had been fully preserved in writing. Some prophets, such as Jeremiah and Ezekiel, had a priestly education (Jer 1:1; Ezek 1:3).

The wise men of Israel reflect another educational tradition. Some scholars deny that the sages were a professional class, but others have made a reasonable case for the existence of wisdom schools in ancient Israel. Though much of the wisdom literature may be postexilic in compilation, many of its teachings are preexilic in origin. Parallels in other ancient Near Eastern wisdom literature support this contention. In the wisdom schools, children of the more well-to-do families were taught pragmatic maxims by the sages concerning the good life. Qoheleth, the wise man who speaks in the first person throughout the book of Ecclesiastes, is said to have "imparted knowledge to the people" (Eccl 12:9). The book of Proverbs appears to have been used as a kind of "textbook" for reciting the observations of the wise. Job and Ecclesiastes, however, mainly present a kind of "speculative" wisdom that reflects on perplexing issues of life such as the suffering of the righteous and the meaning of existence. Just as the headmaster in Sumerian schools was addressed as "father" and the pupil as "son," so in the OT a sage might address the learner as "son" (Prov 1:8, 10, 15; cf. 2 Kgs 2:12). Proverbs advocates discipline in inculcating lessons: "Whoever spares the rod hates their children, but the one who loves their children is careful to discipline them" (Prov 13:24); "Folly is bound up in the heart of a child, but the rod of discipline will drive it far away" (Prov 22:15). The discipline involved in learning (cf. Prov 23:12–14) is reflected in the root meaning of the OT verb *lāmad* ("to learn"). The verb originally carried the idea of to "train" or "exercise in," and by extension to "discipline," "practice," or "correct."

Teaching of children was far from monolithic in its approach. Parents had the obligation to provide ethical and moral instruction rooted in the fear of the Lord and the obligation to keep his commandments (cf. Prov 1:7; Eccl 12:13). Some texts, however, may suggest teaching practices that allowed for respect of the individual circumstances, disposition, abilities, and station of the child, with the instruction and learning opportunities adjusted accordingly. Prov 22:6 states, "Train up a child in the way he should go" (KJV; Heb. *ḥănōk lanna'ar 'al pî darkô*, lit., "Train up a child according to his [the child's?] way").

According to Ezra 7:25, Artaxerxes I empowered Ezra, upon his returning from Babylon to Palestine, to appoint judges and to teach the "laws of your God" to all who did not know them. Ezra read from the law before a solemn assembly that included "men and women and all who were able to understand" (Neh 8:2). The last phrase, which literally means "all who understood to hear," is rendered by the JB as "children old enough to understand." In ancient Israel, fathers were not commanded to teach daughters the Torah, and women did not participate in ordinary religious meetings. But they were included in solemn assemblies such as the one mentioned in Neh 8 (cf. Deut 31:12; Josh 8:35; 2 Kgs 23:2).

Though only the Levites sang in the temple services, there are several references in the OT to female singers (2 Sam 19:35; 2 Chr 35:25; Ezra 2:65; Neh 7:67; Eccl 2:8), who must have received some specialized training.

After the reign of Solomon, when Israel became the pawn of contending empires, some of its scribes must have had to learn Egyptian and its hieratic script, Akkadian and its cuneiform script, and, in the Persian era, Aramaic, which was written in the same alphabet as Hebrew.

B. THE NEW TESTAMENT

The Virgin Mary, who was no doubt but a teenager at the time of her betrothal, revealed her knowledge of the OT Scriptures in her Magnificat (Luke 1:46–55). Jesus spoke Aramaic (Mark 15:34), as did Paul (Acts 21:40) and other early disciples (as is indicated, for example, by the Aramaic phrase *marana tha*, "Come, Lord!," in 1 Cor 16:22). Jesus could read the Hebrew Scriptures, as is evidenced by his doing so in the synagogue at Nazareth (Luke 4:16–19). The only reference to Jesus writing comes in the pericope of the woman caught in adultery (John 8:6), a passage that is not in our earliest Greek NT manuscripts.

During NT times the landscape was dotted with itinerant teachers and their disciples. Jesus was one such teacher in the scribal tradition (cf. Matt 13:52). In the Gospels Jesus is referred to as *didaskalos*, "teacher," over forty times and as "rabbi" twelve times. Like one of the scribes, he teaches in synagogues (Mark 1:21) and expounds Scripture (Matt 5:17–48). In Jesus's day the word "rabbi" was a popular term of honor meaning "my master," "my great one." It was not until the second century that "rabbi" became an official title and term of formal address, with the institution at the time of Johanan ben Zakkai of the rite of ordination (the laying on of hands).

Most of Jesus's disciples were fishermen, with the exception of the tax collector Matthew, and possibly also of Judas Iscariot, who was entrusted with the money box. The Sanhedrin dismissed Peter and John as *anthropoi agrammatoi . . . kai idiōtai*, "unschooled, ordinary men" (Acts 4:13).

All of the NT books were written in the *koinē* ("common") Greek that had been spread throughout the Near East by the conquest of Alexander and his generals. The Greek of the books of the NT varies from that of the Apocalypse, whose grammar is non-standard and contains many "Semitisms," to the polished rhetoric of the book of Hebrews. The majority of the citations of the OT in the NT follow the text of the Septuagint, the Greek translation of the Hebrew Scriptures.

Paul, who was from the city of Tarsus, was a Roman citizen; perhaps his father had earned citizenship either for service to the Romans or as a liberated slave. Paul was able to earn his living as a tentmaker (Acts 18:3; cf. 1 Cor 4:12). He came to Jerusalem to sit at the feet of the famous Pharisaic teacher Gamaliel (Acts 5:34; 22:3). Paul's claim that he was "brought up" (*anatethrammenos*) in Jerusalem (Acts 22:3) implies that he probably came there before he was thirteen. Paul points out in his letter to the Galatians that before his encounter with Christ and special calling on the road to Damascus he had advanced in the traditions of the fathers more than his peers (1:14).

While in Ephesus, Paul preached daily for two years at the *scholē* (KJV "school"; NIV, NEB "lecture hall"; RSV "hall") of Tyrannus (Acts 19:9). NT manuscripts of the "Western text-type" add that he did this "from the fifth hour to the tenth," that is, from 11 a.m. to 4 p.m. If this reflects a sound tradition, Paul would have worked making tents in the early morning and would then have preached at a time of day when others would have had leisure to listen to him. An early third-century AD Greek inscription found on a pillar of the Gate of Mazaeus and Mithridates near the Library of Celsus at Ephesus contains the word *audeitōrion* (which is the only known transliteration, rather than providing a cognate, of the Lat. *auditorium* in ancient Greek), which refers to a lecture hall that would have been in view from the inscription and was used for the recitations and speeches of professors, rhetors, and poets.

Though Paul eschewed the use of crowd-pleasing "wisdom and eloquence" (1 Cor 1:17), scholars have detected numerous rhetorical forms in his letters, such as chiasmus (Rom 2:6–10), euphemism (1 Cor 5:1–2), litotes (Rom 1:28), meiosis (Rom 3:9), *epanaphora* (Phil 4:8), *captatio* (Rom 9:1–5), climax (Rom 5:3–5), zeugma (1 Cor 3:2), oxymoron (2 Cor 6:9), and paronomasia (2 Cor 3:2). Some scholars have therefore inferred that Paul may have received advanced rhetorical training, either at Tarsus or at Jerusalem, but others regard this as unlikely. Paul's three citations of classical authors (of Epimenides's statement, "For in him we live and move and have our being" [Acts 17:28]; of Menander's *Thais*, "Bad company corrupts good character" [1 Cor 15:33]; and of Epimenides's *De oraculis*, "Cretans are always liars, evil brutes, lazy gluttons" [Titus 1:12]) are not sufficient evidence for an advanced education, inasmuch as these were commonplace quotations.

The Greek word for "to educate" or "to train" is *paideuō*, which is related to the Greek word *pais*, "child." In Eph 6:4, Paul provides this exhortation: "Fathers, do not exasperate your children; instead, bring them up in the training [*paideia*] and instruction [*nouthesia*] of the Lord." In 2 Tim 3:16 Paul declares that "all Scripture is God-breathed and is useful for teaching [*didaskalian*], rebuking, correcting and training [*paideian*] in righteousness."

In Gal 3:24, Paul likens the OT law to a *paidagōgos*, "child-attendant," "tutor," or "guide" (cf. "pedagogy," which is derived from this Gk. term). In this context the reference is not to a teacher but to a slave who accompanied a young boy to school, saw that he was not molested, sat with him in classes, and brought him home. He had the authority to discipline the lad. Paul may be alluding to the temporary nature of this tutor's authority, which lasted until the boy was allowed to be on his own.

The word *paideuō* can have the sense of "punish," as in Luke 23:16, 22. Outside of the texts cited above (Eph 6:4; 2 Tim 3:16) the word *paideia*, "training," occurs in the NT only in Heb 12, where it always refers to "discipline" (Heb 12:5, 7, 8, 11). (The word *paideia* is also used in the sense of "punishment" or "chastisement" in the LXX of Isa 53:5.) The word *paideutēs*, "instructor, one who disciplines," occurs in Heb 12:9.

Scholars are divided over how to interpret and apply Paul's injunction in 1 Tim 2:11–12: "A woman should learn in quietness and full submission. I do not permit a woman to teach or to assume authority over a man; she must be quiet." On the one hand, in light of the subsequent verses' reference to the creation of Adam and Eve, many regard this command as generally applicable even today. Others believe that this injunction was called forth by a particular situation in Ephesus, where some wealthy and exceptionally educated women were attempting to "usurp" the authority of the male leaders.

C. THE NEAR EASTERN WORLD

Mesopotamia

In Mesopotamia students generally came from the upper classes of society, as parents had to pay the teachers. Many followed in the footsteps of their fathers, who were themselves scribes. Students were primarily trained to serve in the bureaucracy of the palace and of the temples.

The school was called in Sumerian the É.DUBBA (Akk. *bīt ṭuppi*), "the house of tablets." The student was known as the DUMU É.DUBBA, "the son of the tablet house," and the head of the school was the ADDA É.DUBBA, "the father of the tablet house," who was also called the UMMIA. The UMMIA, "headmaster," had under him specialized assistants, such as the DUBŠAR.NIŠID ("the scribe of counting") and the DUBŠAR.KENGIRA ("the scribe of Sumerian"). Much of the actual supervision lay in the hands of an older student, the ŠEŠ.GAL ("older brother").

The scribe's education involved the arduous process of learning cuneiform script, which consisted of hundreds of different signs used to represent syllables or used as ideograms. The pupil learned them by copying
tablets prepared by the teacher, writing with a stylus on a moist, clay tablet.
Typically the clay tablet was plano-convex and could fit into the student's
hand. The teacher inscribed a model text on the flat side. We have an example on which an apparently exasperated teacher crossed out all of the
student's clumsy copy.

After the second millennium BC Sumerian was no longer a living language, but in schools Sumerian continued to be the language of instruction. We read comments such as "A student boasts: 'Having been in school
for the required period, I am now an expert in Sumerian, in the scribal
art, in interpretation, and in budgeting. I can even speak Sumerian'" (COS
1.186:593). Another derides his fellow student: "You are slow of understanding and hard of hearing; you are but a novice in the school! You are
deaf to the scribal art, and silent in Sumerian" (COS 1.184:589).

Scribes (sing. Sum. DUB.SAR, Akk. ṭupšarru, "tablet writer") had to
memorize bilingual lists of Sumerian signs and words and their Akkadian
equivalents. The earliest example of such a list dates to 2700 BC. Such lists
have been found in numerous locations, including Ur, Nippur, Isin, Uruk,
Girsu, Sippar, Ebla, Susa, and Babylon. A comprehensive list, known in
Sumerian as HAR.RA and in Akkadian as ḫubullu, consisted of twenty-
four tablets that contained the following categories: (1–2) legal and administrative terminology, (3–7) trees and wooden artifacts, (8–9) reeds and
reed artifacts, (10) pottery, (11) hides and copper, (12) other metals, (13)
domestic animals, (14) wild animals, (15) parts of the body, (16) stones,
(17) plants, (18) birds and fish, (19) textiles, (20–22) geographic terms, and
(23–24) food and drinks. A second bilingual (Sumerian and Akkadian) list,
known as nâqu, consisted of forty-two tablets with about fourteen thousand entries. We have trilingual lists (Sumerian, Akkadian, Hittite), and
even quadralingual lists (Sumerian, Akkadian, Ugaritic, Hurrian).

Students memorized grammatical paradigms such as "I kneaded, I will
knead, I will not knead, knead now, he will not knead, [etc.]." They would
also copy excerpts of literary texts. The study of mathematics included abstract and practical aspects of the discipline; in addition to learning about
multiplication, reciprocals, squares, and square roots, and learning coeffi-
cient lists, a student also would learn how to make pay allotments, balance
accounts, and divide property.

Those who were destined to serve as temple personnel studied music;
they learned Sumerian technical terms and were to master the playing of
several instruments. A writer criticized a rival's incompetence in music as
follows: "Even if he had a zami-instrument, he, the most backward among

(his) classmates; he has not been able to make a beautiful tremolo . . . he cannot sing a song, cannot open his mouth" (Lucas, 317).

Classes were probably quite small. Most of the school tablets that have been found were discovered in domestic areas. The early schools may have been associated with the temples. A schoolroom at the palace at Mari had rows of benches of baked brick together with a collection of writing materials. Schools must have had provisions for keeping a supply of wet clay to form into tablets.

We have no information about the age at which students began their studies, nor about how long they pursued them. The student woke up early in the morning, fearful of being late, and took with him two rolls of bread for lunch. He studied until sunset. As to his schedule, one pupil recalled:

> My holidays were three every month;
> Various feasts averaged three per month;
> With all that, there were 24 days per month
> That I spent in school. (COS 1.186:592)

As one Sumerian schoolboy's narrative of his day at school makes clear, the learning environment was regimented and peppered with corporal punishment:

> My headmaster read my tablet, said:
> "There is something missing," caned me. . . .
> The fellow in charge of neatness (?) said:
> "You loitered in the street and did not straighten up (?) your clothes (?)," caned me. . . .
> The fellow in charge of silence said:
> "Why did you talk without permission," caned me. . . .
> The fellow in charge of good behavior said:
> "Why did you rise without permission," caned me.
> The fellow in charge of the gate said:
> "Why did you go out from (the gate) without permission," caned me. . . .
> The fellow in charge of Sumerian said:
> "Why didn't you speak Sumerian," caned me.
> My teacher (ummia) said:
> "Your hand is unsatisfactory," caned me. (Kramer, 238–39)

Women were generally not educated in the scribal art. In an analysis of 464 Ur III scribes, not a single female name appears. But there were some notable exceptions. In fact, the earliest named author in world literature is Enheduanna (2285–2250 BC), the daughter of Sargon of Agade, who composed the 153-line poem "The Exaltation of Inanna." The wife of Ur-Nammu (ca. 2100 BC) may have composed a lament after her husband's death, and the wife of Shulgi may have composed a lullaby for her sons. Over a dozen female scribes are known from Sippar, and about ten from Mari.

Most kings were probably illiterate and relied on scribes to read and write for them, but some were well educated. The Sumerian king Shulgi, of the Ur III Dynasty (r. 2029–1982 BC), boasted:

> As a youth, I studied the scribal art in the EDUBBA,
> From the tablets of Sumer and Akkad;
> Of the nobility, no one was able to write a tablet like me,
> In the place where the people attend to learn the scribal art,
> Adding, subtracting, counting, and accounting—I completed all [of their courses];
> The fair Nanibgal-Nisaba (goddess of scribes)
> Endowed me generously with wisdom and intelligence.
>   (Shulgi B, 13–20; *CANE*, 2.853)

This king established scribal schools at Ur and Nippur. Another literate ruler was the last great Neo-Assyrian king, Ashurbanipal (668–627 BC), who claimed,

> Marduk, master of the gods, granted me as a gift a receptive mind (lit., wide ear) and ample (power of) thought. Nabû, the universal scribe, made me a present of his wisdom (lit., the possession, grasp, of his wisdom). . . . I have read the artistic script of Sumer (and) the dark (obscure) Akkadian, which is hard to master, (now) taking pleasure in the reading of the stones (i.e., stelas) (coming) from before the flood. (*ARAB*, 2.378–79)

Egypt

Egyptian education prepared a scribal class of civil servants. During the Old Kingdom only sons of officials had access to education, but after the turmoil of the First Intermediate Period an effort was made, during the Middle Kingdom, to recruit able students from the lower classes to create a bureaucracy loyal to the pharaoh. Students from humble beginnings were able to advance to eminent positions by virtue of their education. A portion of Papyrus Chester Beatty IV declares: "Be a scribe, that your limbs may be smooth and your hands languid, that you may go out dressed in white, being exalted so that the courtiers salute you" (Williams, 218). Moreover, teachers often reminded their pupils that education meant a life free from taxes, poverty, and physical labor. Khety wrote the popular *Satire on the Trades* to encourage his son, Pepi, by pointing out the disadvantages of non-scribal occupations, such as that of the gardener, the washerman, the mat maker, the potter, the messenger, and other individuals the boy encountered routinely on his way to school (*ANET*, 432–34).

The Egyptian word for "instruction," *sb3jt*, comes from the root *sb3*, "to chastise, punish," and was written with a hieroglyphic determinative of a man holding a stick. The teacher's motto was: "A boy's ear is indeed upon his back, and he hearkens to the beating of him" (Papyrus Anastasi 3.13; Caminos, 83).

The child went to school with rolls of bread and a jug of beer. School lasted for only half the day. When noon came, the children left shouting for joy. No texts mention girls as students, but royal princesses, such as Hatshepsut's daughter, were taught by private tutors. The title for a female scribe appears occasionally in Middle Kingdom contexts, but there are no such references from the New Kingdom.

Boys began to attend school at the age of four or five. Bakenkhons, the son of a priest, reported that he attended school for eleven years, training to become a stable master for Seti I's breeding stable. He also became a junior priest (Frood, 41; cf. Jansen-Winkeln, 222). Schools were held in the open air, and at times next to a temple. We learn of a school next to the Ramesseum. Temples had attached to them a scriptorium, called a *pr-ʿnḫ*, "house of life," where texts would be copied. Instruction included reading, writing, abstract and applied mathematics, and geography. Some students also had lessons in archery, wrestling, and swimming.

The young student's first efforts at writing were made on ruled limestone flakes or potsherds. He learned to use a wooden palette in his left hand and a rush pen in his right hand. He would advance to writing on palimpsests, papyrus that had already been used. Only later would he write on unused papyrus. Pupils first learned the cursive hieratic script, writing words as a whole rather than spelling out texts sign by sign. (In the late fourth century BC, the demotic script replaced the hieratic.) Only special artisans who worked on the royal monuments would learn the pictographic hieroglyphic script. Students copied classic texts from the Middle Kingdom, and memorized them. Judging from the number of copies, the most popular texts included the *Book of Kemit*, the *Tale of Sinuhe*, and the *Satire on the Trades*, of which more than a hundred copies have been found. The *Instruction of Amenemhet* was copied over seven centuries. It appears that strategies for memorization included repeating the texts aloud. The Egyptian word for "reading" implies recitation. The *Instruction for Merikare* advises: "Do not kill anyone whose good side you know, with whom you once chanted the writings" (*ANET*, 412).

The scribe would study geography, mathematics, geometry, and related subjects, such as accountancy, architecture, and surveying. Each student had to learn the specialized vocabulary of his intended profession: for example, the names of ninety-six Egyptian cities, or of forty-eight different baked meats. If he planned to work with the army, he had to learn the geography of Palestine, the organization of a military campaign, and the distribution of provisions. This is made clear in the satirical letter written to Amen-em-Opet by Hori: "Let me tell thee of another strange city, named Byblos. What is it like? And its goddess? Once again—[thou] hast not trodden it. Pray, instruct me about Beirut, about Sidon and Sarepta" (*ANET*, 477).

In spite of the rewards of a scribal career, there were delinquents. One teacher bemoaned a former pupil's behavior, telling him:

> I am told that you have abandoned writing and whirl around in pleasures, that you go from street to street. . . . If only you knew that wine is an abomination . . . you would not set the beer-jar in your heart, you would forget *tnrk*-wine. . . . Now you are seated (still) in the house, and the harlots surround you, now you are standing and bouncing. . . . Now you are seated in front of the wench, soaked in anointing-oil, your wreath of *ištpn* at your neck, and you drum upon your belly. Now you stumble and fall upon your belly, anointed with dirt.
> (*Papyrus Anastasi* IV, 11.9–12.5; Caminos, 182)

D. THE GRECO-ROMAN WORLD

Greece

Sparta

After Sparta conquered Messenia in the southwestern Peloponnese, it made its population into helots, slaves of the state, to do all the agricultural work. In order to control the helots, who outnumbered the Spartans by a large ratio, Sparta became a militarized state with a unique system of education, overseen by an individual called the *paidonomos*. Unlike the situation in other cities, education in Sparta was sponsored by the state. This unique education (*paideia*), known as the *agōgē*, "guidance," was attributed anachronistically by Plutarch to the legendary Lycurgus (8th c. BC): "In the matter of education, which he [Lycurgus] regarded as the greatest and noblest task of the law-giver, he began at the very source by carefully regulating marriage and births" (*Lyc.* 14).

Girls received athletic training with the goal of making them robust mothers; they learned to run, wrestle, and throw the javelin. At the age of seven, boys were separated from their homes to live in barracks under strict discipline intended to make them tough and obedient soldiers. They were assigned to age classes, *bouai*, each with its own *bouagos*, "oxen leader." Between the ages of eight and eleven they were considered by the Spartans to be *paides*; from twelve to fifteen, *paidiskoi*; and from sixteen to twenty, *hēbōntes*. In a practice known as *krypteia*, the boys were encouraged to hunt and kill helots at night. Competing bands fought each other for the possession of an island. Youths underwent the *diamastigōsis*, a severe ritual beating at the altar of Artemis Orthia, which sometimes led to death; this practice continued into the Christian era.

As a result of their intense physical and military training, the Spartans dominated the Panhellenic athletic games and became unrivaled soldiers. Much less emphasis was placed on other types of learning. Spartans were taught only the rudiments of reading and writing; the Athenians considered them uneducated. Their musical training was solely for martial purposes. From their being discouraged from speaking, we derive the world "laconic," as Spartans came from Laconia.

Athens

In his famous funeral speech, Pericles contrasted the Spartan way of life with his own Athenian culture: "And again in the matter of education [*paideiais*], whereas they [the Spartans] from early childhood by a laborious discipline make pursuit of manly courage, we with our unrestricted mode of life are none the less ready to meet any equality of hazard" (*Thuc.* 2.39.1). The great Athenian statesman concluded with this boast: "In a word, then, I say that our city as a whole is the school of Hellas [*tēs Hellados paideusin*]" (*Thuc.* 2.41.1). What Pericles meant by this famous statement is that, in contrast to the xenophobic society of Sparta, Athens, with its openness to *metics* (non-Athenian immigrants) and intellectual innovation, fostered the Golden Age of Greece, which included unparalleled achievements in architecture (the Parthenon), drama (Aeschylus, Sophocles, Euripides, Aristophanes), and history (Herodotus, Thucydides).

The Athenian reformer Solon (638–558 BC) insisted that a father must teach his son a skill so that the son could support the father in his old age. Xenophon lists as a father's chief preoccupations his prosperity of his *oikos* (household), his daughter's virginity, and his son's education (*Mem.* 1.5.2).

Boys started school between the ages of five and seven (see Beck 1964, 95). How long a student stayed depended on his family's economic status. A few city-states subsidized teachers (Teos, Miletus, and Delphi), but in most city-states parents had to pay the teachers' salaries. According to Plato, "This is what people do, who are the most able; and the most able are the wealthiest. Their sons begin school at the earliest age, and are freed from it at the latest" (*Protag.* 326c). Poorer children left school after they attained literacy, typically in three to four years. Poorer families could not afford to educate their children beyond the attainment of basic literacy. The English word "school" is derived from the Greek word *scholē*, "leisure." Educated Greeks looked down upon the *banausoi*, those who had no free time for learning because they had to work with their hands or worked for hire or profit.

The pay and status of the *grammatistēs*, the elementary school teacher, was low. Demosthenes taunted an opponent as follows:

> In my boyhood, Aeschines, I had the advantage of attending respectable schools: and my means were sufficient for one who was not to be driven by poverty into disreputable occupations. . . . But do you—you who are so proud and so contemptuous of others—compare your fortune with mine? In your childhood you were reared in abject poverty. You helped your father in the drudgery of a grammar-school, grinding the ink, sponging the benches, and sweeping the school-room, holding the position of a menial, not of a free-born boy. (*Cor.* 257–258)

Most families would have a *paidagōgos*, usually an elderly slave, who carried a boy's equipment, accompanied him to school, protected him from those who would molest him, and quizzed him on his lessons. The *paidagōgos* had the authority to discipline the child by twisting his ears or by beating him with a *narthex* ("cane"). Though many young boys grew up resenting their *paidagōgos*'s authority, some grew fond of their "minders" and later, after they had grown to manhood, manumitted them from slavery.

The pupil went to school at daybreak accompanied by his *paidagōgos*, who carried a lamp on dark winter mornings. Pupils sat on benches (*bathra*) with their waxed writing tablets on their knees. The teacher sat on a chair (*kathedra*) on a platform. From illustrations on pottery we see that at times the children brought pet cats, dogs, and even leopards to class. Classes ended a half hour before dusk. Although there were no summer vacations, as many as one hundred days were set aside for feasts, pageants, and dramatic spectacles.

The children would learn the *stoicheia*, the twenty-four letters of the Greek alphabet, by rote. Then they learned to form these letters into syllables and into words that formed simple sentences. An emphasis was laid upon calligraphy in writing out the *grammata*, "letters," with a pointed stylus that had a flattened end for erasures.

All books were papyrus scrolls, and students always read them aloud; the ancients never read silently. One difficulty about learning to read Greek was that there was no punctuation or word separation. Homer was the preeminent text, especially the first two books of the *Iliad*. After the fourth century BC, other authors, such as Herodotus, Thucydides, Euripides, Demosthenes, and Menander, would be added to the curriculum.

The pupil was taught basic mathematics, learning to count with his fingers and to use the twenty-four letters of the alphabet to stand for numbers, plus three now-obsolete symbols: the *digamma* (which stood for 6), the *koppa* (90), and the *sampi* (9900). He learned simple fractions, and could use an abacus for addition, subtraction, multiplication, and division.

To stimulate interest, teachers relied on competition. To maintain order, they relied on the threat of corporal punishment, which they administered with a stick, switch, sandal, or leather strap. We have numerous depictions of students being whipped on their backs, in some cases while hoisted onto another student's back. In one of the mimes of Herondas (3rd c. BC) we learn what could happen to truant boys. A mother named Metrotime complains that her son would rather play knucklebones than go to school. He is not able to spell from dictation and can read only hesitantly. When he is scolded, he runs away to his grandmother. Metrotime therefore brings her son, Kottalos, to his teacher with this instruction: "As you wish for any pleasure from the dear Muses, Lampriskos . . . , and to enjoy your life, so do you beat this fellow a-shoulder, till his life [*psyche*, spirit, soul]—curse it—remain hanging on his lips" (Mime 3.1–4; translation Knox, cited in Will, 62). The schoolmaster then addresses his pupil: "I'll make you more orderly than a girl—he says to Kottalos—stirring not a twig, if that's what you are after. Give me my stinging whip, the ox-tail, with which I flog the 'gaol-birds' and the disgraced. Put it into my hand before I choke with choler" (Mime 3.66–70; translation Knox, cited in Will, 62).

The word *gymnastikē* is derived from the word *gymnos*, "naked"; boys exercised while unclothed. They were taught in private *palaistrai*, "wrestling arenas," by *paidotribēs* (lit., "boy-rubbers," from the practice of rubbing the body with oil and dust before exercising). Boys were taught first to wrestle; later, as teenagers, they received instruction in boxing. Running and hurling the javelin would be practiced in public gymnasiums.

The public *gymnasion* was a key center of civic life. Typically it would contain many specialized rooms, such as a court for wrestling (*palaistra*), a running track (*dromos*), colonnades, a cloakroom (*apodytērion*), rooms for playing with a ball (*sphairistēria*), a room for the punching bag (*kōrykeion*), loggia fitted with seats (*exedrai*), halls (*oikoi*), and lecture rooms (*akroatēria*). Preparation of the body with oil and dust before exercise took place in an anointing room (*aleiptērion*) and a dusting room (*konistērion*); the *gymnasiarchos*, superintendent of the *gymnasion*, was responsible for providing the oil. In the Hellenistic period the Greeks established gymnasiums in every city they founded in the Near East; this served as the primary means of preserving the Hellenic tradition and of assimilating non-Hellenes into Hellenic society.

When a boy reached the age of sixteen and became of age, he was at last freed from the restrictive care of his *paidagogos*. He could then enjoy several years of pleasure, amusing himself at festival competitions and going on hunts. Starting in 335 BC, at Athens youths underwent a compulsory, state-sponsored course of military and athletic training between the ages of eighteen and twenty. They were called *ephēbeioi*. In an "ephebic school" they practiced sword fighting, built fortifications, and patrolled frontier areas. Later, in the third century BC, the Macedonian kings employed mercenary soldiers, and enrollment as an *ephēbeios* became voluntary. But the institution retained its prestige, because its graduates formed the upper class of Hellenic society.

The so-called "Old Education" emphasized *gymnastikē*, "athletics," and *mousikē*, which included not only music but also poetry and dance. Boys were taught how to play the *kithara*, "lyre," by the *kitharistēs*, and also the *aulos*, "flute." Aristotle believed that music was the cornerstone of a liberal education. After about 450 BC the "New Education" was introduced into Athens by "sophists" who came from Magna Graecia (Sicily, southern Italy) in the west and Ionia (western Turkey) in the east. They rejected the emphasis on athletics and music, concentrating instead on intellectual pursuits. They taught on many subjects, asserting that there are two opposed arguments on any issue. They especially emphasized rhetoric, the art of persuasive speech. Aristophanes, a conservative, decried the "New Education" as undermining the manhood of Athenian youth. In his comedy *The Clouds* (423 BC), Aristophanes contrasts the Old Education (*tēn archaian paideian*) with the New Education (*tēn kainēn paideian*) (*Nub.* 961–1023).

Protagoras of Abdera (490–420 BC) was the first sophist to teach for money. According to Sextus Empiricus,

> Protagoras also holds that "Man is the measure of all things, of existing things that they exist, and of non-existing things that they exist not"; and by "measure" he means the criterion, and by "things" the objects, so that he is virtually asserting that "Man is the criterion of all objects, of those which exist that they exist, and of those which exist not that they exist not." And consequently he posits only what appears to each individual, and thus he introduces relativity. (*Pyr.* 1.216)

Sextus Empiricus writes of Gorgias of Leontini (483–375 BC):

> In his book entitled *Concerning the Non-existent* or *Concerning Nature* he tries to establish successively three main points—firstly, that nothing exists; secondly, that even if anything exists it is inapprehensible by man; thirdly, that even if anything is apprehensible, yet of a surety it is inexpressible and incommunicable to one's neighbour. (*Against the Logicians* 65)

Gorgias's student Isocrates (436–338 BC) established an important school in 392 in Athens for the teaching of rhetoric. He charged 1,000 drachmas for a course that would last three to four years. (A drachma was worth a day's pay.) He established the model for the *rhētōr* or *sophistēs*, the teacher of tertiary education, which only the most advanced students achieved. Students were asked to compose *progymnasmata*, preparatory compositions. They were then taught how to compose and present different types of speeches, including those that were judicial (*dikanikos*), advisory (*symbouleutikos*), and celebratory (*epideiktikos*).

Socrates (469–399 BC) taught by a method of interrogation. He asserted that he was impelled to do so by a Delphic oracle that proclaimed him "the wisest man"; he denied, however, that he knew anything. He did not charge a fee to students, which irritated his irascible wife, Xanthippe. Socrates, who was critical of the sophists for their amoral attitude, was ironically depicted as a sophist by Aristophanes in his play *The Clouds*. This was a calumny, which in Plato's *Apology* Socrates claimed contributed to his conviction of "atheism," that is, disrespect for the traditional gods, which led to his condemnation to death in 399 BC by a trial by 501 jurors.

Socrates's disciple Plato (ca. 429–347 BC) established his school at the gymnasium known as the Academy in about 385 BC. He rejected book learning but asserted: "For it [i.e., philosophy] does not at all admit of verbal expression like other studies, but, as a result of continued application to the subject itself and communion therewith, it is brought to birth in the soul on a sudden, as light that is kindled by a leaping spark, and thereafter it nourishes itself" (*Ep.* 7.341d).

Reacting against the democracy of Athens, which had condemned to death his beloved teacher, Plato was inspired by Spartan education. He proposed the supremacy of a state's authority over the child and compulsory education for all. He asserted that

> no father shall either send his son as a pupil or keep him away from the training-school at his own sweet will, but every "man jack" of them all (as the saying goes) must, so far as possible, be compelled to be educated, inasmuch as they are children of the State even more than children of their parents.
> (*Leg.* 7.804d)

In the *Timaeus* Plato advocated the teaching of arithmetic, geometry, astronomy, and music rather than rhetoric. He proposed that in an ideal city-state, the philosopher-rulers' education would concentrate upon one subject at a time: on literature from the ages of ten to thirteen, on music from thirteen to sixteen, and on mathematics from sixteen to eighteen. Plato wished to censor Homer because of the immoral examples of the gods he depicted. Plato was critical of learning by memorization and wished rather to arouse in students the latent ideas that he considered to be the archetypes of reality in the soul. His most radical proposal was equal education for females: "For females, too, my law will lay down the same regulations as for men, and training of an identical kind" (*Leg.* 7.804e).

Two women were students at the Academy: Lasthenia of Mantinea, and Axiothea of Phlius, who dressed like a man.

After they reached puberty, respectable Athenian girls did not attend schools; they prepared for marriage and learned homekeeping skills. Menander expressed a typically misogynistic point of view when he wrote: "He who teaches letters to a woman ... provides poison for a powerful asp" (*Fragments* 702K). Non-Athenian women (who were not eligible for a legitimate marriage to an Athenian man, but who functioned as *hetairai*, "companions," serving as entertainers and courtesans at male banquets) were sometimes highly educated; one example of such a woman is Aspasia, the mistress of Pericles.

Aristotle from Stagira (384–322 BC) was the son of a physician at the Macedonian court. He was a member of Plato's Academy from his seventeenth to thirty-seventh year. When Speusippus was named in 347 as Plato's successor, the disappointed Aristotle went to the court of Assos at the invitation of a fellow student, the tyrant Hermeias. He then served as the tutor of the young Alexander (the Great), from 343 to 342. Aristotle returned to Athens in 335 to establish his own school, known as the Lyceum, at the Lykeion gymnasium. His followers became known as *peripatetics*, a word derived from the Lyceum's colonnaded porticos, which were referred to as *peripatoi*.

In contrast to Plato's philosophy, which proceeded from the conviction that there are eternal ideas that the visible world only imperfectly reflects, Aristotle emphasized research encompassing almost every branch of knowledge. In his *Politics* he writes that, to produce virtuous citizens and rulers for the good city, men must be trained in reading, writing, drawing, athletics, and music. He held that *theōria*, "philosophic contemplation," is the highest activity, and that the goal of education should be *scholē*, "leisure." Despite his empirical emphasis, Aristotle was influenced by his male chauvinism to declare that men have more teeth than women, and that men's baldness is evidence that they are more intelligent than women, because their baldness is symptomatic of their intense intellectual activity!

Epicurus of Samos (341–270 BC) arrived in Athens in 306 and established in his house there a unique community called the Garden (*kēpos*), to which he invited many friends, including women and a slave. He based his philosophy on the atomistic materialism of Democritus, denying that humans have a soul. Epicurus renounced traditional education, asserting that to be ignorant of Homer was not a source of shame but was rather an advantage. He promoted the memorization of his forty *Kyriai Doxai* (*Authoritative Opinions*), the first four of which were the *tetrapharmakos*, "fourfold remedy": (1) god is not to be feared, (2) death is not to be suspected, (3) the good is easy to acquire, and (4) terrible things are easy to endure. The goal of the Epicureans was the pursuit of *hēdonē*, "sweetness" or "pleasure," not in the sense of sensual indulgence but rather in the pleasant calm of friendship achieved by the avoidance of politics.

Zeno of Kition in Cyprus (350–260 BC) came to Athens in 314. He became a follower of Crates the Cynic. In 304 Zeno began teaching in the *Stoa Poikilē*, "The Painted Porch" in the Agora. His followers were called "Stoics" because of their association with this colonnaded porch. Zeno was a pantheist who conceived of god as somewhat like a material gas that pervades the universe, including humans. He advocated the pursuit of *apatheia*, which does not mean "apathy," but rather imperturbility or indifference to what one cannot control.

Cleanthes of Assos came from a poor family and had to work as a porter so that he could attend Zeno's lectures. He became the head of the Stoa in 262 BC. Cleanthes saw the universe as a living being with the sun at its center. He composed forty poems, most notably the "Hymn of Zeus." Some scholars regard this poem, rather than Aratus, as the source of Paul's statement "for we are also his offspring" in his Areopagus speech (Acts 17:28).

Succeeding Cleanthes in 232 BC as the head of the Stoa was Chrysippus, who was born in Soli, just west of Tarsus in Cilicia. He was a prolific author and is credited with over seven hundred works, though only fragments of them have survived. His great achievement was to systematize Stoic doctrines. He was succeeded by Zeno of Tarsus. Many noted Stoic philosophers lived and taught in Tarsus in the first century AD.

Rome

Even before Greece became a Roman province in 146 BC, its cultural influence was felt at Rome. Cato the Elder (234–149 BC), who opposed Greek learning, is said to have learned Greek at the end of his life. Quintilian (AD 40–118), the great authority on Roman education, held that Roman children should be taught Greek before Latin.

As Rome expanded and conquered Greece in the Macedonian Wars of the second century BC, Rome acquired a large number of Greek slaves to serve either as private pedagogues or as public teachers. This influx of educated Greek slaves transformed Roman education. Some conservatives were critical of Greek mores, but by the first century BC every educated Roman was expected to know the Greek language. The pragmatic Roman outlook introduced some striking differences with Greek education. Mathematics, geometry, and music were taught only insofar as they had practical applications. Architecture and engineering were taught through apprenticeships and by the study of manuals.

Rhetoric, not philosophy, was the subject that ranked supreme in higher studies. The Romans had little liking for the nudity of Greek athletics, which they felt were conducive to effeminacy and homosexuality. More to their taste were the horse races of the hippodrome and the gladiatorial games of the amphitheater.

The Roman word *educatio* referred to the training of a child to instill in him respect for the *mos maiorum*, the custom of the ancestors. A boy was in the care of his mother until the age of seven, when the father took over. According to Plutarch, Cato, who was a paragon of the Roman virtues, undertook to teach his son everything:

> As soon as the boy showed signs of understanding, his father took him under his own charge and taught him to read, although he had an accomplished slave, Chilo by name, who was a school-teacher, and taught many boys. Still, Cato thought it not right, as he tells us himself, that his son should be scolded by a slave, or have his ears tweaked when he was slow to learn, still less that he should be indebted to his slave for such a priceless thing as education. . . . His History of Rome, as he tells us himself, he wrote out with his own hand and in large characters, that his son might have in his own home an aid to acquaintance with his country's ancient traditions. (*Cat. Maj.* 20.3–5)

But Cato was exceptional. After about 250 BC most parents would pay fees to teachers for their children's education. At the age of seven, both boys and girls would enter the *ludus litterarius* ("elementary school"), where they would learn basic reading and writing from the *ludi magister*. A *calculator* would teach elementary mathematics using *calculi* ("pebbles"). A *citharoedus magister* would teach music.

Pupils would memorize and copy the twenty-four letters of the Latin alphabet on their *tabulae*, waxed writing tablets, with a stylus of metal or wood. As was the case with Greek, there was no word division or punctuation, so reading remained a challenging task. When the son of Herodes Atticus had difficulty learning the letters, Herodes Atticus provided twenty-four slaves, each of whom carried a letter as a placard on his back.

Teachers, most of whom were Greek slaves or freedmen (former slaves), received grudging payment and little respect. Juvenal wrote: "Just so you get some pay—but for that it takes a court order. . . . 'That's your job,' they [the parents] say, and your pay, at the end of a twelve month, equals a jockey's fee if he's ridden only one winner" (*Sat.* 7.224, 242–243; Humphreys, 99–100).

The *grammaticus* sometimes taught in a *pergula* ("balcony") or on the street level, with a tent-cloth partition. Students sat on benches, and the teacher on a chair. School began early—too early for Martial, who complained: "What have you to do with me, cursed schoolmaster, creature hateful to boys and girls? The crested cocks have not yet broken silence and already you make a din with your savage roaring and your thwacks" (*Ep.* 9.68).

The school year began in March, after the *quinquatrus* holiday dedicated to Minerva. Students would have the summer off, from July to October, and extensive holidays in December and in March. Every *nundinae* ("ninth day") was a market day and also a school holiday. Some students who did not find one day off in nine sufficient would pretend illness in order to play hooky, rubbing their eyes with olive oil or taking cumin to make themselves pale.

At the close of the elementary school years, girls' institutional education ended. Boys went on to secondary school, which they attended between the ages of twelve and fifteen. The teacher was called a *grammaticus*. His main subjects were technical grammar and literature, primarily Homer and other Greek texts. Latin texts such as Virgil, Horace, and Cicero were introduced in 25 BC. Lessons had three formal structural elements: the teacher began with *lectio* (expressive reading), followed it with *enarratio* (explanation), and concluded with a *partitio* (analysis of the text).

Boys took on the toga of manhood between the ages of fifteen and seventeen. Only a select few would go on at the age of sixteen to receive training from *rhetores* to prepare for a career in politics or the courts. Rhetoric was taught almost entirely in Greek. Students were taught to construct speeches following principles that went back to Aristotle's *Rhetoric*:

(1) *Inventio* (Gr. *heuresis*), the discovery of things to say to meet the question at issue.

(2) *Dispositio* (Gr. *oikonomia*), which included prescriptions for the division of the subject matter.

(3) *Elocutio* (Gr. *phrasis*), how to use various figures, word order, rhythm, and euphony.

(4) *Memoria* (Gr. *mnēmē*), how to memorize the speech, using associations. It was considered very bad form to read from a text in court.

(5) *Actio* (Gr. *hypokrisis*), how to use inflection, gestures, and facial expressions. Cicero declared: "Demosthenes was right, therefore, in considering delivery [*actioni*] to be the first, second and third in importance. If, then, there can be no eloquence without this, and this without eloquence is so important, certainly its rôle in oratory is very large. Therefore the one who seeks supremacy in eloquence will strive to speak intensely with a vehement tone, and gently with lowered voice, and to show dignity in a deep voice, and wretchedness by a plaintive tone" (*De or.* 17.56).

Students were asked to declaim on either *suasoria* (which proposed some action, such as "Should Agamemnon sacrifice his daughter?") or *controversia* (which dealt with some far-fetched case involving a conflict of laws). Juvenal mocked this artificial practice: "Do you teach rhetoric? Vettius must have a heart of steel, when his crowded class slays 'The Cruel Tyrant.' You know how it is: what they've just read sitting down each in turn will repeat standing up, chanting the same things in the same lines. All that rehashed cabbage kills the poor teachers" (*Sat.* 7.150–154).

Corporal punishment was common. The phrase *manum ferulae subducere*, "to withdraw the hand from the rod," meant to leave school. Horace called Orbilius a teacher who was *plagosus*, "fond of flogging" (*Ep.* 2.1.70). A teacher wrote on a school exercise in Egypt, "Work hard, boy, lest you be thrashed" (Cribiore 2001, 67). The emperor Claudius hated his pedagogue, who had whipped him when he was a child. Quintilian is a noted voice of reason protesting this universal practice:

> Flogging a pupil is something I do not at all like, though it is an accepted practice. . . . In the first place, it is humiliating and proper only for slaves; and certainly it is an infringement of rights. . . . Secondly, if a boy is so lacking in self-respect that reproof is powerless to put him right, he will even become hardened to blows, like the worst type of slave. (*Inst.* 1.3.14)

Quintilian also commented:

> Give me a boy who is encouraged by praise, pleased by success, and who cries when he has lost. He is the one who will be nourished by ambition, hurt by reproof, and excited by honour. In him I shall never have to fear laziness. However, everyone must be given some relaxation, not only because there is nothing that can stand perpetual strain—even things which are without sense or life need to be relaxed by periods of rest in order to preserve their strength—but also because study depends on the will to learn, and this cannot be forced. (*Inst.* 1.3.7–8)

Some teachers gave out as rewards cookies, ivy wreaths, books, or small busts of the poets.

Although elementary education of girls was widespread, opinions differed regarding their higher education. After completing elementary school at about age twelve, girls remained at home to prepare for marriage. Some in wealthy homes could continue their education with private tutors. Pliny the Younger wrote about Minicia, a young girl who died before the age of fourteen: "She loved her nurses, her attendants and her teachers, each one for the service given her; she applied herself intelligently to her books and was moderate and restrained in her play" (*Ep.* V 16.3). Of Pompey's fifth wife, Cornelia, Plutarch wrote: "She was well versed in literature, in playing the lyre, and in geometry, and had been accustomed to listen to philosophical discourses with profit. In addition to this, she had a nature which was free from that unpleasant officiousness which such accomplishments are apt to impart to young women" (*Pomp.* 55).

Musonius Rufus (1st c. AD), a Stoic who believed in coeducation, was challenged about his views. He noted:

> But, by Zeus, some say that women who associate with philosophers are generally headstrong and brash, when they abandon their house-keeping and go around in public with men and practice arguments, act like sophists, and analyze syllogisms. These women, they say, should be sitting at home spinning wool. (Lecture 3.6; King, 29)

Juvenal voiced displeasure with educated woman who showed off their learning in the company of men:

> But she's much worse, the woman who as soon as she's taken her place at dinner is praising Virgil and forgiving Elissa on her deathbed, who pits the poets against one another and assesses them, weighing in her scales Maro [i.e., Virgil] on this side and Homer on the other. . . . I loathe the woman who is forever referring to Palaemon's *Grammar* and thumbing through it, observing all the laws and rules of speech, or who quotes lines I've never heard, a female scholar. Do men bother about such things? . . . Husbands should be allowed their grammatical oddities. (*Sat.* 6.434–456)

Repeated Roman efforts to eliminate abstract intellectual academic disciplines in favor of practical instruction failed, and in time, Roman leaders personally and institutionally supported such fields of study and even enacted laws that supported teachers on a number of fronts. In 161 BC the Senate decreed the expulsion of all Greek teachers of rhetoric and philosophy, but given that Athens sent three philosophers to Rome in 155 BC, it appears this had little effect. In 92 BC Roman censors banned the teaching of rhetoric in Latin schools; again, this was counterproductive. Julius Caesar decreed that all teachers of the liberal arts be given citizenship. The emperor Vespasian was the first to endow professors of Greek and Latin rhetoric. Quintilian was the first to hold the latter chair.

When Pliny the Younger visited his hometown in northern Italy, he discovered that the son of his friend was going away to Mediolanum (Milan) because there was no school in Comum (Como). Pliny, who was childless, offered to pay a third of the cost of hiring a teacher, if the parents of the town would get together and pay the rest. He wrote to his friend Tacitus, the historian, to ask him to recommend one of his students for the post (*Ep.* 4.13).

Antoninus Pius, who was the emperor from AD 138 to 161, granted immunities from obligations to certain professions, as noted in the *Digest of Justinian*:

> An extract from a rescript of Antoninus Pius, quoted in a *constitutio* of the Emperor Commodus. . . . The actual words are as follows: "In all those cases my deified father . . . confirmed in a *constitutio* all existing offices and immunities, providing that philosophers, rhetoricians, grammarians, and doctors were to be immune from the function of gymnasiarch, aedile, chief priest, billeting soldiers, corn buying or oil buying, nor were they to be adjudicators nor ambassadors nor compulsorily enlisted in military service nor forced into other provincial duties nor anything else." (*Dig. Just.* 27.1.8; Watson, 2.325)

Antoninus Pius's successor, Marcus Aurelius, who reigned from 162 to 180, endowed four chairs of philosophy and one chair of rhetoric for the "university" in Athens.

E. THE JEWISH WORLD

Following the exile (which began in 586 BC), scribes assumed a leading position in religious instruction. Ezra, a scribe, priest, and "teacher well versed in the Law of Moses" (Ezra 7:6), did much to shape the scribal tradition. Within newly established scribal schools, attention was given to studying, interpreting, and copying the Scriptures (Ezra 7:10; Neh 8:8). During this time much of the editing of the OT took place. Before the NT period, the scribes held a recognized position as the official teachers of Israel's spiritual heritage.

Under the Hellenizing high priest Jason (175–171 BC), a gymnasium was established in Jerusalem (1 Macc 1:1–15; 2 Macc 4:9–10; Jos. *Ant.* 12.240–241). This provoked an anti-Hellenistic Maccabean revolt, which threw off the Seleucid yoke and established an independent Jewish state that would last until the Roman conquest by Pompey in 63 BC.

One of the earliest uses of the word "school" in postbiblical Jewish literature occurs in Ben Sira, also known as Ecclesiasticus (ca. 180 BC), a manual of ethical maxims and the oldest of the apocryphal books. Ben Sira declares that, in contrast to those who worked with their hands, such as the farmer, the craftsman, the seal maker, the smith, and the potter—all necessary crafts, to be sure—the scribe must be free to pursue wisdom only, as Ben Sira emphasizes through the following chiasm: "The wisdom of the scribe depends on the opportunity of leisure; and he who has little business may become wise" (Sir 38:24). The book encourages special attentiveness to the discourse of old men, who in turn learned wisdom from their fathers (Sir 8:8–9). Ben Sira invited students to come and learn in his *bēt hammidrāš*, or "house of study" (Sir 51:23). Other sages established their own "houses" for instruction in the law. However, the synagogue gradually became the focal center for study in the community, and in NT times the synagogue became known as the "house of study."

Philo (20 BC–AD 50), a Jewish philosopher who lived in Alexandria and whose voluminous writings were influenced by Hellenistic culture and philosophy, asserted in his report on his embassy to the emperor Gaius Caligula: "For all men guard their own customs, but this is especially true of the Jewish nation. Holding that the laws are oracles vouchsafed by God and having been trained in this doctrine from their earliest years, they carry the likenesses of the commandments enshrined in their souls" (*Legat.* 210).

The historian Josephus (AD 37–ca. 100) was educated in Greek. He writes:

> For my compatriots admit that in our Jewish learning I far excel them. I have also laboured strenuously to partake of the realm of Greek prose and poetry, after having gained a knowledge of Greek grammar, although the habitual use of my native tongue [i.e., Aramaic] has prevented my attaining precision in the pronunciation. (*Ant.* 20.263)

Josephus reports: "Above all we pride ourselves on the education of our children" (*Ag. Ap.* 1.60). Contrasting Jewish with Greek education, he declares: "All schemes of education [*paideias*] and moral training [*ēthē kataskeuēs*] fall into two categories: instruction is imparted in the one case by precept, in the other by practical exercising of the character" (*Ag. Ap.* 2.171–172). Josephus claims that, in contrast with the Athenians, who stressed the former, and the Spartans, who stressed the latter, Moses combined both systems. Josephus boasts: "But, should anyone of our nation be questioned about the laws, he would repeat them all more readily than his own name" (*Ag. Ap.* 2.178).

The Qumran community, which many identify as Essenes, stipulated the following:

> From [early ch]ildhood each boy is to be instructed in the Book of Meditation. As he grows older, they shall teach him the statutes of the Covenant, and [he will receive] [in]struction in their laws. For ten years he is to be considered a youth. Then, at a[ge] twenty, [he shall be enrolled] [in] the ranks and take his place among the men of his clan, thereby joining the holy congrega[tion]. (1QSa I, 6–9)

In its so-called *Manual of Discipline*, the sect ordained that,

> in any place where is gathered the ten-man quorum, someone must always be engaged in study of the Law, day and night, continually, each one taking his

turn. The general membership will be diligent together for the first third of every night of the year, reading aloud from the Book, interpreting Scripture, and praying together. (1QS VI, 6–8)

According to a rabbinic tradition, the Pharisees established the first district school system for youths, though some scholars consider this to be an anachronism. Simeon ben Shetach (ca. 75 BC) declared that children should attend the *bēt sēper*, or "house of the book [i.e., the Torah]" (*y. Ketub.* 8:11). The next significant leader in the development of an educational system was Joshua ben Gamala, who was high priest ca. AD 65. The Talmud indicates that he decided that teachers should be appointed for boys six to seven years of age in every province and town of Palestine (*b. B. Bat.* 21a).

Up to the start of their teen years Jewish boys attended elementary school. Classes met in the synagogues, with the *ḥazzān*, the attendant in charge of the scrolls, as the teacher. Children would sit on the floor before him. The teacher had to be a married man; no women were allowed to teach. Elementary school had two divisions. The earliest years were spent in the *bēt sēper*, where the reading of the written law was taught. By the age of ten, the students moved on to the *bēt talmûd*, the "house of learning," where study of the oral law (later codified in the Mishnah) began (cf. *m. 'Abot* 5:21). It is said that before AD 70, 480 synagogues existed in Jerusalem, each with its own *bēt sēper* and *bēt talmûd* (*y. Meg.* 3:1).

Girls did not attend elementary school, but they did attend the synagogues, and some gained a good knowledge of the Scriptures. Opinions differed about the instruction girls should receive at home. In the context of a discussion about the administering of the bitter drink to a suspected adulteress, the following disagreement arose:

> Ben Azzai says: A man ought to give his daughter a knowledge of the Law so that if she must drink [the bitter water] she may know that the merit [that she had acquired] will hold her punishment in suspense. R. Eliezer says: If any man gives his daughter a knowledge of the Law it is as though he taught her lechery. (*m. Soṭah* 3:4)

It was also stated in the Talmud that daughters should not be taught, because Deut 11:19 commands that sons should be taught the Scriptures, with no explicit mention of also teaching daughters (*b. Qidd.* 29b; see also *Sifre Deut* 46). Girls were often betrothed at the age of twelve or thirteen.

Young boys' schooling began at daybreak and often continued until sundown. Some have questioned whether students took time out for a noon meal! During the hot months of July and August, the school day was shortened to four hours. School was even held on the Sabbath, but no new materials were taught on that day. The day before the Sabbath was a half day, and school did not meet during religious festivals.

According to a statement of Judah ben Tema (2nd c. AD) in the Mishnah, boys began to study the Scriptures at the age of five, the Mishnah (oral traditions) at ten, and the Talmud (which contains commentaries on the Mishnah) at fifteen. They were expected to be responsible for keeping the Torah at age thirteen and to marry at age eighteen (*m. ʾAbot* 5:21). The rabbinic council at Usha in Galilee (2nd c. AD) counseled fathers to have patience with their sons learning Torah until the age of twelve. Most parents could not afford to allow their sons to have more than an elementary education. Some rabbis were contemptuous of those who had studied only the Scriptures, regarding them as ignorant ʿam hāʾareṣ, "people of the earth."

The Hebrew Scriptures were originally written to be read aloud. Hence learning centered on oral instruction. The lesson consisted entirely of repetition. (*Mishnah* means "repetition, a review.") Students would begin by reading the Torah, beginning at Leviticus. Some books, such as the Song of Solomon, would not be presented to immature students. Individually, or in groups, students often chanted passages aloud. The following Talmudic saying reflects this practice: "He that repeated his chapter a hundred times is not to be compared with him who repeated it a hundred and one times" (*b. Ḥag.* 9b). The Talmud records that one teacher, R. Pereda, had a student who needed to have the lesson repeated four hundred times before he could absorb it (*b. ʿErub.* 54b). Absolute precision was demanded. Accordingly, an accurate and retentive memory was the greatest aid to learning.

The various aids to memory that were employed included mnemonic devices such as alliteration, paronomasia, and alphabetic acrostics (e.g., Prov 31:10–31). Music was also utilized from earliest times (Exod 15; Deut 32; 2 Sam 1:18–27). In addition, parables were commonly used. Jewish teachers' frequent use of parables is illustrated by the prevalence of this rhetorical device in the teachings of Jesus and by the occurrence of nearly five thousand parables in early rabbinic literature.

Though students were expected to memorize the Scriptures and to be able to recite them to their fathers, they were prohibited from writing the Scriptures down from dictation. Writing was a specialized skill that only those destined to serve as scribes were expected to master.

Gifted and diligent pupils might continue their studies in their spare time at a *bēt hammidrāš*, "house of study." Graduates of this institution would be ordained as "rabbis" at about the age of twenty-two. As a rule, rabbis were not compensated for teaching; they supported themselves by working as millers, shoemakers, tailors, potters, etc. A father was obligated to teach a son a trade (*t. Qidd.* 1:11).

The "academies" were conducted by teachers of the law, some of whom were of outstanding reputation, such as Hillel and Shammai. Paul was a student of Hillel's grandson, the famed Gamaliel (Acts 22:3). Gamaliel was one of the few scholars to permit students to study Greek learning (*ḥokmâ yābānît*). The substance of many of the discussions held in the academies was eventually reduced to writing and used by the rabbis in the formulation of the Talmud. After the destruction of the temple in AD 70, Vespasian allowed the rabbinical academy to move to Jamnia (Yavneh). By the second century, other centers of Jewish learning were established in Galilee, such as those at Usha, Tiberias, and Sepphoris.

Flogging was used with recalcitrant students. According to Sir 30:1, "He who loves his son will whip him often, in order that he may rejoice at the way he turns out." The Hebrew word for instruction, *mûsār*, comes from the verb *yāsar*, which sometimes means "to discipline." Abba Saul absolved from guilt a teacher who chastised a pupil who died as a result (*m. Mak.* 2:2).

F. THE CHRISTIAN WORLD

The *Apostolic Fathers*, the earliest and most important Christian texts after the NT, assert the following precepts: fathers *and* mothers were to instruct sons *and* daughters in one subject, "the fear of God," using physical discipline if necessary. Clement exhorts: "Let us instruct the young with instruction [*paideusōmen tēn paideian*] that leads to the fear of God" (*1 Clem.* 21.5). Similarly, Polycarp writes: "Then instruct your wives . . . to teach their children with instruction [*paideian*] that leads to the fear of God" (*Phil.* 4.2). The *Didache* exhorts, "You shall not withhold your hand from your son or your daughter, but from their youth you shall teach [*didaxeis*] them, the fear of God" (4.9). Nearly identical words are also found in *Barnabas* (19.5).

By the second century educated Christian converts who were fully conversant with Greco-Roman mythology and philosophy were offering rational defenses of Christianity, distinguishing it from Judaism and denouncing paganism. The earliest and one of the most important of these Apologists was Justin Martyr (ca. 100–165). His *First Apology* was addressed to the emperor Antonius Pius (138–161) and his adopted sons, Marcus Aurelius and Lucius Verus. In Justin's writings are found numerous citations of Euripides, Xenophon, and, above all, Plato's *Apology*, *Republic*, and *Timaeus*. Justin's *Second Apology* is a passionate protest against the execution of a Christian teacher, Ptolemy, who had been denounced to the prefect of Rome by the pagan husband of a Christian woman. Justin was executed for his faith. His disciple Tatian, in his *Oration to the Greeks*, written in 167, used Greek rhetoric to denounce Greek myths.

The first great Latin Apologist, Tertullian of Carthage (ca. 160–225), was thoroughly trained in rhetoric, and refers to Demosthenes and Cicero with respect (*Apol.* 11.15–16). Tertullian makes a distinction between Christian children studying in pagan schools and Christians teaching in them:

> If a believer teach literature, while he is teaching doubtless he commends, while he delivers he affirms, while he recalls he bears testimony to, the praises of idols interspersed therein. . . . But when a believer learns these things, if he is already capable of understanding what idolatry is, he neither receives nor allows them. . . . To him necessity is attributed as an excuse, because he has no other way to learn. (*Idol.* 10.5–7)

Tertullian vehemently opposed almost all aspects of pagan beliefs and practices. In his most famous statement he declared:

> What indeed has Athens to do with Jerusalem? What concord is there between the Academy and the Church? What between heretics and Christians? Our instruction comes from "the porch of Solomon." . . . Away with all attempts to produce a mottled Christianity of Stoic, Platonic, and dialectic composition! (*Praescr.* 7)

Despite his protestations, Tertullian's theology was unconsciously influenced by Stoicism.

In contrast with Tertullian and Tatian, but following the lead of Justin in accepting the view that Greek philosophers such as Plato had expressed truths before the time of Christ, were the great Christian thinkers of Alexandria. In his church history, Eusebius reports that ca. AD 180 "Pantænus, a man highly distinguished for his learning, had charge of the school of the faithful in Alexandria. A school of sacred learning, which continues to our days, was established there in ancient times" (*Hist. eccl.* 5.10.1). This was known as a catechetical school (from Grk. *katēchēsis*, "oral instruction").

Pantænus's student Clement of Alexandria was born in Athens and studied in Greece, Syria, and Palestine before settling in Egypt. In his work the *Protrepticus* (*Exhortation to the Greeks*), Clement quotes Homer thirty-nine times and Euripides nine times. Heavily influenced by Plato and the Stoics, Clement wrote an important treatise on Christian ethics, called the *Paedagogus* (*The Instructor*). Christ, Clement taught, is the only true teacher: "The Instructor being practical, not theoretical, His aim is thus to improve the soul, not to teach, and to train it up to a virtuous, not to an intellectual life" (*Paed.* 1.1).

Clement's successor, Origen (ca. 185–254), became the greatest Christian scholar of antiquity. As a young boy he wished to follow his father as a martyr, but providentially for posterity, his mother hid his clothes. Origen studied under the pagan Ammonius Saccus, who also taught the founder of Neo-Platonism, Plotinus. When Origen was but seventeen, Demetrius, the bishop of Alexandria, appointed Origen to head the catechetical school, which met in Origen's home. As Origen attracted large numbers of students, he had to move to other homes. Females were attracted to his teaching, and to prevent succumbing to temptation, Origen, in an excess of zeal, secretly castrated himself.

Origen taught secular subjects such as geometry, arithmetic, music, grammar, rhetoric, and philosophy because he believed that his students should have a general education before learning the profundities of Christian doctrine. After about fifteen years, he obtained an assistant, Heraclas, who taught the beginners, while Origen lectured to the advanced students. As Origen's fame spread, he was invited to Athens and to Jerusalem, where he was ordained a priest, much to the chagrin of his bishop in Alexandria. Origen finished his career in Caesarea in Palestine (230–254). He laboriously compiled the *Hexapla*, which set the Hebrew Scriptures next to several Greek translations. Origen's literary production, which was funded by a wealthy patron, Ambrose, was prodigious: "He dictated to more than seven amanuenses, who relieved each other at appointed times. And he emloyed no fewer copyists, besides girls who were skilled in elegant writing" (Eus. *Hist. eccl.* 6.23).

Gregory "Thaumaturgus" (The Wonder-Worker), who originally planned to study at the famed law school in Berytus (Beirut), came under the spell of Origen and studied under him for eight years, starting at the age of fourteen. Gregory recalled his master's approach as follows:

> For he deemed it right for us to study philosophy in such wise, that we should read with utmost diligence all that has been written, both by the philosophers and by the poets of old, rejecting nothing, and repudiating nothing (for, indeed, we did not yet possess the power of critical discernment), except only the productions of the atheists. . . . Therefore to us there was no forbidden subject of speech; for there was no matter of knowledge hidden or inaccessible to us, but we had it in our power to learn every kind of discourse, both foreign and Greek, both spiritual and political, both divine and human; and we were permitted with all freedom to go round the whole circle of knowledge, and investigate it, and satisfy ourselves with all kinds of doctrines, and enjoy the sweets of intellect.
>
> (Gregory Thaumaturgus, *Panegyric Addressed to Origen*, 13, 15)

Lactantius (ca. 250–320), who was from North Africa, was appointed by Diocletian, the last pagan Roman emperor, to teach Latin rhetoric at his capital city of Nicomedia in northwest Asia Minor (Turkey), but he lost his position when he converted to Christianity. After Constantine converted to Christianity, he appointed Lactantius to serve as the tutor to his son Crispus. Lactantius wrote *The Divine Institutes* in superb Latin, and was admired as the Christian "Cicero." To educated pagans who despised Christianity because it was not a formal philosophic system, Lactantius countered that Christian education was superior to pagan education since it was accessible to all, not just to an elite minority.

In speeches addressed to the Christian emperors Constantius (r. 337–361) and Thedosius (r. 379–395), the pagan rhetorician Themistius (317–390) contended that pagan traditions could offer spiritual satisfaction and ethical teachings that were important to rulers. Theodosius, who is noted for ending the Olympic Games in 393, appointed Themistius to serve as the tutor to his son Arcadius.

The emperor Julian "the Apostate" (r. 361–363), who was raised as a Christian but who reverted to paganism and became a follower of Neo-Pythagorean mysticism, passed a law in 362 that barred Christians from teaching positions, declaring:

> I hold that a proper education results, not in laboriously acquired symmetry of phrases and language, but in a healthy condition of mind, I mean a mind that has understanding and true opinions about things good and evil, honourable and base. Therefore, when a man thinks one thing and teaches his pupils another, in my opinion he fails to educate exactly in proportion as he fails to be an honest man. (*Rescript on Christian Teachers* 422B)

He was indignant that Christians were teaching the classical authors:

> What! Was it not the gods who revealed all their learning to Homer, Hesiod, Demosthenes, Herodotus, Thucydides, Isocrates and Lysias? Did not these men think that they were consecrated, some to Hermes, others to the Muses? I think it is absurd that men who expound the works of these writers should dishonour the gods whom they used to honour. (ibid., 423A)

He advised Christians:

> If, however, they think that those writers were in error with respect to the most honoured gods, then let them betake themselves to the churches of the Galilaeans to expound Matthew and Luke, since you Galilaeans are obeying them when you ordain that men shall refrain from temple-worship.
>   (ibid., 423D)

On the other hand, Julian did not prevent Christian children from attending pagan schools:

> Any youth who wishes to attend the schools is not excluded: nor indeed would it be reasonable to shut out from the best way boys who are still too ignorant

to know which way to turn, and to overawe them into being led against their will to the beliefs of their ancestors. Though indeed it might be proper to cure these, even against their will, as one cures the insane, except that we concede indulgence to all for this sort of disease. For we ought, I think, to teach, but not punish, the demented. (ibid., 424A)

In reaction to this ban, two well-trained Christian educators, a father and son known as the Apollinarii, composed substitute texts. According to Socrates Scholasticus (ca. 379–ca. 450),

The imperial law which forbade Christians to study Greek literature, rendered the two Apollinares of whom we have above spoken, much more distinguished than before. For both being skilled in polite learning, the father as a grammarian, and the son as a rhetorician, they made themselves serviceable to the Christians at this crisis. For the former, as a grammarian, composed a grammar consistent with the Christian faith: he also translated the Books of Moses into heroic verse; and paraphrased all the historical books of the Old Testament, putting them partly into dactylic measure, and partly reducing them to the form of dramatic tragedy. He purposely employed all kinds of verse, that no form of expression peculiar to the Greek language might be unknown or unheard of among Christians. (*Eccl. Hist.* 3.16)

After the death of Julian, these substitute texts were no longer needed.

Gregory of Nazianzus (ca. 330–390) was from Cappadocia in eastern Turkey. He studied in Caesarea in Palestine, in Alexandria, and then, for nine years, in Athens, where he was joined by his friend Basil. Another of his fellow students in Athens was the future emperor Julian, whose apostasy Gregory denounced in his orations. Because of his oratorical gifts, Gregory was called to become the preacher of the Church of the Anastasis in Constantinople, where he played a key role at the Council of Constantinople (AD 381) in affirming the deity of the Holy Spirit. But he despised the politics of his position and resigned to return to Nazianzus. In his panegyric for his friend Basil, who died in 379, Gregory argued that pagans have no exclusive right to the language and literature of Greece. Gregory also declared: "We must not then dishonour education, because some men are pleased to do so, but rather suppose such men to be boorish and uneducated, desiring all men to be as they themselves are, in order to hide themselves in the general, and escape the detection of their want of culture" (*Or. Bas.* 43.11). Gregory has been considered the most important figure in the synthesis of Christianity and classical rhetoric.

Basil (330–379) became apologetic about the time he had spent in Athens in rhetorical studies: "Much time had I spent in vanity, and had wasted nearly all my youth in the vain labour which I underwent in acquiring the wisdom made foolish by God" (*Ep.* 223.2). He composed a treatise for his nephews called *To Young Men, On How They Might Derive Profit from Pagan Literature*. He condemned pagan values such as ancestral renown, bodily strength, physical beauty, and honors. But he praised Greek philosophy, and advised that Christian students can be like the bees, who gather what is useful from flowers.

Libanius (314–ca. 404) was the greatest pagan teacher of rhetoric of his day. He wrote encomiums to Constantine's sons Constantius and Constans. Although Libanius admired Julian and decried the destruction of pagan temples by monks, he avoided attacking Christianity. He taught at Constantinople, and, starting in 354, at Antioch. His most famous student was the renowned Christian preacher John "Chrysostom" (The Golden Mouth). According to Sozomen (ca. 375–ca. 447), "When this sophist [Libanius] was on his death-bed he was asked by his friends who should take his place. 'It would have been John,' replied he, 'had not the Christians taken him from us'" (*Eccl. Hist.* 8.2).

John Chrysostom (347–407) received a secular education and then lived for a time as a hermit in the desert, where he memorized the Bible. But his extreme asceticism ruined his health and forced him to return to Antioch. There he was ordained as a priest. His great eloquence as a preacher in Antioch between 386 and 397 attracted so much attention that in 397 the emperor Arcadius forced him to become the bishop of Constantinople. Subsequently John's rebuke of the wealthy, including the empress Eudoxia, led to his exile.

John scolded his congregation when they applauded his sermons, but even his rebukes brought forth applause. Hundreds of his sermons have been preserved and are still well worth reading. In his important address on "Vainglory and the Right Way for Parents to Bring up Their Children," John counsels:

> Have not recourse to blows constantly and accustom him not to be trained by the rod; for if he feel it constantly as he is being trained, he will learn to despise it. And when he has learnt to despise it, he has reduced thy system to nought. Let him rather at all times fear blows but not receive them.
> (*Inan. glor.* 30; Laistner, 99–100)

Jerome (347–420) had a superb Latin education and studied under leading Greek theologians such as Gregory of Nazianzus. Jerome aspired to live as a hermit in Syria, while still harboring his love for the classics. One night he had a terrifying dream in which he appeared before the Supreme Judge. When asked what he was, Jerome answered that he was a Christian. The Judge answered, "Thou liest, you are a follower of Cicero and not of Christ." At that moment, Jerome vowed, "Lord, if I ever have secular books, if I ever read them, I have denied thee" (*Ep.* 22.30). As Je-rome was the only Christian scholar since Origen to have mastered He-brew, Pope Damasus commissioned him to produce a new translation of the Bible into Latin from the Hebrew OT and the Greek NT; the resulting translation became known as the Vulgate. Jerome, who was disappointed that he was not named Damasus's successor, left Rome for Bethlehem with his friend Paula. They established two monasteries there, one for men and the other for women. In a letter written in 403 to Laeta, the mother of Paula's granddaughter (also called Paula), Jerome gives extensive advice as to the young girl's education:

> Get for her a set of letters made of boxwood or of ivory and called each by its proper name. Let her play with these, so that even her play may teach her something. . . . Offer prizes for good spelling and draw her onwards with little gifts such as children of her age delight in. . . . And let it be her task daily to bring to you the flowers which she has culled from scripture. Let her learn by heart so many verses in the Greek, but let her be instructed in the Latin also.
> (*Ep.* 107)

Augustine of Hippo (354–430) was born in the rural North African town of Thagaste (now in Algeria), where he had his elementary education. He recalls in his *Confessions*: "But why, then, did I dislike Greek learning which was full of like tales? . . . For not a single word of it did I understand, and to make me do so, they vehemently urged me with cruel threatenings and punishments" (1.14). But Latin he learned to love. He studied rheto-ric at Madaura, and later at Carthage. He was then appointed to the chair of rhetoric in Milan, where through the preaching of bishop Ambrose he experienced a dramatic conversion in 386. Augustine became a priest and returned to Africa, where in 395 he became the bishop of Hippo (now in Algeria). In his *De doctrina christiana* (*On Christian Teaching*), completed near the end of his life, Augustine discusses how learning such subjects as history, natural science, mathematics, logic, and philosophy can help one understand the Bible. He writes: "If those who are called philosophers, and especially the Platonists, have said anything that is true and in harmony with our faith, we are not only not to shrink from it, but to claim it for our own use from those who have unlawful possession of it" (*Doctr. chr.* 2.40).

Christian women, like their pagan counterparts, generally did not ad-vance beyond elementary education, since most prepared for marriage at the age of twelve or a little later. But with the growth of the monastic movement, some, like little Paula, whose mother was counseled by Je-rome, rejected marriage and prepared for a life of prayer and devotion. Among the *Sayings of the Desert Fathers* (*Apophthegmata Patrum*) from the fourth to fifth centuries are the sayings of three women: Theodora, Sarah, and Syncletica.

The most famous pagan female teacher of antiquity was Hypatia of Alexandria, a Neo-Platonist who taught astronomy and mathematics. She was the daughter of a famous philosopher, Theon. Though, unlike the Neo-Platonist Porphyry, Hypatia did not attack Christianity, Bishop Cyril instigated monks to attack and kill her in 415. One of her devoted students, Synesius, became the bishop of Ptolemais in Cyrenaica (Libya).

After the fourth century, civil authorities' regulation of education was expanded. According to the Theodosian Code, students who came from abroad to Rome in the late fourth century had to bring documents from their provincial judges and register with the tax assessor. "Nor," the Code went on,

> shall the students attend shows too frequently nor commonly take part in unseasonable carousals. We furthermore grant to you as prefect the authority that, if any student in the City should fail to conduct himself as the dignity of a liberal education demands, he shall be publicly flogged, immediately put on board a boat, expelled from the City and returned home.
> (*Cod. Theod.* 14.9.1; Pharr, 414)

In 425 the emperor Theodosius II established the so-called University of Constantinople, with thirty-two chairs for grammarians, orators, philosophers, and teachers of law. Each of these teachers was assigned his own lecture hall. The emperor forbade professors who did not hold an official appointment from teaching.

The "University of Athens" is a modern designation for the group of sophists who taught in this city from the fourth to the sixth century. In addition to the three official professors who were subsidized, there were as many as ten other teachers of philosophy. There was a great rivalry between those teachers; students were sworn to be loyal to their master, and some students were kidnapped by a rival teacher. In 529 Justinian closed this institution.

BIBLIOGRAPHY: F. A. G. Beck, *Bibliography of Greek Education and Related Topics* (1986); F. A. G. Beck, *Greek Education 450–350 B.C.* (1964); A. Booth, "Elementary and Secondary Schooling in the Roman Empire," *Florilegium* 1 (1979), 1–14; A. Booth, "Punishment, Discipline and Riot in the Schools of Antiquity," *Echos du Monde Classique* 17 (1973), 107–14; B. Burrell, "Reading, Hearing, and Looking at Ephesus," in *Ancient Literacies: The Culture of Reading in Greece and Rome*, ed. W. A. Johnson and N. H. Parker (2009); R. Byrne, "The Refuge of Scribalism in Iron I Palestine," *BASOR* 345 (2007), 1–31; R. A. Caminos, trans., *Late Egyptian Mis-*

cellanies (1954); M. Civil, "Education (Mesopotamia)," *ABD* 2.301–5; R. R. Clark, Jr., "Schools, Scholars, and Students: The Wisdom School, *Sitz im Leben* and Proverbs," *ResQ* 47 (2005), 161–77; J. L. Crenshaw, *Education in Ancient Israel: Across the Deadening Silence* (1998); R. Cribiore, *Gymnastics of the Mind: Greek Education in Hellenistic and Roman Egypt* (2001); R. Cribiore, *The School of Libanius in Late Antique Antioch* (2007); A. C. Dionisotti, "From Ausonius' Schooldays? A Schoolbook and Its Relatives," *JRS* 72 (1982), 83–125; R. Doran, "Jewish Education in the Seleucid Period," in *Second Temple Studies III: Studies in Politics, Class and Material Culture*, ed. P. R. Davies and J. M. Halligan (2002), 116–32; J. Ducat, *Spartan Education* (2006); J. T. Fitzgerald, "Proverbs 3:11–12, Hebrews 12:5–6, and the Tradition of Corporal Punishment," in *Scripture and Traditions*, ed. P. Gray and G. R. O'Day (2008), 291–317; J. L. Foster, "Some Comments on Khety's Instruction for Little Pepi on His Way to School (Satire on the Trades)," in *Gold of Praise: Studies on Ancient Egypt in Honor of Edward F. Wente*, ed. E. Teeter and J. A. Larson (1999), 121–29; E. Frood, *Biographical Texts from Ramessid Egypt* (2007); I. Gildenhard, *Paideia Romana: Cicero's Tusculan Disputations* (2007); R. C. Gregg, *Consolation Philosophy: Greek and Christian Paideia in Basil and the Two Gregories* (1975); J. R. Harrison, "Paul and the Gymnasiarchs," in *Paul: Jew, Greek, and Roman*, ed. S. E. Porter (2008), 141–78; E. A. Hemelrijk, *Matrona Docta: Educated Women in the Roman Elite from Cornelia to Julia Domna* (1999); R. W. Hibler, *Life and Learning in Ancient Athens* (1988); R. F. Hock, "Homer in Greco-Roman Education," in *Mimesis and Intertextuality in Antiquity and Christianity*, ed. D. R. MacDonald (2001), 56–77; R. Humphreys, trans., *The Satires of Juvenal* (1958); K. Jansen-Winkeln, "The Career of the Egyptian High Priest Bakenkhons," *JNES* 52 (1993), 221–25; M. Joyal, I. McDougall, and J. C. Yardley, ed., *Greek and Roman Education: A Sourcebook* (2009); G. A. Kennedy, *Greek Rhetoric under Christian Emperors* (1983); C. King, trans., *Musonius Rufus* (2011); A. D. Knox, trans., *Herodas: The Mimes and Fragments* (1922); C. Laes, "School-Teachers in the Roman Empire," *Acta Classica* 50 (2007), 109–27; M. L. W. Laistner, *Christianity & Pagan Culture in the Later Roman Empire together with an English Translation of John Chrysostom's* "Address on Vainglory and the Right Way for Parents to Bring Up Their Children" (1951); M. L. W. Laistner, "Pagan Schools and Christian Teachers," in *Liber Floridus: Mittellateinische Studien*, ed. B. Bischoff and S. Brechter (1950), 47–61; N. Lazaridis, "Education and Apprenticeship," *UCLA Encyclopedia of Egyptology* (2010); J. P. Lynch, *Aristotle's School* (1972); H. I. Marrou, *A History of Education in Antiquity*, trans. G. Lamb (1982); C. J. Lucas, "The Scribal Tablet-House in Ancient Mesopotamia," *History of Education Quarterly* 19 (1979), 305–32; A. Mendelson, *Secular Education in Philo of Alexandria* (1982); C. Osiek, "The Education of Girls in Early Christian

Ascetic Traditions," *Studies in Religion* 41 (2012), 401–7; O. Padilla, "Hellenistic παιδεία and Luke's Education: A Critique of Recent Approaches," *NTS* 55 (2009), 416–37; C. Pharr, trans., *The Theodosian Code and Novels and the Sirmondian Constitutions* (1952); J. J. Pilch, " 'Beat His Ribs While He is Young' (Sir 30:12)," *BTB* 23 (1993), 101–13; A. Pitts, "Hellenistic Schools in Jerusalem and Paul's Rhetorical Education," in *Paul's World*, ed. S. E. Porter (2008), 19–50; K. Robb, *Literacy and Paideia in Ancient Greece* (1994); C. A. Rollston, "Scribal Education in Ancient Israel: The Old Hebrew Epigraphic Evidence," *BASOR* 344 (2006), 47–74; R. S. Schellenberg, *Rethinking Paul's Rhetorical Education: Comparative Rhetoric and 2 Corinthians 10–13* (2013); Å. Sjöberg, "The Old Babylonian Eduba," in *Sumerological Studies in Honor of Thorkild Jacobsen on His Seventieth Birthday*, ed. S. Lieberman (1975), 159–79; S. Tinney, "Texts, Tablets, and Teaching: Scribal Education in Nippur and Ur," *Exped* 40.2 (1998), 40–50; Y. L. Too, ed., *Education in Greek and Roman Antiquity* (2001); H. L. J. Vanstiphout, "On the Old Babylonian Eduba Curriculum," in *Centres of Learning*, ed. J. W. Drijvers and A. A. MacDonald (1995), 3–16; N. Veldhuis, "On the Curriculum of the Neo-Babylonian School," *JAOS* 123.3 (2003), 627–33; C. Wassen, "On the Education of Children in the Dead Sea Scrolls," *SR* 41 (2012), 350–63; A. Watson, trans. and ed., *The Digest of Justinian* (4 vols., 1985); D. F. Watson, "Education: Jewish and Greco-Roman," in *Dictionary of New Testament Background*, ed. C. A. Evans and S. E. Porter (2000), 308–13; D. F. Watson, "The New Testament and Greco-Roman Rhetoric: A Bibliography," *JETS* 31 (1988), 465–72; F. Will, *Herondas* (1973); R. J. Williams, "Scribal Training in Ancient Egypt," *JAOS* 92 (1972), 214–21; M. R. Wilson, "The Jewish Concept of Learning," *CSR* 5 (1976), 350–63; C. E. Woods, "Bilingualism, Scribal Learning, and the Death of Sumerian," in *Margins of Writing, Origins of Cultures*, ed. S. L. Sanders (2006), 91–120; N. H. Young, "The Figure of the *Paidagōgos* in Art and Literature," *BA* 53.2 (1990), 80–86.

MRW and EMY

See also ATHLETICS, CHILDBIRTH & CHILDREN, LITERACY, and WRITING & WRITING MATERIALS.

EUNUCHS

A eunuch is a male who has been emasculated either by having his testicles damaged or removed (castration) and/or by having his penis removed. Eunuchs were highly prized by rulers as harem or court personnel, though they were despised by the public. In a few religious movements priests were required to be eunuchs.

A. THE OLD TESTAMENT

The Hebrew word *sārîs*, which occurs forty-five times in the OT and which was almost always translated *eunouchos* in the LXX (hence the typical English translation "eunuch"), is derived from the Akkadian term *ša rēši*, literally, "he who is at the head," that is, a courtier. During the Neo-Assyrian, Neo-Babylonian, and Persian periods, individuals referred to by this title were often but not always eunuchs. When the term *sārîs* is used of Potiphar (Gen 37:36; 39:1) and Joseph's fellow prisoners (Gen 40:2), it is unlikely that the term means "eunuch," since Potiphar was married and there is no credible extrabiblical evidence for eunuchs in pharaonic Egypt.

Samuel warned that a king would take tithes of the people's produce and give these to his servants and eunuchs (1 Sam 8:15). Jehu enlisted the help of two or three eunuchs to throw Jezebel out of a window (2 Kgs 9:31–33). The Lord proclaimed that Hezekiah's sons would serve as eunuchs at the palace in Babylon (2 Kgs 20:18||Isa 39:7). One of the chief military officers at Sennacherib's siege of Jerusalem in 701 BC, Rab-saris, was a chief eunuch; Rab-saris was not his proper name but his title. Eunuchs are found in the lists of captives, after categories such as men, women, and children (2 Kgs 24:15; Jer 41:46).

One of the three Neo-Babylonian officers who controlled Jerusalem after Nebuchadnezzar's conquest of the city, Nebo-Sarsekim, was a chief eunuch (Jer 39:3, 13). His name and title in Akkadian, *Nabū-šarrussu-ukin* ("May [the god] Nabu establish his king") *rēš šarri*, have been found in a cuneiform tablet from the reign of Nebuchadnezzar dated to 595 BC and a tablet of his successor, Evil-Merodach (Akk. Amel-Marduk), dated to 561 BC. A Cushite eunuch named Ebed-melek came to Jeremiah's rescue when the latter was placed in a pit (Jer 38:7).

A chief of the eunuchs (Heb. *śar haśśārîsîm*) figures prominently in the story of Daniel and his three friends (Dan 1:3, 7–11, 18) and eunuchs are mentioned repeatedly in the book of Esther (Esth 1:10, 12, 15; 2:3, 14, 21; 4:4–5; 6:14; 7:8). Some scholars believe that Nehemiah, the cupbearer of the Persian king Artaxerxes I, was a eunuch, since some Assyrian cupbearers were eunuchs and since eunuchs were very prominent at Persian courts. In place of *oinochoos*, "cupbearer," the reading of the LXX Codex Alexandrinus at Neh 1:11, both the Codex Vaticanus and the Codex Sinaiticus have *eunouchos*, "eunuch." Because of the Jewish aversion to eunuchs (see Deut 23:1, quoted below), it is most unlikely that Nehemiah was a eunuch.

In ancient Israel, castrated animals, or animals whose testicles were otherwise damaged, were considered unfit as offerings (Lev 22:24), and eunuchs were banned from the public worship of the Lord: "No one who has been emasculated by crushing or cutting may enter the assembly of the LORD" (Deut 23:1). But there was a promise for eunuchs in the messianic age:

> And let no eunuch complain, "I am only a dry tree." For this is what the LORD says: "To the eunuchs who keep my Sabbaths, who choose what pleases me and hold fast to my covenant—to them I will give within my temple and its walls a memorial and a name better than sons and daughters; I will give them an everlasting name that will endure forever." (Isa 56:3–5)

B. THE NEW TESTAMENT

In a discussion of marriage and divorce, Jesus (Matt 19:12) refers to three types of "eunuchs": (1) those who are eunuchs from birth, (2) those "who have been made eunuchs by others," and (3) those who have made themselves eunuchs "for the sake of the kingdom of Heaven," perhaps an allusion to himself and John the Baptist, who may have been derided as "eunuchs" for remaining unmarried. Some have speculated that Jesus may also have been referring to celibate Essenes.

The "Ethiopian eunuch" who was converted by Philip while reading the book of Isaiah in the Septuagint was the treasurer of Candace, the queen of the kingdom of Meroe south of Egypt (Acts 8:27–40).

In exasperation against the "Judaizers" who insisted that Gentile converts be circumcised, Paul exclaims: "As for those agitators, I wish they would go the whole way and emasculate themselves!" (Gal 5:12). In decrying continued emphasis on circumcision, Paul describes the act as "mutilation" (Phil 3:2).

C. THE NEAR EASTERN WORLD

As noted above, the Hebrew word for "eunuch" is derived from Akkadian *ša rēši*, which is written in Sumerian logograms as LÚ.GAL.SAG. Eunuchs seem to be associated with the cult of Ishtar. In the Sumerian *Descent of Inanna*, which was later developed as the Akkadian *Descent of Ishtar*, the goddess descends to the underworld, where she is killed by her sister. In the Sumerian version, Enki creates two asexual beings, the *kurgarru* and the *kalaturru*, whom he sends to revive Inanna; in the Akkadian version, Ea creates a eunuch, *Asushunamir*, to revive Ishtar. It is debated whether lower temple personnel associated with Ishtar such as the *assinnu*, *kurgarru*, and *kulu'u* were eunuchs. One text may indicate that such personnel wore female dress when it refers to "*kurgarrû*'s; *assin*[*nu*'s], who for making the people reverent, Ištar turned their masculinity to fem[ininity]" (*The Poem of Erra* IV.55; Peled, 288).

The Middle Assyrian Laws punished adultery and sodomy with castration. Law 15 decrees that if the husband of an adulterous wife chooses not to put his wife to death but prefers to cut off her nose, he can spare the adulterer death and castrate him instead. Law 20 punishes a homosexual relationship with castration.

Eunuchs who were intended for service at the court were generally made eunuchs by having their testicles crushed before puberty. These boys were dedicated to the king and were separated from their families. They were richly rewarded with land and other rewards.

Eunuchs are first attested in the Middle Assyrian period serving under Tukulti-Ninurta I (13th c. BC). They were influential at the Assyrian court of Adad-nerari III (9th c. BC). Eunuchs at the Assyrian court functioned as governors, army commanders, heralds, personal attendants, cooks, bakers, cupbearers, drivers, guards, doorkeepers, and scribes. In processions, the last person before the king was a eunuch. Among the seals of Neo-Assyrian officials, those of eunuchs are quite numerous. Since one of the results of castration is that eunuchs cannot grow beards, beardless officials in Assyrian reliefs have been identified as eunuchs, and the totality of officials could be expressed as *ša rēši* and *ša ziqni*, "(from) the eunuch" to "the bearded one." There is less lexical and iconographic evidence for eunuchs during the Neo-Babylonian era than for earlier periods.

Eunuchs were especially prominent at the court of the Achaemenid kings in Persia. Herodotus reports that Babylon and the rest of Assyria gave Darius five hundred boys to serve as eunuchs (*Hist.* 3.92). Xenophon explains why Cyrus chose eunuchs to serve him:

> But as he observed that eunuchs were not susceptible to any such affections, he thought that they would esteem most highly those who were in the best position to make them rich and to stand by them, if ever they were wronged. . . . Besides, inasmuch as eunuchs are objects of contempt to the rest of mankind, for this reason, if for no other, they need a master who will be their patron. (*Cyr.* 7.5.60–61)

Artoxares, the favorite court eunuch of Artaxerxes I (464–424 BC) and of Darius II (424–404 BC), had an artificial beard made for himself and unsuccessfully plotted to become king. The eunuch Bagoas became the commander of the Persian army under Artaxerxes III (358–338 BC). He killed the king and installed Darius III, the last Achaemenid king, only to be poisoned himself, because he had tried to poison Darius III.

D. THE GRECO-ROMAN WORLD

The Greek word *eunouchos* is derived from the words *eunē*, "bed," and *echō*, "hold"; that is, a eunuch was originally "a guardian of the bed." Because such servants in harems were castrated slaves, the term came to be used to refer to any castrated or otherwise emasculated man. Greek synonyms for *eunouchos* are *apokopos*, *ektomias*, and *spadōn*.

Herodotus narrates that Panonius of Chios would procure beautiful boys, castrate them, and then sell them at Sardis and Ephesus (*Hist.* 8.105). Hermotimus, one who had been castrated by Panonius, carried out a terrible vengeance when he later had Panonius castrate his own sons and had them castrate their father.

In the Hellenistic age, after Alexander's conquests, eunuchs played prominent roles in the successor kingdoms. Seleucus I ordered a statue of his faithful eunuch Combabos to be set up in the temple of the goddess Atargatis. Eunuchs were prominent in Ptolemaic Egypt, and some were governors, military commanders, tutors, guardians, and advisors.

Toward the end of the Second Punic War against Hannibal, the Romans in desperation invited Cybele, the Magna Mater, from Asia Minor to Rome. She was served by *galli*, eunuch priests who had emasculated themselves in imitation of Attis, Cybele's lover, who was driven by the jealous goddess to castrate himself. Other eunuch priests are attested in the worship of the Dea Syria, Hecate, Aphrodite of Aphaca in Syria, and the Scythian mother goddess.

Despite literary references (Strabo and Quintilian) that the high priests of the temple of Artemis at Ephesus were eunuch priests called Megabyzoi, the lack of this title among the four thousand inscriptions recovered from Ephesus casts doubt on their existence. Writers such as Plautus, Juvenal, Lucian, and Apuleius made fun of eunuchs.

The first attested eunuch in the Roman court was Lydus, a slave of Drusus, the son of Tiberius. Eunuchs played prominent roles in the household of Claudius. Nero's eunuch Anicetus became the commander of the Roman fleet and was employed by the emperor to kill his mother. Another eunuch, Sporus, was the emperor's lover.

According to Ammianus Marcellinus, Domitian "won distinction by a most highly approved law, by which he had under heavy penalties forbidden anyone within the bounds of the Roman jurisdiction to geld a boy; for it this had not happened, who could endure the swarms of those whose small number is with difficulty tolerated?" (*Res. G.* 18.4.5).

Hadrian made both performing castration and being castrated capital offenses. At the same time, Hadrian appointed his favorite eunuch, Favorinus, to a prominent position in the priesthood. Cassius Dio, speaking of the emperor Septimius Severus (AD 193 to 211), wrote: "Nor was it boys or youths alone that he castrated, but grown men as well, some of whom had wives. His purpose was that Plautilla, his daughter, ... should have only eunuchs as her attendants in general, and especially as her teachers in music and other branches of art" (*Hist. rom.* 76.14.4–5). Sempronius Rufus, who was a eunuch, was a high-ranking official under Septimius Severus's son Caracalla. Over a hundred court eunuchs have been catalogued from the four centuries of the Roman Empire.

Roman law classified eunuchs as follows: *spadones*, those who are infertile from birth; *thlibiae*, those whose gonads have been "pressed"; *thladiae*, those whose gonads have been "crushed"; and *castrati*, those whose penises have been detached. Juvenal and Martial report that wealthy women had as their paramours eunuchs who still had penises so they could enjoy sex without bearing children.

E. THE JEWISH WORLD

According to Sirach: "So is he who is afflicted by the LORD; he sees with his eyes and groans, like a eunuch who embraces a maiden and groans" (Sir 30:19–20). The Wisdom of Solomon promises, "Blessed also is the eunuch whose hands have done no lawless deed, and who has not devised wicked things against the LORD; for special favor will be shown him for his faithfulness, and a place of great delight in the temple of the LORD" (Wis 3:14).

Philo interpreted as allegorical the reference to Potiphar, the baker, and the butler in the story of Joseph as "eunuchs," writing that "all these three were shewn to be eunuchs and unable to beget wisdom" (*Ebr.* 220; cf. *Ios.* 153). He likens "the multitude which purchases the statesman" to eunuchs, because, just as a eunuch possesses regenerative organs but cannot use them for this purpose, such a "multitude is unproductive of wisdom, though it seems to practise virtue" (*Ios.* 58–59).

Josephus notes that Herod the Great had three eunuchs who served as chamberlains at his court (*J. W.* 1.488). He also reports of Herod: "The king had some eunuchs of whom he was immoderately fond because of their beauty. One of them was entrusted with the pouring of his wine, the second with serving his dinner, and the third with putting the king to bed and taking care of the most important matters of state" (*Ant.* 16.230). A eunuch named Bagoas was involved in a conspiracy against Herod. The most trusted servant of Herod's wife Mariamne was a eunuch.

The rabbis made a distinction between two classes of eunuchs: (1) *srys ḥmh,* "a eunuch of heat," that is, one who is a eunuch from birth, and (2) *srys ʾdm,* "a eunuch of man," one who has been made a eunuch. The Mishnah records debates concerning whether a eunuch can take part in the *halisah* (i.e., "drawing off of the shoe") ceremony of levirate marriage attested in Ruth 4:7 (*m. Yebam.* 8:4–6). The eunuch from birth was not barred from either the priesthood or marriage. Accordingly, the Mishnah states, "If a priest that was a eunuch by nature married the daughter of an Israelite, he gives her the right to eat of Heave-offering" (*m. Yebam.* 8:6).

F. THE CHRISTIAN WORLD

Montanus, who began an important millenarian movement (known as Montanism) in western Asia Minor in the second century BC, was reputed to have been a castrated priest of Cybele before his conversion to Christianity.

Justin Martyr refers to a young Christian in Alexandria who asked the Roman governor for permission to be castrated in order to refute the charge of sexual immorality against Christians, but who was denied permission (*1 Apol.* 29). Tertullian believed that Paul was a eunuch (*Mon.* 3.1), but denounced those in his own day who made themselves eunuchs as being inspired to do so by a Marcionite loathing of marriage (*Marc.* 4.11).

Clement of Alexandria observed of hairdressers: "Many are eunuchs; and these panders serve without suspicion those that wish to be free to enjoy their pleasures, because of the belief that they are unable to indulge in lust" (*Paed.* 3.4.26). In Alexandria young men who played the passive homosexual role (*kinaidoi*) castrated themselves as a reflection of the fact that their role in sexual activity was akin to the one normally played by women.

Origen of Alexandria's literal interpretation of Matt 19:12 led him to extreme action. According to Eusebius,

> While Origen was conducting catechetical instruction at Alexandria, a deed was done by him which evidenced an immature and youthful mind, but at the same time gave the highest proof of faith and continence. For he took the words, "There are eunuchs who have made themselves eunuchs for the kingdom of heaven's sake," in too literal and extreme a sense. And in order to fulfill the Saviour's word, and at the same time to take away from the unbelievers all opportunity for scandal,—for, although young, he met for the study of divine things with women as well as men,—he carried out in action the word of the Saviour. He thought that this would not be known by many of his acquaintances. But it was impossible for him, though desiring to do so, to keep such an action secret. (*Hist. eccl.* 8.1–2)

Canon 1 of the Council of Nicaea decrees:

> If any one has been obliged to undergo a surgical operation from disease, or has been castrated by barbarians, let him continue in the clergy. But if any one in good health has so mutilated himself, it is right that, if he be enrolled amongst the clergy, he should cease from his ministrations; and that from henceforth no such person should be promoted. As, however, it is plain that this is said with reference to those who dare to mutilate themselves, therefore, if any persons have been so mutilated by barbarians, or by their own masters, and in other respects are found worthy, the canon allows them to be admitted to the clerical office. (Stevenson 1960, 358)

The so-called *Apostolic Constitutions* decreed: "Let an eunuch, if he be such by the injury of men, or his *virilia* were taken away in the persecution, or he was born such, and yet is worthy of episcopacy, be made a bishop." But this text then adds: "Let not him who has disabled himself be made a clergyman; for he is a self-murderer, and an enemy to the creation of God" (8.21–22). In his treatise *On the True Integrity of Virginity*, Basil of Ancyra (ca. AD 336–358) condemns the many self-made eunuchs in churches. In 395 Pope Leo I forbade voluntary emasculation. Chrysostom also preached in Antioch against those who had castrated themselves, as did Cyril of Alexandria.

Valesius (ca. AD 240) founded a sect that required men to be castrated. Epiphanius commented on this Transjordanian sect as follows:

When they take someone as a disciple, as long as he has not yet been castrated he does not partake of animal flesh. But once they have persuaded or forced him to be castrated, then he partakes of everything whatever, as though he had already retired from the contest and were no longer in danger of being roused by the foods to the enjoyment of passion. It is not just their own people that they treat like this, but often they do the same to strangers who pass through and stay with them as guests, as is frequently reported.

(*Pan.* 58.1.5–6; Amidon, 202)

Of the same group, Augustine said, "the Valesians castrate both themselves and their guests, thinking that in this way they ought to serve God" (*Haer.* 37; Müller, 79).

Despite the general Christian aversion to eunuchs, even after the conversion of Constantine in AD 312 such men served at the Byzantine court, playing major roles both in domestic politics and in military conquests. Eunuchs also occupied such posts as "superintendent of the sacred bedchamber" and "chief steward of the sacred palace." Indeed, chief eunuchs at Byzantium, such as Eutropius and Chrysaphius, sometimes exercised more power than the emperor himself.

When boys are castrated before puberty, they retain a uniquely high voice. Eudoxia, the empress of Arcadius (AD 395–408), is the first person known to have employed a eunuch singer. During the millennium that followed, eunuch choirs were common in the Byzantine church.

BIBLIOGRAPHY: D. C. Allison, Jr., "Eunuchs Because of the Kingdom of Heaven (Matt. 19:12)," *TSFB* 8.2 (1984), 2–5; P. R. Amidon, trans., *The Panarion of St. Epiphanius, Bishop of Salamis* (1990); C. Bernabé, "Of Eunuchs and Predators: Matthew 19:1–12 in a Cultural Context," *BTB* 33.4 (2003), 128–34; P. Briant, *From Cyrus to Alexander: A History of the Persian Empire*, trans. P. T. Daniels (2002); D. F. Caner, "The Practice and Prohibition of Self-Castration in Early Christianity," *VC* 51.4 (1997), 396–415; C. Daniel, "Esséniens et Eunuques (Matthieu 19, 10–12)," *RevQ* 6.3 (1968), 353–90; K. Deller, "The Assyrian Eunuchs and Their Predecessors," in *Priests and Officials in the Ancient Near East*, ed. K. Watanabe (1999), 303–11; J. Everhart, "Hidden Eunuchs of the Hebrew Bible," *SBL Seminar Papers* 41 (2002), 137–55; N. S. Fox, *In the Service of the King: Officialdom in Ancient Israel and Judah* (2000); A. K. Grayson, "Eunuchs in Power: Their Role in the Assyrian Bureaucracy," in *Vom Alten Orient zum Alten Testament*, ed. M. Dietrich and O. Loretz (1995), 85–97; C. Grottanelli, "Faithful Bodies: Ancient Greek Sources on Oriental Eunuchs," in *Self, Soul and Body in Religious Experience*, ed. A. I. Baumgarten, J. Assmann, and G. G. Stroumsa (1998), 404–16; P. Guyot, *Eunuchen als Sklaven und Freigelassene in der griechisch-römischen Antike* (1980); M. Heltzer, "On the Akkadian term *rēšu* in Ugarit," *IOS* 4 (1974), 4–11; K. Hopkins, *Conquerors and Slaves* (1978); M. Horstmanshoff, "Who Is the True Eunuch? Medical and Religious Ideas about Eunuchs and Castration in the Works of Clement of Alexandria," in *From Athens to Jerusalem: Medicine in Hellenized Jewish Lore and in Early Christian Literature*, ed. S. Kottek et al. (2000), 101–18; G. H. Johnson, "6247. *sārîs*," *NIDOTTE* 3.288–95; G. E. Kadish, "Eunuchs in Ancient Egypt?" *Studies in Honor of John A. Wilson* (1969), 55–62; L. G. Müller, trans., *The De Haeresibus of Saint Augustine* (1956); A. D. Nock, "Eunuchs in Ancient Religion," in *Essays on Religion and the Ancient World*, ed. Z. Stewart (1972), 7–15; A. L. Oppenheim, "A Note on *ša rēši*," in *JANESCU* 5 (1973), 324–34; I. Peled, "*assinnu* and *kurgarrû* Revisited," *JNES* 73.2 (2014), 283–97; R. Péter-Contesse, "Was Potiphar a Eunuch? (Genesis 37.35; 39.1)," *BT* 47.1 (1996), 142–46; J. E. Reade, "The Neo-Assyrian Court and Army: Evidence from the Sculptures," *Iraq* 34.2 (1972), 87–112; F. P. Retief, J. F. G. Cilliers, and S. P. J. K. Riekert, "Eunuchs in the Bible," *Acta Theologica* 26.2 (2010), 247–58; G. Sanders, "Les galles et le gallat devant l'opinion chrétienne," in *Hommages à Maarten J. Vermaseren*, ed. M. B. de Boer (1978), 3.1062–91; P. O. Scholz, *Eunuchs and Castrati: A Cultural History* (2001); J. O. Smith, "The High Priests of the Temple of Artemis at Ephesus," in *Cybele, Attis and Related Cults*, ed. E. N. Lane (1996), 323–35; J. Stevenson, ed., *A New Eusebius* (1960); W. Stevenson, "The Rise of Eunuchs in Greco-Roman Antiquity," *Journal of the History of Sexuality* 5.4 (1995), 495–511; H. Tadmor, "Was the Biblical *sārîs* a Eunuch?" in *Solving Riddles and Untying Knots*, ed. Z. Zevit, S. Gitin, and M. Sokoloff (1995), 317–25; G. Taylor, *Castration: An Abbreviated History of Western Manhood* (2000); S. Tougher, *The Eunuch in Byzantine History and Society* (2008); E. F. Weidner, "Hof- und Haremserlässe assyrischer Könige aus dem 2. Jahrtausend v. Chr.," *AfO* 17 (1954–1956), 257–93; F. Williams, trans., *The Panarion of Epiphanius of Salamis* (1987); J. L. Wright and M. J. Chan, "King and Eunuch: Isaiah 56:1–8 in Light of Honorific Royal Burial Practices," *JBL* 131.1 (2012), 99–119; E. Yamauchi, "The Descent of Ishtar," in *The Biblical World*, ed. C. Pfeiffer (1966), 196–200; E. Yamauchi, "Was Nehemiah the Cupbearer a Eunuch?" *ZAW* 92.1 (1980), 132–42; E. Yamauchi, "Why the Ethiopian Eunuch Was Not from Ethiopia," in *Interpreting the New Testament Text: An Introduction to the Art and Science of Exegesis*, ed. B. Fanning and D. Bock (2006), 351–65.

EMY

See also BARBERS & BEARDS, CELIBACY, and MARRIAGE.

FISH & FISHING

Along with hunting, fishing has been part of human activity since the beginnings of settled habitation. The Mediterranean and its adjoining seas, the Nile of Egypt, and the inland waters of Palestine provided an abundant variety of fish for consumption. While fishing and hunting were usually inseparable in antiquity, hunting was sometimes glorified and reserved for royalty, whereas fishing was often carried out by the middle and lower classes.

A. THE OLD TESTAMENT

The word "fish" (Heb. *dāgâ*, *dāg*) appears in the Bible for the first time in Gen 1:26, when humankind is given dominion over the fish of the sea. According to Gen 1:21, fish were created during the fifth day of creation and they were part of "the great creatures of the sea and every living thing with which the water teems." No specific variety of fish is mentioned in the Bible, and the words *dāgâ* and *dāg* have a wide semantic range, referring to shellfish, crustaceans, and even sea mammals.

The Israelites ate fish, probably from the Nile (Exod 7:18), while living as slaves in Egypt (Num 11:5). According to the Mosaic law, only fish with fins and scales were allowed for consumption (Lev 11:9–12; Deut 14:9–10). Images or idols, including those of "any fish in the waters below," were forbidden (Deut 4:18); such images would have been an enticement to false worship and even tantamount to returning to the bondage of Egypt, a land that deemed several types of fish sacred to deities. The OT uses several Hebrew words to refer to nets used to catch fish: *mikmōret* (Isa 19:8; Hab 1:15–16, where the term is translated "dragnet" in the NIV), *ḥērem* (Hab 1:15–16; Ezek 32:3), and *rešet* (Ezek 32:3).

Fishermen who fished in the Nile River used hooks (Isa 19:8), as was probably the case in eighth-century BC Israel (Amos 4:2). The God of Israel refers to his ability to destroy the environment in which fish live as an aspect of his power: "By a mere rebuke I dry up the sea, I turn rivers into a desert; their fish rot for lack of water and die of thirst" (Isa 50:2). The book of Ezekiel mentions the existence of fish in Egyptian streams (Ezek 29:4) and also prophesies of a time when the Dead Sea, like the Mediterranean Sea, will be teeming with a great variety of fish (Ezek 47:10).

During the reign of Solomon, a period characterized by international contacts, leisurely pursuits, and a shared wisdom tradition, the king expounded on plants and animals, including "birds, reptiles and fish" (1 Kgs 4:33). The OT historical books state that the city of Jerusalem had a Fish Gate, suggesting either that fish were brought into the city through this gate or that a fish market was located near it (2 Chr 33:14; Neh 3:3; 12:39; 13:16; see also Zeph 1:10). The transportation of fish was only possible after processing by smoking, pickling, or drying and salting.

The books of wisdom literature allude to fishing by means of fishhooks (Job 41:1), harpoons and fishing spears (Job 41:7), and nets (Eccl 9:12). Iron fishhooks from the tenth century BC have been found at Ezion Geber, Solomon's seaport on the Red Sea.

B. THE NEW TESTAMENT

Jesus's first disciples were fishermen from Galilee, whom he cleverly regarded as fishers of men (Matt 4:19). The importance of the Sea of Galilee for fish and the fishing industry is reflected in the place name Bethsaida (Aram. "house of hunting [fishing]," Mark 6:45; Luke 9:10; John 1:44), the home of Peter, Andrew, and Philip. The fishing town of Capernaum (Mark 1:29) became the headquarters for Jesus's extended ministry. Magdala (cf. Matt 15:39, "Magadan"; 27:56), on the western shore of the sea, was widely known by its Greek name, Taricheae, that is, "place where fish are salted" (from Gk. *tarichos*, lit., "preserved fish"). Shortly before Jesus launched his public ministry, the geographer Strabo observed that at Taricheae, "the lake supplies excellent fish for pickling" (*Geogr.* 16.2.45).

First-century fishermen could join together to become *koinōnoi*, "partners" or "associates" (Luke 5:10; cf. John 21:2–3). Thus, they were able to bid for fishing contracts. Similar to tax farming, the owner of a fishing business would doubtless pay taxes to the Roman Empire through a local tax collector. Most fishermen would have been considered part of the middle class; fishermen were ranked with the artisans and craftsmen in that they made nets from flax and had perfected the art of fishing.

The disciples used both hooks (Matt 17:27) and nets (Luke 5:6) to fish on the Sea of Galilee. Nets came in different sizes. A net for casting (Gk. *amphiblēstron*, Matt 4:18) was approximately fifteen to twenty feet across, was circular, and had small weights set around the perimeter. The large, industrial dragnet, or seine (Gk. *sagēnē*, Matt 13:47), could reach six hundred feet in length. Weights made of metal or stone were used as net sinkers. They were typically perforated or grooved and varied in size (stone weights tended to be bigger) and shape (from round to square to pyramidal). Metal weights could also be coiled or folded in various manners. Fishing hooks ranged between 3.1 and 6.1 centimeters in length, and were made of iron or bronze.

Fishermen would sometimes fish from the shore, while at other times they would use fishing boats (John 21:3). These boats had oars and/or sails and would be about twenty-five feet long. When not in use, they could be anchored with irregularly shaped basalt stone anchors or drawn up onto the shore. In 1986, a well-preserved wooden boat from around the NT period was discovered buried in mud and silt near Magdala and the modern Kibbutz Ginnosar.

Fishing nets required maintenance. Fish often got caught by their gills in the netting, sometimes tearing the threads and leaving the net in need of repair. Once fishermen disentangled the fish, the nets were washed (Luke 5:2) and folded. The fish were sorted into baskets, which served as an excellent image for the kingdom of heaven (Matt 13:48).

Fish was an important part of the diet of the common first-century Jew (Matt 14:17; John 21:12–13). There are over twenty-five native species of fish in the Sea of Galilee, including tilapia, bleak, barbell, catfish (while catfish had non-scaly skin, they were likely eaten by Gentiles rather than Jews), and the grey mullet. The edible fish found in the greatest numbers in the Sea of Galilee is the *Tilapia galilaea*, also known as "St. Peter's fish." The largest fish native to the Sea of Galilee is the catfish, which can weigh as much as twenty pounds. Before consumption, fish would be broiled (Luke 24:42–43) or cooked over a charcoal fire (John 21:9). Fishing was often done at night, when the water was cool and when the fish, unable to see the meshes of the nets, would come to the surface (Luke 5:5).

C. THE NEAR EASTERN WORLD

Mesopotamia

Fishing is not limited to people living along the shores of lakes, larger seas, or the oceans, but is encountered wherever there are fish, in moving bodies of water, rivers, brooks, and streams, and in other places, such as marshes and even man-made ponds, to which the fish may be intentionally introduced. Fish was an important part of the diet of the Assyrian people. The Tigris and the Euphrates Rivers, along with their man-made canals, provided around fifty types of freshwater fish. The identification of specific species of fish from reliefs is very difficult, but among those that have been identified are types of barbell, from the cyprinid family to which the carp belongs. Fish ponds are represented in Mesopotamian art. Gudea, a Sumerian governor who lived ca. 2100 BC, is said to have put fish in ponds. A bas-relief from Nineveh from the seventh century BC depicts an Assyrian fishing in a pond, holding a short fishing line; around his shoulder is a basket containing fish (*ANEP*, fig. 114). Sinkers to weight down the line were ceramic or were made of stone or lead. The Assyrians ate both fresh and dried fish. According to Herodotus, several Mesopotamian tribes subsisted on dried fish alone (*Hist.* 1.200).

In Sumer, fishing was often referred to as an occupation. However, fishermen had to pay temple priests or civic rulers for the right to fish. Those living on canals would get the rights to fish there in exchange for their work maintaining the canals.

Egypt

The Nile, its Delta, connecting canals, and lakes provided a rich source of fish. The high average water temperature, combined with intense irrigation practices, provided an environment in which the more than one hundred species of fish found within its waters could flourish. When the Nile's waters receded after the annual fall floods, some fish became trapped in the mud and could be gathered by hand. The Nile perch could grow as large as one hundred pounds. The well-known importance of the Nile as a source of fish, as well as the methods used to fish in it, can be observed in a prophetic oracle of judgment from the book of Isaiah: "The fishermen will groan and lament, all who cast hooks into the Nile; those who throw nets on the water will pine away" (Isa 19:8). Sometimes fishermen used a dragnet stretched between two papyrus boats equipped with oars; at other times a net was manually dragged from the water to the shore. Egyptians also speared fish from above using a small, flat-bottomed boat. Wealthy officials would sometimes fish for amusement, an activity termed *shmḥ-ib*, "distraction of the heart."

Some fish were considered sacred: the eel was dedicated to the gods of Heliopolis, the mormyrus fish was worshipped in Oxyrhynchus, and the perch was dedicated to the early goddess Neith of the western Delta region. The *Satire on the Trades*, an Egyptian papyrus dating to 2000 BC, alludes to the fact that although fishing was common in Egypt, it was dangerous because of the presence of crocodiles. Tomb art from a number of periods in Egyptian history suggests that once caught, fish were scaled and gutted either in the boat or on the shore.

During the Old Kingdom (2545–2120 BC) fish were considered unclean food, and thus were rejected by nobility. A person who ate fish was not permitted to enter a funerary chapel. The ancient Egyptian word for "abomination" was written with a fish sign.

Fish was also used as medicine. The Ebers Medical Papyrus, dating to 1550 BC, shows how nine varieties of fish were used in prescriptions for external applications dealing with different ailments. Gout, for example, was treated with Nile electric catfish and honey. In addition to being eaten and being used as medicine, fish was used as payment or for exchange. In the *Story of Wenamun*, Ramesses XII sends an emissary with thirty baskets of preserved fish to the Prince of Byblos as partial payment for cedar wood needed for ship construction. According to the historian Diodorus Siculus (1st c. BC), a profitable fishery in the Faiyum area provided Pharaoh Moeris (Amenemhat III, 12th Dyn.) with funds to pay for the queen's perfumes, ointments, and personal items of adornment (*Bib. hist.* 1.52).

D. THE GRECO-ROMAN WORLD

Greece

Fish was a staple feature in the diet of ancient Greeks, especially among those living along the coasts. The Greeks ate shellfish, tuna, pike, and carp from early times. Crabs, lobsters, and prawns were common as well. Even the tentacles of the sea anemone were eaten, generally fried. The Greeks viewed octopus as a delicacy, and enjoyed eating anything taken from the sea, from barnacles to whales. Even though the Greeks viewed fishing as a far less noble pursuit than hunting, the fish industry was well organized both economically and technologically. Fishermen's knowledge of fish migration and the breeding habits of fish helped them develop booming fisheries. The government held a state monopoly on the fishing industry, with only a small margin of profit going to the fishermen themselves. Fishing was done with hook and line, as well as with nets. The cast net was funnel-shaped and was fitted with lead weights. The tow net was long, rectangular, and needed to be pulled by several boats. The Greeks also used the harpoon for medium-sized and large fish. The Zodiac sign Pisces, "Fish" (Gk. *ichthys*; Lat. *pisces*), is one of the signs of early Greek mythology and was sometimes depicted by two fish swimming in opposite directions.

Rome

The Mediterranean Sea yielded a variety of fish species, ranging from anchovies and sardines to tuna, swordfish, and sharks. As in ancient Greece, fishing was a monopoly held by the state during the Roman Empire. Thus, fishing in rivers, harbors, or lakes did not result in the fisherman's direct ownership of the catch. Fishing in seas was, however, free of taxation. In Roman Africa, the serving of fish was the preeminent sign of a rich table. In some areas fish was three times more expensive than meat. Roman aristocrats had *piscinae*, or fish tanks, that served not just as decorative ornaments but also as fish hatcheries. Cleopatra had such a rock-cut tank at Caesarea Maritima that measured 35 x 15 meters. The water in the tank would lead to secondary tanks, via channels cut in rock, that ultimately led to the sea. Roman ships could have carried live fish to buyers across the Mediterranean Sea via onboard fish tanks. These tanks were part of an ingenious onboard pumping system designed to provide the fish tanks with a continuous supply of oxygenated water.

A red-figured plate from Italy for serving fish (ca. 350 BC) depicts several types of fish, including bass, cuttlefish, mullet, and sargus. The center of fish plates often held a small container either for oil or for *garum*, a fermented fish sauce that was used as a condiment. At Pompeii a *garum* factory was discovered. *Garum* was such a popular culinary amenity that it was shipped in large quantities throughout the Roman provinces to political leaders, businessmen, and soldiers.

Oppian (ca. AD 175), in his work *Halieutica* ("Fishing"), mentions four methods of fishing: using hook and line, nets, wicker baskets, and spears (3.72–91). He further states that fish were sometimes caught with the bare hand (4.593–634) or were poisoned (4.647–693). The poison used for this purpose, which was derived from the cyclamen flower, bloats fish but does not harm humans (see Lytle, 165–66).

E. THE JEWISH WORLD

The Pseudepigrapha link fish and fishing to the blessing given by Jacob in the book of Genesis to his son Zebulun, which says, "Zebulun will live by the seashore and become a haven for ships" (Gen 49:13). In the *Testament of the Twelve Patriarchs*, Zebulun declares, "I was in Canaan catching fish by the sea for our father, Jacob" (*T. Zeb.* 5:5). He further states, "The LORD made my catch to be an abundance of fish" (*T. Zeb.* 6:6). The book of *Jubilees* describes how the "angel of the presence" commands Moses to write down the story of creation, which includes the fish being created on the fifth day (*Jub.* 2:11). Reflecting Gen 9:2–3, *Jubilees* states that God gives Noah and his family the fish of the sea for food (*Jub.* 6:6). The fish, furthermore, are named as part of all that God will destroy on account of humanity's great iniquity (*Jub.* 23:14–18). According to the final chapter of *Jubilees*, which deals with Sabbath regulations, "any man . . . who snares any beast or bird or fish" on the Sabbath should die (*Jub.* 50:12). In the book of *1 Enoch*, the giants sin against birds, animals, reptiles, and fish, and in response the earth brings judgments against the giants (*1 En.* 7:5). Fish are also part of the language of restoration about what will occur on "the day of the Elect One," when those who were devoured by the fish of the sea, and others who have been killed, will return (*1 En.* 61:5).

In the apocryphal book of Tobit, at the river Tigris an angel tells the boy Tobias to seize a large fish that has jumped out of the river. In response, Tobias throws the fish on land and cuts it up; they then cook and eat it (Tob 6:1–5). The burned heart and liver of the fish is to be used to chase away evil spirits (6:7, 16–17; 8:2–3) and the gall used to cure white films over the eyes (6:8).

Josephus affirms that the Sea of Galilee "contains species of fish different, both in taste and appearance, from those found elsewhere" (*J.W.* 3.509). He describes the habitat of the fish as fresh and clear water (*J.W.* 3.507–508) and states that in his day (late 1st c. AD) a total of 230 boats were on the Sea of Galilee (*J.W.* 2.635).

The rabbis believed that Joshua set forth a rule (upon entering Israel) against fishing in the Sea of Galilee from boats with spread sails, which would interfere with navigation (*b. B. Qam.* 81a). However, it was permissible to fish from the shore or from a boat without spread sails. Fishing was accomplished with hooks, nets, and traps (*b. B. Qam.* 81b).

The Talmud confirms that Babylonia's rivers, canals, and ponds were well stocked with fish. The rabbis record that on a certain day, at a canal on the northern Euphrates, "everybody engaged in fishing and they brought in fish, and [the sage] Raba allowed to put them in salt" (*b. Mo'ed Qaṭ.* 11a). Fresh fish were often broiled, but salt allowed any that went uneaten to be preserved for future consumption. The Mishnah comments on the need for rinsing "old salted fish" (*m. Šabb.* 22:2).

Just as water is essential for fish, so the rabbis considered the study of the Torah and Talmud essential for life. Reflecting on Hab 1:14, which says that God has "made people like the fish in the sea," the Talmud states, "Just as the fishes of the sea, as soon as they come on to dry land, die, so also man, as soon as he abandons the Torah and the precepts [incurs destruction]" (*b. 'Abod. Zar.* 3b). Similarly, in response to Roman oppression against Torah study, R. Akiba told a parable about a fox entreating fish to flee a net onto dry land. Though the net imposed an immediate danger,

Akiba noted that fish can no more live without water than Jews can without Torah study (*b. Ber.* 61b). Moreover, the Talmud was likened to a sea due to its unfathomable wisdom.

In one of the minor tractates of the Talmud (*'Abot de Rabbi Nathan* 40), the first-century AD Rabbi Gamaliel the Elder compares his disciples to different types of fish. He likens a poor youth who studies the Torah and Mishnah without comprehension to an unclean fish and he compares a rich youth who studies the Torah and Mishnah with comprehension to a clean fish. A scholar who studies the Torah and Mishnah but does not have the talent for debate and discussion is like a fish from the Jordan, yet a scholar who studies the Torah and Mishnah and does have the talent for debate and discussion is like a fish from the Mediterranean Sea, which is of the greater quality.

F. THE CHRISTIAN WORLD

The fish became an established symbol of Christianity because the five letters of the Greek word *ichthys* formed an acronym for the phrase *Iēsous Christos theou huios sōtēr*, "Jesus Christ, Son of God, Savior." The fish appears as a Christian symbol on paintings, gravestones, sarcophagi, and a variety of other objects from the church's inception until the sixth century AD. Most of the early church fathers interpreted fish and fishing language (as found, e.g., in Jer 16:16 and Mark 1:17) allegorically.

Origen interprets the majestic Leviathan of Job 41 allegorically as the devil (due to its physical and spiritual attributes), affirming that Christians can defeat this creature through divine virtue: "with the favor of divine virtue, they can bear not only a piece of the skin of his tail but also his entire body, and [they can] mortify it" (*Fragments on Job* 28:85; Simonetti and Conti, 214). In one of his hymns on the nativity, Ephrem the Syrian reflects on Jesus's role as the ultimate "fisher of men": "out of the stream the fish whereof Simon took, out of it the Fisher of men came up, and took him. With the Cross which catches all robbers, He caught up unto life that robber!" (*Hymns on the Nativity* 3). Origen correlates Jesus's comparison of the kingdom of heaven with a net that is thrown into the sea (Matt 13:47) with the OT, writing that, "before our Saviour Jesus Christ this net was not wholly filled; for the net of the law and the prophets had to be completed by Him who says, 'Think not that I came to destroy the law and the prophets, I came not to destroy but to fulfil'" (*Comm. Matt.* 10.12). Cyril of Alexandria interprets the miraculous fishing related in Luke 5:4–11 allegorically, noting: "For still is the net drawn, while Christ fills it, and summons unto conversion those in the depths of the sea, according to the Scripture phrase; those, that is to say, who live in the surge and waves of worldly things" (Homily 12 on Luke; Smith, 105).

After his resurrection, Jesus appears to the disciples by the Sea of Galilee and at Jesus's instruction the disciples cast their net and catch a large number of fish (John 21:1–14). Augustine allegorizes this incident and suggests that

> the Lord indicated by an outward action the kind of character the Church would have in the end of the world, so in the same way, by that other fishing, He indicated its present character. In doing the one at the commencement of His preaching and this latter after His resurrection, He showed thereby in the former case that the capture of fishes signified the good and bad presently existing in the Church; but in the latter, the good only, whom it will contain everlastingly, when the resurrection of the dead shall have been completed in the end of this world. (*Tract. Ev. Jo.* 122.7)

Both Jerome and Chrysostom affirm that Jesus ate fish with the disciples in order to prove the resurrection. Jerome writes that the risen Lord ate to "prove the resurrection: not to give your palate the pleasure of tasting of honey. He asked for a fish broiled on the coals that he might confirm the doubting Apostles, who did not dare approach Him because they thought they saw not a body, but a spirit" (*To Pammachius against John of Jerusalem* 35). Regarding the 153 fish Simon Peter hauls out of the Sea of Galilee in John 21:11, Augustine reasons that "when to the number of ten, representing the law, we add the Holy Spirit as represented by seven, we have seventeen; and when this number is used for the adding together of every several number it contains, from 1 up to itself, the sum amounts to one hundred and fifty-three" (*Tract. Ev. Jo.* 122.8). That is, $1+2+3+ \ldots +16+17 = 153$. Scholars have suggested that, if this number has any allegorical meaning, it might point to 153 major churches or 153 territories in which the gospel was preached.

BIBLIOGRAPHY: G. C. Aalders, "The Fishers and the Hunters," *EvQ* 30.3 (1958), 133–39; R. Arav and R. A. Freund, ed., *Bethsaida: A City by the North Shore of the Sea of Galilee* (1995); P. Ariès, G. Duby, and P. Veyne, ed., *A History of Private Life I: From Pagan Rome to Byzantium*, trans. A. Goldhammer (1987); E. F. F. Bishop, "Jesus and the Lake," *CBQ* 13 (1951), 398–414; O. Borowski, *Every Living Thing: Daily Use of Animals in Ancient Israel* (1998); G. W. Bowersock, P. Brown, and O. Grabar, ed., *Late Antiquity: A Guide to the Postclassical World* (1999); B. Brier and M. V. L. Bennett, "Autopsies on Fish Mummies," *JEA* 65 (1979), 128–33; G. S. Cansdale, *All the Animals of the Bible Lands* (1970); A. Dalby, *Siren Feasts: A History of Food and Gastronomy in Greece* (1996); J. D. M. Derrett, "ΗΣΑΝ ΓΑΡ ἉΛΙΕΙΣ

(MK. I 16): Jesus's Fishermen and the Parable of the Net," *NovT* 22.2 (1980), 108–37; S. J. R. Ellis, "The Rise and Re-organization of the Pompeian Salted Fish Industry," in *The Making of Pompeii*, ed. S. J. R. Ellis (2011), 59–88; R. Flacelière, *Daily Life in Greece at the Time of Pericles*, trans. P. Green (2002); A. Flinder, *Secrets of the Bible Seas: An Underwater Archaeologist in the Holy Land* (1985); K. C. Hanson, "The Galilean Fishing Economy and the Jesus Tradition," *BTB* 27.3 (1997), 99–111; J. Higginbotham, *Piscinae: Artificial Fishponds in Roman Italy* (1997); G. H. R. Horsley, *New Documents Illustrating Early Christianity* (1989); R. H. Isaacs, *Animals in Jewish Thought and Tradition* (2000); E. Lytle, *Marine Fisheries and the Ancient Greek Economy* (2006); M. Nun, "Cast Your Net Upon the Waters: Fish and Fishermen in Jesus' Time," *BAR* 19.6 (1993), 46–56, 70; M. Nun, "Fishing," *OEANE* 2.315–17; J. P. Oleson, *The Harbours of Caesarea Maritima: Results of the Caesarea Ancient Harbour Excavation Project 1980–85* (1994); S. M. Paul, "Fishing Imagery in Amos 4:2," *JBL* 97.2 (1978), 183–90; A. Salonen, *Die Fischerei im alten Mesopotamien nach sumerisch-akkadischen Quellen* (1970); J. Scarborough, *Facets of Hellenic Life* (1976); B. Schwank, "Vom Fisch und den Fischen," *Erbe und Auftrag* 73.3 (1997), 222–24; C. W. Smith, "Fishers of Men," *HTR* 52.3 (1959), 187–203; R. P. Smith, trans., *Commentary on the Gospel of Saint Luke* (1983); S. P. Toperoff, "Fish in Bible and Midrash," *Dor le Dor* 16 (1987/88), 46–50.

TR and MRW

See also FOOD CONSUMPTION, HARBORS, and WILD ANIMALS & HUNTING.

FOOD CONSUMPTION

The consumption of foodstuffs is essential for maintaining human life, and can be engaged in on an individual or communal level within either a secular or religious context. In the ancient world, how and with whom one ate, and even the posture of eating, could carry great social or religious significance.

A. THE OLD TESTAMENT

The Heb. word for food, *ʾōkel*, "food," is derived from the verb *ʾākal*, "to eat," which occurs over eight hundred times in the OT. According to Gen 2:9, "The LORD God made all kinds of trees grow out of the ground—trees that were pleasing to the eye and good for food." After the flood, God declared that "everything that lives and moves about will be food for you. Just as I gave you the green plants, I now give you everything," but included this proviso, "But you must not eat meat that has its lifeblood still in it" (Gen 9:3–4).

According to Psalm 104, God provides food for all living creatures (cf. Eccl 3:13). Ordinarily God does this by natural processes, but while the Israelites were sojourning in the wilderness he provided them miraculously with "bread from heaven" called manna (Exod 16:31; Ps 105:40–41; Neh 9:15).

Three agricultural products that are mentioned together on a number of occasions in the OT and that were an important part of the ancient Israelite diet are *dāgān*, "grain," *tîrôš*, "new wine," and *yiṣhār*, "olive oil." As a reward for Israel's covenantal obedience, God promises his people the following: "I will send rain on your land in its season, both autumn and spring rains, so that you may gather in your grain, new wine, and oil" (Deut 11:14; cf. 2 Kgs 18:32; 2 Chr 31:5; Neh 5:11; Jer 31:12; Hos 2:8; Joel 1:10; Hag 1:11).

Though the OT contains no *kashrut* (i.e., kosher) regulations regarding cereals, fruits, and vegetables, aside from the banning of leaven from the holy sanctuary, it does contain elaborate laws regarding the flesh of animals, which could be either *ṭāhôr,* "clean," or *ṭāmēʾ,* "unclean" (Lev 11:2-47; cf. Deut 14:3-21). The OT bans the eating of blood (*dām*) (Gen 9:4-6; Lev 17:10-15; Deut 12:15-25) and animal carcasses (Deut 14:21; cf. Ezek 4:14). Animals such as cattle, sheep, and goats, and sea creatures that had scales and fins, were permitted to be eaten (Lev 11:12); by implication, such creatures as shrimp and crabs were not. Omnivores, such as pigs, carnivores, and birds that were raptors, were forbidden, as were creatures that swarmed on the ground, like rodents and lizards. Although certain flying insects were unfit for food, the "locust, katydid, cricket or grasshopper" could be consumed (Lev 11:20-23).

The sacrifice and consumption of meat formed an important part of the festival of Booths (Tabernacles), which was celebrated after the harvest ingathering. During the eight-day period of the celebration seventy-one bulls, fifteen rams, 105 lambs, and eight goats were offered sacrificially to the Lord (Num 29:12-34). In contrast to non-Israelite concepts that regarded such sacrifices as food for the gods, Yahweh did not regard such offerings as meals (Ps 50:12-13).

An enigmatic command that one should not "cook [KJV: seethe] a young goat in its mother's milk" (Exod 23:19; 34:26; Deut 14:21), which was the basis of the later kosher prohibition of mixing meat and dairy dishes together, has been variously interpreted. The attempt to read this prohibition as aimed at a Canaanite practice on the basis of a fragmentary Ugaritic text has now been abandoned. Some scholars have interpreted this text as an expression of Israelite humanitarian concern for animals. J. Sasson has argued for revocalizing the word *ḥālāb,* "milk," as *ḥēleb,* "fat." S. Schorch interprets the text to mean, "You shall not boil a young goat which is at its mother's milk"—that is, a kid not yet weaned.

While the poor subsisted on the grapes and grain that were deliberately left for them to glean (Deut 23:24-25; Ruth 2), kings and the wealthy seized the produce of farmers, as Samuel warned: "He will take your daughters to be perfumers and cooks and bakers. He will take the best of your fields and vineyards and olive groves and give them to his attendants. He will take a tenth of your grain and of your vintage and give it to his officials and attendants" (1 Sam 8:13-15). According to 1 Kgs 4:22-23, "Solomon's daily provisions were thirty cors [= 195 bushels] of the finest flour and sixty cors [= 390 bushels] of meal, ten head of stall-fed cattle, twenty of pasture-fed cattle and a hundred sheep and goats, as well as deer, gazelles, roebucks and choice fowl." The prophet Amos denounced the wealthy who feasted while the poor hungered: "You lie on beds adorned with ivory and lounge on your couches. You dine on choice lambs and fattened calves. . . . Therefore you will be among the first to go into exile; your feasting and lounging will end" (Amos 6:4, 7).

Voluntary fasting took place as a sign of mourning, repentance, or earnest petition (Deut 26:14; 1 Sam 7:6; 31:13; Ezra 8:21; Esth 4:3). Because of drought food shortages were common, which raised the cost of food and caused hardship among the majority of the populace, who would have had no reserves (Gen 12:10; 26:1; 41:54; Ruth 1:1; 2 Sam 21:1; 1 Kgs 18:1–2; 2 Kgs 8:1; Jer 14:1–6).

In the extreme case of starvation caused by the Aramean siege of Samaria, the head of a donkey, an unclean animal, was sold for eighty shekels of silver, and even doves' dung (2 Kgs 6:25, KJV) was consumed as food. The privations caused by this siege even provoked the horrific situation of a mother, along with another woman, eating her own child (2 Kgs 6:26–29), which is forecast in Deut 28:53–57, where the Lord states that this would be an effect of his bringing enemies to besiege the cities of the disobedient children of Israel.

B. THE NEW TESTAMENT

In NT Palestine the basic diet of the poor consisted of bread and fish (John 6:9; Matt 7:9–10). Many of Jesus's disciples were fishermen from the Sea of Galilee. Fish could be preserved by salting or they could be eaten immediately by being roasted on a fire (Luke 24:42; John 21:9). Jesus's reference to an *ornis*, "hen" (Matt 23:37||Luke 13:34), and to an *ōon*, "egg" (Luke 11:12), indicates that poultry and their eggs were available. His Parable of the Prodigal Son (Luke 11:15–32) illustrates the extremes of the *moschon ton siteuton*, "the calf fattened with grain" (vs. 23) provided the repentant son and his earlier longing to feed on the *keratiōn*, "carob pods" (vss. 15–16) fed to pigs. The story of the expulsion of the multitude of demons from the Gadarene demoniac (Matt 8:28–34||Mark 5:1–20||Luke 8:26–39) demonstrates that large herds of pigs were raised by Gentiles east of the Sea of Galilee.

John the Baptist, who lived in the wilderness of Judea, subsisted on an unusual diet of locusts and wild honey (Matt 3:4||Mark 1:6). The only other reference to honey in the NT concerns John's vision of a scroll that tasted like honey to him when he ate it but turned sour in his stomach (Rev 10:9–10).

Because salt was useful for seasoning and preserving, it serves as a useful metaphor in different NT passages. For example, Jesus calls his disciples "the salt of the earth" (Matt 5:13), and exhorts them, "Have salt among yourselves, and be at peace with each other" (Mark 9:50). Paul exhorts his followers, "Let your conversation be always full of grace, seasoned with salt, so that you may know how to answer everyone" (Col 4:6).

Because Jesus ate with "tax collectors and sinners" (cf. Mark 2:15), his enemies accused him of being "a glutton and a drunkard" (Matt 11:19||Luke 7:34). He was also criticized when a woman poured perfume on his head (Mark 14:3), and on another occasion when a woman anointed his feet, while he was dining (Luke 7:36–50). Women of the family did not normally dine with the men but served them (Mark 1:31; Luke 10:38–42).

In all the references to Jesus as dining (e.g., Mark 14:18; Luke 7:36; 22:14), he is said to be reclining (*katakeimai, kataklinō*), the position (in which one rested on one's left hand) that males assumed at dinner in the Greco-Roman world. In contrast, for example, to the depiction in Da Vinci's painting *The Last Supper*, Jesus and his twelve disciples were probably on this occasion reclining on three couches (*klinai*) arranged in an upside-down U-shape, so that servants could set up tables with food through the opening. Diners would rest on their left elbows and reach for the food with their right arms. As the host, Jesus would have taken the top position on the left table, with "the beloved disciple" leaning on his bosom (John 13:23), and with Peter perhaps below him. Judas apparently had the place of honor in the central couch (John 13:26).

Jesus's disciples were criticized for eating without washing their hands (Mark 7:1–5). Reacting to the Pharisaic concern about the contagion of uncleanness that was manifested in their "washing of cups, pitchers and kettles," (Mark 7:4), Jesus declared: "Don't you see that nothing that enters a person from the outside can defile them? For it doesn't go into their heart but into their stomach, and then out of the body" (Mark 7:18–19a). The Greek phrase that follows this statement, *katharizōn panta ta brōmata*, "cleansing all foods," was considered by the translators of the KJV to refer to the process of digestion (hence that translation's "purging all meats"). Most modern translations interpret this phrase instead as Mark's commentary, for example, the NIV, which reads: "In saying this, Jesus declared all foods clean."

One effect of observant Jews' careful observation of OT food laws was that it prevented them from eating with non-observant Jews, and, even more so, with Gentiles. To overcome Peter's traditional concerns about food, God sent him a dramatic vision while he was hungry and on the roof of Simon the Tanner's home in Joppa, before his encounter with the Roman centurion Cornelius.

> [Peter] saw heaven opened and something like a large sheet being let down to earth by its four corners. It contained all kinds of four-footed animals, as well as reptiles and birds. Then a voice told him, "Get up, Peter. Kill and eat." "Surely not, Lord!" Peter replied. "I have never eaten anything impure or unclean." The voice spoke to him a second time, "Do not call anything impure that God has made clean." (Acts 10:11–15)

With the conversion of Gentiles, especially through the ministry of Paul, the issue of commensality or table fellowship between Jews, who observed OT purity laws, and Gentiles, who did not, became an even more divisive issue. This was addressed by a council in Jerusalem ca. AD 50 under the leadership of James, which commanded that Gentile believers "abstain from food sacrificed to idols, from blood, from the meat of strangled animals and from sexual immorality" (Acts 15:29; cf. Acts 21:25).

Later, however, when Peter, under pressure from stricter Jewish Christians, withdrew from table fellowship with Gentile Christians, Paul rebuked him to his face (Gal 2:11–14). A problem that arose at Corinth concerned the eating of meat sold at the *macellum* or meat market, which may have come from sacrifices (1 Cor 8 and 10). While Paul forbade the eating of such meat in ritual contexts (1 Cor 8:10; 10:21), he allowed it in private contexts (1 Cor 10:27). In his epistles Paul declared that "food does not bring us near to God; we are no worse if we do not eat, and no better if we do" (1 Cor 8:8), but he counseled believers to abstain from eating foods that "weaker" (that is, more sensitive) Christians would find objectionable.

At the Last Supper, which took place during the week of Passover, Jesus declared that the bread that he was breaking represented his body that would be broken, and the wine he was drinking represented his blood that he would shed for humankind (Matt 26:26–29; Mark 14:22–25; Luke 22:19–20; cf. 1 Cor 11:23–25). Christians at Corinth celebrated the Lord's Supper in connection with a communal meal (1 Cor 11:21–22, 33–34) that the church fathers (Ignatius, Tertullian) called an *agapē* ("love") meal. But there were divisions because of the disparity between the foods that were available to the owner of the house where the church met and those that were provided to the majority of the guests (1 Cor 11:17–22): the host and his friends would have dined on superior food in the *triclinium* (dining room) of a villa, whereas "the many" (*hoi polloi*) would have had inferior food in the villa's atrium.

Paul warned that false teachers had arisen who

> forbid people to marry and order them to abstain from certain foods, which God created to be received with thanksgiving by those who believe and who know the truth. For everything God created is good, and nothing is to be rejected if it is received with thanksgiving, because it is consecrated by the word of God and prayer. (1 Tim 4:3–5)

Though on one occasion Jesus was asked why John the Baptist's disciples fasted and his did not (Luke 5:33–34), Jesus himself fasted (Luke 4:2) and commanded his disciples to fast without making it obvious to others that they were doing so (Matt 6:16–18). After Jesus's death, the early Christians fasted and prayed when they sought special guidance (Acts 13:2; 14:23).

C. THE NEAR EASTERN WORLD

Mesopotamia

Our knowledge of the food consumed in ancient Mesopotamia comes primarily from textual evidence such as lists of food offered to the gods, though occasionally, such as at Ur (ca. 2500 BC), actual remains of food offerings have been preserved, including bread, date stones, dried apple rings, and sheep and goat bones. Some bread made from fine flour was found preserved in the tomb of Queen Puabi at Ur.

Ration tablets for royal messengers list as basic provisions beer, bread, onions, oil, and fish, which were provided by the palace. A diet made up predominantly of barley and wheat would provide carbohydrates but would be lacking in protein and vitamins. A deficiency in vitamin A could lead to blindness (xerophthalmia) and a lack of vitamin C could result in scurvy. Protein was supplied not only by meat but also by legumes, and vitamins by vegetables and fruits.

Fifty types of fish were available from the Euphrates River, some reaching two hundred pounds in weight. Other fish were caught in the irrigation canals, or raised in fish ponds. After the Kassite era (ca. 1200 BC), fish became less popular. Fish were split and grilled over charcoal grills. Turtles were also eaten.

The Sumerians enjoyed hunting and eating gazelles. Some gazelles were captured and fattened by being fed barley. There was even a month named MAŠ.DA.KU, the month of "gazelle eating." Also hunted were wild boar, hares, large rodents, and francolins (wild hens). The inhabitants of Nuzi were exceptional in that they ate horse meat. Reliefs of skewered locusts at Ashurbanipal's palace indicate that these were considered delicacies in Assyria.

Fowl such as ducks, geese, pigeons, and partridges were caught and eaten. Ostrich eggs have been found at Mari. Domestic fowl from the east appeared in Mesopotamia in the seventh century BC.

City-dwellers looked with contempt on nomads of the steppe, who dug up truffles, ate uncooked meat, and did not know barley. The first use of fire for the preparation of meats was ascribed to Lugalbanda, the mythical ruler of Uruk. The so-called "Assyrian Encyclopedia" lists at least one hundred different stews and soups. The Yale Culinary Tablets (ca. 1700 BC) contain thirty-five detailed recipes, primarily for stews. One instructs the cook to start with mutton or poultry boiled in a pot with water and fresh sheep fat and then to add vegetables and a variety of condiments, such as leeks, garlic, onion, and cumin. Malted barley was also used to thicken the broth. There are recipes for broths featuring venison, gazelle, goat meat, lamb, and pigeons. Cooks in the royal kitchens were men.

While the gods of Sumer were fed four times a day, the Sumerians themselves seem to have eaten only two meals per day, one early in the morning and the other at sunset. (Later texts from Mari also refer to only two meals, one in the morning and one in the evening.) A simple breakfast would consist of emmer groats. According to a Sumerian composition, a schoolboy said to his mother, "'Give me my lunch, I want to go to school!' My mother gave me two rolls . . . and I went to school" (Kramer, 238). The word for the evening meal, KIN.SIG, signifies "twilight." The Akkadian phrase for "lunch," *naptan muṣlāli*, consists of *naptan*, "meal," and a word that is cognate with *ṣalīlu*, "nap," implying that midday was not only a time for a meal but also a time for lying down for a nap.

A Sumerian proverb relates: "When he [a poor man] had bread he had no salt, when he had salt he had no bread, When he had meat he had no condiment, when he had the condiment he had no meat" (Kramer, 263). A character in the Akkadian *Dialogue about Human Suffering* says, "Let me enter house after house, control my hunger . . . Let me enter like a beggar" (*ANET*, 440). The *Tale of the Poor Man of Nippur* graphically describes the desperate state of Gimil-Ninurta:

> His storage bins lacked pure grain,
> His insides burned, craving food, and
> His face was unhappy, craving meat and first-class beer;
> Having no food, he lay hungry every day, and
> Was dressed in garments that had no change. (Cooper, 170)

Palaces such as the Old Babylonian one at Mari hosted sumptuous banquets. Guests were given special robes. Food was placed in large vessels, with everyone helping himself, using his fingers. Slaves poured water over the hands of guests. The greatest banquet in antiquity was probably that hosted by the Assyrian king Assurnasirpal II (883–859 BC), who hosted 69,574 guests for ten days. The menu included

> 1,000 fattened head of cattle, 1,000 calves, 10,000 stable sheep, 15,000 lambs . . .
> 1,000 spring lambs, 500 stags, 500 gazelles, 1,000 *ducks*, 500 *geese* . . . 10,000
> other (assorted) small birds, 10,000 (assorted) fish . . . 10,000 (assorted) eggs;
> 10,000 loaves of bread, 10,000 (jars of) beer, 10,000 skins with wine.
> (*ANESTP*, 560)

According to an Assyrian medical text, "[If a person's] insides are continually colicky, his palate continually gets dry, . . . he belches, he has plenty of appetite (for food), but when [he sees it], it does not please him . . . [the] 'hand' of a ghost is pursuing that person" (Scurlock, 491).

Egypt

We have multiple sources of evidence for the food that was eaten in ancient Egypt, including texts, mortuary paintings, models for the after-life, and actual food remains preserved on account of the low humidity in Egypt. Among the texts that can inform us about this topic are lists of offerings to the gods.

In Egypt bread was baked on an open fire over ashes, on preheated conical molds on low braziers, or in cylindrical ovens. Egyptian texts list fifty-seven types of bread and thirty-eight types of cakes. Loaves were baked in a variety of shapes: round, oval, pyramidal, crescent, and triangular. Some had a hole in the center to hold a garnish; others were sprinkled with seeds. Actual examples have been preserved in a number of tombs. The daily requirement of barley for the palace in Memphis during the reign of Seti I (13th c. BC) was 100–180 sacks, which was required to produce 2,000–4,000 loaves of bread. On one occasion in the thirteenth century BC, preparations for the arrival of a pharaoh required 9,200 loaves of eight varieties of bread and 20,000 biscuits of two varieties. Excavators have uncovered mass baking facilities near Giza that provided the bread to feed the workers who built the pyramids there.

Onions and garlic formed part of the wages of the builders of the Great Pyramid of Khufu (Cheops). Vegetables were grown in garden plots, which were irrigated by a *shaduf*, a bucket attached to a leveraged pole. Among the most popular vegetables in ancient Egypt were leeks (Egy. sing. *iwrj.t*, which also served as a general word for vegetables), onions, and garlic (cf. Num 11:5). Pulses (edible legume seeds) included lentils, fava beans, peas, and chickpeas, which were ground into a paste (like modern hummus). Root vegetables included radishes, turnips, and carrots. The Egyptians enjoyed cucumbers, squash, and pumpkins, and ate leafy vegetables including celery, parsley, spinach, and lettuce. Lettuce was associated with the fertility god Min. Its leaves were considered an aphrodisiac, and its milky juice a cure for impotence. The Egyptians ate the roots of lotus plants and gnawed papyrus stalks, which were sweet like sugarcane. When ground and mixed with milk, sweet carob beans jelled into a kind of chocolate pudding.

The poor in Egypt seldom ate meat, subsisting on a diet of bread, dried fish, fruit, and vegetables. Royalty, on the other hand, feasted on cuts of beef and mutton, and ducks and geese. One famous scene shows Akhenaten munching on a shoulder of beef, while his wife Nefertiti gnaws on a bird she holds in her hand. Since Egyptians ate with their fingers, servants were on hand to pour water over their hands when they had finished eating. The *Teaching of Khety* (also known as the *Satire on the Trades*) comments: "How wretched it is, the belly which thou heedest! If three loaves should satisfy thee, and the swallowing of two *hin* of beer, (but) there is (still) no *limit* [to] the belly, fight against it" (*ANET*, 434).

D. THE GRECO-ROMAN WORLD

Greece

The Greek word for a meal, *opson,* was used to describe anything that was eaten with bread, including meat, fish, fruits, and vegetables. As in most cultures, the staple foods in ancient Greece were grains, vegetables, and legumes. Bread was eaten at every meal. Soldiers ate a lot of garlic, onions, and cheese. Olive oil was the main source of fat in the Greek diet. Legumes such as beans, lentils, peas, chickpeas, and broad beans, which could be dried and stored, were eaten as purées or in soups. One legume, *thermos* (lupine), had to be boiled because it was toxic if eaten raw. The flowering asphodel provided a poor man's diet; he could eat its fried stalk, its roasted seed, and its root. Medical authorities valued the lettuce for its soporific white juice. Greeks celebrated a bean festival in honor of Apollo. Pythagoras, who believed in reincarnation, forbade the eating of beans; he thought the flatulence they caused was evidence that bean plants contained the souls of the deceased.

The eating of fish is not mentioned by Homer, but fish in fact formed such a major portion of the *opson,* food taken with bread, that the modern Greek word for fish, *psari,* is derived from *opsarion,* the diminutive of *opson.* The poor ate small and salted fish, such as sardines and anchovies. Wealthy Athenians preferred larger species such as the turbot and the bream, and fish imported from the Black Sea such as mackerel, sturgeon, tuna, and mullet. The Greeks also enjoyed shellfish, cuttlefish, squid, and octopi. Fishmongers (*ichthyopōlai*) had a very poor reputation: they were reputed to sell inferior and even rotten fish at inflated prices, as many passages in Athenaeus attest (*Deipn.* 6.224d–228f).

A Greek gourmet named Archestratus (ca. 330 BC), who came from Gela in Sicily, a region noted for its cooking traditions, traveled widely throughout the Greek world in the eastern Mediterranean. He recorded his experiences in a comic poem called *Hedypatheia* ("The Experience of Sweet Things"). Of the sixty-two preserved fragments, forty-eight deal with the cooking of fish. Greeks who could afford them also ate eels, which were praised as a delicacy. Archestratus writes, "I praise every eel [*egchelyn*]; but it is far and away the best when caught in the sea-strait opposite Rhegium. . . . I believe that the king of everything associated with a feast and the foremost in pleasure is the eel, the only fish with a naturally minimal bone-structure" (quoted in Athen. *Depn.* 7.298f). Eels from Lake Copais in Boeotia were expensive but were readily available in Athens.

Greeks also ate all kinds of fowl, including pelicans, cranes, owls, pigeons, thrushes, larks, jays, nightingales, swans, ducks, and geese. They even force-fed geese with figs; such an animal was known as *sykōtos* ("stuffed with figs"). The practice was followed by the Romans to produce *ficatum*, a precursor to French *foie gras* ("fatted liver" of a goose).

In the idealized heroic age described by Homer, the heroes dine almost entirely on roast beef. Numerous passages discuss the slaughter and consumption of cattle both for human meals and as sacrifices to the gods. In addition to beef, Greeks ate mutton and goat meat. They also ate wild game such as boar, deer, and foxes. A hare could serve as a lover's gift to his beloved.

Pigs were also an important source of meat in ancient Greece. Among the livestock listed in the Mycenaean tablets from Pylos are *si-a$_2$-ro* (*sialos*), fatted pigs. In Homer's *Odyssey*, when Odysseus returns to Ithaca after a twenty-year absence, he encounters his faithful swineherd Eumaeus, who, Homer records, keeps 360 fatted hogs in his master's large pigsty (*Od.* 14.19–20). In Greek cities large numbers of pigs were killed at certain fertility festivals, for example, for the goddess Demeter. The offal was minced and placed in the casings of the intestines to make sausages, which were popular since they were tasty, and soft to eat, even for those who had few teeth left. Black puddings (sausages made with blood) were also popular. The Spartans were famous for their "black broth," a highly seasoned stew made from pork, pig's blood, vinegar, and salt.

Only wealthy Greeks could afford to eat meat on a regular basis. The Athenian comic poet Eubulus (fl. 370 BC) expressed his preference for meat and his disdain for the vegetables eaten by the poor:

> As for me [i.e., Heracles], I have not come here to browse on kale or silphium or sacrilegious bitter dishes or bulbs. But on what counts first as real food, promoting health and the full vigor of physical strength, I have always been wont to feed—beef boiled and unspoiled, in huge quantity, with a generous portion of foot and snout, and three slices of young pork sprinkled with salt.
> (*Amaltheia*, quoted in Athen. *Deipn.* 2.63de)

Greeks ate their *ariston* or breakfast soon after sunrise. It could consist of *akratisma*, bread dipped in vinegar. A light lunch was often eaten outdoors, or might be skipped altogether. The *deipnon* or *dorpon*, dinner, was the main meal of the day, and was served at home and included several courses. The first course of *paropsides* or appetizers could consist of barley bread or a thick soup. The main course was meat cut into fillets or served on the bone. Dessert (*tragēmata*) could include dates, raisins, chestnuts, or honey cakes.

Although spoons were used for soup and knives for meat, Greeks mainly used flat bread to scoop up food or used their fingers. Fingers were either wiped clean with bread, which was then thrown to the ground for dogs, or they were washed by water poured by slaves.

At dinner parties, men reclined on couches in the *andrōn* ("men's room"), a practice that is first attested in the writings of the poet Alcman (ca. 7th c. BC). The typical dining room was furnished with three couches arranged in an inverted U-shape known as the *triklinion* (lit., "three couches"). Slaves served food to the guests through the open fourth side or arranged dishes on low tables. After dinner, the slaves would remove the tables, sweep the floors, and bring in wine and garlands for the *symposion*, or evening drinking banquet. The only women who could be present at a *symposion* were *hetairai*, professional entertainers who also provided sexual services. *Parasitoi* ("parasites") were guests who were invited for their willingness to flatter the host and to entertain other guests with humor (Athenaeus, *Deipn.* 6.235f–237f).

Greek women and children ate separately from the men. In the fourth century BC, the orator Isaeus commented, "nor do married women accompany their husbands to banquets or think of feasting in the company of strangers, especially mere chance comers" (*On Pyrrhus' Estate* 14). In the preface to his *Lives of Eminent Commanders*, the Roman writer Cornelius Nepos (1st c. BC) wrote: "But in Greece the case is far otherwise; for a wife is neither admitted to a feast, except among relatives, nor does she sit anywhere but in the innermost apartment of the house, which is called *gynaeconitis* and into which nobody goes who is not connected with her by near relationship" (Watson, 307).

Greek physicians strongly believed in the connection between diet and health, and often prescribed detailed regimens for their patients. The Hippocratic School of medicine held that health depended on the balance of four "humors" or fluids in the body: blood, phlegm, yellow bile, and black bile. Dietetics was an important way of correcting imbalances of the humors, which the members of this school believed led to illness. Foods were classified as (1) hot and dry, (2) hot and moist, (3) cold and dry, and (4) cold and moist. Hot and moist people were advised to eat similar foods except when they became unbalanced, in which case they were to eat cold and dry foods. The Hippocratic author of *Regimen III* (68) recommended only one meal a day!

Greeks were also no strangers to special diets, whether for athletes or based on philosophic principles. Cynic philosophers, who defied tradition and custom, slept on the ground, drank only water, and ate only what they could find or beg. On the other hand, athletes ate heartily, none more pro-digiously than the wrestler Milo of Croton (6th c. BC), who according to Theodorus of Hierapolis, "used to eat 20 minas [about twenty pounds] of meat, along with an equal amount of bread, and would drink three pitch-ers of wine. At Olympia he put a four-year-old bull on his shoulders and walked around the stadium carrying it, and afterward he butchered it and ate the whole thing in a single day, all by himself" (*On Athletic Contests*, quoted in Athen., *Deipn.* 10.412e–f)!

Rome

We have three important sources that give detailed information on the preparation and consumption of food in ancient Rome:

(1) Galen (AD 129–199), who began as a physician for the gladiators in Pergamum and then became the physician to the emperor Marcus Au-relius, was the most important Roman proponent of Hippocratic medicine. His treatise *On the Powers of Foods* gives a comprehensive review of what the Romans ate, commenting on the relative values of different foods.

(2) Athenaeus (early 3rd c. AD), a Greek author who was originally from Naucratis in Egypt, provides a Hellenic perspective on Roman food and meal customs. In his *Deipnosophistae*, Athenaeus claims to record a lengthy dinner conversation between twenty-three learned men, including Galen, at a banquet in Rome. In fact, Athenaeus uses his erudite characters to display his own exhaustive knowledge of Roman customs and Greek lit-erature; their conversation includes citations from around seven hundred earlier Greek authors.

(3) *Apicius*, or *De re coquinaria* (*The Art of Cooking*), is a Roman cook-book that contains 468 recipes. It was compiled in about AD 400 and is named after a famous gourmet who lived during the reign of Tiberius (AD 14–37).

Like the ancient Greeks, the Romans enjoyed eating fresh fish such as anchovies, mackerel, sprat, tuna, and red mullet, as well as mussels, oys-ters, sea urchins, and octopus. Salted fish could keep for about a year and were eaten during winter and early spring, when fresh food became scarce. The Romans also had fishponds, *piscinae*, where they fattened up lampreys, bream, and eels caught in the sea.

The distinctively Roman seasoning called *garum* was usually served with fish and was also served with many other dishes. It was made from the guts of small fish such as smelts, sprats, or anchovies, which were al-lowed to rot in large open tanks for one to three months, mixed with salt and herbs. Combined with honey and vinegar, it became a sweet-and-sour sauce. Though some brands were expensive, evidence from Pompeii indicates that it was enjoyed by all levels of society. Much of it came from Spain. Not everyone liked it. Seneca complained: "Do you not think that the so-called 'Sauce [*garum*] from the Provinces,' the costly extract of poisonous fish, burns up the stomach with its salted putrefaction?" (*Ep.* 95.25).

The Romans also enjoyed eating fungi: the best mushroom was the porcini (*Boletus edulis*). *Apicius* has four recipes for truffles. Taking advantage of the emperor Claudius's love of mushrooms, his wife Agrippina hastened her son Nero's advancement by feeding her husband poisoned mushrooms (*boleti*; Suet. *Claud.* 44).

Commenting on the varieties of meat, Galen lists pork as the most nutritious, then beef and goat meat, then lamb and hares. His medical opinion certainly suited Roman tastes. Pork (*porcus*) was inexpensive and tasty. Pigs were easy to feed with acorns and figs. They were prolific; a sow could have two litters with ten piglets each in a year. Many Romans kept pigs, and killed them in the late summer to have ham and bacon for the fall and winter. Pigs were the most frequently sacrificed animal in Rome, and pork was the most common meat available at the butchers' shops. We have over ninety Roman recipes for a variety of pork dishes. Pigs' lard was used for cooking, and minced pork flavored with spices was stuffed into the casings made from their intestines to form sausages. *Apicius* advised,

> Pound pepper, cumin, savory, rue, parsley, mixed herbs, laurel-berries, and *liquamen* [a fish sauce], and mix with this well-beaten meat, pounding it again with the ground spice mixture. Work in *liquamen*, peppercorns, plenty of fat and pine-kernels, insert into a sausage-skin, drawn out very thinly, and hang in the smoke. (Flower and Rosenbaum, 73)

Suckling pigs (*porcelli*) and sow's udder and vulva were considered delicacies.

In contrast to the many Roman recipes for pork, *Apicius* lists only four recipes for beef or veal (*vitulinum*). Goat meat was roasted. As a delicacy, the Romans also raised rodents known as dormice, which they fattened with walnuts, acorns, and chestnuts. They served them sprinkled with honey and poppy seed.

In Book 3 of *The Powers of Foods*, Galen declares:

> Of all foods, therefore, pork is the most nutritious. . . . Beef furnishes nourishment which is substantial and not easily digested, although it generates thicker blood than is suitable. . . . Lambs have moist and phlegmatic flesh. The flesh of sheep, on the other hand, is even more ecrementitious and unwholesome (than sucking pigs). The flesh of nanny-goats combines unwholesomeness with bitterness. . . . As for dogs, what can I say? In some countries they are often eaten when young and plump, and particularly after they have been castrated. (cited in Grant, 154–55)

Just as there were huge disparities in wealth and status, there were also huge differences in the types of food that were available to different classes. As in ancient Greece, Roman farmers and workers rarely ate meat. For slaves working on a country estate, Cato suggests the following rations: "The chain-gang should have a ration of four pounds of bread through the winter, increasing to five when they begin to work the vines, and dropping back to four when the figs ripen" (*Agr.* 56). He also recommends that they be given olives that have fallen on the ground, fish sauce, and vinegar. Cato indicates that the staple diet of peasants and working-class folk consisted of bread, wine, salt, and olives. These items would be supplemented by vegetables, especially onions, and fruits. In *Moretum*, a poem attributed to Virgil, a peasant goes into his garden to pick four heads of garlic, parsley, rue, and coriander. He pounds these into a paste with water, olive oil, vinegar, salt, and hard cheese, which he then eats with bread.

A few Romans also eschewed meat for philosophical rather than economic reasons. Following the example of the Greek philosopher Pythagoras, the Roman Stoic philosopher Musonius Rufus and the later Neo-Platonist Porphyry rejected the eating of flesh in favor of eating vegetables. Musonius "argued that a meat-based diet was too crude for humans and more suitable for wild beasts. He said that it was too heavy and that it impeded mental activity. The fumes which come from it, he said, are too smoky and darken the soul" (*Lectures* 18.A; King, 72).

Most Romans ate three meals a day, beginning with a breakfast (*iantaculum*) upon rising that consisted of bread, cheese, and leftovers from the night before. Lunch (*prandium*) was eaten between noon and 2 p.m. Boys would eat bread, olives, cheese, dried figs, and nuts at school. A quick lunch would be available from *tabernae* (shops and taverns), *cauponae* (restaurants and hotels), and *popinae* (bars), where wine and hot food were sold. As illustrated by several examples from Pompeii, food shops had counters on the streets stocked with *dolia*, large vessels that contained mainly dry foods such as legumes, beans, grains, and nuts. Liquids were probably kept in small amphoras. Prices were posted at one facility (IX.7.24–25): cheeses from 1 to 2 asses (the "as" [pl. "asses"] was a Roman monetary unit), onions 5 asses, dates 1 as, sausages 1 as.

Pompeii had 158 bars with counters, 85 percent of which were located on its main roads and intersections. Of these, 81 percent had cooking facilities either on the counter itself or nearby. Recent excavations by Ellis of drains at two facilities have revealed striking differences in their menus: at one drain remains included relatively inexpensive foodstuffs such as grains, olives, lentils, local fish, and some chicken eggs (VIII.7.1–4); on the other hand, the drain at a second *popina* included some imports and expensive food such as meat, shellfish, sea urchin, dormice, and even a leg joint of a giraffe (VIII.9–11)!

The main Roman meal was the *cena*, or dinner, which was served at the eighth hour during the winter and the ninth hour in summer (i.e., between 4 and 6 p.m.). This consisted of three courses, *ab ovo usque ad mala*, "from the egg to the apple": (1) the *gustatio*, or appetizer, which consisted of eggs, raw vegetables, and fish (cf. Martial, *Ep.* 5.78; 11.52; Pliny the Younger, *Ep.* 1.15); (2) the *prima mensa*, or main course, which included cooked vegetables, roasted or boiled meat, poultry, sausages, etc.; and (3) the *secunda mensa*, or dessert, which was comprised of fruit or sweet pastries, egg custards, and also shellfish, oysters, and snails.

In wealthy homes cooks (*coqui*) were slaves who worked in dark and poorly ventilated kitchens (*culinae*). Other slaves included the *structor*, who carved and served the meat; the *ministrator*, who served the guests; and the *cellarius*, who served the wine. At times wealthy Romans ate from plates made of silver and gold. They were handed knives and spoons by their slaves as needed, but they mainly ate with their hands. Slaves brought bowls of water for the frequent washing of hands. It was acceptable to toss unwanted scraps of food on the floor, which would later be cleaned up by the slaves or eaten by dogs. Belching after eating was also acceptable, but only a few would go so far as to use emetics or vomit into pots held by slaves so they could gorge themselves again.

In Rome adult males adopted the Greek custom of reclining on couches to dine, a posture denoting leisure (*otium*) and privilege. Women and children ate on chairs. According to both Varro and Valerius Maximus, even after men were reclining to dine, women continued to sit, as this was regarded a more modest posture; this distinctive pose is depicted on funerary monuments.

But unlike Greek women, Roman wives dined in the company of their husbands. In the preface to his *Lives of Eminent Commanders*, Cornelius Nepos (1st c. BC) writes: "For what Roman is ashamed to bring his wife to a feast, or whose consort does not occupy the best room in the house, and live in the midst of company?" (Watson, 307). And some women did recline to eat with men, though this posture conveyed erotic possibilities. The Roman comic playwright Plautus describes prostitutes reclining with men. Ovid describes how such close quarters afforded opportunities for sexual intimacy. A painting on the walls of a newly discovered *triclinium* room at Pompeii (IX.12.6–8) depicts intoxicated women reclining against males with bared chests.

Invited guests were expected to have bathed and to have changed into loose dining garments (*vestis cenatoria*) before the *cena*. When entering the house, they took care to step over the threshold with their right foot first. Their shoes would be removed by slaves before they reclined on the couches. The host and guests reclined propped up on their left elbows on couches; there were typically three couches in a *triclinium*, or dining room, usually with three people to a couch.

It was not uncommon for different qualities of food to be served to guests, depending upon their social standing. As Juvenal complained,

> The greatest houses are always full of arrogant slaves: here's another. Grumbling audibly, he proffers bread that is hardly breakable, hunks of solid dough that are already mouldy, to keep your molars busy without letting you bite. But for the master is reserved soft snowy-white bread kneaded from fine flour.
> (*Sat.* 5.66–71; cf. Martial, *Ep.* 3.60; Pliny the Younger, *Ep.* 2.6.1–2)

The host would often give out *apophoretae*, small gifts such as pins, combs, and vases, for guests to take home. Guests were also allowed to take home leftover food in the napkins they brought with them, although this custom could be abused. Martial protested:

> Whatever is served, you sweep it up from this side and that; teats of sow's udder, rib of pork, a woodcock meant for two, half a mullet and a whole pike, side of lamprey, leg of fowl, pigeon dripping with its gravy. When these have been secreted in a greasy cloth, they are handed to your boy to be taken home!
> (*Ep.* 2.37)

Not all wealthy Romans were quite so decadent, however. The emperor Augustus (27 BC–AD 14) was a light eater who preferred plain food. According to Suetonius, "He particularly liked coarse bread [*secundarium panem*], small fishes, hand-made moist cheese, and green figs of the second crop; and he would eat even before dinner, wherever and whenever he felt hungry" (*Aug.* 76). Augustus often ate alone before a dinner party.

Other emperors, such as Claudius and Nero, were known as gluttons. Especially egregious was Vitellius, one of a series of four emperors who held the throne in AD 69 after Nero's suicide. According to Suetonius,

> Being besides a man of an appetite that was not only boundless, but also regardless of time or decency, he could never refrain, even when he was sacrificing or making a journey, from snatching bits of meat and cake amid the altars, almost from the very fire, and devouring them, on the spot; and in the cookshops along the road, viands smoking hot or even those left over from the day before and partly consumed. (*Vit.* 13)

Clodius Albinus (r. AD 196–197) was also remarkable for his ravenous appetite:

> Albinus was a glutton—so much so, in fact, that he would devour more fruit than the mind of man can believe. For Cordus says that when hungry he devoured five hundred dried figs ... one hundred Campanian peaches, ten Ostian melons, twenty pounds weight of Labican grapes, one hundred figpeckers, and four hundred oysters! (*S.H.A.* [Clodius Albinus 11])

E. THE JEWISH WORLD

For Jewish homes bread was essential for meals; "to eat bread" meant "to have a meal." It was forbidden to set a pitcher of water on bread or to throw away crumbs if they were "as large as an olive." Bread was not to be cut, but had to be broken by hand.

The rabbis held that "one must not taste anything until he has [first] recited a benediction [over it], as Scripture states, *The earth is the Lord's and all that it contains* (Ps 24:1). One who derives benefit from this world [by eating its produce] without first having recited a benediction has committed sacrilege" (*t. Ber.* 4:1). Disputes arose over whether separate blessings were required for each item and whether a blessing needed to be said out loud (*b. Ber.* 15b). The host was not to break bread until the guests had finished saying the "Amen." Nor were the guests to begin eating until the one who had first broken the bread had tasted it (*b. Ber.* 47a).

All vegetables, both cultivated and wild, were considered kosher. At least thirty kinds of vegetables were known in Palestine. Pulse, or edible seeds, such as lentils, chickpeas, and vetch, are frequently mentioned in the Talmud. Cabbage, onions, and garlic were popular. According to the Talmud, "Our Rabbis taught: Five things were said of garlic: It satiates, it keeps the body warm, it brightens up the face, it increases semen, and it kills parasites in the bowels. Some say that it fosters love and removes jealousy" (*b. B. Qam.* 82a). Husbands were advised to eat garlic as an aphrodisiac prior to performing their conjugal duty on Friday night.

Observant Jews' refusal to eat pork led to their martyrdom during the persecution led by Antiochus IV (1 Macc 1:47; 2 Macc 6:18–19; 7:1). But archaeologists have found some pig bones at settlements in Galilee that were predominantly Jewish in the Hellenistic and Roman eras: 18 to 20 percent of the bones were pig bones at Tel Anafa. It is possible that some non-observant Jews ate pork.

Following the traditions of the Pharisees (the main Jewish sect that survived the destruction of the temple in AD 70), the rabbis considered food that came into contact with a source of impurity to be impure; in addition, they considered one who ate impure food also to have become impure. The Pharisees formed dining circles known as *ḥăvûrôt*, whose members, the *ḥăvērîm*, did not associate with those they considered to be common and ignorant (whom they referred to as *ʿam hāʾāreṣ*, lit., "people of the land"), since such persons might not observe proper rules, e.g., those related to tithing. The Mishnah declares: "He that undertakes to be trustworthy must give tithe from what he eats and from what he sells and from what he buys [to sell again]; and he may not be the guest of an *Am-haaretz*" (*m. Demai* 2:2).

Those who were poor scavenged for food or begged. They ate inferior bread made with bran and could not afford meat or even vegetables, except wild plants. The Talmud speaks of a poor man who after work comes home to eat his bread with salt (*b. Ber.* 2b). Some communities provided a "soup kitchen" for the poor: "A poor man that is journeying from place to place should be given not less than one loaf worth a *pondion*. . . . If he stays over the Sabbath he should be given food enough for three meals. If a man has food enough for two meals he may not take aught from the [Paupers'] Dish" (*m. Pe'ah* 8.7). On the other hand, the wealthy ate meat, white bread, and sweets.

Jewish women, children, and slaves often dined separately from men, but there were occasions when women dined with men. Sirach warns, "Never dine with another man's wife, nor revel with her at wine; or your heart may turn aside to her, and in blood you may be plunged into destruction" (Sir 9:9). Jewish men adopted the Greco-Roman custom of reclining at the evening meal. Reclining, which symbolized freedom from slavery, became obligatory for men when celebrating the Passover. The Hebrew verb *sbb*, "recline," is used in the Tannaitic corpus only once with reference to a woman.

The Talmud decrees: "A woman in her husband's [house] need not recline; but if she is an important woman she must recline" (*b. Pesaḥ.* 108a). In a discussion of liquids made impure through contact with Gentiles,

> Raba said: If Israelites were reclining at table with a Gentile harlot, the wine is permitted because while lust would be strong in them a desire for *yen nesek* [wine part of which had been offered to an idol] would not be strong in them. If, however, Gentiles were reclining at table with an Israelite harlot the wine [which belongs to her] is prohibited. Why?—Because she would be held in contempt by them and be influenced to follow them. (*b. ʿAbod. Zar.* 69b–70a)

This teaching was based on the likelihood in each case that the wine might be made impure by being used in the Greco-Roman rite of libation. In the first case, although Jewish men might dine with a "Gentile harlot," they would still have kept kosher by refraining from touching the wine. On the other hand, the rabbis assumed that a "Jewish harlot" dining with Gentile men would have been pressured to drink the defiled wine.

On the whole, Jewish sources strongly stressed the role that *kashrut* (observance of kosher rules about clean and unclean foods) play in keeping the Jews from interacting with idolatrous heathens. In the apocryphal Additions to Esther, Esther proclaims: "And thy servant has not eaten at Haman's table, and I have not honored the king's feast or drunk the wine of the libations" (Add Esth 14:17). When Holofernes orders his own food and wine to be served to the Jewish woman Judith, she says, "I cannot eat it lest it be an offense; but I will be provided from the things I have brought with me" (Jdt 12:1–2). Tobit claims, "Now when I was carried away captive to Nineveh, all my brethren and my relatives ate the food of the Gentiles [*tōn artōn tōn ethnōn*]; but I kept myself from eating it, because I remembered God with all my heart" (Tob 1:10–12).

The *Letter of Aristeas*, which relates the miraculous translation of the Hebrew Scriptures into Greek, reports that the high priest Eleazar explained to Ptolemy II: "So, to prevent our being perverted by contact with others or by mixing with bad influences, he [Moses] hedged us in on all sides with strict observances connected with meat and drink and touch and hearing and sight, after the manner of the Law" (*Let. Aris.* 142–43).

Greek and Roman authors were thus correct in their perception that Jewish food customs erected a barrier against their interaction with non-Jews. Tacitus observed that "they sit apart at meals" (*Hist.* 5.5). According to Philostratus,

> The Jews cut themselves off long ago, not only from the Romans, but from all mankind, since people who have devised an unsociable way of life, with no meals, libations, prayers, or sacrifices in common with other men, have moved further away from us than Susa, Bactria, and the Indians beyond that. (*Vit. Apoll.* 5.33)

Despite the Roman perception that fasting was a characteristic trait of the Jews (Martial, *Ep.* 4.4; Suetonius, *Aug.* 76.2; Tacitus, *Hist.* 5.4), apart from fasting on the Day of Atonement, Jewish sources advocated moderation in eating and counseled against extreme fasting. Fasting was forbidden on the Sabbath. One rabbi counseled: "Eat a third and drink a third and leave a third for when you get angry, and then you will have had your fill." Another taught: "In a meal which you enjoy indulge not too freely, and do not wait too long to consult nature" (*b. Giṭ.* 70a). Furthermore, the rabbis ruled that "a scholar may not afflict himself by fasting because he lessens thereby his heavenly work," and "the young scholar who would afflict himself by fasting let a dog devour his meal!" (*b. Taʿan.* 11b).

In addition to normal Jewish moderation and *kashrut* observance, Jewish sects such as the Therapeutae in Egypt described by Philo, the Essenes in Judea described by Josephus, and the Qumran community revealed by the Dead Sea Scrolls, whom many scholars identify with the Essenes, had their own distinctive rules about what and how they ate.

In a sharp contrast to the gluttony of Romans, Philo describes a remarkable community of celibate and ascetic Jewish men and women in Egypt, called the *Therapeutae* (*Contempl.* 53–55). He writes, "None of them would put food or drink to his lips before sunset" (ibid., 34). Furthermore, "they eat nothing costly, only common bread with salt for a relish flavoured further by the daintier with hyssop, and their drink is spring water. . . . Therefore they eat enough to keep from hunger and drink enough to keep from thirst but abhor surfeiting as a malignant enemy both to body and soul" (ibid., 37).

The Qumran texts stipulate that a prospective member of the community had to undergo a year of probation before he could "touch the pure food of the general membership" (1QS VI, 16), and a second year before he could touch the "the drink of the general membership" (1QS VI, 20–21). The members evidently immersed themselves in water and put on white garments before eating. For every meal a *minyān* (quorum) of ten men and a priest to bless the bread and the wine was required (1QSa II, 17–22). The discovery of hundreds of small plates, bowls, and cups in the pantry of the Qumran community indicates that members ate from individual dishes rather than from a common bowl. The lack of couches also indicates that they sat rather than reclined. The community looked forward to an eschatological banquet presided over by the priestly and Davidic messiahs.

According to Josephus, the Essenes worked until the fifth hour (about 11 a.m.) before they broke their fast. The initiated members bathed in cold water and donned linen clothes and then gathered to dine in a refectory. "When they have taken their seats in silence, the baker serves out the loaves to them in order, and the cook sets before each one [a] plate with a single course. Before meat the priest says a grace, and none may partake until after the prayer" (*J. W.* 2.130–131). In the evening they would eat supper in the same manner.

F. THE CHRISTIAN WORLD

Food and eating came to bear important theological significance for several different reasons during the early history of Christianity. In the centuries before Christianity was recognized as a tolerated religion in the empire (AD 313), Christians lived and ate in a polytheistic context where foods like meat and wine were commonly offered to the gods.

The *Didache*, one of the earliest Christian texts, exhorts believers: "Now concerning food, bear what you are able, but in any case keep strictly away from meat sacrificed to idols [*eidōlothyton*], for it involves the worship of dead gods" (*Did.* 6.3). Many Christians appear to have obeyed this injunction, as indicated by one of the earliest Roman witnesses to Christianity, a letter sent to the emperor Trajan by Pliny the Younger, who was the governor of Bithynia (AD 112–114) in northwest Anatolia. Pliny had made inquiries about Christianity, which had many adherents in his province. In one passage, he reports to the emperor:

> It is not only the towns, but villages and rural districts too which are infected through contact with this wretched cult. I think though that it is still possible

for it to be checked and directed to better ends, for there is no doubt that people have begun to throng the temples which had been almost entirely deserted for a long time; the sacred rites which had been allowed to lapse are being performed again, and flesh of sacrificial victims is on sale everywhere, though up till recently scarcely anyone could be found to buy it. (*Ep. Tra.* 10.96)

That is, until the governor's persecution, the numerous Christians in his province had abstained from buying meat that had been offered in pagan sacrifices.

The refusal to eat meat offered to idols or to pour libations in honor of the emperors led to the martyrdom of numerous Christians. Christians in Carthage in Tertullian's day (ca. AD 200) refused to eat blood, as we learn from his *Apology*, which is addressed to Roman officials: "You tempt Christians with sausages of blood, just because you are perfectly aware that the thing by which you thus try to get them to transgress they hold unlawful" (*Apol.* 9.13–14).

Christian opposition to sacrifices was so widespread that the emperor Decius (AD 250) used sacrifice as a test of religious loyalty to the Rome. To escape the penalty of death imposed by this emperor, Christians needed to have a document called a *libellus*, which certified: "I have always sacrificed to the gods, and now in your presence in accordance with the edict I have made sacrifice, and poured a libation, and partaken of the sacred victims" (Stevenson, 228). Some Christians tried to compromise by purchasing *libelli* without having actually sacrificed and eaten the meat of the victims.

Some pagans accused Christians of "atheism," claiming that they committed immorality and even cannibalism at their communal meals. Tertullian relates: "We are accused of observing a holy rite in which we kill a little child and then eat it; in which, after the feast, we practise incest" (*Apol.* 7.1). Tertullian responds to the erroneous charge by contrasting the drunken orgies of pagan banquets with the simplicity and sobriety of the Christian *agapē* meal:

> Whatever it costs, our outlay in the name of piety is gain, since with the good things of the feast we benefit the needy; not as it is with you, do parasites aspire to the glory of satisfying their licentious propensities, selling themselves for a belly-feast to all disgraceful treatment—but as it is with God himself, a peculiar respect is shown to the lowly. . . . As much is eaten as satisfies the cravings of hunger; as much is drunk as befits the chaste. . . . After manual ablution, and the bringing in of lights, each is asked to stand forth and sing, as he can, a hymn to God, either one from the holy Scriptures or one of his own composing—a proof of the measure of our drinking. (*Apol.* 39.16–18)

The *agapē* ("love") meal (cf. Jude 12) was originally linked with the Eucharist, but by the third century the Eucharist was celebrated without the meal, and the meal served a primarily social function.

Clement gives detailed instructions as to how Christians should eat:

> From all slavish habits and excess we must abstain, and touch what is set before us in a decorous way; keeping the hand and couch and chin free of stains; preserving the grace of the countenance undisturbed, and committing no indecorum in the act of swallowing; but stretching out the hand at intervals in an orderly manner. (*Paed.* 2.1)

He also advises:

> Be the first to stop for the sake of regimen; and, if seated in the midst of several people, do not stretch out your hand before them. You must never rush forward under the influence of gluttony nor must you, though desirous, reach out your hand till some time, inasmuch as by greed one shows an uncontrolled appetite. Nor are you, in the midst of the repast, to exhibit yourselves hugging your food like wild beasts; nor helping yourselves to too much sauce, for man is not by nature a sauce-consumer, but a bread-eater.
> (*Paed.* 2.7)

If one must hiccup, Clement advises, let him do it silently (*Paed.* 2.2). And servants, in his opinion, should be summoned by words and not by whistling (*Paed.* 2.7).

Fasting from certain foods was an important part of early Christian asceticism, a term that derives from the Greek word for athletic training. Some early Christians chose to abstain from all but the poorest fare as a way of training themselves to embrace humility and suffering, or in order to learn self-control. For some, this meant eschewing meat and other animal products such as milk and eggs, as well as wine, whether for their entire life or on certain days of the week. Eusebius, citing Hegesippus, claimed that James, the brother of Jesus, "drank no wine or strong drink, nor did he eat flesh" (*Hist. eccl.* 2.23.5). The Encratites, ascetic followers of Tatian, renounced both meat and wine. Like several other Christian authorities, Clement of Alexandria praised vegetarianism. He cited the tradition that Matthew the Evangelist "partook of seeds, and nuts, and vegetables, without flesh" (*Paed.* 2.1).

One of the earliest references to fasting after the NT appears in the *Didache*, where Christians are exhorted: "But do not let your fasts coincide with those of the hypocrites [the Jews]. They fast on Monday and Thursday, so you must fast on Wednesday and Friday" (*Did.* 8.1). It is noteworthy that the voluminous writings of the Alexandrian fathers Clement and Origen do not mention fasting at all. Clement, however, does exhort Christians not to "live that they may eat," and recommends moderation as a way of conquering gluttony, explaining that "the Instructor [Christ] enjoins us to eat that we may live. For neither is food our business, nor is pleasure our aim; but both are on account of our life here, which the Word is training up to immortality" (*Paed.* 2.1).

Other Christians went beyond the practice of moderation, engaging in extreme fasts. Tertullian, after his conversion to the rigorist Montanist sect, wrote (ca. AD 208) a spirited defense of their practice of compulsory and prolonged fasting and xerophagy, the eating of "food unmoistened by any flesh, and by any juiciness, and by any kind of specially succulent fruit" (*Jejun.* 1). He held that fasting could atone for sins (*Jejun.* 3).

Later on, the ascetic life came to be particularly emphasized by the influential monastic movement that arose in Egypt in the late third and fourth centuries AD. This movement was partly inspired by the example of the solitary hermit St. Antony and by the establishment of cenobitic (communal) monasteries for men and women by St. Pachomius. *The Life of Antony*, written by Antony's contemporary Athanasius (ca. AD 295–373), inspired many Christians, including Jerome, to follow Antony's ascetic example by living in the desert as an eremite (from Gk. *erēmos*, "desert"). There the early monks and nuns kept an extreme fasting regimen. According to Athanasius, Antony "ate once a day, after sunset, sometimes once in two days, and often even in four. His food was bread and salt, his drink, water only" (*Vit. Ant.* 7). Despite his extremely abstemious diet, Antony lived to be over a hundred (ca. AD 251–356). Jerome claimed: "I have seen and still see in . . . the desert . . . monks of whom one was shut up for thirty years and lived on barley bread and muddy water, while another in an old cistern . . . kept himself alive on five dried figs a day" (*Vita Pauli*, 6).

After his conversion from paganism, Pachomius (ca. 286–346) lived at first with an older monk, Palamon. His biography records, "Sometimes they ate charlock [field mustard] without oil and vinegar and many times they mixed ashes into the salt" (*Vita Pachomii*, 7; Athanassakis, 11). Later, in the numerous monastic communities for men and for women that Pachomius established in the Nile Valley, it was customary to have two meals: the main meal during the working day, and a lighter one in the evening. The basic diet consisted of bread and cooked vegetables, which were eaten in silence. *Tragēmatia*, a dessert of dried fruit, was also distributed to the monks after supper.

Palladius, who observed the Egyptian monasteries later in the fourth century, noted that, in addition to bread and vegetables, monks and nuns were allowed to eat olives, cheese, and figs. Some monks, however, abstained from what was available. Evagrius said to Palladius: "I did not touch lettuce or any vegetable greens, or fruit" (Palladius, *Hist. Laus.*, Evagrius, 12; cited in Meyer, 114).

Monks, who fasted twice a week, believed that a satisfied stomach might lead to lust, and therefore promoted fasting as an exercise that frightened the devil and brought one close to God. One of the most ardent defenders of monasticism and the celibate life, Jerome, was also a proponent of ascetic practices. In a polemical work entitled *Adversus Jovinianum* (*Against Jovinian*), he contested the views of a former monk who claimed that celibacy was not superior to marriage and who held that fasting was no better than eating food with thanksgiving. Jerome conceded that God had allowed the eating of flesh after the flood (*Jov.* 1.18), for those who needed physical strength, but he argued, "But our religion does not train boxers, athletes, sailors, soldiers, or ditchers, but followers of wisdom, who devote themselves to the worship of God, and know why they were created and are in the world from which they are impatient to depart" (*Jov.* 2.6). Jerome linked satiety to sexuality (*Jov.* 2.7).

Jerome wrote a series of letters encouraging women, young and old, to embrace celibacy and to fortify their resolve by discipline in their diets. In a letter to Eustochium, written in AD 384, Jerome declared: "Not that the Creator and Lord of all takes pleasure in a rumbling and empty stomach, or in fevered lungs; but . . . these are indispensable as means to the preservation of chastity" (*Epist.* 22.11). Writing to a widow named Furia in AD 394, Jerome explained: "In saying this, I do not of course condemn food which God created to be enjoyed with thanksgiving [1 Tim 4:40], but I seek to remove from youths and girls what are incentives to sensual pleaure" (*Epist.* 54.9).

In AD 403, in a letter to Laeta to advise her on the education of her young daughter Paula, Jerome wrote:

> Let her food be herbs and wheaten bread with now and then one or two small fishes. . . . Let her meals always leave her hungry and able on the moment to begin reading or chanting. I strongly disapprove—especially for those of tender years—of long and immoderate fasts in which week is added to week and even oil and apples are forbidden as food. (*Ep.* 107.10)

Gnostic Christians incorporated ritual feasts into their religious life. Manichaeanism was an important Gnostic movement founded by Mani (AD 216–276), a Persian living in Mesopotamia. His teachings spread widely, as far east as China and as far west as North Africa. Manichaean cosmology held that Light and Darkness are intermingled and can become separated once more through the actions of the faithful. The Manichaeans had two separate categories of disciples: (1) the elect, who were celibate, and who did not eat meat or drink wine, and (2) the auditors, or laymen. The auditors offered daily gifts of fruit, cucumbers, and melons, which they believed contained trapped particles of light, to the elect, who were believed to release these particles into the Milky Way by burping!

BIBLIOGRAPHY: A. N. Athanassakis, trans., *The Life of Pachomius* (1975); M. Beer, *Taste or Taboo: Dietary Choices in Antiquity* (2009); J. Bottéro, *Textes culinaires mésopotamiens* (1995); A. Brenner and J. W. van Heuter, ed., *Food and Drink in the Biblical Worlds* (Semeia 86; 2001); D. Brothwell and P. Brothwell, *Food in Antiquity: A Survey of the Diet of Early Peoples* (exp. ed., 1998); J. D. Brumberg-Kraus, "Meals as Midrash: A Survey of Ancient Meals in Jewish Studies Scholarship," in *Food and Judaism*, ed. L. J. Greenspoon, R. A. Simkins, and G. Shapiro (2005), 297–317; J. Burton, "Women's Commensuality in the Ancient Greek World," *GR* 45.2 (1998), 143–65; A. T. Cheung, *Idol Food in Corinth: Jewish Background and Pauline Legacy* (1999); J. S. Cooper, "Structure, Humor and Satire in the Poor Man of Nippur," *JCS* 27.3 (1975), 163–74; K. E. Corley, *Private Women, Public Meals: Social Conflict in the Synoptic Tradition* (1993); R. I. Curtis, "In Defense of Garum," *CJ* 78.3 (1983), 232–40; A. Dalby, *Siren Feasts: A History of Food and Gastronomy in Greece* (1995); W. J. Darby, P. Ghalioungui, and L. Grivetti, *Food: The Gift of Osiris* (2 vols., 1977); A. W. Day, "Eating Before the Lord: A Theology of Food According to Deuteronomy," *JETS* 57.1 (2014), 85–98; M. Delcor, "Repas cultuels esséniens et thérapeutes," *RevQ* 6.3 (1968), 401–25; G. Feeley-Harnik, *The Lord's Table: The Meaning of Food in Early Judaism and Christianity* (1994); B. Flower and E. Rosenbaum, trans., *The Roman Cookery Book* (1958); J. Fotopoulos, *Food Offered to Idols in Roman Corinth* (2003); B. K. Gold and J. F. Donahue, ed., *Roman Dining* (AJP 124.3; 2005); P. D. Gooch, *Dangerous Food: 1 Corinthians 8–10 in Its Context* (1993); M. Grant, *Galen on Food and Diet* (2000); V. E. Grimm, *From Feasting to Fasting, The Evolution of Sin: Attitudes to Food in Late Antiquity* (1996); C. Grocock and S. Grainger, *Apicius: A Critical Edition* (2006); C. King, trans., *Musonius Rufus: Lectures and Sayings*, ed. W. B. Irvine (2011); S. N. Kramer, *The Sumerians: Their History, Culture, and Character* (1963); N. MacDonald, *What Did the Ancient Israelites Eat?* (2008); R. T. Meyer, trans., *Palladius: The Lausiac History* (1964); J. Moskala, "Categorization and Evaluation of Different Kinds of Interpretation of the Laws of Clean and Unclean Animals in Leviticus 11," *Biblical Research* 46 (2001), 5–41; D. E. Neel, *The Food and Feasts of Jesus* (2012); D. Newton, *Deity and Diet: The Dilemma of Sacrificial Food at Corinth* (1998); I. Nielsen and H. S. Nielsen, ed., *Meals in a Social Context* (2001); F. Rosner, "Eating Fish and Meat Together: Is There a Danger?" *Tradition* 35.2 (2001), 36–44; S. Schorch, " 'A Young Goat in Its Mother's Milk'? Understanding An Ancient Prohibition," *VT* 60.1 (2010), 116–30; J. Scurlock, *Sourcebook for Ancient Mesopotamian Medicine* (2014); D. Sharon, "The Literary Functions of Eating and Drinking in Hebrew Bible Narrative," PhD diss., Jewish Theological Seminary of America (1995); S. Sherratt, "Feasting in Homeric Epic," *Hesperia* 73.2 (2004), 301–37; F. J. Simoons, *Eat Not This Flesh: Food*

Avoidances from Prehistory to the Present (2nd ed., 1994); D. E. Smith and H. E. Taussig, ed., *Meals in the Early Christian World: Social Formation, Experimentation, and Conflict at the Table* (2012); C. Spencer, *The Heretic's Feast: A History of Vegetarianism* (1995); J. Stevenson, ed., *A New Eusebius: Documents Illustrative of the History of the Church to A.D. 337* (1960); U. Verhoeven, *Grillen, Kochen, Backen im Alltag und im Ritual Altägyptiens* (1984); J. S. Watson, trans., *Justin, Cornelius Nepos, and Eutropius* (1853); J. Wilkins and S. Hill, trans., *Archestratus: Fragments from the Life of Luxury* (2011); J. C. Wright, *The Mycenaean Feast* (2004); E. Yamauchi, "The 'Daily Bread' Motif in Antiquity," *WTJ* 28 (1966), 145–56.

RKH and EMY

See also ALCOHOLIC BEVERAGES, ANIMAL HUSBANDRY, BANQUETS, BIRDS, DWELLINGS, FISH & FISHING, FOOD PRODUCTION, MILK & MILK PRODUCTS, and WILD ANIMALS & HUNTING.

FOOD PRODUCTION

The availability of cereals, vegetables, fruits, and meat varied greatly throughout the ancient world, though methods of processing such foods remained similar throughout the centuries.

A. THE OLD TESTAMENT

The largest source of carbohydrates in antiquity was cereal grains. The KJV employs the word "corn" to render various Hebrew and Greek terms referring to grain, and this usage of the word continues in British English. In the United States, however, "corn" refers to Indian maize, which was unknown in the ancient Near East.

The Heb. word *ḥiṭṭâ*, identified with *Triticum aestivum*, was the ordinary summer or winter wheat. Heb. *kussemet* (pl. *kussĕmîm*), which occurs only in three passages (Exod 9:32; Isa 28:25; Ezek 4:9), should not be translated "spelt," but should be identified with emmer wheat (*Triticum sativum* or *Triticum dicoccum*), which is a hulled variety of wheat (as opposed to a "naked" variety); that is; even after threshing and winnowing, it needed pounding to separate the grains from their hulls. Wheat, which needs twenty to twenty-five inches of rain to grow, was sown in November and harvested in May or June. The completion of the wheat harvest was celebrated by the Festival of Weeks (Deut 16:1–12).

Barley (Heb. *śĕ'ōrâ*, pl. *śĕ'ōrîm*) was a cereal that ranked in importance second only to wheat. Because barley had a shorter growing season than wheat, and could flourish in a less fertile environment, it was also considerably cheaper to buy. There were several species of barley in the Near East, with the spring barley (*Hordeum vulgare* L.) being most common. The harvest of this kind of barley was mentioned in the tenth-century BC Gezer Calendar ("his month is barley harvest," line 4; cf. Ruth 1:22) as occurring in April and May, about two weeks before the wheat harvest. But a winter barley (*Hordeum hexastichon*) produced good crops in the Jordan Valley and on the uplands of Transjordan to the east of Palestine. Like emmer wheat, barley was a hulled grain. Being less expensive than wheat (2 Kgs 7:1, 16), barley was used to feed animals (1 Kgs 4:28). It was sufficiently cheap for the poor to be able to afford it for making bread (Lev 23:22; Ruth 3:15), and was used in Israelite religious rites as a cereal offering (Num 5:15). The very poor used barley for this purpose (cf. 2 Kgs 4:42), but when possible they mixed it with other grains of rather better quality (cf. Ezek 4:9). Under ordinary circumstances barley was the normal food for horses and mules.

Millet (Heb. *dōḥan*), which is referred to once in the OT, was the grass that bore the smallest grains that could be used for flour. Being of comparatively poor quality, millet was often mixed with better-quality grains before being used as flour for bread. God commanded Ezekiel to use millet as an ingredient in a symbolic bread that would illustrate the conditions the Judahites would experience in exile (Ezek 4:9).

Grains could be roasted (*qālî*) and eaten (Ruth 2:14; 1 Sam 17:17), but they were ordinarily ground as flour for use as porridge or as dough for bread. The process of grinding wheat or barley into flour, which could occupy as many as three or four hours early in the morning, was usually done by women, who, kneeling on the ground, would do the grinding using a saddle quern, moving a loaf-shaped upper stone (usually of basalt) back and forth over a large flat lower stone. So necessary were millstones for everyday life in Israel that the law forbade them to be taken by creditors (Deut 24:6), lest a family should be deprived of food. A woman hurled the upper millstone, *pelaḥ rekeb* "the rider," upon Abimelech's head, crushing his skull (Judg 9:53).

Only in the fifth century BC was the more elaborate rotary mill, which consisted of two circular stones placed one above the other, developed. The upper stone had a concave surface that fit over the convex outer face of the lower stone, which for convenience was sometimes fixed to the ground. The two stones were connected by a central shaft, and the outer edge of the upper stone had a handle that enabled it to be rotated. The finished flour emerged from an opening in the upper stone, and tended to have fewer impurities than flour produced by the saddle quern, which was mostly used at ground level.

The common Hebrew word *leḥem* specifically denotes "bread" but can also refer to food in general. Leavened bread could only be made from wheat, which has sufficient gluten, a nitrogenous substance that captures the gas produced when dough with yeast is baked, to make the bread rise. The loaves eaten by the ancient Israelites were round and fairly flat. Though bread could remain edible for up to four days, it was baked daily (Jer 37:21). Unleavened bread (*maṣṣâ*) was required for the Passover week

(Exod 12:18–20). Such bread could be made relatively quickly by mixing flour, water, and some salt (Gen 18:6; 1 Sam 28:24). Yeast for leavened bread could come from the brewing of beer or fermented grape skins.

A day's supply of bread could be baked in about an hour's time with a clay oven called a *tannûr* (cf. modern Arab. *tabūn*). Such ovens, which are about three feet high, have been used in the Near East from the second millennium BC to the present. The fuel for heating the oven, which included kindling, leftovers from the pressing of olives, and often sun-dried animal-dung cakes (Ezek 4:12–15), was placed on the floor. Lumps of dough were slapped on the interior or exterior walls of the heated oven.

The bread that Ezekiel was commanded to eat included "wheat and barley, beans and lentils, millet and spelt" (Ezek 4:9). The Lord condemned the apostate women of Judah who kneaded dough and made cakes (*kawwānîm*) to offer to the Queen of Heaven (Jer 7:18). By the time of Jeremiah (6th c. BC), there were commercial bakeries in Jerusalem (Jer 37:21).

The twelve loaves (representing the twelve tribes of Israel) of the so-called "shewbread" (KJV), or, more accurately, "the bread of the presence" (Heb. *leḥem (hap-)pānîm*), were placed each Sabbath on a table in the tabernacle (Exod 25:30), and, later, in the holy of holies in the temple. The loaves were to be eaten by the priests (Lev 24:8–9), though on one occasion David requisitioned them from the priest Ahimelek for his hungry men (1 Sam 21:1–6).

Olive trees (Heb. sing. *zayit*), which take five years to mature and bear fruit only every other year, flourished in ancient Palestine despite its low precipitation and rocky soil. Olives were harvested from October to January. It is unlikely that the olives themselves were eaten in the OT era, as they were bitter unless they underwent proper processing, which only developed in the Hellenistic age. There is no reference to the eating of olives in the OT. Olive oil, however, was valuable as an element in cooking; in some cases it was mixed with flour in the baking of bread (Ezek 16:13). Olive oil was also used for lamps, and as an ointment. Palestine exported its valuable oil to Egypt and to Mesopotamia.

The OT contains no term for an olive press and only two references to the production of olive oil (Joel 2:24; Mic 6:16), but excavations have uncovered numerous structures for the pressing of oil, for example, at Tel Dan, Tel Beit Shemesh, and Tel Beit Mirsim. At the Philistine city of Ekron more than one hundred presses were discovered, which could have processed one thousand tons of oil for export.

Olives placed in bags or baskets were crushed with a beam anchored to a niche in a wall and weighted with a stone. The first pressing yielded the best or "virgin" oil, which was skimmed as it floated on the surface of the hot water poured on the mash. Less desirable oils were produced by subsequent pressings.

When the twelve Israelite spies explored the land of Canaan, at the valley of Eshkol (which means "cluster") "they cut off a branch bearing a single cluster of grapes. Two of them carried it on a pole between them, along with some pomegranates and figs" (Num 13:23). In addition to being pressed for wine, grapes were also eaten fresh (Num 6:3; Jer 31:29) or dried and eaten as raisins (1 Sam 25:18; 2 Sam 16:1; 1 Chr 12:41). Those consecrated as Nazirites were prohibited from drinking wine and from eating grapes and raisins (Num 6:1–3).

Figs (Heb. sing. *tĕʾēnâ*) were an important source of sweet nourishment for the ancient Israelites. Because they had broad leaves, fig trees were valued for the shade they provided (1 Kgs 4:25). They produced several crops, in June, August, and November. Figs could be eaten fresh (Jer 24:2) or dried and made into cakes, which the biblical text records being eaten, for example, by travelers and warriors (1 Sam 25:18; 1 Sam 30:12; 1 Chr 12:40). According to the biblical portrait of the messianic age, each man will be able to sit under his own vine and his own fig tree (Mic 4:4; Zech 3:10). The inferior figs of the wild sycamore tree (Heb. *šiqmâ*) served as food for the poor. Part of Amos's profession was to incise sycamore figs to hasten their ripening (Amos 7:14).

Another source of sweetness in ancient Israel was the date, the fruit of the date palm (Heb. *tāmār*). Dates could be processed to produce both honey and wine. The main sweetener in antiquity, however, was honey from either wild or domesticated bees.

Palestine was an abundant source of fruits (cf. Deut 8:8). So valuable were the trees on which fruits grew that the Mosaic law prohibited their destruction in time of war (Deut 20:19–20). On account of their many seeds, pomegranates (Heb. sing. *rimmôn*) were a symbol of fertility (Song 4:3, 13), and they were also a popular religious symbol (Exod 28:33; 39:24–26). The OT also mentions apples and apple trees (Heb. *tappuaḥ*) in several places (e.g., Prov 25:11; Song 2:5; 8:5; Joel 1:12).

Only three kinds of nut are mentioned in the OT. Two of these, pistachios (*boṭnîm*) and almonds (*šĕqēdîm*), were sent as part of a gift package by Jacob to an Egyptian official, who, unbeknownst to him, was his son Joseph (Gen 43:11). Almonds also appear as the product of Aaron's budding staff (Num 17:23). The almond tree (*šaqēd*; Ecc 12:5; Jer 1:11) was noteworthy for blossoming as early as January. The walnut (*ʾĕgôz*) is referred to but once in the OT, in Song 6:11.

Vegetables provide vitamins, and legumes proteins, that are important to the human diet. The famished Esau sold his birthright to Jacob in exchange for red lentil stew (*nĕzîd ʿădāšîm*; Gen 25:34). Lentils, which could be dried and also used in cooking, were an important kind of pulse, or edible seed, as they provided essential nutrients. When the Israelites were provided manna in the wilderness, they recalled with regret "the cucumbers, melons, leeks, onions and garlic" that they had eaten in Egypt (Num 11:5; cf. Deut 11:10–11). In Palestine the Israelites had beans (*pôl*) in addition to lentils (2 Sam 17:28; Ezek 4:9).

Proverbs 15:17 ("Better a small serving of vegetables with love than a fattened calf with hatred") compares ordinary food with the highly valued but rare treat of meat by stressing that love with the former is to be esteemed more than the latter without love. In order not to be defiled by the food and wine of Nebuchadnezzar's court, Daniel and his companions asked to be served only vegetables and water, and as a result of this diet they "looked healthier and better nourished than any of the young men who ate the royal food" (Dan 1:16).

References to nets and snares (Job 18:8–10) indicate that wild game such as deer and gazelles were trapped in ancient Israel. Isaac loved the tasty meat that Esau acquired for him with his bow and arrow (Gen 27:3–4). Traps were set to capture birds (Amos 3:5). "Choice fowl" are listed among the foods served at Solomon's table (1 Kgs 4:23), perhaps a reference to fattened geese. The eggs of birds such as partridges were gathered and eaten (Isa 10:14; Jer 17:11). There are no references in the OT to hens, but a seal found at Tell en-Nasbeh, dated ca. 600 BC, depicts a fighting cock.

Abraham served veal to his mysterious guests (Gen 18:7) and Gideon served the angel of the Lord who visited him goat meat (Judg 6:19). A lamb was slaughtered for each family during the celebration of Passover (Exod 12:3–5). Meat was normally boiled as part of a stew (1 Sam 2:13–14), but the Passover lamb had to be roasted and not boiled (Exod 12:9). In sharp contrast to the prevalence of the remains of pigs along the Philistine coast, there is a notable absence of pig bones in the Judean highlands, which reflects the biblical prohibition on pork.

Salt (*melaḥ*) could be used to flavor food (Job 6:6), and it was to be added to all grain offerings (Lev 2:+13). It could be readily obtained from the Salt Sea (Heb. *yām hammelaḥ*), now known as the Dead Sea. Covenants were sealed by meals that included salt, hence the expression "covenant of salt" (Num 18:19; 2 Chr 13:5). The phrase "we are under obligation to the palace" (NIV) in Ezra 4:14 literally reads "we eat the salt of the palace."

Only a few other spices are mentioned in the OT. The Bible describes manna as appearing white like coriander (Heb. *gad*) (Exod 16:31). Isaiah 28:27 refers to the processing of caraway (*qeṣaḥ*) and cumin (*kammōn*). Other spices such as saffron (*karkōm*) and imported cinnamon (*qinnāmôn*) (Song 4:14) were used as aromatics in perfumes rather than as condiments in food. The primary sweetener in antiquity was honey (*dĕbaš*). Boiling grape juice or date juice could also produce a sweet syrup.

In ancient Israel the women of the house would get up early (cf. Prov 31:15) to grind the grain for flour, to bake bread for the day. Breakfast might have consisted of porridge made of grain mixed with ground chickpeas, and lunch might have consisted of parched grain, with bread dipped in vinegar (Ruth 2:14). The main meal was dinner, which took place after work and which might consist of *nāzîd* "stew" with vegetables and some meat (Gen 25:29; 2 Kgs 4:38–40; Hag 2:12).

B. THE NEW TESTAMENT

In the Sermon on the Mount Jesus teaches his disciples not to be anxious since their heavenly Father, who feeds the birds of the sky, will all the more care for their needs (Matt 6:25–27; cf. vss. 31–32). In the Lord's Prayer Jesus teaches his followers to ask for their "daily (*epiousios*) bread" (Matt 6:11‖Luke 11:3). Since the word *epiousios* only occurs in these two verses, its meaning is debated. Some have suggested on the basis of possible etymologies that the word may have meant either "super-substantial" or "bread for the morrow," pointing to the eschatological banquet. But since bread was baked daily, the term probably implied food that was necessary for subsistence.

When Jesus, after having fasted for forty days, was tempted by the devil to transform stones into bread, he responded, "Man shall not live on bread alone, but on every word that comes from the mouth of God" (Matt 4:4; cf. Luke 4:4) citing Deut 8:3. After miraculously feeding five thousand men and additional women and children, Jesus declared that he was the "bread of life" (John 6:35, 48, 51).

Jesus spoke of the growth of seeds (Mark 4:26–29) and the (wheat) seed dying to produce new life (John 12:24; cf. 1 Cor 15:37). A number of Jesus's parables deal with the process of growing food, such as the Parable of the Sower (Matt 13:3–8), and the Parable of the Tares (Matt 13:24–30). Jesus's disciples were criticized for plucking grains of wheat or barley (Matt 12:1–2) on the Sabbath. Jesus defended them by citing the example of David, who was given consecrated bread to eat (Matt 12:3–4).

By NT times, rotary stone mills and mills using levers had replaced stone querns, but women were still responsible for operating the mills (Matt 24:41). Women also kneaded dough with yeast (Luke 13:21). One of Jesus's parables deals with leaven (Luke 13:20–21). The poor in this period ate barley loaves, which were not leavened (John 6:9). In antiquity bread was never sliced, but was always broken into pieces (Luke 24:35; Acts 20:7).

On one occasion, when Jesus was hungry and found only leaves on a fig tree, he cursed it and caused it to wither (Matt 21:18–21). On another occasion, he used the development of the fig tree as a sign of the dawning of future events (Matt 24:32–33).

Cinnamon is mentioned in the OT (Heb. *qinnāmôn*; Exod 30:23; Prov 7:17; Song 4:14) as a spice used for its odor. Its one occurrence in the NT is as an import (Gk. *kinnamōmon*; Rev 18:13), which may have been for its use as a condiment, as noted in Roman cookbooks. This fragrant and flavorable spice was obtained from the inner bark of an evergreen that grew in Ceylon and Malaysia. Its name comes from the Malay *kayu*, "wood" + *manis*, "sweet" (Skeat, 91).

C. THE NEAR EASTERN WORLD

Mesopotamia

The massive development by various city-states of irrigation canals fed by the Tigris and Euphrates Rivers made possible bountiful harvests of grain. The hot climate, however, caused the increased salinity of the soil, which especially reduced the production of wheat. The heat caused water in the soil to rise up and deposit salts on the surface, rendering it increasingly less arable, especially for wheat, a process that has been documented over the centuries by cuneiform texts.

The dominant wheat in Mesopotamia was emmer, which, because of its low level of glutens, was baked as unleavened bread. Since emmer is a hulled wheat, it took considerable labor to pound, grind, and sieve it to produce flour. The common flat bread was baked either on the outside or inside of clay ovens or in ashes. More than two hundred types of breads and cakes are known to have existed in ancient Mesopotamia, some of which were made in molds, such as the fifty or so molds found at Mari.

Barley, on the other hand, was capable of thriving in relatively saline soil. Barley grains could also be boiled with a little water, parched, stored, and then used to make *burghul*, a kind of porridge to be eaten with oil and vegetables. A favorite dish was *mersu*, which was made by mixing flour, oil, dates, dried fruits, clarified butter, date juice, and garlic, all of which was then baked.

Barley was essential for the brewing of beer, the main beverage in Mesopotamia. After barley was soaked and allowed to sprout, the sprouted grain was dried out in the sun. This produced diastase enzymes in the resulting malt that converted cereal starches into sugar, which was then converted to alcohol by the addition of yeast.

Before the Neo-Assyrian period (8th c. BC), payments to workers were made by the palace and the temple with rations of barley. Men were given forty to sixty silas (= liters) of barley, women were given thirty silas, and children were given ten silas per month. Such rations would have provided men with about 3,000 calories per day for men and women with about 2,200 calories per day, which would meet the standard currently set by the Food and Agricultural Organization of the United Nations.

Kings such as Merodach-Baladan and Nebuchadnezzar of Babylon were able to establish irrigated gardens to grow numerous varieties of vegetables and orchards with many kinds of fruit and nut trees. Among the vegetables Mesopotamians ate were beans, chickpeas, lentils, peas, vetch, garlic, leeks, onions, lettuce, cucumbers, melons, pumpkins, cabbage, beets, carrots, and radishes.

Since olive oil was not available in Mesopotamia, the main cooking oil was derived from sesame. In addition to salt (Akk. *ṭabtu*), seasoning from aromatic herbs such as mint, basil, saffron, coriander, rue, and thyme was used. The English word "cumin" goes back ultimately to the common Semitic word for this herb (cf. Akk. *kamūnu*; Heb. *kammōn*). The Mari texts record large quantities of coriander and black and white cumin. A clove that was native to the Spice Islands of Indonesia was found at Terqa near Mari on the Euphrates River. Honey and concentrated grape and date syrup were used as sweeteners.

The most important source of sweetness was the dates grown in southern Mesopotamia. Date palms could flourish in relatively saline soil. Other known fruits are apples, apricots, figs, grapes, melons, pears, plums, and pomegranates. Nut trees included the almond and the pistachio. The Assyrian king Tiglath-pileser I (1114–1076 BC) boasted: "I took rare garden fruits not found in my own land and caused them to flourish in the gardens of Assyria" (*ARAB*, 1.87).

Because of the lack of meadowlands in Mesopotamia, cattle were scarce. The primary meat was mutton. Goats provided milk that could be used for butter and cheese. Pigs were plentiful in the marshlands of the south and also roamed cities as scavengers. Those who raised pigs were held in low esteem; pigs were not offered to the gods.

Egypt

As illustrated in the story of Joseph in Genesis, no region in the ancient world rivaled Egypt for its abundance and variety of food. The source of the fertility of the narrow Nile Valley was the river's annual floods, which provided dependable water for irrigation. At some times, however, the Nile flood would fall below its usual level, which could result in a year of famine.

Six-row barley (*Hordeum hexastichum*), which in Egyptian was called *šr.t*, was cultivated as early as 4000 BC. It was essential not only for making flat bread, but also for making beer, the Egyptians' main beverage. Models show the brewery located next to the bakery; lightly baked loaves would be soaked and then mixed with malted barley to produce beer. The ideal funerary offerings were the daily provisions of "a thousand (loaves) of bread, a thousand (jars) of beer" (Frankfort, 241).

Emmer wheat (*bd.t*) was grown in Egypt from the Neolithic era onward (5th millennium BC). Barley was more important in drier Upper Egypt (that is, in the south), and wheat was more important in Lower Egypt (that is, in the north). During the earlier epochs of Egyptian history barley was more important, but after the New Kingdom (1570 BC) wheat became more significant. Salaries were paid to workers in grain (*psw*) during the entire period of Dynastic Egypt, as coinage was not adopted until the Hellenistic era. The rations given to soldiers posted at the Middle Kingdom (ca. 2000 BC) fortress at Uronarati in Kush (Sudan) amounted to a half pound of grain per day, which would have provided about two thousand calories per man. This would have been supplemented by beer and vegetables.

As both barley and emmer were hulled grains, after they were threshed and winnowed they still needed to be pounded to separate the grains from their hulls. Kneeling women originally milled the grain using saddle querns made of a variety of hard stones (basalt, granite, and limestone). Later, stone mortars about three feet high were developed, which enabled the women to stand and use pestles to pound the grain. In the process, grit and sand entered the flour, and this had deleterious results upon the enamel of teeth, even those of the pharaohs, as demonstrated by x-rays of their mummies.

Grain would be stored in tall, beehive-shaped silos. In one scene a workman on a ladder pours in grain from an upper window, and a door is depicted on the ground floor for the removal of the grain when this was needed. Flour was mixed with water and then kneaded into dough. In a wall painting from the tomb of Ramesses III, two men are depicted kneading dough with their feet. Dough was at times enriched with the addition of milk, eggs, honey, or dates. The earliest possible evidence of leavened bread comes from the Predynastic Gerzean period. Leaven was obtained from day-old dough, which naturally bred yeast (hence sourdough). Allowing dough to stand for a day would attract the omnipresent yeast cells to leaven the mix, creating "sour dough," which has a slightly acidic taste. Other sources of leaven could be obtained from grape leaves. Leavened bread became more customary after 1500 BC.

Although Akhenaten (14th c. BC) is depicted presenting a branch laden with olives to the god Aten, and though olive leaves have been found in tombs, the olive tree did not flourish in Egypt, which imported olive oil from Palestine. Edible oils were produced from linseed, safflower, and sesame, and from the seeds of flax, lettuce, and radishes. Castor oil was used for lighting and for medicine.

The Egyptians ate figs, sycamore figs, grapes, and watermelons. From the New Kingdom (1570 BC) there is pictorial and archaeological evidence of apples and pomegranates. The Egyptians also had access to the tasty nuts of the dom palms that grew in the south. The funerary garden of the scribe Ani included 170 date palms. The tomb of Tutankhamun (14th c. BC) contained almonds and a basketwork container of raisins.

The Egyptians maintained fishing fleets both in the Delta and in the area of the Faiyum, where there was a large lake fed by a tributary flowing from the Nile. At the time of the annual inundation of the Nile, some fish could be caught by hand in the irrigation canals. Among the species that were caught were catfish and perch; one giant specimen of perch that was depicted was so large that it had to be carried by two men. Roe (fish eggs) were considered a delicacy, and fish cakes a treat. Fish were preserved by drying them in the sun or pickling them in brine. Egypt exported salted fish.

Egypt had abundant sources of salt from salt pans located in oases in the Sahara and along the Mediterranean Sea and the Red Sea. The Egyptians also used a variety of spices including anise, mint, dill, and marjoram. The location where the architect Khe was buried contained a basket of cumin seeds, and black peppercorns (from India) were found stuffed in the nostrils of the mummy of Ramesses II.

The Egyptians hunted animals like the oryx, gazelle, and ibex, and trapped many species of migratory birds, such as ducks, geese, quails, and cranes. Once such birds were captured, they would be force-fed. There are twenty-four different hieroglyphic signs for varieties of fowl. Tuthmosis brought back some roosters from Syria, and a graffito of a rooster was found in Tutankhamun's tomb. Roosters were prized for fighting, and not for their meat. The Egyptians ate the eggs of ducks, geese, pigeons, and ostriches.

The Egyptians raised large herds of long-horned cattle. From as early as the Old Kingdom (ca. 2500 BC), cattle were force-fed balls of dough. They were ready for slaughter only when they were so fat that they could scarcely walk. During his long sixty-seven-year reign, Ramesses II donated half a million cattle to various temples. Mutton was provided by reddish mouflon sheep. With few exceptions, Egyptians did not eat lamb. To celebrate a wedding, common people might slaughter a goat, which were valued at one-sixteenth the worth of a cow.

Though a mythological text that associates the pig with Seth, the enemy of Horus, explains, "This is how the pig became an abomination to the gods, as well as their followers, for Horus' sake" (*ANET*, 10), and though pig bones are absent from Egyptian tombs, there is abundant textual and archaeological evidence that the pig was not universally considered an unclean animal in ancient Egypt. Pigs were especially important in Lower Egypt, and workers at Deir el-Medina raised a large number of them. Pigs were bred on the temple grounds of Osiris at Abydos in the reign of Seti I. Amenhotep III offered pigs at the temple of Ptah at Memphis, and Ramesses III did the same in offerings to Ptah Sokar at Medinet Habu.

In the Ptolemaic era, after the conquest of Egypt by Alexander, two varieties of wheat became more prevalent than emmer wheat: *Triticum durum*, a "hard" wheat that is high in protein but low in gluten, and *Triticum aestivum*, "bread wheat." These varieties had "free-threshing" grains, that is, grains that separated from the chaff during the threshing process. It was also during the Hellenistic period that rotary mills for grinding grain were introduced in Egypt.

D. THE GRECO-ROMAN WORLD

Greece

Because of Greece's mountainous terrain, only 20 percent of its land was arable. On the other hand, its long indented coastline meant that few city-states were far from the sea. Prior to the Classical Age (5th c. BC) the Greeks were known to be modest eaters and were described by such terms as *mikrotrapezoi*, "small-table people," and *phyllotrōges*, "leaf chewers."

Barley (Gk. *krithē*), which could grow with low rainfall in the thin limestone soil of Greece, was used in religious rituals as it was believed to be the earliest food. Barley grains were soaked overnight, roasted, and ground into *alphita*, barley meal, which could be made into a porridge. Barley flour was kneaded with water, milk, or oil to be made into *maza*, a barley cake, which was eaten without being baked. The poor sometimes ate only black *maza*, wild herbs, and acorns. Peasants survived on *kykeon*, a mixture of barley and water or wine that was spiced with herbs such as pennyroyal, mint, and thyme.

Barley meal and wheat flour are referred to by Homer as "the marrow of men [*myelon andrōn*]" (*Od.* 20.108). Wheat (*sitos*) could be grown only in the few areas that had adequate rainfall and fertile land: Boiotia, Thessaly, and Euboea. The variety of wheat grown in these regions was emmer. The grain was grown not by the city-states but by individual farmers. In times of shortages the authorities did little to intervene. After the Greeks repulsed the Persian invasion and as Athens established a maritime empire in the fifth century BC, Athens began to import grain from its colonies and allies in the Black Sea region. During the Peloponnesian War (432–404 BC), the Spartans established a garrison at Decelea to cut off grain supplies to Athens from Euboea, while the Athenian navy sought to intercept grain imports to the Peloponnese from Crete, Cyprus, and Egypt.

Originally, the tasks of grinding grain (with wooden mortars and pestles) and baking bread belonged to individual households. Early in the fifth century BC, Solon decreed that those who dined at the city's expense should receive barley *maza*s on ordinary days, and *artos*, leavened bread made from wheat, only during festivals. Dough was leavened by either wine yeast or by *nitron* (baking soda). By the middle of the fifth century BC commercial mills and bakeries in Athens were providing both *maza* and *artos*. In some cases the dough was placed in earthenware pots (Gk. *klibanoi*) and covered with embers (bread baked in this way was known as *klibanitēs*). Bread baked under ashes was known as *spoditēs*; bread baked in an oven was known as *ipnitēs*. Flat bread soaked with honey was called *plakous*.

Homer lists a number of fruit trees in his description of the orchard of Alcinous: "Therein grow trees, tall and luxuriant, pears and pomegranates and apple-trees with their bright fruit, and sweet figs, and luxuriant olives" (*Od.* 7.113–116).

In a lengthy passage of Aristophanes's comedy *The Acharnians* (lines 719–1234), which was first presented in 425 BC, Dicaeopolis, who has made his private peace with the Spartans, sets up his market (*agora*) in which a variety of food items are for sale, including wheat (*sitos*), pigs (*choiridioi*), salt (*halas*), garlic (*skoroda*), geese (*chanas*), hares (*lagōs*), and eels (*egcheleis*). Other, unusual animals are for sale as well, such as otters, hedgehogs, weasels, moles, and cats! In a dialogue found in this text, locusts (*akrides*) are declared tastier than thrushes (*kichlai*) (lines 1115–1117).

Honey from Mount Hymettus north of Athens was prized and expensive. Good salt pans were available in Megara and Boiotia. Spices imported into the Aegean from the Near East are already attested in the Linear B texts (1400–1200 BC), such as *ku-mi-no*, "cumin," *ko-ri-a-da-na*, "coriander," and *sa-sa-ma*, "sesame." Anise and coriander seeds were found in Late Bronze (1500–1200 BC) Thera. Pepper (*peperi*), probably long pepper from northwest India, was used as a medicinal ingredient in Greece as early as the fifth century BC. Black pepper from southwest India, which was less spicy than long pepper, was known by the fourth century BC. Diphilus of Siphnos (2nd c. BC) is the first known to refer to pepper as a condiment.

Food was originally prepared outdoors by women or by slaves using either a brazier (*eschara*), an open hearth with cauldrons suspended from a chain, or cooking vessels set on gridirons or trivets. Separate kitchens, with vents for smoke, were not developed until the fourth century BC. The professional *mageiros*, who was a butcher and cook, did not appear until the fourth century BC. The Platonic dialogue *Gorgias* mentions "Thearion, the baker [*artokopos*]" and "Mithaecus, the author of the book on Sicilian cookery [*opsopoian*]" (*Gorg.* 518B).

Rome

Our knowledge of food in the Roman Republic and Empire comes from inscriptions, papyri from Egypt, and numerous other historical and literary sources, as well as some extraordinary remains preserved at Herculaneum and Pompeii in AD 79 by the eruption of Vesuvius.

Barley (Lat. *hordeum*) was considered food for animals and slaves. Barley groats were eaten by the poor, and barley gruel was fed to invalids. Antony (in 36 BC) and Octavian (in 34 BC) punished their troops by forcing them to eat barley bread rather than wheat bread. Gladiators were nicknamed *hordearii*, as they were fed barley porridge to bulk up their flesh.

As was the case in Mesopotamia and Egypt, emmer (Lat. *far*, whence Lat. *farina*, "flour") was the variety of wheat grown in Italy, especially in the areas of Etruria and Campania and in the Po Valley. According to Pliny the Elder, "Varieties of wheat are not the same everywhere. . . . The most widely known of them and the most prevalent are emmer [*far*] (the old name for which was adoreum), common wheat [*siligo*], and hard wheat [*triticum*]" (*Nat.* 18.19.81). He further comments: "It is evident, too, that the Romans subsisted for a long time upon pottage, and not bread [*pane*]; for we find that from its name of 'puls,' certain kinds of food are known, even at the present day, as 'pulmentaria'" (*Nat.* 18.19.83–84). The hulled grain was pounded with a wooden pestle in a wooden mortar to separate the hulls from the grain, and was then pounded again to turn the grain into groats to be used as porridge.

Emmer was the only variety of wheat raised by the Romans until the second century BC. As it was the most ancient, meal sacrifices were made of emmer pottage (*puls fitilla*). As Rome expanded its power through the Mediterranean, including North Africa and Egypt, it was able to import durum wheat (*Triticum turgidum*), which could be used to produce *similago*, flour for unleavened bread, and bread wheat (*Triticum aestivum*) for leavened bread.

Those who were poor would use grain as pottage; if they did not have enough money to have it milled and baked, they would give a portion of their grain for these services. The vast majority of Rome's population, who lived in *insulae*, multistoried apartment buildings, did not have separate kitchen facilities; they could bake bread using a *clibanus*, or covered pot upon a brazier. Professional millers (*molinarii*) and bakers (*pistores*, lit., "pounders") are attested in Rome by the second century BC. The millers would use stone hourglass mills that had an upper stone with a hole for the grain and a lower half in the form of a cone set in a base. The upper millstone would be rotated by a blindfolded animal. Apuleius's *Metamorphoses* (*The Golden Ass*) tells the tale of a man who was transformed into a donkey and who had to perform this laborious task.

At Herculaneum the mill and bakery of Sextus Patulcus Felix was preserved. The skeletons of two asses were found by his mills. In addition to his ovens, which would have been heated by charcoal, Felix had twenty-five bronze pans for the baking of cakes.

The Romans ate various types of bread, including *panis sordidus* (the cheapest), made of coarse grain; *semidalis*, unleavened bread made from durum wheat; and *siligineus* (which only the wealthy could afford), white, sweet, expensive leavened bread made from bread wheat. Bread was leavened with either sourdough, sour grape juice, or brewer's yeast. Loaves were flat, about two inches thick, and weighed about a pound.

To support the burgeoning population of Rome, in 122 BC the tribune Gaius Gracchus established a monthly distribution of grain (*frumentum*) at a reduced price for all male citizens resident in the city. In 58 BC, Publius Clodius Pulcher made such a distribution that was free. By 5 BC, the number of recipients had risen to three hundred twenty thousand; three years later Augustus reduced the number to two hundred thousand.

In order to receive an allotment one needed a ticket (*tessara*). These tickets could be given by patrons to their clients. The monthly ration of five *modii* (a bushel and a quarter) was sufficient to supply the caloric needs of a citizen, but not sufficient for his family. As there was no means test, the grain was given to wealthy as well as poor citizens. It was only in the reign of Septimius Severus (AD 193–211) that the dole developed into a distribution of grain and olive oil for the urban poor, regardless of their citizenship status. Around the year 270, the emperor Aurelian offered a daily issue of bread, supplemented with pork and cheap wine.

An equestrian official known as the *praefectus annonae* was in charge of the import of the grain from Sicily, Sardinia, the province of Africa (Tunisia), and Egypt, and its storage in warehouses (*horrea*). By the reign of Nero (AD 54–68), about one hundred fifty thousand tons of wheat were being imported annually from Egypt alone. From time to time grain shortages developed, causing riots and accusations that the wealthy were hoarding grain (cf. Philostratus, *Vit. Apoll.* 1.15; Dio Chrysostom, *Orations* 46.8–10).

In AD 32, during the reign of Tiberius, Tacitus reported: "The excessive price of corn [i.e., grain] all but ended in rioting; and large demands were for several days made in the theatre with a freedom not usually employed towards the sovereign" (*Ann.* 6.13). About two decades later, in AD 51, Suetonius wrote of Claudius that

> when there was a scarcity of grain because of long-continued droughts, he was once stopped in the middle of the Forum by a mob and so pelted with abuse and at the same time with pieces of bread, that he was barely able to make his escape to the Palace by a back door; and after this experience he resorted to every possible means to bring grain to Rome, even in the winter season. (*Claud.* 18)

The olive tree, which was imported from Greece, was not widely cultivated in Italy until the sixth century BC. Olives were pickled in brine, must (new wine), or vinegar for eating. Olive oil was used in many dishes. Rome imported olive oil from Spain, transported in large clay amphoras (two-handled jars), which were discarded at the wharf on the Tiber River. Their remains form Monte Testaccio, a mound that is over one hundred feet high and has a circumference of a kilometer. It is estimated that this mound contained the remains of fifty-three million amphoras.

Fruits were served as the most common dessert. Columella listed about fifty different fruits; Pliny the Elder knew more than a hundred varieties, including apples and pears. Figs were extremely popular among all classes. They were grown in Italy and were also imported from Africa and Syria. Dried figs were an important food source in the winter for those who lived in the countryside. Farmers mixed dried figs with anise, cumin, and fennel seed. Balls of this mixture, wrapped in fig leaves, would then be stored in jars. Pomegranates were known as *mala punica*, "Punic fruits," because they were imported from Carthage, a Phoenician (Punic) colony. Pliny the Elder reported that Lucullus brought the cherry tree to Rome from Pontus (northern Turkey) after his war against Mithridates in 74 BC. Dates, which were imported from Jericho, were included in many recipes found in a recipe collection known as *Apicius*. The Romans called the almond the "Greek nut," the pistachio the "Syrian nut," and the walnut the "Persian nut."

Vegetables (sing. *holus*) were a most important source of food for those in the countryside and for the urban poor. The poor ate a lot of turnips. Cato the Censor highly praised cabbage (*brassica*), which was eaten raw or cooked and was also recognized to have medicinal value. The greens of the leek (*porrum*) were used in salads and its bulbs were cooked. Nero, who ate great quantities of leeks, believing that this was beneficial for his voice, was known as a *porrophagus*, or "leek eater"; on the other hand, he avoided apples, as he thought that they would have a deleterious effect (Suet. *Nero*

20). Legumes such as fava beans, field beans, peas, chick peas, cow peas, lupines, and lentils were important sources of protein. Legumes were ground up and used in bread and porridge; they were seasoned with oil and salt and sold by street vendors.

Pliny the Elder declared, "Heaven knows, a civilized life is impossible without salt [*sal*]" (*Nat.* 31.41.88). The English word "salary" is derived from *salarium*, the money given to soldiers to obtain salt. The extraction and distribution of salt was supervised by an imperial procurator, who leased out contracts. The word "spice" is derived from the Latin *species*, which could designate a commodity of special value.

The Romans disliked bland food, preferring food that was sour and spicy. Unlike the Greeks, the Romans did not tend to flavor their food with onions and garlic. The most important spice was pepper (*piper*, a word derived from the Indian *pippali*), especially black pepper (*Piper nigrum*) from the Malabar coast of southwestern India. Remarks made by Pliny the Elder in his *Natural History*, which was written around AD 77, indicate that at this time pepper was still rare and expensive:

> It is remarkable that the use of pepper has come so much into favour, as in the case of some commodities their sweet taste has been an attraction, and in others their appearance, but pepper has nothing to recommend it in either fruit or berry. To think that its only pleasing quality is pungency and that we go all the way to India to get this! (*Nat.* 12.14.29)

But a few years later pepper had become so popular that Domitian (AD 81–96) had to build special warehouses (*horrea piperatoria*) to store imported pepper. It was used in 349 of the 468 recipes in *Apicius*.

Among other imported spices were cassia from China, cinnamon from Malaysia, and cloves from the "Spice Islands" of the Moluccas, which are today part of Indonesia. A popular pungent spice was silphium, which was used as a vegetable in pickles and sauces. It was obtained from the rhizome of an umbelliferous plant that only grew in Cyrenaica in North Africa. When it became extinct, the Romans used *asafoetida*, the product of another fennel plant from Afghanistan. As its name implies, the plant has a rather unpleasant (fetid) odor.

E. THE JEWISH WORLD

Among activities the Mishnah prohibits on the Sabbath are several related to food production: "sowing, ploughing, reaping, binding sheaves, threshing, winnowing, cleansing crops, grinding, sifting, kneading, baking" (*m. Šabb.* 7:2).

Barley was the grain for the poor, and the wealthy ate wheat (cf. Jos. *J. W.* 5.427). A Mishnaic tractate reflects a situation in which wheat was considered to have twice the value of barley: "If a husband maintained his wife at the hands of a third person, he may not grant her less than two *kabs* of wheat or four *kabs* of barley [every week]" (*m. Ket.* 5:8; one *kab* = 1.2 liters).

It was a wife's primary duty to prepare the grain and bake the bread for the family. According to the Mishnah: "These are works which the wife must perform for her husband: grinding flour and baking bread and washing clothes and cooking food. . . . If she brought him in one bondwoman she need not grind or bake or wash" (*m. Ket.* 5:5). Housewives were expected to rise early to bake the daily bread.

Grain was also ground by rotary mills turned by animals, and even in some cases by water mills (*b. Šabb.* 18a). Grains of spelt were boiled, dried in the sun, and then used as groats. Coarsely ground wheat was used as porridge at harvesttime or during voyages.

Bread was baked in a *tabūn*, a domed clay oven, usually found in the courtyard. The most common fuel was animal dung or olive pits. Women from several families could share an oven. According to the Mishnah, "Rabban Gamaliel says: Three women may knead dough at the same time and bake it in the same oven one after the other. But the Sages say: Three women may occupy themselves [at the same time] with the dough, one kneading, one rolling it out, and one baking" (*m. Pesaḥ.* 3:4).

In a discussion of how one should determine the probable owner of a loaf of bread that one has found in a city, the rabbis suggest that the answer might depend on whether Jews or Gentiles have more bakeries in that place or who prefers "bread of pure flour" or "bread of coarse meal" (*m. Makš.* 2:8). White bread, which was preferred for Sabbath meals, was made of the finest flour, leavened with yeast.

The Talmud has a discussion of an incident in which a Gentile presents a loaf of bread to Judah ha-Nasi in a field, whereupon he exclaims, "How fine this loaf is, Why do the Rabbis forbid it?" (*b. ʿAbod. Zar.* 35b). Though some argued that it might be permissible to eat bread baked by Gentiles where Jewish bakeries were scarce, the general conclusion was that Jews should not eat such bread, in order to prevent "intermarriage."

All fruits were considered kosher. There were thirty different kinds of fruit trees in Palestine, the most important of which was the fig tree. The citron, which became one of the four kinds necessary for the Feast of the Booths according to later rabbinic tradition, originated in the Indus Valley and is first attested in Palestine at Ramat Rahel (ca. 500 BC). The dates of Jericho were renowned as far away as Rome. A mixture of dates, figs, raisins, and vinegar known as *ḥărōset* became part of the Passover feast (*m. Pesaḥ.* 2:8; 10:3).

Salted fish was a staple of the Jewish diet, especially on the Sabbath. Fish salted with a brine called *muries* was prepared in a city named Magdala, which Josephus refers to as Tarichaeae, "Fish Salter" (*J.W.* 1.180), and was known as far as Rome. Numerous fish bones from the Roman and Byzantine eras have been found at inland sites. A relatively small number of species is represented: tuna, mackerel, groupers, mullets, and sea bream. According to the Talmud, "A fish [*bînita'*] was roasted [i.e., baked] together with meat [*bíśra'*], [whereupon] Raba of Parzikia forbade it to be eaten with kutah. Mar b. R. Ashi said: Even with salt too it is forbidden, because it is harmful to [one's] smell and in respect of 'something else'" (*b. Pesaḥ.* 76b).

Careful rules for the slaughter of animals (sheep, goats, cows) are laid down in the Mishnaic tractate *Ḥullin*. Animal destined for slaughter had to be without defect, and had to be killed by using a knife to cut the esophagus and trachea with one swift cut. All the organs and the skull, spinal column, ribs, and legs were examined for defects. The liver, lungs, and other organs were sliced to allow all the blood to drain. The veins were removed, and the meat was soaked and salted. If the meat was not salted and drained within seventy-two hours, it could only be eaten if it was roasted over an open flame. According to the beginning of this tractate, "What is slaughtered by a gentile is deemed carrion, and it conveys uncleanness by carrying" (*m. Ḥul.* 1:1).

In an attempt to honor the OT prohibition against "cook[ing] a young goat in its mother's milk" (Exod 23:19; 34:26; Deut 14:21), the rabbis required a strict separation of meat and milk dishes: "No flesh may be cooked in milk excepting the flesh of fish and locusts; and no flesh may be served up on the table together with cheese excepting the flesh of fish and locusts" (*m. Ḥul.* 8:1). Locusts were cooked in salt water. Sometimes their heads and legs were dried in the sun and then ground into powder. They could be flavored with vinegar or honey.

According to the Mishnah,

> These things that belong to gentiles are forbidden, and it is forbidden to have any benefit at all from them: wine, or the vinegar of gentiles that at first was wine. . . . Flesh that is entering in unto an idol is permitted, but what comes forth is forbidden, for it is as *the sacrifices of the dead*. . . . The grape-stones and grape-skins of the gentiles are forbidden and it is forbidden to have any benefit at all from them. (*m. ʿAbod. Zar.* 2:3–4)

Also forbidden was cheese of the Gentiles, "because they curdle[d] it with rennet from a carcase" (*m. ʿAbod. Zar.* 2:5). Milk that a gentile milked when an Israelite watched was permitted (*m. ʿAbod. Zar.* 2:7). While the Mishnah categorically bans the eating of Gentile bread (*m. ʿAbod. Zar.* 2:6), the Tosefta forbids the eating of "a loaf of bread which a gentile baked, not in the presence of an Israelite" but allows the eating of bread whose dough is kneaded by a Gentile as long as a Jew bakes it (*t. ʿAbod. Zar.* 4:11).

F. THE CHRISTIAN WORLD

Christians in the Roman world engaged in the production of food in the same way as their pagan neighbors. Those who were farmers were subject to oppressive taxation, which was required whether the harvests were good or poor. Many in Egypt fled to the desert regions to join monasteries, which were self-sustaining communities that were exempt from such taxation. The burden of taxation fell disproportionately on rural farmers, as authorities relied on land taxes but never had income taxes.

Clement of Alexandria deplored the extravagant efforts that wealthy Romans expended to procure their expensive foods, declaring:

> For my part, I am sorry for this disease, while they are not ashamed to sing the praises of their delicacies, giving themselves great trouble to get lampreys in the Straits of Sicily, the eels of the Maeander, and the kids found in Melos, and the mullets in Sciathus, and the mussels of Pelorus, the oysters of Abydos, not omitting the sprats found in Lipara, and the Mantinican turnip . . . (*Paed.* 2.1)

He was also opposed to the culinary arts:

> We must therefore reject different varieties [of food], which engender various mischiefs, such as a depraved habit of body and disorders of the stomach, the taste being vitiated by an unhappy art—that of cookery, and the useless art of making pastry. For people dare to call by the name of food their dabbling in luxuries, which glides into mischievous pleasures. (*Paed.* 2.1)

Rather, Clement counseled a spare and simple diet:

> Wherefore we must guard against those articles of food which persuade us to eat when we are not hungry, bewitching the appetite. For is there not within a temperate simplicity a wholesome variety of eatables? Bulbs, olives, certain herbs, milk, cheese, fruits, all kinds of cooked foods without sauces; and if flesh is wanted, let roast rather than boiled be set down. (*Paed.* 2.1)

BIBLIOGRAPHY: J. P. Alcock, *Food in the Ancient World* (2006); R. I. Curtis, *Ancient Food Technology* (2001); A. Dalby, *Food in the Ancient World from A to Z* (2003); W. J. Darby, P. Ghalioungui, and L. Grivetti, *Food: The Gift of Osiris* (2 vols., 1977); D. Eitam and M. Heltzer, ed., *Olive Oil in Antiquity: Israel and Neighbouring Countries from the Neolithic to the Early*

Arab Period (1996); R. Ellison, "Methods of Food Preparation in Meso-potamia," *JESHO* 27 (1984), 89–98; P. Erdkamp, *The Grain Market in the Roman Empire* (2005); H. Frankfort, "The Cemeteries of Abydos: Work of the Season 1925–26," *JEA* 14 (1928), 235–45; P. Garnsey, *Cities, Peasants and Food in Classical Antiquity* (1999); F. F. Leek, "Further Studies Concerning Ancient Egyptian Bread," *JEA* 59 (1973), 199–204; J. I. Miller, *The Spice Trade of the Roman Empire 29 B.C. to A.D. 641* (1969); R. L. Miller, "Counting Calories in Egyptian Ration Texts," *JESHO* 34 (1991), 257–69; M. Renfrew, "Vegetables in the Ancient Near Eastern Diet," *CANE*, 191–202; W. W. Skeat, *A Concise Etymological Dictionary of the English Language* (1963); J. Wilkins, D. Harvey, and M. Dobson, ed., *Food in Antiquity* (1995).

RKH and EMY

See also AGRICULTURE, ANIMAL HUSBANDRY, BUTCHERS & MEAT, INSECTS, MILK & MILK PRODUCTS, PLANTS & FLOWERS, THRESHING & WINNOWING, and TREES.

Furniture

Movable objects that accommodate human activity, usually in indoor space, are called furniture. These objects are reflections of cultural identity, resources, and values. This overview seeks to locate and describe the principal forms of furniture used in antiquity, giving special attention to domestic contexts.

A. THE OLD TESTAMENT

Furniture, as envisioned by the Western mind, appears rarely in the literature of the OT. This is likely due, in part, to the nature of Hebrew narrative, but it may also be a reflection of lifestyles in a temperate, Mediterranean climate, where squatting, sitting, or reclining outdoors was possible for much of the year. Indoor furnishings were a luxury, largely unnecessary in domiciles equipped with courtyards, masonry niches, benches, roofs, lofts, and platforms.

Vocabulary from the text of the OT that reflects contemporary ideas of furniture includes the following.

(1) *Bed.* The *miškāb* is simply a place for lying down. It may be as simple as a mat on the ground or a fleece on an elevated bench. It can be associated with a room inside a structure (2 Sam 13:5, 10; 1 Kgs 1:47; 2 Kgs 6:12) or an outside bivouac (2 Sam 17:28; Judg 6:37). The *miškāb* can be set up, made, spread, enlarged, shared, given as a gift, or even seized by a creditor (Ezek 32:25; 2 Sam 11:13; Isa 57:7–8; Prov 22:27). For the living, a *miškāb* is a bed; for the dead, it is a grave (e.g., Isa 57:2; 2 Chr 16:14). Quiet meditation is encouraged here, not evil scheming (Pss 4:4[5]; 36:4[5]; Mic 2:1). Job sought relief in his bed, but instead experienced nightmares (Job 7:13). The *miškāb* is a place of weeping for the unfaithful (Hos 7:14), while the sick (or those pretending to be so) use it for recuperation (2 Sam 13:5). Treasonous thoughts are discouraged in the bedroom, which is not as secret as one might suspect (Eccl 10:20). Not surprisingly, the *miškāb* is

where nakedness is revealed, and sex, adultery, or even murder can take place (Gen 49:4; 2 Sam 13:10–14; Song 3:1; Ezek 23:17). The promiscuous woman of Proverbs offers a bed of ruinous rapture to the naive that is sprinkled with myrrh, aloes, cinnamon, and, not surprisingly, death (Prov 7:17, 27).

While not considered "furniture" per se, mats, rugs, tapestries, or garments (*śĕmîkâ*, *marbād*, *śalmâ*, and possibly *śimlâ*) could function as "beds," or better, "spreads," and should be considered part of a household's furnishings (e.g., Gen 9:23; Deut 22:17; 24:13; Judg 4:18; Prov 31:22). These textiles were rolled up during the day to yield space for other activities.

(2) *Cot* or *litter*. At times, the *miškāb* parallels the more mobile *miṭṭâ*, possibly a litter or palanquin (cf. 2 Sam 4:7 with 4:11). Jacob died on a *miṭṭâ* (Gen 47:31; 49:33), as did Ahaziah (2 Kgs 1:4). Michal deceived her father by placing a mannequin of a sleeping David in a *miṭṭâ*. The ruse was topped with a goat-haired pillow and the whole thing was carried to Saul (1 Sam 19:16). Saul later sat upon a *miṭṭâ* to eat (1 Sam 28:23). Solomon arrived on the day of his wedding on a *miṭṭâ*, borne aloft, seemingly, by a cadre of armed warriors (Song 3:7). Elisha was given a furnished room, complete with *miṭṭâ*. Later, he raised a dead boy from that very bier (2 Kgs 4:10, 32), an act reminiscent of the work of his master (1 Kgs 17:19). Amos railed against those feasting on "beds adorned with ivory" (Amos 6:4); such beds were taken from Hezekiah by Sennacherib as booty (Taylor Prism III, 43–44). Ezekiel describes an elegant *miṭṭâ* as a place of prostitution (Ezek 23:41). The royal palace in the book of Esther had *miṭṭôt* (pl. of *miṭṭâ*) made from precious metals and stones (Esth 1:6). Haman fell upon the *miṭṭâ* of Esther and begged for his life, a move that, ironically, precipitated his death (Esth 7:8).

(3) *Couch*. The *yāṣûaʿ*, "couch," is treated as a synonym of "bed" (Gen 49:4). This term, which is derived from the verbal idea of "stretching" or "spreading out" (Job 17:13; Pss 63:7; 139:8), is used relatively rarely by OT writers. A slightly more common noun that is usually translated "couch" is *ʿereś*. Amos condemned those who sprawl on an *ʿereś* to drink and sing (Amos 6:4) and predicted that in the wake of God's judgment on Samaria only scraps of such furniture would remain in that place (Amos 3:12). The psalmist uses the term *ʿereś* synonymously with *miṭṭâ* (Ps 6:6[7]), and the author of Proverbs links the *ʿereś* to the *miškāb* of the adulteress (Prov 7:16). Her couch is sensual, draped with tapestries and fine Egyptian linen. The lovers in the Song of Songs celebrate their love in a more natural *ʿereś*; their sanctuary has green grass below and tree branches above (Song 1:16). In Ps 132:3, David, who is pictured speaking, declares that until he finds a dwelling place for the Lord he will not recline on *ʿereś yĕṣûʿāy*, lit., "the couch of my couch," which possibly refers to "a (final) stretching couch

(= deathbed?).” Elsewhere the Psalter declares that the Lord sustains the blessed man while the latter is lying on his *ʿereś dĕway*, “couch of sickness,” i.e., sickbed (Ps 41:3[4]).

A unique marvel was the monstrous *ʿereś* (usually translated “bed,” but which context indicates may be a sarcophagus) of King Og of Bashan, which according to Deut 3:11 was displayed at Rabbah of the Ammonites: “His bed was decorated with iron [lit., “his bed was an iron bed”] and was more than nine cubits long and four cubits wide.” That is, it was about thirteen feet long and nearly six feet wide! Millard has pointed out that prior to the later Iron Age, iron was considered a precious metal, citing as a parallel a Hittite text that mentions a “throne of iron,” that is, one decorated with iron as a royal gift.

(4) *Chair/Throne.* The term *kissēʾ* normally refers to the chair of a divine or earthly king. It is often used figuratively, to represent the locus of power, though on occasion it refers to a physical seat. The most celebrated instance of the latter is found in 1 Kgs 10:18–20, which depicts the seat of Solomon constructed of gold-foiled ivory. The pedestal beneath had six decorated steps, and the chair itself, which had armrests flanked by lions, was mounted on a platform. This description is surpassed only by Ezekiel’s vision of the seat of God, which, given its otherworldly origin, is described as appearing *like* a throne made of something *like* sapphire (1:26). Nebuchadnezzar’s throne had a spreading canopy or carpet (Jer 43:10).

In Neh 3:7 the phrase “under the authority” of the Persian governor of Trans-Euphrates is literally *lĕkissēʾ*, “to the chair.” Fragments of a lion’s paw and a bronze cylinder that belonged to the foot of a Persian chair similar to those depicted on the Persepolis reliefs were found at Samaria (see Tadmor).

Rarely is the *kissēʾ* found outside of these royal or divine contexts. Three exceptions occur. In the first, Elisha’s furnished room is equipped with its own *kissēʾ* (2 Kgs 4:10). In the second, the high priest Eli perches on such a piece of furniture precariously (possibly because it lacked a back), and from it he falls and dies (1 Sam 1:9; 4:13, 18). Finally, the thuggish Eglon perished beside his *kissēʾ*. A satirical reading of this text indicates that Eglon’s “throne” may have been a toilet (Judg 3:20).

The generic term *kĕlî*, often translated “tool,” is suggestive of any manufactured thing, but in least one instance it may refer to a seat. In the legal context of Leviticus 15, which indicates that a *kĕlî* may be rendered unclean by a menstruating woman (Lev 15:4, 6, 22–23, 26), the word is used in parallel with *miškāb* (“bed”) and may therefore represent a kind of seat. In other texts, however, the term *kĕlî* refers to containers, implements, weapons, or even ideas. A *kĕlî* may be precious (e.g., Exod 22:7[6]; Hos 13:15; Nah 2:9[10]) or not (Jer 22:28; Hos 8:8). It may be made of wood (Num 31:20), hide (Lev 13:49–59), bronze (1 Kgs 7:45), or other materials.

It may be numbered among the household objects (Gen 31:37) or be a part of a cultic assemblage (Exod 25:9; Num 3:31; Jer 27:19–21; 1 Chr 9:28–29).

(5) *Footstool.* In the OT, the word *hădōm*, "footstool," often appears as part of a dramatic anthropomorphism. It suggests the royal furniture of God. The deity's *kissē'*, "throne," is the sky, which towers over the plain of earthly existence. The ground is his *hădōm*, or "footstool" (Isa 66:1; Acts 7:49), the place from which he is worshipped (Pss 99:5; 132:7). Those who oppose God are vanquished underfoot and become a footstool for his feet (Ps 110:1). On the other hand, God's chosen city, Zion (Lam 2:1), and the ark of the covenant (1 Chr 28:2), the place where his presence dwells, are also referred to as his footstool.

(6) *Table.* Often translated as "table," the *šulḥān* is an eating place. The etymology of this term may suggest nothing more than a hide spread on the ground, though this has been questioned (Mitchell, 51). This is one way to understand Isa 21:5, which may depict a table(-cloth) being "unrolled" for a meal. In ancient Israel, people did not generally eat sitting on chairs; rather, meals were a reclining affair (Ezek 23:41; see also Ps 78:19; Isa 21:5). Down on the floor, the table(-cloth) could ensnare the feet of the awkward (Ps 69:22[23]) or become filled with vomit (Isa 28:8)!

In other texts, the table surface is described as being elevated from the ground by means of legs. This seems to be the case in contexts describing the dining place of God or the king. The "table of showbread" within the tabernacle/temple was made of gilded wood (Exod 25:23–30; 1 Kgs 7:48). This may also have been the case for the "king's table," as suggested by ancient Near Eastern parallels, though this phrase may simply be an expression of royal provision (e.g., Judg 1:7; 1 Sam 20:29).

B. THE NEW TESTAMENT

As in the case of the OT, the pool of NT terms that refer to furniture is relatively small. Theological expressions, ancient contextualizations, and figurative uses may cloud contemporary readings. Still, glimpses into life in the NT world are possible.

(1) *Throne.* The word *thronos* appears more than sixty times in the NT. Like Hebrew *kissē'*, Greek *thronos* represents the locus of power, and is almost exclusively used of God's throne. Occasionally the term is associated with others, whether David (Acts 2:30), human rulers (Col 1:16), or Satan (Rev 2:13). The book of Revelation offers glimpses into God's throne room (Rev 4) but provides little description of the throne itself.

(2) *Bench/Chair.* Drawn from a family of terms connected with the act of seating, the *kathedra* is a bench or chair. The seats of those selling birds

in the temple are overturned by Jesus (Matt 21:12‖Mark 11:15). Elsewhere, the disciples are warned about hypocrites who sit in the *kathedra* of Moses (Matt 23:2) and claim authority to interpret the Scriptures.

The *bēma* was originally a raised platform used for oration. In time, a chair came to be used on this platform. By metonymy, the entire fixture of steps, platform, and chair became known as a "judgment seat." Pilate sat in such a place (Matt 27:19; John 19:13), as did Herod (Acts 12:21), Gallio (Acts 18:12, 16), and Festus (Acts 25:6, 10, 17). According to Rom 14:10 and 2 Cor 5:10, God himself will one day render judgment from his *bēma*.

(3) *Table*. The *trapeza* is a table, lit., a "fourfooted" structure. In the NT it is associated with food and money. As a dining table, the *trapeza* appears in the account of, for example, the Last Supper (Luke 22:21), as a place from which crumbs fall (Matt 15:27; Luke 16:21), as the table on which the showbread lay (Heb 9:2), and as the eschatological table at which Christ's followers will dine (Luke 22:30). As a money table, the *trapeza* is overturned in the temple cleansing (Matt 21:12). Elsewhere, the word may connote financial investment (Luke 19:23) or the idea of business or administration in general (Acts 6:2).

A host of NT expressions for reclining, such as *anakeimai, katakeimai, kataklinō*, or *anapiptō*, are of interest here, as they are sometimes rendered in English with a phrase involving the word "table," despite the fact that they are not always accompanied by the word *trapeza* (e.g., Matt 9:10; 26:7; Mark 14:3; Luke 7:36–37; 14:10; 17:7; John 12:2). As an example of how one must be cautious in translating such terms, consider how *anapiptō*, "to sit down," and *anakeimai*, which in some texts is translated "to recline at a table," appear in the feeding of the five thousand narrative of John 6 (vv. 10, 11), where people cluster, recline, and eat on the grass of an open Galilean field. This suggests that care is needed in deciding when, if ever, *anakeimai* and like terms should be interpreted as referring to people sitting at a table. It is possible for cultural misreadings of "reclining texts" to color one's understanding of NT dining scenes.

(4) *(Marriage) bed*. Mentioned only a few times in the NT, the *koitē* can refer to a bed generally, but also to the sexual intercourse that occurs there. The related word *koitōn*, which occurs once in the NT (Acts 12:20), refers to the bedchamber. In Luke 11:7, the man awakened in the night hesitates to help because he is already in bed with his family. The author of Hebrews urges that the marriage bed be kept pure (Heb 13:4). In the LXX, the term *koitē* is often used to gloss the Hebrew word *miškāb*, "resting place."

(5) *Pallet*. The *krabattos* is a lightweight cot or stretcher. In Mark 2:4 a paralytic is lowered on such a portable platform through a hole in a roof. Once healed, he picks up his portable *krabattos* and walks out. Elsewhere, those who are ill may be carried on a *krabattos* (Mark 6:55; John 5:8; Acts

5:15; 9:33–34). The *klinarion* (a diminutive of *klinē*, "bed, couch"), a "small bed" that is referred to just once in the NT, is also used as a litter for the sick (Acts 5:15).

(6) *Bed or couch.* The *klinē* is occasionally used in contexts where a stretcher for the sick is expected (e.g., Matt 9:2, 6; Luke 5:18). Apart from these examples, the word suggests a sleeping place for one child (Mark 7:30) or for two persons (Luke 17:34). According to Jesus, a lamp could, but should not, be placed under a *klinē* (Mark 4:21; cf. Luke 8:16). One may infer that such a *klinē* was elevated above the floor.

Interestingly, Mark 7:4 indicates that the ritually observant person washes hands, cups, copper pots, and *klinōn* ("couches"). This context indicates that the couch could function not only as a place for sleeping, but as a place for eating as well, possibly in *symposion* style. Such a reading empowers the reversal of Rev 2:22: the "Jezebel" here, known for her feasting and whoring with others (on couches?), will be pitched into a *klinēn . . . eis thlipsin megalēn*, "a bed . . . of great suffering."

The *triklinion* (Gk.) or *triclinium* (Lat.), a "three-couch" feasting arrangement, is well known in classical contexts. These arrangements do not appear explicitly in the Bible, but they may be suggested in John 2:8–9, where the master of the wedding feast is dubbed the *architriklinos*, literally, the "leader of the *triklinion*." On the other hand, John's choice of vocabulary could be an adaptation for Greco-Roman readers. The extent to which this style of luxury dining filtered down from elite urbanites in Jewish Palestine to village folk is unknown.

C. THE NEAR EASTERN WORLD

Sources from which we can learn about ancient furniture in the Fertile Crescent include literary references, artistic images, and recovered remains. Because furniture was often constructed from perishable materials, the latter kind of data surely represent only a very small fragment of what once existed. Nevertheless, when such remains as have been preserved are considered together with pictorial representations and the literary references, a remarkable continuity emerges.

(1) *Literary references.* Booty, tribute, and dowry lists from the ancient Near Eastern world demonstrate the value of pieces of furniture. Such objects could be treasures of state: prestige items that were hoarded, exchanged, or stolen. A few examples from the second and first millennia BC may serve as illustrations.

From tablets recovered at Tell el-Hariri (Mari) in Syria, one learns of carpenters and their projects. Thrones, beds, chairs, and stools are mentioned.

Production notes reveal the use of sinews and glue for furniture assembly, and of leather for upholstery (*CANE* III.1654). In a letter found at Amarna from Amenhotep III to Kadašman-Enlil, the king of Babylon, the pharaoh enumerated among his greeting gifts the following: "1 bed of ebony, overlaid with ivory and gold; 3 beds of ebony, overlaid with gold . . . 1 lar[ge] chair [o]f ebony, overlaid with gold . . . 10 footrests of ebony . . ." (Moran, 11). Assyrian booty lists list tribute items, such as those received by Sennacherib: "couches (inlaid) with ivory, *nîmedu*-chairs (inlaid) with ivory, . . . ebony-wood, boxwood (and) all kinds of valuable treasures" from "Hezekiah, the Jew" (*ANET*, 288).

(2) *Artistic representations.* Visual depictions of furniture appear for the first time toward the end of the fourth millennium BC. These may be found on seals and statuary from Mesopotamia as well as paintings and models from Egypt. Clearer depictions than those just mentioned are found in second-millennium BC artistic presentations. From Mesopotamia, a bed model reveals a couple locked in an embrace. Their bed appears to be made of woven material stretched across a square frame (*CANE* III.1651). In statuary, gods and men sit stiffly on rush stools. A particularly stunning bronze model of a chair was found in Enkomi on Alashiya (Cyprus) (Schaeffer, pl. 73).

Richer yet are late-second-millennium tomb paintings from New Kingdom Thebes. The Tomb of Rekhmire (18th Dyn.), whose painted scenes depict various kinds of furniture and techniques of furniture production, is most illustrative. Cabinetmakers shape boards with pull saws and adzes. Holes are bored with bow drills. Chiselers engrave surfaces, while specialists work with joinery, hot glue, thin veneer, and stone inlay.

Depictions of furniture continue into the first millennium BC. Assyrian carved relief is conventional, yet instructive. A relief of Ashurbanipal shows his queen seated on a chair with her feet on a footstool, while the king himself reclines on a couch—the first depiction of a style of dining that spread to many cultures over the centuries (see Dentzer). On obelisks and palace walls, soldiers march stiffly as they carry off furniture as booty on their shoulders. Tables have lion's-paw feet on tapered casters. Struts appear to be lathe-turned (*ANEP*, 350). Elsewhere, emperors of Assyria, Babylon, and Persia recline on elevated and ornate thrones, their feet comfortably resting on footstools.

Palestine has yielded depictions of furniture in clay. Small models of chairs, beds, benches, and tables have been recovered from many sites. The *Ashdoda*, an oddly shaped chair with female features, is a particularly mysterious class of artifact. The purpose of the *Ashdoda*, as well as of other furniture models, is not fully understood.

(3) *Physical remains.* As furniture was usually constructed of perishable materials, few remains survive. However, isolated finds—which

mostly come from tombs—are surprisingly sophisticated in form and design. These bear witness to the skill of ancient artisans.

Remains of chairs, a table, and a cupboard door were recovered from a third-millennium palatial context at Tell Mardikh (Ebla), in Syria (Crawford, 34–35). Wood joints in the table and chair were held together with bone studs and dowels. Second-millennium contexts from Tell Baghouz, in Syria, and Jericho, in Palestine, yielded wooden furniture as well. Beds, stools, and three-legged tables were found in the latter (Parr, 42, 45–47).

In 1925 archaeologists discovered the site of the reburial of Queen Hetepheres in a 100-foot-deep shaft at Giza, which included her gilded carrying chair, another chair, a bed with a headrest, and a gold-covered canopy frame, all of which have been meticulously restored and are on display at the Museum of Fine Arts in Boston. (See Aldred.)

Assemblages from New Kingdom Egypt reflect the high end of the economic ladder. From the famous tomb of King Tutankhamun (KV 62) came about fifty pieces of furniture, ranging from elaborately decorated beds and throne chairs to ordinary stools, all of which were jumbled together when the tomb was opened by Howard Carter in 1922 (see Desroches-Noblecourt). From tomb KV46, the burial site of Yuya and Thuya, the parents of the wife of Amenhotep III, were recovered three carved and gilded chairs, two decorated cabinets, three beds, and a number of storage chests. The tomb of the architect Kha yielded thirty-two pieces of furniture, including stools, chests, beds, chairs, tables, and a lamp on a stand. In contrast, furniture pieces recovered from the workmen's village at Deir al-Medina in Egypt are less elaborate.

The Egyptian carpenters who manufactured this furniture used some native woods, such as acacia, date palm, and sycamore fig, but preferred imported wood, such as cedar and cypress from Lebanon and ebony from Kush (that is, Sudan). In addition to the assemblage from the burial of Hetepheres mentioned above, the Museum of Fine Arts in Boston has a floor lamp from Kha's tomb, as well as chairs, stools, folding stools, tables, and headrests (see Brovarski, Doll, and Freed).

A spectacular collection of furniture emerged from the site of Yassıhüyük (Gordion) in Turkey. Here more than fifty pieces of wooden furniture were recovered within the tumuli (artificial [burial] mounds) of Phrygia's ancient nobility. These pieces of furniture are unique in style, date to the eighth century BC, and were preserved due to the mounds of clay that sealed the burial chambers. The assemblages include inlaid screens, simple tripod tables, an extravagant "pagoda" table, beds with mattresses, and stools. Advanced techniques of wood joining, turning, bending, and laminating are evident. These finds at Gordion reflect the acme that the woodworking craft reached in ancient times, and, given their rarity, serve as a reminder of the great degree of loss that this class of artifacts from the ancient Near Eastern world has undergone with the passage of the centuries.

D. THE GRECO-ROMAN WORLD

Our knowledge of furniture among elites in the Greco-Roman world is fairly comprehensive, despite the paucity of recovered remains. This is due to the wealth of textual references and artistic representations that survive from the elite culture of ancient Greece and Rome. From the lower strata of society, however, the situation is more bleak.

(1) *Textual references.* Inscriptions, narratives, poetry, and even plays provide evidence for furniture names and uses from the Greco-Roman world. A series of Linear B texts from the Mycenaean palace at Pylos provide inventories of furniture, including the mention of eleven tables, five chairs, and fifteen footstools. One clay tablet (TA642) lists "One *stone* table, of *spring* type, inlaid with 'aquamarine' and *kyanos* and *silver* and gold, a nine-*footer*. One *crescent*-shaped *stone* table, inlaid with ivory carved in the form of *pomegranates* and helmets" (Ventris and Chadwick, 339).

The oral tradition of Homer's *Odyssey* (8th c. BC) remarkably preserved memories of the palatial furniture of the Mycenaeans over four centuries. The poem describes Odysseus's home in Ithaca in rich detail. In one passage, Telemachus invites a goddess into his house without recognizing her: "Athene herself he led and seated on a chair [*thronon*], spreading on it a linen cloth—a beautiful chair, richly wrought [*kalon daidaleon*], and below was a footstool [*thrēnys*] for the feet. Beside it he placed for himself an inlaid seat" (*Od.* 1.130–132). Odysseus returns home disguised as a beggar after a twenty-year absence. "Then wise Penelope [Odysseus's wife] came forth from her chamber, . . . and for her they set by the fire, where she was accustomed to sit, a chair inlaid with spirals of ivory and silver [*elephanti kai argyrō*], . . . and had set beneath it a footstool for the feet, that was part of the chair" (*Od.* 19.53–58). In the climactic scene, Odysseus proves his identity to his wife by describing the secret of their bed, which he made himself: "Beginning with this, I made smooth the timbers of my bed, until I had it done, inlaying it with gold and silver and ivory, and I stretched on it a thong of oxhide, bright with purple" (*Od.* 23.199–202).

Two later sources stand out from the mass of textual data on furniture from the Mediterranean world. The first is a list of confiscated property from the late fifth century BC. The Attic Stelai detail the sale of many different kinds of goods from southern Greece and the Troad. Domestic objects such as the *klinē* ("bed"), *koitē* ("marriage bed"), *anaklisis* ("chair with a back"), and *trapeza* ("table") are listed along with their contemporary values. These inscriptions give us a sense of the typical Aegean furniture assemblage.

A second source for furniture terms is the work of Athenaeus, a second-century AD author whose *Deipnosophistae* ("The Learned Banquet") provides a wealth of evidence about meals and domestic life in the Greco-Roman world. In this work, the reader eavesdrops on an aristocratic symposium. The banqueters discuss culinary habits, recipes, feasting paraphernalia, and dining-room furniture, among other topics.

(2) *Artistic representations.* Funerary stelae, wall paintings, vase paintings, and terra-cotta reliefs are important sources that portray furniture forms and uses in the Greco-Roman world. Funerary stelae memorialize the dead by depicting them in lifelike scenes. Sometimes individuals are portrayed standing alone, sometimes they sit or recline in groups. Chairs, such as the elegant *klismos* or the more stolid *diphros*, are often represented on stelae in Greek contexts; the *curule* seat and the *lectus* couch-bed are common on stelae of the Roman period. These latter displays likely have roots in Etruscan funerary traditions and functioned as a display of wealth.

Roman wall paintings depicting furniture have been found in public buildings and private homes. Bold colors were used to enliven indoor spaces and transport viewers to intimate or faraway places. The best examples of Roman wall-painting are preserved at Pompeii. Pompeii's buildings are decorated with a wide range of subjects, including initiation scenes inside the Villa of the Mysteries, banquet scenes from the House of the Chaste Lovers, and erotic scenes from the Stabian Baths.

Greek vase paintings vividly capture life and depict a wide repertoire of furniture forms, including chairs, stools, couches, tables, and chests. Equally informative are small terra-cotta relief plaques, famous from Melian (Greece) or Locrian (South Italy) contexts, that were used as wall hangings. In one scene, a woman lifts the lid of a chest and places a neatly folded garment inside. The chest is used as a closet (Richter, fig. 505).

(3) *Physical remains.* While furniture is a familiar element of Greco-Roman artwork, relatively few artifacts have survived. Wood was the primary material for the bulk of furniture in the Greco-Roman world, and only under special conditions could it be preserved over centuries.

The fragmentary state of the data set makes the finds at the Roman village of Herculaneum all the more stunning. Like nearby Pompeii, Herculaneum was buried by the eruption of Mt. Vesuvius in AD 79. More than forty pieces of furniture, preserved in part or in whole, have been found at the site. As reported by Mols (1993, 489; 2007–2008, 148–49), the wooden inventory recovered to date includes bed-couches, a cradle with curved rockers, small tables and other table legs, benches, assorted chairs and chair pieces, a stool, cupboards, racks, chests, and shrines. All but one of the tables have small disk tops supported by three legs that resemble those of animals. Among the bed-couches at Herculaneum, the "bed with boards," or *pluteus* style, is the most common. These have high boards on two or three sides (akin to a modern sleigh bed) surrounding a cushioned seat.

This style of bed-couch is common in Roman funerary reliefs as a resting platform for one or two persons. The sideboards held the mattresses in place and offered the occupant(s) some degree of privacy.

More appropriate for communal banqueting (Lat. *convivium*) is the open bed-couch known as "bed with fulcrum [a board at one end]." These could either be constructed of masonry and built into a dedicated room or be constructed of wood to be mobile. Pressed into the shape of the Greek letter *pi*, open bed-couches could accommodate a group of reclining adults. At Herculaneum, for example, two bed-couches (*biclinia*) joined at right angles have been preserved. The standard arrangement of three bed-couches (*triclinia*) is well established in Roman art by the turn of the millennium and formed a part of the fabric of cultivated behavior. Unfortunately, apart from metal sockets, leg sheathings, and ornamentation in the form of corners, inlays, and headboard (*fulcra*) medallions from these open bed-couches, artistic and literary representations are far better known than the realia themselves. This may be changing, however, as a recent study of *klinē* tombs from Anatolia by Elizabeth Baughan suggests.

There are no examples of mattresses or cushions from Herculaneum, but the bed frames that have been preserved suggest that mattresses were probably supported by wooden slats or ropes. In the House of the Gem-Cutter an adolescent boy's skeleton still remained on an elegantly inlaid bed (Deiss, 100). Among other noteworthy furnishings preserved at Herculaneum were a bronze charcoal brazier supported by ithyphallic satyrs and a folding chair with bronze legs in the form of bird beaks. Chamber pots were also recovered.

E. THE JEWISH WORLD

Jewish communities living in a predominantly Greco-Roman context would have been familiar with the styles of furniture mentioned in the previous section. This is reflected in two loanwords preserved in Jewish texts: the *triclinium* of the Greco-Roman period evolved into the *ṭraqlîn* of Talmudic literature, and the *qîṭôn*, or bedroom, is likewise derived from the Greek word *koitos*. Both spaces reflected accommodations to Greco-Roman social and material culture. With respect to the social aspect, however, it would be simplistic to assume that upper-class urban Jews readily embraced Greco-Roman feasting practices while rural folk rejected them (a social division that characterized Roman culture); some variegated fusion is more likely. With respect to the material aspect, furniture fragments from the early centuries of the first millennium AD continue to surface. Rabbinic literature also regularly references common furniture pieces, if only as props for the application of legal code to the endless variety of life-situations. A few examples may be listed.

Places where one sat, such as couches, stools, cushions, mats, and benches, are often mentioned in rabbinic literature. One rabbi sits on cushions while teaching (*b. Mo'ed Qaṭ.* 16b); another, on a "golden couch" (*b. Yebam.* 16a). The question of liability in the case of a broken bench is raised (*b. B. Qam.* 10b). The purity of a stool is debated (*m. 'Ed.* 1:11), as is that of furniture that loses a leg or a door (*m. Kelim* 22:1–10).

With respect to reclining or sleeping, references to beds, cots, and even canopy beds (for protection against insects) can be found in rabbinic texts. The Shema should be recited on one's bed (*b. Ber.* 5a). An orphan who asks for assistance to be married must be given a bed; it is a necessity (*b. Ketub.* 67b). Similarly, a couch and a mat/mattress must not be taken as pledge articles (*b. B. Meṣ.* 113b). Beds with frames and canopies and even "bridal beds" are mentioned in a discussion of "booths" (*b. Sukkah* 10b–11a). The Tosefta addresses the etiquette of ranked position for reclining diners (*t. Ber.* 5:5); this is a clear indication of a Jewish adaptation of the Greek symposium.

Needless to say, a large repertoire of furniture is envisioned in this literary world. The specific identity of many words used for furniture remains uncertain and continues to be studied.

Excavations by N. Avigad in the Upper City of Jerusalem, where the wealthy high priestly families resided, uncovered several stone tables in the "Burnt House" and the "Mansion." There were rectangular tables with a single central column, and smaller round tables that presumably had three legs. The former were generally rectangles of about eighteen by thirty-three and a half inches, and stood about twenty-eight to thirty-one and a half inches high. The round tables were about twenty inches in diameter. The tabletops were generally made of limestone, but some used imported granite. The edges and columns are highly decorated. Tables with three legs and with one leg are mentioned in rabbinic texts (*m. Kelim* 22:2; *b. B. Bat.* 3.4).

One item of furniture from a Jewish context has proved difficult to interpret. Excavations at Qumran revealed the remains of a narrow table about sixteen feet long. Made of mud-brick and covered with plaster, it was recovered from the debris of a second-floor collapse. With the table were two inkwells, two smaller tables, and the remains of a plastered mud-brick bench. The excavator, R. de Vaux, interpreted this room as a collapsed "scriptorium," possibly a place where the famed Dead Sea Scrolls were written. Metzger disputed the initial assumption that scribes sat on the benches to write on the tables. He suggested that a scribe would sit on the so-called "table," and, using the "bench" as a footstool, write on his lap. Clark has pointed out that the presentation of the assemblage in the modern museum offers a false impression of the height of the furniture. The table is only seventeen-and-a-half inches high. Relying on depictions of scribes in late antiquity, Clark has proposed that the scribes sat on the bench, wrote on their knees, and possibly used the tables to display the exemplars to be copied.

F. THE CHRISTIAN WORLD

In 1938, striking evidence of a possible Christian chapel was uncovered in the upper room of the House of the Bicentenary in Herculaneum. On one wall, a white stucco panel bore the impression of what was evidently a wooden cross that had been nailed there. Below it was an unusually large wooden cabinet that may have been used to store Christian texts, with a platform in front that perhaps functioned as a place for prayer (Deiss, 64–69; cf. Finegan, 374–75). When Paul landed at nearby Puteoli in the Bay of Naples (Acts 28:13–14), he was greeted by Christians from the area, so it would not be surprising to find Christians in Herculaneum decades later, in AD 79.

Continuities and discontinuities in furniture style can be observed as one moves into the Late Roman or Byzantine period. One cannot overlook an exceptional collection of furniture fragments recovered from the port of Kenchreai, near Corinth, Greece. The place of manufacture for these fragments is debated, although a date prior to the early fifth century is certain. Much of the mass consists of broken wooden chairs, crossed-leg in style (*thronos*), a common form but unique on account of ivory and bone veneers that grace their surfaces (Stern and Thimme). Parts of at least one cupboard, or *armarium*, are also a part of this collection.

The word for *kathedra* continued to be used in the Christian period as the normal word for "chair," but also found new application in reference to the seat of the bishop, and eventually to the place of the bishop's seat (hence the term "cathedral"). Perhaps the most celebrated example of a bishop's seat is the Throne of St. Peter in Rome, known today as Bernini's Cathedra. Hidden under the gold sheet of Bernini's elaborate reliquary is a wooden relic with origins in the Byzantine period. The chair is exceptional; apart from chancel screens and tables in stone, ecclesiastical furniture from late antiquity is rarely encountered. What has been recovered is largely drawn from reliquaries or annex rooms.

There is, however, some artistic evidence that Greco-Roman dining arrangements continued to evolve during this period. Mosaics and miniature paintings suggest that the *triclinium* arrangement of group feasting gave way to a new semicircular arrangement toward the end of the fourth century. Catacomb frescoes feature the *stibadium* couch, highly ornamented and bolstered, centered on a *sigma*-shaped table sitting in the center of the room (Vroom, 320–25). In Carthage and elsewhere, aristocrats return to a more upright and "barbarian" position in artistic representations, dining on benches (Mols 2007–2008, 153). How much of this, if any, is a Christian reaction to the paganism of Rome is a question worth exploring. Needless to say, the table is still set for elite company.

BIBLIOGRAPHY: C. Aldred, *Egypt to the End of the Old Kingdom* (1965), 93–95; D. Andrianou, "Chairs, Beds, and Tables: Evidence for Furnished Interiors in Hellenist Greece," *Hesperia* 75 (2006), 219–66; N. Avigad, *Discovering Jerusalem* (1980); H. S. Baker, *Furniture in the Ancient World* (1966); E. P. Baughan, *Couched in Death: Klinai and Identity in Anatolia and Beyond* (2013); E. Brovarski, S. K. Doll, and R. E. Freed, ed., *Egypt's Golden Age: The Art of Living in the New Kingdom 1558–1085 B.C.* (1982); K. W. Clark, "The Posture of the Ancient Scribe," *BA* 26.2 (1963), 63–72; H. Crawford, "The Earliest Evidence from Mesopotamia," in Herrmann and Parker, 33–39; P. M. M. Daviau, *Houses and Their Furnishings in Bronze Age Palestine* (1993); J. J. Deiss, *Herculaneum: Italy's Buried Treasure* (1966); J.-M. Dentzer, *Le motif du banquet couché dans le Proche-Orient et le monde grec du VIIe au IVe siècle avant J.-C.* (1982); C. Desroches-Noblecourt, *Life and Death of a Pharaoh: Tutankhamen* (1963); J. Finegan, *The Archaeology of the New Testament* (rev. ed., 1992); E. Gubel, *Phoenician Furniture* (1987); G. Herrmann and N. Parker, ed., *The Furniture of Western Asia, Ancient and Traditional* (1996); Y. Hirschfeld, *The Palestinian Dwelling in the Roman-Byzantine Period* (1995); A. E. Killebrew, "Wooden Artifacts," in *Encyclopedia of the Dead Sea Scrolls*, ed. L. H. Schiffmann and J. C. VanderKam (2000), II.987–89; G. Killen, *Ancient Egyptian Furniture* (2 vols., 1980, 1994); G. Killen, *Egyptian Woodworking and Furniture* (1994); G. Killen, "Furniture," in *The Oxford Encyclopedia of Ancient Egypt*, ed. D. B. Redford (2001), I.580–86; K. Kirshenbaum, *Furniture of the Home in the Mishnah* (2013) (in Hebrew); H. A. Liebowitz, B. A. Nakhai, and E. Stern, "Furniture and Furnishings," *OEANE* 2.352–58; B. M. Metzger, "The Furniture in the Scriptorium at Qumran," *RevQ* 1 (1958–59), 509–15; A. R. Millard, "King Og's Iron Bed: Fact or Fancy?" *BRev* 6.2 (1990), 16–21, 44; T. C. Mitchell, "Furniture in the West Semitic Texts," in Herrmann and. Parker, 49–60; S. Mols, "Ancient Roman Household Furniture and its Use," *Anales de Universidad de Murcia* 23–24 (2007–2008),

145–60; S. Mols, *Wooden Furniture in Herculaneum* (1999); W. L. Moran, trans. and ed., *The Amarna Letters* (1992); P. Parr "Middle Bronze Age Furniture from Jericho and Baghouz," in Herrmann and Parker, 41–48; G. M. A. Richter, *Ancient Furniture* (1926); G. M. A. Richter, *A Handbook of Greek Art* (1959); S. Safrai, "Home and Family," in *The Jewish People in the First Century,* ed. S. Safrai and M. Stern (1976), I.728–92; C. F.-A. Schaeffer, *Enkomi-Alasia* (1952); E. Simpson, "Furniture," in *The Oxford Encyclopedia of Ancient Greece and Rome,* ed. M. Gagarin and E. Fantham (2010), III.252–55; E. Simpson, *The Furniture from Tumulus MM I: The Gordion Wooden Objects* (2010); E. Simpson, "Furniture in Western Asia Minor," *CANE* III.1647–71; W. O. Stern and D. H. Thimme, *Kenchreai VI: Ivory, Bone, and Related Wood Finds* (2007); M. Tadmor, "Fragments of an Achaemenid Throne from Samaria," *IEJ* 24 (1974), 37–43; R. Ulrich, *Roman Woodworking* (2007); M. Ventris and J. Chadwick, *Documents in Mycenaean Greek* (2nd ed., 1973); J. Vroom, "The Archaeology of Late Antique Dining Habits in the Eastern Mediterranean," in *Objects in Context, Objects in Use: Material Spatiality in Late Antiquity,* ed. L. Lavan, E. Swift, and T. Putzeys (2007), 313–61; R. S. Young, *Three Great Early Tumuli (The Gordion Excavations Final Reports* 1, 1981).

MSZ

See also BANQUETS, DWELLINGS, FOOD CONSUMPTION, and TOOLS & UTENSILS.

GAMES & GAMBLING

Children's games and playing are universal to all cultures. Running games, jumping games, and hide and seek have been played since the beginning of time. Little girls "played house" and had dolls with moving limbs, preparing them for motherhood and domestic chores. Boys dressed like their conquerors who often were occupying forces, as counterintuitive as this may seem. Ball games that used balls constructed of hard, stuffed hides were also popular. Board games that used pieces and *astragaloi* (Gk. for the knucklebones of sheep or goats) or dice to move them were played in many societies over the millennia. Often these games involved gambling.

A. THE OLD TESTAMENT

Games and gambling are mentioned very rarely in the OT. Samson makes a wager with the Philistines, offering them "thirty linen garments and thirty sets of clothes" if they can solve his riddle (Judg 14:12–13). Zechariah 8:5 declares that when God returns to Jerusalem, "the city streets will be filled with boys and girls playing there." Though the biblical text does not mention dolls and toys, numerous examples of these have been uncovered in archaeological excavations in Palestine. Excavators have also found gaming pieces at sites such as Bethel and Tel Beit Mirsim. An ivory game board with fifty-eight holes was found at Megiddo; a stone game board and a terra-cotta game plaque came from Gezer. Dice dated to the early second millennium BC have been found at Gaza and Tell Beit Mirsim.

B. THE NEW TESTAMENT

Like the OT, the NT refers to games and gambling infrequently. Jesus compared those of his generation to "children sitting in the marketplaces and calling out to others: 'We played the pipe for you, and you did not dance; we sang a dirge, and you did not mourn'" (Matt 11:16–17). Scholars have speculated that the Roman soldiers who clothed and crowned Jesus as king may have done so as a cruel extension of the children's game of "king," where a child would be robed and crowned (Matt 27:27–30). After crucifying Jesus, the soldiers cast lots to see who would get Jesus's garment (Matt 27:35; Mark 15:24; John 19:24).

In 1856 a priest named Father Ratisbonne, a Jewish convert to Catholicism, came to Palestine, and in 1857 he bought the area near the so-called Ecce Homo Arch (named for Pilate's declaration "Behold, the man," in John 19:5), which is located at the beginning of the Via Dolorosa in Jerusalem. In 1865 he built the adjoining Convent of the Sisters of Sion over the Herodian Antonia Fortress, which overlooked the temple. Excavations by L. H. Vincent under the building of the convent uncovered a stone pavement of the Fortress Antonia on which Roman soldiers had carved games. This led Vincent and others to conclude that this was the *Lithostrōtos*, "Stone Pavement," or *Gabbatha*, mentioned in John 19:13 (see de Sion). Astragaloi, which were probably used by the soldiers in gambling, were also at the site. But excavations in 1966 revealed that the pavement and the "Ecce Homo" arch both date to the emperor Hadrian's rebuilding of Jerusalem after the suppression of the Second Jewish Revolt in AD 135 (Finegan, 256–58).

C. THE NEAR EASTERN WORLD

The Indus River Valley

A great urban civilization that included the cities Harappa and Mohenjo-Daro and that had extensive trade contacts with Mesopotamia flourished in the Indus River Valley (now in Pakistan) from 2500 to 1800 BC. The earliest known cubical dice (Sanskrit sing. *akṣa*), which were made of terra-cotta, stone, and faience, were recovered from the two cities just mentioned. Unlike modern dice, in which each set of opposing sides adds up to 7 (1+6, 2+5, 3+4), these dice had dots in various combinations (1+2, 2+4, 3+4, 5+6, etc.).

The Indus Valley Civilization was brought to an end by ecological factors and an invasion of Aryans (Indo-Europeans) from the north. One of the great Hindu scriptures, the Rig Veda (which dates prior to 1000 BC), testifies to the popularity of gambling among the Aryans. In the Vedic "Gamester's Lament," we read:

The gambler goes to the hall of assembly.
"Shall I win?" he wonders. His body trembles.
The dice run counter to his hopes,
and gives his opponent the lucky throws.

The dice are armed with hooks and piercing,
they are deceptive, hot and burning.
Like children they give and take again, they strike back at their conquerors.
They are sweetened with honey through the magic they work on the gambler.

The forsaken wife of the gambler sorrows,
and the mother of the son who wanders afar.
In debt, in fear, in need of money,
he goes by night to the house of others.
   (Rig Veda 10.34; cited in Basham, 404)

According to the Laws of Manu (dated 200 BC to AD 200), the king was to outlaw gambling:

Gambling and betting let the king exclude from his realm; those two vices cause the destruction of the kingdoms of princes. (221)

Let the king corporally punish all those (persons) who either gamble and bet or afford (an opportunity for it). (224; Bühler, 380–81)

The earliest known gambling games in the world were played with small hard nuts; later, four-sided, oblong dice known by the name *pāsā* (which date to the third millennium BC) were used. A gambling hall was attached to the king's palace. The royal consecration ceremony, the *rājasūya*, involved a liturgical act of gambling with five dice (Heesterman; Bowley, 6). The obligation for the king to gamble and the dangers of gambling are central to the Vedic epic the *Mahābhārata* (composed between 300 BC and AD 300), which recounts the struggle between two sets of royal cousins, the Pandavas and the Kauravas, over the throne of a kingdom, whose capital was at Hastinapura on the Ganges River in north central India. King Yudiṣṭhira (a Pandava) gambles with Śakuni (Kaurava) in a game of dice, which proceeds through twenty throws. The king keeps losing, first one hundred thousand gold pieces, then his chariots, one thousand elephants, one hundred thousand slave girls, one hundred thousand male slaves, one hundred thousand chariots, his army, his treasury, etc., and finally his wife, Draupadī. He and his followers are then sent into exile, and only after many years and bloody conflicts does he regain his kingdom (*Mahābhārata* 2.43–65; van Buitenen, 106–54).

The *Brahmajāla Sutta* (5th c. BC), which purports to record the words of Gautama Buddha, has him decry the amusements that preoccupy the thoughts of men, including playing a number of games:

> Whereas some ascetics and Brahmins remain addicted to such games and idle pursuits as eight- or ten-row chess, "chess in the air," hopscotch, spillikins, dicing, hitting sticks, "hand-pictures," ball-games, blowing through toy pipes, playing with toy ploughs, turning somersaults, playing with toy windmills, measures, carriages, and bows, guessing letters, guessing thoughts, mimicking deformities, the ascetic Gotama refrains from such idle pursuits.
> (*Brahmajāla Sutta* 1.14; Walshe, 70)

In India in the early centuries AD, a military board game was played on an 8 x 8 board of squares; this was known as *caturanga*, "four corps." Adopted in turn by the Persians, the Arabs, and the Crusaders, it evolved into the game of chess. Both "chess" and the word "check" that is said while playing this game are derived from Old French *esches*, the plural of *eschec*, which in turn comes from Arabic *esh-shāg*, reflecting Persian *shāh*, "the king."

Mesopotamia

Many children's toys have been found in Mesopotamia, including dolls (Akk. sing. *passu*) and miniature weapons, furniture, and chariots. Seals depict jugglers and balls. Rattles, spinning tops, and jump ropes (Akk. sing. *keppû*) were used (jump rope was called "the game of Ishtar"). Children, like adults, also played with knucklebones (Akk. sing. *kiṣallu*). Terra-cotta dice similar to Indian examples have been found at Tell Chuera, Tepe Gawra, Tell Asmar (Eshnunna), and Ur.

From earliest times, people have played board games, and such games are found in virtually every ancient archaeological setting. Evidence for board games dates as early as 9000 BC. Board games were inexpensive to make and easy to transport. They required only a board (which could be as simple as a flat surface); playing pieces; and a die, knucklebones, or throwing sticks to determine how many spaces a piece could be moved. Boards could be scratched into the dirt or etched in pavement stones. Many elegant game sets made of beautiful inset wood, shell, ivory and semi-precious stones have survived in burial contexts.

Board games required strategy, chance, and speed in moving pieces. They were usually played by two persons. The games that have been discovered typically fall into three groups: games of twenty holes (or squares), games of fifty-eight holes, and games of eighty-four holes.

Four gaming boards dating to the third millennium BC were recovered during Leonard Woolley's excavation of the Royal Cemetery at Ur. The most exquisite of these board games dates to 2700 BC. It is made of red limestone and lapis lazuli with beautifully handcrafted inlaid shell. The board has a storage space for seven circular pieces of black shale inlaid with five white spots, and seven of white shell inlaid with five lapis lazuli spots. It accompanied a princess to the grave to provide entertainment in the afterlife. Each of the boards discovered at Ur from this early period is configured with twenty squares, comprising four sets of five squares that are designated by different designs that represent lucky and unlucky spaces. A game of twenty squares was scratched into the pedestal of one of the winged bull statues guarding Sargon's palace at Khorsabad; this was apparently used by the guards to while away their time.

These games involved speed. Two players competed by attempting to advance their playing pieces across the finish line first. The outcome was a mix of luck and strategy. Merchants, soldiers, ambassadors, and slaves carried these games west to Crete and as far east as India.

Seldom do rules accompany ancient game boards. An exception is the rules that were found inscribed on the back of a game board with eighty-four squares dating to 177 BC. While they appear to form more of a sort of treatise, they also provide random details about the game. The fact that this text is preserved in Akkadian and in Sumerian has led some to conclude that it may provide clues as to how the Royal Board Game of Ur (the game exemplified by the twenty-square boards referred to above that were discovered at Ur) was played.

Two game boards that have eighty-four squares and that date to the Parthian Period (250 BC–AD 225) were discovered in Mesopotamia. The game these boards represent has been called the "Pack of Hounds." A set of rules is inscribed on the verso of one of the boards, though the other contains an inscription claiming the game has no rules! In addition to recreation, these may have been used for divination for the purpose of determining one's course in life.

Egypt

Egyptian children's toys included puppets of dwarves and mice with articulated extremities that could be moved with strings. In the town of Kahun excavators found a shop of a toy maker. Tomb scenes from Beni Hasan from the 11th Dynasty (ca. 2000 BC) depict girls juggling balls; one scene shows girls riding on other girls and tossing balls to each other. Boys jump over a seated companion, who, with his eyes closed, tries to trip the jumper. Girls play a whirling game with boys, as they spin with their feet on the ground and their hands are grasped by the boys. In the tomb of Mereruka, boys are depicted playing tug-of-war, with the opposing captains holding each other's hands and two boys behind them. One side cries out, "Your arm is stronger than his, don't give way!" The other responds, "My group is stronger than yours. Hang tight, comrade!" (Brier and Hobbs, 119).

The hieroglyphic sign for a gaming board (having diagonal mark-ings similar to a modern checker board), *mn*, gives us the name of Menes, the pharaoh who first united Upper and Lower Egypt at the beginning of the first Dynasty. The fact that this hieroglyphic sign was the name of the "founder of the nation" highlights the important role that gaming boards already played at the beginning of Egyptian history. Evidence for the Egyp-tian board game Senet ("Passing") has been found in burials dating to the middle of the fourth millennium BC (Predynastic period). A Senet game board is depicted on a wall painting from a tomb dating between 3300 and 2700 BC and in a tomb dating to 2500 BC. The board is a grid of thirty squares divided into three parallel rows of ten squares called *peru* ("houses"). Some of the squares were decorated to indicate lucky and unlucky events. The fifth square from the end was marked *nefer* ("good"); the sixth square was called *per heb* ("the house of humiliation"). The playing pieces for the game of Senet were called *ibau* ("dancers"). Each player received the same number of pieces, usually seven. Although the rules for this game have not survived, it was a race the objective of which was to move one's pieces to the end of the board before one's opponent. The movements were effected by the casting of marked sticks or of astragaloi.

By the New Kingdom, Senet was associated with powerful magic and with well-being in the afterlife. According to the Middle Kingdom Coffin Texts, the dead could play Senet with those on earth. As attested in hieratic texts of the 20th Dynasty and in a Theban tomb (#359), the board game be-came a contest with an invisible adversary to gain passage into the Realm of the Dead (Morris and Papadopoulos, 233). The successful player over-came fate and was under the protection of Ra, Thoth, and Osiris. Three Senet boards were buried with Tutankhamun (see Desroches-Noblecourt, 95, 232). The most elaborate was a box made of ivory and ebony and set on four animal-shaped legs, with a drawer to contain the pieces. The game of Senet was popular with all classes, from the royalty to the commoners. More than forty sets have been found in New Kingdom tombs.

Tjau, the game of "Twenty Squares," which is first attested in the 17th Dynasty, is found on the reverse side of many Senet board boxes. In this game, each player received five playing pieces, which were moved along by the casting of astragaloi. This game resembles the Indian game of *pachisi* (cf. Parcheesi). A humorous papyrus depicts a lion and an ibex playing this game.

Mehen (Egy. *mḥn*, "The Coiled One") was another Egyptian board game popular from 3000 to 2300 BC. Mehen is the name for a snake-god who protects Ra in the hours of darkness. Mehen appears, for example, on a wall painting in the Middle Kingdom (ca. 2600 BC) tomb of Hesy-Re. The Mehen game board depicts a coiled snake with its body divided into segments that vary in number. Some of the segments are decorated, perhaps indicating something special. The game was played with lion-shaped pieces in sets of between three and six pieces, along with a few marbles. The rules of the game are unknown.

"Hounds and Jackals" was another popular Egyptian board game that first appears in tombs of the 9th through 12th Dynasties. The board for this game is rectangular and is sometimes found with the long sides concave, thus causing the board to resemble an ax blade. The board has fifty-eight holes, twenty-nine on each side. A palm tree is etched in the center, with a hole marked by the a hieroglyphic sign that meant "to encircle," which may have symbolized the sun's perceived circumnavigation around the earth. An exquisite example of the game of "Hounds and Jackals" was found in the Middle Kingdom (ca. 1800 BC) tomb of Reny-Seneb. The board measures 15 x 10 centimeters and is made of ivory and ebony. The game pieces are short, pointed sticks, five with the heads of hounds and five with the heads of jackals. The board has short legs in the shape of four cloven-hooved oxen's feet. A drawer fitted under the board was used to store the playing pieces. Although the rules of this game have not survived, it was undoubtedly a race game. It appears that a playing piece could skip ahead or fall back, landing on certain holes.

We have archaeological evidence for ninety-seven twenty-square boards and sixty-eight fifty-eight-hole boards. The games of "Twenty Squares" (*Tjau*) and "Fifty-Eight Holes" (Hounds and Jackals) were transmitted from Egypt to Palestine, Cyprus, Anatolia, Mesopotamia, and Iran, and were played over the course of two millennia. (See Voogt et al.)

D. THE GRECO-ROMAN WORLD

Greece

At the beginning of the twentieth century, Arthur Evans uncovered, at the palace of Knossos on the island of Crete, a unique game board decorated in gold, silver, and rock crystal, that dates to the Middle Minoan Era (2000–1500 BC). This board has been compared to the royal gaming board found at Ur. (See Brumbaugh.)

In Greece a child's earliest toy was a *krotalos*, "rattle." Later, a child's *paignia*, "toys," might include a top (*strobilos*), a ball, and a drum. Most toys were made at home and were constructed of wood. Girls had their dolls (*korai*). In a game called *ōmilla* or *delta*, either a circle or a triangle was traced on the ground and children attempted to pitch nuts into the shape. Whoever succeeded gained all the other nuts. Children played "odd or even" with small bronze coins (*chalkinda*) and also played with yo-yos and stilts. In *psēlaphinda*, "blind man's bluff," a blindfolded child tried to capture one of his playmates, saying that he was hunting a bronze fly (*chalkē muia*). His friends circled round and hit him. In a game called *chytrinda*, "cooking pot," one child who was thus designated sat down while others circled round and hit him. If he succeeded in touching someone with a foot, that person took his place as the pot. In the game of *ephedrismos*, "sat upon," boys aimed an object at a target. The one whose object was farthest away was blindfolded and made to grope his way to the target while carrying another boy on his back.

A marble base of a *kouros* (male nude) statue found in the Themisto-clean Wall and now in the National Museum at Athens (ca. 500 BC) de-picts naked young men facing off with curved sticks over a ball. In a rural festival in honor of Dionysus, young men tried to see who could stay bal-anced on a greased skin filled with wine. The winner was awarded the skin of wine as his prize.

The suitors of Penelope played a game of draughts (*pessoi*), that is, dice, before the doors of her house (*Od.* 1.107). After doing the laundry and eating a picnic lunch, Nausicaa and her handmaids "threw off their head-gear and fell to playing at ball [*sphaira*]" (*Od.* 6.100). With his dying breath, Patroclus confesses to Achilles his one regret, namely, that as a youth, "I slew Amphidamus' son in my folly, though I willed it not, in wrath over the dice [*astragaloi*]" (*Il.* 23.87–88). Ajax and Idomeneus nearly came to blows over a wager on a chariot race (*Il.* 23.485–491).

The ankle bones (or knucklebones) of sheep and goats have four differ-ent sides: one flat, one concave, one convex, and one irregular. These sides represented the values 1, 3, 4, and 6, respectively. When throwing four as-tragaloi, the luckiest throw, which was called "Aphrodite," occurred when all four values appeared; conversely, the worst throw, the "Chian" throw, occurred when each bone registered a 1.

According to a tale related by Herodotus, the Lydians "invented the games of dice and knuckle-bones and ball and all other forms of game ex-cept dice" during a siege as a means of distraction from their lack of food (*Hist.* 1.94). The Greek word for the cubical die was *kybos* (which also could simply mean "cube"). Circular counters included the *klēros* (lit., "lot") and *pettos* (or *pessos*), "an oval-shaped stone." Loaded dice were not unknown.

A famous black-figure amphora created by the painter Exekias (ca. 550–530 BC) depicts the helmeted Achilles playing a game of draughts (*pessoi*) with the bareheaded Ajax in the camp before Troy. Achilles has thrown a 4, while Ajax, the perpetual loser, has thrown a 3. This scene, with some variations, was repeated on many vases. The board was divided into thirty-six squares. The central line dividing the board was the *hiera grammē*, "the sacred line." This game, which was also called *poleis*, "cities," was a battle game. Each player had five pieces of different colors. The goal was to take the other's piece by enclosing it between two of one's own pieces. Plato held that skill in draughts and dice had to be acquired from childhood.

A favorite game at the men's symposium, or banquet, was *kottabos*. While still reclining on their left elbows, the diners tossed the last drops of wine, or the lees, at a target, which could be saucers floating in water or an object that could be toppled. Women also played this game at their own parties. Women also played tops, striking them with whips. We have numerous statues and paintings of women and children playing with knucklebones. Artificial knucklebones were made of gold, silver, bronze, and glass. At a cave near Delphi, twenty-three thousand bone astragaloi were recovered, probably the dedications of boys and girls who relinquished their childhood toys when they came of age.

An activity that involved much betting was cockfighting, in which the birds' spurs were tipped with bronze barbs. An annual cockfighting jamboree was sponsored by the city officials of Athens. Even children attended these fights.

Rome

Roman children played with colorful balls. They tossed coins, calling "heads" or "ships." They had terra-cotta dolls, hobby horses, hoops, push carts, and tops (*turba*). Virgil describes how children played with the latter: "As at times a top, spinning under the twisted lash, which boys intent on the game drive in a great circle through an empty court—urged by the whip it speeds on round after round" (*Aen.* 7.378–380). Horace lists as children's activities building toy houses, playing odd and even, and even harnessing mice to a small cart (*Sat.* 2.3.247–248).

The Romans learned their gambling games from the Greeks. They called the knucklebones *tali* and the dice *tesserae*; the dice box was the *fitullus*. Games played with dice were *aleae*; they were played with pieces (*calculi*) on boards (sing. *tabula*, *abacus*, or *alveus*). A game board was a *tabula lusoria*. Hundreds of the latter were carved on pavements in Rome in the Forum, the Colosseum, and the House of the Vestal Virgins, as well as abroad at Corinth, Ephesus, Jerusalem, and at Hadrian's Wall in England, as such games with boards and dice were especially popular with soldiers.

The *latrunculi* "soldiers game" was played on a space marked by an 8 x 8 grid of squares. Each player had fifteen pieces, which included the *ordinarii*, who could move a square at a time; the *vagi*, who could move freely in any direction; and the *inciti*, who guarded the *mandra* or home base. If one landed on an enemy's space, his piece had to go back to its base. A piece surrounded by two opposing pieces was removed. The victor was hailed as *imperator*, "leader." The *Laus Pisonis* (1st c. AD) praises the skill of an individual named Piso in playing this game: "Cunningly the pieces are disposed on the open board, and battles are fought with soldiery of glass, so that now white blocks black, now black blocks white. But every foe yields to thee, Piso: marshalled by thee, what piece ever gave way?" (cited by Austin, 30).

Another popular game was *ludus duodecim scriptorum*, "the game of twelve letters," which was played with the throw of three dice. On some game boards were written expressive sentiments, such as this example from Timgad in North Africa:

V E N A R I L A V A R I
L V D E R E R I D E R E
O C C E S T V I V E R E

"Hunting, bathing,
playing, laughing,
this is living."

As in the throwing of the Greek *astragaloi* related above, in throwing the *tali* (knucklebones), the highest throw, Venus, occurred when all four possible surfaces appeared; the lowest throw was *canes*, "dogs," when all four showed the number 1. *Senio*, a combination that added up to 6, was also a bad throw. In throwing three *tesserae* (dice), the Venus throw was all 6s, and the dogs throw was all 1s. Cicero writes: "Nothing is so uncertain as the cast of dice, and yet there is no one who plays often who does not sometimes make a Venus-throw and occasionally twice or thrice in succession. Then are we, like fools, to prefer to say that it happened by the direction of Venus rather than by chance?" (*Div.* 2.59).

Young children learned early how to gamble, if only with nuts. According to Persius, "If it's ruinous gambling that is the old man's pleasure, his heir is a player, too, while still a boy, rattling the very same weapons in his tiny dice-shaker" (*Sat.* 14; cf. *Sat.* 3). Persius recalls that when he was little, "The thing I wanted most of all back then was to know what a lucky treble six would win and how much the losing dog throw would claw back" (*Sat.* 3.44–51).

Ovid advised prospective lovers to deliberately lose at dice to gain favor with the women they were courting. When in exile by the Black Sea, he recalled: "Others have written of the arts of playing at dice—this was no light sin in the eyes of our ancestors—what is the value of the *tali*, with what throw one can make the highest point, avoiding the ruinous dogs" (*Tristia* 2.471–474).

In Republican Rome there was a law forbidding gambling except during the December holidays of the Saturnalia. As Martial notes: "Now the schoolboy sadly leaves his nuts, recalled by the clamorous (school) master, and the boozy gambler, betrayed by an all too alluring dice box and just hauled out of a secret tavern, is pleading with the aedile. The Saturnalia are over and done with" (*Ep.* 5.84).

Taverns such as the *popinae* in Pompeii would have an inner room to serve as a gambling den, with waitresses who also served as prostitutes. A wall painting (Pompeii VI.10.1) depicts two quarreling gamblers. The first cries out: *exsi*, "I'm out" (i.e., "I win"); but the other objects: *non tria; duas est*, "That's not a three, it's a two!" The two come to blows, as the first man claims: *noxse a me tria ego fui*, "You've wronged me, it was a three; I was (out)." The second retorts: *orte fellator, ego fui*, "Son of a cocksucker! I was (out)." The proprietor shoves both of them to the door, saying: *itis foris rixiatis*, "Get out, do your fighting outside!" (translated by P. Foss, cited in DeFelice, 485, n. 56).

Julius Caesar risked his patrimony in gambling. Even more significantly, when Pompey and the Senate ordered Caesar to lay down his arms before entering Italy proper, he hesitated at the Rubicon stream, which was the limit of his authority in Transalpine Gaul, knowing that crossing it meant civil war. Then, wading across it with his troops, he cried out, according to Plutarch, "Let the die be cast!" (*anerriphthō kybos*: Plu. *Caes.* 22; cf. *Pomp.* 60.2), or, according to Suetonius, "The die is cast!" (*iacta alea est*: Suet. *Jul.* 32).

All of the Julio-Claudian emperors except Tiberius were addicted to gambling. Augustus informed Tiberius: "We gambled like old men during the meal both yesterday and to-day; for when the dice were thrown, whoever turned up the 'dog' or the six, put a denarius in the pool for each one of the dice, and the whole was taken by anyone who threw the 'Venus'" (Suet. *Aug.* 71). Augustus wrote to his daughter: "I send you two hundred and fifty denarii, the sum which I gave each of my guests, in case they wished to play at dice or at odd and even during the dinner" (Suet. *Aug.* 71). (A denarius was a day's wage.)

Gaius Caligula cheated at gambling (Suet. *Cal.* 41), and even played during the period of mourning for his sister, with whom he was rumored to have had an incestuous relationship. Claudius wrote a book on gambling, and even had a gaming board installed on his carriage (Suet. *Claud.* 33). In his absentmindedness he summoned those he had just executed to play dice with him (Suet. *Claud.* 39). After this emperor's death, Seneca mocked him as a frustrated gambler in the hereafter: "Then Aeacus decreed he should rattle dice for ever in a box with holes in the bottom. At once the poor wretch proceeded to his fruitless task of hunting for the dice, which for ever slipped away" (*Apoc.* 15).

Nero wagered as much as four hundred thousand sesterces a point in a game (Suet. *Nero* 30), which would have been the equivalent of over 1.5 million dollars (one sestertius equals about four dollars). With many other Romans, he was a fanatical follower of the four-horse chariot races held in the Circus Maximus, which could accommodate two hundred fifty thousand spectators. When Nero's pregnant wife Poppaea nagged him for coming home late after the races, he kicked her and caused her death (Suet. *Nero* 35). The charioteers were organized in four factions identified by their colors, Red, White, Blue, and Green. It has been estimated that the Blues and Greens both won about a third of the races. Juvenal recalls the excitement of these races:

> The shouting is earshattering—and this tells me that the Green jackets have won. If they'd lost, you know, you'd see this Rome of ours dumbstruck and in mourning, as when the consuls were defeated in the dust of Cannae. The races are a fine sight for our young men, who are fit for the noise and bold betting, with a chic young woman at their side. (*Sat.* 11.196–202)

When Ammianus Marcellinus, a historian and admirer of Julian the Apostate (r. AD 361–363), first visited Rome in 357, he observed with disgust the obsession of the urban poor with gambling and their passion for the chariot races (see Faris, 203).

E. THE JEWISH WORLD

Jewish children played with toy carts, animals, and even with locusts (*m. Šabb.* 9:7). Children played with toy helmets and shields. The Tosefta deals with playing with balls in a public area during the Sabbath: "In a case of those who play ball in public domain, if the ball went from the hand of one of them beyond a distance of four cubits [about six feet], he is liable" (*t. Šabb.* 10:10). That is, he is liable for breaking the Sabbath. The Talmud discusses the possibility of fatal accidents during a ball game (*b. Sanh.* 77b).

Rabbinic literature recognizes the importance of fathers playing with their children, even if one was a famous sage (*b. Šabb.* 154b). The best kind of play, as far as the rabbis were concerned, was play acting as sages.

Archaeological evidence indicates that some wealthy Jews may have engaged in gambling. A bone die was uncovered in excavations of the Upper City of Jerusalem conducted by N. Avigad, in an area associated with the dwellings of the Sadducean high priests. Another die was found in the Armenian Gardens, where Herod's palace stood. There was even a "loaded" die found in the tomb of Jason. A die was also found at Masada, as well as some wooden gaming counters in the "Cave of Horrors," where Jews hid during the Bar Kochba Revolt. A number of dice as well as games inscribed in pavement slabs were uncovered at Sepphoris, a largely Jewish city. Two circular games were carved in the pavement to the east of the synagogue at Capernaum.

Few Jews were involved in gambling since they regarded it as a vice, and also because most lacked the wealth to indulge in such amusement. According to the Mishnah, "These are they which are not qualified [to be witnesses or judges]: a dice-player [*hmśḥq bqwbyh*], a usurer, pigeon-flyers [*wmpryḥy ywnym*], or traffickers in Seventh Year produce. R. Judah said: This applies only if they have none other trade, but if they have some other trade than that they are not disqualified" (*m. Sanh.* 3.3). Pigeon-flyers were connected with gambling.

According to the Tosefta, a gambler must break up his *psĕpāsîm* (gaming pieces) and tear up his (gambling) notes before he can be accepted as a witness (*t. Sanh.* 5:2). While the Talmud does not condemn occasional gambling for amusement, it presents a more stringent attitude toward professional or compulsive gambling.

The Romans had a top known as a teetotum, which had letters on its four sides: T = *totum*, "all"; A = *aufer*, "take away"; D = *depone*, "pay"; N = *nihil*, "nothing." This is the ancestor of the dreidel, which Jewish children play with at Hanukkah. The letters on the sides of the dreidel are an acronym for "a great miracle happened there," referring to the miraculous provision of oil for the temple that is commemorated by Hanukkah. But according to Yiddish legend, the letters on a dreidel actually signify "all," "half," "pay up," and "nothing," corresponding to the meanings of the letters on the Roman tops.

F. THE CHRISTIAN WORLD

With the triumph of Christianity, gladiatorial games were finally stopped in AD 404, after a monk who tried to personally intervene was killed. But chariot races continued unabated, especially at Rome, Carthage, Antioch, and Constantinople.

Tertullian condemns the chariot races at Carthage and their attendant gambling:

> Since, then, all passionate excitement is forbidden us, we are debarred from every kind of spectacle, and especially from the circus, where such excitement presides as in its proper element. See the people coming to it already under strong emotion, already tumultuous, already passion-blind, already agitated about their bets. The prætor is too slow for them: their eyes are ever rolling as though along with the lots in his urn; then they hang all eager on the signal; there is the united shout of a common madness. (*Spec.* 16.1)

The earliest-known Latin Christian text against gambling is a sermon entitled "De Aleatoribus" ("Against the Dice-Throwers"), which dates to the second century and condemns bishops who gamble with offerings intended for the work of the church. This important text was traditionally ascribed to Cyprian, but has more recently been attributed to Pope Victor I. The sermon declares: "O noxious gamblers, you are pernicious and filled with indolent iniquity! O cruel hands, which turn their own arms against themselves, ruining with disgraceful zeal the estate which their ancestors have amassed by the sweat of their brow" (Carroll, 91).

Canon 79 of the Council of Elvira in Spain (AD 306) declares: "If one of the faithful plays dice, that is, on a playing board, for money, he shall be kept away; if, having reformed, he stops, he may be reconciled to communion after a year" (Laeuchli, 135). In Justinian's Code clergy were forbidden "from playing at the tables" (*ad tabulas ludere*) (1.6.17).

Some Byzantine-era gambling chips have been found with Christian symbols such as the fish. A Greek inscription has been found in Rome that constitutes an invocation to Jesus to help in a game of dice (*CIG* 8983). A mosaic of a gaming board dating to ca. AD 400 has been uncovered at Antioch. In a sermon delivered at Constantinople in 399, John Chrysostom assailed church members who preferred to watch the races at the nearby hippodrome to attending Good Friday services. Instead of reflecting on Christ's sacrifice, these so-called Christians, in his view, were jumping up and down and screaming themselves hoarse.

The great Byzantine emperor Justinian (r. 527–565) was responsible for codifying Roman laws in the *Digest*. Book 11.1, which deals with gamblers, reports a *senatus consultum* "forbidding playing for money, except when one is competing at spear or javelin-throwing, jumping, wrestling, or boxing, which are contests of strength" (Watson, 1:346).

Justinian issued new edicts to forbid the playing of dice (*alea*). In 529 he declared: "Desiring, therefore, to look after the interests of our subjects, we ordain by this general law, that no one shall be permitted to play in private or public places, either in appearance or in earnest." However, betting on sports was permitted, but limited; the law continues: "They shall further arrange for five games: leaping, pole-vaulting, throwing javelins or pikes, wrestling and show fighting. But no one shall, even in these games, risk more than a gold piece, although he is very rich, so that when anyone happens to be best, the loss may not be great" (*Corp.* 3.43; cited in Faris, 214).

BIBLIOGRAPHY: J.-M. André et al., *Jouer dans l'Antiquité* (1992); R. G. Austin, "Greek Board Games," *Antiq* 14 (1940), 257–71; R. G. Austin, "Roman Board Games. I," *GR* 4.10 (1934), 24–34; R. G. Austin, "Roman Board Games. II," *GR* 4.11 (1935), 76–82; J. P. V. D. Balsdon, *Life and Leisure in Ancient Rome* (1969); A. L. Basham, *The Wonder That Was India* (1954); R. Bell, *The Boardgame Book* (1983); P. Bowley, "Kings Without Authority: The Obligation of the Ruler to Gamble in the *Mahābhārata*," *SR* 20 (1991); B. Brier and H. Hobbs, *Daily Life of the Ancient Egyptians* (1999); R. S. Brumbaugh, "The Knossos Game Board," *AJA* 79 (1975), 135–37; G. Bühler, trans., *The Laws of Manu* (1967); J. Carcopino, *Daily Life in Ancient Rome* (1966); S. Carroll, "An Early Church Sermon Against Gambling (CPL 60)," *SecCent* 8 (1991), 83–95; G. F. Dales, "Of Dice and Men," *JAOS* 88 (1968), 14–23; H. Daniel-Rops, *Daily Life in Palestine at the Time of Christ*, trans. P. O'Brian (1962); W. Decker, *Sports and Games of Ancient Egypt*, trans. A. Guttmann (1993); J. DeFelice, "Inns and Taverns," in *The World of Pompeii*, ed. J. J. Dobbins and P. W. Foss (2008), 474–86; M. A. de Sion, *La Forteresse Antonia à Jérusalem et la question du prétoire* (1955); C. Desroches-Noblecourt, *Tutankhamen* (1963); A. Dundes, ed., *The Cockfight: A Casebook* (1994); S. B. Faris, "Changing Public Policy and the Evolution of Roman Civil and Criminal Law on Gambling," *UNLV Gaming Law Journal* 3 (2012), 199–219; J. Finegan, *The Archeology of the New Testament* (rev. ed., 1992); I. L. Finkel, *Ancient Board Games in Perspective: Papers from the 1990 British Museum Colloquium* (2007); W. W. Hallo, "The First Purim," *BA* 46 (1983), 19–29; W. W. Hallo, "Games in the Biblical World," *ErIsr* 24 (1993), *83–*88; J. C. Heesterman, *The Ancient Indian Royal Consecration* (1957); A. J. Hoerth, "Games People Played: Board Games in the Ancient Near East," in *Life and Culture in the Ancient Near East*, ed. R. E. Averbeck, M. W. Chavalas, and D. B. Weisberg (2003), 471–89; U. Hübner, "Games," *OEANE* 2.379–82; U. Hübner, *Spiele und Spielzeug im antiken Palästina* (1992); T. Kendall, *Passing through the Netherworld: The Meaning and Play of Senet, an Ancient Egyptian Funerary Game* (1978); S. Laeuchli, *Power and Sexuality: The Emergence of Canon Law at the Synod of Elvira* (1972); L. Landman, "Jewish Attitudes toward Gambling I: The Professional and Compulsive Gambler," *JQR* 57 (1967), 298–318; T. J. Leary, "Some Roman Board Games," *Akroterion* 35 (1990), 123–25; R. May, "Les jeux de table dans l'antiquité," *Les dossiers d'archéologie* 168 (1992), 18–33;

S. P. Morris and J. K. Papadopoulos, "Of Granaries and Games: Egyptian Stowaways in an Athenian Chest," in *Charis: Essays in Honor of Sara A. Immerwahr*, ed. A. P. Chapin (2004), 225–42; H. J. R. Murray, *A History of Board-Games Other than Chess* (1952); J. Neils and J. H. Oakley, ed., *Coming of Age in Ancient Greece: Images of Childhood from the Classical Past* (2003); P. A. Piccione, *In Search of the Meaning of Senet* (1980); N. Purcell, "Literate Games: Roman Urban Society and the Game of *Alea*," *Past & Present* 147 (1995), 3–37; G. Reith, *The Age of Chance: Gambling in Western Culture* (1999); A. Sasson, "Corpus of 694 Astragali from Stratum II at Tel Beersheba," *TA* 2 (2007), 171–81; J. Schwartz, "Aspects of Leisure-Time Activities in Roman Period Palestine: The Evidence of the Talmud Yerushalmi," in *The Talmud Yerushalmi and Greco-Roman Culture*, ed. P. Schäfer (1998), 1.313–25; J. Schwartz, "Ball Playing in Ancient Jewish Society: The Hellenistic, Roman and Byzantine Periods," *Ludica* 3 (1997), 139–61; J. Schwartz, "Pigeon Flyers in Ancient Jewish Society," *JJS* 48 (1997), 105–19; J. Schwartz, "Play and Games," *OHJDL* 641–53; W. J. Tait, *Game Boxes and Accessories from the Tomb of Tutʿankhamūn* (1982); D. W. Thompson, "Games and Playthings," *GR* 2 (1933), 71–79; J. P. Toner, *Leisure and Ancient Rome* (1995); J. Tyldesley, *Egyptian Games and Sports* (2007); J. A. B. van Buitenen, trans., *The Mahābhārata, Book 2: The Book of the Assembly Hall; Book 3: The Book of the Forest* (1975); L.-H. Vincent, "Le Lithostrotos évangelique," *RB* 59 (1952), 513–30; A. de Voogt, A.-E. Dunn-Vaturi, and J. W. Eerkens, "Cultural Transmission in the Ancient Near East: Twenty Squares and Fifty-Eight Holes," *Journal of Archaeological Science* 40 (2013), 1715–30; M. Walshe, trans., *The Long Discourses of the Buddha; A Translation of the Digha Nikaya* (1995); A. Watson, ed., *The Digest of Justinian* (1985); S. Woodward, "Ajax and Achilles Playing a Game on an Olpe in Oxford," *JHS* 102 (1982), 173–85; C. L. Woolley, "Excavations at Ur," *University of Pennsylvania Museum Journal* 23.3 (1933), 193–248.

STC

See also ATHLETICS, DIVINATION & SORTITION, DRAMA & THEATERS, and SPECTACLES.

HAIR

The literature and art of the Bible lands reveals a wide range of hairstyles. The style and length of a person's hair were not simply matters of individual taste or local custom. Frequently, the way a person chose to wear his or her hair—including the shaving of hair—was closely tied to a religious rite, social grouping, or particular lifestyle. Thus, depending upon the specific culture and period of time, the appearance of an individual's hair in public sometimes also carried a message with it.

A. THE OLD TESTAMENT

The Hebrews, like other Semites, considered well-kept hair something to be desired, a matter of personal beauty. Indeed, in the OT attractive hair was worthy of poetic eulogy (Song 4:1; 5:11). Among the finds at Beni Hassan in Middle Egypt dating to the early nineteenth century BC is a fresco depicting a group of Semites—probably from the Sinai or Negeb— who have come to an Egyptian frontier post to trade. The men are depicted with thick, dark hair trimmed at the top of the neck and thin, pointed beards without a moustache. It was typical in ancient Near Eastern art to display a full head of hair on gods, kings, and heroic figures. This reflected the fact that thick, lengthy hair was considered a sign of vitality and strength. Absalom, handsome claimant to David's throne, is described as cutting his luxuriant hair from time to time and weighing it when it became too heavy for him (2 Sam 14:25–26). Baldness, on the other hand, was disliked. It was often related to mourning or catastrophe (Isa 3:17–24), as was unkempt or disheveled hair (Lev 10:6). The prophet Elisha experienced ridicule in connection with his baldness (2 Kgs 2:23). The dread of baldness sometimes was due to its association with leprosy, a defiling skin disease that required the afflicted person to shave off all his hair (Lev 13:1–46; 14:8–9).

Hairstyles varied in Hebrew society. Women's hair was usually at least shoulder length, and often longer, as the Beni Hassan fresco indicates. The attractiveness of hair flowing down from the head catches the eye of the lover in the Song of Songs (4:1; 7:5). Women usually plaited or braided their hair (cf. 2 Kgs 9:30), and they rarely cut their hair except in times of deep mourning (Deut 21:12; Mic 1:16). Women usually concealed their hair with veils or scarfs as a sign of modesty or of betrothal (Gen 24:65; Song 4:1, 3).

Men's hair was trimmed periodically—especially the hair of men of the working classes, who could not afford the time or money often required to maintain slightly longer styles. Samson, a judge and Nazirite, was an exception and wore his hair in seven braids, a rare mention of specific hairstyle in the OT (Judg 16:13, 19). According to the law of Moses, if an Israelite trimmed his hair, he was to leave the hair at the sides of the head (i.e., the forelocks around the edges of the temple) uncut (Lev 19:27). The Torah proscribes cutting of the hair around the forehead since this appears to have been a pagan practice (Deut 14:1).

A few depictions of Israelites can be found in the Assyrian reliefs of the first millennium BC. The Lachish Reliefs of the Assyrian king Sennacherib depict events that happened in Judea in 701 BC. Most of the Israelite men depicted on these reliefs have their head covered by turbans or helmets, but the ones who are not wearing anything on their heads are depicted with short, curly hair and beards. By way of contrast, the Assyrian soldiers are depicted with hair down to their shoulders and long beards. It is not possible to see the hair of the women on the Lachish Reliefs since they are wearing long head shawls. The boys on the reliefs have short hair and the girls, like their mothers, cover their hair with long shawls. On the Black Obelisk of Shalmaneser III, King Jehu (or one of his officials) is depicted as paying homage to the Assyrian king. He is depicted with a long beard, hair down to his shoulders, and a pointed hat that resembles a nightcap.

According to the OT, priests were not allowed to shave their hair; neither were they permitted to let their hair grow uncut like the Nazirites (Lev 21:5; Ezek 44:20; cf. Num 6:5). Hair offerings in the Semitic world betokened the sacrifice of the life of a person to a deity, for hair, like blood, represented life. Thus, when a Nazirite ended his vow, he shaved his hair and burned it in the fire as an offering (Num 6:18).

Several OT legal passages describe the manipulation of women's hair. In the ritual involving a wife accused of unfaithfulness, the woman is required to stand before the Lord and then the priest must loosen her hair (Num 5:18). Apparently, this dramatic act was meant to signify her openness before the community. Another legal text involves a woman who has been taken captive in war. The captor is allowed to bring the woman into his house as a wife, but before they can come together she has to shave her head, cut her nails, and mourn her parents for a month (Deut 21:10–14).

Hair oil was used frequently in the OT period. It helped condition the hair and eliminate vermin and dryness of the scalp. Sometimes the oil was perfumed. To anoint the hair of a guest at a banquet was a sign of honoring that person (Ps 23:5). The psalmist compares the pleasantness of unity among brothers to "precious oil poured on the head, running down on the beard" (Ps 133:1–2). Qoheleth wishes that his head might always be anointed with oil (Eccl 9:8).

Black or dark hair was considered beautiful on both sexes (Song 5:11). The attractiveness of the beloved's hair in the Song of Songs is likened to the dark color of goat's hair (Song 4:1). Gray hair was considered a crown of splendor for the old (Prov 16:31; 20:29). Old age and gray hair go together (1 Sam 12:2; Job 15:10; Ps 71:18; Isa 46:4), and with them comes respect and wisdom (Lev 19:32; cf. Wis 4:8–9). White hair symbolized the wisdom and dignity of the divine presence (Dan 7:9; cf. Rev 1:14; cf. 2 Macc 15:13).

Biblical literature does not mention the use of wigs among the Hebrews. Furthermore, the Bible is silent about professional hairdressers and only once mentions the term "barber" (Ezek 5:1). It would seem likely, however, that every town in Israel must have employed the services of at least one person who specialized in the trimming of hair and/or beards.

B. THE NEW TESTAMENT

Hair is only rarely discussed in the NT. The comments on hair that do exist in the NT indicate, for example, that in the Jewish society of the first century women had long hair. The woman who cleaned Jesus's feet with her tears and her hair obviously had hair long enough to use as a sort of towel (Luke 7:37–38, 44). Later in Jesus's ministry, Mary the sister of Lazarus similarly cleaned Jesus's feet by pouring ointment on them and wiping them with her hair, so she too must have had long hair (John 11:2; 12:3).

Gentile women are also described in the NT as having long hair. Similar to other Greek women, it was customary for Greek women in the church to have long hair, and Paul describes such hair as a glory and a covering (1 Cor 11:15). Paul also mentions in this passage that it was a disgrace for a woman's hair to be cut off (1 Cor 11:6). It is debated whether Paul is addressing the length of women's hair or their use of head coverings in 1 Cor 11, but there is good evidence from Greek literature that married Greek women typically wore a veil when they left their home. There is also evidence from Greek literature that the purpose of this veil was, at least in part, to accentuate a woman's beauty, perhaps as a visual extension of her long hair (cf. 1 Cor 11:14–15). Another way women beautified their hair at this time was through braiding (1 Tim 2:9; 1 Pet 3:3). In contrast to the practice of other women in Greco-Roman society who adorned themselves with elaborate hairstyles, the NT emphasizes the inward spiritual adornment of the heart as being more important.

The observation made by Paul to the Corinthians about men having short hair rather than long (1 Cor 11:14) is confirmed by studies of the iconography of the Greek world. Typically Jewish men and Gentile men alike kept their hair cut short, so the standard depiction of Jesus with long hair is probably incorrect. One exception in the Jewish culture to men's keeping their hair short was the practice of the Nazirite vow (Num 6:5), which included growing the hair out and then cutting it at the end of the vow period. Paul himself had his hair cut due to such a vow (Acts 18:18).

Hair oil continued to be used by Jews in the NT era, especially on joyous occasions (Matt 6:17). To anoint the hair of a guest with oil was a token of hospitality (Luke 7:46).

C. THE NEAR EASTERN WORLD

Mesopotamia

Our knowledge of Mesopotamian hair styles comes largely from representations in art, especially statues, reliefs, and cylinder seals. Many of the archaeological remains from the last half of the third millennium depict Sumerians, a non-Semitic people, as bald and beardless. However, this was not the norm for most of the peoples of Mesopotamia. Such shaving by the Sumerians of the hair on both head and face, and possibly the shaving of the rest of the body, probably was prompted by an understanding of ritual purity that required a worshipper to appear before his god naked. In addition, since lice and vermin were so prevalent in the ancient world, Sumerians may have sought relief from their itchy scalps by shaving the hair rather than by delousing it. Delousing was usually carried out by combing and/or treating the affected area with oil.

Unlike the Sumerians, most Semitic men of Mesopotamia wore a full head of hair and a beard. Exceptions to this rule were slaves, priests, and, apparently, doctors, each group being marked by a certain form of tonsure. A variety of hairstyles existed in Mesopotamia. Local inhabitants tended to follow the fashion displayed by those in high authority. Foreigners, however, usually opted for less elaborate styles.

During the third millennium, both men and women had long hair hanging below the neck. Sometimes the hair was worn down, in one bunch, held together by two or three plaits. Other times the hair was brought back from the face and coiled about the head turban-wise. During the closing centuries of the third millennium the style was curly or wavy hair, parted in the middle. Women typically did their hair up into a bun that ran from the neck to the crown of the head. A headband usually held the hair in place. Hairpins made of bone, copper, silver, and gold have been uncovered in archaeological digs. Remains of women found in the Royal Cemetery of Ur show that when preparing the body for burial, the hair was arranged with gold hairnets, gold and silver ribbons, silver hairpins, strings of gold willow leaves, and beads made of gold, lapis lazuli, and carnelian.

The reliefs found in the course of excavations at several Assyrian palaces have shed considerable light on Mesopotamian hairstyles. Semitic kings and warriors from the start of the Old Assyrian period (1850 BC) through the end of the Neo-Assyrian period (612 BC) are normally depicted in Mesopotamian art with beautiful curly beards and long, wavy hair extending neatly over the shoulder. Assyrian soldiers are depicted with similar features. Most of the time the hair hung down the back but occasionally it was doubled up and tucked into the soldier's headband. Attendants typically had clean-shaven faces, and a few of the warriors also are depicted as beardless. Priests had shaved heads and faces. Assyrian beards were typically square shaped but there were a few exceptions. Foreigners are sometimes depicted with pointed beards and sometimes with squared beards. In general, there seems to have been a principle of longer beards depicting a higher status in the society, so the king often had the longest beard of all.

An Old Babylonian terra-cotta figurine of a woman from ca. 1900 BC depicts her hair as parted down the middle, with braids arranged in loops on either side of the head, and arranged with a fillet. Women are not depicted nearly as often as men on the Neo-Assyrian artwork. When they do occur, they usually are depicted with long hair that is often arranged in fancy plaits. Some foreign women are depicted with full head coverings, such as the Judean women on the Lachish Reliefs mentioned above. One relief from the time of Ashurbanipal (669–629 BC) shows the king and queen seated together. They both have shoulder-length, wavy and curly hair that is held in place by a thick headband. Naturally, the king is distinguished by his long beard, but otherwise their hairstyles are very similar.

Mesopotamian physicians had remedies for hair loss for both men and women. A Mesopotamian treatment for graying hair consisted of applying lotion and reciting an incantation.

Egypt

In general, Egyptian men kept their hair shorter and their bodies smoother than most other peoples in the ancient Near East. It was the custom of Egyptian men to shave the head and beard (Her. *Hist.* 2.36).

Thus, we see Joseph having to shave before appearing before Pharaoh (Gen 41:14). Similarly, in the 12th Dynasty an Egyptian named Sinuhe who had spent much of his life living in exile in Palestine had to be shaved when he returned to Egypt and started living in the pharaoh's palace (*The Story of Sinuhe*; *ANET*, 18–22). Shaving, however, normally seems to have entailed a very short haircut; it did not mean all men were shaved bald. Certain statues, for example, reveal small locks of natural hair poking out from under wigs. In addition, Egyptian physicians provided prescriptions for balding heads and for hair turning white (see below). Monuments, on the other hand, often depict priests cleanly shaven or with a long lock on the side of their head. Herodotus indicates that several times a week priests shaved their entire bodies (Her. *Hist.* 2.37). From early childhood the heads of boys were shaved or closely cropped so that only a long tuft or curl remained, usually over the right temple (cf. Her. *Hist.* 2.65; 3.12). The hair removed was typically dedicated to an Egyptian deity at a local shrine. During periods of mourning, men refrained from shaving the head.

Women generally wore their hair long, with it often falling in two tresses on their shoulders and neck. Furthermore, long hair was the fashion for goddesses. Numerous female mummies have been uncovered with the hair remarkably well preserved. Animal fat or resin would be used to hold the hair in place on the mummy. During the Old Kingdom, the tendency was toward simple hairstyles. In the New Kingdom, however, styles became more elaborate; women sometimes added flowers, ribbons, or perfumed oil to their hair. Hairdressing scenes depicted on panels and reliefs suggest that hairdressers especially frequented the presence of royalty and people of wealth. The Egyptians used wooden hair combs, sometimes decorated with animal motifs, such as an ibex. Examples of hairpins decorated with animals have also been found. There was some variety in the hairstyles of Egyptians girls: artistic representations can be found of girls with either short hair, a large braid, one or more pigtails in the back, or a side-lock similar to those worn by boys. Girls and young women were also known to use hair pendants, sometimes shaped like a fish.

Men and women of all but the poor classes wore wigs both indoors and out. Occasionally, close-fitting caps were worn. Wigs provided needed protection from the sunny Egyptian climate. Wig makers usually plied their art by using human hair, although sometimes vegetable fibers or sheep's wool was mixed with the hair. Beeswax would be used to help hold the plaited locks together. Wigs worn by men were of two kinds. One was made to imitate short, wooly hair and thus reflected a typically African style. This wig was constructed by placing little curls in overlapping horizontal rows that, like a modern bathing cap, usually covered the forehead, ears, and back of the neck. The other type of male wig was made of long hair that fell from the crown of the head over the shoulders. In one example of a long-haired wig, the hair at the top of the wig was styled with bushy, curly hair while the hair underneath was braided in long strands. Wigs made for women during the Old Kingdom largely consisted of long, straight hair in two tresses that hung in front. During the Middle Kingdom, however, the two tresses were formed into a sort of fringe. Sometimes the fringe was plaited or curled. Either it covered the upper part of the body or was combed back so as to hang behind. There is literary evidence that wigs were considered an essential aspect of a woman's beauty and were even worn during intercourse. In anticipation of the afterlife, Egyptians often placed wigs in boxes to accompany them to the next world.

Like Mesopotamian physicians, Egyptian physicians prescribed various remedies for those with hair problems. The Ebers Papyrus, a sixteenth-century BC Egyptian medical document, states that one can prevent the hair from turning white by anointing it with the blood of a black calf that has been boiled in oil. The same medical treatise prescribes, for the renewal of hair that has fallen out, the application of a mixture of six fats, namely, those of the lion, the hippopotamus, the crocodile, the cat, the snake, and the ibex. For strengthening hair, the Ebers Papyrus recommends that a person anoint it with the tooth of a donkey crushed in honey.

D. THE GRECO-ROMAN WORLD

Greece

In the Homeric period, men's hair was worn long. The epic poetry of the *Iliad* uses the recurring epithet *karēkomoōntes*, "long haired," to describe the Achaeans. The Abantes, however, were one people during the early age of Greece who deviated from this custom. A warlike group used to hand-to-hand combat, the Abantes are said to have cut the front of their hair so the enemy could not take hold of it. Early Greek statues depict long-haired men and long-haired gods, such as Zeus, Dionysus, and Apollo. Greek mythology held that magic power and superhuman strength resided in the unshorn locks of its legendary heroes. Two of the titles of Apollo are *chrysokomēs*, "golden haired," and *akersekomēs*, "never shorn," i.e., ever young, an explanation why Greek youths wore long hair until they reached maturity. When the Theban king Pentheus threatened to cut off Dionysus's hair, the latter objected that his hair had been dedicated to a god (Euripides, *Bacch.* 493–496). Thus, a Greek custom seems to have developed of growing one's hair following an oath and dedicating it to a god. Young women were known to sacrifice their hair to a deity at marriage, sailors after surviving a storm at sea, and warriors after victory in battle. Hygieia, the goddess of health, was presented offerings of the hair of women before or after they gave birth to a child. Greek boys typically had long hair, with the exception of the boys in Sparta, who had short haircuts and who were already undergoing military training by age seven. When an Athenian youth became a citizen, his childhood locks were dedicated to a god.

Before the Persian Wars, toward the middle of the first millennium BC, Athenian men tied up their long hair in a kind of "knot" or "bun" on the top of their head called a *krōbylos*. The knot was fastened with a gold brooch or pin that resembled a grasshopper (Thucydides, *Hist.* 1.6). By the start of the fourth century BC, the knot was largely discarded in favor of a shorter style of hair that normally fell somewhere around, or slightly below, the natural hairline at the back of the neck. This change brought most Athenian men to the barbershop on a regular basis. Though the hair of most men was much shorter than that of the earlier period, their hair was not as close cropped as that of athletes and slaves. In addition, class distinctions and particular occupations sometimes affected the particular hairstyle worn. Some scholars, on the basis of Philo and other early writers, argue that homosexuals let their hair grow longer than most men. The Greeks often ridiculed baldness.

Greek women's hairstyles varied through the centuries. In general, the styles moved from allowing the hair to hang down, in the seventh and sixth centuries BC, to arranging it up on the head, in the late fifth century and onwards. Women cared for their own hair rather than visiting a local hairdresser, but slaves often assisted women of means in the arrangement of hair. It was the custom for Greek women to have long hair (cf. 1 Cor 11:15), with the exception of female slaves, who had short hair. The hair was usually parted in the middle and either wrapped around the head in plaits or wound into a knot in back of the head. Some women wore braided or twisted strands running to the forehead and back of the head in a type of raised, looped ridge. Other women styled their hair with seven or eight braided strands on either side of the middle parting. Sometimes a head covering would be worn, but the practice does not seem to have been widespread. At Corinth, hundreds of bone and ivory hairpins have been excavated. Greek women also used pins of bronze, silver, and gold. In addition to pins, ornamental headbands or fillets were worn to hold the hair in place. Sometimes a simple ribbon was used. On other occasions, women anchored their coil of hair by use of a wider band made of cloth or leather, sometimes decorated with gold. Hair combs were also employed. Only on rare occasions, such as during certain religious rites and at marriage ceremonies, did women appear in public with their hair unbound, i.e., flowing over the shoulders. Dio Chrysostom, a Greek philosopher of the first century AD, points out that a woman found guilty of adultery was subject to the humiliating act of having her hair cut off (*2 Fort.* 3).

Rome

Until ca. 300 BC, Roman men wore their hair long. After this date, with the formal introduction of barbering, the hair was worn short with no part. Writing around AD 65, Musonius Rufus encouraged men to cut off hair that is useless, similar to trimming a vine, and to cut their hair short so that they would not be mistaken for women. The aristocrats and people of wealth had their hair cared for at home by slaves. Men of the middle class made their way to one of the many city barbershops. The hair was usually combed straight down to the forehead from the crown. Boys had long hair that was not cut until they experienced a rite of passage allowing them to wear the toga. Many fashion-conscious Roman men made use of curling tongs. In addition, they often applied various kinds of oil and grease to the hair and scalp. These concoctions were derived from such substances as the marrow of deer bones, the fat of bears and sheep, and the excrement of rats.

Roman women displayed a bewildering array of hairstyles. In general, simple styles were used in the early periods of Roman history and they developed into elaborate hairstyles in the later periods. It was popular for young girls to comb the hair straight back and to bring it together in a knot at the back of the neck. Young women often used a similar style but with the addition of a plait running over the top of the head in front. Matrons and women of social standing commonly wore their hair in a mass on the crown of the head. A number of elaborate styles were employed. On their wedding day, brides had special attention given to their hair arrangement. It was divided into six locks, likely braided and tied with ribbons.

Roman women arranged and secured their hair by the use of hairpins, hairnets, ribbons, and combs. The combs were made of boxwood, tortoise-shell, or ivory. Hairdressers also employed needles and thread to accomplish some of the more complex hairstyles of the Roman world. Long, thick needles of bone and ivory (and sometimes more costly materials such as gold and glass) have been found in archaeological excavations, measuring ten to fifteen centimeters long and one-half to one centimeter wide. Such needles would have been well suited to hairdressing purposes, but would have been impractical for other uses. One such needle (as well as a spindle) was found in the "beauty case of Cumae" along with other hairdressing tools, and a needle and cosmetic spatula are paired together on the frieze of the *mundus muliebris* tomb, showing a close connection between these two beautification tools. Garlands of flowers and crown-like ornaments containing jewels were also used by wealthy women to enhance the beauty of their hair. The Romans used a primitive curling iron called a *calamistrum*. It consisted of a hollow, iron rod and a thinner solid rod. The hollow rod would be heated over coals, and then the hair would be wrapped around the smaller rod and inserted into the hollow rod. It is likely that elaborate hairstyles were a marker of social status: only a wealthy woman would have the means and the leisure time available for such complex hair arrangements. However, it was a sign of modesty for women to cover their head when they were outside, so many of these elaborate hairstyles would have been covered by a part of the woman's mantle when she left the home.

Both men and women used various substances to dye their hair. Black was a popular color for men, but sometimes they used a blond dye. Women also used black dye. Henna was also quite popular. Women were known to either pluck out gray hairs or use hair dye to cover them up. Hair oil is also mentioned in Roman literature. As in ancient Egypt, wigs were worn by both sexes. Blond wigs were especially in demand. Many were imported from Germany and were made from the naturally blond hair of Germans captured in battle.

E. THE JEWISH WORLD

There is some indication that the Jewish world of the first century AD was influenced by the shorter hairstyles adopted by Greek and Roman men some three centuries earlier. Indeed, Jewish art from the Roman period—particularly the synagogue wall paintings at Dura-Europos on the Euphrates—generally depicts well-trimmed beards and rather short hair that follows the contour of the head. Likewise, in Talmudic times, rabbinic authorities permitted Jews who had frequent dealings with Roman authorities to clip their hair in the Gentile fashion (*b. B. Qam.* 83a). Thus, in Jewish society, the length of hair and style of beards was, to some degree, determined by the accepted custom of the time.

Jewish women are known to have plaited or braided their hair (Jdt 10:3). The braided hair of a woman dating to the first century was found by archaeologists in the Judean wilderness at the fortress of Masada. The Mishnah forbids women plaiting hair on the Sabbath (*m. Šabb.* 6:5), and dyeing one's hair is discouraged in the Babylonian Talmud (*b. Ketub.* 54a).

In Talmudic times it was required that married women conceal their hair in public. The reasons given for this by the rabbis are because the beauty associated with women's hair is likely to seduce men (or at least distract them from their prayers) and because it was Eve who first sinned and thus brought shame on all those who share her gender. Covering the hair was accomplished through use of a head scarf or a part of the woman's mantle, or less frequently a hairnet (*śĕbākâ*) or cap (*kippâ*). Remains of hairnets, hairpins, and possibly even head scarves are part of the archaeological record. According to Tertullian, Jewish women could be easily identified in Carthage because they wore veils (*Cor.* 4.2). A wife going out in public with her hair "unbound" was sufficient grounds for divorce (*m. Ketub.* 7:6), but, conversely, a man had to pay a fine if he uncovered a woman's hair in public, since he had shamed her (*m. B. Qam.* 8:6). It is possible that the covering of a girl's hair marked her coming of age, but there is no strong evidence that a head covering was necessarily a marker of womanhood.

Although women were required to wear coverings (*b. Ned.* 30b), men were not. Only in the Babylonian Talmud are men said to sometimes cover their heads, and this was only on special occasions or by personal choice (*b. Ned.* 51a; *b. Moʿed Qaṭ.* 24a; *b. Ber.* 51a; *b. Šabb.* 156b). Scholars, however, typically covered their heads (*b. Qidd.* 31a; *b. Pesaḥ.* 11b). The practice of all Jewish men covering their heads, a custom followed by observant Jews today, was a later development.

As mentioned above, Nazirite vows were still practiced in early Judaism, including growing the hair and offering it as a sacrifice when the temple was still standing (Num 6:18; cf. *m. Naz.* 4:7). Philo explains that since this offering was a type of firstfruits offering and the Nazirite was offering himself as the sacrifice, his hair had to be used since human blood was not allowed on the altar (*Spec.* 254).

As in the OT period, among early Jews gray hair continued to signal respect and wisdom (Wis 4:8–9; Philo, *Spec.* 238; cf. Lev 19:32). Contrary to the practice of the Romans of the same period, wigs were not used by Jewish men or women, and dyeing the hair was discouraged by the rabbis in the Babylonian Talmud (*b. Ketub.* 54a). Josephus states that Herod the Great dyed his hair black to conceal signs of aging, but even in the passages where he discusses this it is implied that dyeing the hair was a mark of poor taste (Jos. *Ant.* 233; *J. W.* 490).

F. THE CHRISTIAN WORLD

In the first few centuries of the church, Christian men typically had short hair and left it uncovered, and Christian women typically grew their hair long and covered it with some sort of head covering. When factions of the church deviated from these norms, we see the church fathers discussing hair practices and arguing on biblical and moral grounds for the normal practices to be observed.

Clement of Alexandria (d. ca. AD 214) taught extensively about the proper use of hair. For men, his ideal hairstyle was relatively short so that the hair would not get into one's eyes, but if one did not have curly hair, he advised having the head shaved (*Paed.* 3.11). In either situation, he strongly advocated growing a long beard. However, he also advised that the hair on the upper lip should be trimmed so that it would not get dirty while eating. He discouraged Christian men from participating in a common practice of the day whereby hair was forcibly removed by applying plaster or some other adhesive to the skin and then ripping it off (*Paed.* 3.3). He found smooth skin, produced through either this practice or just shaving with a razor, to be effeminate and contrary to the will of God for men, since, in his view, God created men to grow hair all over their bodies. Overall, Clement viewed masculine hair as a gift from God and encouraged Christian men to let it grow as much as possible.

In his writings, Clement did not spend as much time preaching against the vices of women in their hair practices as he did discussing men's hair fashion, but his opinions on woman's hairstyles were no less strong than his views on men's hair. He advised Christian women to have a simple hairstyle that involved arranging the hair up with a hairpin (*Paed.* 3.11), and he spoke out strongly against spending a lavish amount of time arranging the hair in exotic fashions (*Paed.* 3.2). Clement also discouraged both men and women from dyeing their hair and wearing wigs (*Paed.* 2.8, 11; 3.2, 11). He even went so far as to call these practices lying since they involve changing one's appearance for the purpose of deceiving others.

Tertullian (ca. 160–200) preached against women dyeing their hair blond with saffron (*Cult. Fem.* 6.1). This was to be avoided, he felt, since it changed the color that God had given to the woman who dyed her hair in this way, it was harmful to the hair, and saffron was offered to idols in pagan religions. He also was shocked that some people would thwart God's design by dyeing their gray hair black again. Another issue that Tertullian faced was that of a faction of Christian women who forsook wearing a head covering in order to show that they had devoted themselves to the Lord and that they were committing to sexual abstinence. For these reasons, they believed, they were no longer bound by traditional cultural conventions; that is, since they were not going to marry, they asserted that they no longer needed to follow the dress code of married women. Tertullian strongly argued that even women who had vowed to remain virgins still needed to wear a veil.

Like Clement, Jerome (ca. 347–420) and Paulinus of Nola (ca. 353–431) also preached against elaborate hairstyles. Around the same time, Chrysostom (ca. 347–407) advised that boys should have their hair cut short so that they would not become sinfully conceited by their good looks. Instead, they were to be encouraged to enjoy a simpler way of life. Chrysostom, in one of his sermons (*Hom. 1 Cor. 11.2–16*), and Epiphanius of Salamis (ca. 315–403), in his work *Panarion*, interpreted 1 Cor 11 as teaching that men should not have long hair since it would be considered a head covering.

Monks in the early church generally wore their hair short, as was the custom among other Christian men of the time. However, Augustine of Hippo (354–430) had to deal with a situation in which some monks claimed that they were eunuchs and that therefore they were neither male nor female (*Op. mon.* 40). To show that they were not bound to the customary restrictions of other Christian men, they grew their hair long. Augustine preached strongly against this practice, arguing that men who have chosen to become eunuchs by choosing a life of sexual abstinence are still considered males in the eyes of both God and men, and therefore they should not adopt a feminine practice such as growing their hair long.

BIBLIOGRAPHY: L. Adkins and R. Adkins, *Handbook to Life in Ancient Greece* (1997); P. Bienkowski, "Hair Dressing," *DANE* 137; B. Brier and H. Hobbs, *Daily Life of the Ancient Egyptians* (1999); L. Bronner, "From Veil to Wig: Jewish Women's Hair Covering," *Judaism* 42 (1993), 465–77; A. P. Brown, "Chrysostom and Epiphanius: Long Hair Prohibited as Covering in 1 Corinthians 11:4, 7," *BBR* 23 (2013), 365–76; D. Collon, "Clothing and Grooming in Ancient Western Asia," *CANE* 1.503–15; A. T. Croom, *Roman Clothing and Fashion* (2000); M. E. Doerfler, "'Hair!': Remnants of Ascetic Exegesis in Augustine of Hippo's *De Opere Monachorum*," *JECS* 22 (2014), 79–111; A. Erman, *Life in Ancient Egypt*, trans. H. M. Tirard (1894); R. Flacelière, *Daily Life in Greece at the Time of Pericles*, trans. P. Green (1966); J. Fletcher, "Hair," in *Ancient Egyptian Materials and Technology*, ed. P. T. Nicholson and I. Shaw (2000), 495–501; R. Garland, *The Greek Way of Life: From Conception to Old Age* (1993); D. W. J. Gill, "The Importance of Roman Portraiture for Head-Coverings in 1 Corinthians 11:2–16," *TynBul* 41 (1990), 245–60; C. R. Hallpike, "Hair," in *The Encyclopedia of Religion*, ed. M. Eliade (1987), 6.154–57; J. B. Hurley, "Did Paul Require Veils or the Silence of Women? A Consideration of I Cor. 11:2–16 and I Cor. 14:33b–36," *WTJ* 35 (1973), 190–220; P. J. King and L. E. Stager, *Life in Biblical Israel* (2001); K. R. MacGregor, "Is 1 Corinthians 11:2–16 a Prohibition of Homosexuality?" *BSac* 166 (2009), 201–16; T. A. Madhloom, *The Chronology of Neo-Assyrian Art* (1970); P. T. Massey, "Long Hair as a Glory *and* as a Covering: Removing an Ambiguity from 1 Cor 11:15," *NovT* 53 (2011), 52–72; O. Margalith, "Samson's Riddle and Samson's Magic Locks," *VT* 36 (1986), 225–34; J. Morgenstern, *Rites of Birth, Marriage, Death and Kindred Occasions Among the Semites* (1966); K. Y. Mumcuoglu and J. Zias, "How the Ancients De-Loused Themselves," *BAR* 15.6 (1989), 66–69; J. Murphy-O'Connor, "Sex and Logic in I Corinthians 11:2–16," *CBQ* 42 (1980), 482–500; S.-A. Naguib, "Hair in Ancient

Egypt," *AcOr* 51 (1990), 7–26; K. R. Nemet-Nejat, *Daily Life in Ancient Mesopotamia* (1998); K. Olson, *Dress and the Roman Woman: Self-presentation and Society* (2008); A. Padgett, "Paul on Women in the Church: The Contradictions of Coiffure in I Corinthians 11.2–16," *JSNT* 20 (1984), 69–86; E. Riefstahl, "Two Hairdressers of the Eleventh Dynasty," *JNES* 15 (1956), 10–17; D. Shlezinger-Katsman, "Clothing," *OHJDL* 362–81; J. Stephens, "Ancient Roman Hairdressing: On (Hair)pins and Needles," *JRA* 21 (2008), 110–32; C. L. Thompson, "Hairstyles, Head-coverings, and St. Paul: Portraits from Roman Corinth," *BA* 51.2 (1988), 99–115; H. Trau, N. Rubin, and S. Vargon, "Symbolic Significance of Hair in the Biblical Narrative and in the Law," *Koroth* 9 (1988), 173–79; D. Ussishkin, *The Conquest of Lachish by Sennacherib* (1982); Y. Yadin, *Masada: Herod's Fortress and the Zealots' Last Stand*, trans. M. Pearlman (1966).

MRW & SMR

See also AGE & THE AGED, BARBERS & BEARDS, and COSMETICS.

H̲ARBORS

A harbor is a sheltered body of water where boats and ships can moor or anchor. A harbor can be natural or man-made. A good harbor provides easy access to open water, sufficient depth, protection from high waves and storms, and a suitable bottom for anchorage (that is, one that is not overly rocky, sandy, or mucky). In antiquity, most harbors were natural and were located at the mouth of a river or sheltered by a bay or an offshore island. Construction of breakwaters and jetties (docks) could improve natural harbors. Moles (man-made breakwaters) made of massive stone walls were used to enclose a harbor. Quays were built along the shore of a harbor to facilitate the loading and unloading of vessels. These would at times be equipped with bollards, posts on which hawsers, the ropes used to moor ships, could be tied.

A. THE OLD TESTAMENT

Though there is a Hebrew word for "ship," ʾŏniyyâ, there is no distinct Hebrew word for "harbor" or "port." The OT refers about a half dozen times to the "coast" or "shore" (Heb. ḥôf), always that of the Mediterranean Sea (Deut 1:7; Josh 9:1; Judg 5:17; Jer 47:7; Ezek 25:16), and on one occasion uses the phrase ḥôf ʾŏniyyôt (Gen 49:13), which the NIV translates "a haven for ships." The word māḥôz, "haven," which occurs once (Ps 107:30), is a loanword from Akkadian (cf. Akk. māḥāzu, "harbor").

While the OT does not manifest a particular interest in harbors per se, the text does mention port cities for various reasons. Ur, which in antiquity was situated along the coast of the Persian Gulf, was the birthplace and original home of Abraham (Gen 11:28, 31). Isaiah (19:13), Jeremiah (2:16), Ezekiel (30:13), and Hosea (9:6) all mention Memphis in Egypt, another port city, in negative terms. Jeremiah may have had personal contact with this city, as well as with the eastern delta city of Zoan (Tanis), which is mentioned in a number of places in the OT (e.g., Num 13:22; Ps 78:12, 43; Isa 19:11; Ezek 30:14).

Arvad, which is on the Levantine Coast, is mentioned, along with Sidon and Byblos, by Ezekiel in his oracle against and lament over Tyre (Ezek 27:8–11). Arvad was captured by Tiglath-pileser III (8th c. BC) and, because it resisted, its inhabitants were deported. Tyre, which surrendered, was allowed to pay tribute.

Of all the ancient port cities, Tyre is the one mentioned most frequently in the OT (about four dozen times). Its king Hiram I (10th c. BC) was a strong ally of both David and Solomon, supplying the latter with cedar beams and craftsmen, and cooperating with him in maritime ventures in the Red Sea (1 Kgs 10:22). Tyre originally consisted of two islands, which were joined by Hiram. Its main harbor, which was natural, was situated to the north and was known as the "Sidonian" harbor. Ithobaal I (9th c. BC) created another, artificial harbor, the "Egyptian" harbor, to the city's south.

Zarephath was a small fishing port located between Tyre and Sidon. Its Hebrew name, ṣārĕpat, may be related to the Akkadian verb ṣarāpu, "to dye red," which was a specialization of the Phoenicians, who processed dye derived from *murex* mollusks. Zarephath (Gk. *Sarepta*) was the home of the widow Elijah helped in a time of famine (cf. Luke 4:25–26). Excavations at this site conducted by J. B. Pritchard revealed important Iron Age Phoenician materials that had been lacking from Tyre and Sidon. Among the discoveries were clay lamps with two spouts, mushroom-lip jugs, and, most significantly, a symbol of Tanit, the chief goddess of Carthage. He also uncovered a Roman quay dated to the first century AD.

Joppa (Heb. *yāpô*, Akk. *yapu*, Egy. *ypw*, Gk. *Ioppē*, present-day Jaffa), whose name is related to a Hebrew word meaning "beauty," was a port city on the coast of Palestine. In view of the straight coastline of Palestine, which has been formed by the deposition of silt from the Nile River borne by the counterclockwise current, this region lacked the deep, well-protected harbors of the Phoenicians to its north. Joppa's harbor was protected only by a breakwater of rocks located 90 to 120 meters offshore. Located thirty-five miles west-northwest of Jerusalem, it was the city's closest port. The cedars of Lebanon for the building of both the temple of Solomon (2 Chr 2:8, 16) and the second temple (Ezra 3:7) were floated along the Mediterranean coast, perhaps to Tell Qasile at the mouth of the Yarkon River, just north of Joppa.

Joppa was the port of embarkation for Jonah (Jonah 1:3), who was heading for a distant Phoenician port called Tarshish. The name Tarshish occurs twenty-eight times in the Hebrew Bible. It occurs eight times in the phrase *ʾŏniyyôt taršîš*, "ships of Tarshish," which designates long-distance ships. The name may possibly be derived from a Phoenician word for "smeltery." It may possibly designate a distant Phoenician port, such as Tartessus in Spain. The Phoenician inscription found at Nora in Sardinia indicates that Phoenicians had penetrated into the western Mediterranean by the tenth century BC.

First Kings 9:26–28 refers to the joint Solomonic-Phoenician naval activities at Ezion Geber, which was near Elath, at the north end of the Gulf of Elath on the Red Sea. Trade with Ophir, a site located somewhere on the Arabian Peninsula, motivated these efforts. Later, Jehoshaphat failed in an attempt to conduct a similar enterprise (2 Chr 20:35–37). The only natural harbor in the area of Ezion Geber and Elath is on a small island off the Coral Island known as the *Jezīrat Faraʿūn* ("Pharaoh's Island"), which is located seven and a half miles southwest of Elath and 250 meters off the coast, in a protected bay. A small, artificially closed basin was found on the island, with a quay on the opposite, mainland shore.

B. THE NEW TESTAMENT

Jesus and his disciples knew the Sea of Galilee harbors for small vessels. It is recorded in Mark 7:24 that Jesus visited the coastal region of Tyre on the Mediterranean. It remained for his followers to exploit sea routes and seaports in the expansion of the early church, as recorded in the book of Acts.

The Ethiopian eunuch was en route to Gaza when Philip met him (Acts 8:26), but since he was returning home in a chariot, it is unlikely that he planned to board a ship at that port. Saul departed from Caesarea to return to Tarsus (Acts 9:30). Tarsus, now nine miles from the sea due to silting, was originally a seaport on a lagoon at the mouth of the Cydnus River (also known as the Berdan River).

On their first missionary journey, Paul, Barnabas, and Mark departed Antioch, an inland city, by sailing from its coastal port, Seleucia Pieriea, which was located at the mouth of the Orontes River (Acts 13:4). They disembarked in the port of Salamis on eastern Cyprus (Acts 13:5). They then traveled overland to (Nea) Paphos in western Cyprus, the seat of the Roman governor Sergius Paullus. The harbor of Paphos was located in the lee of a natural headland. The eastern mole, which was six hundred meters long and between six and ten meters wide, was constructed of ashlars, and may have had a lighthouse at its end. The group sailed from Paphos (Acts 13:13) to the southern Turkish coast, to Perga in Pamphylia, where Mark left the mission. After evangelizing the area of Galatia, Paul and Barnabas departed from Attalia, modern Antalya, just west of Perga (Acts 14:26).

Attalia was the major harbor of Pamphylia. Hadrian's Gate commemorates the emperor's visit here in AD 130.

The second missionary journey of Paul was overland to Alexandria Troas (Acts 16:8), which lay south of the historic site of Troy. Ruins of its man-made harbor are still visible, as are remains of a stoa that once circled the harbor. At Troas Paul was evidently joined by Luke, as the "we" section of Acts begins right after Paul's arrival in Troas is mentioned (Acts 16:10). Their ship anchored overnight in a harbor on the north side of the island of Samothrace, which was protected from the southwest winds (Acts 16:11).

Paul and his companions then sailed north to Neapolis, which was built on a promontory and which had both east and west harbors. They then traveled to Philippi. Next they continued west on the Via Egnatia to Thessalonica, at the head of the Thermaic Gulf, a city that had an excellent natural harbor. After his time in Berea, Paul probably went alone to Athens by sea from Thessalonica. Disappointed by the meager reception he experienced in Athens, Paul left for Corinth to the south (Acts 17:34–18:1).

Corinth had two ports, Lechaion (Lat. *Lechaeum*) and Cenchreae, which in Hellenistic times were the most active ports in the Aegean, if not the entire eastern Mediterranean. Corinth occupied a narrow isthmus that connected the Peloponnesus with mainland Greece. Instead of risking the hazards of circumnavigating the dangerous Cape Malea in the south, ship goods were loaded onto carts at one coast and were hauled, along with the boat, about four miles overland to the opposite coast. The land passage, a section of which was discovered in 1956 (Vanderpool, pl. 83, fig. 3), was called the *diolkos* (a word that has to do with "drawing along" or "hauling"). Much of the east-west traffic across the Mediterranean passed through Corinth.

Lechaion, which was but a quarter mile north of the city, was Corinth's western harbor, on the Corinthian Gulf. It was connected to the city by walls. The foundations of an exceptionally large basilica dating to the fourth or fifth century have been excavated adjacent to the Lechaion harbor. The region around a large lagoon is presently being excavated.

Paul departed from the region of Achaia from the port of Cenchreae (Acts 18:18), which was located on the Saronic Gulf, six miles to the east of Corinth. Phoebe, the deaconness from the church at Cenchreae, carried Paul's letter to the church at Rome (Rom 16:1). This small harbor, with its protected basin of about three hectares, was probably first built after Caesar, in 44 BC, refounded Corinth as a new Roman colony. At Cenchreae, two moles extend from a natural bay; these were broad enough to support warehouses. From the southern mole archaeologists recovered unique panels of *opus sectile* glass (that is, glass cut and inlaid in floors or walls) from the inundated floor of a temple of Isis. Panels 16 and 18 depict the harbor, with temples on the ends of its two moles. These may have been the temples to Aphrodite and to Isis known from textual sources.

Paul's third missionary journey was on foot from Antioch to Ephesus (Acts 19:1), which had three harbors located at the mouth of the Cayster River. The major commercial center of Asia Minor on the Aegean, Ephesus, which had a population of two hundred fifty thousand, was probably the fourth greatest city of the Roman world, after Rome, Alexandria, and Antioch. The deposition of sediment at the mouth of the Cayster River was a constant problem. Thus, in AD 129, Hadrian diverted the course of the river further north to reduce silt deposition. Today the site of ancient Ephesus is three miles from the sea.

The original harbor of Ephesus was close to the Artemisium, the temple of Artemis, which was regarded as one of the Seven Wonders of the World. Known as the "Sacred Harbor" (due to its proximity to the temple), this original harbor eventually filled with silt from the Cayster River to the north. In the early third century BC, Lysimachus, one of the successors (*diadochi*) of Alexander the Great, relocated the city closer to the present shoreline, which had progressed further north and west, and he had a substantial harbor built. In the first century BC, the Arcadian Street was constructed, which was a great paved road that was five hundred meters long and eleven meters wide that ran from the city's theater to the Middle Harbor Gate. According to Livy, the second harbor once sheltered eighty-nine warships (*Rom. Hist.* 37.14, 30). It has been conjectured that at one time moles extended 170 meters to protect the harbor.

Excavations conducted by G. Langmann and H. Zabehlicky between 1987 and 1989 revealed new details of the Roman harbor at Ephesus. A quay, which was two meters wide, was made up of immense slabs of limestone whose dimensions were 1.5 x 1 meters. The quay culminated in a jetty that extended into the bay. Remains of an original wooden scaffolding were uncovered from the sea.

Paul traveled on through Macedonia, leaving Philippi for Troas (Acts 20:6). Later, he went by himself on foot from Troas to Assos, where he rejoined his party aboard a ship (Acts 20:13–14). At the foot of the hill on which Assos was built were two small harbors. Aristotle once resided at this city, which has some of the best-preserved Hellenistic fortifications.

After brief stops at the island harbors of Chios and Samos, the ship arrived at Miletus (Acts 20:15), which was originally located on the south shore of the Gulf of Latmos, on a peninsula east of the island of Lade. On the north shore of this gulf was the estuary of the Meander River. The deposition of silt has been so great that the gulf has been filled in, transforming a portion of the gulf into a lake, called Lake Bafa, and attaching the island of Lade to the coast. By the fourth century AD, Miletus was no longer on the coast, and now it is five miles from the coast (see Yamauchi 2003, 116–17). Miletus once had four harbors, including a bay west of the peninsula, called the Theater Harbor. The Lion Harbor was so named for two marble lions that once flanked its entrance, which could be closed off by chains. In the Archaic Age (8th–6th c. BC) Miletus was famed as the mother city of scores of colonies around the Black Sea, and also as the home of many of the leading pre-Socratic philosophers, such as Thales, Anaximander, and Anaximenes.

Paul's voyage to Jerusalem took him to the island of Cos and to the large island of Rhodes, both off the southwest coast of Turkey. Today tourists are shown "St. Paul's Bay" at the city of Lindos, which is on the east coast of the island of Rhodes. But it is more probable that his ship would have stopped at the city of Rhodes, with its multiple harbors, at the northern end of the island. After the unsuccessful year-long siege of this city by Demetrius Poliorcetes in 305–304 BC, its citizens paid for a 105-foot bronze statue of their god Helios from the sale of the siege works. This Colossus was one of the Seven Wonders of the World. It did not bestride the harbor, as shown in popular illustrations, but was located on a hill, where it stood for fifty-six years before being toppled by an earthquake in 226 BC.

Paul's ship then sailed on to Patara (Acts 21:1). This was the main harbor of Lycia in southwestern Asia Minor, located near the mouth of the Xanthus River. On the west mole of the harbor was a set of eight *horrea*, or warehouses, each twenty-seven meters deep. An inscription credits the emperor Hadrian (AD 128) with the construction of these storage facilities for grain from Egypt, for its transfer to other ships. Paul and his party boarded a larger ship that stopped at Tyre, then proceeded south to Ptolemais (Akko), and then on to Caesarea (Acts 21:7–8).

The prevailing northwesterly winds in the central Mediterranean and the Aegean facilitated a direct voyage from Rome to Alexandria, but they hindered the return voyage, on which a ship had to proceed slowly and hug the coast, passing under Cyprus to the southern shore of Anatolia. Wilson observes that "a typical return voyage from Alexandria to Rome took approximately 50 days: 9 to Myra, 10 to Rhodes, 15 to western Crete, 13 to the Straits of Messina, and 3 to Puteoli" (Wilson, 90).

It is noteworthy that in his three missionary travels Paul always traveled by land while going westward and by sea when going eastward (Yamauchi 1995). The exception came when Paul, while a prisoner of the Romans, departed with other prisoners from Caesarea on a ship from Adramyttium, a port in Mysia in northwest Anatolia (Acts 27:2), for Rome, stopping first at Sidon (Acts 27:3). The second port reached was Myra on the Lycia coast

(Acts 27:5). This city was located about three and a half miles inland from its port, Andriace, located at the mouth of the Myrus River. Myra and Andriace were transit points for the grain bound for Rome. A set of eight warehouses, each of which was thirty-two meters deep, was built at Myra by the emperor Hadrian (AD 128).

Changing ships, Paul and his fellow travelers headed west and reached Fair Havens, a bay on the south coast of Crete that was the port for Lasea (Acts 27:8). According to Acts 27:12, "Since the harbor was unsuitable to winter in, the majority decided that we should sail on, hoping to reach Phoenix and winter there. This was a harbor in Crete, facing both southwest and northwest." The ship never reached Phoenix, however: as Luke has so vividly described, the ship was suddenly borne westward by a violent Northeaster and for many days those on board had no sight of the sun or stars (Acts 27:13–26). The ship went aground on the small island of Malta east of Sicily and broke up in what is today called St. Paul's Bay, some eight miles northwest of modern Valletta (Acts 27:41). Valletta is the main Maltese harbor and is located on a peninsula with protected bays on either side.

From there, Paul sailed on a new ship to Syracuse, on the eastern shore of Sicily (Acts 28:11–12). Syracuse had two excellent harbors in protected bays on either side of the city. Rhegium, a port on the southwest coast, in the "toe" of Italy, was the next brief stop. The ship reached the destination at Puteoli (Acts 28:13).

On the basis of the Pastoral Epistles (1 Timothy, 2 Timothy, and Titus), scholars assume that Paul was released from his first imprisonment at Rome and that he traveled with Titus to Crete (Titus 1:5) and with Timothy to Ephesus (1 Tim 1:3). Paul later wintered in Nicopolis, where he asked Titus to meet him (Titus 3:12). Nicopolis, whose name means "the city of victory," was established by Augustus in northwestern Greece to commemorate his victory over Antony and Cleopatra at the bay of Actium in 31 BC. The sockets for the bronze beaks of the warships (*rostra*) that he displayed as trophies of his victory can still be seen there.

C. THE NEAR EASTERN WORLD

Mesopotamia

Mesopotamia lay between the Tigris and Euphrates Rivers. Of the two rivers, the Euphrates was much easier to navigate. The identification and use of adequate harbors was concurrent with the expansion of water transportation in the ancient world. In the great riverine civilization of the Mesopotamian valley, river-craft traffic predominated. Wharves along the riverbanks accommodated riverboats and, in some cases, sea-going vessels.

Based on the assumption that the present coastlines of Iraq and Kuwait were formed by the deposition of sediment from the Tigris and Euphrates Rivers over the millennia, some atlases locate the ancient coastline of this region close to Ur (which is now inland). However, geological studies have revealed an uplift in the Zagros Mountains with a corresponding depression in the Persian Gulf, thus indicating that the ancient coastline might have corresponded to the current coastline (Beek, 9).

All cities in southern Mesopotamia were situated on the Tigris, the Euphrates, or canals. According to legend, Eridu was considered the oldest city in Mesopotamia. Its present-day ruins, however, are miles from the coastline. Nevertheless, its mythological foundations place it on the sea-coast, and bones from saltwater and brackish-water fish have been found around the city. Eridu was sacred to the Sumerian water-god Enki (Akk. Ea), whose temple was thought to sit on the primordial waters that surrounded the earth.

Ur, now many miles from the mouth of the Euphrates, once served as the seaport of Mesopotamia. It had two harbor areas on the Euphrates and one on a canal. The Akkadian word for the sites where goods were unloaded was *kārum*, "port, quay."

Imports and exports between the Indus Valley and Mesopotamia were transported via the Indian Ocean and the Persian Gulf. Mesopotamian texts speak of Dilmun, Magan, and Meluḫḫa in this connection. Though Samuel N. Kramer believed that Dilmun referred to the Harappan civilization of the Indus River, scholars today believe that it designated the island of Bahrain off the eastern coast of Saudi Arabia. The islands of Failaka and Bahrain served as stations along the route down the Persian Gulf. Magan is now believed to have referred to Oman in southeast Arabia, and Meluḫḫa to the Indus Valley.

The trade that took place between Mesopotamia and the Indus Valley (now in Pakistan), where the urban centers of Harappa and Mohenjo-Daro flourished during the reign of Sargon of Agade (2340–2284 BC), was extensive. Sargon boasted that ships of Meluḫḫa docked at Agade, a site that has not yet been identified but which was presumably in the rough vicinity of Babylon. There is even textual evidence from Ebla in northwest Syria of trade with Meluḫḫa, which was supervised by a harbor master (LÚ.KAR) there. Further evidence of the trade between Mesopotamia and the Indus Valley has come in the form of eighteen square seals with the as-yet-undeciphered Indus script found at Ur and a round seal with an origin in Bahrain found at the Indus Valley site of Lothal. Trade items from the east included copper, ivory, pearls, and carnelian beads.

Particularly striking is the sophisticated Harappan harbor uncovered at Lothal, which is located about twelve miles from the sea on a tributary of the Sabarmati River, in the Bay of Cambray. This included a large rectangular brick enclosure that measured 215 x 37 meters, with a depth of 3.3 meters. This enclosure had a unique sluice gate to regulate the depth of water during tides. Seven stone anchors were found on the edge of the enclosure. To the west, along the Makran coast, harbors have been identified at Sotka-Koh and Sutkagen-dor.

Egypt

River travel on the Nile was possible in both directions—south to north by floating downriver, and north to south by sailing with prevailing winds that blow from the Delta to the First Cataract at Aswan (ancient Syene). Sea trade between Egypt and the Syro-Palestinian coast began as early as the mid-third millennium BC. The earliest traffic was via short-haul coastal craft traveling in sight of land and docking at night in harbors. Access to Memphis and other Egyptian landings was gained upriver from the Delta rather than at coastal seaports. In the eastern Delta, Tanis (biblical Zoan) on Lake Menzaleh served as a sheltered port through the second millennium BC, particularly during the Ramesside era.

Excavations by Manfred Bietak at Tell el-Dabʿa have demonstrated that the Hyksos capital of Avaris (ca. 1650–1540 BC) and the later city of Pi-Ramesses were not located at Tanis, as scholars had previously thought, but at Qantir on the Pelusiac branch of the Nile River. The city of Avaris attained a huge size of 250 hectares (2.5 sq. km.).

Ports for military purposes were first developed under Tuthmosis III, who wished to ship his soldiers by sea for campaigns in Palestine and Syria. He built his fleet at a site called Peru-nefer, which was located on the Nile River near Memphis, not near the coast.

A long route to the Red Sea through the eastern desert started at Qift (or Coptos), north of Luxor, then went through the Wadi Hammamat to Quseir on the coast of the Red Sea at Elim. An inscription of an 11th Dynasty official called Henu records that he set out from Gebelein to Qena with three thousand men to build so-called Byblos ships (i.e., long-distance ships) to bring back incense from Punt. He constructed water reservoirs in the desert for this arduous journey (Kees, 111).

Following the lead of an earlier discovery of an Egyptian stela by Abdel Monem Sayed of the University of Alexandria, Kathryn Bard and Rodolfo

Fattovich recently uncovered an Egyptian port at Mersa Gawasis (Arab. "Harbor of the Spies"), known from Egyptian texts as *Saww*, on the Red Sea. Mersa Gawasis, which lies thirty-three miles north of Quseir, became the departure for naval expeditions to the fabled land of Punt, which scholars previously located on the coast of Somalia but which they now locate further north, in southern Sudan and northern Eritrea. Punt was a source of incense, ivory, ebony, and exotic animals such as baboons. A related land called Bia-Punt is also mentioned in texts; this may have been a gold-mining region in the interior of Kush (Sudan).

Ships would be constructed in the Nile Valley, then taken apart for transport ninety miles across the eastern desert through the Wadi Qena to the Red Sea, where they would be reassembled. Mersa Gawasis housed temporary contingents for possibly fifteen expeditions over two centuries during the 12th Dynasty (1985–1773 BC). A stela of Intef-iker, the vizier of Senwosret I, describes an expedition to Punt that employed 3,756 men. Some objects from the New Kingdom era may well have been left behind by Hatshepsut's famous expedition to Punt, which is depicted in detail on her mortuary tomb at Deir el-Bahri.

The harbor at Mersa Gawasis was an open bay protected from the northerly winds by a coral terrace. Ships could pass into a lagoon through a channel that was ten meters deep and 140 meters wide. Evidence was found of five ramps where the ships were dragged onto the land. The excavators of the site also found eight man-made caves there that included shrines and sailing equipment. In one of the caves (Cave 5), sixteen large, intact coils of rope were preserved. Outside the entrance of another cave (Cave 6), remains of nine wooden cargo boxes were uncovered. One of these boxes reads in part: "wonderful things of Punt." Stone anchors and timbers from ships, including two large rudder oars, have also survived.

The *Tale of Wenamun*, which is about an official of the Temple of Amun at Karnak (11th c. BC), provides fascinating details about a trip along the Mediterranean coast to Byblos to obtain wood for the construction of the ceremonial boat of the god. When Wenamun reaches Dor, a town occupied by the Tjekker, one of his seamen absconds with eleven *deben* (7.5 lbs.) of silver and five *deben* (1.2 lbs) of gold. Wenamun goes to the ruler of Dor and declares: "I have been robbed in your harbor. Now you are the prince of this land, and you are its investigator who should look for my silver" (*ANET*, 26). When, after nine days, the thief has not been found, Wenamun sails on past Tyre to Byblos, where he spends an additional twenty-nine days. Every day the Prince of Byblos sends a messenger, saying: "Get out (of) my harbor!" (*ANET*, 26). But, after his priest falls into an ecstatic trance, the prince has a change of heart and allows Wenamun to explain his mission. However, since Wenamun lacks documentation and the funds to purchase the wood, he must send back to Egypt for additional silver. Finally, after two years, just when he is about to succeed in his mission, ships from Dor appear to arrest him for having stolen silver from the Tjekker. A storm subsequently sends the ship on which Wenamun sailed adrift to Cyprus, where he has further adventures (*ANET*, 25–29).

Syria/Palestine

The Levant, the lands and islands that lie at the eastern end of the Mediterranean (toward the "rising" of the sun, in French, whence the term), is bordered by narrow coastal plains. Consequently, the Canaanites became seafarers at a very early time, and commerce by sea continued among their successors, the Phoenicians.

As the prevailing winds along the Levantine coast come from the southwest, the best harbors are on the northern, or lee, side of promontories. Furthest to the north along the coast, the site of Ugarit (modern Ras Shamra) lies ca. nine miles north of the Syrian port of Latakia. The city proper was located about a half mile from the sea, while its port, Minet el-Beida, lay on the coast, where a small bay provided a protected anchorage.

Proceeding south along the coast, Arwad (Aradus), by contrast, was a city built on a small island that measures about 900 meters long by about 550 meters wide and that is located about two miles offshore about ninety-four kilometers south of Ras Shamra. The island is U-shaped, with a fishing harbor at its open, southern end. The city on the mainland near the island was called Antaradus, then later Tartus. Tripoli was established on the tip of a small peninsula just north of Byblos.

Byblos, the major port through which goods flowed to and from Egypt, was first known as Gebel, "mountain," a term descriptive of the mountain that loomed above the coastal plain on which the city was built. At its base was a well-protected bay. Egyptian objects from the 2nd Dynasty have been discovered there. The fact that Greece imported its Egyptian papyrus from Byblos gave rise to the Greek word for "book," namely, *biblos*.

Sidon was built on a rocky cape with harbors on both the north and the south, which were available for use according to the direction of the winds. As the more protected of the two, the northern harbor was the main commercial and military harbor. The Sidonian navy was the key component of the Persian fleet that attacked Greece in 480 BC.

Tyre, which was the southernmost harbor in Phoenicia, being located just north of Israel, also had north and south harbors, the latter of which was sheltered, in part, by a man-made breakwater. The city was originally located on a rocky island that was isolated from the mainland, but it was connected to the mainland by Alexander the Great, who built a causeway to the island in order to capture the city.

Acco (NT Ptolemais) is situated on the north side of Haifa Bay. A small cape extending southward provided a protected harbor. The harbor town was the outlet for the ancient city situated approximately one thousand yards inland.

Moving south from Acco toward Egypt, natural harbors are extremely rare. Atlit, which is located fifteen miles south of Haifa, at the mouth of Nahal Oren, has a Phoenician harbor on the northern side of a peninsula, which has been investigated by the Institute of Maritime Sciences at the University of Haifa. A bay in the south could have been used only for small boats during calm weather. At this site the Phoenicians built moles, using blocks two to three meters long, which they laid on foundations of pebbles brought south from Syria or Cyprus. Wooden wedges used in the construction of these moles have been dated, using radiocarbon dating, to the ninth to eighth centuries BC. A bronze battering ram belonging to a Greek warship (4th–3rd c. BC) was recovered from the sea just north of the harbor.

At Dor, ten miles south of Atlit, offshore reefs and small islands served as breakwaters for sheltered anchorages at bays that are known as the North Bay, the Love Bay, and the South Bay. Quays ten meters wide were uncovered at the South Bay. A purple-dye factory was found at the site north of the city, as well as fish ponds to the east of it.

Ashdod, which lay further south, was situated some three miles inland from Tel Mor, which likely served as its port. Tel Mor lies about one-half mile inland from an estuary, at the mouth of the Lachish River. By NT times, the site was abandoned and replaced by Ashdod-Yam (Azotus Paralius) a few miles to the south, where large stones were used to build a breakwater.

Though numerous shipwrecks and anchors have been found off the coast of Ashkelon, recent excavations have not revealed any evidence of a harbor there. Ships must therefore have anchored in the open sea and have had their goods transshipped on smaller boats to shore. Ten miles south of Ashkelon, Gaza was the last stop in Canaan before the desert land route to Egypt. Its harbor was also the last one before Egypt via the coastal sea route.

D. THE GRECO-ROMAN WORLD

The Mediterranean is enclosed except for the Straits of Gibraltar. The warm winds blowing off the Sahara in North Africa drew in a current from the Atlantic, which proceeded around the entire sea in a counterclockwise fashion. The virtual lack of tidal action throughout the Mediterranean meant that harbors built at the mouths of rivers would eventually have to be abandoned, because the sediment deposited by the rivers would build up a marshy delta that would not only obstruct boat traffic but would often become malarial.

About three thousand harbors around the Mediterranean have been catalogued. The invention in 1942 by Jacques Cousteau and his colleagues of scuba (self-contained underwater breathing apparatus) made possible underwater exploration and archaeology. Though this apparatus is limited to a depth of two hundred feet, it has enabled investigators to identify more than 1,500 wrecks in the Mediterranean. Aerial and satellite photography has subsequently greatly enhanced our knowledge of ancient harbors.

Greece

The Minoans (2000–1500 BC) and the Mycenaeans (1500–1200 BC) used such natural features as bays and offshore islands as their harbors. Following the so-called Dark Age (1200–800 BC), during which overseas commerce virtually ceased, the Greeks engaged in a burst of maritime activity during the Archaic Age (800–500 BC), which involved both the establishment of trading outposts in Egypt and the Levant and the planting of innumerable colonies around the Black Sea, as well as in Sicily and western Italy.

Around 800 BC, Greeks from the Cyclades planted outposts at Al Mina near the mouth of the Orontes River in the Lebanon. Judging from the numerous Greek wares found there, Al Mina probably functioned as the main entry port for goods from Greece to the Near East and for Near Eastern goods going west to Greece.

The city of Naucratis on the Canopic Branch of the Nile in the Western Delta was given to the Greeks by the pharaoh Amasis II (570–526 BC). The Greeks even set up a factory here to manufacture Egyptian scarabs to sell in Greece.

The Corinthians established a key colony on the island of Corcyra (modern Corfu) in the Adriatic northwest of Greece, and following that, in 733 BC, they established a major colony at Syracuse (in southeastern Sicily), because of its extensive natural harbor. During the Peloponnesian War, an Athenian fleet led by Nicias was trapped in this harbor when he decided to take no action because of the interpretation of a lunar eclipse. The Syracusans then "began at once to close the entrance to the Great Harbour, which was about eight stadia wide [about a mile], with triremes ranged broadside and with large and small boats, mooring them at anchor"

(Thucydides, *Hist.* 7.59). The destruction of the 170 ships of the Athenian fleet and the capture of all their men was the greatest calamity Athens suffered during this war.

Early Greek colonists settled all along the west coast of Italy but avoided the east (Adriatic) coast, which lacked fertile farmlands and harbors. An early colony was established at the island of Ischia (ca. 760 BC) and at Cumae (750 BC), north of the extensive bay of Naples (Gk. *Neapolis,* "New City"). The Greeks also established a key colony in southern France at Massilia (600 BC), which became the city of Marseilles. This was located in a well-sheltered gulf to the east of the mouth of the Rhone River. Later Roman harbor installations have been uncovered by the docks of Marseille.

During the Classical Age of Greece (5th c. BC), the two dominant city-states were Sparta and Athens. Sparta had a small harbor at Gythion at the mouth of the Eurotas River. It was about twenty-five miles from Sparta to the mouth of the Eurotas River, which was not navigable. As the Spartans satisfied their need for land by conquering Messenia in the southwestern Peloponnesus, they did not engage in colonizing efforts overseas. They only became a naval power in the later stages of their war against Athens through the financial aid of the Persians.

Athens at first relied on a beach at Phaleron, but then fortified larger harbors to the west at Piraeus, a peninsula that was about 4.5 miles southwest of Athens. According to Pausanias:

> Their port was Phalerum, for at this place the sea comes nearest to Athens, and from here men say that Menestheus set sail with his fleet for Troy. . . . But when Themistocles became archon [493 BC], since he thought that the Peiraeus was more conveniently situated for mariners, and had three harbours as against one at Phalerum, he made it the Athenian port. (*Descr.* 1.1.2)

As a protective measure the Athenians built walls from their city proper (*asty*) to both Phaleron and Piraeus. In the case of the latter, two parallel walls were built that were about 450 meters apart. During the siege of Athens by Sparta during the Peloponnesian War, which began in 431 BC, fleeing families from the countryside crowded into this space, which only aggravated the disastrous plague that struck the Piraeus in 430 BC.

The Piraeus had three bays: Kantharos, Mounychia, and Zea. The Kantharos, situated furthest west, was the largest of the three and was therefore called the "Grand Harbor" (*megas limēn*). The Zea was the main military port, and the tiny Mounychia was a secondary naval port. According to Demosthenes, there were 196 ship sheds in Kantharos. These stone slipways were three meters wide and thirty-seven meters long, the length of a trireme.

Triremes had three banks of oars (hence their name) and were rowed with a crew of 170. Because of their need for speed, they did not have the lead sheathing of merchant vessels to protect their hulls from damage caused by sea worms. On campaigns, triremes would normally be beached.

The small island of Delos, located about ninety miles southeast of Athens, in the middle of the Cyclades Islands, held the treasury of the Athenian League. It had an excellent harbor on its western coast that was protected by two natural, enclosing peninsulas. After the Romans made Delos a free port in 177 BC, it became the main center for the selling and buying of slaves, and attracted merchants from many lands, such as Italy and Egypt.

In Egypt, there was a port east of Alexandria that was called Thonis by the Egyptians and Heracleon by the Greeks, which flourished from the sixth to the fourth century BC. All trace of it had been lost until it was found in 2000, by Franck Goddio, submerged in the sea about 6.5 kilometers north of the coast. Goddio's underwater excavations have revealed a number of fascinating aspects of maritime trade. Statues for export, sarcophagi, over seven hundred different types of anchors, weights, and evidence of coin designs and other goods were found among the remains of sixty-four ships. Some of these items appear to have been intentionally sunk in a ships graveyard. This may have been a means of blocking enemy ships from gaining entrance to the port city. Greek papyri from Egypt preserve several extensive records of shipments to the port of Heracleon.

After Alexander conquered Egypt in 331 BC, he founded the city of Alexandria on Pharos, an island north of Lake Mareotis, in the western Nile delta. A bridge called the Heptastadion (seven stadia = 0.8 miles) connected the island to the mainland and separated its two harbors. The western harbor was known as *Eunostos*, "Good Return"; the Grand Harbor was to the east, leeward, with its entrance at the eastern end of the island.

The main boulevard of the city was laid out parallel to the coast and was 3.5 miles long and 200 feet wide. The city was divided into five districts; Jews occupied two of these areas. The wealth of the Ptolemies enabled them to establish the *Mouseion*, which housed the greatest library in the ancient world, attracting leading Greek intellectuals from Athens such as Theophrastus, the disciple of Aristotle.

Beginning around 280 BC, Ptolemy II erected a great lighthouse at the eastern end of the island that was known as the Pharos and that was considered one of the Seven Wonders of the World. It was four hundred feet high and its light, which was reflected by bronze mirrors, could be seen as far as four miles away. Images on coins indicate that that the Pharos had three levels: a quadrangular base, then an octagonal section, and finally a cylindrical tower. It was necessary to constantly provision the tower with firewood for the lamps. The Pharos was topped with a statue of Zeus Soter, "Zeus Savior." Parts of the lighthouse survived until the fourteenth century AD. Its site is today occupied by a fort built by the Mamluk sultan Qait Bey. Underwater excavations near the site of the Pharos lighthouse begun in 1997 by Jean-Yves Empereur have recovered huge Egyptian and Ptolemaic statues from the harbor including an obelisk of Seti I, a sphinx of Psammetichus II, and a statue of a Ptolemaic queen represented as Isis (Empereur, 63–79).

Around 275 BC, after beginning construction on the Pharos, Ptolemy II established a major harbor on the Red Sea at Berenike, 512 miles south of Suez and 162 miles east of Aswan. This harbor was to function for eight centuries. Excavations were conducted at the site by Steven Sidebotham from 1994 to 2001. Thus far, only Roman harbor seawalls have been identified, but inland in the Ptolemaic industrial zone the expedition recovered lead sheets and copper nails that were used to cover the hulls of merchant vessels. In addition to an elephant tooth found in the Ptolemaic industrial zone that witnesses to the elephant trade, a papyrus refers to the outfitting of an *elephantago*, "an elephant transport," at Berenike.

North Africa

The great city of Carthage, founded by the Phoenicians in Tunisia in North Africa south of Sicily around 800 BC, had two headlands, which faced east and northeast. The deposition of the Medjerda River's sediment had created a tombolo, or land bridge, that connected a former island to the mainland. The Carthaginians carved out two harbors in the fourth century BC, a rectangular harbor and, to the north of this, a *kōthōn*, an artificially created, circular inner harbor. Appian gives us this description:

> The harbours had communication with each other, and a common entrance from the sea seventy feet wide, which could be closed with iron chains. The first port was for merchant vessels, and here were collected all kinds of ships' tackle. Within the second port was an island, and great quays were set at intervals round both the harbour and the island. These embankments were full of shipyards which had capacity for 220 [military] vessels. (*Roman History* 8.96)

Because the prevailing winds were from the north and northeast, the harbor was entered from the south.

Carthage was Rome's main military rival during the three Punic Wars, the first of which began in 264 BC and the last of which culminated in the destruction of Carthage, in 146 BC. At first the Carthaginians had total command of the sea, since the Romans initially had no navy, but in 160 BC the Romans captured a Punic vessel and made 120 copies of it in sixty days. The Romans also invented a device called the *corvus*, a plank that enabled them to board enemy ships.

A well-preserved Roman harbor was built by the Roman emperor Septimius Severus (AD 193–211) in his hometown of Lepcis (Leptis) Magna in Libya near the mouth of the Lebda River (the Wadi Lebda in present-day Al-Khums and about 105 kilometers east of Tripoli). It was protected by an eighty-meter-long seawall built of ashlars that had an adjacent quay. There was a lighthouse on the right as ships entered the bay. A tower to the left of the entrance would have been staffed by officials who regulated the traffic of the ships. This was the last major seaport built by the Romans. The well-preserved ruins of the city, which include a magnificent theater overlooking the sea, are among the most impressive of all Roman sites.

Italy and Rome

The Etruscan port of Populonia, on the Italian coast opposite the northern part of Corsica, has been excavated by Anna McCann and her colleagues, beginning in 1965. Evidence was found of the ancient breakwater, and the remains of an ancient ship dated to 840 BC were also discovered. Iron ore was brought to the site from the island of Elba, lying about sixteen kilometers to the southwest of Populonia. Slag indicates that about ten million tons of ore were transported each year. McCann also worked at the site of Cosa, an Etruscan site that became a Roman port in 273 BC. Abundant evidence of fishing activity was recovered in an adjacent lagoon, indicating that in antiquity it was full of fish.

The city of Rome is situated at a crossing point of the Tiber River, some fifteen miles from its mouth at Ostia. Beginning in 150 BC, the main harbor for the unloading of grain from abroad was at Puteoli, which is located to the northeast of the Bay of Naples and about 180 miles from Rome. This harbor is sheltered by a peninsula (Cape Misenum) and an offshore island. An additional man-made breakwater enhanced the protection of the port. Seneca vividly describes the excitement of the populace at the safe arrival of a grain ship:

> Suddenly there came into our view to-day the "Alexandrian" ships,—I mean those which are usually sent ahead to announce the coming of the fleet; they are called "mail-boats" [*tabellarias*]. The Campanians are glad to see them; all the rabble of Puteoli stand on the docks, and can recognize the "Alexandrian" boats, no matter how great the crowd of vessels, by the very trim of their sails.
> (*Ep.* 77.1)

The Roman emperors assumed personal responsibility for the *annona*, the essential supply of grain from Egypt and elsewhere. According to Suetonius, on one occasion,

> As he [Augustus] sailed by the gulf of Puteoli, it happened that from an Alexandrian ship which had just arrived there, the passengers and crew, clad in white, crowned with garlands, and burning incense, lavished upon him good wishes and the highest praise, saying that it was through him they lived, through him that they sailed the seas, and through him that they enjoyed their liberty and their fortunes. (*Aug.* 98)

The port of Misenum, located about five kilometers south of the port of Puteoli, housed the imperial fleet that was commanded by Pliny the Elder when Vesuvius erupted in AD 79.

It was from the region of Puteoli that the Romans secured *pozzolana*, the volcanic ash required for making concrete. The development of a hydraulic concrete that would set underwater was Rome's great contribution to the construction of artificial harbors. According to Vitruvius, a Roman authority on architecture who wrote ca. AD 30,

> There is also a kind of powder which, by nature, produces wonderful results. It is found in the neighbourhood of Baiae and in the lands of the municipalities round Mount Vesuvius. This being mixed with lime and rubble, not only furnishes strength to other buildings, but also, when piers are built in the sea, they set under water. (*De architectura* 2.6.1)

The construction of a harbor (*portus*) at Ostia was envisioned by Caesar (Plu. *Caes.* 58.8) and was begun by Claudius in AD 42 (Suet. *Claud.* 5.20). Though the harbor was already functioning before Claudius died, it was officially dedicated by Nero in AD 64. The site is a few kilometers north of the actual mouth of the Tiber River. Construction of the Fiumicino-Leonardo da Vinci International Airport in 1957–1960 uncovered much of this ancient harbor. Two channels connected the harbor to the river. Two long moles (750 m.) enclosed a circular harbor. The maximum area enclosed was about a third of a square mile and the harbor was about seventeen feet deep. A vessel by which Caligula had transported an obelisk to Rome was sunk to serve as the base for a lighthouse on the northern mole. This lighthouse is prominently portrayed on coins. On the opposite side of the entrance, harbor officials were posted to check the cargos and to collect the *portoria* taxes. Grain would be stored in *horrea* until it could be transported the fifteen miles up to Rome.

After a storm in AD 62 wrecked two hundred ships in this harbor (Tac. *Ann.* 15.18.3), the Romans realized they needed an inner harbor. This was built, in a hexagonal shape, by Trajan in AD 104. Each of the six sides was

335 meters long and the harbor was about fifteen feet deep. A commemorative coin dating to AD 112 depicts this hexagonal harbor with warehouses and statues, and bears the title PORTUS TRAIANI, "Trajan's Harbor."

E. THE JEWISH WORLD

Philo, who was a leading Jewish resident of Alexandria, proudly described its harbor as follows:

> For there is elsewhere no precinct like that which is called the Sebasteum, a temple to Caesar on shipboard, situated on an eminence facing the harbours famed for their excellent moorage, huge and conspicuous . . . the whole a hope of safety to the voyager either going into or out of the harbour. (*Legat.* 151)

In recounting the riots that broke out at Alexandria upon the arrival of Herod Agrippa I, Philo describes a mob that attacked Jewish ships in the harbor: "They boarded the vessels and carried out the cargo before the eyes of the owners, whom they pinioned and burnt, using for fuel rudders, tillers, poles and the planks on the decks" (*Legat.* 129).

Herod the Great (r. 37–4 BC) built the most impressive artificial harbor in the Mediterranean. As Josephus notes, "the whole sea-board from Dora to Joppa . . . was without a harbour, so that vessels bound for Egypt along the coast of Phoenicia had to ride at anchor in the open when menaced by the south-west wind" (*J.W.* 1.409). Herod chose a site called Strato's Tower. The harbor was named Sebastos (the Gk. equivalent of Lat. Augustus), and the port city of Caesarea was designated Caesarea Maritima to distinguish it from other Caesareas.

Herod built Sebastos using Roman hydraulic cement that had probably been provided to him by the Roman architect Marcus Agrippa, a close friend. According to Josephus, Herod used only imported materials for this project (*Ant.* 15.331–341). Josephus provides an extensive description of this project, which was the most ambitious of all of Herod's numerous building endeavors:

> Notwithstanding the totally recalcitrant nature of the site, he grappled with the difficulties so successfully, that the solidity of his masonry defied the sea, while its beauty was such as if no obstacle had existed. Having determined upon the comparative size of the harbour as we have stated, he had blocks of stone let down into twenty fathoms of water. . . . Numerous inlets in the wall provided landing-places for mariners putting in to harbour, while the whole circular terrace fronting these channels served as a broad promenade for disembarking passengers. (*J.W.* 1.411–413)

Josephus further remarks: "On an eminence facing the harbour-mouth stood Caesar's temple, remarkable for its beauty and grand proportions; it contained a colossal statue of the emperor, not inferior to the Olympic Zeus" (*J.W.* 1.414; cf. *Ant.* 15.333). Begun in 22 BC, Sebastos was probably functioning by 16 BC.

Numismatic evidence and underwater excavations at Caesarea Maritima begun in 1982 have confirmed the general accuracy of Josephus's descriptions. The great mole to the south was originally about 540 meters (one-third of a mile) long and 600 meters wide. A mole 245 meters long and 50 meters wide protected the harbor on the north. The entrance to the harbor in the northwest was 30 meters wide. The explorations identified huge blocks of hydraulic concrete, which had been poured into wooden frames and then lowered to the sea bottom. Each of these blocks, which were ca. 15 x 12 x 2 meters in size, weighed approximately ninety tons. The moles were built with stone rubble packed between piers composed of these great concrete blocks.

A story is told in the Jerusalem Talmud concerning a strange event at the harbor of Jaffa. The polished bronze gates on the eastern forecourt of the temple had been donated by a wealthy patron named Nicanor, whose ossuary has been found in Jerusalem. This is probably the "beautiful gate" mentioned in Acts 3:2. According to the Mishnah, "Miracles had befallen the gates of Nicanor and his memory was kept in honour" (*m. Yoma* 3:10). The Jerusalem Talmud explains:

> When Nicanor was bringing them from Alexandria, in Egypt, a gale rose in the sea and threatened to drown them. They took one of them and tossed it into the sea, and they wanted to throw in the other, but Nicanor would not let them. He said to them, "If you throw in the second one, throw me in with it." He was distressed all the way to the wharf at Jaffa. Once they reached the wharf at Jaffa, the other door popped up from underneath the boat. (*y. Yoma* 3:8)

The Babylonian Talmud has the sailors tossing Nicanor overboard, which causes the storm to cease, and has the door washing up at Akko (*b. Yoma* 38a).

One is struck with the relative paucity of Greco-Latin nautical terms in the Talmud, which indicates the lack of direct involvement of Palestinian rabbis in maritime activities. This accords also with Josephus's remark that "ours is not a maritime country; neither commerce nor the intercourse which it promotes with the outside world has any attraction for us. Our cities are built inland, remote from the sea" (*Ag. Ap.* 1.60).

There certainly were Jews present at coastal cities like Akko (Ptolemais), Dor, Caesarea, Joppa, and Ashkelon. Yavneh (Jamnia) became a major refuge for the rabbinical leaders of the Pharisees who survived the First Jewish Revolt against Rome. The rabbis disputed whether the port of

Caesarea should be considered to be "abroad" and not part of the land of Israel (*y. Giṭ.* 1:1). If so, then Jews living there would be free from the tithes and rules of the Sabbath.

F. THE CHRISTIAN WORLD

Constantine moved his capital from Rome to the site of the ancient Greek city of Byzantium, located on a peninsula on the north shore of the Propontis (the Sea of Marmara) just west of the Bosphorus, the entrance to the Black Sea from the Mediterranean Sea. On the northern shore of this peninsula was an inlet five miles long known as "The Golden Horn," where the Harbor of Phospherion was located. The Kontoskelion Harbor and the Eleuterios Harbor were located on the southern shore.

Not only seas and major rivers such as the Nile had harbors, but significant lakes did as well. Among the most popular saints in the Coptic Church in Egypt is St. Menas (Mina), a Christian soldier (ca. AD 285–309) who was martyred. Because of stories of miraculous cures connected with his burial site, which is located southwest of Lake Mareotis (located inland near Alexandria), pilgrims streamed to his shrine beginning in the fourth century. There is evidence that holy water from the site was carried away in terra-cotta flasks made so as to depict St. Menas between two camels. Recent excavations at Philoxenite on the south shore of Lake Mareotis have uncovered long breakwaters, six stone jetties each ten meters long, and a quay 1.5 miles long. These harbor facilities could have accommodated numerous boats and were likely built to accommodate pilgrims coming to the shrine of St. Menas.

The city of Aradus on the Phoenician coast was subject to a major program of rebuilding under Constantius II in AD 346, probably because of a shrine there dedicated to the Virgin Mary. It was for a time renamed Constantinia, before reverting to its ancient name of Tartus. Much later, during the Crusades, when it was named Tortosa, it became one of the main headquarters of the Knights Templar.

Port cities, even smaller ones, frequently figure in the lives of well-known ancient individuals. St. Nicholas, patron saint of sailors and of Russia, was born about AD 300 in the port city of Patara on the southwest coast of present-day Turkey. He would later become the bishop of the city of Myra, another port city just to the east of Patara. Late sources allege that he was present at the Council of Nicaea in AD 325. By the mid-fifth century, literary references attest to his heightened popularity. His church, probably built in the sixth century, became a noteworthy pilgrimage center. The site of Myra, which was inundated by mud from the Myrus River in antiquity, was only cleared in 2013.

BIBLIOGRAPHY: S. H. A. Al Khalifa and M. Rice, ed., *Bahrain through the Ages: The Archaeology* (1986); J. Baines and J. Málek, *Atlas of Ancient Egypt* (1980); K. A. Bard and R. Fattovich, ed., *Harbor of the Pharaohs to the Land of Punt* (2007); M. A. Beek, *Atlas of Mesopotamia* (1962); B. J. Beitzel, *The New Moody Atlas of Bible Lands* (2009); M. Bietak, *Avaris, the Capital of the Hyksos: Recent Excavations at Tell el-Dabʿa* (1996); D. J. Blackmann, "Ancient Harbours in the Mediterranean I," *International Journal of Nautical Archaeology* 11 (1982), 79–104; R. G. Bullard, "The Berbers of the Maghreb and Ancient Carthage," in *Africa and Africans in Antiquity*, ed. E. M. Yamauchi (2001), 180–209; J.-Y. Empereur, *Alexandria Rediscovered* (1998); A. Flinder, "The Island of Jezirat Faraʾun: Its Ancient Harbour, Anchorage and Marine Defence Installations," *International Journal of Nautical Archaeology* 6 (1977), 127–39; A. Flinder, *Secrets of the Bible Seas: An Underwater Archaeologist in the Holy Land* (1985); R. Garland, *The Piraeus: From the Fifth to the First Century B.C.* (1987); B. Giardina, *Navigare necesse est: Lighthouses from Antiquity to the Middle Ages* (2010); F. Goddio, "Heracleion-Thonis and Alexandria: Two Ancient Egyptian Emporia," in *Maritime Archaeology and Ancient Trade in the Mediterranean*, ed. D. Robinson and A. Wilson (2011), 121–37; F. Goddio, *The Topography and Excavation of Heracleion-Thonis and East Canopus (1996–2006): Underwater Archaeology in the Canopic Region in Egypt* (2007); A. de Graauw, *Ancient Ports and Harbours* (4th ed.; 2014); D. Harden, *The Phoenicians* (rev. ed., 1963); R. K. Harrison, ed., *Major Cities of the Biblical World* (1985); J. Hawkes, *Atlas of Ancient Archaeology* (1974); R. L. Hohlfelder, ed., *The Maritime World of Ancient Rome* (2008); K. G. Holum and R. L. Hohlfelder, ed., *King Herod's Dream: Caesarea on the Sea* (1988); N. Jidejian, *Beirut through the Ages* (1973); N. Jidejian, *Byblos through the Ages* (1968); N. Jidejian, *Sidon through the Ages* (1971); N. Jidejian, *Tyre through the Ages* (1969); N. Kashtan, ed., *Seafaring and the Jews* (2001); H. Kees, *Ancient Egypt: A Cultural Topography*, trans. I. F. D. Morrow (1961); E. Lipiński, *Phoenicia and the East Mediterranean in the First Millennium B.C.* (1987); A. M. McCann et al., *The Roman Port and Fishery of Cosa* (1987); J. McRay, *Archaeology and the New Testament* (1991); S. Moscati, ed., *The Phoenicians* (1988); J. Murphy-O'Connor, *St. Paul's Corinth: Texts and Archaeology* (1983); J. Murphy-O'Connor, *St. Paul's Ephesus: Texts and Archaeology* (2008); C. F. Pfeiffer, *Baker's Bible Atlas* (1961); A. Raban, ed., *Harbour Archaeology* (1985); A. Raban et al., ed., *The Harbour of Sebastos (Caesarea Maritima) in its Roman Mediterranean Context* (2009); S. R. Rao, "Shipping and Maritime Trade of the Indus People," *Exped* 7.3 (1965), 30–37; C. G. Rasmussen, *Zondervan NIV Atlas of the Bible* (1989); D. Robinson and F. Goddio, ed., *Thonis-Heracleion in Context* (2014); J. Rougé, *Ships and Fleets of the Ancient Mediterranean*, trans. S. Frazer (1981); D.

Sperber, *Nautica Talmudica* (1986); O. Testaguzza, *Portus: Illustrazione dei porti di Claudio e Traiano e della città di Porto a Fiumicino* (1970); M. K. and R. L. Thornton, *Julio-Claudian Building Programs* (1989); S. L. Tuck, *Creating Roman Imperial Identity and Authority: The Role of Roman Imperial Harbor Monuments* (1997); E. Vanderpool, "News Letter from Greece," *AJA* 57 (1953), 281–86; M. Wilson, *Biblical Turkey: A Guide to the Jewish and Christian Sites of Asia Minor* (2010); L. Woolley, *A Forgotten Kingdom* (1953); E. M. Yamauchi, *Greece and Babylon: Early Contacts between the Aegean and the Near East* (1967); E. M. Yamauchi, *New Testament Cities in Western Asia Minor* (repr., 2003); E. M. Yamauchi, "On the Road with Paul: The Ease and Dangers of Travel in the Ancient World," *CH* 14.3 (1995), 16–19; H. Zabehlicky, "Preliminary Views of the Ephesian Harbor," in *Ephesos: Metropolis of Asia*, ed. H. Koester (1995), 201–15.

STC and KNS

See also BOATS & SHIPS, COMMUNICATIONS & MESSENGERS, and TRADE.

HEATING & LIGHTING

People use heating and lighting to adjust their environmental circumstances in order to gain security, comfort, and increased hours of productivity, as well as to produce food and to transform materials. In antiquity, the main source of heating and lighting was fire.

The climate was temperate in most centers of ancient societies in the Mediterranean region, as they were located between 25 and 40 degrees north latitude. Longer summer days provided considerable natural lighting and warmth. Shorter winter days tended to be cooler, but were typically sunny. When darkness fell in arid regions where there was little cloud cover, cooling was rapid, and therefore daily temperature variation could be significant. Extreme climates existed in this region as well, however, at locations that lay beyond moderating maritime influences or at high elevations. The peoples of the ancient world developed a number of creative responses to adverse conditions, including producing heat to combat the cold and light to counteract the darkness.

A. THE OLD TESTAMENT

The ancient Hebrews and their neighbors were concerned with heating and lighting. The account of creation in Gen 1 records that God made the sun to provide light by day and the moon to provide light by night (Gen 1:14–19). No concerns for heating and lighting are noted in Genesis's account of the Edenic paradise, which portrays an idyllic environment where clothes were not needed and where there was time to walk and talk at the end of the day when work was done. After the fall, Adam and Eve benefited from the protection of garments (Gen 3:21), cities were built (Gen 4:17), and pyrotechnical processes were employed by Tubal-Cain in metallurgy (Gen 4:22). In the postdiluvian period, the continued use of industrial pyrotechnology is reflected in the use of fired bricks in the Tower of Babel (Gen 11:3).

In the patriarchal period, the Hebrews, who were pastoralists, resided in tents. The heat of the day and the cool of the night were part of the travails they experienced (Gen 31:40). Direct and reflected sunlight illuminated the interiors of tents by day, and fires provided nocturnal illumination and heating for food and individuals. When darkness fell and the temperature cooled, people could socialize in the starlight around fires, but they soon went to bed in order to conserve their limited fuel; human activity was largely dictated by the sun. Tents provided shelter from the sun, dew, rain, and winds. Tents made of long panels woven from black goat hair (Song 1:5) absorbed heat, and lighter goat-hair panels were used in summer to reflect heat. When it grew too hot during summers, the tent curtain walls were stretched wide, creating extra shade and a cooler micro-climate in which air could move through the tent. As the people inside the tent perspired from the heat, such small breezes caused the sweat to evaporate and cooled their bodies. Abraham's location at the entrance of his tent as the day grew hot (Gen 18:1) served to give him control of the tent, a commanding view of outside activities, and the additional benefit of cooling breezes.

In both tents (Gen 18:6) and houses (Gen 19:3), fires were kept burning and could be employed in cooking meals for guests at short notice. While pastoralists generally maintained modest cooking fires, and sedentary residents of urban houses had small ovens (Heb. sing. *tannûr*), craftsmen used furnaces (Heb. sing. *kibšān*) in larger metalworking and pottery-firing operations, which were characterized by massive fuel consumption and plumes of smoke (cf. Gen 19:28). Pottery kilns required considerable fuel to achieve the sustained heat of 800 degrees centigrade (ca. 1500 Fahrenheit) needed to transform clay into hard ceramics. The heat in kilns had to be raised slowly to avoid having residual moisture in the clay vaporize and explode the pieces. Pottery could also be deformed by getting too hot and melting.

In the time of the patriarchs, oil lamps in the Levant were made in the form of small, shallow bowls with gently pinched sides that formed wick holders. In the account of the establishment of the Abrahamic covenant, a smoking firepot (Heb. *tannûr ʿāšān*) and flaming torch (Heb. *lappîd ʾēš*) are light sources that represent the divine presence (Gen 15:17). Torches were used for lighting exteriors and firepots were employed in heating interiors or transporting fire. Part of the plight of the poor in the patriarchal period was their inability to light and heat their homes, though ironically they often worked in the olive oil production processes that generated the best lighting fuel (Job 24:7–17). As a result, the poor suffered from exposure and were vulnerable to the predation of thieves.

Fire was important to the Israelites during the wilderness period. The "pillar of fire" illuminated the night and reminded the people of God's presence and providence (Exod 13:21). Under the Mosaic law, the lighting of fires in dwellings was prohibited on the Sabbath (Exod 35:3), but fires and lights that had already been ignited were allowed to continue to burn. The restriction of oxygen to a fire supplied with a large quantity of fuel allowed Sabbath fires to burn for an extended period. Olive oil, a treasured commodity, was collected as a clean burning fuel for the illumination of the tabernacle (Exod 25:6; 35:28). Its illumination was provided especially by the lamps on the multibranched lampstand (Heb. *měnôrâ*) located on the south side of the holy place (Exod 25:31–36). Oil lamps (Heb. sing. *nēr*) placed on or by the lampstand were to burn perpetually (Exod 27:20). These ritual flames in the tabernacle continued to be maintained during the period of the judges (1 Sam 3:3).

As the Israelites took possession of Canaan, the majority of the populace built and occupied houses. (Some pastoral nomads, however, continued to employ tents as they exploited marginal lands during the time of the conquest and on into later periods, as did the Rechabites.) The Israelite houses were usually made of thick mud-brick walls built on stone foundations. The rooms of a typical four-room Israelite house were narrow, as the Israelites did not have significant supplies of large-dimension timber to span wide roofs. The exterior walls of these homes had few openings and these were located high on the walls to maintain security. As a result, most light came through upper-level windows or was reflected through doorways leading from an open central courtyard. Thick roofs made with packed clay were supported on timber frames and reed beds. The thick mud-brick walls and roofs absorbed solar radiation during the day and protected occupants from the heat. At night, the thick walls served as a thermal bank radiating heat that helped to keep occupants warm. In summer evenings, when residents sought to escape the heat of their houses, they socialized on the flat rooftops, which were illuminated by the moon and starlight. The interior cooling of homes was achieved through the creation of shade, which dropped the temperature and raised the air pressure, which in turn generated air movement toward the lower pressure on the sunny exterior. As clay floors were daily sprinkled with water and swept to maintain compaction, the evaporating water also helped to cool the interiors.

In winter, the narrow rooms of Israelite homes would have become cold and therefore their occupants would have appreciated auxiliary heating. Fires could be ignited in courtyards using timber and twigs as fuel for cooking or warmth (cf. Isa 44:15–16). Fixed fire pit installations were occasionally located in lower-level interior rooms, but more frequently the Israelites used moveable firepots and metal braziers. Hot coals could be taken from an open fire outside and brought inside in fire-resistant ceramic or metal containers to warm sedentary residents (Isa 47:14) without creating an eye-watering smoky atmosphere. King Jehoiakim used such a device (Heb. *'aḥ*) to dispose of Jeremiah's scroll while in his winter quarters in the month of Kislev (Jer 36:22–23). The Israelite architectural repertoire did not include chimneys that could create a draft and draw combustion fumes outside. Smoke from firepots and lamps escaped through windows (Hos 13:3), doors, and ventilation openings in the walls.

While people tended to stay close to the lamplight and fires of home at night, lamps (Ps 119:105) and flaming torches (Heb. *zîqôt*) illuminated the paths of nocturnal Israelite travelers (Isa 50:11). In the period of the judges, torches concealed in ceramic jars played a key role in Gideon's defeat of the Midianites, who were frightened because they thought each torch represented a company of warriors (Judg 7:19–25). Torches made of sticks ending in a resinous knot or wrapped at one end with twisted fibers like flax, and dipped in tallow, could be easily ignited and would emit considerable light. Large flames from such devices were not as susceptible to being extinguished by the wind as the small flame at the end of a small twisted-fiber wick in the typical saucer-shaped lamp. In order to protect ignited wicks from wind, small lamps and even larger light sources could be carried in heat-tolerant ceramic and metal containers. Perforated side walls allowed oxygen into such lanterns to feed the flame and allowed light to shine out.

During the period of the united monarchy, David instructed Solomon to brighten the temple with lamps on silver stands (1 Chr 28:15). In addition to the other temple furnishings, Solomon is said to have made ten golden lamps to be placed "in front of the inner sanctuary" in order to illuminate the Holy Place (1 Kgs 7:49; 2 Chr 4:7).

The OT wisdom literature uses the burning lamp as a metaphor for a person's life or a nation's existence, which are under the control of God (2 Kgs 8:19; Job 18:5–6; 21:17; Prov 13:9; 20:20). The book of Isaiah prophesies that the Servant of the Lord will not destroy the spiritually broken, declaring: "a smoldering wick [Heb. *pištâ*] he will not snuff out" (Isa 42:3). In the period of the Judean Restoration, when the returned exiles were under Persian rule, Zechariah envisions renewed worship in a new temple with a golden lampstand holding a seven-spouted lamp flanked by two olive trees (Zech 4:1–3), which, as the angel speaking with him tells him, represent anointed ones, apparently a reference to political and religious leaders (vs. 14).

Pyrotechnology is reflected throughout the OT in allusions to cooking food and the industrial production of ceramic and metal artifacts. In the book of Daniel, which recounts the experiences of Daniel and his companions during the period of the Babylonian captivity, a superheated brick kiln plays a key role in demonstrating the unflinching faith of Shadrach, Meshach, and Abednego (Dan 3:1–27). In the period of Persian domination, the restored city of Jerusalem appears to have had concentrated industrial activity in its northwest quadrant (Neh 3:11; 12:38), where the draft of prevailing winds helped to make smelting fires hotter. The smoke from these fires did not blow over most of the residents of the city and was easily dissipated.

B. THE NEW TESTAMENT

Lighting receives greater attention than heating in the NT. In Palestine, illumination was a nightly concern, while environmental heating was more of an occasional, seasonal concern. During the NT period, the generation of heat for lighting, cooking, and the processing of materials continued to be dependent on fires.

Jesus frequently uses light metaphors and references to lighting devices (Gk. *lampas, lychnos*) in his teachings as they are preserved in the Synoptic Gospels (Matt 5:15; Mark 4:21; Luke 15:8). It is especially in the Gospel of John, however, that the image of Jesus himself as light is most prominent. According to this Gospel, in Jesus "was life, and that life was the light of all mankind" (John 1:4; cf. vss. 5, 7–9), but those who love darkness reject that light (John 3:19–21). John the Baptist is also portrayed as a light. Jesus says: "John was a lamp that burned and gave light, and you chose for a time to enjoy his light" (John 5:35). At the Feast of Tabernacles, which featured ceremonies involving water and light, Jesus declares, "I am the light of the world. Whoever follows me will never walk in darkness, but will have the light of life" (John 8:12; cf. 9:4–5; 11:9–10; 12:35–36, 46).

In the NT and contemporary Greek literature, there is little differentiation between the variety of devices that employed a reservoir of fuel and a burning wick to create illumination. Jesus's use of the Greek word *lychnos* likely refers to small Herodian-style lamps that had a wheel-made reservoir and an affixed short-flared spout (these kinds of lamp were small enough to be covered with measuring bowls [Matt 5:15; Mark 4:21; Luke 11:33] or hidden under beds [Mark 4:21; Luke 8:16] when light was not wanted). His use of the Greek word *lampas* refers to larger light sources (Matt 25:1–13). In interpreting Jesus's Parable of the Virgins (Matt 25:1–13), one should not envision the women carrying small ceramic oil lamps, since these would not have run out of fuel as the women waited for the bridegroom: well-trimmed single-wicked oil lamps can typically burn for over an hour on one tablespoon (ca. 15 ml.) of olive oil, and thus the typical small lamp could burn for a couple of hours. What should be envisaged in this parable, rather, are larger lanterns and flaming torches, which would not have blown out during the festive nocturnal procession to the wedding venue, which would have contributed appropriate illumination for this procession, and which—unlike smaller oil lamps—would be expected to need fuel replenishment. The "lanterns" (Gk. sing. *lampas*) carried by the arresting party that followed Judas to Gethsemane were no doubt also bright torches (John 18:3).

The King James Version (1611) rendering of *lychnos*, which refers to a lamp, as "candle" (e.g., Matt 5:15; Mark 4:21; Luke 6:16; 11:33–34) and of *lychnia*, which refers to a lampstand, as "candlestick" (e.g., Matt 5:15; Mark 4:21; Luke 8:16; 11:33; Heb 9:2; Rev 1:12) reflects the fact that in early modern England candles rather than lamps were used for illumination.

Heating occasionally appears as a minor contextual detail in NT narratives. Peter and the guards and servants warmed themselves near a charcoal fire in the courtyard of the high priest on the cold spring evening when Jesus was in custody (Mark 14:54; John 18:16), and after his resurrection Jesus prepared a cooking fire on the shore of Galilee (John 21:8). Paul and his fellow shipwreck survivors gathered around a fire kindled by the inhabitants of Malta on a cold, wet winter night (Acts 28:2). Living in the warm province of Palestine, Jesus expressed concern that needy persons be supplied with clothing (Matt 25:32–45), but in the NT accounts he makes no allusions to domestic heating.

The cultural elites of the NT world were able to afford a greater number of responses to uncomfortable environments. The wealthy had clothes to layer on themselves when it was cold and could pay for fuel for heating fires and lighting. The Herodian palaces at Masada, Jericho, and Herodium show that the Roman client-kings could afford the cooling of large swimming pools and the heating of bathhouses even in arid places where there were no substantial local fuel supplies.

The Christian assemblies of the apostolic period employed lights when they met at night (Acts 20:8). Apostolic-era Christians used light metaphors in explaining their relationship to a sin-darkened world (2 Cor 4:6; Phil 2:14–15). In the opening vision of the Apocalypse, John sees "seven golden lampstands," which represent the seven churches of Asia Minor (Rev 1:12–20). The early Christian vision of heaven was of a place perpetually illuminated by the radiance of God's presence (Rev 21:23).

C. THE NEAR EASTERN WORLD

Ancient Near Eastern peoples who lived in higher latitudes would have had more of a need to heat their homes than those who lived close to the tropical zones. For example, the Egyptians needed to spend fewer resources on heating in the winter than did residents of Anatolia and Upper Mesopotamia.

In Pharaonic Egypt, a wide variety of local vegetable oils, such as castor oil, linseed oil, and safflower oil, as well as animal fats, were burned in order to provide illumination. The physical environment of Egypt limited olive cultivation. Although olive products such as oil for unguents and cooking were available domestically on a limited scale in northern New Kingdom Egypt, most olive oil was imported, so while olive oil could be used as a fuel, cheaper domestic fuels existed. In Mesopotamia, the environment was similarly not conducive to oleoculture. As a result, sesame seed oil was what was most commonly used for lamps in that region.

The flammable properties of crude oil and tar were known in ancient times and these materials were used in contexts where smoky fires were acceptable, such as for torches to illuminate exteriors. Apiculture was practiced in ancient Egypt, Mesopotamia, and Canaan, which meant that beeswax was available as a fuel, but because it was highly prized for other uses, such as modeling for metal casting, it was not used commonly for fuel.

Floating wicks were a distinctive feature of lighting devices in Pharaonic Egypt. Any fire-resistant reservoir could thus serve as a lamp. Two ornate floating-wick lamps that were found in the tomb of Tutankhamun and that were carved from translucent calcite in the form of locust blossoms demonstrate the artistry that was sometimes invested in decorative lighting pieces for the affluent. In the same tomb, thirty-centimeter-long wicks made of twisted linen supported by anthropomorphic Ankh symbols formed torches that would have burned more brightly than the floating-wick lamps. Such torches would have served to make nocturnal rituals and those inside dark tombs and temples visible.

Herodotus reports that the Egyptians used lights in their religious rituals. He describes in particular an annual Festival of Lights during which salt was added to oil used to generate light that illuminated the night across the country (*Hist.* 2.62). While some have speculated that salted oil created a brighter or less smoky light, it was more likely a symbolic matter of purification. In Egypt, frog-shaped lamps and lamps decorated with frog motifs were associated with burials and the idea of regenerative power.

Mesopotamia, Canaan, and Anatolia shared common lighting techniques. The most common material from which lamps were made was clay. Potters developed utilitarian forms that changed over time and that also reflected local aesthetics. Generally, ceramic lamps developed from those that contained open reservoirs of fuel and had wicks made of absorbent flax fibers around their sides to those with increasingly closed reservoirs and pronounced nozzles for the wicks.

In the earliest human settlements, where people used stone tools, flames fed by fuels in stone and shell containers were employed to provide light in dark places. As ceramic techniques developed, lamps changed. Clay formed by potters into hand-molded bowls and baked in kilns created fire-resistant reservoirs from which fibrous wicks could draw fuel to feed a flame. As the slow wheel was developed during the Early Bronze Age, clay bowls became more symmetrical, and wicks were kept from falling into the fuel or out of the lamp by the creation of wick holders; the latter were made by deforming the rim of a bowl with a finger before it dried. A popular form adopted towards the end of this period had four wick holders, which the potter made by compressing the rim of the leather-hard bowl between two fingers from each hand.

In the Middle Bronze Age, wheel-made round-bottomed saucer lamps became common in the Levant. These lamps had a more tightly compressed wick holder than the typical Early Bronze Age saucer lamp. Saucer lamps continued to be made through the Late Bronze and Iron Ages. Generally, the rims of saucer lamps became more pronounced and everted, the bases became more stable, and the wick holders became increasingly tighter.

In the Iron Age, the Assyrians developed a distinctive "pipe lamp." This type of small lamp was formed by raising a bowl on the potter's wheel and closing the rim to form a little jar with a flattened base. The side of the wet clay jar was punctured with a finger and a nozzle of clay was formed around the finger. The end of the "pipe" thus created was left open for the wick, which drew fuel through it from the reservoir.

In time, the advantages of a lamp with a more restrictive reservoir were recognized and the two opposing rims of small wheel-thrown saucers were pinched together, leaving a small hole for a protruding wick and a rim that could serve as a handle on the opposite side away from the flame. This form was easily made and helped to keep wicks in place and the oil from spilling.

In Mesopotamia and Egypt, large-dimension timber (with the exception of palm trees) for fuel heating and cooking fires had to be imported; because such timber was expensive, it was not widely used. Indigenous dry plant matter and animal dung fueled most small fires. Most cooking was conducted outside of the rooms of a home, in exterior courtyards, since the heat was not usually needed indoors. When interiors needed to be warmed, glowing coals contained in fireproof vessels were carried in from outside. Such coals produced less smoke in rooms without chimneys than did open flames.

Cooking fires in the ancient Near East ranged from open campfires that heated food directly to more sophisticated and efficient enclosed oven installations. Cooking facilities were a typical feature of most Egyptian and Mesopotamian households (Exod 8:3). Most domestic ovens in the Near East were formed from clay mixed with straw, which acted as a binding agent. The typical family oven was circular and had a footprint of less than one meter (about three feet) in diameter. The floors of such ovens were generally formed of cobblestones, and ovens were formed by rounded clay walls that rose about sixty centimeters and came together to form a dome. In areas poor in timber, the typical cooking fuels used in such ovens, which were very fuel-efficient, were straw, brush, and dried animal dung. An opening at one side of the ovens allowed fuel to be inserted and oxygen to come in to feed the flames in the interior. The ovens' tops had an opening through which smoke could escape, into which pieces of bread dough could be inserted to be cooked on the heated interior surface, and over which items could be heated in ceramic or metal vessels. The size of the openings at the tops of ovens varied according to the anticipated cooking techniques. It appears that bread was sometimes also baked on the hot exteriors of the ovens.

Industrial kilns and furnaces used in making ceramic and metal items were situated in strategic places where they could catch prevailing winds and where the smoke they created would not offend the cultural elite. Images of industrial pyrotechnical processes have been preserved from Assyria and Egypt. The painted images from the Tomb of Rekhmire in Thebes illustrate that air blown by mouth or forced from pot-bellows through pipes and tuyeres was used to increase the heat of such operations.

D. THE GRECO-ROMAN WORLD

The early Greek author Hesiod attributed humanity's knowledge of the use of fire to the titan Prometheus, whom Zeus punished for his kindness to people (*Op.* 42–105; *Theog.* 56). The Greeks celebrated Prometheus's legendary contribution with lighted processions and torch races in the Panathenaic festival (Pausanius, *Descr.* 1.30.2). Fire ignited on Mt. Olympus was reverently taken to the Olympic Games as a gift from the gods. The Olympian god Hephaestus was known as the patron of pyrotechnology.

The use of fire in heating and lighting technology is attested from an early period in the Aegean area. Early Minoan lamps were bowl forms made from carved stone or of ceramic manufacture, and sometimes used beeswax as a fuel. The Mycenaeans used painted lamps fueled by olive oil. The Archaic Era Greek stories of Homer use fire in many metaphors and descriptions. In the *Iliad*, for example, the Trojans use the light of bonfires to help them observe the movements of the Achaean fleet during the night (*Il.* 8.495–565). The excavations of earlier Mycenaean palaces at Mycenae, Tiryns, and Pylos reveal that all had large circular hearths in their throne rooms.

As in other societies, in ancient Greece the cultural elite invested in artistic lighting devices. An example of the splendor of royal Macedonian lighting devices is a bronze lantern, about thirty centimeters tall, found in the main chamber of Tomb II at Vergina and now displayed in the Archaeological Museum of Thessalonike. The silvered walls of the vessel are perforated in geometric and grapevine patterns to let the light from the clay lamp in the interior shine through. The Greeks' greatest innovation in decorative lighting was the development of molded clay lamps during the second century BC. Such lamps were commonly made by using two soft limestone molds. One mold had a depression for the top of the lamp and the other had a depression in the shape of the lamp base. Carefully levigated (refined) clay was then pressed into each mold. After a brief period of drying, potters removed the leather-hard halves of the lamp from the molds, dampened the edges with clay slurry, and pressed them together to make thin-walled, pear-shaped lamps that had an oil reservoir and decorated surfaces. Once the molds for a lamp were carefully carved out, it was possible to easily replicate lamps that had intricate designs and shapes. While single-wicked lamps were most common, the Greeks later made lamps with multiple spouts as well. With superior fuels, Hellenistic-era kilns could be raised to higher temperatures that produced more vitrified lamps that held oil without leaking.

The Romans appear to have been significantly influenced by their neighbors in Magna Graecia (Greek colonies in southern Italy and the Adriatic coast) and the Etruscans in regard to lighting techniques. The Etruscans used fire to craft their famous metalwork, but few lamps have been found. Artifacts that have been discovered point to the Etruscans' use of beeswax candles.

The pre-Republican Romans adopted the oil-saucer lamp, and during the period of the later Republic the Romans adopted Hellenistic mold-made lamps. In the Late Republic period, Roman craftsmen created their own "discus lamp." This two-piece molded lamp was round with a small projecting wick hole. The top of the lamp was otherwise closed, with the exception of a filling hole. The top of these lamps was made with a circular depression that funneled oil into the reservoir and provided a frame that could focus attention on a raised image or design. During the period of the Roman Empire, many mass-produced lamps like these were made inexpensively and not fired hot enough to vitrify the clay. Metal and glass lamps came to be favored since they were not susceptible to leaking, as porous ceramic lamps were.

The Greeks and Romans developed simple coastal beacons into taller lighthouses as a means of directing ships safely to ports. These structures were towers with fires maintained at the top. The most famous of these structures was the Pharos, built by the Ptolemies at Alexandria, which Josephus asserted could be seen more than thirty miles (about 50 km.) out to sea (*J.W.* 4.10.5). Polished metal reflectors were used by Archimedes to defend Syracuse against the Roman siege, but at this time large, light-concentrating glass lenses such as those used in modern lighthouses had not yet been perfected.

Greek homes were similar to those of the Levant, with a central court-yard that provided light to the rooms during the daytime. These structures' mud-brick walls helped to moderate interior temperatures. Exterior walls were often whitewashed to reflect heat. As in the Levant, larger fires were relegated to the courtyards and hot coals held in metal or ceramic contain-ers were used to heat interiors. The Greeks also employed ceramic ovens and cooking surfaces that were heated over fires.

The Romans were similarly concerned with controlling the tempera-ture of their homes and used architectural elements that modified daily and seasonal temperature fluctuations. The earliest Romans lived in thatched huts with a single room called an *atrium* that had a central hearth around which cooking and other family activities took place. Vitruvius describes four styles of later *atria* adopted by the Romans that were open to the sky (*De architectura* 6.2). These *atria* are best seen in homes of the wealthy at Pompeii, where the *atrium* functioned largely as a formal receiving area that was illuminated by day with sunlight through a hole in the roof called the *compluvium*. Rainwater that fell through the opening collected in a shallow pool called the *impluvium*. This water reflected sunlight into adja-cent covered rooms and helped to cool the space. In the kitchens of Roman villas a variety of brick ovens and stoves were used for cooking. *Triclinia*, or rooms for formal dining, were located adjacent to the *peristyle* (a columned porch) so as to benefit from the air. The interiors of Roman villas were il-luminated at night by lamps set on stands called *monopodia*, which were suspended by metal chains from the ceiling or placed in elevated niches in the walls. Windows allowed light into upper-story rooms but first floors had few exterior openings to allow light.

In southern Italy the greater concern was for cooling. Residential heat-ing only became a serious consideration as the Romans moved northward into cooler regions. Making fires in metal braziers was the common way to heat rooms in the winter. These braziers were metal boxes raised off the floor on legs; they could be moved around the room using attached handles. Live-coal heaters like these brought with them the dread of fire for Romans like the poet Juvenal, who lived in a cheap apartment at the top of a multistory residential structure in Rome (*Sat.* 3.192–202). Cen-tral heating was first used in bath complexes called *thermae* (from Gk. *thermos*, "hot"). After about 200 BC the Romans heated their baths using hypocausts (subfloor heating systems): a "furnace area" near the room(s) to be heated would provide its hot exhaust gases to a low chamber (sup-ported by numerous pillars) under a room's floor and the hot gases would then pass through specialized ceramic flue pipes (*tubulae*) embedded in the walls and vent safely out of the roof. The truly wealthy in cold places like Britain used this technique to warm the floors of their homes.

The Greeks and Romans frequently used lights in their religious rituals. Pausanius highlights a golden oil lamp of considerable size that provided a continuous light in the Parthenon of Athens. This lamp had a wick made of asbestos that needed no trimming, and was refueled annually (*Descr.* 1.26.6).

E. THE JEWISH WORLD

Jews quite naturally embraced and modified lighting and heating devices and techniques from surrounding societies. In late antiquity Jews decorated the tops of their molded lamps with religious symbols in raised relief.

More concern, however, was given to the proper use of such devices than to their design or modification. Religious considerations proscribed the use of fuels like lard and the lighting of fires on the Sabbath (Exod 35:3). Jews used a variety of vegetable and animal oils as fuels, but those with a disagreeable odor were avoided on the Sabbath, when using olive oil with flax wicks was preferred (*m. Šabb.* 2:2–3). The requirement of Sabbath observance resulted in many rabbinic opinions that constrained lighting and heating. Vessels with large fuel reservoirs could burn for a long time, but the addition of auxiliary reservoirs—such as an eggshell filled with oil that would slowly fill a lamp by draining through a pin hole, or wicking oil from an additional, taller container—was disputed among the rabbinate (*m. Šabb.* 2:4).

The menorah, the seven-branched golden lampstand located in the holy place of the tabernacle (Exod 25:31–40; 26:33–34), and then in the temple, later became the preeminent symbol of Judaism. Philo interpreted the menorah allegorically, with the central lamp signifying the sun, and the six other lamps the planets (*Mos.* 2.102–105). Josephus interpreted the seven lamps as representing seven planets (*J. W.* 5.217). When the temple was destroyed by Titus in AD 70, the Romans carried off the menorah found therein as booty. They prominently memorialized the capture of this Jewish treasure on the inner panel of the so-called Arch of Titus erected by Domitian.

In Rabbinic Judaism, some rituals of light recall earlier practices. The perpetual light of the oil lamps located in the holy place of the temple was continued by the *nēr tāmîd*, "perpetual light" (cf. Exod 27:20; Lev 24:2), located above the Scripture repository in the synagogue. Other large metal and glass lamp fixtures that could burn through the Sabbath without needing attention were suspended from synagogue ceilings and placed on elevated stands. Three passages in the Talmud (*b. Menah.* 28b; *b. ʿAbod. Zar.* 43a; *b. Roš Haš.* 24a–b) forbid the making of a house like the temple and the making of a menorah like that in the temple. Despite this prohibition, after the destruction of the temple the menorah became the most frequently used symbol in Jewish synagogues and cultural artifacts.

The Jewish world annually recalls the miraculous provision of oil in the Jerusalem temple during the Maccabean Wars against the Seleucids (1 Macc 4:36–58) in Hanukkah, the Festival of Lights. Rabbinic Judaism took the lights of the festival outside of public religious venues and into personal settings (cf. *m. B. Qam.* 6:6). Special ceramic oil lamps with seven wicks were precursors to later festive menorahs with eight branches and a ninth igniting candle. The ignition of Sabbath lamps or candles was another rabbinic practice. The rabbinic custom emerged for the woman of a house to ignite lights prior to nightfall and the beginning of a Sabbath. Jewish tradition asserts that women's failure to observe the Sabbath lamp-lighting rituals correctly can lead to their death in childbirth (*m. Šabb.* 2:6). Rabbinic interpretations constrain the ignition, fueling, extinguishing, and transfer of fire used in illumination, heating, and cooking on the Sabbath. If a fire was burning on the Sabbath, it was left burning but could not be tended. On the Sabbath, efforts were made to keep prepared food warm in hot ovens (*m. Šabb.* 1:10–3:6).

F. THE CHRISTIAN WORLD

Because the Christian world sprang from multiple cultures, the use of lighting and heating devices in the home paralleled their use in the various surrounding cultures. But the use of light in religious activity and within religious structures (in due time) is worthy of note.

Before the conversion of Constantine in the early fourth century, lighting was a vital issue during gatherings of Christians, since they often met at night (Acts 20:8; Pliny, *Ep.* 10.96) and used darkened venues such as catacombs. Those gathering for such meetings after dark employed torches as they traveled to find fellowship and needed to use less smoky lamps to illuminate their meetings in closed spaces. Apologists responded to allegations that these nocturnal rendezvous that took place out of public sight involved Christian "brothers and sisters" putting out the lights and engaging in ritual orgies (Tertullian, *Nat.* 16).

The lamp-lighting song *Phōs Hilaron*, translated into English as *O Gladsome Light*, is one of the earliest and most enduring pieces of Christian music. According to the fourth-century *Apostolic Constitutions*, the liturgical singing of this song, which had mistakenly been believed to have been promoted by James the Brother of Jesus as a first-century apostolic tradition, should instead be attributed to the late-third-century martyr Athenogenes, who died in the Diocletianic persecution (Basil, *On the Holy Spirit* 29). There is no evidence that ritual illumination activities were a common practice of the apostolic church, and lamps do not appear in extant collections of early Christian symbols. The theologian Tertullian ridiculed the ceremonial use of candles and lamps by pagans in daylight hours. He observed that pagans, lost in spiritual darkness, needed all the light they could get, both day and night (*Apol.* 35, 44; *Idol.* 15). The North African rhetorician Lactantius, who had converted to Christianity, found the pagan offerings of candles and wax tapers a senseless gift to the Author of Light (*Inst.* 6.2).

Torches and lamps became a standard part of funerary celebrations of the life of Christians. Some Christians, like their pagan neighbors who left funerary offerings for the dead, left burning lamps when they visited polyandrous family tombs and honored champions of their spiritual family who had finished their temporal race. At the beginning of the fourth century, the bishops of the Council of Elvira, in Spain, decided that the practice of Christians lighting wax candles at cemeteries in honor of martyrs during daylight was unacceptable (*Canons of Elvira* 34), but they accepted the lighting of candles as a regular part of worship services (*Canons of Elvira* 37).

The proliferation and enlargement of ecclesiastical structures generated a greater need for, and interest in, lighting. Emperor Constantine's support of Christianity helped to promote a flood of converts from paganism, who could identify similarities in their former light rituals with the lighting of candles and lamps in fourth-century Christian liturgy. Greater illumination of basilicae was achieved through the admission of sunlight through wall openings in facades and clerestory windows. Glazed windows allowed daytime illumination while maintaining the interior environment and reducing drafts, dust, and birds flying into the building.

At the end of the fourth century, Gregory of Nazianzus, the Archbishop of Constantinople, cautioned against the ceremonial use of lights in churches since this had come to resemble pagan practices (*Or. Bas.* 5.35), but he also affirmed the action of Christians whose light displays and procession the night before his Paschal Sermon in AD 383 had illuminated the night (*Or. Bas.* 45.2). In the fourth century, lamps were commonly given to newly immersed converts to symbolize the spiritual light that they were to shine in the world as they awaited the coming of the "bridegroom" Jesus Christ (Zeno of Verona, *Tractate* 1.14.4; Gregory of Nazianzus, *Or. Bas.* 40.46). Tensions arose as the practice of offering candles in church buildings together with prayers to God and saints increased, as evidenced, for example, in the vitriolic epistolary disputation in AD 406 between Vigilantius in Spain and Jerome in Bethlehem over the embrace of light rituals. The Spanish monk found candle-lighting to be syncretistic, while Jerome maintained that lighting tapers for saints was innocuous and that lighting a candle when the Gospel was read was a time-honored practice (Jerome, *Vigil.* 61.7).

In the fifth century, candle-lighting became a standard feature of the Byzantine and Latin liturgies. Ornamented bronze lamps and lampstands were placed in chancel areas and on altars, and multiple glass reservoirs of oil in polycandelaria were suspended from ceilings with fireproof bronze chains and other hanging devices, to illuminate interiors and icons. Byzantine pilgrims to Jerusalem secured special oil lamps as *eulogia* that carried the inscription "Christ is the light of the world." Christians commonly decorated their almond-shaped lamps with symbols like crosses and Greek letters carrying religious significance, *chi/rho* (the first two letters of the name "Christ" in Gk.) and *alpha/omega* (signifying that Jesus Christ is "the beginning and the end"). While Christians embraced their own ritual lighting activities, they were prohibited, under threat of excommunication, from joining in Jewish and pagan festival activities that used lights (*Apostolic Constitutions* 8.5.47.71).

BIBLIOGRAPHY: D. M. Bailey, *A Catalogue of Lamps in the British Museum* (1975–1996); R. J. Forbes, *Studies in Ancient Technology VI: Heat and Heating* (1966); E. R. Goodenough, "The Menorah," in idem, *Jewish Symbols in the Greco-Roman Period* (1954), IV.71–98; S. Loffreda, *Lucerne Bizantine in Terra Sancta con iscrizioni in Greco* (1989); A. Lucas and J. R. Harris, *Ancient Egyptian Materials and Industries* (1999); C. Meyers, "Lampstand," *ABD* IV.141–43; T. Oziol and R. Rebuffat, *Les lampes de terre cuite en Méditerranée: Des origines à Justinien* (1987); E. Parisinou, "Lighting Practices in Early Greece (from the End of the Mycenaean World to the 7th Century BC)," *Oxford Journal of Archaeology* 17 (1998), 327–43; C. N. Reeves, *The Complete Tutankhamun* (1990); R. Rosenthal and R. Sivan, *Ancient Lamps in the Schloessinger Collection, Qedem* 8 (1978); W. E. Scudamore, "Lights, The Ceremonial Use of" in *A Dictionary of Christian Antiquities,* ed. W. Smith and S. Cheetham (1880), I.993–98; M. Serpico and R. White, "Oil, Fat and Wax," in *Ancient Egyptian Materials and Technology,* ed. P. T. Nicholson and I. Shaw (2000), 390–429; R. H. Smith, "Lamps," *OEANE* 3.326–30; G. F. Snyder, *Ante Pacem: Archaeological Evidence of Church Life before Constantine* (1985); N. Yalouris, M. Andronikos, and K. Rhomiopoulou, *The Search for Alexander: An Exhibition* (1980).

RKH and RWS

See also BELLOWS & FURNACES, BOTTLES & GLASS, CERAMICS & POTTERY, DWELLINGS, FOOD PRODUCTION, and METALLURGY.

HORSES

The horse is a magnificent animal that in ancient times was especially important for its military functions, specifically in chariotry and in cavalry. The horse was not generally used as a draft animal, nor was it eaten.

A. THE OLD TESTAMENT

Horses (Heb. sing. *sûs*; cf. Akk. *sisû*; Egy. *ssm.t*) are mentioned 140 times in the OT, many times in symbolic contexts. They are first mentioned in the story of Joseph, who gives the Egyptians grain in exchange for their horses and other livestock (Gen 47:17). Following the defeat of Hadadezer, David kept enough horses for a hundred chariots (2 Sam 8:4) and hobbled the rest. In the time of Solomon, the ancient restriction against a king's acquiring a large number of horses (Deut 17:16; cf. Josh 11:4–9) was disregarded in favor of building up a large force of chariotry for the Israelites, fulfilling Samuel's dire warning (1 Sam 8:11) and tempting Israel to trust in horses and not on the Lord (Ps 33:17; Hos 1:7). Job describes the magnificence of the war horse (Job 39:19–25).

Solomon imported horses from Kue (i.e., Cilicia) and also from Egypt (1 Kgs 10:28–29||2 Chr 1:16–17). He paid 150 shekels for each horse. He had four thousand chariot horses (stallions) and twelve thousand other horses (mares). Structures at Megiddo that probably served as stables (though their function is disputed) were originally dated by scholars to the time of Solomon but are now ascribed to Ahab's reign. As these have been left in situ, however, it is possible that Solomonic structures may lie underneath them.

Josiah removed horse statues from the temple that earlier kings had dedicated to the sun (2 Kgs 23:11). Excavations in Jerusalem have yielded objects probably associated with this cult. Over half of the 1,300 ceramic figurines that were primarily found in Jerusalem (dated to the 8th–6th c. BC) were horse figurines.

The warnings of Jeremiah against "foes from the north" may refer to horse-mounted Scythian archers (Jer 4–5, 8–9). The horses of the Chaldeans are described as swifter than leopards and fiercer than wolves (Hab 1:8). Their power and fearsomeness are also described by Jeremiah (Jer 8:16; 47:3).

Equids, including asses, mules, and horses, figure prominently in the prophecies of Zechariah. The meaning of the Hebrew terms for two of the colors of the four horses described in this book (Zech 1:8, 6:2–3)—the colors other than "black" and "white"—has been disputed. The most realistic renderings for these disputed colors seem to be "brown" and "gray."

B. THE NEW TESTAMENT

Over the thousands of miles that Paul traveled, the only time that the NT reports him possibly using a horse was when he was escorted by soldiers from Jerusalem to Caesarea (Acts 23:23–24), though the word used here is *ktēnos*, a generic term that can simply mean "animal." With the exception of the reference in James to the bridling of a horse as an illustration of the difficulty of taming the tongue (Jas 3:3), all of the explicit references to the horse (Gk. *hippos*) in the NT are found in symbolic contexts in the book of Revelation, such as ch. 6, which speaks about the four apocalyptic horses: a white horse, whose rider was "bent on conquest" (Rev 6:2); a red horse, whose "rider was given power to take peace from the earth and to make people kill each other" (Rev 6:4); a black horse, whose "rider was holding a pair of scales in his hand," which portended inflated prices because of shortages of food (Rev 6:5); and a pale horse, whose "rider was named Death" (Rev 6:8).

C. THE NEAR EASTERN WORLD

The wild tarpan (*Equus ferus ferus*) lived north of the Black Sea. The horse (*Equus caballus*) was indigenous to the plains of Central Asia. Horses are able to survive in areas covered with snow where cattle and sheep cannot. Equid bones and evidence of mare's milk dating to 3500 BC have been found at the site of Botai in northern Kazakhstan. Horse bones from the third millennium BC have been found in northern Syria and in the Negev at Arad. Horses are mentioned in the texts from Ebla, in Syria (24th c. BC).

The Sumerians called the horse the "donkey from the mountains." Shulgi, a Sumerian king of the Ur III Dynasty, declared: "A princely donkey set for the road am I, a horse of the highway that swishes (his) tail am I" (*ANESTP*, 585). An Ur III seal depicts a rider on a horse.

The use of horses to pull war chariots became widespread in the second millennium BC, but riding only became common in the first millennium BC. The Hurrians of Mitanni (15th–14th c. BC) became excellent horse handlers, as is revealed by the training manual of Kikkuli found at the Hittite capital. We also have veterinary manuals that discuss horses from Ashur (in Akkadian) and from Ras Shamra (in Ugaritic).

Price lists from Ugarit list the cost of a sheep as one shekel of silver, that of a bull as seventeen shekels, that of a mare as seventy shekels, and that of a stallion as 200 shekels. In a notable Ugaritic letter (RS 16.402), a chieftain protests the demand that he provide two thousand horses for the king's service.

Though the invading Hyksos may have introduced the chariot into Egypt, in 1958 excavators discovered the skeleton of a horse at an earlier, Middle Kingdom level in a fortress at Buhen in the Sudan (1675 BC). This was a large horse with a height of one and one-half meters at its withers. Two equine molars were found in the excavations of the Hyksos capital of Avaris in the Delta region. In 2009 the burial of a mare in the palace was discovered. The first known Egyptian textual reference to the horse comes from the reign of Kamose, as the native Egyptians started to expel the Hyksos from their land. Horse-drawn chariots became prominent in the New Kingdom. One painting from this period depicts a few scouts on horseback. Senenmut, the chief advisor of Hatshepsut, had a prize horse buried in his tomb chapel.

Tuthmosis III captured 2,041 mares, 191 foals, and six stallions at the battle of Megiddo (1490 BC). One of his officers, Amuemhab, related how he foiled the ruse of the king of Kadesh, who had sent a mare in heat to distract the stallions pulling the Egyptian chariots, when he managed to kill the mare.

Amenhotep II boasted of himself, "Now when he was (still) a lad, he loved his horses and rejoiced in them. It was a strengthening of the heart *training* them, and to enter into their ways" (*ANET*, 244). The Amarna Letters, which were sent between Amenhotep III and Amenhotep IV and other kings of the Near East, make reference to gifts of horses, and even include wishes for the welfare of a king's horses.

Horses from Kush (Sudan) were highly valued. King Piye (Piankhy) from the Kushite 25th Dynasty was outraged that an Egyptian nomarch had allowed horses to starve: "I swear, as [Ra] loves me . . . that my horses were made to hunger pains me more than any other crime you committed in your recklessness!" (*AEL*, 3.73). Piye and other Kushite pharaohs had richly caparisoned (i.e., ornamented) horses buried with them.

At the end of the seventh century BC, the Scythians, mounted nomads from the Russian steppes, attacked the Assyrians and overran Media, before they were expelled from the region. As depicted in the ninth-century BC reliefs of Ashurnasirpal and Shalmaneser III, the example of these horsemen induced the Assyrians to develop their own cavalry, at first with two men riding as a pair, with one holding the reins as the other shot arrows. In the Assyrian invasion of Judah in 701 BC, Sennacherib's general taunted Hezekiah by offering him two thousand horses, "if you can put riders on them" (2 Kgs 18:23).

The Assyrians first became acquainted in the ninth century BC with the Medes, who lived in the valleys of the Zagros Mountains, as a source for horses. A rare horse protome (sculptured column capital) was found at Pasargadae, the capital of Cyrus. A text of Darius from Persepolis declares: "This country Persia which Ahuramazda bestowed upon me, good, possessed of good horses, possessed of good men—by the favor of Ahuramazda and of me, Darius the King, does not feel fear of (any) other" (Kent, 136). He established the so-called "Royal Road" and instituted a courier system consisting of riders and horses posted at twenty-mile intervals. By means of this system, messengers could cover the seventeen-hundred-mile distance from Susa to Sardis in a week. The Persians taught their boys to ride and to shoot arrows from their youth. A Persian satrap of Egypt, Arsham, wrote a letter requesting an artist to make an equestrian statue of himself in addition to one that had already been made.

D. THE GRECO-ROMAN WORLD

In the Aegean area horses first appear in Greece and Troy ca. 1800 BC, concurrent with the influx of Indo-Europeans into Greece. It was because horses were so venerated by the Trojans that the ruse of the Trojan Horse enabled the Greeks to capture Troy. Horses are depicted at the Mycenaean shaft graves (1650–1550 BC) and are listed on the Linear B chariot tablets from Knossos. The Mycenaean Greek spelling of horse was *i-qo*, for Greek *hippos* (cf. Lat. *equus*). The name Philip (Gk. *Philippos*) means "lover of horses."

The two main horse-raising areas in Greece were the plains of Boeotia and the plains of Thessaly. It was therefore a calamitous turn of events for the Athenians, the Spartans, and their allied city-states that both of these areas "Medized," that is, supported the Persian invasion of Xerxes in 480 BC. Darius had transported horses by boat from Ionia in western Turkey to Marathon. Scholars still debate why they were not utilized. (See Yamauchi 1990, 167–68.)

The most prestigious event of the Olympic Games, which were first held in 776 BC, was the chariot races, which were sponsored by the wealthy. In 648 BC the first known racing of ridden horses occurred at Olympia. As much as 1200 drachmae (one drachma was a day's wage) was paid for the purchase of a race horse in 421 BC.

In the Classical Age (5th c. BC), the Greeks mainly used horsemen as scouts. Xenophon, who in his *Anabasis* describes his leading of the "Ten Thousand" mercenaries, later wrote a manual on horsemanship. The Macedonian king Philip II developed a professional cavalry armed with long spears. His son Alexander brilliantly led the cavalry in a series of victories, beginning at Chaeronea in 338 BC. As a young boy, Alexander managed to tame an unruly horse, Bucephalus, which he rode in his famous campaign that led all the way to India.

Horses were well known among the pre-Etruscan Villanovan folk (8th c. BC). In the early Roman Republic, a group of six hundred *equites* was provided horses at public expense. Later this group of cavalrymen was increased to eighteen hundred. This became the origin of the equestrian class, a social group that was second in wealth only to the senators. Only the wealthy could afford to own horses for their private transport.

In the second Punic War, Hannibal used Numidian cavalry to great effect, until Scipio Africanus won over the Numidian king to the Roman side. The Parthians, who employed mounted archers, inflicted a massive defeat on the Romans at Carrhae in 53 BC. By the first century BC, foreign horsemen performed most of the cavalry functions for the Romans. One *ala* ("wing") of cavalry was stationed in Judea.

Romans enjoyed the sport of chariot racing in the huge Circus Maximus. The best horses were from North Africa. By the second century AD, the demand for racehorses was such that the cavalry was hard-pressed to obtain its horses. Caesar was an accomplished rider. According to Plutarch,

> Horsemanship, moreover, had been easy for him from boyhood; for he was wont to put his hands behind his back and holding them closely there, to ride his horse at full speed. And in the Gallic campaigns he practised dictating letters on horseback and keeping two scribes at once busy, or, as Oppius says, even more. (*Caes.* 17.4)

An extraordinary feat of riding was accomplished by Tiberius in 9 BC, when he rode on relays of horses from Ticinum in northern Italy five hundred miles in three days to reach his mortally wounded brother Drusus in Germany. The imperial post relied on a relay of fresh horses. Unlike the Persian system, which employed relays, in Rome the same rider continued on until he had reached his destination.

For traveling under certain conditions, such as on difficult or icy ground, the Romans provided their horses with iron "hipposandals," shoes outfitted with leather thongs. Nailed shoes are known only from the Celtic area of the Empire.

E. THE JEWISH WORLD

A commentary on the book of Habakkuk found at Qumran interprets the horses mentioned in Hab 1:8 to be those of the Kittim, i.e., the Romans: "'Swifter than panthers their horses, faster than desert wolves. Their horses, galloping, spread out, from afar they fly like a vulture intent on food, all of them bent on violence. . . .' [This refers to] the Kittim, who trample the land with [their] horses and with their beasts" (1QpHab III, 6–10). According to the Qumran *War Scroll*, which describes the eschatological battle between the Sons of Light and the Sons of Darkness, the cavalry of the Sons of Light are described as follows:

> The horsemen, with the cavalry of the men of the entire army, will be six thousand; five hundred to a tribe. All the cavalry that go out to battle with the infantry shall ride stallions; swift, responsive, unrelenting, full-grown, trained for battle, and accustomed to hearing noises and seeing all kinds of scenes.
> (1QM VI, 11–13)

Philo praises the creation of the horse:

> Nay, even the horse, most spirited of all animals, is easily controlled by the bit to prevent his growing restive and running away. He hollows his back, making it a convenient seat, takes his rider on it and bearing him aloft gallops at a great pace intent on bringing himself and his rider to the destination which the latter is eager to reach. (*Opif.* 86)

He also interprets horses allegorically as "desire and high spirit" (*Agr.* 73), which recalls Plato's famous exposition (*Phaedr.* 247B).

As to what a horse can carry on the Sabbath, the Mishnah declares: "the horse [may go out] with its chain" (*m. Šabb.* 5:1). The Talmud recognizes the following characteristics of a horse: "Six things were said of a horse: it loves promiscuity, it loves battle, it has a proud spirit, it despises sleep, eats much and excretes little. Some say: it also seeks to slay its master in battle" (*b. Pesaḥ.* 113a). Rab counsels one of his students not to live in a town "where horses don't neigh" (*b. Pesaḥ.* 113a), presumably since the neighing of horses could warn of the approach of an enemy.

F. THE CHRISTIAN WORLD

To escape from Galerius, the Augustus of the East, who had been holding him as a hostage in Constantinople, Constantine used horses to travel across Europe to reach his father Constantius I, the Augustus of the West, in England. Constantine later provided horses to the bishops traveling to the Council of Nicaea in AD 325. Eusebius describes a coin depicting Constantine as a charioteer drawn up to heaven by four horses, an image that followed in the tradition of the Roman iconography of deified emperors.

In his *Banquet of Ten Virgins*, Methodius (d. AD 311) urges young men to cultivate virtue from boyhood and likens the Lord to "the Rider who guides with pure mind" the youth (*Symp.* 5:3). John Cassian (ca. AD 365–ca. 433) describes the anxieties of a covetous monk as follows:

> With such strides then in a downward direction he goes from bad to worse, and at last cares not to retain I will not say the virtue but even the shadow of humility, charity, and obedience; and is displeased with everything, and murmurs and groans over every work; and now having cast off all reverence, like a bad-tempered horse, dashes off headlong and unbridled. (*Institutes* 7.8)

In his *Institutes*, Cassian, speaking of passion, writes, "I mean that those faults will at once appear on the surface which were lying hid, and, like unbridled horses diligently fed up during too long a time of idleness, dash forth from the barriers the more eagerly and fiercely to the destruction of their charioteer" (*Institutes* 8.18).

The eastern Germanic tribes that in the fifth century overran much of the Roman Empire in Europe and even devastated North Africa were accustomed to fighting on horseback.

BIBLIOGRAPHY: A. Afshar and J. Lerner, "The Horses of the Ancient Persian Empire at Persepolis," *Antiq* 53 (1979), 44–47; J. K. Anderson, *Ancient Greek Horsemanship* (1961); D. W. Anthony, "Horse, Wagon and Chariot: Indo-European Languages and Archaeology," *Antiq* 69 (1995), 554–65; D. W. Anthony, "Horses and Prehistoric Chronology of Eastern Europe and Western/Central Asia," *JANESCU* 21 (1992), 131–33; D. R. Ap-Thomas, "All the King's Horses?," in *Proclamation and Presence*, ed. J. I. Durham and J. R. Porter (1970), 135–51; J. B. Burns, "Solomon's Egyptian Horses and Exotic Wives," *Forum* 7 (1991), 29–44; D. J. Clark, "Red and Green Horses?" *BT* 56 (2005), 67–71; J. Clutton-Brock, "The Buhen Horse," *Journal of Archaeological Science* 1 (1974), 89–100; J. Clutton-Brock, *Horse Power: A History of the Horse and the Donkey in Human Societies* (1992); C. Cohen, "The Ugaritic Hippiatric Texts and *BAM* 159," *JANESCU* 15 (1983), 1–12; C. Cohen and D. Sivan, *The Ugaritic Hippiatric Texts* (1983); S. Dalley, "Foreign Chariotry and Cavalry in the Armies of Tiglath-Pileser III and Sargon II," *Iraq* 47 (1985), 31–48; G. I. Davies, "Solomonic Stables at Megiddo after All?" *PEQ* 120 (1988), 130–41; G. I. Davies, "*ʾUrwōt* in I Kings 5:6 (EVV. 4:26) and the Assyrian Horse Lists," *JSS* 34 (1989), 25–38; T. Donaghy, *Horse Breeds and Breeding in the Greco-Persian World* (2014); M. A. Hahlen, "The Background and Use of Equine Imagery in Zechariah," *SCJ* 3 (2000), 243–60; F. Hančar, *Das Pferd in prähistorischer und früher historischer Zeit* (1956); K. Hanson, "Collection in Ancient Egyptian Chariot Horses," *JARCE* 29 (1992), 173–79; L. Heidorn, "The Horses of Kush," *JNES* 56 (1997), 105–14; J. S. Holladay, Jr., "The Stables of Ancient Israel," in *The Archaeology of Jordan and Other Studies*, ed. L. T. Geraty and L. G. Herr

(1986), 103–65; A. Hyland, *Equus: The Horse in the Roman World* (1990); Y. Ikeda, "Solomon's Trade in Horses and Chariots in Its International Setting," in *Studies in the Period of David and Solomon and Other Essays*, ed. T. Ishida (1982), 215–38; A. Kammenhuber, *Hippologia Hethitica* (1961); A. Kammenhuber, "On Hittites, Mitanni-Hurrians, Indo-Aryans and Horse Tablets in the IInd Millennium B.C.," in *Essays on Anatolian Studies in the Second Millennium B.C.*, ed. T. Mikasa (1988), 35–51; O. Keel, "Hyksos Horses or Hippopotamus Deities?" *Levant* 25 (1993), 208–12; R. G. Kent, *Old Persian: Grammar, Texts, Lexicon* (1953); G. A. Klingbeil, " 'Man's Other Best Friend': The Interaction of Equids and Man in Daily Life in Iron Age II Palestine as Seen in Texts, Artifacts, and Images," *UF* 35 (2003), 259–89; M. A. Littauer and J. H. Crouwel, *Wheeled Vehicles and Ridden Animals in the Ancient Near East* (1979); H. A. McKay, "Through the Eyes of Horses: Representation of the Horse Family in the Hebrew Bible," in *Sense and Sensitivity*, ed. A. G. Hunter and P. R. Davies (2002), 127–41; J. W. McKay, "Further Light on the Horses and Chariot of the Sun in the Jerusalem Temple (2 Kings 23:11)," *PEQ* 105 (1973), 167–69; P. R. S. Moorey, "Pictorial Evidence for the History of Horse-Riding in Iraq before the Kassite Period," *Iraq* 32 (1970), 36–50; E. O. Negahban, "Horse and Mule Figurines from Marlik," in *Archaeologia Iranica et Orientalis*, ed. L. de Meyer and E. Haerinck (1989), 287–309; A. Nyland, "*Penna-* and *parḫ-* in the Hittite Horse Training Texts," *JNES* 51 (1992), 293–96; D. Odell, "Images of Violence in the Horse in Job 39:18–25," *Prooftexts* 13 (1993), 163–73; D. Owen, "The 'First' Equestrian: An Ur III Glyptic Scene," *Acta Sumerologica* 13 (1991), 259–73; M. H. Pope, "A Mare in Pharaoh's Chariotry," *BASOR* 200 (1970), 56–61; A. H. Potratz, *Die Pferdetrensen des Alten Orient* (1966); J. B. Pritchard, "The Megiddo Stables: A Reassessment," in *Near Eastern Archaeology in the Twentieth Century*, ed. J. A. Sanders (1970), 268–76; P. Raulwing, *Horses, Chariots, and the Indo-Europeans* (2000); A. Salonen, *Hippologica Akkadica* (1955–56); A. R. Schulman, "Egyptian Representations of Horsemen and Riding in the New Kingdom," *JNES* 16 (1957), 263–71; J. M. C. Toynbee, *Animals in Roman Life and Art* (1973); E. D. Van Buren, *The Fauna of Ancient Mesopotamia as Represented in Art* (1939); P. Vigneron, *Le cheval dans l'antiquité gréco-romaine* (1968); E. Yamauchi, *Foes from the Northern Frontier* (1982); E. Yamauchi, *Persia and the Bible* (1990); D. W. Young, "The Ugaritic Myth of the God Ḥōrān and the Mare," *UF* 11 (1979), 839–48.

EMY

See also ARMIES, ATHLETICS, CAMELS, COMMUNICATION & MESSENGERS, DONKEYS & MULES, and SPECTACLES.

HUMAN SACRIFICE

In the narrow sense, human sacrifice is the sacrifice to a deity of people in place of animals. In a broader sense, the ritual killing of humans in the ancient world involved a variety of practices, including the killing of family members and retainers to accompany a leader and to serve him in the afterworld, the killing of humans to fulfill a vow or to avert a disaster, and the killing of an enemy to avenge the death of one's comrade.

Human sacrifices play a prominent role in mythology and in some historical texts. In a few cases we have artistic representations of human sacrifice, and some archaeological evidence exists as well, most notably from the infamous Tophet of Carthage.

A. THE OLD TESTAMENT

The most notable situation in the Bible in which a human was nearly sacrificed involves God's command to Abraham to sacrifice his son Isaac: "Take your son, your only son, whom you love—Isaac—and go to the region of Moriah. Sacrifice him there as a burnt offering on a mountain I will show you" (Gen 22:2). Abraham obeyed God, but at the last moment the angel of the Lord stayed Abraham's hand and told him to spare his son, saying, "Now I know that you fear God, because you have not withheld from me your son, your only son" (Gen 22:12). A ram caught in a nearby thicket providentially appeared, and Abraham offered this animal as the burnt offering instead of Isaac. Because Abraham was willing to sacrifice his only son, God promised: "I will surely bless you and make your descendants as numerous as the stars in the sky and as the sand on the seashore. Your descendants will take possession of the cities of their enemies, and through your offspring all nations on earth will be blessed, because you have obeyed me" (Gen 22:17–18).

Some scholars have speculated that the redemption of the firstborn son (Exod 13:2; 22:28–29) was a mitigation of a primitive sacrifice of first-born sons, but there is no evidence of such a practice among the Hebrews or any other peoples. Indeed, the stated reason for the redemption of first-born sons and the firstborn male of animals is gratitude that the Lord had punished the Egyptians with the death of their firstborn men and animals at the time of the exodus (Exod 13:12–15).

After the capture of Jericho, Joshua pronounced a curse upon anyone who would attempt to rebuild the city: "At the cost of his firstborn son he will lay its foundations; at the cost of his youngest he will set up its gates" (Josh 6:26). Elsewhere the Bible depicts the rebuilding of Jericho by Hiel of Bethel (during the reign of Ahab, around 860 BC) as occurring "at the cost of his firstborn son Abiram, and . . . at the cost of his youngest son Segub, in accordance with the word of the LORD spoken by Joshua son of Nun" (1 Kgs 16:34). This text may refer to an act of sacrifice in which the bodies of infants were placed in jars that were placed in the city's foundation. Hiel may have undertaken such a cost in order to gain access to fertile land watered by the ʿAin es-Sultan spring and a strategic location. According to J. Bartlett, Jericho controlled one of the routes used to cross the Jordan River, thus connecting Jerusalem and Ammon (Bartlett, 24).

When Jephthah, the leader of the Gileadites, fought against Sihon, the king of the Ammonites, he made a rash vow: "If you give the Ammonites into my hands, whatever comes out of the door of my house to meet me when I return in triumph from the Ammonites will be the LORD's, and I will sacrifice it as a burnt offering [ʿôlâ]" (Judg 11:30–31). After Jephthah won the victory, the first person to meet him was, much to his distress, his only daughter (Judg 11:34–35). Although a few scholars have explained Judg 11:37–39 as indicating that Jephthah fulfilled his vow not by sacrificing his daughter but by consigning her to a life of perpetual celibacy, most interpreters believe that the expression "he did to her as he had vowed" in verse 39 indicates that Jephthah did sacrifice his daughter as a burnt offering. Despite this cruel act, Jephthah was celebrated as a mighty deliverer in both the OT (1 Sam 12:11) and the NT (Heb 11:32).

When Mesha, the king of Moab, was besieged in his city of Kir-Haresheth (el-Kerak), he resorted to a desperate measure: "Then he took his firstborn son [běnô habběkôr], who was to succeed him as king, and offered him as a sacrifice on the city wall" (2 Kgs 3:27). The act was successful, as his enemies withdrew. In Mesha's famous Moabite inscription (ANET, 320–21), dating to ca. 830 BC, he mentions his devotion to his god Chemosh and his conflicts with Omri and Ahab, but not the sacrifice of his son.

After Samaria fell to Shalmaneser V in 722 BC, Sargon II deported the leading members of Israelite society to Mesopotamia and brought in peoples from Mesopotamia to replace them. Among them were the Sepharvites from northern Syria, who "burned their children in the fire as sacrifices to Adrammelek and Anammelek, the gods of Sepharvaim" (2 Kgs 17:31).

Ahaz, the king of Judah (741–725 BC), is accused of sacrificing his son "in the fire" (2 Kgs 16:3), which may refer (though the text does not say this) to an event that occurred when Rezin king of Aram and Pekah king of Israel besieged Jerusalem (2 Kgs 16:5). Manasseh, the longest reigning king of Judah (696–642 BC), was accused of adopting all kinds of pagan practices, including child sacrifice (2 Kgs 21:5–6): "In the two courts of the temple of the LORD, he built altars to all the starry hosts. He sacrificed his own son in the fire, practiced divination, sought omens, and consulted mediums and spiritists."

The Torah bans the sacrificing of sons and daughters in fire ($b\bar{a}$'$\bar{e}\check{s}$) (Deut 12:31; 18:10). Also condemned are sacrifices of children to Molek (Lev 18:21; 20:2–5; cf. Isa 57:9; Jer 32:35). Following O. Eissfeldt, some scholars have denied that the consonants m-l-k in these texts should be considered the name of a god, arguing instead, on the basis of Punic inscriptions from Carthage, that the word refers to the sacrificial offering itself. However, there are extrabiblical parallels from Ebla, Mari, and Ugarit of a god whose name was spelled with these consonants, and the contexts appear to indicate that the offerings were to a god.

Though some have tried to explain the phrase $l\check{e}ha$'$\check{a}b\hat{i}r \ldots b\bar{a}$'$\bar{e}\check{s}$, "to make (someone) pass through the fire," which in 2 Kgs 23:10 refers to an activity associated with the Molek cult, as merely a reference to making individuals pass between two rows of fire, it is clear from other texts (e.g., 2 Kgs 16:3; 21:6; 2 Chr 33:6) that this refers to the sacrifice of children in fire. This took place in an area south of Jerusalem, the Valley of Ben Hinnom, which later was called Gehenna: "He [Josiah] desecrated Topheth, which was in the Valley of Ben Hinnom, so no one could use it to sacrifice their son or daughter in the fire to Molek" (2 Kgs 23:10). According to J. Day, the name Topheth may originally be derived from the Hebrew verbal root '$\bar{a}p\hat{a}$, "bake" (Day, 24–28). Many scholars, however, consider the etymology of Topheth to be uncertain and explain it as a cult site associated with fire and human sacrifice, based on the context of the biblical references (cf. Isa 30:33; Jer 7:31–32).

Other OT texts uniformly condemn human sacrifice as an abominable deed practiced by the Canaanites and apostate Israelites (Ps 106:37–38). Prophets such as Isaiah (57:5–9), Jeremiah (19:4–6; 32:34–35), Ezekiel (16:21; 20:26; 23:39), and Hosea (13:2) passionately condemned the practice.

B. THE NEW TESTAMENT

Abraham's near sacrifice of his son Isaac is mentioned directly in two NT passages, both of which highlight Abraham's faith. In Heb 11:17–19, we read:

> By faith Abraham, when God tested him, offered Isaac as a sacrifice. He who had embraced the promises was about to sacrifice his one and only son, even though God had said to him, "It is through Isaac that your offspring will be reckoned." Abraham reasoned that God could even raise the dead, and so in a manner of speaking he did receive Isaac back from death.

James 2:21–23 declares:

> Was not our father Abraham considered righteous for what he did when he offered his son Isaac on the altar? You see that his faith and his actions were working together, and his faith was made complete by what he did. And the scripture was fulfilled that says, "Abraham believed God, and it was credited to him as righteousness," and he was called God's friend.

The close parallel between the wording *ouk epheisō tou huiou sou tou agapētou*, "you [Abraham] did not spare your beloved son," in the LXX translation of Gen 22:16 and the statement *hos ge tou idiou huiou ouk epheisato*, "he [God] who did not spare his own son," in Rom 8:32 suggests that in the latter text Paul is drawing an analogy between Abraham's sacrifice of Isaac and God the Father's sacrifice of Jesus on the cross.

Some scholars (Daly, Schoeps, Vermes) have seen the influence of the Jewish tradition of the Akedah (the "Binding" of Isaac) in a number of NT passages, such as John 1:29; 3:16; Rom 3:25; 4:18–25. However, although some elements of the Akedah tradition antedate the NT, the full development of this complex and important tradition occurred only after the destruction of the temple in AD 70 (Davies and Chilton, 545).

C. THE NEAR EASTERN WORLD

From 1926 to 1930 C. L. Woolley uncovered spectacular royal tombs at Ur (ca. 2500–2400 BC) that provided clear evidence of the sacrifice of numerous retainers, including soldiers, musicians with lyres, and numerous women adorned with gold, silver, and lapis lazuli jewelry. One of the burial areas, PG ("Private Grave") 1157, contained a death pit with fifty-eight bodies; this was perhaps the tomb of King Meskiagnuna. In the so-called "Great Death Pit" (PG 1237), there were bodies of six armed men, and sixty-eight young girls or women arranged in four rows. Woolley commented:

It is most probable that the victims walked to their places, took some kind of drug—opium or hashish would serve—and lay down in order; after the drug had worked, whether it produced sleep or death, the last touches were given to the bodies and the pit was filled in. There does not seem to have been anything brutal in the manner of their deaths. (Woolley, 60)

Based on recent CT scans of the skulls from the royal tombs at Ur in the University of Pennsylvania Museum of Archaeology and Anthropology, however, scholars now attribute the death of the victims to blunt force trauma caused by "a forceful blow to the skull by a sharp, weighted weapon" (Baadsgaard, Monge, and Zettler, 144).

The only Mesopotamian text that might possibly refer to the sacrifice of retainers to accompany a ruler to the afterlife is a small fragmentary tablet from Uruk, the Death of Gilgamesh, part of which reads:

> His beloved wife, [his] be[loved] son,
> ... [his] be[loved] concubine,
> His musician, [his beloved] *entertainer*,
> [His] beloved chief valet, ...
> ..., the palace *attendants*,
> His beloved *caretaker*.
>   (*ANET*, 51)

Texts from the Neo-Assyrian period (9th–7th c. BC) contain penalty curses stipulating that one who fails to keep a contract or one who effaces the royal name will burn his eldest son to Adad and his eldest daughter to Bēlet-ṣeri (Ishtar). Esarhaddon sacrificed the murderers of his father, Sennacherib, at an altar where the latter was killed.

In order to avert the death of an Assyrian king portended by an eclipse, the reigning king would abdicate his throne temporarily and a substitute king (*šar pūḫi*), who might be a criminal or a prisoner of war, would take his place, only to be executed at the end of the period of danger. However, in the case where the gardener Enlil-bani became a substitute king for Irra-imitti, the latter "died in his palace because he had swallowed boiling broth. Enlil-bani who was upon the throne did not relinquish it and was installed as king" (Green, 88).

In 1955 a Late Bronze Age temple (13th c. BC) was discovered at the airport in Jordan (Hennessy). In addition to yielding pottery from the Mycenaean IIA to IIIB periods, the temple contained several thousand small bone fragments that belonged to humans who had been killed and bled and who were then burned.

In 1978 a text from Ugarit in Syria (RS 24.266) was published in which some scholars have discerned a reference to human sacrifice (in the word "firstborn"), though this interpretation is by no means universal, nor is it necessitated by context. This text, which contains a ritual prayer for a city under siege, reads in part:

> When a strong (foe) attacks your gate, a warrior your walls,
>   You shall lift your eyes to Baꜥlu (and say):
> O Baꜥlu, if you drive the strong one from our gate,
>   the warrior from our walls,
> A bull, O Baꜥlu, we shall sanctify,
>   a vow, (O) Baꜥlu, we shall fulfill;
> a firstborn, (O) Baꜥlu, we shall sanctify, . . .
>   (*COS* 1.88:284–85)

Eusebius cites Philo of Byblos, who wrote about AD 100, as follows: "It was a custom of the ancients in the great crises of danger for the rulers of a city or nation, in order to avert the general destruction, to give up the most beloved of their children for sacrifice as a ransom to the avenging daemons: and those who were so given up were slain with mystic rites" (*Praep. ev.* 4.16; translation Gifford, 156d). According to the Roman historian Quintus Curtius Rufus, at Tyre "some even proposed renewing a sacrifice which had been discontinued for many years . . . of offering a freeborn boy to Saturn—this sacrilege rather than sacrifice, handed down from their founders, the Carthaginians are said to have performed until the destruction of their city" (*History of Alexander* 4.3.23).

In Egypt there is considerable evidence of the sacrifice of servants to accompany the pharaohs to the afterlife in the Predynastic era (3500–3100 BC) and during the 1st Dynasty (3100–2700 BC). In the Naqada II (or Gerzean) period, numerous retainers were killed and buried at tomb T-5 at Naqada, and also at Hierakonpolis and Adaïma. At Naga ed-Deir, chiefs were buried with their wives and concubines surrounding them, a practice that some have described as a *suttee* (from Sanskrit *sati*, "true woman") burial, after the custom in India where a wife would be immolated on the funeral pyre of her husband (a practice that was not abolished until 1829, after the British had occupied parts of India).

During the Archaic Era (1st and 2nd Dyn.), in addition to tombs at Saqqara in Lower Egypt near Memphis, kings also had cenotaphs (empty tombs) at Abydos, a city associated with Osiris that was located midway up the Nile River. Whereas the Saqqara burials of the pharaohs were associated with relatively few retainer sacrifices and simultaneous burials, the massive mastabas at Abydos had enormous numbers of these. The graves of these women and servants, who had evidently died before they were buried, were roofed over at the same time as those of their pharaohs. The following chart (adapted from Hoffman, 276) lists such human sacrifices at Abydos:

Ruler	Probable Cases	Possible Cases	Maximum Total
Djer	63	99	162
Meryet-nit	33	0	33
Uadji	14	99	113
Udimu	40	83	123
Enezib	0	14	14
Semerkhet	68	0	68
Ka'a	26	0	26

After the Archaic Era the practice of human sacrifice in Egypt disappeared. Some believe that this was replaced by the burial of *ushabti* ("answerer") figurines that were expected to perform menial tasks in the afterlife.

The skeleton of a decapitated prisoner dating to the Middle Kingdom was found, along with statuettes of handcuffed enemies, at the fortress of Mirgissa in Kush (biblical Cush) in Sudan. This may be evidence of human sacrifice or simply of the execution of enemies. In recent excavations at Tell el-Dabʿa in the northeast Delta (ancient Avaris), M. Bietak found in a cemetery dated to the seventeenth century BC not only the burial of donkeys but also of servants, "usually girls with strong bones" (Bietak, 45).

The practice of human sacrifice reappeared on a massive scale ca. 2000 BC at the site of Kerma, the capital of the kingdom of Kush. In the cemetery east of the city are four massive tumuli (artificial mounds), each about ninety meters in diameter. The retainers buried there evidently went to their deaths voluntarily and were buried alive in these mounds to accompany their kings. W. Y. Adams comments: "To complete the picture of barbarian magnificence it may be added that the number of human sacrifices in Tumulus X at Kerma—322 by actual count, and perhaps as many as 400 before plundering—is larger than in any other known tomb of any civilization" (Adams, 203; cf. Yamauchi 2004, 71–73).

From the New Kingdom we have vivid depictions of the inhabitants of cities besieged by pharaohs attempting to ward off capture by the sacrifice of young children. From a temple at Beit el-Wali in Kush, a scene from the reign of Ramesses II portrays a woman lowering a child, possibly still alive, over the ramparts. At the Karnak temple, we have a depiction of the besieging of Ashkelon by Ramesses's successor, Merneptah, in which a child is being tossed over the walls of both sides of the city (Spalinger, 50). In the Medinet Habu reliefs of Ramesses III, one of the inhabitants of a Syrian city lowers a child over the rampart as Ramesses attacks (Spalinger, 51).

D. THE GRECO-ROMAN WORLD

Greece

There are numerous references to human sacrifice in Greek mythology, drama, and historical texts, but there are few credible examples. Most Greek sources describe the practice of sacrificing human victims to the gods as belonging to the distant past. According to Pausanias, the Delphic oracle instructed the people of Potniae that "they must sacrifice a boy in the bloom of youth" in order to avert an outbreak of pestilence (*Descr.* 9.8.2).

One notable myth was that of the Minotaur, a man with the head of a bull who lived in the labyrinth at Knossos on Crete. In order to atone for their murder of a Cretan prince, the Athenians had to send an annual tribute of young boys and girls as human sacrifices to be devoured by the Minotaur. The Athenian prince Theseus, originally one of the intended victims, slew the Minotaur and managed to escape from the labyrinth with the aid of the Cretan princess Ariadne.

Striking evidence of human sacrifice was discovered in 1979 at a temple (ca. 1700 BC) at Arkhanes near Anemospila on Crete. Among the four skeletons found in this temple, which was destroyed by an earthquake, was that of an eighteen-year-old male found on a low altar-like structure, with a bronze knife on his body. While the bones of his lower right side were black, those of his upper left side were white, as they had been drained of blood. He was apparently bound before he was killed.

Some scholars have also interpreted the deposit of human (and dog) bones at a Late Bronze *tholos* (beehive-shaped) tomb at Dendra in the northeastern Peloponnesus as evidence of human sacrifice. Other scholars have interpreted a Mycenaean Linear B tablet (Pylos TN 316) dated ca. 1200 BC as possible evidence for human sacrifice. The tablet lists dedications of thirteen golden vessels, eight women, and two men to twelve deities, including Zeus, Hera, and Potnia. (See Chadwick and Ventris, 172, 460.)

In Homer's *Iliad*, Achilles vows to avenge his friend Patroclus's death at the hands of the Trojan Hector (*Il.* 18.333–337), a vow that he duly fulfills: "Hail, Patroclus, even in the house of Hades, for now I am bringing to fulfillment all that I promised you before: that I would drag Hector here and give him raw to dogs to devour, and of twelve glorious sons of the Trojans would I cut the throats before your pyre in my wrath at your slaying" (*Il.* 23.19–23). In addition, Achilles also sacrifices two of Patroclus's nine dogs (*Il.* 23.173–176).

The Trojan War was said to have begun and ended with human sacrifices, although neither is directly referenced in Homer's *Iliad*. The sacrifice of the Trojan princess Polyxena, the daughter of Priam and Hecuba, by Achilles's son Neoptolemus to appease the ghost of his father and permit the Greeks to sail home from Troy was noted by many poets (Ibycus, Simonides, Stesichorus) and is the theme of Euripides's play *Hecuba*: "Was it Fate that induced them to perform human sacrifice at a tomb, a place where the sacrifice of a bull is more fitting? Or if Achilles wished to pay back those who killed him, is it right for him to murder her? She has done him no harm" (260–264).

Though it was omitted by Homer, the most famous human sacrifice in Greek drama was the Greek captain Agamemnon's slaying of his daughter Iphigenia. According to the Myth, the Greek forces had outraged the goddess Artemis, who would not allow them to sail to Troy until they had appeased her by sacrificing Iphigenia. According to the tragic playwright Aeschylus (*Ag.* 199–249), Agamemnon slew his daughter at Aulis before the fleet departed:

> And when he put on the yokestrap of necessity,
> his mental wind veering in a direction that was impious,
> impure, unholy, from that point
> he turned to a mindset that would stop at nothing;
> for men are emboldened by miserable Infatuation,
> whose shameful schemes are the beginning of their sufferings.
> In short, he brought himself to become
> the sacrificer of his daughter, to further
> a war of revenge over a woman
> and as a preliminary rite to the fleet's departure.
> Her pleas, her cries of "father!,"
> and her maiden years, were set at naught
> by the war-loving chieftains.
>   (*Ag.* 218–230)

Iphigenia's sacrifice gains Agamemnon safe passage to Troy but has disastrous consequences for his family. Aeschylus presents Iphigenia's death as the beginning of the cycle of revenge he depicts in his *Oresteia* trilogy of plays. The tragic sacrifice embitters the girl's mother, Clytemnestra (*Ag.* 1412–1417), who then has an affair and kills her husband, Agamemnon, upon his return to Mycenae. This forces Agamemnon's son, Orestes (for whom the trilogy is named), to avenge his father's death.

On the other hand, Euripides's play *Iphigenia in Tauris* has Artemis replace the girl with a deer at the last moment and remove her to serve as her (Artemis's) priestess in Tauris (Crimea), where Iphigenia has the gruesome task of sacrificing strangers who arrive there. The historian Herodotus reports that "the Tauri have the following customs: all ship-wrecked men, and any Greeks whom they take in their sea-raiding, they sacrifice to the Virgin goddess" (*Hist.* 4.103).

The site of Mt. Lykaion in Arcadia in the central Peloponnesus was dedicated to Zeus, whose shrine there was lauded by the Archaic poets Alcman and Pindar. Persistent rumors of human sacrifice at this shrine are noted, for example, by Plato (*Resp.* 565d–e), who relates the *mythos* that one who ate the entrails of the sacrificed human victim would be turned into a wolf.

The biographer Plutarch records several instances of human sacrifice during the Classical Era. According to Plutarch, the Athenian commander Themistocles sacrificed three young Persian prisoners to Dionysus at the battle of Salamis (480 BC) during the Persian invasion of Greece (*Them.* 13.2–5). Scholars have questioned this incident since it is not mentioned by fifth-century BC sources such as Herodotus and Aeschylus.

In his *Life of Pelopidas*, which is named for a commander of the Theban forces who fought against the Spartans at the battle of Leuctra (371 BC), Plutarch writes that before the battle Pelopidas had a dream advising him to sacrifice "a virgin with auburn hair" in order to win the battle. When he reported this dream to his commanders and seers, some urged him to obey, citing numerous examples, including Themistocles's sacrifice of the Persian youths. "Others, on the contrary, argued against it, declaring that such a lawless and barbarous sacrifice was not acceptable to any one of the superior beings above us" (*Pel.* 21.4). Just then a young horse appeared, and this served as an acceptable sacrifice.

In contrast to Plutarch's late accounts, the early Greek historian Herodotus (5th c. BC) ascribes only one human sacrifice to the Greeks: that of two boys by the Spartan king Menelaus, which he offered as he attempted to sail away from Egypt (*Hist.* 2.119). But Herodotus does attribute the practice of human sacrifice to a number of non-Greek barbarians. He claims that Amestris, the wife of the Persian king Xerxes, "buried fourteen sons of notable Persians, as a thank-offering on her own behalf to the fabled god of the nether world" (*Hist.* 7.114).

The Thracians, who lived in the area of Bulgaria, were polygamous. When a Thracian man would die, Herodotus reports,

> there is great rivalry among his wives, and eager contention on their friends' part, to prove which wife was best loved by her husband; and she to whom the honour is adjudged is praised by men and women, and then slain over the tomb by her nearest of kin, and after the slaying she is buried with the husband. (*Hist.* 5.5)

The Scythians were a nomadic tribe from Central Asia who had invaded the Near East and then settled north of the Black Sea (in modern-day Ukraine). Herodotus traveled to the Greek colony of Olbia in that region and there he obtained first-hand information about Scythian customs. He records that they sacrificed one out of a hundred of their enemies to the god "Ares," slitting their throats and collecting their blood (*Hist.* 4.62). When a chief died, he was buried in a mound. "They bury, after strangling, one of the king's concubines, his cupbearer, his cook, his groom, his squire, and his messenger, besides horses" (*Hist.* 4.71). On the anniversary of the chief's death a year later, they strangled fifty more of his servants and also sacrificed fifty of the best horses. Herodotus explains that the Scythians used stakes to set the embalmed bodies of these sacrificed horses and riders up as a perpetual guard around the chief's tomb (*Hist.* 4.72).

Herodotus's account has been confirmed by the excavation of numerous Scythian burials. A survey of sixty-two Scythian kurgans (burial mounds) revealed evidence of human sacrifice in about a third of the tombs. In one tomb, seventeen retainers were buried. Four skeletons of servants were found in the *dromos* (doorway) of the kurgan in Jelisavetinskaya. The skeletons of thirteen servants sacrificed over their master's grave were found in a barrow near Lake Sevan. In 1954 the excavation of a barrow at Melitopol revealed a Scythian warrior in one tomb, and in an adjoining tomb the remains of his wife and a female slave. Investigations in 1969 and 1970 at Gaimanovo Mogila revealed the remains of six individuals: two men, their wives, and two servants. In the Arzhan Kurgan, excavated between 1971 and 1974, the chieftain was buried with his wife, fifteen attendants, and at least 150 riding horses.

The Scythians also had such bizarre habits as being tattooed, smoking hemp, and drinking wine neat (undiluted with water), as well as such barbarous customs as scalping their enemies and using their skulls as drinking vessels. It was no doubt their reputation for savagery that influenced Paul to include them as an extreme example of what the grace of God could accomplish (Col 3:11).

Rome

The Etruscans to the north of Rome sacrificed prisoners of war to the shades of their fallen soldiers. In the sixth century BC the people of Etruscan Caere (Cerveteri) stoned to death the Greek and Carthaginian prisoners they had captured in a sea battle off the coast of Alalia (*Hist.* 1.167). Tarquinius Superbus, the last Etruscan king of Rome (d. 509 BC), was said to have practiced human sacrifice (Macrobius, *Sat.* 1.7.28–35). Later, during the Roman-Etruscan wars, the people of Etruria were said to have sacrificed Roman prisoners. "In 358 BC, three hundred and seven Roman prisoners of war were slaughtered as human sacrifices in the forum of Tarquinii" (Grant, 9). The Roman gladiatorial games may have originated in the funeral games that the Etruscans sponsored to honor their dead warriors (cf. Athenaeus, *Deipn.* 4.153f).

The traditional date of the founding of Rome (A.U.C. = *ab urbe condita*) corresponds to 753 BC. Three burials dated to approximately this time were discovered at the site of the later *carcer*, or prison, of Rome. One male victim, whose hands appear to have been bound behind his back, had been killed by a blow to the head. Some archaeologists speculate that this killing was intended as a human sacrifice; others, however, suggest that the man was executed as a criminal.

Virgil, the great poet of the Augustan age, has the Trojan hero Aeneas imitating Achilles's sacrifice for Patroclus: "He had bound behind their backs the hands of those whom he meant to send as offerings to the Shades, sprinkling the flames with the blood of the slain" (*Aen.* 11.81–82; cf. 10.517–520).

Octavian (later the emperor Augustus), who was to be Virgil's patron, is said to have performed a similar sacrifice. Suetonius records that upon the capture of the city of Perusia (Perugia) in 40 BC, Octavian severely punished the rebels who had supported Julius Caesar's assassination: "Some write that three hundred men of both orders were selected from the prisoners of war and sacrificed on the Ides of March like so many victims at the altar raised to the Deified Julius" (Suet. *Aug.* 15).

The Romans are also said to have resorted to human sacrifices to propitiate the gods on three historic occasions when Rome was threatened. According to Plutarch, when the Gauls from the north threatened the city in 226 BC, the Romans "were constrained to obey certain oracular commands from the Sibylline books, and to bury alive two Greeks, a man and a woman, and likewise two Gauls, in the place called the 'forum boarium,' or cattle-market" (*Marc.* 3.4). Livy records that after the disastrous defeat at Cannae by Hannibal in 218 BC, the Romans resorted to the same practice:

> In the meantime, by the direction of the Books of Fate, some unusual sacrifices were offered; amongst others a Gaulish man and woman and a Greek man and woman were buried alive in the Cattle Market, in a place walled in with stone, which even before this time had been defiled with human victims, a sacrifice wholly alien to the Roman spirit [*minime Romano sacro*].
> (*Rom. Hist.* 22.57.6)

R. Drews notes that "whether there was a repetition of popular pressure for human sacrifices when the Cimbri and Teutones imperiled Italy we do not know, but the senatorial ban on human sacrifice in 97 B.C. suggests that calls for such sacrifice were still to be heard" (Drews, 298).

Nevertheless, as Livy's comment demonstrates, these three instances of human sacrifice were considered exceptional in their own day. While the

Romans condoned the killing of enemies and rebels during war, and enjoyed spectacles of gladiators killing each other, they condemned ritual human sacrifices as the barbaric acts of non-Romans. Cicero wrote: "How many peoples, such as the Taurians on the shores of the Euxine, the Egyptian king Busiris, the Gauls, and the Carthaginians, have believed human sacrifice both pious and most pleasing to the immortal gods!" (*Rep.* 3.15). Pliny the Elder relates that the Senate passed a law in 97 BC forbidding human sacrifice. He declares: "It is beyond calculation how great is the debt owed to the Romans, who swept away the monstrous rites, in which to kill a man was the highest religious duty and for him to be eaten a passport to health" (*Nat.* 30.13).

The Romans associated human sacrifice with their enemies the Carthaginians in particular. Carthage was a colony established by Phoenicians from Tyre on the coast of North Africa (in present-day Tunisia) around 800 BC. The Romans were to fight three wars (known as the Punic Wars) against Carthage, finally destroying the city in 146 BC. Greek and Roman authors (Pseudo-Plato, Theophrastus, Cleitarchos, Ennius, Quintus Curtius, Dionysius of Halicarnassus, Porphyry) and Christian authors (Justin Martyr, Tertullian, Lactantius, Eusebius) describe the Carthaginians' sacrifice of infants, which lasted throughout the city's history.

The Greek historian Diodorus Siculus (1st c. BC) records that when Agathocles, the tyrant of Syracuse on Sicily, besieged Carthage in 310 BC, the Carthaginian leaders were alarmed that some had not sacrificed their own children but had secretly bought the children of others to sacrifice to ensure their victory. Diodorus offers a long and detailed account of what happened next:

> When they had given thought to these things and saw their enemy encamped before their walls, they were filled with superstitious dread, for they believed that they had neglected the honours of the gods that had been established by their fathers. In their zeal to make amends for their omission, they selected two hundred of the noblest children and sacrificed them publicly; and others who were under suspicion sacrificed themselves voluntarily, in number not less than three hundred. There was in their city a bronze image of Cronus, extending its hands, palms up and sloping toward the ground, so that each of the children when placed thereon rolled down and fell into a sort of gaping pit filled with fire. (*Bib. hist.* 20.14.5–6)

Plutarch adds these further details of the rite:

> No, but with full knowledge and understanding they themselves offered up their own children, and those who had no children would buy little ones from poor people and cut their throats as if they were so many lambs or young birds; meanwhile the mother stood by without a tear or moan; but should she utter a single moan or let fall a single tear, she had to forfeit the money and

her child was sacrificed nevertheless; and the whole area before the statue was filled with a loud noise of flutes and drums so that the cries of wailing should not reach the ears of the people. (*Superst.* 13.171c–d)

The Roman poet Silius Italicus (*Punica* 4.765–822) reports that the rite of sacrificing children at Carthage was an annual event, and that the children were selected by lot. It is uncertain whether the children were alive or dead at the time their bodies were cremated.

These literary accounts of infant sacrifice at Carthage do not appear to be entirely exaggerated. Burial grounds for infant sacrifices at Carthage, which are known today as the Tophet (a name derived from such OT passages as 2 Kgs 23:10 and Jer 7:31–32), were used for centuries after the founding of the Phoenician colony (ca. 800 BC) until its destruction by the Romans in 146 BC. The incinerated remains of children and animals were contained in urns, normally one infant in an urn. Each urn was covered with a lid.

The Carthaginian Tophet covered sixty-eight thousand square feet (6,000 sq. m.). Three major levels have been identified, which have been designated Tanit I (750/725 to 600 BC), Tanit II (600 to the 3rd c. BC), and Tanit III (3rd c. to 146 BC). Excavations and analysis of the Tophet by L. E. Stager and S. R. Wolff revealed that, rather than declining, the practice of human sacrifice was at its height during the peak of Carthage's prosperity (400–200 BC), when an estimated twenty thousand urns were buried—an average of one hundred per year.

Over seven thousand stelae were erected over the urns. The earlier examples (from ca. 800 to 400 BC) are uninscribed. The later stelae are decorated and incised with inscriptions that list the dedicant, his genealogy, and the god(s) to whom the child was dedicated. The chief god to whom sacrifices were made was Baal-Hammon, also known as Kronos or Saturn. The chief Punic goddess was Tanit (who is identified with Phoenician Astarte). Some inscriptions state specifically that the sacrifice was made in the fulfillment of a vow. One stela from the fourth century BC depicts a priest cradling an infant as he prepares to sacrifice him.

Punic inscriptions from Carthage and from other tophets in Punic sites refer to (1) *mlk ʾmr* (perhaps vocalized *mulk ʾimmor*), the sacrifice of a lamb; (2) *mlk ʾdm* (perhaps *mulk ʾadam*), the sacrifice of a child; and (3) *mlk bʿl* (perhaps *mulk baʿl*), the sacrifice of an upper-class child.

Based on an analysis of 348 burial urns containing the remains of children who died prenatally or up to the ages of five or six months, some investigators (Schwartz et al.) concluded that these children had not been sacrificed. Other scholars (Stager, Smith, Avishai) note that the majority of these children died at from four to six weeks old, and conclude that this indicates not simply an infant cemetery but reflects infant sacrifice.

Other Punic sites around the Mediterranean have similar, if less extensive, evidence of tophets and human sacrifice. At Motya in western Sicily, cremated remains of infants and animals were found below stelae. In 1971 a stone relief dating to 500–490 BC was found at Pozo Moro in southeastern Spain. This relief depicts a two-headed monster with a body of a human holding a bowl with the head of a small child peering over its rim; another figure holds a curved blade, evidently a grim visual image of child sacrifice. Though infant sacrifice at Carthage ended with the city's destruction in 146 BC, the custom continued in North Africa as late as AD 200, as we learn from Tertullian, the Christian apologist from Carthage.

As the Romans expanded their empire throughout Europe, they found other peoples who practiced human sacrifice. One such people were the Cimbri, who dwelled in northern Germany and southern Denmark. Strabo reports that certain women from this group, wearing white tunics and girdles of bronze, would lead prisoners up to a bronze vessel:

> They had a raised platform which the priestess would mount, and then, bending over the kettle, would cut the throat of each prisoner after he had been lifted up; and from the blood that poured forth into the vessel some of the priestesses would draw a prophecy, while still others would split open the body and from an inspection of the entrails would utter a prophecy of victory for their own people. (*Geogr.* 7.2.3)

Archaeological and artistic evidence confirms the practice of human sacrifice in northern Europe. In 1950 the well-preserved body of the Tollund man was found in a peat bog in the Jutland Peninsula of Denmark. Marks on his neck indicate that he had been garroted. Also found in a Danish peat bog was the richly decorated, silver Gundestrup cauldron; in one scene a large figure is immersing a smaller human victim in a vat.

In modern-day France the Romans conquered the Gauls, a Celtic people who practiced human sacrifice. From his encounter with this people, Julius Caesar reported:

> The whole nation of the Gauls is greatly devoted to ritual observances, and for that reason those who are smitten with the more grievous maladies and who are engaged in the perils of battle either sacrifice human victims or vow so to do, employing the Druids as ministers for such sacrifices. . . . They believe that the execution of those who have been caught in the act of theft or robbery or some crime is more pleasing to the immortal gods; but when the supply of such fails they resort to the execution even of the innocent. (*Bell. gall.* 6.16)

Strabo commented: "They used to strike a human being, whom they had devoted to death, in the back with a sabre, and then divine from his death-struggle" (*Geogr.* 4.4.5). In a similar vein, Diodorus Siculus reports:

"They devote to death a human being and plunge a dagger into him in the region above the diaphragm, and when the stricken victim has fallen they read the future from the manner of his fall and from the twitching of his limbs, as well as from the gushing of the blood" (*Bib. hist.* 5.31.3).

In his defense of M. Fonteius, the governor of Cisalpine Gaul in northern Italy, the Roman orator Cicero defamed his Gallic accusers as follows: "For who does not know that to this very day they retain the monstrous and barbarous custom of sacrificing men? What then, think you, is the honour, what the piety, of those who even think that the immortal gods can best be appeased by human crime and bloodshed?" (*Font.* 31).

Archaeological evidence of human sacrifice has also been preserved in the peat bogs of Britain, e.g., at Lindow Moss, Cheshire, where the body of a young man who had been garroted and buried naked was discovered. At Verulamium (St. Alban's), north of London, the remains of a British chieftain who was cremated in about AD 50 have been discovered, along with the bodies of three women who were probably sacrificed to attend him in the next world.

Julius Caesar invaded Britain twice, but it was not until the emperor Claudius's (r. AD 41–54) campaign that the Romans were able to make the island a province. When the British Celts under the leadership of the Druids rebelled, they were defeated in AD 60 by Suetonius Paulinus in a famous battle at the island of Mona (Anglesey) off the north coast of Wales. According to Tacitus, Paulinus destroyed "the groves consecrated to their savage cults: for they considered it a pious duty to slake the altars with captive blood and to consult their deities by means of human entrails" (*Ann.* 14.30).

According to Suetonius, Claudius "utterly abolished the cruel and inhuman religion of the Druids among the Gauls, which under Augustus had merely been prohibited to Roman citizens" (*Claud.* 25.5). Later, Hadrian (AD 117–138) abolished human sacrifice throughout the Roman Empire.

The Neo-Platonic philosopher Porphyry (3rd c. AD), who was a critic of both Christianity and traditional paganism, presented in his *De abstinentia* (2.56) a long list of sixteen examples of human sacrifice, of which only the Carthaginian practice has been verified by archaeological evidence.

E. THE JEWISH WORLD

Because the Jews' religious practices set them apart from their Greek and Roman neighbors, they were sometimes accused of outrageous practices such as human sacrifice. The Jewish philosopher Philo of Alexandria quotes one such accusation from his contemporary Apion (ca. 20 BC–AD 45). Apion had asserted that when Antiochus IV captured the temple in Jerusalem, he found a Greek prisoner who related that the Jews "would kidnap a Greek foreigner, fatten him up for a year, and then convey him to a wood, where they slew him, sacrificed his body with their customary ritual, partook of his flesh, and, while immolating the Greek, swore an oath of hostility to the Greeks" (*Ag. Ap.* 2.95–96). The Suda cites a first-century AD historian, Damocritus, who also related that the Jews worshipped an ass's head and sacrificed a stranger every seventh year, cutting up his flesh into small pieces.

Jewish sources from the time expand on the OT prohibition against human sacrifice. The apocryphal Wisdom of Solomon (1st c. BC) explicitly describes God's anger at the Canaanites' human sacrifices as justification for the Hebrews' conquest of the land of Israel:

> Those who dwelt of old in thy holy land thou didst hate for their detestable practices, their works of sorcery and unholy rites, their merciless slaughter of children, and their sacrificial feasting on human flesh and blood. These initiates from the midst of a heathen cult, these parents who murder helpless lives, thou didst will to destroy by the hands of our fathers, that the land most precious of all to thee might receive a worthy colony of the servants of God.
> (Wis 12:3–7)

After the OT period, the sacrifice of Isaac developed into a central motif of Jewish tradition. Over centuries, Jewish teachers reflected and elaborated on the Akedah, the "Binding" of Isaac (Gen 22:9), as an atoning act, stressing not so much Abraham's obedience but Isaac's willingness as a human sacrifice.

Fourth Maccabees (dated to the latter part of the 1st c. AD) describes the courage of the Jews who became martyrs at the hands of Antiochus IV. One of seven sons cried out to his brothers: "Remember whence you came, and the father by whose hand Isaac would have submitted to being slain for the sake of religion" (4 Macc 13:12). The mother of these sons exhorted them, "For his sake also our father Abraham was zealous to sacrifice [*sphagiasai*] his son Isaac, the ancestor of our nation; and when Isaac saw his father's hand wielding a sword and descending upon him, he did not cower" (4 Macc 16:20).

The OT pseudepigraphical work *Jubilees*, copies of which were found at Qumran, precisely dates Isaac's birth in the 1988th year after creation and his binding in the year 2003, when he was fifteen. Like the case of Job in the book of Job, in *Jubilees* the testing of Abraham is not ascribed directly to God but rather to Mastema, that is, Satan:

> And Prince Mastema came and said before God: 'Behold, Abraham loves Isaac, his son. And he is more pleased with him than everything. Tell him to

offer him (as) a burnt offering upon the altar. And you will see whether he will do this thing. And you will know whether he is faithful in everything in which you test him. (*Jub.* 17:16)

Implicit in the time frame established in *Jub.* 17:15, the sacrifice was to take place, significantly, at the very time of the Passover meal.

The fragmentary *Paraphrase of Genesis* from Qumran, which some have called "Pseudo-Jubilees," also names Mastemah as the instigator of the Akedah: "Now the Prince of Malevolence (Mastemah) approached [G]od and displayed his anger against Abraham on account of Isaac" (4Q225 2 I, 9). The text adds the detail that as Isaac was about to be sacrificed, the angels of Mastemah were rejoicing, but the holy angels were weeping (4Q225 2 II, 5–7).

Philo defends Abraham's willingness to offer up Isaac in his treatise on the patriarch's life (*De Abrahamo*). In the course of describing other acts of human sacrifice, Philo comments in passing on the Indian practice of suttee: "And the womenfolk when the husbands die before them have been known to hasten rejoicing to share their pyre, and allow themselves to be burned alive with the corpses of the men" (*Abr.* 182). He interprets Isaac's name as equivalent to the Greek word *geloia*, "laughter," suggesting that the wise man should be willing, as was Abraham, to surrender his "laughter" to God.

Pseudo-Philo (late 1st c. AD) relates that after God had given Abraham a son, "all the angels were jealous of him, and the worshiping hosts envied him" (*Liber antiquitatum biblicarum* 32.1). He also notes that Abraham bound the feet of Isaac, a detail not found in the Masoretic Text but added by the Septuagint. This version of the story also adds that after the Lord prevented Abraham from slaying his son, he told him: "For now I have appeared so as to reveal you to those who do not know you and have shut the mouths of those who are always speaking evil against you" (*Liber antiquitatum biblicarum* 32.4).

In recounting the story of Gen 22, the Jewish historian Josephus indicates that Isaac was twenty-five years old at the time. He records the tradition that Abraham built the altar on "that mount whereon king David afterwards erected the temple" (*Ant.* 1.226–227). Josephus explains that after God observed Abraham's willingness to sacrifice his son, "it was, He said, from no craving for human blood that He had given command for the slaughter of his son, nor had He made him a father only to rob him in such fashion of his offspring; no, He wished but to test his soul and see whether even such orders would find him obedient" (*Ant.* 1.233).

The earliest of the Targumim (Aramaic paraphrases of the OT), *Targum Neofiti* (possibly 2nd c. AD), relates that Isaac was thirty-seven years of age at the time of the Akedah. It offers a vivid elaboration of Isaac's willingness to be sacrificed:

Abraham stretched out his hand and took the knife to kill Isaac his son. Isaac answered and said to Abraham his father: Bind my hands properly that I may not struggle in the time of my pain and disturb you and render your offering unfit and be cast into the pit of destruction in the world to come. The eyes of Abraham were turned to the eyes of Isaac, but the eyes of Isaac were turned to the angels of heaven. . . . In that hour the angels of heaven went out and said to each other: Let us go and see the only two just men in the world. The one slays, and the other is being slain. The slayer does not hesitate, and the one being slain stretches out his neck.

(*Tg. Neof.* on Gen 22:10; cited in Vermes 1961, 194–95)

Elsewhere *Targum Neofiti* (on Lev 22:27) explicitly presents the binding of Isaac as the prototype of the Passover lamb.

In a sermonic midrash in *Genesis Rabbah* (5th c. AD), Rabbi Isaac says:

When Abraham wished to sacrifice his son Isaac, he said to him: "Father, I am a young man and am afraid that my body may tremble through fear of the knife and I will grieve thee, whereby the slaughter may be rendered unfit and this will not count as a real sacrifice; therefore bind me very firmly." Forthwith, he bound Isaac: can one bind a man thirty-seven years old (another version: twenty-six years old) without his consent? (*Gen. Rab.* 56.8)

The Akedah is referred to briefly in the Mishnah (*m. Taʿan.* 2:4) and the Babylonian Talmud (*b. Šabb.* 89b). It is also featured in the art of the Beth Alpha and Sepphoris synagogues.

F. THE CHRISTIAN WORLD

The Christian apologists of the second and third centuries AD defended their faith against charges of human sacrifice and cannibalism, though we lack any evidence of such accusations in the pagan texts that have been preserved. Such accusations were probably made publicly in orations such as the lost speech "Against Christians" by Fronto, the tutor of Marcus Aurelius (cf. Minucius Felix, *Oct.* 31.2). Pliny, the governor of Bithynia in northwestern Anatolia, investigated such charges and even tortured women *ministrae* (deaconesses) to ascertain the truth of such rumors. He reported to the emperor Trajan that the Christians met regularly before dawn on a fixed day to chant verses to Christ as to a god (*quasi deo*), and that "after this ceremony it had been their custom to disperse and reassemble later to take food of an ordinary, harmless kind" (*Ep. Tra.* 10.96.7), not to perform human sacrifices or engage in cannibalism.

In their own responses to these accusations, the Christians contrasted their behavior with that depicted in earlier Greek and Roman accounts of human sacrifices to their gods. To Christian apologists, ancient and even mythological accounts of such sacrifices symbolized the cruelty of the Greek and Roman deities. Many of the apologists also accused pagan worshippers of carrying out such sacrifices in their own day.

The earliest Christian apologist, Justin Martyr, accused the Romans and other pagans of human sacrifice, and denied that Christians committed such offenses. If Christians did sacrifice humans victims, he asked,

> why did we not even publicly profess that these were the things which we esteemed good, and prove that these are the divine philosophy, saying that the mysteries of Saturn are performed when we slay a man, and that when we drink our fill of blood, as it is said we do, we are doing what you do before that idol you honour, and on which you sprinkle the blood not only of irrational animals, but also of men, making a libation of the blood of the slain by the hand of the most illustrious and noble man among you? (2 *Apol.* 12)

Justin's disciple Tatian recounted how his disgust at pagan religion, including human sacrifice, influenced him to consider the claims of Christianity:

> Wherefore, having seen these things, and moreover also having been admitted to the mysteries, and having everywhere examined the religious rites performed by the effeminate and the pathic, and having found among the Romans their Latiarian Jupiter delighting in human gore and the blood of slaughtered men, and Artemis not far from the great city sanctioning acts of the same kind, and one demon here and another there instigating to the perpetration of evil—retiring by myself, I sought how I might be able to discover the truth. (Tatian, *Or.* 29.1)

In his *Exhortation to the Greeks*, Clement of Alexandria (d. AD 215) lists many examples of human sacrifices to Greek and Roman gods and concludes that these gods are in fact demons:

> For a murder does not become a sacrifice by being committed in a particular spot. You are not to call it a sacred sacrifice, if one slays a man either at the altar or on the highway to Artemis or Zeus, any more than if he slew him for anger or covetousness . . . but a sacrifice of this kind is murder and human butchery. (*Protr.* 3)

The debate between Christians and pagans on the subject of human sacrifice is captured in the dialogue *Octavius* by the apologist Minucius Felix (ca. AD 160–250). In this work, the pagan character Caecilius recounts the apparently common belief that Christians sacrificed and feasted on infants in a ritual meal. He alleges:

Now the story about the initiation of young novices is as much to be detested
as it is well known. An infant covered over with meal, that it may deceive the
unwary, is placed before him who is to be stained with their rites: this infant is
slain by the young pupil, who has been urged on as if to harmless blows on the
surface of the meal, with dark and secret wounds. Thirstily—O horror!—they
lick up its blood; eagerly they divide its limbs. (*Oct.* 9.5)

Minucius has the Christian character Octavius respond:

No one can believe this, except one who can dare to do it. . . . For Saturn did
not expose his children, but devoured them. With reason were infants sacrificed to him by parents in some parts of Africa, caresses and kisses repressing
their crying, that a weeping victim might not be sacrificed. Moreover, among
the Tauri of Pontus, . . . it was a sacred rite to immolate their guests, and for
the Galli to slaughter to Mercury human, or rather inhuman, sacrifices. The
Roman sacrificers buried living a Greek man and a Greek woman, a Gallic
man and a Gallic woman; and to this day, Jupiter Latiaris is worshipped by
them with murder. . . . To us [Christians] it is not lawful either to see or to
hear of homicide; and so much do we shrink from human blood, that we do
not use the blood even of eatable animals in our food. (*Oct.* 30)

In his rhetorically brilliant *Apology,* Tertullian of Carthage promises
not only to refute the charges of human sacrifice made against Christians
but to demonstrate that their accusers themselves are guilty of this very
crime. First, he relates the charge: "Monsters of wickedness, we are accused
of observing a holy rite in which we kill a little child and then eat it" (*Apol.*
7.1). Then he declares:

That I may refute more thoroughly these charges, I will show that in part openly,
in part secretly, practices prevail among you which have led you perhaps to
credit similar things about us. Children were openly sacrificed in Africa to
Saturn as lately as the proconsulship of Tiberius, who exposed to public gaze
the priests suspended on the sacred trees overshadowing their temple—so
many crosses on which the punishment which justice craved overtook their
crimes, as the soldiers of our country still can testify who did that very work
for that proconsul. And even now that sacred crime still continues to be done
in secret. (*Apol.* 9.1–3)

Lactantius, who also came from North Africa, was a teacher of rhetoric
who converted to Christianity. He comments on human sacrifice as follows:

What benefit do they who offer such sacrifices implore from the gods? Or
what are such deities able to bestow on the men by whose punishments they
are propitiated? But this is not so much a matter of surprise with respect
to barbarians, whose religion agrees with their character. But are not our

countrymen, who have always claimed for themselves the glory of gentleness and civilization, found to be more inhuman by these sacrilegious rites? For these ought rather to be esteemed impious, who, though they are embellished with the pursuits of liberal training, turn aside from such refinement, than those who, being ignorant and inexperienced, glide into evil practices from their ignorance of those which are good. And yet it is plain that this rite of immolating human victims is ancient, since Saturn was honoured in Latium with the same kind of sacrifice; not indeed that a man was slain at the altar, but that he was thrown from the Milvian bridge into the Tiber. (*Inst.* 1.21)

During the persecution of the Christians in Lugdunum (Lyon) in France in AD 177, a woman named Biblis was tested:

But she recovered under torture, and, as it were, woke up out of deep sleep, being reminded through this transitory punishment of the eternal torments in hell, and contradicted the blasphemers, saying, "How would such men eat children, when they are not allowed to eat the blood even of irrational animals?" And after this she confessed herself a Christian and was added to the ranks of the martyrs. (Eus. *Hist. eccl.* 5.1.26)

BIBLIOGRAPHY: W. Y. Adams, *Nubia: Corridor to Africa* (1977); M. Aldhouse-Green, *Caesar's Druids: Story of an Ancient Priesthood* (2010); A. Baadsgaard, J. Monge, and R. Zettler, "Bludgeoned, Burned and Beautified: Reevaluating Mortuary Practices in the Royal Cemetery of Ur," in *Sacred Killing: The Archaeology of Sacrifice in the Ancient Near East,* ed. A. Porter and G. Schwartz (2012), 125–58; J. Bartlett, *Jericho* (1982); M. Bietak, *Avaris, the Capital of the Hyksos: Recent Excavations at Tell el-Dabʿa* (1996); L. Bodoff, "The Tragedy of Jephthah," *JBQ* 28 (2000), 251–55; S. Brown, *Late Carthaginian Child Sacrifice and Sacrificial Monuments in Their Mediterranean Context* (1991); R. B. Chisholm, Jr., "The Ethical Challenge of Jephthah's Fulfilled Vow," *BSac* 167 (2010), 404–22; R. J. Daly, "The Soteriological Significance of the Sacrifice of Isaac," *CBQ* 39 (1977), 45–75; P. R. Davies and B. D. Chilton, "The Aqedah: A Revised Tradition History," *CBQ* 40 (1978), 514–46; T. S. Davis, "The Condemnation of Jephthah," *TynBul* 64 (2013), 1–16; J. Day, *Molech: A God of Human Sacrifice in the Old Testament* (1989); P. Derchain, "Les plus anciens témoignages de sacrifices d'enfants chez les Sémites occidentaux," *VT* 20 (1970), 351–55; R. de Vaux, *Studies in Old Testament Sacrifice* (1964); R. Drews, "Pontiffs, Prodigies, and the Disappearance of the 'Annales Maximi,'" *CP* 83.4 (1988), 289–99; D. Edelman, "Biblical Molek Reassessed," *JAOS* 107 (1987), 727–31; O. Eissfeldt, *Molk als Opferbegriff im Punischen und Hebräischen, und das Ende des Gottes Moloch* (1935); W. B. Emery, *Archaic Egypt* (1961); S. Farron, "Aeneas' Human Sacrifice," *Acta Classica* 28 (1985), 21–33; K. Finsterbusch, A. Lange, and K. F. D. Römheld, ed., *Human Sacrifice in Jewish and Christian Tradition* (2007); E. H. Gifford, trans., *Eusebius: Preparation for the Gospel* (2 vols., 1981); M. Grant, *Gladiators* (1967); A. R. W. Green, *The Role of Human Sacrifice in the Ancient Near East* (1975); J. G. Griffiths, "Human Sacrifices in Egypt: The Classical Evidence," *Annales du Service des Antiquités de l'Égypte* 48 (1948), 409–23; G. C. Heider, "Molech," *ABD* IV.895–98; J. B. Hennessy, "Thirteenth Century B.C. Temple of Human Sacrifice at Amman," in *Phoenicia and Its Neighbours*, ed. E. Gubel and E. Lipiński (1985), 85–104; M. Hoffman, *Egypt Before the Pharaohs: The Prehistoric Foundations of Egyptian Civilization* (1979); D. D. Hughes, *Human Sacrifice in Ancient Greece* (1991); I. Kalimi, " 'Go, I Beg You, Take Your Beloved Son and Slay Him!': The Binding of Isaac in Rabbinic Literature and Thought," *The Review of Rabbinic Judaism* 13 (2010), 1–29; J. D. Levenson, *The Death and Resurrection of the Beloved Son: The Transformation of Child Sacrifice in Judaism and Christianity* (1993); H. Lloyd-Jones, "Artemis and Iphigeneia," *JHS* 103 (1983), 87–102; A. Logan, "Rehabilitating Jephthah," *JBL* 128 (2009), 665–85; B. Margalit, "Why King Mesha of Moab Sacrificed His Oldest Son," *BAR* 12.6 (1986), 62–63, 76; P. G. Mosca, *Child Sacrifice in Canaanite Israelite Religion: A Study in Mulk and Molech* (1975); A. Nagy, "La forme originale de l'accusation d'anthropophagie contre les chrétiens, son dévelopement et les changements de sa représentation au IIe siècle," *REAug* 47 (2001), 223–49; E. Noort and E. Tigchelaar, ed., *The Sacrifice of Isaac: The Aqedah (Genesis 22) and Its Interpretations* (2002); J. Reade, "The Royal Tombs of Ur," in *Art of the First Cities*, ed. J. Aruz and R. Wallenfels (2003), 93–132; J. B. Rives, "Human Sacrifice among Pagans and Christians," *JRS* 85 (1995), 65–85; J. B. Rives, "Tertullian on Child Sacrifice," *Museum Helveticum* 51 (1994), 54–63; T. C. Römer, "Why Would the Deuteronomists Tell about the Sacrifice of Jephthah's Daughter?" *JSOT* 77 (1998), 27–38; J. S. Rundin, "Pozo Moro, Child Sacrifice, and the Greek Legendary Tradition," *JBL* 123 (2004), 425–47; Y. Sakellarakis and E. Sapouna-Sakellaraki, "Drama of Death in a Minoan Temple," *National Geographic* 159.2 (1981), 204–22; H. J. Schoeps, *Paul: The Theology of the Apostle in the Light of Jewish Religious History*, trans. H. Knight (1961), 141–49; J. H. Schwartz, F. Houghton, R. Macchiarelli, and L. Bondioli, "Skeletal Remains from Punic Carthage Do Not Support Systematic Sacrifice of Infants," *PLOS ONE* (Feb. 17, 2010); A. F. Segal, "The Sacrifice of Isaac in Early Judaism and Christianity," in *The Other Judaisms of Late Antiquity* (1987), 109–30; A. J. Spalinger, "A Canaanite Ritual Found in Egyptian Reliefs," *Journal of the Society for the Study of Egyptian Antiquities* 8 (1978), 47–60; W. D. Spencer, "Christ's Sacrifice as Apologetic: An Application of Heb 10:1–18," *JETS* 40 (1997), 189–97; L. E. Stager and S. R. Wolff, "Child Sacrifice at Carthage—Religious Rite or Population Control?"

BAR 10.1 (1984), 30–51; J. Swetnam, *Jesus and Isaac: A Study of the Epistle to the Hebrews in the Light of the Aqedah* (1981); M. Todd, *The Northern Barbarians: 100 BC–AD 300* (rev. ed., 1987); B. L. Twyman, "*Metus Gallicus*: The Celts and Roman Human Sacrifice," *AHB* 11 (1997), 1–11; J. C. VanderKam, "The *Aqedah*, *Jubilees*, and PseudoJubilees," in *The Quest for Context and Meaning*, ed. C. A. Evans and S. Talmon (1997), 241–61; J. Van Dijk, "Retainer Sacrifice in Egypt and in Nubia," in *The Strange World of Human Sacrifice*, ed. J. N. Bremmer (2007), 135–55; G. Vermes, "Redemption and Genesis XXII: The Binding of Isaac and the Sacrifice of Jesus," in *Scripture and Tradition in Judaism: Haggadic Studies* (1961), 193–227; G. Vermes, "New Light on the Sacrifice of Isaac from 4Q225," *JJS* 47 (1996), 140–46; J.-P. Vernant et al., ed., *Le sacrifice dans l'Antiquité* (1981); M. Weinfeld, "The Worship of Molech and of the Queen of Heaven and Its Background," *UF* 4 (1972), 133–54; L. Woolley, *Ur of the Chaldees: A Record of Seven Years of Excavation* (1965); E. Yamauchi, *Africa and the Bible* (2004); E. Yamauchi, "The Scythians—Who Were They? And Why Did Paul Include Them in Colossians 3:11?" *Priscilla Papers* 21.4 (2007), 13–18.

EMY

See also INFANTICIDE & EXPOSURE.

SELECT BIBLIOGRAPHY

A. THE BIBLICAL WORLD

Barton, J., ed. *The Biblical World.* 2 vols. London: Routledge, 2002.

Blaiklock, E. M. and R. K. Harrison, ed. *The New International Dictionary of Biblical Archaeology.* Grand Rapids: Zondervan, 1983.

Bromiley, G. W., ed. *The International Standard Bible Encyclopedia.* 4 vols. Rev. ed. Grand Rapids: Eerdmans, 1979–1988.

Buttrick, G. A., ed. *The Interpreter's Dictionary of the Bible.* 4 vols. New York: Abingdon Press, 1962.

Crim, K., ed. *The Interpreter's Dictionary of the Bible: Supplementary Volume.* Nashville: Abingdon Press, 1976.

Douglas, J. D. and N. Hillyer, ed. *The Illustrated Bible Dictionary.* 3 vols. Leicester: Inter-Varsity Press, 1980.

Freedman, D. N., ed. *Anchor Bible Dictionary.* 6 vols. New York: Doubleday, 1992.

Freedman, D. N., ed. *Eerdmans Dictionary of the Bible.* Grand Rapids: Eerdmans, 2000.

Gower, R. *The New Manners and Customs of Bible Times.* Chicago: Moody Press, 1987.

Master, D. M., ed. *The Oxford Encyclopedia of the Bible and Archaeology.* 2 vols. Oxford: Oxford University Press, 2013.

Matthews, V. H. *Manners and Customs in the Bible.* Peabody, MA: Hendrickson, 1988.

Pfeiffer, C. F., ed. *The Biblical World: A Dictionary of Biblical Archaeology.* Grand Rapids: Baker Book House, 1966.

Ryken, L., J. C. Wilhoit, and T. Longman III, ed. *Dictionary of Biblical Imagery.* Downers Grove: InterVarsity Press, 1998.

Thompson, J. A. *Handbook of Life in Bible Times.* Leicester: Inter-Varsity Press, 1986.

Toorn, K. van der, B. Becking, and P. van der Horst, ed. *Dictionary of Deities and Demons in the Bible*. 2nd ed. Leiden: Brill; Grand Rapids: Eerdmans, 1999.

The Old Testament

Arnold, B. T. and H. G. M. Williamson, ed. *Dictionary of the Old Testament: Historical Books*. Downers Grove: InterVarsity Press, 2005.

Avi-Yonah, M., ed. *Encyclopedia of Archaeological Excavations in the Holy Land*. 4 vols. London: Oxford University Press, 1975–1978.

Borowski, O. *Daily Life in Biblical Times*. Atlanta: Society of Biblical Literature, 2003.

Borowski, O. *Every Living Thing: Daily Use of Animals in Ancient Israel*. Walnut Creek, CA: Altamira Press, 1998.

Botterweck, G. J. and H. Ringgren, ed. *Theological Dictionary of the Old Testament*. 15 vols. Grand Rapids: Eerdmans, 1974–2008.

De Vaux, R. *Ancient Israel: Its Life and Institutions*. Trans. John McHugh. New York: McGraw-Hill Book Co., 1961.

Dever, W. G. *The Lives of Ordinary People in Ancient Israel*. Grand Rapids: Eerdmans, 2012.

Ebeling, J. R. *Women's Lives in Biblical Times*. London: T & T Clark, 2010.

Harris, R. L., G. L. Archer, and B. K. Waltke, ed. *Theological Wordbook of the Old Testament*. 2 vols. Chicago: Moody Press, 1980.

Hoerth, A. J., G. L. Mattingly, and E. M. Yamauchi, ed. *Peoples of the Old Testament World*. Grand Rapids: Baker Books, 1994.

Isserlin, B. S. J. *The Israelites*. London: Thames and Hudson, 1998.

King, P. J. and L. E. Stager. *Life in Biblical Israel*. Louisville: Westminster John Knox Press, 2001.

Matthews, V. H. and D. C. Benjamin. *Social World of Ancient Israel: 1250–587 BCE*. Peabody: Hendrickson, 1993.

Stern, E., ed. *The New Encyclopedia of Archaeological Excavations in the Holy Land V: Supplementary Volume*. Jerusalem: Israel Exploration Society; Washington, DC: Biblical Archaeological Society, 2008.

VanGemeren, W. A., ed. *New International Dictionary of Old Testament Theology & Exegesis*. 5 vols. Grand Rapids: Zondervan, 1997.

Wiseman, D. J., ed. *Peoples of Old Testament Times*. Oxford: Clarendon Press, 1973.

The New Testament

Bell, A. A. *Exploring the New Testament World*. Nashville: Thomas Nelson, 1998.

Bouquet, A. C. *Everyday Life in New Testament Times.* New York: Charles Scribner's Sons, 1954.

Charlesworth, J. H., ed. *Jesus and Archaeology.* Grand Rapids: Eerdmans, 2006.

Daniel-Rops, H. *Daily Life in Palestine at the Time of Christ.* London: Phoenix Press, 1962.

Deissmann, A. *Light from the Ancient East: The New Testament Illustrated by Recently Discovered Texts of the Graeco-Roman World.* Grand Rapids: Baker Book House, 1965 repr.

Evans, C. and S. E. Porter, ed. *Dictionary of New Testament Background.* Downers Grove: InterVarsity Press, 2000.

Green, J. B. and L. M. McDonald, ed. *The World of the New Testament: Cultural, Social, and Historical Contexts.* Grand Rapids: Baker Academic, 2013.

Hall, J. F. and J. W. Welch, ed. *Masada and the World of the New Testament.* Provo: Brigham Young University Press, 1997.

Hawthorne, G. F., R. P. Martin, and D. G. Reid, ed. *Dictionary of Paul and His Letters.* Downers Grove: InterVarsity Press, 1993.

Jeffers, J. S. *Greco-Roman World of the New Testament Era.* Downers Grove: InterVarsity Press, 1999.

Kittel, G., ed. *Theological Dictionary of the New Testament.* 10 vols. Grand Rapids: Eerdmans, 1964.

Rousseau, J. J. and R. Arav. *Jesus & His World: An Archaeological and Cultural Dictionary.* Minneapolis: Fortress Press, 1995.

Tenney, M. C. *New Testament Times.* Grand Rapids: Eerdmans, 1965.

Yamauchi, E. M. *Harper's World of the New Testament.* San Francisco: Harper & Row, 1981.

B. THE NEAR EASTERN WORLD

Averbeck, R. E., M. W. Chavalas, and D. B. Weisberg, ed. *Life and Culture in the Ancient Near East.* Bethesda: CDL Press, 2003.

Gates, C. *Ancient Cities: The Archaeology of Urban Life in the Ancient Near East and Egypt, Greece and Rome.* 2nd ed. London: Routledge, 2011.

Meyers, E. M., ed. *The Oxford Encyclopedia of Archaeology in the Near East.* 5 vols. New York: Oxford University Press, 1997.

Pritchard, J. B., ed. *The Ancient Near East in Pictures Relating to the Old Testament.* Princeton: Princeton University Press, 1954.

Pritchard, J. B., ed. *Ancient Near Eastern Texts Relating to the Old Testament.* 3rd ed. Princeton: Princeton University Press, 1969.

Pritchard, J. B., ed. *The Ancient Near East: Supplementary Texts and Pictures Relating to the Old Testament.* Princeton: Princeton University Press, 1969.

Sasson, J., ed. *Civilizations of the Ancient Near East.* 4 vols. New York: Charles Scribners, 1995; repr. 2 vols. Peabody: Hendrickson, 2000.

Mesopotamia

Bertman, S. *Handbook to Life in Ancient Mesopotamia.* New York: Facts On File, 2003.

Bienkowski, P. and A. Millard, ed. *Dictionary of the Ancient Near East.* Philadelphia: University of Pennsylvania Press, 2000.

Bottéro, J. *Everyday Life in Ancient Mesopotamia.* Baltimore: Johns Hopkins University Press, 2001.

Gelb, I. J. et al., ed. *The Assyrian Dictionary of the Oriental Institute of the University of Chicago.* 20 vols. Chicago: University of Chicago Press, 1956–2010.

Hallo, W. W. *Origins: The Ancient Near Eastern Background of Some Modern Western Institutions.* Leiden: Brill, 1996.

Leick, G., ed. *The Babylonian World.* New York: Routledge, 2007.

Nemet-Nejat, K. R. *Daily Life in Ancient Mesopotamia.* Westport: Greenwood Press, 1998.

Saggs, H. W. F. *Everyday Life in Babylonia & Assyria.* New York: Dorset Press, 1965.

Snell, D. C., ed. *A Companion to the Ancient Near East.* Oxford: Blackwell Pub., 2007.

Snell, D. C. *Life in the Ancient Near East.* New Haven: Yale University Press, 1997.

Egypt

Brier, B. and H. Hobbs. *Ancient Egypt: Everyday Life in the Land of the Nile.* New York: Sterling, 2009.

Bunson, M. *A Dictionary of Ancient Egypt.* New York: Oxford University Press, 1991.

Casson, L. *Everyday Life in Ancient Egypt.* Baltimore: Johns Hopkins University Press, 1975.

David, R. *Handbook to Life in Ancient Egypt.* Oxford: Oxford University Press, 1998.

Erman, A. *Life in Ancient Egypt.* New York: Dover Publications, 1971.

Freed, R. E., ed. *Egypt's Golden Age: The Art of Living in the New Kingdom, 1558–1085 B.C.* Boston: Museum of Fine Arts, 1982.

Lucas, A. and J. R. Harris. *Ancient Egyptian Materials and Industries.* Mineola: Dover Publications, 1999 repr.

Mertz, B. *Red Land, Black Land: Daily Life in Ancient Egypt.* New York: Harper, 1978.

Montet, P. *Everyday Life in Egypt in the Days of Ramesses the Great.* London: Edward Arnold, 1958.

Nicholson, P. T., and I. Shaw, ed. *Ancient Egyptian Materials and Technology.* Cambridge: Cambridge University Press, 2000.

Redford, D. B., ed. *The Oxford Encyclopedia of Ancient Egypt.* Oxford: Oxford University Press, 2001.

Silverman, D. P., ed. *Ancient Egypt.* London: Piatkus, 1997.

Szpakowska, K. *Daily Life in Ancient Egypt.* Oxford: Blackwell Publishing, 2008.

Wilkinson, T., ed. *The Egyptian World.* London: Routledge, 2007.

C. THE GRECO-ROMAN WORLD

Aldrete, G. S. and A. *The Long Shadow of Antiquity: What Have the Greeks and Romans Done for Us?* London: Continuum, 2012.

Avi-Yonah, M. and I. Shatzman, ed. *Illustrated Encyclopaedia of the Classical World.* New York: Harper & Row, 1975.

Cary, M. and T. J. Haarhoff, ed. *Life and Thought in the Greek and Roman World.* London: Methuen & Co., 1963 repr.

Connolly, P. and H. Dodge. *The Ancient City: Life in Classical Athens & Rome.* Oxford: Oxford University Press, 2001.

Gates, C. *Ancient Cities: The Archaeology of Urban Life in the Ancient Near East and Egypt, Greece and Rome.* 2nd ed. London: Routledge, 2011.

Grant, M. and R. Kitzinger, ed. *Civilizations of the Ancient Mediterranean.* 3 vols. New York: Charles Scribner's Sons, 1988.

Hornblower, S. and A. Spawforth, ed. *The Oxford Classical Dictionary.* Oxford: Oxford University Press, 1996.

Hornblower, S. and A. Spawforth, ed. *The Oxford Companion to Classical Civilization.* Oxford: Oxford University Press, 1998.

Humphrey, J. W., J. P. Oleson, and A. N. Sherwood, ed. *Greek and Roman Technology: A Sourcebook.* London: Routledge, 1998.

Lefkowitz, M. R., and M. B. Fant, ed. *Women's Life in Greece and Rome: A Source Book in Translation.* 3rd ed. Baltimore: Johns Hopkins University Press, 2005.

Greece

Adkins, L. and R. A. *Handbook to Life in Ancient Greece.* New York: Facts On File, 1994.

Devambez, P., R. Flacelière, P.-M. Schuhl, and R. Martin, ed. *The Praeger Encyclopedia of Ancient Greek Civilization*. New York: Frederick A. Praeger, 1966.

Flacelière, R. *Daily Life in Greece at the Time of Pericles*. New York: Macmillan Company, 1966.

Garland, R. *The Greek Way of Life*. Ithaca: Cornell University Press, 1993.

Hooper, F. *Greek Realities: Life and Thought in Ancient Greece*. New York: Charles Scribner's Sons, 1967.

Powell, A., ed. *The Greek World*. London: Routledge, 1995.

Sacks, D. *Encyclopedia of the Ancient Greek World*. New York: Facts On File, 1995.

Scarborough, J. *Facets of Hellenic Life*. Boston: Houghton Mifflin, 1976.

Wace, A. J. B., and F. H. Stubbings. ed. *A Companion to Homer*. London: MacMillan & Co., 1962.

Rome

Adkins, L. and R. A. *Handbook to Life in Ancient Rome*. New York: Oxford University Press, 1997.

Bunson, M., ed. *Encyclopedia of the Roman Empire*. New York: Facts On File, 1994.

Carcopino, J. *Daily Life in Ancient Rome*. New Haven: Yale University Press, 1960.

Casson, L. *Everyday Life in Ancient Rome*. Rev. ed. Baltimore: Johns Hopkins University, 1998.

Dobbins, J. J. and P. W. Foss, ed. *The World of Pompeii*. London: Routledge, 2008.

Dupont, F. *Daily Life in Ancient Rome*. Oxford: Blackwell, 1994.

Freeman, C. *The World of the Romans*. New York: Oxford University Press, 1993.

Gardner, J. F. and T. Wiedemann, ed. *The Roman Household: A Sourcebook*. London: Routledge, 1991.

Levick, B., ed. *The Government of the Roman Empire: A Sourcebook*. 2nd ed. London: Routledge, 2000.

Lewis, N. and M. Reinhold, ed. *Roman Civilization I: The Republic and the Augustan Age*. 3rd ed. New York: Columbia University Press, 1990.

Lewis, N. and M. Reinhold, ed. *Roman Civilization II: The Empire*. 3rd ed. New York: Columbia University Press, 1990.

Parkin, T. G. and A. J. Pomeroy. *Roman Social History: A Sourcebook*. London: Routledge, 2007.

Rodgers, N. *Life in Ancient Rome*. London: Southwater, 2008.

Shelton, J., ed. *As the Romans Did: A Sourcebook in Roman Social History.* 2nd ed. New York: Oxford University Press, 1998.

D. THE JEWISH WORLD

Ausubel, N. *The Book of Jewish Knowledge.* New York: Crown Publishers, 1964.

Collins, J. J. and D. C. Harlow, ed. *The Eerdmans Dictionary of Early Judaism.* Grand Rapids: Eerdmans, 2010.

Hezser, C., ed. *The Oxford Handbook of Jewish Daily Life in Roman Palestine.* Oxford: Oxford University Press, 2010.

Jacobs, J., ed. *The Jewish Encyclopedia.* 12 vols. New York: Funk & Wagnalls, 1901–2006.

Magness, J. *Stone and Dung, Oil and Spit: Jewish Daily Life in the Time of Jesus.* Grand Rapids: Eerdmans, 2011.

Neusner, J. and W. S. Green, ed. *Dictionary of Judaism in the Biblical Period.* Peabody: Hendrickson, 1999.

Schürer, E. *The History of the Jewish People in the Age of Jesus Christ (175 B.C.-A.D. 135),* rev. and ed. G. Vermes and F. Millar. 3 vols. Edinburgh: T. & T. Clark, 1973–1987.

Skolnik, F., ed. *Encyclopaedia Judaica.* 16 vols. New York: Macmillan, 1971–1972.

E. THE CHRISTIAN WORLD

Bowersock, W., P. Brown, and O. Grabar, ed. *Late Antiquity: A Guide to the Postclassical World.* Cambridge: Belknap Press, 1999.

Cohick, L. H. *Women in the World of the Earliest Christians.* Grand Rapids: Baker Academic, 2009.

Cross, F. L. and E. A. Livingstone, ed. *The Oxford Dictionary of the Christian Church.* Oxford: Oxford University Press, 1997.

Daniélou, J. *Primitive Christian Symbols.* Baltimore: Helicon Press, 1961.

Di Berardino, A., ed. *Encyclopedia of Ancient Christianity.* 3 vols. Downers Grove: IVP Academic, 2014.

Ermatinger, J. W. *Daily Life of Christians in Ancient Rome.* Westport: Greenwood Press, 2007.

Esler, P. F., ed. *The Early Christian World.* 2 vols. London: Routledge, 2000.

Ferguson, E., ed. *Encyclopedia of Early Christianity.* New York: Garland Publishing, 1990.

Forell, G. W. *History of Christian Ethics I: From the New Testament to Augustine.* Minneapolis: Augsburg Publishing House, 1979.

Guy, L. *Introducing Early Christianity: A Topical Survey of Its Life, Beliefs & Practices.* Downers Grove: InterVarsity Press, 2004.

Lee, A. D., ed. *Pagans and Christians in Late Antiquity: A Sourcebook.* London: Routledge, 2000.

MacMullen, R. and E. N. Lane, ed. *Paganism and Christianity 100–425 C.E.: A Sourcebook.* Minneapolis: Fortress Press, 1992.

Mitchell, M. M. and F. M. Young, ed. *The Cambridge History of Christianity I: Origins to Constantine.* Cambridge: Cambridge University Press, 2006.

Robinson, T. A. *The Early Church: An Annotated Bibliography of Literature in English.* Metuchen: Scarecrow Press, 1993.

Stevenson, J., ed. *A New Eusebius: Documents Illustrative of the History of the Church to A.D. 337.* London: S.P.C.K., 1960.

Thomson, B. *A Bibliography of Christian Worship.* Metuchen: Scarecrow Press, 1989.

Veyne, P., ed. *A History of Private Life I: From Pagan Rome to Byzantium.* Cambridge: Harvard University Press, 1987.

Volz, C. A. *Faith and Practice in the Early Church.* Minneapolis: Augsburg Publishing House, 1983.

Young, F., L. Ayres, and A. Louth, ed. *The Cambridge History of Early Christian Literature.* Cambridge; Cambridge University Press, 2004.

Figure 1. The Stela of Katumuwa decreeing offerings for his soul. Courtesy of the Oriental Institute of the University of Chicago / Photo: Anna Ressman.

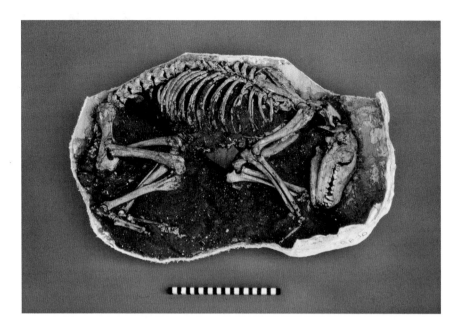

Figure 2. One of over one thousand dog burials found at Ashkelon (5th–4th c. BC). Courtesy of the Leon Levy Expedition to Ashkelon / Photo: Carl Andrews.

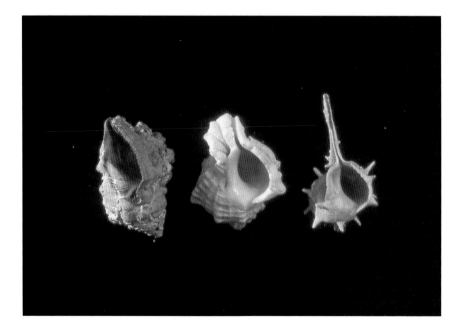

Figure 3. Murex shells, a main source of purple dye. Courtesy of Nira Karmon and Ehud Spanier, Leon Recanati Institute for Maritime Studies, University of Haifa, Israel.

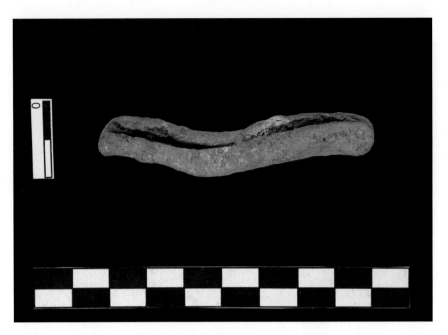

Figure 4. Lead net weight from Bethsaida. Courtesy of the Consortium
for the Bethsaida Excavations Project / Photo: Christine Dalenta.

Figure 5. An Egyptian bread mold. Courtesy of the Oriental Institute
of the University of Chicago / Photo: Anna Ressman.

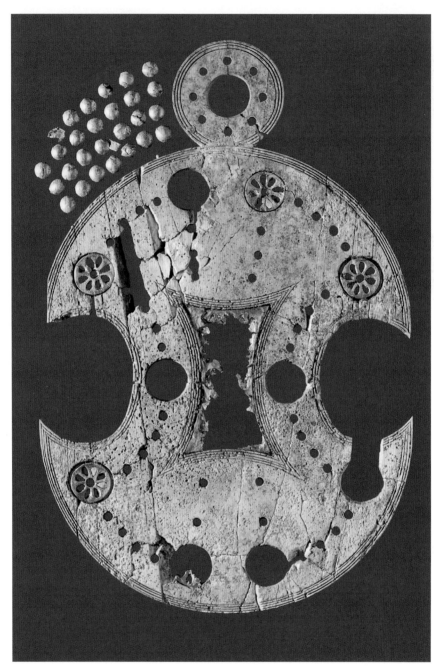

Figure 6. Ivory game board of fifty-eight holes found at Megiddo. Courtesy of the Oriental Institute of the University of Chicago.

Figure 7. The harbor of Cenchreae, Greece. Courtesy of Steven L. Tuck.

Figure 8. Remains of the ancient mole, Cenchreae. Courtesy of Steven L. Tuck.

Figure 9. Cargo box from the Red Sea port of Mersa Gawasis, inscribed "Wonderful things of Punt." Courtesy of the UNO/BU Archaeological Expedition Archive.

Figure 10. A coil of rope from the Red Sea port of Mersa Gawasis (20th–19th c. BC). Courtesy of the UNO/BU Archaeological Expedition Archive.

Figure 11. The harbor of Caesarea Maritima, Israel. Courtesy of Todd Bolen/BiblePlaces.com.